BRITISH WRITERS

Edited under the auspices of the British Council

IAN SCOTT-KILVERT

General Editor

VOLUME I

WILLIAM LANGLAND

TO

THE ENGLISH BIBLE

CHARLES SCRIBNER'S SONS / NEW YORK

Library of Congress Cataloging in Publication Data

Main entry under title:

British writers.

   Includes bibliographies and index.
   CONTENTS: v. 1. William Langland—the English
Bible.
   1. English literature—History and criticism.
2. English literature—Bio-bibliography. 3. Authors,
English—Biography. I. Scott-Kilvert, Ian. II. Great
Britain. British Council.

PR85.B688   820'.9   78-23483
ISBN 0-684-15798-5

3 5 7 9 11 13 15 17 19   V/C   20 18 16 14 12 10 8 6 4
PRINTED IN THE UNITED STATES OF AMERICA

Editorial Staff

List of Subjects in Volume I

Introduction

British Writers is designed as a work of reference to complement *American Writers*, the six-volume set of literary biographies of authors past and present, which was first published in 1974. In the same way as its American counterpart, which first appeared in the form of individual pamphlets published by the University of Minnesota Press, the British collection originates from a series of separate articles entitled *Writers and Their Work*. This series was initiated by the British Council in 1950 as a part of its worldwide program to support the teaching of English language and literature, an activity carried on both in the English-speaking world and in many countries in which English is not the mother tongue.

The articles are intended to appeal to a wide readership, including students in secondary and advanced education, teachers, librarians, scholars, editors, and critics, as well as the general public. Their purpose is to provide an introduction to the work of writers who have made a significant contribution to English literature, to stimulate the reader's enjoyment of the text, and to give students the means to pursue the subject further. The series begins in the fourteenth century and extends to the present day, and is printed in chronological order according to the date of the subject's birth. The articles are far from conforming to a fixed pattern, but speaking generally each begins with a short biographical section, the main body of the text being devoted to a survey of the subject's principal writings and an assessment of the work as a whole. Each article is equipped with a selected bibliography that records the subject's writings in chronological order, in the form both of collected editions and of separate works, including modern and paperback editions. The bibliography concludes with a list of biographical and critical publications, including both books and articles, to guide the reader who is interested in further research. In the case of authors such as Chaucer or Shakespeare, whose writings have inspired extensive criticism and commentary, the critical section is further subdivided and provides a useful record of the new fields of research that have developed over the past hundred years.

British Writers is not conceived as an encyclopedia of literature, nor is it a series of articles planned so comprehensively as to include every writer of historical importance. Its character is rather that of a critical anthology possessing both the virtues and the limitations of such a grouping. It offers neither the schematized form of the encyclopedia nor the completeness of design of the literary history. On the other hand it is limited neither by the impersonality of the one nor the uniformity of the other. Since each contributor speaks with only one voice out of many, he is principally concerned with explaining his subject as fully as possible rather than with establishing an order of merit or making "placing" comparisons (since each contributor might well "place" differently). The prime task is one of presentation and exposition, rather than of assigning critical praise or censure. The contributors to the first volume consist of distinguished scholars and critics—later volumes include contributions by poets, novelists, historians, and biographers. Each writes as an enthusiast for his subject, and each sets out to explain what are the qualities that make an author worth reading.

Volume I opens with essays on Langland, the last notable poet writing in the ancient Anglo-Saxon alliterative measure, and on Chaucer, whose genius in mastering the new Continental forms of rhyme and meter and applying them to the English language shaped the whole subsequent course of English poetry. The volume closes with the Archbishop of Canterbury's study of the evolution of the English Bible, and in particular of the Authorized Version of 1611, one of the supreme products of the period when the English language attained, in G. M. Trevelyan's words, "its brief perfection."

Critical fashions and methods have changed significantly during the past three decades, and part of the attraction of the series may be found in the diversity of critical approaches that it now provides. In some articles, such as Nevill Coghill's *Langland* and *Chaucer*, much attention is necessarily paid to the civilization and social history of the medieval era; in others, such as Frank Kermode's *Donne*, the treatment is primarily analytical. Sergio Baldi brings to the discussion of Wyatt's writing an expert knowledge of the Italian poetry of the period, which vitally influenced the development of English lyrical verse at that moment. Peter Green on *Skelton* and Agnes Latham on *Ralegh* present their subjects to an important extent in biographical terms, the former in stressing the sturdy eccentricity of the poet, and the latter in sketching Ralegh's preeminence as a man of action. M. C. Bradbrook on *Chapman* and Alastair Fowler on *Spenser* both emphasize the value of the recent development of iconographical study in understanding the poetry of their subjects.

Finally, a word of explanation is due concerning the treatment of Shakespeare in the present volume. The *Writers and Their Work* series contained ten essays by different contributors dealing with the various groupings of the plays and poems. A survey of this size would inevitably have upset the balance of the present volume, and, accordingly, Stanley Wells, editor of the Oxford Shakespeare, was invited to contribute a new, shorter critical appreciation dealing with Shakespeare's writings, and a review of the theatrical history of the plays, the publication and editing of the texts, and the development of Shakespeare criticism, together with a compendious select bibliography.

The series was founded by Laurence Brander, then director of publications, at the British Council. The first editor was T. O. Beachcroft, himself a distinguished writer of short stories. His successors were the late Bonamy Dobree, formerly Professor of English Literature at the University of Leeds; Geoffrey Bullough, Professor Emeritus of English Literature, King's College, London, and author of *The Narrative and Dramatic Sources of Shakespeare*; and since 1970 the present writer. To these founders and predecessors *British Writers* is deeply indebted for the design of the series, the planning of its scope, and the distinction of their editorship, and I personally for many years of friendship and advice, and invaluable experience, generously shared.

—Ian Scott-Kilvert

Chronological Table

ca. 1325	John Wycliffe born
	John Gower born
1327–1377	**Reign of Edward III**
ca. 1332	William Langland born
1337	Beginning of the Hundred Years' War
ca. 1340	Geoffrey Chaucer born
1346	The Battle of Crécy
1348	The Black Death (further outbreaks in 1361 and 1369)
ca. 1350	Boccaccio's *Decameron*
	Langland's *Piers Plowman*
1351	The Statute of Laborers pegs laborers' wages at rates in effect preceding the plague
1356	The Battle of Poitiers
1360	The Treaty of Brétigny: end of the first phase of the Hundred Years' War
1362	Pleadings in the law courts conducted in English
	Parliaments opened by speeches in English
1369	Chaucer's *The Book of the Duchess*, an elegy to Blanche of Lancaster, wife of John of Gaunt
1369–1377	Victorious French campaigns under du Guesclin
ca. 1370	John Lydgate born
1371	Sir John Mandeville's *Travels*
1372	Chaucer travels to Italy
1372–1382	Wycliffe active in Oxford
1373–1393	William of Wykeham founds Winchester College and New College, Oxford
1376	Death of Edward the Black Prince
1377–1399	**Reign of Richard II**
ca. 1379	Gower's *Vox clamantis*
ca. 1380	Chaucer's *Troilus and Criseyde*
1381	The Peasants' Revolt
1386	*The Canterbury Tales* begun
	Chaucer sits in Parliament
	Gower's *Confessio amantis*
1399–1413	**Reign of Henry IV**
ca. 1400	Death of William Langland
1400	Death of Geoffrey Chaucer
1408	Death of John Gower
1412–1420	Lydgate's *Troy Book*
1413–1422	**Reign of Henry V**
1415	The Battle of Agincourt
1420–1422	Lydgate's *Siege of Thebes*
1422–1461	**Reign of Henry VI**
1431	François Villon born
	Joan of Arc burned at Rouen
1440–1441	Henry VI founds Eton College and King's College and King's College, Cambridge
1444	Truce of Tours
1450	Jack Cade's rebellion
ca. 1451	Death of John Lydgate
1453	End of the Hundred Years' War
	The fall of Constantinople
1455–1485	The Wars of the Roses
ca. 1460	John Skelton born
1461–1470	**Reign of Edward IV**
1470–1471	**Reign of Henry VI**
1471	Death of Sir Thomas Malory
1471–1483	**Reign of Edward IV**
1476–1483	Caxton's press set up: *The Canterbury Tales*, *Morte d'Arthur*, and *The Golden Legend* printed
1483–1485	**Reign of Richard III**
1485	The Battle of Bosworth Field: end of the Wars of the Roses
1485–1509	**Reign of Henry VII**
1486	Marriage of Henry VII and Elizabeth of York unites the rival houses of Lancaster and York
	Bartholomew Diaz rounds the Cape of Good Hope

vii

CHRONOLOGICAL TABLE

1492 Columbus' first voyage to the New World

1493 Pope Alexander VI divides undiscovered territories between Spain and Portugal

1497–1498 John Cabot's voyages to Newfoundland and Labrador

1497–1499 Vasco da Gama's voyage to India

1499 Amerigo Vespucci's first voyage to America

Erasmus' first visit to England

1503 Thomas Wyatt born

1505 John Colet appointed dean of St. Paul's: founds St. Paul's School

1509–1547 Reign of Henry VIII

1509 The king marries Catherine of Aragon

1511 Erasmus' *Praise of Folly* published

1513 Invasion by the Scots defeated at Flodden Field

1515 Wolsey appointed lord chancellor

1516 Sir Thomas More's *Utopia*

1517 Martin Luther's theses against indulgences published at Wittenberg

Henry Howard (earl of Surrey) born

1519 Charles V of Spain becomes Holy Roman Emperor

1519–1521 Magellan's voyage around the world

1525 Cardinal College, the forerunner of Christ Church, founded at Oxford

1526 Tyndale's English translation of the New Testament imported from Holland

1529 Fall of Cardinal Wolsey

Death of John Skelton

1529–1536 The "Reformation" Parliament

1531 Sir Thomas Elyot's *The Governour* published

1532 Thomas Cranmer appointed archbishop of Canterbury

Machiavelli's *The Prince*

1533 The king secretly marries Anne Boleyn

Cranmer pronounces the king's marriage with Catherine "against divine law"

1534 The Act of Supremacy constitutes the king as head of the Church of England

1535 Sir Thomas More executed

Thomas Cromwell appointed vicar general of the Church of England

1536 The Pilgrimage of Grace: risings against the king's religious, social, and economic reforms

Anne Boleyn executed

The king marries Jane Seymour

1537 The dissolution of the monasteries: confiscation of ecclesiastical properties and assets; increase in royal revenues

Jane Seymour dies

1538 First complete English Bible published and placed in all churches

1540 The king marries Anne of Cleves

Marriage dissolved

The king marries Catherine Howard

Fall and execution of Thomas Cromwell

1542 Catherine Howard executed

Death of Sir Thomas Wyatt

1543 The king marries Catherine Parr

Copernicus' *De revolutionibus orbium coelestium*

1546 Trinity College, Cambridge, refounded

1547 The earl of Surrey executed

1547–1553 Reign of Edward VI

1548–1552 Hall's *Chronicle*

1552 The second Book of Common Prayer

ca. 1552 Edmund Spenser born

1553 Lady Jane Grey proclaimed queen

1553–1558 Reign of Mary I (Mary Tudor)

ca. 1554 Births of Walter Ralegh, Richard Hooker, and John Lyly

1554 Lady Jane Grey executed

Mary I marries Philip II of Spain

Bandello's *Novelle*

Philip Sidney born

ca. 1556 George Peele born

1557 Tottel's *Miscellany*, including the poems of Wyatt and Surrey, published

ca. 1558 Thomas Kyd born

1558 Calais, the last English possession in France, is lost

Mary I dies

1558–1603 Reign of Elizabeth I

1559 John Knox arrives in Scotland

Rebellion against the French regent

ca. 1559 George Chapman born

CHRONOLOGICAL TABLE

1561 Mary Queen of Scots (Mary Stuart) arrives in Edinburgh

Thomas Hoby's translation of Castiglione's *The Courtier Gorboduc*, the first English play in blank verse

Francis Bacon born

1562 Civil war in France

English expedition sent to support the Huguenots

1562–1568 Sir John Hawkins' voyages to Africa

1564 Births of Christopher Marlowe and William Shakespeare

1565 Mary Queen of Scots marries Lord Darnley

1566 William Painter's *Palace of Pleasure,* a miscellany of prose stories, the source of many dramatists' plots

1567 Darnley murdered at Kirk o'Field

Mary Queen of Scots marries the earl of Bothwell

1569 Rebellion of the English northern earls suppressed

1570 Roger Ascham's *The Schoolmaster*

1571 Defeat of the Turkish fleet at Lepanto

ca. 1572 Ben Jonson born

1572 St. Bartholomew's Day massacre

John Donne born

1574 The earl of Leicester's theater company formed

1576 The Theater, the first permanent theater building in London, opened.

The first Blackfriars Theater opened with performances by the Children of St. Pauls.

1576–1578 Martin Frobisher's voyages to Labrador and the northwest

1577–1580 Sir Francis Drake sails around the world

1578 Holinshed's chronicles

1579 John Lyly's *Euphues: The Anatomy of Wit*

Thomas North's translation of *Plutarch's Lives*

1581 The Levant Company founded

Seneca's *Ten Tragedies* translated

1582 Richard Hakluyt's *Divers Voyages Touching the Discoverie of America*

1584–1585 Sir John Davis' first voyage to Greenland

1585 First English settlement in America, the "Lost Colony" comprising 108 men under Ralph Lane, founded at Roanoke Island, off the coast of North Carolina

1586 Kyd's *Spanish Tragedy*

Marlowe's *Tamburlaine*

William Camden's *Britannia*

The Babington conspiracy against Queen Elizabeth

Death of Sir Philip Sidney

1587 Mary Queen of Scots executed

Birth of Virginia Dare, first English child born in America, at Roanoke Island

1588 Defeat of the Spanish Armada

Marlowe's *Dr. Faustus*

1590 Spenser's *The Faerie Queen*, Cantos I–III

1592 Outbreak of plague in London: the theaters closed

1593 Death of Christopher Marlowe

1594 The Lord Chamberlain's Men, the company to which Shakespeare belonged, founded

The Swan Theater opened

Death of Thomas Kyd

1595 Ralegh's expedition to Guiana

Sidney's *Apology for Poetry*

1596 The earl of Essex's expedition captures Cadiz

The second Blackfriars Theater opened

ca. 1597 Death of George Peele

1597 Bacon's first collection of *Essays*

1598 Jonson's *Every Man in His Humor*

1598–1600 Richard Hakluyt's *Principal Navigations, Voyages, Traffics, and Discoveries of the English Nation*

1599 The Globe Theater opened

Death of Edmund Spenser

1600 Death of Richard Hooker

1601 Rebellion and execution of the earl of Essex

1602 The East India Company founded

The Bodleian Library reopened at Oxford

1603 John Florio's translation of Montaigne's *Essays*

1603–1625 Reign of James I

1605 Bacons' *Advancement of Learning*

Cervantes' *Don Quixote*, Part 1

CHRONOLOGICAL TABLE

The Gunpowder Plot

1606 Death of John Lyly

1607 The first permanent English colony established at Jamestown, Virginia

1609 Kepler's *Astronomia nova*

1610 Galileo's *Sidereus nuncius*

1611 The Authorized Version of the Bible

1613 The Globe Theater destroyed by fire

1614 Ralegh's *History of the World*

1616 Deaths of Shakespeare and Cervantes

1618 Ralegh executed

1626 Death of Francis Bacon

1631 Death of John Donne

1634 Death of George Chapman

1637 Death of Ben Jonson

List of Contributors

SERGIO BALDI. Professor of English, University of Florence. Publications include *La Poesia di Sir Thomas Wyatt; Il Primo Petrarchista Inglese*. **Sir Thomas Wyatt.**

JOHN BERNARD BAMBOROUGH. Principal, Linacre College, Oxford, and Pro-Vice Chancellor, Oxford University. Editor of *Review of English Studies*. Publications include *Ben Jonson* and editions of *Volpone* and *The Alchemist*. **Ben Jonson.**

MURIEL CLARA BRADBROOK. Mistress of Girton College, Cambridge (1968–1976); Professor of English, University of Cambridge (1965–1976). Publications include *Themes and Conventions of Elizabethan Tragedy; The Rise of the Common Player;* and *Shakespeare: The Poet in His World*. **George Chapman; Sir Thomas Malory.**

MOST REVEREND AND RIGHT HONORABLE FREDERICK DONALD COGGAN, PC. Archbishop of Canterbury since 1974. Publications include *A People's Heritage; Five Makers of the New Testament; The Prayers of the New Testament;* and *Convictions*. **The English Bible.**

NEVILL HENRY KENDAL AYLMER COGHILL. Merton Professor of English Literature, University of Oxford (1957–1966). Publications include *The Poet Chaucer; Visions of Piers Plowman;* and *The Canterbury Tales* (in modern English). **Geoffrey Chaucer; William Langland.**

A. S. G. EDWARDS. Associate Professor of English, University of Victoria, British Columbia. Publications include *George Cavendish's Metrical Vision* and *John Skelton: The Critical Heritage*. **Henry Howard, Earl of Surrey.**

PHILIP WALTER EDWARDS. King Alfred Professor of English Literature, University of Liverpool. Publications include *Sir Walter Ralegh; Shakespeare and the Confines of Art;* and an edition of *The Spanish Tragedy*. **Thomas Kyd and Early Elizabethan Tragedy.**

ALASTAIR DAVID SHAW FOWLER. Regius Professor of Rhetoric and English Literature, University of Edinburgh. Publications include *Spenser and the Numbers of Time; Conceitful Thought*. Editor of C. S. Lewis' *Spenser's Images of Life* and *The Poems of John Milton* (with John Carey). **Edmund Spenser.**

PETER MORRIS GREEN. Professor of Classics, University of Texas at Austin. Publications include *The Sword of Pleasure* (novel); *Kenneth Grahame; Essays in Antiquity;* and *Alexander of Macedon*. **John Skelton.**

PHILIP HENDERSON. Publications include *Christopher Marlowe; Swinburne; The Portrait of a Poet;* and *William Morris*. **Christopher Marlowe.**

GEORGE HUNTER. Professor of English, Yale University. Publications include *John Lyly* and editions of John Marston's *Antonio and Mellida* and *Antonio's Revenge* and Shakespeare's *Henry IV*, Pts. 1 & 2, *King Lear*, and *Macbeth*. **John Lyly and George Peele.**

JOHN FRANK KERMODE. King Edward VII Professor of English, University of Cambridge. Publications include *The Romantic Image; John Donne; Puzzles and Epiphanies; Shakespeare; Spenser; Donne; Modern Essays;* and an edition of *The Tempest*. **John Donne.**

AGNES LATHAM. Formerly Reader in English, Bedford College, University of London. Editor of *The Poems of Sir Walter Ralegh* and an edition of *As You Like It*. **Sir Walter Ralegh.**

KENNETH MUIR. King Alfred Professor of Literature, University of Liverpool (1951–1974). Editor of Shakespeare Survey. Publications include *Shakespeare and the Tragic Pattern; Shakespeare's Tragic Sequence; Shakespeare The Professional; Life and Letters of Sir Thomas Wyatt.* Co-editor of *Collected Poems of Sir Thomas Wyatt* (with Patricia Thomson) and *A New Companion to Shakespeare Studies* (with S. Schoenbaum); and editions of *Macbeth; King Lear; Othello;* and *The Winter's Tale.* **Sir Philip Sidney.**

DEREK PEARSALL. Professor of Medieval English Literature, University of York. Publications include *John Lydgate; Landscapes and Seasons of the Medieval World* (with Elizabeth Salter); *Old English and Middle English Poetry;* and editions of *The Floure and the Leaf; The Assembly of Ladies;* and *Piers Plowman: An Edition of the C-text.* **John Gower; John Lydgate.**

ARTHUR POLLARD. Professor of English, University of Hull. Publications include *Charlotte Brontë; Trollope;* and *Mrs. Gaskell.* Editor of *The Letters of Mrs. Gaskell* (with J. A. V. Chapple). **Richard Hooker.**

STANLEY WELLS. Head of the Shakespeare Department, Oxford University Press. General Editor of the Oxford Shakespeare. Publications include *Literature and Drama; Shakespeare: An Illustrated Dictionary;* and editions of *The Comedy of Errors; A Midsummer Night's Dream;* and *Richard II.* **William Shakespeare.**

BRIAN VICKERS. Professor of English Literature and Director, Centre of Renaissance Studies, Swiss Federal Institute of Technology, Zurich, Switzerland. Publications include *Francis Bacon and Renaissance Prose; The Artistry of Shakespeare's Prose; Classical Rhetoric in English Poetry; Towards Greek Tragedy;* and an edition of H. Mackenzie's *The Man of Feeling* and of Hooker's *Laws of Ecclesiastical Polity* (with A. S. McGrade). Editor of *Shakespeare: The Critical Heritage* (5 vols.). **Francis Bacon.**

WILLIAM LANGLAND: PIERS PLOWMAN

(ca.1332-ca.1400)

Nevill Coghill

The writer of short studies, having to condense in a few pages the events of a whole lifetime, and the effect on his own mind of many various volumes, is bound, above all things, to make that condensation logical and striking. . . . It is from one side only that he has time to represent his subject. The side selected will be either the one most striking to himself, or the most obscured by controversy.

Robert Louis Stevenson, *Men and Books*

AUTHORSHIP AND DATE

Piers Plowman, the greatest Christian poem in the English language, comes from the second half of the fourteenth century and is thought, although not unanimously, to be the work of an unbeneficed cleric, probably in minor orders, named William Langland. Nothing certain is known about him; even his name comes doubtfully to us through a late tradition. All we know of his personal life is what he tells us of it in the poem, and that is little enough and open to doubt. In these uncertainties, it is best to begin by setting out such facts as there are, for they shed a light helpful to criticism on the poem, on the man who wrote it, and on how it was written and received.

It has survived in fifty-one manuscripts of the fourteenth and fifteenth centuries—a very large number, although *The Canterbury Tales* tops it with eighty-three—and in one early printed text (1550). The poem is cast in the form of a series of dream-visions told in the first person, as if dreamer and poet were one; and no sensitive reader can escape some impression of his personality and genius, or fail to wonder at the spiritual range and intensity of a mind that can generate a ferociously satirical laughter, a compassion as humane as Lear's, and a mystical sense of glory in God's love as expressed in the passion and resurrection of Christ. Here and there, among these greater effects, there are other touches that tell us something about the accidents, rather than the substance, of his life. To these touches can be added a few marginal comments with which later fifteenth-century hands annotated one or two manuscripts, and the brief jottings, gathered by Robert Crowley and set down in the 1550 printed text, of which he was the editor. Another version of the same information, more garbled than before, appears in the later catalog of John Bale, *Scriptorum illustrium maioris Britanniae catalogus* (1559).

Before we can consider the author and what is said of him, there is something further to be said of the texts, for they present a complication that bears directly on the author's methods and on the poem's date. The manuscripts fall into three clear classes offering three distinct versions of the work; they are known as the A, B, and C texts. Seventeen manuscripts support the first, fifteen and Crowley's text the second, and nineteen the third. A study of these three versions makes it abundantly clear that B is a revision of A, and C of B. It has been doubted whether all three were the work of one mind; and, beginning in 1908, a number of scholars, led by J. M. Manly of the University of Chicago, persuaded themselves that they had reason to believe that no fewer than five different poets had had a hand in it. But reason that could convince was never shown, and critics have now ceased to saw the poet asunder.

1

WILLIAM LANGLAND: PIERS PLOWMAN

The A and B texts can be dated with some certainty, from references within the poem to contemporary events; the A text, for instance, refers unmistakably (A,V,14) to the famous storm that started to blow on the evening of Saturday, 15 January 1362, which the chronicle writers also record; it follows that the first version of the poem was later than that. The B text, which is three times as long as the A text, describes, with baleful satire, the coronation of Richard II (B, Prologue,112–209), an event that took place in 1377. The date of the C text cannot be so clearly established, but Sister Mary Aquinas has shown that it strongly influenced another work of the late fourteenth century, *The Testament of Love* by Thomas Usk; since he was put to death in 1387, it follows that the C text must have largely been in being by then. The picture that emerges from these datings is one of a lifetime's work-in-progress, seen in its three major stages; they bridge a period of twenty-five years. The poet may have continued to work on it until his death, no date for which is known. He seems not to have written anything else; he was a one-poem man.

When we attack the problem of who and what he was, we have to push through quagmires of even deeper uncertainty, for the records are late and conflicting. In his own day the poem was famous enough; there is reason to think it had some of the effect of a rallying cry on the insurgents in the Peasants' Revolt of 1381, for John Ball's famous letter to his followers seems to allude to it. In the extract below, I have italicized the relevant phrases; Ball calls himself Schep (a shepherd) to signify his leadership:

Iohon Schep, som tyme Seynte Marie prest of York, and now of Colchestre, greteth well Iohan Nameles, and Iohan the Mullere, and Iohon Cartere, and biddeth hem that thei bee war of gyle in borugh [tell them to beware of guile in town] and stondeth togidre in Godes name, *and biddeth Peres Ploughman go to his werk,* and chastise wel Hobbe the Robbere, and taketh with yow Iohan Trewman and alle hiis felawes, and no mo, and loke schappe you to on heved, and no mo [see that you form together under one head, and no more].

Iohan the Mullere hath ygrounde smal, smal, smal;
The Kynges sone of hevene schal paye for al.
Be war or ye be wo; knoweth your freend fro your
  foe;

Haveth ynow, and seith "Hoo!"
And do wel and bettre, and fleth synne. . .

[John the miller has ground fine, fine, fine;
The Son of the King of Heaven shall pay for all.
Beware before you are sorry; know your friend from
  your foe;
Have enough and say "Ho!"
And do well and better, and flee from sin. . . .]

This would be enough to make a poet cautious in the use of his name and avoid blowing himself up with his own gunpowder; but in any case anonymity was then a common fate for poets. The author of *Sir Gawain and the Green Knight* is unknown; and even Chaucer, though careful to put himself by name into *The Canterbury Tales,* was mentioned in the official records of his times only because he was a trusted servant of the court whose work and wages had to be set down in the accounts. William Langland also put his name into his poem, but under the veils of allegory and anagram. There is an ambiguity in the name William when it is shortened to Will, especially in poems that are involved in moral issues; and even the name Langland or Longland (they are the same) can be played with:

"I have lyved in *londe,*" quod I, "my name is *Longe Wille*"[1]
["I have lived in the country," said I, "my name is Long Will."] (B,XV,148)

The Laud manuscript, now in the Bodleian Library, bears a scribal comment at this line, "Nota, the name of th'auctour." The fullest scribal note, however, is found in a Trinity College, Dublin, manuscript, in a late fifteenth-century hand:

Memorandum quod Stacy de Rokayle pater Willielmi de Langlond, qui Stacius fuit generosus, et morabatur in Schypton vnder Whicwode, tenens domini le Spenser in comitatu Oxon., qui predictus Willielmus fecit librum qui vocatur Perys ploughman.

[1] All quotations from the A text are taken, with slight typographical modification, from the edition by G. Kane (1960). Quotations from the B and C texts are taken, similarly modified, from the editions by W. W. Skeat (Early English Texts Society, 1869, 1873).

WILLIAM LANGLAND: PIERS PLOWMAN

[To be remembered that Stacy de Rokayle (was) the father of William of Langlond, and this Stacy was a gentleman, and lived at Shipton-under-Wychwood in the county of Oxford, a tenant of Lord Despenser, and this aforesaid William made the book called Piers Plowman.]

This seems circumstantial; the Rokayles are known to have been involved with the Despensers, who were lords of Malvern Chase; business might easily have brought Stacy from Shipton-under-Wychwood to Malvern. It is odd that his son William should have taken the name Langland if his father's name was de Rokayle; but in the fourteenth and fifteenth centuries "there is abundant precedent for younger sons not taking the father's name," as R. W. Chambers reminds us. It is possible, too, that William Langland was illegitimate, and that he took his name from the place of his birth. This last possibility will be further considered, but let us first turn to the testimony of Robert Crowley and John Bale.

This was gathered more than 150 years after the poet's death, a long stretch for the linkages of human memory; a man born in (say) 1380 might have had personal knowledge of Langland and have lived until (say) 1460; another born in 1450 might have met him in his last years and learned from him of the author of *Piers Plowman*, then a famous poem, and have passed the information on, in turn, to Robert Crowley in his own old age. I have myself spoken to a lady who knew Charlotte Brontë's aunt, Miss Prunty, and who clearly recalled that old lady's contempt for the change of the family name from Prunty to Brontë, which she regarded as foreign and finicky. And that linkage covers 150 years.

For whatever reason Langland changed his name, both Bale and Crowley assert that he was called Robert Langelande and say he was a Shropshire man, born "about eight miles from the Malvern Hills"—at "Cleybirie," says Crowley, at "Mortymers Clibery," says Bale. Both these authorities, being valiants in the early days of Protestant propaganda, proclaim the poet a champion of their new faith and a follower of Wycliff: "contra apertas Papistarum blasphemias adversus Deum" trumpets Bale; one of those, declares Crowley, who were given the boldness of heart "to open thir mouthes and crye out agaynste the workes of darckenes, as dyd John Wicklyfe."

As Langland's poem shows him to have been one of the most orthodox Catholics who ever took a sacrament, this opinion is clearly an error; but, then, all that they say is erroneous. The poet's name was not Robert, but William; he never calls himself anything else, and the manuscript note cited above confirms this. What is more, the reason for this error is easily found in the line that opens the ninth passus of the A text: "Thus, yrobid in rosset, I rombide aboute," which means "Thus, robed in russet," not "Thus I, Robert, in russet," as Crowley and Bale no doubt conjectured. One manuscript has been found that incorporates this error. Neither Cleobury nor Cleobury Mortimer is eight miles from the Malvern Hills; they are something over twenty. These topographical discrepancies can, however, be reconciled with what appears to be the truth if we suppose that Cleobury was an aural or scribal blunder for Ledbury, which is the right distance from Malvern. This conjecture was first made by A. H. Bright in an exciting book, *New Light on Piers Plowman* (1928). The Bright family had long lived near Ledbury; local knowledge was their specialty.

We learn from this book that in the parish of Colwall, not far from Ledbury, there lies a great flat meadow called Longland; the name, says Bright, can be found to describe it in conveyances as far back as 1681. Anyone who takes the main road from Ledbury to Malvern will come upon it, immediately to the left of the road, just below the Duke of Wellington Inn and Chance's Pitch.

As Bright looked up from this field, he was able to see the Herefordshire Beacon towering above him; a little below and to one side, as his local knowledge told him, there lay the moatlike ditches belonging to a vanished Norman keep known as "Old Castle"; from the Beacon ridge there flowed several streams, the best of which was known as "Primeswell,"[2] and from this brook could be seen a fine stretch of fields between the site of Old Castle and the Hereford-

---

[2] Now no longer visible, having been piped to a table-water factory. Bright believed it to be the "bourne" mentioned in line 8 of the quotation from the opening of the poem, beside which the poet lay down to sleep, and beheld his vision.

shire Beacon. One had only to go there, thought Bright, and stand by the Primeswell, to recognize instantly the whole landscape that unfolds into a magical allegory in the opening lines of *Piers Plowman:*

In a somer sesoun whanne softe was the sonne
I shop me into a shroud as I a shep were;
In abite as an Ermyte, unholy of werkis,
Wente wyde in this world, wondris to here.
But on a May morwenyng on Malverne hilles
Me befel a ferly, of fairie me thoughte;
I was wery, forwandrit, and wente me to reste
Undir a brood bank be a bourne side,
And as I lay and lenide and lokide on the watris
I slomeride into a slepyng, it swiyede so merye.
Thanne gan I mete a merveillous swevene,
That I was in a wildernesse, wiste I nevere where;
Ac as I beheld into the Est, an heigh to the sonne,
I saigh a tour on a toft triyely imakid;
A dep dale benethe, a dungeoun therinne,
With depe dikes and derke and dredful of sight.
A fair feld ful of folk fand I there betwene
Of alle maner of men, the mene and the riche,
Worching and wandringe as the world askith.

[In a summer season when the sun was soft, I got myself into clothes to look like a shepherd; in the habit of a hermit of unholy behavior, I went abroad in the world, to hear of wonders. But on a May morning, on the Malvern Hills, a marvel befell me, it seemed from fairyland; I was weary, having wandered too far, and I went to rest myself under a broad bank by the side of a brook. And as I lay and leaned and looked into the waters, I slumbered into sleep, it rippled so merrily. And then I began to dream a marvelous dream, that I was in a wilderness, I have no idea where; but as I looked toward the east, high up to the sun, I saw a tower on a hilltop, well and truly made, a deep dale beneath with a dungeon in it, with deep ditches and dark ones, and dreadful to see. A fair field full of folk I found between them, all manner of men, the poor and the rich, working and wandering as the world asks.] (A, Prologue, 1–19)

In view of these texts and of this topography, it is not unreasonable to believe, as many scholars now do, that *Piers Plowman* was written by William Langland, born in the parish of Colwall by the Malvern Hills, toward the end of the first half of the fourteenth century. We can even refine on this a little, for twice in the course of the B text (B, XI, 46 and B, XII, 3) he hints that he

is forty-five; and since the date of the B text cannot be earlier than 1377, Langland cannot have been born before 1332, if his hints are to be trusted.

At what date he left the Malverns for London we cannot know; but he did go to London to seek his fortune, for he tells us so. The A text is full of a knowledge of London and its ways, so he had become a Londoner by the time he was thirty at least. It is likely, indeed, that Langland went there soon after finishing the education he may be presumed to have had at Malvern Priory, for he had not the physique for farm work, or so he tells us:

". . . Ich am to waik to worche with sykel other with
    sythe,
And to long, leyf me, lowe for to stoupe,
To worchen as a workeman, eny while to dure."

[I am too weak to work with sickle or with scythe,
And too long in the back, believe me, to stoop low,
Or to last any length of time working as a workman.]
(C, VI, 23–25)

But if he could not work as a workman, he could work as a cleric, for he had had a good education:

"Whanne ich yong was," quath ich," meny yer
    hennes,
My fader and my frendes founden me to scole,
Tyl ich wiste wyterliche what holy wryt menede,
And what is best for the body, as the bok telleth,
And sykerest for the soule. . . ."

["When I was young," said I, "many years ago, my father and my friends paid for my schooling until I assuredly knew what Holy Writ meant, and what is best for the body, as the Book tells, and what surest for the soul. . . ."] (C, VI, 35–39)

Such a young man would naturally enter holy orders; and that Langland did so is a reasonable certainty, not only from the deeply instructed religious cast of the poem but also from what he tells us of how he earned a living:

The lomes that ich laboure with and lyflode deserve
Ys pater-noster and my prymer, *placebo* and *dirige,*
And my sauter som tyme and my sevene psalmes.

Thus ich synge for hure soules, of suche as me
  helpen,
And tho that fynden me my fode vouchen saf, ich
  trowe,
To be welcome whanne ich come other-whyle in a
  monthe. . . .

[The limbs I labor with and earn my living by are my
paternoster and (elementary religious) primer, *Placebo* and *Dirige,* and my psalter sometimes and then
my seven psalms. Thus I sing for the souls of such as
help me, and those that find me my food are kind
enough, I believe, to make me welcome when I come
once or twice a month. (*Placebo* and *Dirige* are
phrases from Psalms 114 and 115 in the Vulgate version and are used as antiphons in the Office for the
Dead. The seven psalms in question are those called
the Penitential Psalms: 6, 32, 38, 51, 102, 130, 143.)]
(C,VI,45–50)

Since no one would pay a layman to do these
offices, it follows that Langland must have taken
holy orders of some kind. Yet it is almost
equally certain that he cannot have been a priest,
for he tells us he had a wife Kitty and a daughter
named Calotte (C,VI,2 and B,XVIII,426), and I
see no reason to disbelieve him. We may conclude he was a *tonsuratus,* an acolyte, who liked
wearing the long robe of his profession in
which he describes himself, and who went
round from patron to patron, praying for them
and for their cherished dead, and perhaps reading to them from his poem now and then.

It is a continual source of wonder to any lover
of Langland how such a spirit—so learned, so
religious, so orthodox and fervent a son of the
church—escaped, or avoided, full priesthood.
Perhaps he knew himself to lack the gift, if it is
a gift, of continence; for he tells how in his wild
youth he gazed into the mirror of middle-earth
that Fortune held out before him, telling him to
make up his mind what thing he wanted among
the wonders of the world, and to go out and
grasp it (B,XI,8–10). Instantly in his dream there
appeared "two faire damoyseles," one called
Concupiscencia Carnis, who "colled him about
the neck" [necked him round the neck], and the
other, *Coveytise-of-eyes.* A third, *Pryde-of-
parfyt-lyvynge,*

badde me, for my contenaunce, acounte clergye lighte

[And bade me, in respect of continence, to take little
notice of holy orders. ("Clergy" means "learning"; but
in this passage it refers to holy orders, for the learned
were generally ordained. Since learning, by itself, is
no bar to incontinence, Langland must here be thinking of ordination.)]

And so (he allows us to think) he gave himself
over to the flesh and to the lust of the eyes
drawn on by "Fauntelté" [childishness]. "*Concupiscencia Carnis* acorded alle my werkes"
(B,XI,42), he confesses, as long as Fortune was
his friend. And then he forgot his youth and
hastened into age, and Fortune became his foe.
Poverty pursued him (B,XI,61); he lost his hair
and his teeth, and was attacked by gout
(B,XX,183,190; C,XXIII,192); he went deaf and
lost his potency; Elde (old age)

. . . hitte me under the ere, unnethe may ich here;
He buffeted me aboute the mouthe and bette out my
  tethe,
And gyved me in goutes, I may noughte go at large.
And of the wo that I was in, my wyf had reuthe,
And wisshed ful witterly that I were in hevene.
For the lyme that she loved me fore, and leef was to
  fele,
On nyghtes namely, whan we naked were,
I ne myght in no manere maken it at hir wille,
So Elde and she sothly hadden it forbeten.

[hit me under the ear, I can hardly hear; he buffeted
me about the mouth and beat out my teeth, and
gyved me with gout, I could not walk about. And my
wife sorrowed for the woe I suffered, and most certainly wished I were in Heaven. For the limb she
loved, and was fond of feeling, especially at night,
when we were naked, I could in no way make behave
in the way she wanted, old age and she, to tell the
truth, had so utterly battered it.]   (B,XX,190–197)

This sardonic glimpse of his latter days is the
last we get of Langland the man, and so we may
leave him to consider Langland the poet.

THE FIRST VISIONS

IT is reasonable and attractive to imagine the
young cross-grained poet, standing in the big
flat field from which he had taken his name and

looking up in the May sunshine at the Malvern Beacon, overcome by a moment of great vision. Suddenly he had seen the whole universe, as he knew it, in the configuration of his parish and the hills about it. He had perhaps been helped to this eye-opening instant by seeing miracle plays; that he had seen some cannot be doubted, for he uses their very language at times. The triple world of the medieval theater, with the mansions of Heaven high on one side and Hell's mouth below and on the other, with man's middle-earth between them, suddenly had bodied itself forth in the Beacon, the ditches of Old Castle, and the intervening fields. This was the setting for the first flight of his poem, his first dream series, known as the *Visio de Petro Plowman;* when it burst upon him, he cannot have foreseen how three further visionary tracts, consequences or sequels to the first, would open up before him and demand to be explored, and would be called the *Vita de Do-wel,* the *Vita de Do-Bet,* and the *Vita de Do-Best.* Into these four large movements the texts are divided.

The first movement gives the poem its name, *Visio de Petro Plowman,* but it is a long time before we meet Piers; Langland had first to depict a world to be saved before he could show a savior for it. The opening vision of the field full of folk is this world as he saw it; it has as much of London in it as of Herefordshire, for we open upon great crowds busy about the maze of their lives, "working and wandering as the world asks." Chaucer shows us England through some thirty sharply individual pilgrims; Langland, through surging crowds of shadowy self-seekers differentiated by their ways of bullying, begging, thieving, tricking, and earning a living out of the Tom Tiddler's ground of the world. Instead of one amiable and distinguished rogue of a friar, such as Chaucer chooses as his exhibit, Langland lumps all the mendicants together, all the four orders, "preaching the people for the profit of their bellies" (A,Prologue,56). We see a swirl of parsons, pardoners and bishops, barons and burgesses, lawyers and businessmen, butchers and brewers, weavers and workmen, with tinkers and tailors and the idle scum of beggars, sham hermits, and common jugglers. We hear the shouts of the tavern keepers' apprentices advertising their masters' wares with "Hot Pies! Good pork and goose! Come and Dine! White wine from Alsace, red wine from Gascony!" (A,Prologue,96–108).

In all this rout there are, however, some that quietly and straitly live by the criterion upon which all Langland's thought is based—the love of our Lord:

> In prayers and in penance putten hem manye,
> Al for love of owre lord lyveden ful streyte,
> In hope forto have hevenriche blisse. . . .

[Many gave themselves to prayer and penance, and lived austerely enough, all for the love of our Lord, in hope to have the bliss of the Kingdom of Heaven.]
(B,Prologue,25–27)

One may say that the whole poem is a search for the true nature of that love. In the last moments of the poem, after all that has been seen and said, when he finds himself beset by old age and death after the attack of Antichrist, and left alone amid universal desolation, the Dreamer turns once more to Kynde, that is, to Nature (and perhaps to God, whose works and will are seen in Nature), which passes by as he sits in helpless grief and terror:

> And as I seet in this sorwe, I say how Kynde passed,
> And Deth drowgh niegh me; for drede gan I quake,
> And cried to Kynde out of care me brynge.
> "Loo! Elde the Hoore hath me biseye,
> Awreke me, if yowre wille be, for I wolde ben hennes."
> "Yif thow wilt ben ywroken, wende into Unité,
> And holde the there evre, tyl I sende for the,
> And loke thow conne somme crafte, ar thow come thennes."
> "Conseille me, Kynde," quod I, "what crafte is best to lerne?"
> "Lerne to love," quod Kynde, "and leve of alle othre."

[And as I sat in this sorrow, I saw how Kynd passed by, and Death drew near me; I began to quake for fear and cried to Kynd to bring me out of care. "Look, Old Age the Hoary One has set eyes on me, avenge me if you will, for I would be out of this." "If you would be avenged, go into Unity (the church), and keep yourself there till I send for you, and see that you learn some craft (trade) before you leave." "Advise me, Kynd," said I, "what craft is best to learn?" "Learn to love," said Kynde, "and leave all other learning."] (B,XX,198–207)

WILLIAM LANGLAND: PIERS PLOWMAN

The Dreamer's first lesson in love opens the poem, when the Prologue is over; it is that truth and love are the same, for God is both. This he learns of Holy Church, the lady lovely of face, who comes down from the Tour on the Toft, Truth's Tower, in the opening vision:

"Whan alle tresores aren tried," quod she, "trewthe
  is the best;
I do it on *deus caritas*, to deme the sothe;
     . . .
For trewthe telleth that love is triacle of hevene;
May no synne be on him sene that useth that spise,
And alle his werkes he wroughte with love as him
  liste;
And lered it Moises for the levest thing, and most like
  to hevene,
And also the plente of pees, moste precious of ver-
  tues.
For hevene myghte noghte holden it, it was so hevy
  of Hym self,
Tyl it hadde of the erthe yeten his fylle,
And whan it haved of this folde flesshe and blode
  taken,
Was nevere leef upon lynde lighter ther-after,
And portatyf and persant as the poynt of a nedle,
That myghte non armure it lette, ne none heigh
  walles. . . ."

["When all treasures are tried," she said, "truth is the best; I prove it by the text 'God is Love'; . . . For truth tells that love is the treacle of Heaven; no sin may be seen on him that uses that spice. And all the works that He created, He created with love, as it pleased Him; and He taught it to Moses as the dearest thing, the thing most like Heaven, and also the plant of peace, most precious of virtues. For Heaven could not hold it, it was so heavy with Himself, till it had eaten its fill of earth. And when of this fold of earth it had taken flesh and blood, never was leaf on linden lighter than it thereafter, and it was portable and piercing as the point of a needle, so that no armor could keep it out, nor any high wall."]

(B,I,85–86;146–156)

Love seen as truth is the rock of Langland's morality; and in the first visions of the poem, he measures the actual, contemporary world presented in them by this unanswerable criterion. Truth and love are the strengths under the rage, under the irony, under the laughter, under the compassion of all his poetry. Opposite to truth is falsehood, which is first pictured for us in the vision of Lady Meed, fountain of bribery and simony, surrounded by a rout of governmental

and ecclesiastical officials, sheriffs, deans, archdeacons, registrars, lawyers and liars; her portrait is drawn in language that suggests the notoriously venal and luxurious Alice Perrers, mistress of Edward III in his senility. She is a colorful figure, robed in scarlet and loaded with jewelry; her wedding present is the lordship of the lands of the Seven Sins. But presently her wedding is challenged and all her grotesque followers are put to ignominious flight, riding on each other's backs. After this sardonic vision of officialdom and the political world has run its course, and Lady Meed has met with the reproof of Conscience before the king—this time an ideal king, certainly not a Plantagenet—Langland takes us once again to the field of folk and shows us Reason, with a cross before him, preaching repentance to the common people. They weep; and the Seven Sins come forward, one after the other, to make their confession, and are absolved.

These sins are no abstractions, but are seen in terms of shop and pub and fair, false weights, wicked words, watered beer, short measure, slander, ignorance, laziness, and a generally sozzled condition. Of the many portraits of the Seven Sins in literature, these are the most lively, the most scrofulous, the most penitent; and, since they show Langland's satiric art at its best, let us pause over the most famous of them—Glutton on his way to church, to make his confession. Before he gets there, Betty the Breweress tempts him into the tavern, where he finds the whole village—Cissy the Shoemaker, Wat the Warrener, Tim the Tinker and two of his apprentices, Hickey and Hackneyman, Clarice of Cockslane, Daw the Ditcher, and a dozen others:

There was laughyng and louryng and "let go the
  cuppe,"
And seten so til evensonge and songen umwhile,
Tyl Glotoun had y-globbed a galoun an a jille.
His guttis gunne to gothely as two gredy sowes;
He pissed a potel in a *pater-noster* while,
And blew his rounde ruwet at his rigge-bon ende,
That alle that herde that horne held her nose after,
And wissheden it had be wexed with a wispe of
  firses.
He myghte neither steppe ne stonde, er he his staffe
  hadde;
     . . .

And when he drowgh to the dore, thanne dymmed
  his eighen,
He stumbled on the thresshewolde an threwe to the
  erthe.
Clement the cobelere caughte hym bi the myddel,
For to lifte hym alofte and leyde him on his knowes;
Ac Glotoun was a gret cherle, and a grym in the
  liftynge,
And coughed up a caudel in Clementis lappe;
Is non so hungri hounde in Hertford schire
Durst lape of the levynges, so unlovely thei
  smaughte.

[There was laughing and scowling and "Let go the
cup!" And they sat so until evensong, singing now
and then, until Glutton had englobed a gallon and a
gill. His guts began to grumble like two greedy sows;
he pissed a pottle (two quarts) in the time it takes to
say a Paternoster and blew his little round horn at his
backbone's end, so that all who heard that horn held
their noses after and wished it had been wiped with
a wisp of gorse. He could neither step nor stand until
he had his staff; . . . and when he drew toward the
door, his eyes dimmed and he stumbled on the
threshold and was thrown to the ground. Clement the
cobbler caught him by the middle, to lift him up, and
laid him across his knees; but Glutton was a great big
fellow, grim in the lifting, and he coughed up a caudel in Clement's lap. There is no hound so hungry in
Hertfordshire that it would dare lap up those leav-
ings, they tasted so unlovely.]   (B, V, 344–363)

To the delinquent world thus pictured in the
Seven Sins a penance is given: the penitents are
to make a pilgrimage to St. Truth. For Langland
saw sin as a failure in truth and love, a failure
for which a sort of bloody-minded ignorance
was partly responsible, it would seem; but a
change of heart could change the bloody mind,
and his sinners showed themselves eager for
their pilgrimage:

A thousand of men tho throngen togideris,
Wepynge and weylyng for here wykkide dedis;
Criede upward to Crist and to his clene Modir
To have grace to seke Treuthe; God leve that hy
  moten!

[A thousand men then thronged together, weeping
and wailing for their wicked deeds; cried upward to
Christ and to His clean Mother, to have grace to seek
Truth. God give them leave to do so!]

                                    (A, V, 251–254)

But their ignorance remains with them; few
are so wise as to know the way, and they "blus-
ter[ed] forth as beasts over hills and streams"
(A, VI, 2), pretty well at random. Presently they
meet a palmer, one of those perpetually globe-
trotting, trophy-laden pilgrim-tourists of the
shrine-collecting type, who seem to have visited
every holy place on earth; they ask him the way
to St. Truth. He is the last of Langland's figures
of satirical comedy in this part of the poem, and
is here introduced, with a technique typical of
medieval art, to make an explosion of derisive
laughter immediately before a moment of solemnity, thus creating the easy step from the ridiculous to the sublime. This is the moment for
the entry of Piers Plowman:

"Knowist thou ought a corseint," quath thei, "that
  men callen Treuthe?
Canst thou wisse us the wey where that wy dwell-
  ith?"
"Nay, so me God helpe," seide the gome thanne.
"I saugh nevere palmere with pik ne with scrippe
Axen aftir hym, er now in this place."
"Petir," quath a ploughman and putte forth his hed,
"I knowe hym as kyndely as clerk doth his bokis.
Clene Conscience and Wyt kende me to his place,
And dede me sure hym sithe to serve hym for evere;
Bothe sowe and sette while I swynke mighte.
I have ben his folewere al this fourty wynter!"

["Do you know a sainted body," said they, "that people call Truth? Can you inform us of the way to where
the creature lives?" "No, so help me God," said the
fellow then, "I never saw a palmer with staff and
scrip ask after him until now and in this place!"
"Peter!" said a plowman, and put forth his head, "I
know him as naturally as a cleric knows his books! Clean
conscience and natural intelligence told me the way and
bound me afterward to serve him forever, both to sow
and to plant as long as I could work. I have been his follower all these forty winters!"]   (A, VI, 21–30)

Piers knows the way to Truth, first in the simplest sense of knowing and doing honest, faithful work; but he also knows the more spiritual
way, through meekness and obedience to the
Commandments, that leads to Langland's grand
criterion, the love of Our Lord. Piers says:

"Ye mote go thorugh meknesse, both men and
  wyves,

8

WILLIAM LANGLAND: PIERS PLOWMAN

Til ye come into consience that crist wyte the sothe,
That ye loue hym levere thanne the lif in youre hertis;
And thanne youre neighebours next in none wise
   apeire
Otherwise thanne thou woldist men wroughte to
   thiselve."

[You must go through meekness, both men and
women, till you come into knowledge that Christ
knows the truth, that you love Him more dearly than
the life in your hearts, and then your neighbors next,
in no way to injure them, or do otherwise than you
would wish people to do unto you.]   (A,VI,48–52)

If you follow this way, says Piers, you shall
come to a court as clear as the sun; its moat is
mercy, its walls are wit to keep out evil will, its
crenellations are Christendom, and its but-
tresses are belief; it is roofed with love and
guarded by grace. The tower in which Truth is,
is up toward the sun:

He may do with the day sterre what hym dere likith;
  Deth dar not do thing that he defendith.

[He may do with the daystar what seems best to him;
death dares do nothing that he forbids. (The daystar,
I think, here means Lucifer.)]   (A,VI,80–81)

And if grace grants that you may enter this
court:

Thou shalt se treuthe himself wel sitte in thin herte
And lere the for to love, and hise lawes holden.

[You shall see Truth himself truly sitting in your
heart, and he shall teach you how to love, and keep
his laws.]   (A,VI,93–94)

Truth is not only in his heavenly tower, but
also in our hearts, for we are made in His image
and it is He who teaches us how to love.

The pilgrims find all this too difficult, and beg
Piers to be their guide; he consents, but asks
them, before they set out, to help him plow his
half-acre. So the poem turns from the problem
of sin to the problem of hunger in a Christian
world, for the "half-acre" is an emblem of England under the threat of famine, as it was after
the black death; and the pilgrims are set to work
to provide food for the community. Work is also

prayer; honest work is truth; feeding the
hungry is love. As a reward for their work,
Hunger is sent away and Piers receives a pardon from Truth Himself, for him and his heirs,
"for evermore aftir" (A,VIII,4), a pardon perpetually available.

Then comes the climax, both in drama and in
significance, of this first great section of the
poem; all critics agree on its striking poetic
force, but no two wholly agree as to its significance. What happens is this. Piers is holding
the document containing Truth's pardon, not
yet unrolled. A priest in the crowd, supposing
him ignorant of Latin, offers to construe it for
him into English:

And Piers at his preyour the pardoun unfoldith,
And I behynde hem bothe beheld al the bulle.
In two lynes it lay and nought o lettre more,
And was writen right thus in witnesse of treuthe:
Et qui bona egerunt ibunt in vitam eternam;
Qui vero mala in ignem eternum.

[And Piers at his prayer unfolds the pardon; and I,
behind them both, saw the whole bull. In two lines it
lay, not a single letter more, and was written exactly
thus, in witness of truth: Those who did good shall
go into eternal life, but those who did evil into eternal fire.]   (A,VIII,91–96)

This baleful statement (which comes from
the end of the Athanasian Creed) is no pardon,
as the priest instantly points out; it demands an
eye for an eye and a tooth for a tooth. So Piers
tears it in pieces.

And Piers for pure tene pulde it assondir
And seide "*Si ambulavero in medio umbre mortis,*
  Non timebo mala, quoniam tu mecum es."

[And Piers, "for pure teen," tore it asunder and said,
"Though I should walk in the midst of the shadow of
death, I shall fear no evil, for thou art with me."]
    (A,VIII,101–103)

What is the meaning of "pure teen"? Why did
he tear the pardon asunder? Here begin the
enigmas, the inward mysteries of this extraordinary poem, upon which hardly two critics can
be found perfectly to agree. "Teen" can mean
almost any shade of feeling of sorrow, distress,

disappointment, anger, or lament. The tearing of the pardon, which, as a piece of imaginative storytelling, seems so superbly, so unexpectedly fitting, as a piece of allegory bursts with ambiguity. Was it a pardon or was it not? Had Truth really sent it, or was it a cunning fraud, like the pardons of so many pardoners? And what did Piers think of it? His gesture of tearing it has invited many explanations, and this may be the reason why it is omitted from the C text; for the changes made by Langland in his last revision seem to be made in order to clarify his meanings. Be that as it may, in all three texts a dispute arises between Piers and the priest. The noise of it awakes the Dreamer, who finds himself "meatless and moneyless in the Malvern Hills," wondering, like his readers, what his vision can have meant.

DO-WEL, DO-BET, DO-BEST

The poem now leads us through a wilderness of disputation that seeks to solve the overwhelming question posed by the pardon. If our salvation depends on our "doing well" (*bona agere*), what does "doing well" involve? On this quest the Dreamer-poet now sets out, but has no Piers to guide him; for Piers vanishes with his first vision and does not return to comfort and instruct him for many a passus.

The first disputants the Dreamer meets are a couple of friars; and they remind him, quoting the Book of Proverbs, that even the just man sins seven times a day. If he sins, how can he be "doing well"? If the just are lost, who can be saved? So what can be the efficacy of the pardon of Truth? Where is the catch? In his triadic mind the Dreamer's first question now multiplies itself by three, and the quest continues not only for doing well, but also for doing better and doing best. Many are the allegorical phantoms and figures he consults, and in their answers and his own conjectures his triple question proliferates into tissues of theological speculation. What are the merits of the active, what of the contemplative life? Can learning save the soul? Does not predestination foredoom us from everlasting to election or to damnation? What are the relative values of faith and works? Are the righteous heathen (like Aristotle and Trajan) saved? Why? How is it that all Nature, except mankind, obeys Reason? And, as he marvels at the natural world, the tediums of disputation (so fascinating to medieval clerisy) are lifted for a moment. We hear a kind of poetry that Wordsworth, had he known it, might have envied:

Briddes I bihelde that in buskes made nestes;
Hadde nevere wye witte to worche the leest.
I hadde wonder at whom and where the pye lerned
To legge the stykkes in whiche she leyeth and
    bredeth;

. . .

Moche mervveilled me what maister thei hadde,
And who taughte hem on trees to tymbre so heighe,
That noither buirn ne beste may her briddes rechen.
And sythen I loked upon the see, and so forth upon
    the sterres. . . .
I seigh floures in the fritthe, and her faire coloures,
And how amonge the grene grasse grewe so many
    hewes. . . .
Ac that moste moeved me and my mode chaunged,
That Resoun rewarded and reuled alle bestes,
Save man and his make. . . .

[Birds I beheld that in bushes made their nests; no man ever had skill enough to make the least of them. I wondered from whom and where the magpie learned to lay the twigs in which she lays her eggs, and breeds. . . . Much I marveled who their master was, who taught them to build their nests so high among the trees, so that neither boy nor beast might reach their young. And then I looked out to sea and upward to the stars. . . . I saw the flowers in the forest and their lovely colors, and saw how many shades of color grew among the grasses . . . but what most moved me, and changed my mood, was that reason rewarded and ruled all animals, except man and his mate.]   (B,XI,336–339;351–362)

Through all these questionings the steady search for a definition of the three good lives continues; gradually their meaning is felt to accumulate into a quite unsystematic yet feeling body of Christian wisdom. In it conscience takes the lead and the virtues of patience, humility, sincerity, and peace of heart have first place; the acceptance of poverty is commended, for it is the gift of God. So we move toward the great virtues Faith and Hope, presented in the shapes of Abraham and Moses, with whom the

WILLIAM LANGLAND: PIERS PLOWMAN

Dreamer has a long colloquy, until it is interrupted by their coming upon the man who fell among thieves; then they meet the Good Samaritan, who is Charity.

Faith and Hope, like the priest and Levite in the parable, draw away ("like duck from falcon"); but the Good Samaritan tends the man wounded by thieves. This wounded man is no other than the human race itself, which fell among thieves in Paradise, having been robbed of Eden by Satan; nothing can cure him:

Neither Feith ne fyn Hope, so festred ben his
   woundis,
Without the blode of a barn, borne of a mayde.

[Neither Faith nor fine Hope, so festered are his wounds, without the blood of a child born of a virgin.]   (B,XVII,92–93)

So, at least, the Samaritan tells the Dreamer; and when he has further instructed him in the trinity-in-unity of God, by images such as that of a candle, its wick, and its flame, he sets spurs to his mule and rides off like the wind, toward Jerusalem.

Now the long inquiry is over and the Dreamer is ready for the supreme vision. It is Lent, and he sleeps; and in dream he hears the singing of children in the streets of Jerusalem on the first Palm Sunday:

Of gerlis and of *gloria laus* gretly me dremed,
And how *osanna* by orgonye olde folke songen.
One semblable to the Samaritan, and some-del to
   Piers the Plowman,
Barfote on an asse bakke botelees cam prykye,
Wythoute spores other spere, spakliche he loked,
As is the kynde of a knyghte that cometh to be
   dubbed,
To geten hem gylte spores, or galoches ycouped.
Thanne was Faith in a fenestre, and cryde "A! fili
   David!" . . .
Olde Jewes of Jerusalem for joye thei songen,
Benedictus qui venit in nomine domini.
Thanne I frayned at Faith what al that fare bemente,
And who sholde Jouste in Jherusalem. "Jesus," he
   seyde,
"And fecche that the fende claymeth, Piers fruit the
   Plowman."
"Is Piers in this place?" quod I, and he preynte on
   me,

"This Jesus of his gentrice wole juste in Piers armes,
In his helme and in his haberioun, *humana natura. . . ."*

[Of children and of glory and praise greatly I dreamed, and how old folk sang Hosanna to the sound of an organ. One similar to the Samaritan, and somewhat to Piers Plowman, came riding, unshod, on the back of an ass, without spur or spear; gallant he looked, as is the nature of a knight coming to be dubbed, to win his gilt spurs and his slashed shoes. Then Faith was in a window and cried, "Ah, Son of David!" . . . Old Jews of Jerusalem sang for joy, "Blessed is he that comes in the name of the Lord!" Then I asked Faith what all this fuss was about and who should joust in Jerusalem. "Jesus," he said, "and he will fetch the fruit of Piers the Plowman which the Fiend claims." "Is Piers in this place?" said I, and he gazed at me. "This Jesus, of his nobility, will joust in Piers's armor, in his helmet and habergeon, human nature. . . ."]   (B,XVIII,8–23)

The sublimity of vision and colloquialism of language unite to carry us vividly to the scene described, and onward to the trial before Pilate and to the crucifixion itself, which has the stamp of a gospel's authority:

"Consummatum est," quod Cryst, and comsed forto
   swowe,
Pitousliche and pale as a prisoun that deyeth;
The lorde of lyf and of lighte tho leyed his eyen togi-
   deres.
The daye for drede with-drowe, and derke bicam the
   sonne,

          . . .

The wal wagged and clef, and al the worlde quaved.
Some seyde that he was goddes sone that so faire
   deyde,
Vere filius dei erat iste, etc.

["It is finished," said Christ, and began to swoon, piteously and pale, like a prisoner dying; the Lord of life and of light laid his eyelids together. Day withdrew in dread and dark became the sun; the wall shook and clef in two, and the whole world trembled. . . . Some said it was God's son that died so fairly, "Truly this was the son of God."]
          (B,XVIII,57–61; 68–69)

But this triumph of eyewitness poetry, which reaches back toward *The Dream of the Rood*, five centuries before, and is, in this description, an equal masterpiece, now moves on to an even

11

greater effort of imagination in picturing the harrowing of Hell. Thither the Dreamer descends, and sees Christ's approach to Hell's barriers as a voice speaking from a light shining upon that darkness. So it is also seen in the pseudepigraphic gospel known as The Acts of Pilate, where Langland undoubtedly found it:

Efte the Lighte bad unlouke, and Lucifer answered,
"What lorde artow?" quod Lucifer, "quis est iste?"
"Rex glorie," the Lighte sone seide,
"And lorde of myghte and of mayne, and al manere
  vertues; dominus virtutum;
Dukes of this dym place, anon undo this yates,
That Cryst may come in, the Kynges Sone of He-
  vene."
And with that breth helle brak, with Beliales barres;
For any wye or warde, wide opene the yatis.
Patriarkes and prophetes, populus in tenebris,
Songen Seynt Johanes songe, Ecce Agnus Dei.
Lucyfer loke ne myghte, so lyghte hym ableynte.
And tho that Owre Lorde loved, into his lighte he
  laughte,
And seyde to Sathan, "Lo! here my soule to amendes
For alle synneful soules, to save tho that ben worthy.
Myne thei be and of me, I may the bette hem
  clayme. . . ."

[Again the Light bade them unlock, and Lucifer answered: "What Lord art thou?" said Lucifer, "who is this one?" "The King of Glory," the Light soon said, "and Lord of might and of power, Lord of all virtues. Dukes of this dim place, open the gates at once, that Christ may come in, Son of the King of Heaven." And with that breath, Hell broke, with Belial's bars; wide open were the gates, in spite of man or guard. Patriarchs and prophets, the people that sat in darkness, sang St. John's song, "Behold the Lamb of God." Lucifer could not look, the Light so blinded him. And those that Our Lord loved, He caught up into His light, and said to Satan, "See here my soul in amends for all sinful souls, to save those that are worthy; mine they are, and of me, I may claim them the better. . . ."]   (B, XVIII, 313–327)

The passus ends with jubilation in Heaven; Mercy and Truth meet, Righteousness and Peace kiss each other, and these four "wenches," as Langland calls them when they first appear, are left dancing until Easter dawns, when the poet wakes, and calls to his wife and daughter:

Tyl the daye dawed this damaiseles daunced,
That men rongen to the resurexioun, and right with
  that I waked,
And called Kitte my wyf, and Kalote my doughter—
"Ariseth and reverenceth goddes resurrexioun,
And crepeth to the crosse on knees, and kisseth it for
  a juwel!
For goddes blissed body it bar for owre bote,
And it afereth the fende, for such is the myghte,
May no grysly gost glyde ther it shadweth!"

[Until the day dawned these damsels danced, and men rang the bells for the resurrection. Instantly I awoke and called Kitty my wife and Calotte my daughter—"Rise, and reverence God's resurrection, and creep to the cross on your knees, and kiss it for a jewel! For it bore God's blessed body for our good, and it puts fear into the fiend; such is its power that no grisly spirit may glide where it overshadows!"]
          (B, XVIII, 424–431)

The eighteenth passus of the B text is the top of Langland's writing in this vein, our greatest Christian poetry; yet, when you compare it with Glutton in the alehouse, you hear the same vigorous voice, uttering things as sharply seen and heard, in the same simple, vigorous speech. The line "Lucyfer loke ne myghte, so lyghte hym ableynte" is in the same tone as that which describes Glutton in a somewhat similar condition:

And whan he drowgh to the dore, thanne dymmed
  his eighen,
He stumbled on the thresshewolde, and threwe to the
  erthe.

The blinding of Lucifer by the blaze of Christ is as realistic a detail, in an apocalyptic mood, as that of Glutton, by mere drunkenness, in a mood of sardonic satire. It is the range of mind supported by an equal strength of speech that makes this poet and his poem unlike any other; he has both lion and lamb in him—and hyena too. To take other examples, he describes the theological sophistries of well-fed dons on their dais at dinner thus:

Thus thei dryvele at her deyse the deite to knowe,
And gnawen god with the gorge when her gutte is
  fulle.

12

WILLIAM LANGLAND: PIERS PLOWMAN

[Thus they drivel on their dais, discussing the deity, and gnaw God in their throats when their gut is full.]
(B,X,56–57)

This triumphant poetical rage issues from the same Christian ferocity as Langland's tenderness, in the same language of colloquial power:

The most needy aren oure neighebores, an we nyme good hede,
As prisones in puttes, and poure folke in cotes,
Charged with children and chef lordes rente,
That thei with spynnyge may spare, spenen hit in hous-hyre,
Bothe in mylk and in mele to make with papelotes,
To a glotye with here gurles, that greden after fode. . . .

[The most needy are our neighbors, if we take careful heed, such as prisoners in pits, and poor folk in hovels, charged with children and rent to their landlords, so that what they can spare out of spinning they must spend on house hire, and on milk and meal to make a sort of porridge with, to glut their children, crying out for food. . . .] (C,X,71–76)

Do-Bet ends with the harrowing of Hell (as it is called), and the poem moves on to the Resurrection; once again Christ is seen in Piers, for the Dreamer, falling asleep, suddenly dreams that he is in church hearing Mass, and that Piers the Plowman comes in, painted in blood, a cross in his hand, before the common people:

. . . And righte lyke in alle lymes to owre lorde Jesu;
And thanne called I Conscience to kenne me the sothe.
"Is this Jesus the Juster?" quod I, "that Juwes did to deth?
Or is it Pieres the Plowman? Who paynted hym so rede?"
Quod Conscience, and kneled tho, "thise aren Pieres armes,
His coloures and his cote-armure, ac he that cometh so blody
Is Cryst with his crosse, conqueroure of Crystene."

[And right like, in all his limbs, to our Lord Jesus; and then I called Conscience to know the truth. "Is this Jesus the Jouster?" I said, "that the Jews did to death? Or is it Piers the Plowman? Who painted him so red?" Said Conscience then, and knelt, "These are Piers's arms, his colors and coat-armor, but he that comes so bloody is Christ with His cross, conqueror of Christians."] (B,XIX,8–14)

And it is by the power of that conquest that the Church is built; Jesus, fighting in the armor of Piers, has done well, done better, and done best. By His victory the sacrament of pardon is established:

And whan this dede was done, Dobest he taughte,
And yaf Pieres power and pardoun he graunted
To alle manere men, mercy and foryyfnes,
And yaf hym myghte to asoylye men of alle manere synnes,*
In covenant that thei come, and knowleche to paye,
To Pieres pardon that plowman, *redde quod debes.*

[And when his deed was done, he taught Do-Best, and gave Piers power, and granted pardon to all manner of men, mercy and forgiveness, and gave power to absolve men of all manner of sins, on condition that they come, and acknowledge to pay the debt that you owe to the pardon of Piers Plowman.]
(B,XIX,177–182. The asterisked line from C,XXII,185, as the B text is here corrupt.)

And so the enigma of the pardon sent to Piers is solved; Truth had bought it on Calvary and had granted it to the race that fell among thieves, to wipe away their sins, *provided* they did their share and paid their debt of confession, and whatever else they owed, to the sacraments and the Church. That done, they would be doing well, however many times a day they, like the just man, had fallen. But they must do their part. Grace would be with them.

After the Ascension comes the descent of the dove, "in the likeness of lightning," upon Piers and his companions; for Christ, having put on Piers "our suit" of human nature, now takes it off, leaving Piers on earth, to build the barn that is to hold his harvest of souls. The Holy Spirit directs the building of this barn, which is to be called "Unity"—Holy Church, in English:

"Ayeines thi greynes," quod Grace, "bigynneth for to ripe,
Ordeigne the an hous, Piers, to herberwe in thi cornes."
"By God! Grace," quod Piers, "ye moten gyve tymbre,

13

WILLIAM LANGLAND: PIERS PLOWMAN

And ordeyne that hous ar ye hennes wende."
And Grace gave hym the crosse, with the croune of
    thornes,
That Cryst upon Calvarye for mankynde on pyned,
And of his baptesme and blode that he bledde on
    rode
He made a maner morter, and Mercy it highte.
And there-with Grace bigan to make a good foun-
    dement,
And watteled it and walled it with his peynes and his
    passioun,
And of al holywrit he made a rofe after,
And called that hous Unité, holicherche on Englisshe.

["Against the time when your grains begin to ripen,"
said Grace, "ordain yourself a house, Piers, to garner
your corn." "By God, Grace," said Piers, "you must
give me timber and ordain that house before you go
away." And Grace gave him the cross with the crown
of thorns on which Christ suffered for mankind on
Calvary; and of his baptism and of the blood that He
bled on the cross, he made a kind of mortar, and it
was called mercy. And with it Grace began to make a
good foundation, and wattled and walled it with His
pains and passion; and of all holy writ he made a roof
afterward and called that house Unity, Holy Church
in English.]   (B,XIX, 324–325).

And so the simple Peter Ploughman of the first
vision, in virtue of the Incarnation and of Pen-
tecost, has become Peter, the rock on which
Christ founded His church, and is to make of it
a barn to store the grain of Christian souls.

With such a climax many poets would have
felt they had reached the end of their vision and
would be ready to lay down their pens. But
Langland saw further; he was not celebrating a
victory but a desolation. For Antichrist was still
to come, with his seven allies, the seven sins,
and with old age and death and all the terrors of
eschatology at his heels, to upturn and destroy
the House of Unity and drive out the fools that
had taken refuge in it. He is the great enemy of
Truth, and the friars are in his following:

. . . A-non ich fel a-sleope,
And mette ful merveilousliche that, in mannes forme,
Antecrist cam thenne, and al the crop of treuthe
Turned tyte up-so-doun, and over-tilte the rote,
And made fals to springe and sprede, and spede
    menne neodes;
In eche contreie ther he cam, he cutte away treuthe,
And gert gyle growe ther as he a god were.
Freres folweden that feonde, for he yaf hem copes,

And religiouse reverencede hym, and rongen here
belles . . . .

[. . . presently I fell asleep, and I dreamed most mar-
velously that, in a man's form, Antichrist then came
and at once turned upside down all Truth's crop, and
overturned the root, and made False to spring and
spread and suffice men's needs. In each country he
came to, he cut away Truth, and caused Guile to grow
there, as if he were a god. Friars followed that fiend,
for he gave them copes and the religious reverenced
him and rang their bells.]   (C,XXIII, 51–59)

In this destruction and betrayal of the church
the poem ends, and Conscience is left to walk
"as wide as the world lasts" to seek Piers Plowman, who once again has vanished from the
poem:

"Bi Cryste," quod Consience tho, "I wil bicome a
    pilgryme,
And walken as wyde as al the worlde lasteth,
To seke Piers the Plowman that pryde may destruye,
And that freres hadde a fyndyng that for nede fla-
    teren,
And contrepleteth me, Conscience; now Kynde me
    avenge,
And sende me happe and hele til I have Piers the
    Plowman!"
And sitthe he gradde after grace, til I gan awake.

["By Christ," said Conscience then, "I will become a
pilgrim, and walk as wide as the whole world lasts to
seek Piers the Plowman, who can destroy Pride, and
that friars may have a maintenance who now must
flatter to supply their needs and counterplead me,
Conscience. Now, Nature, avenge me, and send me
luck and health until I have Piers Plowman!" And
then he cried out for Grace, and I awoke.]
                                    (B,XX,378–384)

It is hard in our days to see friars as Langland
saw them. We need Chaucer's help, and that
chronicler's byword sneer, *Hic est mendicans,
ergo mendax* (This is a friar, therefore a liar). But
the rest of his vision we can see well enough: a
world in moral ruin, seeking some way of good
life, and seeking someone who knows how to
live and teach it. For Langland, at least, all was
to be done again; the pilgrimage to Truth had to
begin once more from the beginning, and Conscience sets about it as the Dreamer awakes.

WILLIAM LANGLAND: PIERS PLOWMAN

It is uniquely fortunate for us that two writers of genius, but of contrasting natures, almost exactly contemporary, should both have given us a portrait of their age in the terms of the two high centers of their culture, the court and the church, that shows us the best things and thoughts of their day in the two languages of English poetry, the old and the new, alliteration and rhyme, at their last and first greatness. Both writers were learned in what most concerned them: Chaucer in all the flowerings of the humane spirit from Ovid to Boccaccio, Langland in all that touched on Holy Writ; Chaucer intent on the evolving nuances of personality, Langland on the needs and qualities of the soul. Chaucer's art centered on romantic love, Langland's utterance on the love of Our Lord. They were both Christians; but Chaucer shows himself as pious rather than religious, with more feeling, let us say, for the Blessed Virgin than for the Holy Ghost; Langland shows little piety or sentiment, but much religious passion. He seeks not comfort but grace. In almost all things each other's opposite, they seem exactly complementary. Together they express a spiritual civilization in being, and they lived the kinds of life they describe. They have passed on the inheritance, enriching it.

They are alike in one rare faculty, though each exercises it in his own manner: the faculty for irony. Chaucer's irony is urbane, sophisticated, *nuancé;* Langland's blazes like a Hebrew prophet's anger saved with laughter. The objects of the great ironists are always the same in their satires—affectation and hypocrisy—and we find the same rogues and frauds held up to unfading mockery in both Langland and Chaucer: monks, friars, pardoners, summoners, and other tricksters and double-talkers. Most of these characters have now disappeared from the English scene, or at least into other professions; but the power to see them as they appeared to the searching secular eye of Chaucer and the no less searching, but mystical, eye of Langland gives us a binocular, stereoscopic vision of the body and soul of their age.

Chaucer, however, has left us no character, among all his many, that embodies the whole duty of man or woman. Rulership may perhaps be seen in his Duke Theseus, wifemanship in his Wife of Bath; a diffused aristocratic principle of largesse runs through all he wrote, less as a principle for us to follow than as a noble infection for us to take, if we are capable of it. He has made no myth for us unless, unknowingly, the myth of "Merry England." In all other ways he has outclassed Langland easily enough during the six centuries between us and them; everything has gone his way—the language, the verse, the literary conventions, the attitudes and interests, secularization, humanism, the cult of character, romance. He is an early modern; Langland, a late medieval wrapped in marvelous but outdated allegories. He seems, at first sight, a poet mainly for medievalists.

Yet these are superficial contrasts, and greatness in poetry is not affected by any of them; Langland is a great poet too, and in one respect has a greater hold on our imaginative attention, in that he faces despair. He ends his poem in a desolation as ruinous as that in *The Waste Land:* the church has tumbled down; the faithful are scattered, bamboozled or seduced; and nothing is left but the individual conscience, by itself, seeking grace "as wide as the world lasts," crying out for Piers Plowman.

What is this enigmatic figure whose identity so strangely merges with that of Christ and of St. Peter? To what reality in experience does it correspond? From the character of the poem and from the number of its manuscripts, one would infer some spiritual need that many felt, but that died away or found satisfaction in some other image in the seventeenth century, when *Piers Plowman* sank into oblivion. Milton knew of it, but its language was too difficult and its matter too Gothic to suit the taste of that time.

It is tempting to think of Piers as a medieval image comparable with the image of *The Dance of Death,* so popular in the fifteenth century, or like those double-decker family tombs of the same period, on which angels support a weight of heraldry in honor of some alabaster lord or lady recumbent on the upper story, while below lies the sculpture of a rotting corpse, to show what six months of death will do, even to princes. If these images are parallel to that of Piers, we may think of him as an emblem from an age gone by that can no longer satisfy any more serious need than a wish to understand the art of the later Middle Ages. And I think that if *Piers Plowman* had never undergone revision, that is how we would think of him. He would seem no more than what he is in the A text, an ideal farmer, a noble peasant, another manifestation of the convention that gave us the virtuous Plowman of Chaucer's *Prologue*, but carried it rather further in its claims for his usefulness to society and for the purity of his vision of God.

But when Langland revised his poem to touch Piers with divinity, he lifted it out of time, so that the convention of an age became a universal and the noble Christian peasant a type of Christ. By this he gave form to an idea often reasserted in his poem: that man is made in God's image of truth and love (their fountainhead His heart), and the corollary faith that at one point in history God was made in man's image. The *imitatio Christi* is a concept to which Western imagination perpetually returns for renewal; it tells us "what we need to be," especially in ages that have a keen sense of spiritual need. The idea of life as a pilgrimage makes good sense with it, for Christians claim that Christ is the Way as well as the Truth; these concepts are embodied in Langland's imagery: Do-Well, Do-Better, and Do-Best, for which Piers stands, are ways of life that Christ Himself had lived, so Langland tells us (B,XIX, 104–189). The pilgrimage toward them is our quest for Piers, under the guidance of Grace.

Chaucer's use of the imagery of pilgrimage is not so urgent: he makes of it a happy human holiday, something in the manner of Chesterton's "The Rolling English Road"; he is casual and confident that it is possible

> To shewe yow the wey, in this viage,
> Of thilke parfit glorious pilgrimage
> That highte Jerusalem celestial,

while not neglecting the fact that "there is good news yet to hear and fine things to be seen, Before we go to Paradise by way of Kensal Green." Langland's urgency has only once been matched, in *The Pilgrim's Progress*. Langland's pilgrimage is a quest, Bunyan's an escape.

From the furthest extremes of Christian theology, these great poets meet in their knowledge of the world and of the soul's need in the struggle of light with darkness. It is a light that harrows Hell, and at the Crucifixion "Lyf and Deth in this derknesse, her one fordoth her other" (B,XVIII,65) [Life and death in this darkness, each is destroying the other]. And it is "Life, life, eternal life" that Christian seeks, as he thrusts his fingers in his ears and flees from the City of Destruction. Both Langland and Bunyan see the world as a wilderness and dream of a remedy, a salvation; many are the parallels and the contrasts between their dreams. Bunyan's pilgrim is allowed to reach and enter the Gate of the Celestial City: "Then I heard in my Dream that all the Bells in the City Rang for Joy." Langland's pilgrims are dispersed in their desolated world, in which Conscience is left alone, calling after Grace in the search for Piers.

For all the differences between them, Langland and Bunyan are natural Christian poets who have an equal urgency and an equal vision of man and his soul in the wilderness of the world that is also Vanity Fair, the field of folk; Langland surpasses Bunyan in showing us Christ in Piers and Piers in Christ, a thing we need to see.

We see a third, and a more modern, picture of the world's wilderness in Samuel Beckett's *Waiting for Godot* (1956), for we are back to that basic vision once again, though the urgency is lost, since the hope is lost. Yet if the old hope is lost, the old criterion remains:

Vladimir: Your boots. What are you doing with your boots?

Estragon: (*turning to look at the boots*) I'm leaving them there. (*Pause*) Another will come, just as . . . as . . . as me, but with smaller feet, and they'll make him happy.

Vladimir: But you can't go barefoot!

Estragon: Christ did.

Vladimir: Christ! What's Christ got to do with it? You're not going to compare yourself to Christ!

Estragon: All my life I've compared myself to him.

It seems that in our age there are others who have Estragon's criterion in mind.

"What do people mean when they say somebody is their personal hero?"

It comes sooner than I expect. "Your hero is what you need to be."

"Then is Jesus your hero?"

"Why do you think that?"

"You say you are scared of dying. Jesus is the one that did not die." . . . "I think your hero has to be a man. Was Jesus a man?"

"No sir. He was God disguised."

"Well, that's it you see. You would not stand a chance of being God—need to or not—so you pick somebody you have got half a chance of measuring up to."[3]

A like, and yet a different, return to the same image can be seen in David Storey's *Radcliffe* (1963).

"But if Christ came to earth as man, why didn't He come as a man we know? Why didn't He use His sex? Isn't it from sex that all our problems and frustrations arise? Yet He refused to acknowledge it by His own example."

Can eighteenth- or nineteenth-century fiction or drama show parallels for these three passages? I do not think so. No one, outside the pulpit, seems to have felt the need for questionings so extreme. *Piers Plowman* was not republished between 1561 and 1842, and was even then considered as little more than an obscure curiosity of literature. It remained so until Skeat's great editions began to make it famous once again. It has reawakened in a world more ready for it; in those glossier days before the twentieth century began, the need for an image of man raised to the power of Christ may not have been so generally felt. But now the time gives it proof.

SELECTED BIBLIOGRAPHY

(Books published in London or New York, unless stated otherwise. Reprints are not recorded. Works are listed chronologically.)

I. EDITIONS. W. W. Skeat, ed., *The Vision of William Concerning Piers the Plowman, Together with Vita de Dowel, Dobet et Dobest by William Langland*, Early Text Society, original ser.: A text, no. 28 (1857), B text, no. 38 (1869), C text, no. 54 (1873); W. W. Skeat, ed., *The Vision of William Concerning Piers the Plowman in Three Parallel Texts, Together with Richard the Redeless* (Oxford, 1886), edited from numerous MSS, with preface,

notes, and glossary (still the standard text for C); T. A. Knott and D. C. Fowler, eds., *Piers the Plowman, A Critical Edition of the "A" Version* (Baltimore, 1952), with introduction, notes, and glossary; G. Kane, ed., *Piers Plowman: The "A" Version* (1960), text with variant readings, also important textual introduction; C. Wilcockson, ed., *Selections from Piers Plowman* (1965), from the B text, with commentary and glossary; E. Salter and D. Pearsall, eds., *Piers Plowman* (1967), selections from the C text, with commentary and glossary; J. A. W. Bennett, ed., *Piers Plowman: Prologue and Passus I—VII of the B Text* (Oxford, 1972), with commentary and glossary. G. Kane and E. T. Donaldson, eds., *Piers Plowman: The "B" Version* (1975), text with variant readings, also important textual introduction; A facsimile ed. is *The Vision of Pierce Plowman 1550* (1976).

II. BIBLIOGRAPHY. J. E. Wells, *A Manual of the Writings in Middle English 1050–1400* (New Haven, 1916)—ninth and last supp. issued in 1952; a revised *Manual* is in progress, covering the period *1050–1500* (Hamden, Conn., 1967–); see also eds. by Wilcockson, Salter and Pearsall, Bennett; studies by Donaldson (to 1949), Saito, Aers; and the relevant section of *The Year's Work in English Studies* (1901–).

III. STUDIES. A. H. Bright, *New Light on Piers Plowman* (1928), an inquiry into the topography of the poem, with a preface by R. W. Chambers; T. P. Dunning, *Piers Plowman, an Interpretation of the "A" Text* (Dublin, 1937), an inquiry into the theology of the poem; G. Hort, *Piers Plowman and Contemporary Religious Thought*, Church History Society Publications, n.s. 29 (1938); R. W. Chambers, "Piers Plowman: A Comparative Study," in his *Man's Unconquerable Mind* (1939); R. W. Chambers, "Poets and Their Critics: Langland and Milton," in *Proceedings of the British Academy*, 27 (1941); N. Coghill, "The Pardon of Piers Plowman," in *Proceedings of the British Academy*, 31 (1945); E. T. Donaldson, *Piers Plowman, the "C" Text and its Poet*, Yale Studies in English, no. 113 (New Haven, 1949; and ed., with new preface, 1966), an authoritative study with a bibliographical index that includes all important articles on the poem published before 1949; G. Kane, *Middle English Literature: A Critical Study of the Romances, the Religious Lyrics, Piers Plowman*, in Methuen's Old English Library (1951); D. W. Robertson and B. F. Huppé, *Piers Plowman and the Scriptural Tradition* (Princeton, 1951); A. G. Mitchell, *Lady Meed and the Art of Piers Plowman* (1956); R. W. Frank, Jr., *Piers Plowman and the Scheme of Salvation*, Yale Studies in English, no. 136 (New Haven, 1957); D. Traversi, "Langland's Piers Plowman," in *Pelican Guide to English Literature* (Harmondsworth, 1959); M. W. Bloomfield, *Piers Plowman as a Fourteenth Century Apocalypse* (New Brunswick,

---

[3] Reynolds Price, *The Names and Faces of Heroes* (New York; London, 1963).

N.J., 1961); D. C. Fowler, *Piers the Plowman, Literary Relations of the "A" and "B" Texts* (Seattle, Wash., 1961).

Further studies are N. Coghill, "Langland's Kind of Poetry," in *English and Mediaeval Studies Presented to J. R. R. Tolkien* (1962); J. Lawlor, *Piers Plowman, an Essay in Criticism* (1962), a detailed interpretation of the poem as a whole, with critical chapters on its rhythms, imagery, and wordplay; E. Salter, *Piers Plowman, An Introduction* (Oxford, 1962); W. Swieckowski, *Word-Order Patterning in Middle English: A Quantitative Study Based on Piers Plowman and Middle English Sermons*, Janua Linguarum, series minor 19 (1962); A. C. Spearing, *Criticism and Medieval Poetry* (Cambridge, 1964; rev. ed., 1972); G. Kane, *Piers Plowman: The Evidence for Authorship* (1965); E. Vasta and G. O'Grady, *The Spiritual Basis of Piers Plowman* (The Hague, 1965); I. Saito, *A Study of Piers the Plowman* (Tokyo, 1966); B. H. Smith, *Traditional Imagery of Charity in Piers Plowman* (The Hague, 1966); E. Salter, "Medieval Poetry and the Figural View of Reality," in *Proceedings of the British Academy*, 54 (1968); R. W. Ames, *The Fulfillment of the Scriptures: Abraham, Moses and Piers* (Evanston, Ill., 1970); P. Calì, *Allegory and Vision in Dante and Langland* (Cork, 1971); E. D. Kirk, *The Dream Thought of Piers Plowman*, Yale Studies in English, no. 178 (New Haven, 1972); C. Muscatine, *Poetry and Crisis in the Age of Chaucer* (South Bend, Ind., 1972); D. Aers, *Piers Plowman and Christian Allegory* (1975); P. S. Taitt, *Incubus and Ideal: Ecclesiastical Figures in Chaucer and Langland*, Salzburg Studies in English Literature, Elizabethan and Renaissance Studies, no. 44 (1975).

IV. COLLECTIONS OF SPECIAL STUDIES. E. Vasta, ed., *Interpretations of Piers Plowman* (South Bend, Ind., 1968); R. J. Blanch, ed., *Style and Symbolism in Piers Plowman* (Knoxville, Tenn., 1969); S. S. Hussey, ed., *Piers Plowman: Critical Approaches* (1969).

V. LITERARY HISTORY AND CRITICISM. J. P. Oakden, *Alliterative Poetry in Middle English*, 2 vols. (Manchester, 1930–1935); E. T. Donaldson, R. E. Kaske, and C. Donahue, "Patristic Exegesis in the Criticism of Medieval Literature," in D. Bethurum, ed., *Critical Approaches to Medieval Literature: Selected Papers from the English Institute, 1958–1959* (1960), discusses the method of Robertson and Huppé (above); G. T. Shepherd, "The Nature of Alliterative Poetry in Late Medieval England," in *Proceedings of the British Academy*, 46 (1970); J. A. Burrow, *Ricardian Poetry* (1971); P. Gradon, *Form and Style in Early English Literature* (1971); D. Pearsall, *Old English and Middle English Poetry* (1977); T. Turville-Petre, *The Alliterative Revival* (Cambridge, 1977).

VI. ALLEGORY. A. S. Fletcher, *Allegory, the Theory of a Symbolic Mode* (Ithaca, N.Y., 1964); G. Clifford, *The Transformations of Allegory* (1974).

VII. HISTORICAL AND OTHER BACKGROUND. J. J. Jusserand, *English Wayfaring Life in the Middle Ages* (1889; repr. many times); D. Chadwick, *Social Life in the Days of Piers Plowman* (Cambridge, 1922); G. R. Owst, *Preaching in Medieval England* (Cambridge, 1926); G. R. Owst, *Literature and Pulpit in Mediaeval England* (Cambridge, 1933); H. S. Bennett, *Life on the English Manor* (Cambridge, 1937); A. H. Thompson, *The English Clergy and Their Organisation in the Later Middle Ages* (Oxford, 1947); W. A. Pantin, *The English Church in the Fourteenth Century* (Cambridge, 1955); M. McKisack, *The Fourteenth Century* (Oxford, 1959), the standard historical survey; J. A. Yunck, *The Lineage of Lady Meed* (South Bend, Ind., 1963); H. A. Oberman, *The Harvest of Medieval Theology* (rev. ed.; Grand Rapids, Mich., 1967); A. R. Myers, ed., *English Historical Documents 1327–1485* (1969); R. W. Southern, *Western Society and the Church in the Middle Ages* (Harmondsworth, 1970).

VIII. TRANSLATIONS. H. W. Wells, trans., *The Vision of Piers Plowman* (1935; repr. 1945), complete, in alliterative verse; N. Coghill, trans., *Visions from Piers Plowman* (1949), selections, in alliterative verse; D. and R. Attwater, trans., *The Book Concerning Piers the Plowman* (1957), in Everyman's Library, complete, in alliterative verse; J. F. Goodridge, trans., *Piers the Plowman* (rev. ed.; Harmondsworth, 1968), in the Penguin Classic series, complete, in prose.

GEOFFREY CHAUCER

(ca.1340-1400)

Nevill Coghill

A shilling life will give you all the facts.
W. H. Auden

In what his father and mother would have regarded as his career—for it was they who had the wit, and the luck, to launch him upon it—Geoffrey Chaucer did remarkably well. His successive appointments, missions, and awards, achieved in the administrative service of three kings, were something better than a mediocre success; and who could have foreseen that his marriage, prudent and suitable as it was—romantic, too, for all we know to the contrary—would ultimately make him brother-in-law to his own best patron, John of Gaunt—that is, to the fourth son of Edward III, the uncle of Richard II and the father of Henry IV, the poet's chief employers?

But it was not as a poet that they employed Chaucer; his poetry was an extra, so far as they were concerned. His career was that of a courtier, as his father and mother had intended; and it was that career that gained him his place in the official records of the time. Except for those records, we should probably know as little about him as we do of the other great poets of his age, the authors of *Piers Plowman* and of *Sir Gawain*.

Yet the recorded facts of this courtier's life, remote from poetry as they may seem, are those upon which the styles of his poetry turn; they mark its progress from his first beginnings, step by step, to his maturities. Being a courtier made a European of Chaucer, and more than that; he became the first great English poet in the general tradition of Christendom, the heir of Ovid, of Vergil, of Boethius, of Saint Jerome, of Guillaume de Lorris and Jean de Meung, of Dante and Boccaccio.

He was not the first great English Christian poet; Langland was before him. But he was the first English poet in the high culture of Europe, then breaking out all over England in a glorious profusion of creative power. There are moments in the lives of nations when they declare their genius: the life of Geoffrey Chaucer fell in the middle of the first such moment in England.

In every art then known, and in some now lost—in architecture, sculpture, carving, and stained glass; in the work of goldsmiths and armorers and the makers of robes for ceremonial and daily use; in manuscript illumination, painting and portraiture, music and dancing—sudden perfections were being achieved all over England. Moreover, they were harmonious, as if they were the particular manifestations of a personal style flowering freely in every field. Grace, strength, freshness of invention, clarity, richness, and a sense of the humane, as well as of the divine, characterize this breeding time of England's first civilization.

Out of the multitude of masterpieces I will name a few to show these qualities: the central tower of Wells Cathedral and the breathtaking inverted arch that supports it, the work of William Joy about the year of Chaucer's birth (*ca.* 1340), and the great octagonally fashioned vault over the transept of Ely Cathedral, the work of Alan of Walsingham and William Hurley not long before—miracles, both, of strength and ingenuity; and the nave of Westminster Abbey, grove of slender stone, built by the greatest English architect before Wren, Henry Yevele. Chaucer, late in his life, knew and worked with him. It was Yevele who, with Hugh Herland, master carpenter, built Westminster Hall (1394).

In portraiture, an art then dawning and of which Chaucer became a master, one may recall the tragic alabaster face of Edward II that haunts the visitor to Gloucester Cathedral, or the knowingly practical visage of Henry IV, carved in Canterbury; less tragic than Edward, more humane than Henry, the painted effigy of Edward le Despenser, kneeling in his chantry roof in Tewkesbury Abbey. Illumination and painting could show pieces as fine as these: for instance, the Wilton diptych that presents the young Richard II to the Blessed Virgin and a host of angels, himself hardly less angelical in beauty, or the greater portrait of him that hangs in Westminster Abbey and shows him against a gold background, in a robe the color of dried blood. From his face, he seems to be thinking Shakespearean thoughts.

In glass the antechapel windows of New College by Thomas of Oxford, with their canopied saints and patriarchs in soft greens and porphyries and blues, seem a silent reproach to the baroque-souled figures and inharmonious tints of a neighboring window by Sir Joshua Reynolds that was somehow allowed to be put there in an age that knew no better. In the same chapel is the crozier of William of Wykenham, a masterwork of the goldsmiths, silversmiths, and enamelers of the fourteenth century.

Harp and flute and social song were part of a gentleman's education, and song was gracefully combined with dance in the "carol"; the art of conversation was so much esteemed that Andreas Capellanus gave it third place among the requirements for a girl worthy to be loved; and Chaucer, in his first considerable poem, ensured that it would be known to have graced the dead patroness he was celebrating, Blanche, duchess of Lancaster:

> And which a goodly, softe speche
> Had that swete, my lyves leche![1]
> So frendly, and so well ygrounded,
> Up al resoun[2] so wel yfounded,
> And so tretable[3] to alle goode . . .

In poetry (our chief concern in this essay) the age was richer than in all else, except architecture. There were the three great poets I have mentioned, of whom Chaucer was chief; there was John Gower, too, and the makers of the miracle plays, then coming to their first fullness in York and elsewhere. *Troilus and Criseyde, The*

Canterbury Tales, Piers Plowman, Sir Gawain, The Pearl, and the Townley or Wakefield Plays may speak for the great achievements of those times in poetry; but there was also a first pouring forth of lyrical writing, by many anonymous hands and one-poem men, of whose work a fragment follows:

> Bytuene Mersh and Aueril,
>   When spray biginneth to springe,
> The lutel foul hath hire wyl
>   On hyre lud to synge.
>   Ich libbe in loue-longinge
>   For semlokest of alle thynge;
>   [S]he may me blisse bringe—
>   Icham in hire baudoun.
>
> An hendy hap ichabbe yhent;
> Ichot from heuene is it me sent;
> From alle wymmen mi loue is lent,
>   And lyht on Alysoun.

[Between March and April, when the spray begins to spring, the little bird has its pleasure to sing in its language. I live in love-longing for the seemliest of all things; may (s)he bring me joy; I am in her power. I have grabbed a lucky chance. I know it has been sent me from Heaven; from all women my love has turned away, and lights on Alison.].[4]

And here is another, in a more "metaphysical" vein:

> Gold & al this werdis wyn
> Is nouth but cristis rode;
> I woulde ben clad in cristis skyn,
> That ran so longe on blode,
> & gon t'is herte & taken myn In—
> Ther is a fulsum fode.

[Gold and all the glory of this world is nought, save Christ's cross; I would be clad in Christ's skin, that ran so long with blood, and go to his heart and make my Inn there, where there is a bounteous food.][5]

This was a mystical age, the age of Richard Rolle of Hampole and Juliana of Norwich; her writings are like the writings of a lover:

---

[1] My life's physician.   [2] Upon all reason.
[3] So tractable.

[4] Kenneth Sisam, ed., *Fourteenth Century Verse and Prose* (London, 1937).
[5] Carleton Brown, ed., *Religious Lyrics of the XIVth Century* (London, 1924; 2nd ed., by G. V. Smithers, 1957).

GEOFFREY CHAUCER

I saw his sweet face as it were dry and bloodless with pale dying. And later, more pale, dead, languoring; and then turned more dead unto blue: and then more brown-blue, as the flesh turned more deeply dead. For his Passion shewed to me most specially in his blessed face, and chiefly in his lips: there I saw these four colours, though it were afore fresh, ruddy, and liking, to my sight.

(Revelations of Divine Love)

It was also an age that loved learning, a founding time of colleges. Nine new ones were added within the century, four at Oxford and five at Cambridge.

Paradoxes are to be understood as best they can. This same age of the first, and in some ways the finest, English culture was also an age preeminent for plague, poverty, rebellion, war (both international and civil), political murder, heresy, and schism. Fissures seemed to be opening in the Catholic church with the ''Babylonish'' captivity of the popes at Avignon, followed by a great schism and war between pope and antipope. To Langland it seemed like the day of Antichrist. Heresies were also raising their terrible heads; the chronicles tell the story of a knight who snatched the consecrated host out of his priest's hand and fled away with it, to devour it with oysters and mustard, thinking (in some obscure way) that this disproved transubstantiation.

There were secular terrors too: the black death began its repeated visitations in 1348, when Chaucer was a child.

Ther cam a privee theef men clepeth Deeth,[6]
That in this contree al the peple sleeth.
(The Pardoner's Tale)

The tyrannies of nature were matched by the tyrannies of man. Mob madness and xenophobia filled London with the shouts and shrieks of massacre when the rebels of the Peasants' Revolt, entering London, fell upon the Flemings there in 1381; Chaucer, in later years, passed it off as a joke, a farmyard flurry:

Certes, he Jakke Straw and his meynee[7]
Ne made nevere shoutes half so shrille,

[6] There came a secret thief that men call death.
[7] And his gang.

Whan that they wolden any Flemyng kille,
As thilke day was maad upon the fox.
(The Nun's Priest's Tale)

This revolt, which was also an attack upon church and law, was suppressed as savagely as it had arisen, with hanging in chains for many a deluded peasant. Their betters were also liable to liquidation; the intrigues that stewed within and seethed outside the court and government led often enough to the scaffold:

The ax was sharpe, the stokke was harde
In the xiiii yere of Kyng Richarde.
(Sisam, Fourteenth Century Verse and Prose)

As a sort of ground bass to all these disturbances, there was an unstanched issue of blood—bitter, barbarous, and futile—in the feuds with France that are now called the Hundred Years' War. No doubt it was conducted with great panache and had moments of thrilling, heraldic heroism; it certainly dazzled the eyes of its chronicler, Jean Froissart, who could write of it in the *Chroniques* with the kind of romantic feeling that stirs in us when we read Chaucer's *The Knight's Tale:*

Thus the knights and squires sparkled abroad in the plain and fought together . . . (Froissart, 1364)
It was great joy to see and consider the banners and the penons and the noble armoury . . . the Prince himself[8] was the chief flower of chivalry of all the world, and had with him as then right noble and valiant knights and squires . . . (1367)
The men of arms beat down the Flemings on every side . . . and as the Flemings were beaten down, there were pages ready to cut their throats with great knives, and so slew them without pity, as though they had been but dogs . . . (1382)

What with Jack Straw and the men of arms, the Flemings met with small mercy, but nationalism knows no restraint and soldiers cannot expect a ransom from a Flemish burgher.

Into this age of extremes, which in every direction forces superlatives from its astonished student, Geoffrey Chaucer, most equable of men, was born.

He was born in the middle of the century and in the middle of society, toward the year 1340,

[8] The Black Prince.

21

in a middle-class cockney home. No record was kept of the event. Round the corner, and half a street away from his father's house, flowed the Thames; a little above towered old Saint Paul's, whose chapter house and cloister, the work of William Ramsey, stood in their brand-new perpendicular beauty. A new style had been born.

EDUCATION IN RHETORIC

The noble rethor poete of brytayne
John Lydgate, *Life of Our Lady*,
referring to Chaucer

NOT far away, in the Vintry, stood Saint Paul's Almonry; and if it is not a fact, it is a likely conjecture, that young Geoffrey was sent there daily to learn his letters and his Latin, through the medium of French:

Children in scole, ayenst the vsage and manere of alle othere naciouns beeth compelled for to leue hire owne langage, and for to construe hir lessouns and here thynges in Frensche, and so they haueth seth the Normans come first to Engelond. Also gentil men children beeth i-taught to speke Frensche from the tyme that they beeth i-rokked in here cradel . . . And vplondisshe men wil likne hym self to gentil men, and fondeth with greet besynesse for to speke Frensche, for to be i-tolde of.

(Ranulf Higden, *Polychronicon*, 1363)

As might be expected from the above, Chaucer's Squire in *The Canterbury Tales*, being of "gentil" birth, was accustomed to speaking French, and confesses:

Myn Englissh eek is insufficient.

And the Franklin, an "vplondisshe" or country-bred man if ever there was one, loudly regrets that his own son lacks the gentle breeding of the Squire, in such a way as to unleash the mockery of the Host, who could see at a glance that there was a penny short in the shilling of the Franklin's gentility:

"Straw for youre gentillesse!" quod oure Hoost.

What was it like to be at school in those days? Children were sent very young: *enfantz* they were called, and their instruction began like that of Chaucer's "litel clergeon" in *The Prioress's Tale*, with the singing of Latin hymns, the easiest way into the difficult language of heaven:

". . . I lerne song, I kan but smal grammeere."
(*The Prioress's Tale*)

At Westminster School, and probably at Saint Paul's, too, a boy who knew Latin and presumed to speak English, or even French, had a cut of the cane for every word so spoken. Rod and birch were frequently applied to the seat of learning and accepted as a rueful joke by the little victims. There is, for instance, a late fifteenth-century poem by—or at least about—a boy who had dared to excuse himself for being late for school on the ground that his mother had told him to go out and milk the ducks:

My master lokith as he were madde:
"wher hast thou be, thow sory ladde?"
"Milked dukkis, my moder badde":
hit was no mervayle thow I were sadde.
  what vaylith it me thowgh I say nay?
My master pepered my ars with well good spede
. . . He wold not leve till it did blede,
Myche sorow haue he for his dede!
(*Babees Book*) [9]

Discipline, if rough, was ready. The day began with prayer, then a recitation of the Creed, the Lord's Prayer, a salutation to the Blessed Virgin, and some psalm singing, which was called "dinging on David." And so to class to learn letters, to do sums with counters, to grammar, to logic, to rhetoric, and to the classic authors: Ovid, Vergil, Lucan, Cicero, Statius, Dionysius Cato, and the rest.

Rhetoric has come to mean a windy way of speech, marked by a pompous emptiness and insincerity, and trotted out as a trick on any occasion calling for solemn humbug. It did not mean this to the Middle Ages. It meant then the whole craft of writing, the arts and devices by which whatever you had to say could best be varied, clarified, and elaborated; it even included the study of appropriate gesture:

[9] *The Babees Book (Early English Poems and Treatises on Manners and Meals in Olden Time)*, F. J. Furnival, ed., Early English Text Society, original ser., XXXII (London, 1868).

And, for his tale sholde seme the bettre,
Accordant to his wordes was his cheere,
As techeth art of speche hem that it leere.

[He suited his action to his words, as the art of speech teaches those that learn it, to do.]

(*The Squire's Tale*)

The word *rethor* had come to be used as the simple equivalent of "good poet"; so Chaucer used it in *The Squire's Tale*, to underline the skill needed to describe the beauty of his heroine:

It moste been a rethor excellent

. . .

If he sholde hire discryven every part.
I am noon swich, I moot speke as I kan.

So it was used of Chaucer by Lydgate and other poets:

O reverend Chaucere, rose of rethoris all,
As in oure tong ane flour imperiall . . .

(William Dunbar, *The Golden Targe*)

The rules of rhetoric are now, for the most part, forgotten; and the enormous effect they had on the formation of Chaucer's style is therefore often not perceived, even by good Chaucerists. Every educated person in the fourteenth century knew them and admired those who knew how to use them, of whom Chaucer was chief. It would be fair to say that an anthology of the finest things in Chaucer could be employed to demonstrate the nature and use of these rules.

They had come down from Roman times, and reached a second flowering in the twelfth and thirteenth centuries. The scholars of that time, notably Matthieu de Vendôme (*ca.* 1170) and Geoffrey de Vinsauf (*ca.* 1210), had assembled all the traditions of rhetoric in a number of prose treatises and illustrative verses; the general heading under which particular devices of style were recommended was that of *amplificatio*, the art of enlarging and embellishing your matter. There were eight or ten principal ways of doing so, each with its high-sounding name, and some with as many as four subdivisions. For instance, there was *circumlocutio*, the art of making a simple statement in a roundabout and decorative way:

The bisy larke, messager of day,
Salueth in hir song the morwe gray,
And firy Phebus riseth up so bright
That al the orient laugheth of the light,
And with his stremes dryeth in the greves[10]
The silver dropes hangynge on the leves.

(*The Knight's Tale*)

The simple statement underlying this lovely and lively passage is "The sun rose brightly." That Chaucer was perfectly conscious of this, and sometimes also amused by it, can be seen from the following:

But sodeynly bigonne revel newe
Til that the brighte sonne loste his hewe;
For th'orisonte hath reft the sonne his lyght,—
This is as muche to saye as it was nyght!—

(*The Franklin's Tale*)

The first twelve magical lines of *The General Prologue* is a simple *circumlocutio* for "In April, people go on pilgrimages."

Another figure of rhetoric, much used by Chaucer, was *interpretatio*; this consisted in repeating an idea in other words: *varius sis et tamen idem.*[11]

A plain example of this would be

Soun ys noght but eyr ybroken,
And every speche that ys spoken,
Lowd or pryvee, foul or fair,
In his substance ys but air . . .

(*The House of Fame*, II)

The last three lines are an *interpretatio* of the first. But the figure could also have a subtler form, as when the idea was not only repeated, but given a new twist. For instance:

Ful swetely herde he confessioun,
And pleasaunt was his absolucioun:
He was an esy man to yeve penaunce,
Ther as he wiste to have a good pitaunce.

(*The General Prologue*)

The last two lines repeat the sense of the first with a dagger thrust of meaning added.

In like manner examples of every figure of rhetoric can currently be found in Chaucer: of

---

[10] Groves.
[11] Be various and yet the same (Vinsauf, *De poetria nova*).

digressio in its two forms, namely, when you digress to matter outside your story in order to illuminate it (as when the Wife of Bath tells the story of Midas to illustrate a point in her own tale) and when you digress by developing an idea within your story, in a manner directly arising from it (as when the Merchant, describing the garden that old January had made, digresses to thoughts of the *Roman de la rose*, Priapus, and Proserpine). Or of *occupatio*, when you explain that you are too busy to go into details; this can be used either to shorten your tale:

> I coude folwe, word for word, Virgile,
> But it wolde lasten al to longe while.
> (*The Legend of Good Women*)

or to lengthen it, by saying you have no time to describe the things that you then proceed to describe:

> And eek it nedeth nat for to devyse
> At every cours the ordre of hire servyse.
> I wol nat tellen of hir strange sewes,[12]
> Ne of hir swannes, ne of hire heronsewes,[13]
> Eeek in that lond, as tellen knyghtes olde,
> Ther is som mete that is ful deynte holde,
> That in this lond men recche of it but smal;[14]
> Ther nys no man that may reporten al.
> (*The Squire's Tale*)

The Squire's use of *occupatio* is tame, however, compared with that of his father, the Knight, who performs a dazzling cadenza of some fifty lines toward the end of his tale, enumerating all the features of Arcite's funeral, which (he says) he has no time to mention. It is a real tour de force.

But Chaucer's favorite rhetorical device was certainly *apostrophatio*. This figure had four subdivisions, of which the commonest was *exclamatio*, a simple exclamation of feeling, of whatever kind; the second and third, *subjectio* and *dubitatio*, were forms of rhetorical question; and the last, *conduplicatio*, was a series of exclamations, each beginning with the same phrase (this Chaucer uses only in his most serious invocations):

> Lo here, of payens corsed olde rites,[15]
> Lo here, what alle hire goddes may availle!
> Lo here, thise wrecched worldes appetites!
> Lo here, the fyn and guerdoun for travaille[16]
> Of Jove, Appollo, of Mars, of swich rascaille!
> (*Troilus and Criseyde*, V)

Chaucer sparkles with apostrophes; he is ever ready to exclaim in sympathy, wonder, indignation, pathos, prayer, and irony, to address his audiences personally with a question not meant to be answered, but that brings them into the story:

> Woot ye nat where there stant a litel toun
> Which that ycleped is Bobbe-up-and-doun,
> Under the Blee, in Caunterbury Weye?
> (*The Manciple's Prologue*)

Or they may be asked to picture an incident in a tale by reminding them of something similar in their own lives, as when Chaucer asks them to imagine the plight of his heroine by recalling the sight of some unhappy criminal on his way to execution:

> Have ye nat seyn somtyme a pale face,
> Among a prees,[17] of hym that hath be lad
> Towards his deeth, wher as hym gat no grace,
> And switch a colour in his face hath had,
> Men myghte knowe his face that was bistad,[18]
> Amonges all the faces in that route?
> So stant Custance, and looketh hire aboute.
> (*The Man of Law's Tale*)

These are rhetorical questions, not exactly of the kinds named above, but of a kind to vary, by an apostrophe to his hearers, Chaucer's means of engaging their attention. Often he will pause in midstory to ask what sort of a universe it can be where such things happen, or to make a general comment on life:

> Allas! allas! that evere love was sinne!
> (*The Wife of Bath's Prologue*)

These were things that Chaucer began to learn in his school days, and in his hands the

[12] Strange broths.
[13] Their young heron (like the swans, a dish to eat).
[14] In this country people think little of it.

[15] Behold the accursed, ancient rites of pagans.
[16] Behold the end and the reward for your labors (given by Jove, etc.).
[17] Crowd.   [18] Set round (with enemies).

rules of the pedants became the instruments of a living and natural style; as with any great virtuoso, the technical rule or accomplishment, artificial and laborious as it may seem, can become the means of a greater freedom of expression, can even prompt a thought that might have been lost without it, for

> . . . Nature is made better by no mean
> But Nature makes that mean: so, over that art
> Which you say adds to Nature, is an art
> That Nature makes.
>
> *(The Winter's Tale)*

Above all, Chaucer's training in rhetoric sharpened his perception of character; no one was his equal in this, because no one had his touch with the rhetorical figure of *descriptio.* This is a figure to which we must return later. At the moment let us pass on from Saint Paul's Almonry (if that indeed was where he had his early schooling) and follow him to the next phase of his upbringing. It was the decisive phase, the true beginning of his career as a courtier and as a poet.

EDUCATION IN COURTESY

> *Let me see if Philip can*
> *Be a little gentleman.*
> Heinrich Hoffman, *Struwwelpeter*

AT some unknown date, but certainly when he was still a boy, Geoffrey was taken from school and put out to service in the household of Elisabeth, countess of Ulster. She was the wife of Lionel, third son of Edward III and later duke of Clarence. For Geoffrey this was an almost unimaginable stroke of good fortune; his parents, no doubt through their slender court connections, had somehow pulled it off.

The countess kept household books on parchment. These books were later torn up and the parchment used to line a manuscript of poems by Lydgate and Hoccleve. A nineteenth-century scholar examining the manuscript discovered the lining. It was found to contain the first known reference to Geoffrey Chaucer. It is dated April 1357 and records that the countess laid out seven shillings on a cloak and a pair of red-and-black breeches for the lad. He had taken the first step in courtiership and was a page in a royal household.

This did not mean that Chaucer's education was interrupted; on the contrary, it was widened, intensified, and given a practical turn. We know almost exactly of what it consisted, thanks to another household book, the *Liber niger* of Edward IV, in which is laid down the traditional curriculum for lads in his position, rising from page to squire. They were known as henxmen or henchmen, a word derived from the older word *hengest,* meaning a horse, for all chivalry (to which Chaucer was now apprenticed) arose from the cult of the horse (*cheval*), as the word implies. It tamed and civilized the lust of battle much in the way that courtly love tamed and civilized the lust of the body; the tournament was the meeting place of both, and it did what it could to impart to the natural Yahoo some qualities of the Houyhnhnm.

Edward IV arranged for "young gentylmen, Henxmen, VI Enfauntes or more, as it shall please the Kinge" to be placed under the tuition of a "Maistyr of Henxmen"

to shew the schooles[19] of urbanitie and nourture of Englond, to lerne them to ryde clenely and surely; to drawe them also to justes [jousting]; to lerne them were theyre harneys [to teach them how to wear their equipment, armor, etc.]; to have all curtesy in wordes, dedes and degrees [i.e., to know who ranks above or below whom, as Griselda did in *The Clerk's Tale,* welcoming her lord's guests "everich in his degree"]. . . . Moreover to teche them sondry languages, and othyr lerninges vertuous, to harping, to pype, sing, daunce, and with other honest and temperate behaviour and patience . . . and eche of them to be used to that thinge of vertue that he shall be moste apt to lerne [i.e., to be encouraged in any personal talent], with remembraunce dayly of Goddes servyce accustumed. This maistyr sittith in the halle, next unto these Henxmen . . . to have his respecte unto theyre demeanynges [attend to their behavior], and to theyre communication [conversation]. . . .

The best results of such a system can be seen in Chaucer's Knight and Squire—and, I think, in Chaucer too.

Courtesy, it will be noticed, is the first thing to be stressed in this schedule of breeding, after

[19] Scholars?

the military essential of horsemanship. Courtesy is behavior proper to a court; and the masters in courtesy fixed their standards by the highest court they knew of, which was the court of heaven. That was the court, they claimed, in which courtesy had its origin:

> Clerkys that canne the scyens seuene,
> Seys that curtasy came fro heuen
> When gabryell owre lady grette,
> And elyzabeth with here mette.
> All vertus be closyde in curtasy,
> An alle vyces in vilony.

[Learned men that know the seven sciences say that courtesy came from Heaven when Gabriel greeted Our Lady and Elizabeth met with her. All virtues are included in courtesy, and all vices in rusticity.[20]]

(Babees Book)

Of all English poets, Geoffrey Chaucer is the most courteous to those who read or listen to him; he seems ever-conscious of our presence and charmed to be in such perceptive company. He never threatens or alarms us, as Milton can, intent upon his great theme; nor does he ignore us, as Wordsworth can, intent upon himself. He addresses his readers as if he could wish for none better, he exchanges experiences with them, consults them, and begs them not to take offense at what he is about to say, touching his show of courtesy with an elegant but ironic wit:

> But first I pray yow, of youre curteisye,
> That ye n'arette[21] it nat my vileynye,
> Thogh that I pleynly speke in this mateere,
> To telle yow hir wordes and hir cheere,
>   . . .
> Whoso shal telle a tale after a man,
> He moot reherce as ny as evere he kan
> Everich a word, if it be in his charge,
> Al speke he never so rudeliche and large,
> Or ellis he moot telle his tale untrewe,
> Or feyne thyng, or fynde wordes newe.
> He may nat spare, althogh he were his brother;
> He moot as wel seye o word as another.

Crist spak hymself ful brode[22] in hooly writ,
And wel ye woot no vilenynye is it.

(The General Prologue)

Chaucer learned his manners not only from those with whom he came in contact, but also from cautionary rhymes, of which there survive a great number, specially written for the education of children. They are too long to quote in full, for they enter into details of table manners, right down to versified instructions for the washing of spoons and the laying of cloths, freely intermingled with moral advice:

> . . . Loke thyne hondis be wasshe clene,
> That no fylthe on thy nayles be sene.
> Take thou no mete tylle grace be seyde,
> And tylle thou see alle thyng arayede . . .
> And at thy mete, yn the begynnyng,
> Loke on pore men that thow thynk,
> For the fulle wombe without any faylys
> Wot fulle lytyl what the hungery aylys.[23]
> Ete not thy mete so hastely,
> Abyde and ete esily . . .

(The Lytylle Childrnes Lytil Boke or
Edyllys be, in Babees Book)

Perhaps the best of these poems is the one called The Babees Book; it is addressed to children of the blood royal and, like other poems in this vein, gives precise instructions how to behave:

> Youre heede, youre hande, your feet, hold yee in
>   reste
> Nor thurhe clowying your flesshe loke yee nat Rent;[24]
> Lene to no poste whils that ye stande present
> Byfore your lorde . . .

And so forth. It ends thus:

> And, swete children, for whos love now I write,
> I yow beseche withe verrey lovande herte,
> To knowe this book that yee sette your delyte;
> And myhtefulle god, that suffred peynes smerte,
> In curtesye he make yow so experte,
> That thurhe your nurture and youre governaunce
> In lastynge blysse yee mowe your self avaunce!

---

[20] Vilony is a difficult word to translate. It is here intended to mean a condition of primitive rustic malice, ignorance, and crudity, to be presumed of a countryman in a savage, semianimal state. Villanus means someone living in the wilds, as opposed to civis, a city dweller versed in "urbanitie" (urbs = a city).

[21] Impute it not.

[22] Very broadly.

[23] For the full stomach, without fail, knows very little of what the hungry one is suffering.

[24] See that you do not tear yourself by scratching.

In opening a window upon the Middle Ages, there is always the danger that it may turn into a stained glass window. Nevertheless, I am forced by all these cautionary verses to believe that the reason for being courteous was a religious reason, namely, that it was pleasing to God and would advance your soul; it was the application of Christianity to social behavior, a practical way of learning to love your neighbor as yourself. Manners makyth Man.

The simple piety of this approach to courtesy was no doubt dinned into the little bourgeois boy from the moment he entered the Ulster household. Although there were rules of thumb for courtesy, the underlying theory had been worked out by the philosophers and poets. Indeed, when he grew up, Chaucer himself, as we shall see, made a significant contribution to it.

The problem was one with which the age was profoundly concerned. What is nobility? How does one become noble? Has it to do with wealth or heredity?

> Whan Adam dalf and Eve span
> Who was tho the gentilman?

This watchword of the Peasants' Revolt had come to them (though they knew it not) from Dante, who had devoted an entire treatise to the subject:

> If Adam himself was noble, we are all noble, and if he was base, we are all base. (*Convivio*, IV, xv)

Dante was arguing that nobility was not inherited. In this he was echoing Boethius, who some eight hundred years before had said:

> . . . yif thou ne have no gentilesse of thiself . . . foreyn gentilesse ne maketh thee nat gentil.
> (*De consolatione philosophie*, III, vi, translated by Chaucer)

Nor, said Dante, had nobility anything to do with wealth. It was wholly a matter of virtue, he argued, following Aristotle in his argument:

> . . . this word "nobleness" means the perfection in each thing of its own proper nature . . . everything is most perfect when it touches and reaches its own proper virtue . . . So the straight path leads us to look for this definition . . . by way of the fruits; which are moral and intellectual virtues whereof this our nobleness is the seed. . . .
> (*Convivio*, IV, xvi)

Chaucer had read, and alludes to, this discussion in the *Convivio*; but in giving his own account of "gentillesse" (or, as we would say, of "nobility") he appeals to higher authority than Dante or Aristotle. To be "gentil," he says, is to imitate Christ, for that is the perfection of our proper natures:

> But, for ye speken of swich gentillesse
> As is descended out of old richesse,
> That therfore sholden ye be gentil men,
> Swich arrogance is nat worth an hen.
> Looke who that is moost vertuous alway,
> Pryvee and apert,[25] and moost entendeth ay
> To do the gentil dedes that he kan;
> Taak hym for the grettest gentil man.
> Crist wole we clayme of hym our gentillesse,
> Nat of oure eldres for hire old richesse.
> (*The Wife of Bath's Tale*)

This, the root of all things, was for Chaucer the root from which the flowers of charity and courtesy both sprang. And, like sainthood, they might be met in every rank of life. The rough-mouthed Host himself was capable of it:

> . . . and with that word he sayde,
> As curteisly as it had been a mayde,
> "My lady Prioresse, by youre leve,
> So that I wiste I sholde yow nat greve,
> I wolde demen that ye tellen sholde
> A tale next, if so were that ye wolde.
> Now wol ye vouche sauf, my lady deere?"

But the finest figure of courtesy in *The Canterbury Tales* is the Knight. Chaucer was very careful to make this noble figure as realistic as any of his rogues; half the details of his career, as it is epitomized in *The General Prologue*, were fresh in Chaucer's mind from the Scrope-Grosvenor trial of 1386, in the course of which the Scrope family, bearing the disputed arms (*azure a bend or*), had been seen in "the great sea," at Satalye, at Alexandria, in Spain, Prussia, and Lithuania (Lettowe). All these place names occur in *The General Prologue*, written in the

---

[25] In private and public.

same year, in the description of the Knight's military career. Nothing said of him could have sounded more likely or authentic to Chaucer's first hearers; his "character" would have sounded equally so, formed as it was on the principles of Christian courtesy dinned into everyone day in and day out from childhood. The entire knightly caste had been brought up that way for some two centuries, and was to be brought up so for at least a century more.

Chaucer's Knight is the embodiment of a whole way of life, a creation whose importance I cannot measure or state; it is the first image of the idea of a gentleman in the language that has given that idea to the world. Chaucer's Knight is to his Plowman as a fourteenth-century cathedral is to a fourteenth-century parish church, and all four of them were the products of the same great style and civilization.

Many things are mocked in Chaucer, but never courtesy; it was the great ideal of his age, upheld by every writer. The poet of *Sir Gawain* builds his poem upon it, to maintain in honor the court of Arthur and the order of chivalry. If the idea was, in its origins, aristocratic, it spread outward and downward through society to a universal acceptance, so that the peasant Langland could think and speak of the Incarnation as the courtesy of Christ.

COURTIER–SOLDIER–SCHOLAR–POET

The courtier's, soldier's, scholar's eye,
tongue, sword . . .
William Shakespeare, *Hamlet*

LIKE many another henxman before and since, Chaucer was presently sent to the wars. It was a foul campaign, bitterly cold, utterly inept, a military fiasco; but it had one important result: it struck a blow for civilization by putting the young genius into direct touch with France and its poetry. For Chaucer's luck held; he was taken prisoner almost at once. We get a glimpse of this over his shoulder, as it were, for he tells us about it in the Scrope-Grosvenor trial already mentioned; he was one among the many witnesses. Indeed, so many and so distinguished were those called on to give evidence, a *Who's*

Who for 1386 could easily be compiled from them. Chaucer deposed:

GEFFRAY CHAUCER ESQUIER del age de xl ans & plus armeez p xxvii ans pduct pr la ptie de mons Richard Lescrop jurrez & examinez demandez si lez armeez dazure ove un bende dor appteignent ou deyvent appteigner au dit mons Richard du droit & de heritage, dist q oil qar il lez ad veu estre armeez en Fraunce devant la ville de Retters . . . & . . . p tout le dit viage tanq le dit Geffrey estoit pris. . . .

[Geoffrey Chaucer Esquire, of the age of forty years and more, having borne arms for twenty-seven years, produced by Sir Richard Le Scrope's party, sworn and examined, asked if the arms of azure with a bend or belonged or should belong to the said Sir Richard by right and inheritance. Said that yes, for he had seen them being armed in France before the town of Retters (probably Rhetel, near Rheims) . . . and . . . during the whole campaign when the said Geoffrey was taken prisoner . . .] (*The Scrope and Grosvenor Roll,* Vol. I, edited by Sir N. H. Nicolas, 1879).

His captivity did not last long; he was no Flemish burgher only fit to have his throat cut, but a negotiable prize. On 1 March 1360, the king paid £16 toward his ransom. It is an old joke among the biographers of Chaucer that this was slightly less than he paid to ransom Sir Robert de Clinton's charger.

From then on, Chaucer led three interweaving kinds of life: a courtier's, a scholar's, and a poet's. Some chronological shape can be given to at least the first of these, the events of which help to date some of his poems, and the accessions of strength, style, and subject to be discerned in them. Many are the subjects he handles; we have already touched upon one, the idea of a gentleman, and I mean to restrict myself in this essay to two more (his greatest, I think) for somewhat detailed consideration, rather than attempt in so small a space to touch on every aspect of his genius. The subjects I have chosen are love and men and women; but before I may come to them, there is the outline of a triple life to be sketched.

For the next seven years there is no record of Chaucer as a courtier, save that he carried letters for the king to Calais at least once. But his poet's life was beginning; he was at work on a translation of the *Roman de la rose,* transplanting an aristocratic and French philosophy of love and a French way of poetry to England. He was also engaged in formal studies at the Inner Temple, if we may believe a late tradition reported by Thomas Speght in his edition of Chaucer (1598), which also asserts that he was "fined two shillings for beatinge a Franciscane Fryer in fletestrete."

Chaucer was growing to manhood; all of a sudden we find him married to a lady-in-waiting to Queen Philippa, perhaps her goddaughter, Philippa de Roet; she became Philippa Chaucer in 1366. Were they in love? We do not know; he has left us no poem to her, though he once refers to her in jest. He compares her voice awakening him in the mornings to the scream of an eagle (*The House of Fame*).

In 1369, Queen Philippa died; the Chaucers went into service with Blanche, duchess of Lancaster, first wife of John of Gaunt. With that began (if it had not begun even earlier) the firm friendship and steady patronage that the duke gave Chaucer ever after. Philippa Chaucer's sister, Catherine, was to become the governess of the duke's children, then his mistress, and at last his wife; thus the duke ended brother-in-law to the poet.

If the duke did much for Chaucer, Chaucer did more for him. He made him a central and romantic figure in his first masterpiece, *The Book of the Duchess*, an elegy on the lady Blanche, who also died in 1369.

It is the first elegy in the English language, drenched in a leisured melancholy that begins with a dream and moves out into a great forest, to the sound of far-off hunting horns; under a tree the poet meets a sorrowful figure in black, singing a lament for his dead lady. It is John of Gaunt, mourning the loss of Blanche, his wife. Though the poem is an elegy, it is imagined as a love story; narrative instinct and a feeling for sexual passion (let it take what form it may) are things we learn to expect in Chaucer. This slow and dreamy poem keeps the memory of Blanche in her living grace, heroine of a tale of courtship and untimely death; the courtier and rhetor has put forth all his young art for his patron and sometime patroness.

Chaucer's career as a man of affairs was now beginning; he was being used as something between a king's messenger and a royal nuncio to France in 1370. But the great events of this kind were his missions to Italy in 1372 and 1378, for it was from these that his poetry took much of its greatest strength.

It is worth pausing on the voyage of 1372; Chaucer went to Genoa and Florence *in nuncio regis in secretis negociis*. He was away for six months, and it is a reasonable conjecture (doubted, however, by some scholars) that he spent a part of them on a private poetical pilgrimage of his own, to visit Petrarch, the most famous living poet of the day, in Padua. It would have been a rough journey, a hundred and fifty miles off course across the Apennines in the cold and windy month of March, through a war-stricken countryside. But all that would have been nothing to a young poet (he was in his early thirties) eager to snatch a chance of meeting the greatest literary figure of his time.

What prompts readers to believe that he did are the lines that Chaucer was later to put into the mouth of the Clerk of Oxford as he broaches the tale of Griselda:

> I wol yow telle a tale which that I
> Lerned at Padowe of a worthy clerk,
> As preved by his wordes and his werk.
> He is now deed and nayled in his cheste,
> I prey to God so yeve his soule reste!
> Fraunceys Petrak, the lauriat poete,
> Highte this clerk, whos rethorike sweete
> Enlumyned al Ytaille of poetrie,
>
>   . . .
>
> (*The Clerk's Prologue*)

Now it is a question whether what an imaginary character says in imagined circumstances is evidence of anything that happened to his imaginer in the actual world. So many authors can be shown to have used their own lives to create the lives of their characters that it is not unreasonable to believe that Chaucer did so on this occasion, that he had indeed heard the story of Griselda from Petrarch's lips and recorded the occasion in this oblique manner. The text of the tale, from which he came to fashion his own version, must have been subsequently acquired by him in some other way, for its date has been established as June 1374, the year of Petrarch's death. For all these possibilities, we have no proof that the two poets ever met, and it may be wisest to say, with the Sage of Cambridge:

Wovon man nicht sprechen kann, darüber muss man schweigen.[26]

In between these Italian journeys Chaucer was promoted; he became comptroller of the customs and subsidies of wools, skins, and tanned hides in London, and had to keep the books in his own fair hand.[27] It was a busy life, and all his recreation was to read:

> For when thy labour doon al ys,
> And hast mad alle thy rekenynges,
> In stede of reste and newe thyngs,
> Thou goost hom to thy hous anoon;
> And, also domb as any stoon,
> Thou sittest at another book
> Tyl fully daswed ys thy look,[28]
>
> . . .
>
> (*The House of Fame*)

So spoke the admonishing eagle (with a voice like his wife's); and what the bird said need not surprise us, for Chaucer read enormously—smatteringly, perhaps, but rememberingly. Almost everything that he read seems to have left its trace upon his poetry, for he delighted in allusion and quotation (whether acknowledged or not) from his favorite authors. He drew easily on the Latin classics: Ovid, Vergil, Statius, Boethius; he was at home in the poetry of France: Deguilleville, Machault, Froissart, Deschamps, and the authors of the *Roman de la rose*. In Italian he was a reader of Dante and of Petrarch; above all he had come to know at least two of Boccaccio's poems, *Filostrato* and *Teseide*. Of these he made two of his own noblest works, *Troilus and Criseyde* and *The Knight's Tale*.

Chaucer was also a considerable student of the sciences, especially of astronomy and mathematics; he was widely read in medicine, psychology, and other natural sciences, including the pseudo science of alchemy. His theology he did not so readily parade, though there is an amusing passage on God's uses for fiends in *The Friar's Tale*. He read Saint Jerome and Saint Bernard, and could quote from almost every book in the Bible and the Apocrypha. Though he may not have been the most learned, he was perhaps the most widely read man of his day; he seems never to have lost the habit and delight of reading:

> On bokes for to rede I me delyte, . . .
> (*The Prologue to The Legend of Good Women*)

There is a passage in Boswell's *Life of Johnson* describing the special powers of mind enjoyed by the doctor; they describe Chaucer's equally well:

> . . . His superiority over other learned men consisted chiefly in what may be called the art of thinking, the art of using his mind; a certain continual power of seizing the useful substance of all that he knew and exhibiting it in a clear and forcible manner; so that knowledge, which we often see to be no better than lumber in men of dull understanding, was, in him, true, evident and actual wisdom. His moral precepts are practical; for they are drawn from an intimate acquaintance with human nature. His maxims carry conviction; for they are founded on the basis of common sense, and a very attentive and minute survey of real life. . . .

It is not surprising that Boswell adds:

> His mind was so full of imagery that he might have been perpetually a poet.

To return to Chaucer's life as a courtier: he had had a windfall in the customs in 1376; he caught a man named John Kent evading duty on an export of wool to Dordrecht, and the culprit was fined for it to the tune of £71 4s. 6d. The whole of this sum (worth £2,000 or £3,000 in modern money) was paid to Chaucer as a reward. He was becoming almost affluent. Foreign missions continued now and then to come his way, as well as civil appointments; in 1382 he was made comptroller of petty customs; in 1385 he was allowed to appoint a deputy and was made a justice of the peace. In October of the following year, he sat in Parliament at Westminster as knight of the shire for Kent.

Then, suddenly, in 1386, fortune deserted him:

---

[26] Ludwig Wittgenstein, *Tractatus Logico-Philosophicus*: "What one cannot speak about, one has to keep quiet about."

[27] And a fair hand it was, if D. J. Price is right in conjecturing that a late fourteenth-century manuscript, *The Equatorie of the Planetis*, brought to light by him at Peterhouse, Cambridge, is a Chaucer holograph.

[28] Till thy look is fully dazed.

For whan men trusteth hire, thanne wol she faille,
And covere hire brighte face with a clowde.
(The Monk's Tale)

John of Gaunt was out of the country; and Chaucer, deprived of his patron, was deprived of his offices. He must live on his pension and on his savings until better times. In the next year Philippa died; he was now a widower with nothing to do. If this was sad for him, it was lucky for us; he began to compose *The Canterbury Tales*.

To take brief stock of Chaucer's career as a writer up to the time of his wife's death, it had produced several long or fairly long poems, ambitiously different from anything ever written before in English, as well as a prose translation of Boethius' *Consolation of Philosophy* and a work of instruction in mathematics—*A Treatise on the Astrolabe*—for "Lyte Lowys, my sone." There is no agreement among scholars about the dating, and little agreement about the order in which his poems were composed. We may be certain that *The Book of the Duchess* was written in 1369–1370 and *The Legend of Good Women* in 1385–1386; it is also sure that *Troilus and Criseyde* and such parts of his translation of the *Roman de la rose* as have survived were written before *The Legend of Good Women*, because it mentions them; it also mentions *The Parliament of Fowls*, "al the love of Palamon and Arcite" (later *The Knight's Tale*), the translation of Boethius, and the *Life of Saint Cecilia* (later *The Second Nun's Tale*).

The Canterbury Tales (it is agreed) were begun as such toward 1386–1387, and remained Chaucer's "work in progress" until the end of his life, never completed. It would seem that toward the end he tired of writing:

For elde, that in my spirit dulleth me,
Hath of endyting al the subtilte
Wel nygh bereft out of my remembraunce; . . .
(The Complaint of Venus)

We need not, however, take this confession too seriously; it had always been Chaucer's way to make fun of himself.

Of his longer poems it only remains to mention *The House of Fame*, of which it can only be said with certainty that it was written after Chaucer had read the *Divine Comedy*; that is, at some time after his first or second visit to Italy.

His very last poem, perhaps, was addressed on the accession (1399) of the new king—*The Complaint of Chaucer to His Purse*:

I am so sory, now that ye been lyght; . . .

It need not be taken too tragically; the poem is almost as light as the purse.

According to the inscription on his tomb, put there by a Tudor admirer, Nicholas Brigham, in 1556, Chaucer died on 25 October 1400. He was buried in Westminster Abbey; it is not known why. Saint Margaret's, Westminster, was his parish church, and that would have been his natural resting-place; perhaps they put him in the Abbey because he had been clerk of the works, or perhaps he slipped in by some oversight when the tumult of the new reign dwindled to a calm, much as George III, according to Lord Byron, slipped into heaven. It was, anyhow, not Chaucer's fame as a poet that made him head of the Poets' Corner; it was not until the late sixteenth century that a corner in the Abbey began to belong to the poets.

THE POET OF LOVE

For I, that God of Loves servantz serve, . . .
Troilus and Criseyde, I

FROM the beginning, as we have seen, Chaucer revealed himself as a love poet and a teller of tales; to commemorate the Duchess Blanche he imagined a story about her death, told by her mourning lover in a dream forest.

Now, in truth, this "lover" represented John of Gaunt, Blanche's widower; they had been married ten years. In the poem, however, they are seen as courtly lovers and the "Man in Black" voices his desire on that ideal courtly plane, in full troubadour style:

"To love hir in my beste wyse,
To do hir worship and the servise
That I koude thoo, be my trouthe,
Withoute feynynge outher slouthe[29]; . . ."
(The Book of the Duchess)

[29] That I then could, by my truth, without pretence or sloth.

Troilus was later to declare his passion in the same key:

> "And I to ben youre verray, humble, trewe,
> Secret, and in my paynes pacient,
> And evere mo desiren fresshly newe
> To serve, and ben ay ylike diligent, . . ."
> (*Troilus and Criseyde,* III)

For a long time, true to the convention, the "Man in Black" dares not confess his love; and when he at last summons the courage to say the hard word, he uses the favorite in the whole vocabulary of courtly love, mercy:

> "I seyde 'mercy!' and no more."

He is refused; it is only after a conventional year of "service" that she understands and is willing to reward his sufferings:

> "So when my lady knew al this,
> My lady yaf me al hooly
> The noble yifte of hir mercy,
> Savynge hir worship, by al weyes,—"[30]

All that was young and romantic in Chaucer had swallowed the dream allegories of France and the philosophy of courtly love in long draughts from the *Roman de la rose,* the *Fontaine amoureuse,* the *Jugement du roi de Behaingne,* and other poems of the sort; and he was trying to do extreme honor to this ordinary Christian marriage by representing it as an idealized amour. All the conventions are beautifully there—the golden hair, the gentle eyes, the neck like a tower of ivory, the long body, the white hands, the round breasts, the tints of her cheek:

> "But thus moche dar I sayn, that she
> Was whit, rody, fressh, and lyvely hewed,
> And every day hir beaute newed."

It was this way of imagining love and of writing poetry that Chaucer brought back from France. Much has been written about "courtly love" and of its sudden appearance in the courts of the nobles of Languedoc in the eleventh and twelfth centuries; some have explained it as a degenerated form of Plato's ideal affection, passed on through Arab hands to France from Africa and, in the process, heterosexualized and allowed the gratification of the body. Be that as it may, this elegant, illicit amorism took all Christendom for its province; and our world began to ring with ballades, rondels, virelays, aubades, and complaints such as the "Man in Black" was singing when Chaucer came upon him in the dream forest.

If in his youth Chaucer thought it a compliment to a bereaved husband to speak of his wife as if she had been a mistress, he came ultimately to change his perspective; his maturest expression of courtly love, *Troilus and Criseyde,* ends in the knowledge of its insufficiency.

Troilus and Criseyde was the greatest yield of Chaucer's Italian journeys; he learned from Boccaccio how to abandon dream and build a story of the waking world with clarity and realism, yet retain within it the delicacies of feeling and convention that prevailed in the visionary, allegorical world of the *Roman de la rose;* the new poem was undergirt by the philosophy of Boethius, who taught Chaucer the shape of tragedy and filled him with thoughts of fortune and free will. For the lovers and their mentor Pandarus, however free they may seem in a thousand decisions, and indecisions, move to the calls of courtly love as surely as they move under fatal stars. On the way to their still-distant doom, they pass through an ecstasy of high sexual passion; and Chaucer rises effortlessly to the great poetry of their long night of first union, which I do not know where to find equaled, except in Shakespeare, for intimacy, tenderness, and noble quality. He reveals himself as engaged by the love he is describing:

> O blisful nyght, of hem so longe isought,
> How blithe unto hem bothe two thow weere!
> Why nad I swich oon with my soule ybought,
> Ye, or the lesste joie that was theere?[31]

Yet he retains his typical attitude of spectator:

This Troilus in armes gan hire streyne,
And seyde, "O swete, as evere mot I gon,[32]

---

[30] My lady gave me all wholly the noble gift of her mercy, saving her honor, of course.

[31] Why had I not bought one such night at the price of my soul, yes, or the least joy that was there?
[32] "As ever I may go (thrive)."

Now be ye kaught, now is ther but we tweyne!
Now yeldeth yow, for other bote is non!"[33]
To that Criseyde answerede thus anon,
"Ne hadde I er now, my swete herte deere,
Ben yold, ywis, I were now nought heere!"[34]

O, sooth is seyd, that heled for to be
As of a fevre, or other gret siknesse,
Men moste drynke, as men may ofte se,
Ful bittre drynke; and for to han gladnesse,[35]
Men drynken ofte peyne and gret distresse;
I mene it here, as for this aventure,
That thorugh a peyne hath founden al this cure.

And now swetnesse semeth more swete,
That bitternesse assaied was byforn;
For out of wo in blisse now they flete;
Non swich they felten syn that they were born.[36]
Now is this bet than bothe two be lorn.
For love of God, take every womman heede
To werken thus, if it comth to the neede.

Criseyde, al quyt from every drede and tene,[37]
As she that juste cause hadde hym to triste,
Made hym swich feste, it joye was to seene,[38]
Whan she his trouthe and clene entente wiste;
And as aboute a tree, with many a twiste,
Bytrent and writh the swote wodebynde,[39]
Gan ech of hem in armes other wynde.

And as the newe abaysed nyghtyngale,
That stynteth first whan she bygynneth to synge,
Whan that she hereth any herde tale,
Or in the hegges any wyght stirynge,
And after siker doth hire vois out rynge,
Right so Criseyde, whan hire drede stente,[40]
Opned hire herte, and tolde hym hire entente.

. . .

Hire armes smale, hir streghte bak and softe,
Hire sydes longe, flesshly, smothe, and white
He gan to stroke, and good thrift bad ful ofte
Hir snowisshe throte, hire brestes round and lite:[41]

Thus in this hevene he gan hym to delite,
And therwithal a thousand tyme hire kiste,
That what to don, for joie unnethe he wiste.[42]

. . .

"Benigne Love, thow holy bond of thynges,
Whoso wol grace, and list the nought honouren,[43]
Lo, his desir wol fle withouten wynges."
                                        (*Troilus and Criseyde*, III)

But from this exaltation the poem has to turn; the fatal moment must come, the lovers must part. Once parted from her lover, Cryseyde lacks the strength to return to him; lacks the strength to resist Diomed; is faithless. Chaucer does not reproach her; he says he would excuse her, "for routhe," that is, for pity. At last Troilus is killed by the fierce Achilles.

Swich fyn hath, lo, this Troilus for love!
Swich fyn hath al his grete worthinesse!
Swich fyn hath his estat real above,[44]
Swich fyn his lust, swich fyn hath his noblesse!
Swich fyn hath false worldes brotelnesse!

It is the insecurity of human love in a world ruled by chance that made Chaucer see the brittleness of the courtly code. Fortune can untie the holy bond of things in human affairs; and if we seek a lasting love, we must look elsewhere, to a region beyond fortune's power:

O younge, fresshe folkes, he or she,
In which that love up groweth with youre age,
Repeyreth hom fro worldly vanyte,
And of youre herte up casteth the visage
To thilke God that after his ymage
Yow made,[45] and thynketh al nys but a faire
This world, that passeth soone as floures faire.

And loveth hym, the which that right for love
Upon a crois, oure soules for to beye
First starf, and roos, and sit in hevene above;
For he nyl falsen no wight, dar I seye,
That wol his herte al holly on hym leye.
And syn he best to love is, and most meeke,
What nedeth feynede loves for to seke?

---

[33] "There is no other remedy."
[34] "Had I not been yielded before now, my dear, sweet heart, indeed I would not now be here."
[35] To have gladness.
[36] None such they felt since they were born.
[37] Quite free of fear and distress.
[38] Made such a feast (welcome) for him.
[39] The sweet honeysuckle engirdles and writhes about.
[40] And as the newly abashed nightingale, that stops, as she begins to sing, when she hears any shepherd speak, and afterwards rings her voice out, just so Criseyde, when her fear ceased.
[41] And begged a blessing on her snowy throat, her breasts, round and small.

[42] He hardly knew what to do for joy.
[43] Whoso desires grace, and cares not to honor thee.
[44] Such an ending had his royal estate above (the earth, after death).
[45] Repair home (i.e., to heaven) from wordly vanity and cast up the countenance of your heart to that God that made you after His image.

[And love him who, exactly because of love, first died upon a cross, to buy our souls, and (then) rose and sits in heaven above; for he will not prove false to any, I dare affirm, that will wholly lay his heart upon him. And since he is the best and meekest to love, what is the need to seek a pretended love?]

(*Troilus and Criseyde*, V)

What the court held to be love, the church held to be sin. It had a contrary love system of its own. Of absolutely sovereign value in the church's scale of sex was virginity; there was no higher kind of life than to be a virgin for the love of God. Saint Jerome expressed the idea in one of his startling epigrams:

Nuptiae terram replent, virginitas paradisum.

[Marriages replenish the earth, virginity replenishes Paradise.]   (*Epistola adversus Jovinianum*)

The preeminence of virginity is asserted by Chaucer in *The Parson's Tale*:

Another synne of Leccherie is to bireve a mayden of hir maydenhede; for he that so dooth, certes, he casteth a mayden out of the hyeste degree that is in this present lyf . . . And forther over, sooth is that hooly ordre [holy orders] is chief of al the tresorie of God, and his especial signe and mark of chastitee . . . which that is the moost precious lyf that is.

It is again asserted by the Prioress, in her apostrophe to the martyred chorister:

O martir, sowded to virginitee,[46]
Now maystow syngen, folwynge evere in oon[47]
The white Lamb celestial—quod she—
Of which the grete evaungelist, Seint John,
In Pathmos wroot, which seith that they that goon
Biforn this Lamb, and synge a song al newe,
That nevere, flesshly, wommen they ne knewe.[48]

(*The Prioress's Tale*)

It is even asserted by the Wife of Bath.:

Virginitee is greet perfeccion
(*The Wife of Bath's Prologue*)

And again:

[46] O martyr, soldered to virginity.
[47] Continually following.
[48] That never knew women after the manner of the flesh.

Crist was a mayde, and shapen as a man,
And many a seint, sith that the world bigan;
Yet lyvved they evere in parfit chastitee.
I nyl envye no virginitee.

Next to virginity, the church esteemed the condition of wedded chastity, which Shakespeare was later to celebrate allegorically in the *Threnos* of his most metaphysical poem, *The Phoenix and the Turtle*; it is a condition to which the Wife of Bath refers, with approval, as

continence with devotion . . .

And one of the first stories Chaucer ever wrote, the story of Saint Cecilia (later *The Second Nun's Tale*), celebrates her sanctity in having persuaded her young and noble husband, on their wedding night and forever after, to forgo the consummation of his love. The same idea is at the back of Chaucer's mind when, in *The Man of Law's Tale*, he feels it incumbent on him to defend his holy-hearted heroine, Constance, for yielding her body to her husband. The passage rings in my ear with a note of comedy; but I am not sure if Chaucer intended it so, for it comes from his most pious period as a writer:

They goon to bedde, as it was skile and right;[49]
For thogh that wyves be full hooly thynges,
They moste take in pacience at nyght
Swiche manere necessaries as been plesynges
To folk that han ywedded hem with rynges,
And leye a lite hir hoolynesse aside,
As for the tyme,—it may no bet bitide.[50]

Griselda is another chaste and patient wife; her story, enormously popular in the Middle Ages, found its fullest eloquence in Chaucer's telling of it. It was an earlyish work of his; and when he came back in later life to shape it as *The Clerk's Tale* for inclusion in *The Canterbury Tales*, he modified the effect of this marriage sermon by adding an ironic tailpiece:

It were ful harde to fynde now-a-dayes
In al a toun Grisildis thre or two; . . .

Still, virginity and chastity and married love of the kind approved by the church were approved

[49] As it was reasonable and right.
[50] And lay aside her holiness a little for the moment, one can do no better.

in these and other of Chaucer's poems, and with no less poetry than he had celebrated courtly love. It is true that there is no sexual ecstasy recorded of the unions of Griselda and of Constance with their husbands; but then, sexual ecstasy, even in marriage, was held suspect:

> And for that many man weneth that he may nat synne for no likerousnesse that he dooth with his wyf, certes that opinion is false.
>
> *(The Parson's Tale)*

Over against what the church taught and what the troubadours taught about women, there were the opinions of the celibate misogynists. They reached in a long tradition from Saint Jerome to Walter Map, and the extremes to which they went in vilifying the fair sex almost outdistanced the extremes of the gynecolaters in the opposite direction; as I have said before, it was an age of extremes.

The Wife of Bath knew all about these scholars, the children of Mercury, the natural enemies of the children of Venus:

> The clerk, whan he is oold, and may noght do
> Of Venus werkes worth his olde sho,
> Thanne sit he doun, and writ in his dotage
> That wommen kan nat keepe hir mariage!

But, for all her low opinion of them as lovers, she admired them as debaters, and put on the whole armor of their abuse to subdue her first three husbands; her method was to anticipate the worst that could be said of women—and here she helped herself freely to Saint Jerome—and fling it back scornfully at her men:

> Thou seist to me it is a greet meschief
> To wedde a povre womman, for costage;
> And if that she be riche, of heigh parage,[51]
> Thanne seistow that it is a tormentrie
> To soffre hire pride and hire malencolie.
> And if that she be fair, thou verray knave,
> Thou seyst that every holour wol hire have;[52]
>   . . .
> And if that she be foul, thou seist that she
> Coveiteth every man that she may se,
> For as a spanyel she wol on hym lepe,
> Til that she fynde som man hire to chepe.[53]

[51] High lineage.   [52] That every lecher will have her.
[53] Some man to make a bid for her.

> Ne noon so grey goos goth ther in the lake
> As, seistow, wol been withoute make.[54]
>   . . .
> Thus seistow, lorel,[55] whan thow goost to bedde;
> And that no wys man nedeth for to wedde,
> Ne no man that entendeth unto hevene.
> With wilde thonder-dynt and firy leven
> Moote thy welked nekke be tobroke![56]

All this, and much more, that she had to say came, almost word for word, from Saint Jerome's *Epistola adversus Jovinianum* and from other "celibate" sources.

She met her match in her fifth husband, a pretty-legged lad half her age called Jankyn (Johnnykin), with whom she was reckless enough to fall in love; this lost her the initial advantage and it was soon he, not she, who was studying the misogynists; they became his favorite reading.

> He hadde a book that gladly, nyght and day,
> For his desport he wolde rede always;
>   . . .
> At which book he lough alway ful faste.

It was a composite volume full of anecdote, proverb, and abuse against women; and the Wife gives us long extracts from it. Here, for instance, is an anecdote borrowed from Walter Map:

> Thanne tolde he me how oon Latumyus
> Compleyned unto his felawe Arrius
> That in his gardyn growed swich a tree
> On which he seyde how that his wyves thre
> Hanged hemself for herte despitus.[57]
> "O leeve brother," quod this Arrius,
> "Yif me a plante of thilke blissed tree,
> And in my gardyn planted shal it bee."

It was in these ways that Chaucer chose to voice the views of the *tertium quid*.

If the wonderful Wife of Bath seems, when we first meet her, to have drawn her philosophy from some Cartesian well of *Copulo ergo sum*, we soon get to know her better and appreciate the complexities of her character; she can hold con-

[54] Will be without a mate.   [55] Thus you say, you wretch.
[56] With a wild thunderbolt and fiery lightning, may your withered neck be dashed in pieces!
[57] Hanged themselves, out of the spite in their hearts.

tradictory beliefs without the slightest inconvenience to herself, such as that virginity is a great perfection and celibacy a thing contemptible. Her bullying methods with her husbands seem at first a matter of mood and idiosyncrasy, but turn out to be employed on principle; and it is this that puts her in a central position in the great sex war of *The Canterbury Tales*. It is fought on the issue "Who is to have the mastery in marriage, husband or wife?"

How she handled her husbands is a lesson to every knowing woman (as she says herself) and to every man about to marry, as Chaucer said in the poem to his friend Bukton, in that momentous situation:

> The Wyf of Bathe I pray yow that ye rede. . . .

In her view, it was right and proper that husbands should submit to their wives; this is not only the moral of her long preamble (the *Prologue* to her tale) but also of the tale itself. The point of the story is to discover what it is that women most wish for, and the surprising answer is:

> "Wommen desiren have sovereyntee
> As wel over hir housbond as hir love,
> And for to been in maistrie hym above."

Women, that is, wish for the same sovereignty over their husbands that they exercise over their lovers—a tall order.

The challenge thus flung down by the Wife of Bath is taken up by the Clerk of Oxford with his tale of patient Griselda and her exemplary obedience to her husband. Other aspects of marriage come before us too: *The Merchant's Tale* of January and May shows what can happen between husband and wife when an old man marries a young girl. *The Shipman's Tale* presents us with the well-known truth that there are always half a dozen things a woman absolutely needs, to keep up with the neighbors, that she cannot very well tell her husband about:

> And well y woot that wommen naturelly
> Desiren thynges sixe as wel as I:
> · · ·
> For his honour, myself for to arraye,
> · · ·

And so she is driven to tell someone else:

> Thanne moot another payen for oure cost,
> Or lene us gold,[58] and that is perilous.

Perhaps the liveliest domestic scene is that between Chanticleer and Pertelote, when with husbandly self-importance he debates the prophetic meaning of a dream he has had that his wife ascribes to constipation.

These are the variations on the theme proposed by the Wife of Bath to which we return for a final statement by the Franklin; his story voices that wise equability and kindliness that is so great an attribute of Chaucer's mind. The Franklin's hero and heroine are married lovers; they had begun their attachment by falling in love in the best courtly manner:

> And many a labour, many a greet emprise[59]
> He for his lady wroghte, er she were wonne.
> · · ·
> But atte last she, for his worthynesse,
> And namely[60] for his meke obeysaunce,
> Hath swich a pitee caught of his penaunce
> That pryvely she fil of his accord
> To take hym for hir housbonde and hir lord,
> Of swich lordshipe as men han over hir wyves.

This fourteenth-century Millamant and her Mirabell had, however, laid down certain provisos and counterprovisos before they agreed to marry; he was to exercise no "maistrie" over her:

> But hire obeye, and folwe hir wyl in al, . . .

And she was to allow him "the name of soveraynetee," so that he should not in public suffer the disgrace of his surrendered authority.

> That wolde he have for shame of his degree.

And, on this happy compromise, the Franklin stops his story for a moment to address the company with a Chaucerian wisdom suiting his sanguine temperament:

> For o thyng, sires, saufly dar I seye,
> That freendes everych oother moot obeye,[61]
> If they wol longe holden compaignye.
> Love wol nat been constreyned by maistrye.

[58] Lend us gold.   [59] Enterprise.   [60] Especially.
[61] Friends must obey one another.

GEOFFREY CHAUCER

Whan maistrie comth, the God of Love anon
Beteth his wynges, and farewel, he is gon!
Love is a thyng as any spirit free.
Wommen, of kynde, desiren libertee,[62]
And nat to been constreyned as a thral;
And so doon men, if I sooth seyen shal.

There was still one other attitude to lovemaking ambient in those times for Chaucer to voice and grace: the attitude of the fabliaux, the low-life oral tales of animal grab[63] that in all ages circulate from person to person, like a limerick. In the typical fabliau, copulation seems to thrive in its cold-blooded way, borne along on strong undercurrents of guilt and hatred. Priests and millers (the most powerful and therefore the most-to-be-humiliated men in the village) are generally the victims; and the very sexuality of the story, which, at one level, they are supposed to enjoy, at another level seems to be a part of their vileness, even of their punishment. The laugh at the end is bitter with triumphant malice.

Chaucer took two such sow's-ear stories and turned them into the silk purses of *The Miller's Tale* and *The Reeve's Tale*. Here, at the bottom of the social scale, the clerical students of Oxford and Cambridge, happy-go-luckies of a saucy sexuality, are seen aping the adulteries of the aristocracy with all the cant of courtly love on their tongues. Nicholas in *The Miller's Tale* woos Alison with

> ". . . Lemman, love me al at ones,
> Or I wol dyen, also God me save!"

It is the argument that Pandarus uses on behalf of Troilus. Absalom, in the same story, goes on his knees (as Troilus did) to receive a kiss. That he got more than he bargained for cured him forever, we are told, of love *par amour*, that is, of courtly love. But Chaucer does more than this to rescue his fabliaux from their beastly dullness. The whole life of the village springs up before us—the rustic conversation, the superstition, the cunning; the impudence and bravado of the young in their gallantries; the rascality of the Miller, the gullibility of the Carpenter; the cottages they live in; and the vivid wenches

[62] Women, by nature, desire liberty.
[63] A children's card game

With buttokes brode, and brestes round and hye

of whose portraits Alison's is the most convincingly fresh and seductive that Chaucer, or anyone else, ever painted.

If, then, we ask ourselves what this "servant of the servants of Love" knew about his masters, and about their Master, a short answer would be that he knew everything; everything that was known and felt on the subject at that time in Christendom. He voiced the whole thought of the Middle Ages, speaking as eloquently for courtly as for Christian love, and as much an expert in marriage as in misogyny; everything came within the power of his pen, right down to the antics of John and Alan, Nicholas and Absalom and their "popelotes." No other English author has a comparable range in such matters. But it is not only a question of range, variety, and subtlety in his art of love; it is the sympathy. Chaucer is all things to all men and women in all their moods and modes of love, able to write as easily of the lowest as of the highest:

O mooder Mayde! O mayde Mooder free!
O bussh unbrent, brennynge in Moyses sighte,
That ravyshedest doun fro the Deitee,
Thurgh thyn humblesse, the Goost that in th'alighte,
Of whose vertu, whan he thyn herete lighte,
Conceyved was the Fadres sapience, . . .

[. . . O bush unburnt, burning in the sight of Moses, thou that didst ravish down, from the Deity, the Spirit that alighted in thee, by thy humbleness; by whose power, when He illumined thy heart, the Sapience of the Father was conceived . . .]

(*The Prioress's Prologue*)

The reason he can do so is that he takes joy in the created world, grasps life affirmatively, and calls nothing that God has made unclean.

MEN AND WOMEN

For the eye altering alters all.
William Blake, *The Mental Traveller*

CHAUCER thought the work of a writer to be something like that of a reaper; and it is with a wondering smile that we hear him say that all

GEOFFREY CHAUCER

the corn of poetry has been reaped already, and that only the gleanings are left for him after the great poets of the past have done their work:

> For wel I wot that folk han here-beforn
> Of makyng ropen, and lad awey the corn;[64]
> And I come after, glenynge here and there,
> And am ful glad if I may fynde en ere[65]
> Of any goodly word that they han left.
> (*The Prologue to The Legend of Good Women*)

The fields that he is thinking of are the fields of "auctoritee," that is, of the ancient writers that he loved so much for their poetry, philosophy, and learning, whence all new learning came:

> For out of olde feldes, as men seyth,
> Cometh al this newe corn from yer to yere,
> And out of olde bokes, in good feyth,
> Cometh al this newe science that men lere.[66]
> (*The Parliament of Fowls*)

But there was another immense field, the field of experience, which Chaucer himself was wont to contrast with "auctoritee." It was the "fair field of folk" of which his great contemporary, Langland, had written, the busy London world of men and women, with whom, whether he was at court or in the customs house, it was his profession and his pleasure to deal.

No one had ever looked at people in the way Chaucer did; it was his eye that altered everything, for it knew what to look for. His was not only an observant, but also an instructed, eye through which he looked out on the world of experience. The instruction had, however, come to him from authority.

There are at least three kinds of books that we can observe directing Chaucer's discovery of human nature: books on rhetoric, books on medicine, and books on astrology. From each of these he learned something that helped to train his eye. To demonstrate this (as I shall now try) is not to offer an explanation of his genius, but to show it at work.

Other men may perhaps have known as much as he about rhetoric, medicine, and astrology; but Chaucer knew how to use his knowledge, how to put his knowledge (so to speak) at the

disposal of his eyes and ears. The result can be seen in the descriptions of the characters in *The General Prologue*.

The rhetoricians were perfectly clear on the subject of how to present a human being; it was a technique or figure known to them as *descriptio*, of which there were at least three equally explicit doctrines current in the Middle Ages. The first was Cicero's.

> Ac personis has res attributas putamus; nomen, naturam, victum, fortunam, habitum, affectionem, studia, consilia, facta, casus, orationes.

> [We hold the following to be the attributes of persons: name, nature, manner of life, fortune, habit, feeling, interests, purposes, achievements, accidents, conversation.] (*De Inventione*, I, xxiv)

As Cicero goes on to paraphrase these eleven attributes, we are able to gloss them, where necessary, as follows:

Name.
Nature. Includes sex, place of origin, family, age, bodily appearance, whether bright or dull, affable or rude, patient or the reverse, and all qualities of mind or body bestowed by nature.
Manner of Life. Includes occupation, trade, or profession, and the character of the person's home life.
Fortune. Includes whether rich or poor, successful or a failure, and rank.
Habit. Includes special knowledge or bodily dexterity won by careful training and practice.
Feeling. A fleeting passion, such as joy, desire, fear, vexation.
Interests. Mental activity devoted to some special subject.
Purposes. Any deliberate plan.
Achievements. What a person is doing, has done, or will do.
Accidents. What is happening to a person, has happened, or will happen.
Conversation. What a person has said, is saying, or will say.

I suppose many readers will agree that the most strikingly described character in *The General Prologue* is that of the Wife of Bath. In some thirty natural, easy lines of seemingly casual observation, she appears in startling completeness. For all that air of unconcern, Chaucer has worked his miracle by remembering his Cicero:

[64] For well I know that folk before now have reaped (the field of) poetry and carried away the corn.
[65] Find an ear (of corn).　　[66] Learn.

GEOFFREY CHAUCER

A good WIF was ther of biside BATHE,   *Nature* (sex, place of origin)
But she was somdel deef, and that was scathe.   (bodily quality)
Of clooth-makyng she hadde swich an haunt,   *Manner of Life* (trade)
She passed hem of Ypres and of Gaunt.   *Habit* (dexterity)
In al the parisshe wif ne was ther noon   *Fortune* (rank)
That to the offrynge bifore hire sholde goon;
And if ther dide, certeyne so wrooth was she,   *Feeling* (vexation)
That she was out of alle charitee.
Hir coverchiefs ful fyne weren of ground;   *Nature* (appearance)
I dorste swere they weyeden ten pound
That on a Sonday weren upon hir heed.
Hir hosen weren of fyn scarlet reed,
Ful streite yteyd, and shoes ful moyste and newe.
Boold was hir face, and fair, and reed of hewe.
She was a worthy womman al hir lyve: *Fortune* (rank)
Housbondes at chirche dore she hadde fyve,   *Manner of Life* (home life)
Withouten oother compaignye in youthe,—
But thereof nedeth nat to speke as nowthe.
And thries had she been at Jerusalem;   *Achievements* (past doings)
She hadde passed many a straunge strem;   and *Accidents*
At Rome she hadde been, and at Boloigne,
In Galice at Seint-Jame, and at Coloigne.
She koude muchel of wandrynge by the weye.   *Habit* (special knowledge)
Gat-tothed was she, soothly for to seye.   *Nature* (bodily quality)
Upon an amblere esily she sat,   *Achievements* (what doing)
Ywympled wel, and on hir heed an hat   *Nature* (appearance)
As brood as is a bokeler or a targe;
A foot-mantel aboute hir hippes large,
And on hir feet a paire of spores sharpe.
In felaweshipe wel koude she laughe and carpe.   *Conversation*
Of remedies of love she knew per chaunce.   *Interests*
For she koude of that art the olde daunce.

The only points demanded by Cicero that are omitted are her name and purposes. We learn later that her name was Alison; as for her purposes, one of them could go without saying—to seek the shrine of Saint Thomas with the other pilgrims. We may perhaps infer another:

> Yblessed be God that I have wedded fyve!
> Welcome the sixte, whan that evere he shal.
> *(The Wife of Bath's Prologue)*

Ciceronian as her portrait is, Cicero cannot claim it all. There is the hint of something learned from Geoffrey de Vinsauf in it, too. Vinsauf's teaching was that a description must start at the top of the head and inch its way downward, detail by detail, to the feet—*poliatur ad unguem*, let it be polished to the toenail. To follow this counsel slavishly would lead to what, in another context, Chaucer calls the "fulsomness of his prolixitee"; but he follows it selectively, beginning with the ten-pound head-dress. His eye is then drawn for an instant from the boldness of her face to her all-too-striking hose, but returns to her face and wimple, glides to her hips, and falls to her spurs.

A third doctrine of *descriptio* was that of Matthieu de Vendôme, who held that a writer must first describe the moral nature and then the physical appearance of his subject. Chaucer moved easily among all these prescriptions, allowing each to point in some direction where the discerning eye could pause, the attentive ear listen. So it comes about that the description of the Prioress in *The General Prologue* begins in the Ciceronian manner (name, sex, profession, social position, special skill, and her prevailing study, "to been estatlich of manere"), then follows Matthieu with an account of her moral sensibilities, her amiable carriage, her charity and tenderness of heart, her charming sentimentality over her pets (which, as a nun, she of course had no business to own), and at last comes to her appearance; here he follows Vinsauf, starting with her wimple and thence to nose, eyes, and mouth, moving downward to the telltale wrist with its ambiguous brooch inscribed *Amor vincit omnia*. Her portrait is a perfect example of how rules obey a genius.

There was also a medical approach to character. Medicine had evolved a theory that the human constitution was fashioned of the four elements: earth, air, fire, and water. Earth had the quality of being cold and dry; air, hot and moist; fire, hot and dry; water, cold and moist. According to the particular proportion and mixture of these elements in the individual man, he was thought to have a predominating "complexion" or temperament. Too earthy, he would be melancholy; too airy, he would be sanguine; too fiery, he would be choleric; too watery, he would be phlegmatic.

To each of these "complexions" or "humors" were attached a number of subsidiary qualities and predispositions, so well known as to be enshrined in popular mnemonic verses, both Latin and English. Here, for instance, is a popular rhyme to remind you what to expect of a sanguine man:

> Or yiftes large,[67] in love hath grete delite,
> Iocunde and gladde, ay of laughyng chiere,
> Of ruddy colour meynt somdel with white;[68]
> Disposed by kynde[69] to be a champioun,
> Hardy I-nough, manly, and bold of chiere.
>   Of the sangwyne also it is a signe
>   To be demure, right curteys, and benynge.
>   (Robbins, *Secular Lyrics of*
>   *the* xivth *and* xvth *Centuries*[70])

The General Prologue tells us that the Franklin was a sanguine man, and that one word is intended to carry all the qualities listed in the rhyme. They fit him very well, not only as we first see him but also as we see him later, during his colloquy with the Squire, and in the tenor of his tale. The Reeve, we are told, was choleric; all that he says and does is in keeping with what medical lore asserted of such men, who were held to be refractory, deceitful, given to anger, full of ruses, lustful, hardy, small and slender, dry of nature, covetous and solemn. Indeed, the

Host rebukes him for solemnity in the prelude to his tale. The Pardoner's moral and physical nature are described in terms from which any doctor (as W. C. Curry[71] has made clear) could at once have diagnosed him as a eunuch from birth, and this fact about him explains much in his subsequent adventures on the pilgrimage. Chaucer helped himself to medical lore in much the way a modern novelist might use his knowledge of Freud or Jung.

Astrology offered yet another approach to the imagining of a character. Curry has also shown that the characters of King Emetrius and King Lycurgus in *The Knight's Tale* are imagined as "personal representatives, in the lists, of the astrological forces" that are involved in the story—namely of Saturn and/or Mars, respectively—and he quotes Ptolemy to show that the description of these kings by Chaucer follows almost exactly the physical details attributed to men born under those planets. Astrology is explicitly invoked by the Wife of Bath to account for the contradictions in her character; they were dictated by the position of the heavenly bodies at her birth:

> For certes, I am al Venerien
> In feelynge, and myn herte is Marcien.
> Venus me yaf my lust, my likerousnesse,
> And Mars yaf me my sturdy hardynesse;
> Myn ascendent was Taur, and Mars therinne.
> Allas! allas! that evere love was synne!
>   (*The Wife of Bath's Prologue*)

Instructed in such ways as these by *auctoritee*, Chaucer looked out with sharpened eyes upon experience, and saw not only how to grasp the essentials of a personality posed for a portrait, but also how to make use of what is latent within a given personality and to draw it forth with a surprising touch of individual or local color. For instance, in *The Miller's Tale*, when the superstitious old carpenter living at Osney, just outside Oxford, peeps into the room of his lodger, Nicholas, to find out what is wrong with him, he sees Nicholas lying gaping on his back on the floor:

> This carpenter to blessen hym bigan,
> And seyde "Help us, seinte Frydeswyde!"

---

[67] Large in his giving.   [68] Mingled somewhat with white.
[69] Disposed by nature.
[70] R. H. Robbins, ed., *Secular Lyrics of the* xivth *and* xvth *Centuries* (London, 1952; 2nd ed., 1955).
[71] W. C. Curry, *Chaucer and the Medieval Sciences.*

In other words, he crossed himself and invoked Saint Frideswide, the local Oxford saint. One can tell that the carpenter was an Oxford man simply from that.

In like manner, in *The Reeve's Tale* the Miller's wife, awakened by the battle between Alan and the Miller, and feeling the sudden weight of her husband's body falling on top of her, cries out:

"Help! hooly croys of Bromeholm" . . .

This relic, the holy cross of Bromeholm, was preserved in East Norfolk, where the Reeve came from. No one else in Chaucer invokes Saint Frideswide or the holy cross of Bromeholm; they are pinpoints of local color latent in the people he was creating, and perceived by him.

This power of seeing the implications in a character or a situation, so as to give a sudden twist or flavor, depth or tone, to his tale is one of the important things that make Chaucer immeasurably superior as a storyteller to his friend and contemporary John Gower, and indeed to all writers of English narrative poetry. The perceptiveness of which I am speaking is continuously, sensitively present throughout *Troilus and Criseyde,* in which there is never a false move or impulse of feeling; and the whole is sensed to be deploying humanly, freely, and yet inevitably under the compulsions latent in the characters, in their struggle with destiny.

On a smaller scale, we may see the operation of this kind of insight in *The Merchant's Tale,* perhaps his most masterly short story. It is characterized by Chaucer's usual moral lucidity. Nothing could be clearer than the never stated motive of rebellious lust present in its three main characters. These are old January, whose senile sexuality is hallowed by matrimony and encouraged by aphrodisiacs; young Damian, with his treacherous animalism; and the "faire fresshe May," who is ready to climb a tree to gratify her desires.

With rarest comment by the narrator, all three are presented through their own eyes, that is, with all the sympathy and self-approval that they all separately feel for the fantasy lives latent within them, which Chaucer elicits. January sees himself as a dear, kind, wise old gentleman, penitent for his past, eager to sin no more,

and seeking the delicious safety and sancity of wedlock; his earnest care in consulting his friends in the choice of a wife (but insisting that she be under twenty), his tender apprehensions lest she be too delicate to endure his amorous heats, his solicitude for the sick squire Damian (who is about to cuckold him) and for the soul of his wife (about to collaborate with the squire) are all presented from the old man's point of view. In his own opinion, he is a generous, romantic figure; his wife will wear mourning forever after his death. We even hear his doting use of troubadour language to entice his wife into the priapic garden of the rose that he had designed for their summery encounters; like Absalom and Nicholas, he would be a courtly lover too, and borrow from the Song of Songs:

"Rys up, my wyf, my love, my lady free!
The turtles voys is herd, my dowve sweete;
The wynter is goon with alle his reynes weete.
Com forth now, with thyne eyen columbyn![72]
How fairer been thy brestes than is wyn!"

At the end of this dithyramb, Chaucer (or his persona, the Merchant) permits himself the remark:

Swiche olde lewed wordes used he.

But the irony does not consist in the bare contrast between this fantasy of courtly love and the nastiness of the old lecher who utters it; he is nothing so simple as a rich, dirty old man—perhaps no one is. He *is* considerate, affectionate, and generous—humble, even ready to admit his dislikable qualities to his girl-wife:

"And though that I be jalous, wyte me noght.[73]
Ye been so depe enprented in my thoght
That, whan that I considere youre beautee,
And therwithal the unlikely elde of me,[74]
I may not, certes, though I sholde dye,
Forbere to been out of youre compaignye
For verray love; this is withouten doute.
Now kys me, wyf, and lat us rome aboute."

In all the irony, there is pathos; and in the pathos, irony. That January should go blind (as he

---

[72] With they dove's eyes.   [73] Blame me not.
[74] My dislikable old age.

GEOFFREY CHAUCER

does in the course of the story) is pathetic, but it is ironic too. He had been blind all along:

> O Januarie, what myghte it thee availle,
> Thogh thou myghte se as fer as shippes saille?
> For as good is blind deceyved be
> As to be deceyved whan a man may se.[75]

In like manner, young Damian, the seducer, is, in his own esteem, a lover-poet; he wears the verses that he writes to May in a silk purse upon his heart, and May, who reads and memorizes his lines in a toilet (down the drain of which, for safety, she consigns them) is a heroine of romance to herself:

> "Certeyn," thoghte she, "whom that this thyng displese,
> I rekke noght, for heere I hym assure
> To love hym best of any creature,
> Though he namoore hadde than his sherte!"

Again the ironical narrator allows himself to intrude:

> Lo, pitee renneth soone in gentil herte!

No moral is pointed at the end of this story; by a perfection of irony, they all lived happily ever after.

There is one character in Chaucer that neither realistic observation nor the authority of ancient books can wholly account for. He comes from some unknown half-world, a visiting presence that some have thought to be the figure of Death, some of the Wandering Jew, some of the old Adam seeking renewal. It may be better to leave him wholly mysterious and unexplained; it is the ancient, muffled man who directs the three rioters of *The Pardoner's Tale* to the heap of gold when they ask him if he knows where Death is to be found. To their rough language, and the question why he is so old, he gives this strange reply:

> "For I ne kan nat fynde
> A man, though that I walked into Ynde,
> Neither in citee ne in no village,
> That wolde chaunge his youthe for myn age;
> And therefore moot I han myn age stille,

[75] For it is as good to be deceived when blind as when you have your sight.

> As longe tyme as it is Goddes wille.
> Ne Deeth, allas! ne wol nat han my lyf
> Thus walke I, lyk a restelees kaityf,[76]
> And on the ground, which is my moodres gate,
> I knokke with my staf, bothe erly and late,
> And seye 'Leeve mooder, leet me in!
> Lo how I vanysshe, flessh, and blood, and skyn!
> Allas! whan shul my bones been at reste?' "

It is a shock to meet with so haunting a figure in the bright Chaucerian world, a figure so loaded with suggestions of supernatural meaning. With slow gravity, he rebukes the three rioters for their discourteous behavior:

> "But, sires, to yow it is no curteisye
> To speken to an old man vileynye. . . ."

And that is the reader's link with this strange phantom and the shadowy world to which he belongs—the huge importance of courtesy. We are never told who our instructor is, nor has he been found in any book that Chaucer studied, save for a few hints in the obscure Latin poet Maximian; the essential creation is all Chaucer's, and it was his "cyclopean eye" that discerned this eerie figure, tap-tapping his invisible way through the crowds at Queenshithe or by the Custom House, and among the courtiers of Richard II at the palace of Eltham or of Shene.

ENVOI

I am sure you are become a good Chaucerist.
Ralph Winwood, *Letter to Sir Thomas Edmondes, 1601*

THE intention here has been to present Chaucer's career as a courtier and to suggest its effect on his career as a poet, rather than to write an all-embracing "honeysuckle life." If this approach leaves much unsaid that needs saying, there are many other studies to supply my deficiencies. More can always be said of any great poet.

Chaucer's greatness was a little impugned by Matthew Arnold, in a celebrated passage, where Chaucer is accused of lacking "high serious-

[76] Like a restless captive.

42

ness." It is clear, however, that Arnold knew very little about Chaucer; he shows only a slight acquaintance with *The Canterbury Tales* and does not appear to have read *Troilus and Criseyde* at all. It need not, therefore, surprise us that he did not perceive Chaucer's moral stature, or that he could not find high seriousness in high comedy; he did not know where to look for it.

There is so much fun in Chaucer, and so little reproof, that his appeal to moralists (who are seldom quite happy about pleasure) is not immediate. Yet he is one of those rare poets who can strongly affect not only our passions and intelligence, but our wills too; he creates generosities in them. A sense of welcome to the created world, to men and women, and to the experience of living flows from his pen.

Chaucer can reach out to a supernal world too; and if, to do so, he has borrowed a little from Dante, he knew what to borrow and how to borrow it:

> Thow oon, and two, and thre, eterne on lyve,
> That regnest ay in thre, and two, and oon,
> Uncircumscript, and al maist circumscrive,
> Us, from visible and invisible foon,
> Defende, . . .

[Thou one and two and three, that livest eternally and reignest ever in three and two and one, uncomprehended, and yet comprehending all things, defend us from visible and invisible foes . . .]
(*Troilus and Criseyde*, V)

Withinne the clositre blisful of thy sydis
Took mannes shap the eterneel love and pees, . . .

[Within the blissful cloister of thy womb, the eternal love and peace took human shape, . . .]
(*The Second Nun's Prologue*)

Victorious tree, proteccioun of trewe,
That oonly worthy were for to bere
The Kyng of Hevene with his woundes newe,
The white Lamb that hurt was with a spere, . . .

[Victorious tree, the protection of all true (souls), that alone wert worthy to bear the King of Heaven . . .]
(*The Man of Law's Tale*)

But it is the mortal world that most exercised his poetical gift, and there he is nearest to Shakespeare as the poet of humane understanding; like him, Chaucer begets a *caritas* in the imagination of his readers. His vision of earth ranges from one of amused delight to one of grave compassion; these are his dawn and his dusk. His daylight is a lively April of fresh goodwill and kindly common sense, and if, here and there, there is a delicate frost of irony, warmth is his great characteristic. He takes deep joy in what we think of as the simple things of nature—birdsong, sunlight, gardens, daisies in the grass, the "ayerissh bestes" of the sky (the ram, the bull, and other signs of the zodiacal zoo), and even in a timid hound puppy, met in a wood:

> And as I wente, ther cam by mee
> A whelp, that fauned me as I stood,
> That hadde yfolowed, and koude no good.
> Hyt com and crepte to me as lowe
> Ryght as hyt hadde me yknowe,
> Helde doun hys hed and joyned hys eres,
> And leyde al smothe doun hys heres.
> I wolde have kaught hyt, and anoon
> Hyt fledde, and was from me goon, . . .
> (*The Book of the Duchess*)

The joy Chaucer seems to experience, he can communicate, or create in others, and that is to create a kind of goodness, or a mood that makes goodness easier; he forges a basic sense of, and desire for, harmony. His universe is not off course, but on the way to a perhaps distant but happy and Christian fulfillment, in which men and women have their generous share. There are plenty of rascals among them, to be sure; he gazes at them evenly with unembarrassed, uncondemning delight, limiting his aspirations to *tout comprendre* and leaving *tout pardonner* to higher authority.

All this is done with laughter not left behind, nor music either. If Matthew Arnold was a little blind where Chaucer was concerned, at least he was not deaf; and he wrote with wonderful discernment and eloquence on the sound of Chaucer's verses:

of Chaucer's divine liquidness of diction, of his divine fluidity of movement, it is difficult to speak temperately. They are irresistible, and justify all the rapture with which his successors speak of his "gold dewdrops of speech."

Chaucer's music was not unrelated to his courtiership. The *Liber niger* of Edward IV ordains that young henxmen shall be encouraged to "harping, to pype and sing." Squires of his household

of old be accustomed, winter and summer, in afternoons and evenings, to draw to Lordes Chambres within Court, there to keep honest company after there Cunninge, in talking of Cronicles of Kinges and other Pollicies, or in pipeing or harpeing, songinges and other actes marcealls, to help to occupie the Court, and accompanie estrangers . . .

In afternoons and evenings, Chaucer's music would be heard in his own voice ("after his cunning"[77]), when he read out his poems. In winter, in a lord's chamber or in the great hall; in summer, in the garden below, where he would "help to occupie the Court, and accompanie estrangers," Jean Froissart, perhaps, among others.

The College of Corpus Christi, Cambridge, owns a fifteenth-century manuscript of *Troilus and Criseyde;* in it there is a full-page illumination of just such a scene. Against a sky of afternoon gold rise the trees and towers of a royal palace—Shene, it may be, or Windsor, or Eltham; a company of young lords and ladies in the richly simple robes of those times are moving down the garden slopes toward a dell where a small pulpit has been set up. It is surrounded by the gathering court: the queen is seated on the grass before it, with her ladies about her. King Richard stands in cloth of gold, a little to the left of her; to the right there stands an older man in blue, with a gold girdle. It might be John of Gaunt. In the pulpit, at which this older man is gazing, Geoffrey Chaucer is reading from a book; he seems to be a youngish man. The hair and eyes are still brown; the eyes also have something of a sad look.

He is reading from his greatest completed poem, the first tragedy in the English language, *Troilus and Criseyde:*

> Go, litel bok, go, litel myn tragedye,
> Ther God this makere yet, er that he dye,
> So sende myght to make in som comedye!
> But litel book, no makyng thow n'envie,

[77] skill

> But subgit be to alle poesye;
> And kis the steppes, where as thow seest pace
> Virgile, Ovide, Omer, Lucan, and Stace.

[Go, little book, go my little tragedy, to that place whence may God likewise yet send thy maker power to make something in the manner of a comedy, before he dies! But, little book, envy no other poetry, but be subject to all poesy, and kiss the steps where thou seest Vergil, Ovid, Homer, Lucan, and Statius pacing.]

The "litel bok" did its errand and the "myght" was duly sent; it gave us our first and freshest comedy, *The Canterbury Tales.*

SELECTED BIBLIOGRAPHY

I. COLLECTED WORKS, ANTHOLOGIES, AND EDITIONS. W. W. Skeat, ed., *The Complete Works of Geoffrey Chaucer,* 6 vols. (Oxford, 1894); R. K. Root, ed., *The Book of Troilus and Criseyde* (Princeton, 1926; 3rd printing, corrected, 1945); F. N. Robinson, ed., *The Complete Works of Geoffrey Chaucer* (Boston, 1933; 2nd ed., 1957), the source of the quotations from Chaucer in the above text; J. M. Manly *et al.,* eds., *The Text of the Canterbury Tales,* 8 vols. (Chicago, 1940), the basic textual ed.; E. T. Donaldson, ed., *Chaucer's Poetry: An Anthology for the Modern Reader* (New York, 1958); D. S. Brewer, ed., *The Parlement of Foulys* (London, 1960, corrected 2nd ed., Manchester, 1972); A. C. Baugh, ed., *Chaucer's Major Poetry* (New York, 1963); R. A. Pratt, ed., *The Tales of Canterbury* (Boston, 1974).

II. CONCORDANCE, SOURCES AND ANALOGUES, DICTIONARIES. J. S. P. Tatlock and A. G. Kennedy, *A Concordance to the Complete Works of Geoffrey Chaucer and to the Romaunt of the Rose* (Washington, D.C., 1927); R. K. Gordon, *The Story of Troilus, as Told by Benoît de Sainte-Maure, Giovanni Boccaccio [translated into English prose], Geoffrey Chaucer and Robert Henryson* (New York, 1934); W. F. Bryan and G. Dempster, eds., *Sources and Analogues of Chaucer's Canterbury Tales* (Chicago, 1941); F. P. Magoun, Jr., *A Chaucer Gazeteer* (Chicago, 1961); T. W. Ross, *Chaucer's Bawdy* (New York, 1972); B. Dillion, *A Chaucer Dictionary: Proper Names and Allusions* (Boston, 1974).

III. REPUTATION. C. F. E. Spurgeon, *Five Hundred Years of Chaucer Criticism and Allusion 1357–1900,* 3 vols. (Cambridge, 1925), first issued in parts by the Chaucer Society between 1914 and 1924, the basic work; J. A. Burrow, ed., *Geoffry Chaucer: A Critical Anthology* (Harmondsworth, 1969); A. Miskimin, *The Renaissance Chaucer* (New Haven, 1975); D. Brewer, *Chaucer: The Critical Heritage,* 2 vols. (London, 1978).

IV. Facsimiles. *The Works 1532: With Supplementary Material from the Editions of 1542, 1561, 1598, and 1602* (London, 1969); *The Canterbury Tales* (London, 1972), Caxton's 2nd ed. of *The Canterbury Tales*, 1484; *Boecius Translated by G. Chaucer* (Norwood, N.J., 1974).

V. Biographical and General Studies. T. R. Lounsbury, *Studies in Chaucer*, 3 vols. (New York, 1892), a pioneering work that remains valuable on the early false biographical accounts and the learning of Chaucer; G. L. Kittredge, *Chaucer and His Poetry* (Cambridge, Mass., 1915; reiss. with intro. by B. J. Whiting, 1970), classic account by a great scholar; J. M. Manly, *Some New Light on Chaucer* (New York, 1926), identifies pilgrims with real people, with varying degrees of certainty; J. M. Manly, "Chaucer and the Rhetoricians," in *Proceedings of the British Academy*, 12 (1926), the pioneer work, although Manly's conclusions are now largely qualified; R. D. French, *A Chaucer Handbook* (New York, 1927; 2nd ed., 1947), includes many summaries and versions of analogues; J. L. Lowes, "The Art of Geoffrey Chaucer," in *Proceedings of the British Academy*, 16 (1930), distillation of a lifetime's work by a great scholar; G. Dempster, *Dramatic Irony in Chaucer* (Stanford, 1932); J. L. Lowes, *Geoffrey Chaucer* (Boston, 1934), contains much valuable intellectual and literary background; B. J. Whiting, *Chaucer's Use of Proverbs* (Cambridge, Mass., 1934); H. R. Patch, *On Reading Chaucer* (Cambridge, Mass., 1939); R. W. Chambers, *Man's Unconquerable Mind* (London, 1939), contains an important essay; H. S. Bennett, *Chaucer and the Fifteenth Century* (Oxford, 1947; repr. with corrections, 1948); N. Coghill, *The Poet Chaucer* (Oxford, 1949; 2nd ed., 1967); K. Malone, *Chapters on Chaucer* (Baltimore, 1951); J. Speirs, *Chaucer the Maker* (London, 1951; 2nd ed., 1960); G. H. Gerould, *Chaucerian Essays* (Princeton, 1952); D. S. Brewer, *Chaucer* (London, 1953, 3rd ed., largely supplemented, 1973); C. Schaar, *The Golden Mirror: Studies in Chaucer's Descriptive Technique and Its Literary Background* (London, 1955; repr. with index, 1967); C. Muscatine, *Chaucer and the French Tradition* (Berkeley–Los Angeles, 1957), the outstanding critical work; B. H. Bronson, *In Search of Chaucer* (Toronto, 1960); Norman Davis and C. L. Wrenn, *English and Mediaeval Studies: Presented to J. R. R. Tolkien on His 70th Birthday* (London, 1962); D. W. Robertson, Jr., *A Preface to Chaucer: Studies in Medieval Perspectives* (Princeton, 1962)—for discussion of the critical issues involved in the methods of Robertson (and of Huppé and Koonce, listed below) see "Patristic Exegesis in the Criticism of Medieval Literature" in D. Bethurum, ed., *Critical Approaches to Medieval Literature* (New York, 1960); R. S. Crane, "On Hypotheses in 'Historical Criticism': Apropos of Certain Contem-

porary Medievalists," in his *The Idea of the Humanities and Other Essays Critical and Historical*, II (Chicago, 1967); and F. L. Utley's review of D. W. Robertson's *Preface*, in *Romance Philology*, 19 (1965).

See also Wolfgang Clemen, *Chaucer's Early Poetry* (London, 1963); R. O. Payne, *The Key of Remembrance: A Study of Chaucer's Poetics* (New Haven, 1963); M. Bowden, *A Reader's Guide to Geoffrey Chaucer* (New York, 1964); H. S. Corsa, *Chaucer: Poet of Mirth and Morality* (South Bend, Ind., 1964); A. C. Spearing, *Criticism and Medieval Poetry* (Cambridge, 1964; rev. ed., 1972); G. Kane, *The Autobiographical Fallacy in Chaucer and Langland Studies* (London, 1965); D. S. Brewer, ed., *Chaucer and Chaucerians* (London, 1966); M. M. Crow and C. C. Olson, eds., *Chaucer Life-Records* (Oxford, 1966), the fundamental work of scholarship on the records of Chaucer's life; John Lawlor, ed., *Patterns of Love and Courtesy* (London, 1966); R. M. Jordan, *Chaucer and the Shape of Creation* (Cambridge, Mass., 1967); J. Lawlor, *Chaucer* (London, 1968); J. J. Mogan, *Chaucer and the Theme of Mutability* (The Hague, 1969); M. Bloomfield, *Essays and Explorations: Studies in Ideas, Language and Literature* (Cambridge, Mass., 1970), reprints some important studies; E. Talbot Donaldson, *Speaking of Chaucer* (London, 1970), a collection of essays, some already published and classic, by an outstandingly witty and penetrating critic and scholar; B. Rowland, *Blind Beasts: Chaucer's Animal World* (Kent, Ohio, 1971); S. S. Hussey, *Chaucer, an Introduction* (London, 1971); J. A. Burrow, *Ricardian Poetry: Chaucer, Gower, Langland and the Gawain Poet* (Boston, 1971), on "the style of the age"; Charles Muscatine, *Poetry and Crisis in the Age of Chaucer* (South Bend, Ind., 1972), refers also to *The Pearl* poet and Langland, and "the relation of poetry to history"; P. M. Kean, *Chaucer and the Making of English Poetry*, 2 vols. (Boston, 1972); S. Knight, *Ryming Craftily: Meaning in Chaucer's Poetry* (Sydney, 1973); J. Norton-Smith, *Geoffrey Chaucer* (London, 1974); J. A. W. Bennett, *Chaucer at Oxford and at Cambridge* (Oxford, 1974); D. S. Brewer, "Towards a Chaucerian Poetic," in *Proceedings of the British Academy*, 60 (1974); D. S. Brewer, *Chaucer and His World* (London, 1978).

VI. Critical Essays. E. Wagenknecht, ed., *Chaucer: Modern Essays in Criticism* (New York, 1959), reprints some classic studies; R. J. Schoeck and J. Taylor, eds., *Chaucer Criticism*, 2 vols.: I, *The Canterbury Tales* (South Bend, Ind., 1960), II, *Troilus and Criseyde and the Minor Poems* (South Bend, Ind., 1961); M. Hussey et al., *An Introduction to Chaucer* (Cambridge, 1965); D. S. Brewer, ed., *Chaucer and Chaucerians: Critical Studies in Middle English Literature* (London, 1966); B. Rowland, ed., *Companion to Chaucer Studies* (Toronto, 1968), essays on different aspects of Chaucer, including biography, meter, learning, rhetoric, with valuable bibliographies; A. C. Cawley, ed., *Chaucer's Mind and Art* (Edinburgh, 1969); L. D. Benson, ed., *The Learned and the Lewed: Studies in Chaucer and Medieval Literature* (Cambridge, Mass., 1974); G. Economou, ed., *Geoffrey Chaucer* (New York, 1975), critical articles with bibliographies.

VII. LANGUAGE, VERSIFICATION. B. ten Brink, *The Language and Metre of Chaucer*, M. Bentinck-Smith, trans. (2nd rev. ed., London, 1901); J. Mersand, *Chaucer's Romance Vocabulary* (London, 1939); H. Kokeritz, *A Guide to Chaucer's Pronunciation* (Stockholm, 1954), excellent elementary guide (see also intros. to eds. by Skeat, Robinson, etc.; P. F. Baum, *Chaucer's Verse* (Durham, N.C., 1961); M. Masui, *The Structure of Chaucer's Rime Words* (Tokyo, 1964); I. Robinson, *Chaucer's Prosody* (Cambridge, 1971); R. W. V. Elliott, *Chaucer's English* (London, 1974).

VIII. STUDIES OF *The Canterbury Tales.* M. Bowden, *A Commentary on the General Prologue to the Canterbury Tales* (New York, 1948; 2nd rev. ed., 1967); W. W. Lawrence, *Chaucer and the Canterbury Tales* (New York, 1950); R. M. Lumiansky, *Of Sondry Folk: The Dramatic Principle in the Canterbury Tales* (Austin, Texas, 1955); B. F. Huppé, *A Reading of the Canterbury Tales* (Albany, N.Y., 1964); T. W. Craik, *The Comic Tales of Chaucer* (London, 1964); P. G. Ruggiers, *The Art of the Canterbury Tales* (Madison, Wis., 1965); B. Bartholomew, *Fortuna and Natura: A Reading of Three Chaucer Narratives* (The Hague, 1966); R. L. Hoffman, *Ovid and the Canterbury Tales* (Philadelphia, 1966); J. Richardson, *Blameth Nat Me: A Study of Imagery in Chaucer's Fabliaux* (The Hague, 1970); J. Mann, *Chaucer and Medieval Estates Satire* (Cambridge, 1973), discussion of the pilgrims as literary-social types; T. D. Cooke and B. L. Honeycutt, eds., *The Humor of the Fabliaux* (Columbia, Mo., 1974); D. R. Howard, *The Idea of the Canterbury Tales* (Berkeley–Los Angeles, 1976).

IX. STUDIES OF *Troilus and Criseyde.* T. A. Kirby, *Chaucer's Troilus: A Study in Courtly Love* (Baton Rouge, La., 1940); I. L. Gordon, *The Double Sorrow of Troilus* (Oxford, 1970); J. M. Steadman, *Disembodied Laughter* (Berkeley–Los Angeles, 1972); H. A. Kelly, *Love and Marriage in the Age of Chaucer* (Ithaca, N.Y., 1975); D. W. Rowe, *O Love O Charite* (Carbondale, Ill., 1976).

XI. STUDIES OF *The Legend of Good Women.* R. W. Frank, Jr., *Chaucer and The Legend of Good Women* (Cambridge, Mass., 1972).

XI. THE SHORTER POEMS. J. A. W. Bennett, *The Parlement of Foulys: An Interpretation* (Oxford, 1966); C. B. Heiatt, *The Realism of Dream Visions* (The Hague, 1967); J. A. W. Bennett, *Chaucer's Book of Fame: An Exposition of "The House of Fame"* (Oxford, 1968); J. Wimsatt, *Chaucer and the French Love Poets* (Chapel Hill, N.C., 1968), on *The Book of the Duchess;* J. Winny, *Chaucer's Dream Poems* (London, 1973).

XII. GENERAL LITERARY BACKGROUND. W. P. Ker, *English Literature Medieval* (Oxford, 1912), inevitably dated but a classic brief account; E. Faral, ed., *Les arts poétiques du XIIᵉ et du XIIIᵉ siècle* (Paris, 1924), collection of medieval treatises on the arts of rhetoric (see also Nims, 1967); C. S. Lewis, *The Allegory of Love* (Oxford, 1936; repr. 1938), an influential and brilliant book; E. R. Curtius, *European Literature and the Latin Middle Ages* (New York, 1953, first published in German, 1948), a work of major significance in medieval literary history; C. S. Lewis, *The Discarded Image* (Cambridge, 1964), how medieval men thought of the world; D. R. Howard, *The Three Temptations: Medieval Man in Search of the World* (Princeton, 1966); M. F. Nims, trans., *Poetria Nova of Geoffrey of Vinsauf* (Toronto, 1967), translation of one of the medieval arts of poetry; D. Mehl, *The Middle English Romances of the Thirteenth and Fourteenth Centuries* (Boston, 1968; rev. and trans. of German ed., 1967); H. Newstead, ed., *Chaucer and His Contemporaries: Essays on Medieval Literature and Thought* (Greenwich, Conn., 1968); P. Gradon, *Form and Style in Early English Literature* (London, 1971); D. S. Brewer, ed., *Geoffrey Chaucer*, Writers and Their Background series (London, 1974; Athens, Ohio, 1975), essays on Chaucer's life, fourteenth-century English manuscripts, French, classical, and medieval Latin, Italian, scientific, religious and philosophical, and artistic backgrounds; A. C. Spearing, *Medieval Dream Poetry* (Cambridge, 1976), discusses general tradition, and Chaucer's dream poems in detail; D. Pearsall, *Old English and Middle English Poetry* (Boston, 1977).

XIII. HISTORICAL, CULTURAL, AND SOCIAL BACKGROUND. J. J. Jusserand, *English Wayfaring Life in the Middle Ages*, Eng. trans. (London, 1889; 4th ed., 1950); S. L. Thrupp, *The Merchant Class of Medieval London* (Ann Arbor, Mich., 1948); E. Rickert, comp., *Chaucer's World*, C. C. Olson and M. M. Crow, eds. (New York, 1948), trans. of interesting contemporary records, contemporary illustrations; A. L. Poole, ed., *Medieval England* (Oxford, 1958); M. M. McKisack, *The Fourteenth Century 1307–1399* (Oxford, 1959), the standard historical work; G. Holmes, *The Later Middle Ages 1272–1485* (London, 1962), a masterly brief account; D. S. Brewer, *Chaucer in His Time* (London, 1963; New York, 1973); R. S. Loomis, *A Mirror of Chaucer's World* (Princeton, 1965), richly illustrated; J. Evans, ed., *The Flowering of the Middle Ages* (London, 1966), historians' essays, splendid illustrations; M. Hussey, *Chaucer's World: A Pictorial Companion* (Cambridge, 1967); D. W. Robertson, Jr., *Chaucer's London* (New York, 1968), excellent historical account of London closely related to Chaucer; B. Cottle, *The Triumph of English 1350–1400* (London, 1969); K. B. McFarlane, *Lancastrian Kings and Lollard Knights* (Oxford, 1972), historian's study of the Lollard knights, some of whom were Chaucer's friends.

XIV. ART AND SCIENCE. A. Hauser, *The Social History of Art*, vol. I (Boston, 1951); G. Henderson, *Gothic* (Harmondsworth, 1967); A. Martindale, *Gothic Art* (London, 1967). See also Jordan, Muscatine, and Robertson, above. W. C. Curry, *Chaucer and the Mediaeval Sciences*, 2nd ed. (New York, 1960); C. Wood, *Chaucer and the Country of the Stars, Poetic Uses of Astrological Imagery* (Princeton, 1970).

XV. RECORDINGS. General recordings include *Music of the Gothic Era*, 3 records (DGG Archive 2723045); *The Art of Courtly Love*, 3 records (HMV SLS 863). Readings in the original pronunciation include *Chaucer Readings* (EVA Lexington LE 5505B); *Troilus and Criseyde*, abridged (Argo ZPL 1003–4); *The General Prologue* (Argo PLT 1001); *The Knight's Tale* (Argo Stereo ZPL 1208–10); *The Miller's Prologue and Tale* (CUP Cassette 211859); *The Wife of Bath* (CUP Cassette 212197); *The Merchant's Prologue and Tale* (CUP Cassette 211875); *The Pardoner's Tale* (Argo Stereo ZPL 1211); *The Nun's Priest's Tale* (Argo RG 466).

XVI. BIBLIOGRAPHIES. E. P. Hammond, *Chaucer: A Bibliographical Manual* (New York, 1908); J. E. Wells, *A Manual of the Writings in Middle English 1050–1400* (New Haven, 1916)—the 9th and last supp. was issued in 1952, and a revision is in progress for the period 1050–1500 (Hamden, Conn., 1967–); D. D. Griffith, *Bibliography of Chaucer 1908–53* (Seattle, 1955); W. R. Crawford, *Bibliography of Chaucer 1954–63* (Seattle, 1967); A. C. Baugh, *Chaucer* (*Golden Tree Bibliography*) (New York, 1968). For articles and annual bibliographies and reports, see *The Chaucer Review* (1966–) and *The Year's Work in English Studies* (Chaucer section) (1901–).

JOHN GOWER

(ca. 1325-1408)

Derek Pearsall

THE head of John Gower's effigy, on his tomb in St. Saviour's Church, Southwark, rests upon three books, the *Speculum meditantis*, the *Vox clamantis*, and the *Confessio amantis*; but his reputation as an English poet rests upon the last of these, the other two poems being in French (Anglo-French, to be precise, which differed somewhat from Continental French) and in Latin, respectively. That Gower wrote in three languages should not surprise us: French was the first language of the English upper classes until the middle of the fourteenth century, and the court language of Edward III and Richard II until the end of the century, while Latin was, and remained, the universal language of learning and serious literature. Gower has been reproached for lacking Chaucer's splendid certainty of Englishness, as if the three-fold phasing of his poetic output were a timid hedging of bets on posterior fame, a safe but unspectacular investment. But Chaucer's certainty was without predecent; and there is a logic in Gower's progress through the languages that reflects the age with great fidelity. The *Mirour de l'omme* (called in Latin the *Speculum meditantis* or *Speculum hominis*) is a moral and didactic survey of the state of man, a handbook of sins, addressed to the thoughtful and literate laity as part of a long tradition of serious, practical, admonitory writing in Anglo-French. The *Vox clamantis* is a calling to account of English society and government before the bar of posterity; its aim is to fix the age's infamy in a context of history, Scripture, and prophecy, and to do so in a language that will endure. The *Confessio amantis*, however, is confessedly a relaxation from these strenuous moral endeavors, a blending of "lore" and "lust"—like Polonius, Gower could not help assuming a hortatory role—in a pattern of sober comedy. As he says, too much moralizing "dulleth oft a mannes wit," and therefore

> I wolde go the middel weie
> And wryte a bok betwen the tweie,
> Somwhat of lust,[1] somwhat of lore,[2]
> That of the lasse or of the more
> Som man mai lyke of that I wryte:
> And for that fewe men endite
> In oure englissh, I thenke make
> A bok for Engelondes sake.
> (Prologue, 17–24)

In this poem Gower found, as if by chance, his natural vocation as a polished and fluent verse narrator. It is this storyteller's gift that is our chief delight in reading Gower, and his chief claim on our attention.

Yet it is not his only claim, nor is it separable from his role as a moralist, for Gower's narratives, however divergent and remote their sources, are staked out in a world of consistent social and moral values, a world of civilized feelings, that Gower can define all the more effectively because he is writing out of imaginative sympathy and not out of admonitory purpose. In some manuscripts of the *Vox clamantis* there is a picture illustrating some Latin verses that begin:

Ad mundum mitto mea iacula, dumque sagitto.[3]

It portrays Gower as an old man, dressed in a long gown, of worn but resolute mien, in the act of shooting an arrow at the globe of the world. It is an image we should remember, of John Gower as the keeper of the nation's conscience

---

[1] pleasure.   [2] teaching.
[3] I hurl my darts at the world and I shoot my arrows.

48

in a brilliant, violent, and corrupt generation, for it is an essential part of the whole man. Chaucer recognized this when he dedicated his *Troilus and Criseyde* to "moral Gower," along with "philosophical Strode,"[4] though he may not have realized how effectively he was entombing his friend's poetic reputation by so doing. The praise lavished by the fifteenth century on Gower, in which he is formally acknowledged, with Chaucer and Lydgate, as one of the three founders of English poetry, is not accompanied by the devotion and enthusiasm that Thomas Hoccleve and Lydgate, for instance, display for Chaucer, or Stephen Hawes for Lydgate. Although the *Confessio* was issued in printed form in 1483, and again in 1532 and 1554, and although both Shakespeare (in *Pericles*) and Ben Jonson (in his *Grammar*) show knowledge of his work, it was generally Gower's fate to remain admired but unread, then to be forgotten (no further edition appeared until 1810), and further to suffer the slings and arrows of Coleridge, James Russell Lowell, and Jean Jules Jusserand before being salvaged by having his morality thrown overboard. Yet, as we have seen, the *Confessio* does not stand alone; some account of Gower's other work is needed before we can see it in perspective.

The *Mirour de l'omme* (the "Mirror of Man") survives incomplete in a single manuscript as a poem of 28,603 lines, in a difficult octosyllabic twelve-line stanza. It is in three parts: the first, occupying 18,000 lines, is a schematic analysis of the seven deadly sins and the opposed seven virtues, each subdivided into five aspects; the second part shows how sin has corrupted the world, by examining the different ranks of society—clergy, secular rulers, knights, lawyers, merchants, craftsmen, tradesmen, and laborers; the third part outlines the way to amendment through repentance and through the intercession of the Virgin, whose life is recounted. The work as a whole is impressively organized as a mechanical structure, and is sustained by the medieval passion for a comprehensive schematization of the moral nature of things, for a summa. Everything is related to the microcosmic combat of passion and reason in fallen man; this combat is reflected in the corruption of nature and society, just as the cathedral is an image of the risen body of man and of the structure of medieval thought, itself a "cathedral of ideas."

Gower is dealing with the same raw material as Chaucer and Langland—hardly a detail of Chaucer's Monk or Friar is absent here—but, although he can demonstrate a lively satiric observation, as when he speaks of the vintner whose samples are so different from what you actually buy (26,065–26,073), and who seems to be able to get a dozen different exotic wines from the same cask (26,089–26,101), Gower always moves toward the general and the abstract. Over some maps one can place a transparent grid so as to make plotting of reference easier: Gower places a moral grid over the map of human experience and reads through it. Every human action is plotted on this grid and given a reference in terms of the enumerated scheme of vices and virtues. Chaucer knew this grid too, but he was not afraid to remove it and look at the map of experience in itself—though he was glad enough to put it back when he had looked hard and long enough, as the epilogue to *Troilus* and the retraction show. Thus Gower, unlike Chaucer, can rarely get beyond the schematic truth of "Les bons sont bons, les mals sont mals," (25,225), except when he is telling a story. Gower is not a philosophical poet, like Boethius or Jean de Meung, the continuator of the *Roman de la rose;* his mind is not stirred and his imagination is not moved by ideas, concepts, or the majestic processes of reason. For Gower, truth is a castle, a castle under constant attack; its walls are crumbling and showing fissures. It is not his duty to make daring exploratory forays into the hinterland of experience, but to shore up these fragments against the world's ruin.

In the *Vox clamantis* (the "Voice of One Crying"), a poem of 10,265 lines, extant in eleven manuscripts, Gower associates himself explicitly, by his title, with the Messianic prophets, Isaiah and John the Baptist, and, in the prologue to Book I, with that other John of the Apocalypse. His vision is of a society rushing toward its doom, driven like Gadarene swine by the sins of the flesh, while God's wrath burns hidden; his call is to the people to repent before

---

[4] Ralph Strode (fl. 1350–1400), logician and Scholastic philosopher.

the inevitable destruction. Book II, the original opening book, offers a credo and, dismissing the idea that Fortune is the author of the world's unhappiness and instability, asserts the essential moral responsibility of man and the subservience of Fortune and Nature to the just man (nothing better illustrates the meaninglessness of experience, in the medieval scheme, in comparison with moral truth).

Having placed man firmly in the dock, Gower proceeds to arraign him, in the next four books, much as in the *Mirour,* by analyzing at length the corruption of all estates of society. There is some powerful writing here, especially against the clergy, often reminiscent of *Piers Plowman* and the clerical portraits of the *Prologue* to the *Canterbury Tales,* though praise of his satiric "realism," as of Chaucer's and Langland's, is perforce inhibited by the fact that much of their material is conventional. Gower also displays an extravagance of rhetoric, as in the description of woman's seductiveness (V, 79ff.), and a savage Roman obscenity of wit, as in the account of the priest's return to "school" (III, 1417ff.; also IV, 603;861), which suggest something of the imaginative and verbal license that Latin provided, when the simple innocence of the laity was not in danger of being corrupted.

Book VI, after dealing with lawyers, turns to the young king and exhorts him to rule with justice and honor, using his father, the Black Prince, as his exemplar. A later revision of this passage (like Langland, Gower was a constant reviser) substitutes stern and menacing reproof for exhortation. Book VII introduces the statue in Nebuchadnezzar's dream, with its head of gold, breast of silver, belly of brass, and feet of iron and clay, as an apocalyptic allegory of the successively degenerating ages of the world. We are now, says Gower, in the age of iron and clay, of hardhearted avarice and fleshly lust—indicted as *Gallica peccata* ("the French sins," the cult of fashionable adultery). The wretchedness of the world is contrasted with God's original purpose for mankind, and Gower's favorite image of the microcosm is given a macabre twist in the comparison of worldly corruption to the corruption of the body after death, in their relation to the indulgence of particular sins (for instance, 848). The poem ends with a *memento mori,* visions of Hell, and a call to repent.

The most interesting part of the *Vox,* however, is Book I, added after the Peasants' Revolt of 1381 had provided Gower and his England with a foretaste of apocalypse. After a brilliant and luxuriant description of terrestrial paradise, as if to symbolize the bounty of Nature now corrupted by man, the poet, in a dream, sees the mob running wild, metamorphosed into animals, engaged in an orgy of destruction, looting, and rape. London is sacked, and the archbishop of Canterbury martyred, in a riot of violent, highly charged imagery and classical allusion, and with the grossest distortion of historical truth. The revolt certainly disturbed Gower, but it was a godsend to him as a fulfillment of his prophecies and as a way of getting his poem off to an explosive start.

Late in his life Gower added a sequel to the *Vox,* called the *Cronica tripertita* (the "Three-Part Chronicle"), in which Richard II is finally exposed and condemned. The first part, *opus humanum,* describes the brave resistance of Gloucester and the lords appellant to Richard's hateful tyranny; the second, *opus inferni,* recounts the treacherous murder of Gloucester and other of the king's infamies; the third, *opus in Cristo,* describes the deposition of Richard and the accession of Henry IV as something, allowing for poetic exaggeration, akin to a secular Second Coming.

There are other minor Latin poems, but it is time to turn now to the *Confessio amantis* ("The Lover's Confession"). The poem was begun about 1386, and Gower tells us that it sprang from a suggestion of King Richard, whom he met on the Thames one day, that he should write "som newe thing." Perhaps the king was tired of being lectured by the stern old moralist—at any rate, Gower's response, in 33,444 lines of octosyllabic couplet (49 MSS), was above and beyond even a sovereign's call to duty. The poem was completed by 1390; but in 1393 Gower, totally disgusted with Richard, revised him out of the prologue and substituted a dedication to Henry, in whom he recognized, even at this early date, England's man of destiny. This was not Gower's only revision of the *Confessio:* in another, a passage in the epilogue in praise of Chaucer was excised. In it Venus addresses the poet Gower:

> And gret wel Chaucer whan ye mete,
> As mi disciple and mi poete:

For in the floures of his youthe
In sondri wise, as he wel couthe,[5]
Of Ditees[6] and of songes glade,
The whiche he for mi sake made,
The lond fulfild is overal. . . .

(VIII, 2941–2947)

Such a change, in view of the long-standing and well-authenticated friendship of the two poets, could hardly have been accidental. Explanations are speculative: it may be that Gower took offense at Chaucer's good-humored sniping in the introduction to the *Man of Law's Tale,* where he makes some ironical play of moral Gower's fondness for tales of incest (77–89), though the irony is directed more at the lawyer's ignorance than at Gower.[7] There are two further passages in the *Tale* (1009, 1086) that may or may not be playfully critical of Gower's telling of the same tale of Constance in Book II of the *Confessio.* A touchy man could have taken them seriously. Perhaps, though, Gower was more generally disillusioned with Chaucer because of the direction the *Canterbury Tales* seemed to be taking in these later years of Chaucer's life. The *Miller's Tale* and the others must have looked to Gower like an appeal to the basest tastes of the public and a betrayal of the high cause of poetry.

The intention of the *Confessio,* as we have seen, is to blend entertainment with instruction; but Gower cannot descend from the pulpit so readily, and in the prologue he therefore recapitulates familiar moral themes—the corruption of the world, analyzed through the three estates; the moral responsibility of man; the insignificance of Fortune; the microcosmic relation of man and Nature; the decay of the age and the coming destruction, embodied again in the allegory of Nebuchadnezzar's dream. In Book I, however, Gower deftly shifts his ground:

I may noght strecche up to the hevene
Min hand, ne setten al in evene
This world, which evere is in balance:
It stant noght in my suffisance
So grete thinges to compasse,
Bot I mot lete it overpasse
And treten upon othre thinges.

Forthi the Stile of my writinges
From this day forth I thenke change
And speke of thing is noght so strange,[8]
Which every kinde hath upon honde,[9]
And whereupon the world mot stonde,[10]
And hath don sithen it began,
And schal whil there is any man;
And that is love, of which I mene
To trete, as after schal be sene.

(I, 1–16)

But it is *reculer pour mieux sauter.* The controlling theme of the Prologue is of division, in man's own nature and in society, as the source of all strife and all evil; the transition to the theme of love is a natural one. For Gower, love is a principle of existence, a blind natural force, in itself neither good nor evil, but providing the strongest motive to good or evil—and therefore for the display of man's moral nature. He recognizes that talk of love and tales of love are interesting in themselves, but that this interest can be used to probe human behavior in its most vulnerable and sensitive areas, that is, where man is passionately involved, and so to quicken moral receptivity. He is not teaching an amorous morality or code of sexual behavior, but evolving patterns of rational morality by reference to sexual passion. There is nothing artificial here, since the art of "fyn lovynge," as Chaucer calls it, and as he and others embody it in their writings, is not so very different from the art of fine living:

Thus wolde Love, yheried be his grace,
That Pride, Envye, and Ire, and Avarice
He gan to fle, and everich other vice.

(*Troilus,* III, 1804–1806)

Like man in general, the lover must eschew the deadly sins, even lechery, for the characteristic theme that Gower develops in the *Confessio* is the control of blind passion through the exercise of reason, and of marriage as the true goal of "fyn lovynge":

It sit[11] a man be weie of kinde[12]
To love, bot it is noght kinde[13]
A man for love his wit to lese . . . .
(*Confessio,* VII, 4297–4299)

[5] knew how.   [6] poems.
[7] W. L. Sullivan, "Chaucer's Man of Law as a Literary Critic," *MLN* 58 (1953).

[8] difficult.   [9] which controls every creature.
[10] must stand.   [11] befits.   [12] in the way of nature.
[13] according to nature.

JOHN GOWER

The dramatic scheme of the *Confessio* is for
Gower to imagine himself as a lover—the fiction
is openly and half-mockingly contrived—and to
appeal to Venus for respite from the pain of
Cupid's fiery dart. Venus, before granting his
request, demands that he be shriven by Genius,
the priest of love, so as to prove his worth and
virtue as a lover. Genius is taken from the
Roman de la rose, but he plays a completely new
part in the *Confessio;* in a superficial sense he is
a product of the fashionable habit of applying
religious terms to love, as is the idea of a
"lover's confession," but essentially he represents the conscience of Love, and comes to represent the conscience of the lover. Gower's technique is to go through the seven deadly sins,
dividing each into five aspects (it sometimes
seems that Gower had only one poem to write,
but had to write it in three languages), to analyze each in both its general and its amorous
manifestations, to question the lover as to his
guilt, and to offer exemplary stories. The
scheme, which is evidently derived from that of
the penitential manual, allows him to speak
with great freedom and to cover the whole
range of human behavior—sometimes, indeed,
he gives but scant attention to the lover's timid
confessions in his pursuit of the larger truths.
Gower makes some wry comedy out of this:
when Genius is expatiating on the evils of sloth,
in particular of *lachesse* (procrastination), the
lover ruefully interjects that he never has the
chance to be late for a date, because his lady
never gives him one (IV, 271); and when Genius
is speaking of idleness, the lover declares his as-
siduity in the service of love, though, as he admits, it never seems to get him anywhere.

> Al is bot ydel ate laste.
> (IV, 1758)

It is idle, but is it idleness? The lover has a
mind of his own, though somewhat overawed
in the presence of his confessor. When Genius
tells the story of Phoebus and Daphne as a
warning against excessive hastiness, the lover
thanks him for his advice, but roundly asserts
that so long as he sees his lady is no tree, he
will continue to pursue her (III, 1730 ff.) Again,
the priest's advocacy of prowess in arms as a
way to win his lady's heart cuts no ice with him
at all:

> What scholde I winne over the Se,
> If I mi ladi loste at hom?
> (IV, 1664–1665)

When questioned about the sin of ingratitude,
the lover suggests with some trepidation that it
is his lady who is ungrateful, half-expecting the
thunders that proceed to roll about his head (V,
5210).

The development of this dry and rueful comedy of the lover is one of the achievements of
the *Confessio*. It is not sufficient to give the
poem the organic quality of growth of the *Canterbury Tales;* it remains a mechanical structure,
a continuing argument rather than a drama.
However, the dramatic scheme gives the whole
poem a buoyancy that other collections of exemplary tales, such as the *Gesta Romanorum* or even
the *Legend of Good Women*, lack. Many delicate
touches enliven the character of the lover, and a
number of longer passages portray his "service"
with fine, gentle sympathy and a kind of wist-
fulness. We hear of his eagerness to please his
lady, how he conducts her to church:

> Thanne is noght al mi weie in vein,
> Somdiel I mai the betre fare,
> Whan I, that mai noght fiele hir bare,
> Mai lede hire clothed in myn arm....
> (IV, 1138–1141)

But the moment of delight is lost in longing:

> ... Ha lord, hou sche is softe,
> How sche is round, hou sche is smal! [14]
> (IV, 1146–1147)

At home, his eyes follow her everywhere; when
she takes up her embroidery:

> Than can I noght bot muse and prie
> Upon hir fingres longe and smale.
> (IV, 1176–1177)

Sometimes he will play with her little dog or
with her caged birds, partly to please her, partly
because they are at least something of hers.
Elsewhere, he tells of his joy in her presence,
especially when dancing gives him the excuse to
hold her hand:

[14] slender.

With such gladnesse I daunce and skippe,
Me thenkth I touche noght the flor;
The Ro, which renneth on the Mor,
Is thanne noght so lyht as I. . . .
(IV, 2784–2787)

At other times he plays "chance" or "love-questions" with her, or reads *Troilus* to her; when he has to leave, he tarries at the door, and sometimes comes back for something he says he has forgotten. And when he reaches his own bedchamber, he torments himself with thoughts of her:

Into hire bedd myn herte goth,
And softly takth hire in his arm
And fieleth hou that sche is warm,
And wissheth that his body were
To fiele that he fieleth there.
(IV, 2884–2888)

Finally he sleeps: "Bot that [what] I dreme is noght of schep" (IV, 2894). This is not passion, but fine feeling refined to the point where it begins to resemble that purification of the will which is the moralist's goal. The ending of the poem describes how Venus promises to heal him of his "unsely jolif wo," and does so by urging that he make a "beau retret" in the face of advancing age:

"That which was whilom grene gras,
Is welked[15] hey at time now.
Forthi mi conseil is that thou
Remembre wel hou thou art old."
(VIII, 2436–2439)

Famous lovers of the past gather round him, wondering at such frostbitten fires, and Cupid gropes his way toward him and pulls out the "fyri Lancegay." The poet begs shamefacedly to be excused from the court and Venus, giving him a necklace of black beads engraved "por reposer" and advising him to return to his moral books, goes to her home, "Enclosid in a sterred sky" (VIII, 2942). It is a strangely moving ending, of which C. S. Lewis writes with deep sympathy, reaching out beyond love to age, to "calm of mind, all passion spent," and to death. Like Chaucer in the *Parlement of Foules*, Gower

---

[15] withered.

begins with a prologue in which the barrenness of prescriptive morality is suggested, and then circles on the central passion and mystery of love, in which the good life is surely hidden somewhere, only to return in the end to his books. Chaucer, however, did find an answer in book III of *Troilus*: Gower's "beau retret" is final.

The lover is sometimes used as a prompt for Genius, who has a penchant for general moral disquisition. Unguarded questions from the lover touch off long discourses on gentillesse, on war and peace, on false and true religion (an especially long one, V, 747–1959), while Book VII consists entirely of a systematic exposition of the bases of medieval knowledge, ending with an account of the duties of a good king, a "regiment of princes," into which Gower concentrates all his political teaching. We must in these passages make some allowance for the medieval pressure toward encyclopedism; but they are not, in the context of the whole work, irrelevant. They function, indeed, not as organic parts of a work of art with its own internal validity, but as the intellectual and informational basis of a program that has validity in its relation to the world of action. The *Confessio*, however, does ultimately become something more than a program, for it passes beyond prescription to a "civilization of the heart," in which fine feeling, humane sensitivity, and gentillesse take over the role of conscience as the source of virtuous action. Sin is made to seem not so much deadly as stupid and low.

It is the stories above all in which this inner "sentence" of the *Confessio* is embodied. There are 133 stories, totaling 17,213 lines, just over half the total for the poem, and ranging in length from exempla of a few lines to the 1738 lines of "Apollonius of Tyre" (Book VIII, not one of the best). The major sources are Ovid, especially the *Metamorphoses*; the *Roman de Troie* of Benoît de Sainte-Maure (completed in 1184); the Bible; and medieval collections of tales such as the *Gesta Romanorum*. The best of these tales ("Mundus and Paulina," "Narcissus," "Albinus and Rosemund," in Book I; "Constantine and Silvester," II; "Canacee," "Pyramus and Thisbe," III; "Pygmalion," "Demephon and Phillis," "Rosiphelee," "Ceix and Alceone," "Iphis and Araxarathen," IV—much the best book; "Jason and Medea," "Adrian and Bardus," "Tereus," V; "Lucrece," VII) display a consummate narrative skill, but they also display the way in which storytelling could release Gower's potential imaginative energy so that he could penetrate to the heart of and realize what elsewhere he could only say.

A simple demonstration is provided by the story of Constantine and Silvester, where Constantine's soliloquy (II, 3243–3273), in which he rejects the barbarous cure prescribed for his leprosy, represents in action the nobility of sentiment and fineness of moral discrimination of which Chaucer speaks—"Pitee renneth soone in gentil herte." More complex is Gower's version of Ovid's tale of Tereus. Ovid orchestrates the tale with great sonority and decks it in all the rich panoply of his rhetoric, dwelling on the details of Tereus' mutilation of the raped Philomena (*Metamorphoses*, VI, 557) and on the dismembering and cooking of Tereus' son by his wife Procne and her sister (640–646). Every gruesome detail is elaborated with a rich and wanton imagination, every speech made the opportunity for a display of emotional rhetoric and wit. Gower, however, turns what is essentially a simple—indeed, a meaningless—tale of lust and revenge into a humanly complex story in which the human emotions of outraged maidenhood and outraged wifehood are given full expression and in which the whole action is related to a significant context of good and evil. Tereus' crime is given a moral context in a finite world by Philomena's prayer to Jupiter (V, 5741 ff.); and Procne's revenge is introduced by her prayers to Venus (5821 ff.), in which she asserts her own truth and fidelity in marriage and the wrong done to her, and then to Apollo (5846 ff.), begging forgiveness for being the indirect cause of it. At every point Gower mutes the horror and invests the action with sentiment of a morally discriminating kind, as if the characters were operating in a civilized environment and not in a world of inhuman passion and violence. For all his artistic simplicity beside Ovid, Gower has a notion of the complex meaningfulness of human behavior, of its "pendulation," to use Erich Auerbach's term, which Ovid does not begin to approach. Chaucer, we may note in passing, tells the story, in *The Legend of Good Women*, as if in an idle daze.

In Pyramus and Thisbe the major change is the development of Thisbe's death speech as a pathetic questioning of justice and divine providence: "Helas, why do ye with ous so?" (III, 1472). The word "deserve," which occurs frequently in Gower's retelling of classical stories, but not in Ovid, is an index to the patterns of moral responsibility he draws from the tales. He makes nothing of the metamorphosis in the Thisbe story (of the mulberry tree); but elsewhere, as in the tale of Tereus and that of Ceix and Alceone, he uses the transformation as a means to poeticize human values. Thus, in the latter tale, he exploits the change of the dead husband and wife into kingfishers, which in Ovid is simply strange (*Metamorphoses*, XI, 742), as an affirmation of the pathetically triumphant endurance of wifely fidelity:

> Hire wynges for hire armes tuo
> Sche tok, and for hire lippes softe
> Hire harde bile, and so fulofte
> Sche fondeth [16] in hire briddes forme,
> If that sche mihte hirself conforme
> To do the plesance of a wif,
> As sche dede in that other lif:
> For thogh sche hadde hir pouer lore, [17]
> Hir will stod as it was tofore,
> And serveth him so as sche mai.
>   (IV, 3106–3115)

Chaucer in *The Book of the Duchess*, has nothing of this—it is not, indeed, to his purpose—and in other respects Gower's telling of the tale is more skillful than Chaucer's. Everywhere, Gower invests his women with humanity and pathos, as in the story of Lucrece, where he dwells at length on Lucrece's openness and hospitality toward her treacherous guest—an episode that Chaucer omits entirely in *The Legend of Good Women*—and portrays her actions after the rape as possessing something of the deliberate ordained quality of a being who has already passed beyond the world, like Clarissa (VII, 4996–5011). So with Medea, who, instead of being harried and lectured at every turn, as was the medieval moralist's wont, is treated with great sympathy, coming vividly alive when her maid brings news of Jason's exploits:

[16] tries.   [17] lost her power.

Sche tolde hire ladi what sche wiste,[18]
And sche for joie hire Maide kiste.
(V, 3799–3800)

Something of the imaginative release that story-telling gave Gower is indicated by the tale of Canacee (Book III), where incest—unmentionable even to Chaucer—is reviewed with a sober and touching lack of outrage as the natural outcome of blind instinctive passion, and where the moral reproof is directed against the father's uncomprehending wrath.

Some of Gower's success with the classical stories is due to his ruthlessness, his readiness to throw overboard the many-storied richnesses of antiquity in favor of a finite moral pattern, which in turn is reinforced by a uniformity of social setting. Ambiguities, fruitful or otherwise, are removed and a clear storyline emerges, often with complete redirection of the original material to a new purpose. The stories of Jason and Medea, and of Paris and Helen, are examples of Gower's skill in cutting the antique moorings and isolating the tellable tale, akin to Malory's technique in handling the polyphonic or interwoven Arthurian narratives. Sometimes, of course, the classical material is intractable to Gower's purposes; there was not much, for instance, that the Christian moralist could make of the story of Orestes (Book III). Sometimes, too, the overt moral runs counter to the inner sense of the story. "Pyramus and Thisbe," for instance, is ostensibly an exemplum against irrational haste; and at one point the story of Troilus and Criseyde is cited as proof that no good can come of flirting in church (V, 7597–7599). What we can assume is that Gower would have come to some less trivial conclusion in actually telling the tale.

Comparison between Gower and Chaucer as narrative artists favors the former until we come to the *Canterbury Tales*, where the dramatic context provides the freedom Chaucer's imagination needs. Here, conventional themes, such as the sermon on the sins of the tavern in the *Pardoner's Tale* or the antifeminist material of the *Wife of Bath's Prologue*, can be placed dramatically off-center so as to explore a new dimension in narrative. Gower's Confessor, however, speaks with a generalized, impersonal, "European" voice, from a calm center of experience; and at times he has the dullness of someone who speaks good sense *all* the time. Even the simplest of the *Canterbury Tales*, such as the *Physician's Tale* (corresponding to Gower's "Appius and Virginia," VII, 5131 ff.) and the *Manciple's Tale* ("Phebus and Cornide," III, 782 ff.—Chaucer's tale may contain some mockery of Gower's here[19]), have a memorableness that Gower's versions lack, while the *Man of Law's Tale* is richer at every point than Gower's tale of Constance (II, 587 ff.).

The truest measure of Chaucer's greatness, however, is in his treatment of a story analogous to Gower's tale of Florent (I, 1407 ff.) in the *Wife of Bath's Tale*. By any normal standards, Gower's realization of the story is much superior to Chaucer's: he actually describes the hag, which seems important to an appreciation of Florent's dilemma; he portrays Florent with great humanity—how he rides away when she first lays down her terms, then drifts back, how he comforts himself with the thought that she cannot live long, how at the court he tries various other answers just in case they will get him off the hook, how he smuggles her unseen into his castle. Throughout he behaves with scrupulous honesty and honor, and the final disenchantment of the hag depends partly upon this. Chaucer, however, puts the knight in the wrong from the first by making the offense a rape, and subtly realigns the story and the question so that the knight gets no chance to choose whether to behave honorably or not. The very tale itself is thus a demonstration of woman's right to sovereignty. When Chaucer is plowing a rich furrow like this, comparison is less favorable to Gower.

One quality of the *Confessio* remains to be mentioned, without which it would be nothing: its verbal artistry. Enough has probably been quoted to show that Gower is indeed a poet, and a poet of the purest kind, one who seeks "the best words in the best order"[20] without fuss or display. Coleridge spoke of the "neutral" style as Chaucer's special achievement; but he

---

[18] knew.

[19] See Bibliography.
[20] See R. Hazelton, "The *Manciple's Tale:* Parody and Critique," *JEGP* 62 (1963).

could well have used Gower as the exemplar of such a style, in which the language never draws attention to itself and in which the long verse paragraph is unfolded with a naturalness that seems—and this is the crown of art—artless. Yet it is a style that can rise, through its integrity and purity, to the demands of the story, as with Jason's return with the Golden Fleece, where the lines seem to embody life, joy, and victory:

> The Flees he tok and goth to Bote,
> The Sonne schyneth bryhte and hote,
> The Flees of gold schon forth withal,
> The water glistreth overal.
>
> (V, 3731–3734)

Brief quotation cannot truly represent Gower's artistry, for his technique is essentially one of diffusion. Perhaps the reader may be directed to the magnificent prayer of Cephalus to the sun (IV, 3197–3237) as the supreme expression of Gower's art.

Late in life, old, blind and semi-invalid, Gower made a collection of fugitive pieces for a presentation volume for Henry IV. He included in it his only other English poem, the stately "To King Henry IV, in Praise of Peace," some Latin verses, and the *Cinkante*[21] *balades*. These last, whether they are actually the work of a man of seventy or whether they are youthful productions gathered for publication, represent the sweetest flowering of "fyn lovyng." They do not describe passion; in fact, the idea that they embody a personal love story is wholly erroneous. They are, rather, a pleasing arrangement of gentle and noble sentiments. Certainly they surpass anything of the kind, in English or French, before the Elizabethans; and through

them we hear a familiar voice speaking, graceful, calm, faintly wry, but perhaps, finally, reconciled: "Armour s'acorde a nature et resoun" (*Balade* 50).

SELECTED BIBLIOGRAPHY

I. Bibliography. G. Watson, ed., *The New Cambridge Bibliography of English Literature*, I (Cambridge, 1974).

II. Editions and Translations: Gower. G. C. Macaulay, ed., *The Complete Works of John Gower*, 4 vols.: I, French works; II and III, English works; IV, Latin works (Oxford, 1899–1902); E. W. Stockton, trans., *The Major Latin Works of John Gower* (Seattle, Wash., 1962); Terence Tiller, trans., *John Gower, Confessio Amantis* (*The Lover's Shrift*) (Harmondsworth, Middlesex, 1963), modern English verse translation, fluent and generally accurate, of excerpts (about 8,000 lines) linked by prose summary; R. A. Peck, *Confessio Amantis* (New York, 1968), about half the poem, in well-chosen extracts; J. A. W. Bennett, ed., *Selections from John Gower*, Clarendon Medieval and Tudor Series (Oxford, 1968).

III. Critical Studies. C. S. Lewis, *The Allegory of Love* (Oxford, 1936), valuable material on Gower (pp. 198–222); R. Weiss, *Humanism in England During the 15th Century* (Oxford, 1941; 2nd ed., 1957); H. S. Bennett, *Chaucer and the Fifteenth Century* (Oxford, 1947); J. H. Fisher, *John Gower: Moral Philosopher and Friend of Chaucer* (New York, 1964), the standard biographical and critical study; D. Pearsall, "Gower's Narrative Art," in *PMLA*, 81 (1966), 475–484; J. Lawlor, ed., *Patterns of Love and Courtesy: Essays in Memory of C. S. Lewis* (London, 1966), essays on Gower by J. A. W. Bennett and J. Lawlor; G. Mathew, *The Court of Richard II* (London, 1968); W. F. Bolton, ed., *The Middle Ages*, Sphere History of Literature in the English Language, I (London, 1970); J. A. Burrow, *Ricardian Poetry* (London, 1971); P. J. Gallacher, *Love, the Word and Mercury: A Reading of John Gower's Confessio Amantis* (Albuquerque, N. M., 1975).

[21] Fifty.

JOHN LYDGATE

(ca. 1370 - ca. 1451)

Derek Pearsall

JOHN LYDGATE is at once a greater and a lesser poet than John Gower. He is a greater poet because of his greater range and force; he has a much more powerful machine at his command. The sheer bulk of Lydgate's poetic output is prodigious, amounting, at a conservative count, to about 145,000 lines. Life at the monastery of Bury St. Edmund's, where he spent most of his life, gave him a leisure that many another poet might have envied, and enabled him to explore and establish every major Chaucerian genre, except such as were manifestly unsuited to his profession, like the fabliau. In the *Troy-book* (30,117 lines), an amplified translation of the Trojan history of the thirteenth-century Latin writer Guido della Colonna, commissioned by Prince Henry (later Henry V), he moved deliberately beyond Chaucer's *Knight's Tale* and his *Troilus*, to provide a full-scale epic. The *Siege of Thebes* (4716 lines) is a shorter excursion in the same field of chivalric epic. The *Monk's Tale*, a brief catalog of the vicissitudes of Fortune, gives a hint of what is to come in Lydgate's massive *Fall of Princes* (36,365), which is also derived, though not directly, from Boccaccio's *De casibus virorum illustrium*.[1] The *Man of Law's Tale*, with its rhetorical elaboration of apostrophe, invocation, and digression in what is essentially a saint's legend, is the model for Lydgate's legends of St. Edmund (3693) and St. Albon (4734), both local monastic patrons, as well as for many shorter saints' lives, though not for the richer and more genuinely devout *Life of Our Lady* (5932).

The allegorical love vision is represented in fine poems like the *Complaint of the Black Knight*, the *Flower of Courtesy*, a Valentine's Day poem in praise of his lady, and the *Temple of Glass*, a highly stylized account of a decorous romantic courtship; and there are many graceful shorter love poems (that these are not autobiographical hardly needs demonstrating). *Reason and Sensuality* (7042) is a translation of the first part of "Les echecs amoureux,"[2] in which Lydgate hit on a happy blend of moralistic and love allegory. The *Pilgrimage of the Life of Man* (24,832) is a good deal less happy, a moral allegory of a type that may have influenced Bunyan's *Pilgrim's Progress*. It is translated from a poem by Guillaume de Deguilleville and, except for the curious literalness of its allegory, which has a weird Bosch-like quality at times, has no claim on our attention—significantly, it is in a genre for which Lydgate found no precedent in Chaucer. The moral beast-fable, which Chaucer transfigured into the *Nun's Priest's Tale*, is represented in the "Churl and the Bird," a poem of some pith; in "The Horse, Goose and Sheep"; and in some poor versions of "Isopes Fabules."

Nor does this exhaust Lydgate's output. There are at least two genres in which he successfully exploits native non-Chaucerian traditions: the Marian hymn (there are minor examples in Chaucer), to which he brings an intensity and verbal luxuriance rare in English, and the gnomic moralizing poem, where, by contrast, he is consciously writing "low style," without aureation or rhetorical elaboration, and achieves a pungent aphoristic compression in poems like "That Now Is Hay Some-tyme Was Grase" and "A Wicked Tunge Wille Sey Amys." In addition there are a large number of occasional and informational pieces in verse. Lydgate was something of a professional court poet, and counted among his patrons not only Henry V but also Humphrey, duke of Gloucester (for the *Fall*), the

---

[1] "Concerning the Falls of Famous Men."

[2] "Love's Game of Chess."

earl of Salisbury (for the *Pilgrimage*), and the countess of Warwick (for a version of *Guy of Warwick*, traditionally regarded as his worst poem). From time to time he also received commissions from Henry VI: the king's title being in question, Lydgate wrote *Title and Pedigree of Henry VI*, and, for the pageant *Henry VI's Triumphal Entry into London*, he produced what we should call now a souvenir program. "Epithalamion for Gloucester" shows how skillfully Lydgate could handle intrinsically unpromising material. Often he was asked for little masques or "mummings" to be performed at convivial gatherings of such companies as the London mercers and the goldsmiths; these pieces have an importance in the history of dramatic literature that is just being recognized.

If such occasional pieces as these have to be written, then Lydgate's are about as good as they can be within their unenviable limits. We have also to appreciate that poetry in the fifteenth century was expected to cover a much wider range of human needs and activities than it does now. There were no "unpoetic" subjects; consequently we find poems in the Lydgate canon on subjects for which we should now consult a history book or encyclopedia, or even a cookbook or "Family Doctor." There is the "Pageant of Knowledge," covering the same ground as book VII of Gower's *Confessio*, a verse tabulation entitled "Kings of England," a "Dietary" or guide to good health (Lydgate's most popular work, to judge by the number of extant manuscripts!), "Treatise for Laundresses," and a book of etiquette for young boys, *Stans puer ad mensam*, full of such imperishable wisdom as "Pike nat thy nase" and "With ful mouth speke nat, list thou do offence." In the *Troy-book* and the *Fall*, too, the encyclopedic tendency is always present: in the former, for instance, when describing the rebuilding of Ilium, Lydgate digresses at length, with only hints of his source, on the origin of chess, the value of *pi*, the nature of classical drama, and the Trojan sewage system (into which he incorporates the latest fifteenth-century thinking on the subject), while the latter shows a strong inclination to become, at times, in its remorseless inventory of the victims of Fortune, a dictionary of universal biography, since the only essential qualification for inclusion is to be dead.

All this, of course, swells the corpus of Lydgate's work enormously, and in a way that is essentially trivial by our standards. But we should be prepared to recognize the narrowing that has taken place in the role of poetry and not blame Lydgate, though it is a human enough reaction, for having written so much. In a deeper sense, however, the massiveness of Lydgate's poetic production is an essential factor in our judgment of him, particularly in the two longest poems, the *Troy-book* and the *Fall*. A Lydgate anthology would be useful, but it can never truly represent him, just as quotation can never do him justice, for he achieves his most powerful effects over vast canvases. There is an ethos of the long poem to which we, with our modern taste for compression and witty intensity, are not readily responsive, one in which the poetic effect is built up by sheer insistence and cumulative iteration. *Richard III* is not Shakespeare's best play, but it looks a lot better at the end of a cycle of three less good plays; and so too the *Troy-book* and the *Fall* depend for a vital part of their power on the colossal sense of panoramic perspective that they develop. Their very size, like that of the Pyramids, is their meaning.

In this sense, then, Lydgate is a greater poet than Gower. But he is a lesser poet too, for in the way in which the word is widely used nowadays he is not a poet at all. What we expect of a poem is that its total meaning should be locally embodied, that the texture of the poem's language and style should be susceptible to the same kind of critical attention and should yield the same critical results as the whole poem. With Chaucer this is true, and with Gower too, but not with Lydgate, except in a special sense that we shall develop, for he is the great example in our literature of the rhetorician. Lydgate has little concern for and little knowledge of the ways in which poetry can release the potentialities of old words or recognize new ones (though he did introduce many words into the language), and his understanding of the function of meter in poetry is naive.

Lydgate took over the decasyllabic couplet and the seven-line stanza ("rhyme royal") from Chaucer, but he seems to appreciate little of his master's handling of them. Instead of attending to the rhythmic counterbalance of syntactical and metrical patterns, and the weaving of line patterns into a continuous paragraph flow, Lydgate appears to have tabulated Chaucer's techniques of variation and then to have used these as metrical standards. In other words, instead of the subtle challenge of the variant to the staple, we have the insistence on the variant as if it were the staple, with the result that Lydgate's verse is full of lines lacking a syllable at the beginning (the "headless" line) and at the caesura (the "broken-backed" line). Such lines, perfectly acceptable in the Chaucerian continuum, give Lydgate's verse the rigidity that is its great defect. So his verse, with its lack of verbal and rhythmical sensitivity, is in its local texture often drab and bare, in just the same way that Thomas Hardy's prose can in itself be exasperating. But this of course is not disabling; a medieval tapestry, upon close investigation, looks coarse and drab, but when one withdraws to take in the full effect, the whole pattern emerges. It is now our task to investigate the kind of patterns that Lydgate's verse makes.

Medieval rhetorical teaching concerns itself almost exclusively with style, and treats "invention" and structure very briefly. Invention is mainly a matter of expanding familiar material through "common-places," like allowing a crystal to grow in solution, while structure is treated from a mechanical rather than a dynamic point of view. Medieval poems are characteristically built up on numerical schemes, like the interwoven patterns of three and ten in Dante's *Divine Comedy* and the seven deadly sins in Gower, or are based on allegorical schemes, like the pilgrimage and the other-world journey, or, simplest of all, are inventories. The *Fall*, for instance, is essentially a catalog, though suggestions of a pageant of the dead are carried over from Boccaccio. The relative neglect of invention and structure is due to the unstated assumption that the material of poetry is all "given"—there is nothing new to be said—and that its form is implied in its very existence. There is no need for Lydgate to "organize" the *Fall*, nor for Langland to "organize" *Piers Plowman*, because the world and all that is in it are already allegorically patterned by their Christian world view.

The task of the poet therefore is not to explore modes of experience and behavior, but to decorate and amplify the infinitely familiar; and it is to decoration and amplification that the medieval rhetorics devote themselves. Geoffrey of Vinsauf, for instance, an early thirteenth-century Anglo-Latin rhetorician well-known in England in the fourteenth and fifteenth centuries, lists in his *Poetria nova* ("The New Poetry") eight forms of amplification (including periphrasis, simile, apostrophe, digression, description); and it would be easy to illustrate how fully Lydgate, in the *Troy-book*, demonstrates these techniques. In fact, amplification is for Lydgate an ingrained habit of mind more than a technique. Comparison with his sources shows how consistently there operates in him a kind of total recall: each move forward disturbs an avalanche and, before further progress can be made, a mass of illustrations, examples, images, and similes has to be shifted. From poem to poem the same stimulus triggers the same response. The ideal, and Lydgate puts it very simply, is not one of compression and economy, but one of expansiveness:

> These ookis grete be nat doun ihewe[3]
> First at a stroke, but bi long processe,
> Nor longe stories a woord may not expresse.
> *(Fall, I, 96–97)*

Lydgate sometimes seems to delight in his power of synonymy, of saying something in as many words as possible without adding to the meaning of what is said. This, for instance, is what he makes of "Constant dripping wears away a stone":

> The rounde dropis off the smothe reyn,
> Which that discende and falle from aloffte
> On stonys harde, at eye as it is seyn,
> Perceth ther hardnesse with ther fallyng offte,
> Al-be in touchyng, water is but soffte;
> The percyng causid be force nor puissance,
> But off fallyng be long contynuance.
> *(Fall, II, 106–112)*

Lydgate amplifies by reflex, except when consciously writing "low style," and subjects even the little moral fable of the "Two Merchants" to the usual barrage of invocation, apostrophe, exclamation, and complaint, with digressions on medicine and Levantine geography for good measure.

---

[3] hewed.

Decoration is handled by the rhetoricians in terms of diction, in which they recommend richness, aureation, and ornate luxuriance above all, and in terms of the tropes, such as metaphor, and the figures, such as repetition in its various forms. The treatment of the figures is fully schematized, and every possible stylistic configuration is classified and analyzed. The image of style is as of some rich brocaded garment that is cast over the naked body of the matter, or as of a form of painting—where the term "colors of rhetoric" lends itself readily to elaborate word play. Thus Peleus attempts to use his powers of persuasion upon Jason:

> And gan with asour and with golde to peynte
> His gay wordys in sownynge glorious.
>
> (*Troy*, I, 384–385)

Elsewhere, interpreting the painting image with the utmost literalness, Lydgate speaks of himself and other followers of Chaucer, the great master rhetorician, "Amonge oure englisch that made first to reyne/The gold dewe-dropis of rethorik so fyne":

> Whan we wolde his stile counterfet,
> We may al day oure colour grynde and bete,
> Tempre our azour and vermyloun:
> But al I holde but presumpcioun.
>
> (*Troy*, II, 4715–4718)

It is not merely an image for Lydgate: for him words are surfaces, colors, bright counters to be arranged in patterns, not instruments for penetrating reality. In some of his Marian poems, the language becomes so aureate and Latinized that it seems to lose touch with referents in reality and to exist solely as a form of hieratic symbolic ritual.

The figures of rhetoric also are used extensively by Lydgate, in ways that suggest that he found in their formal patternings a way of controlling the overwhelming luxuriance of his verbal responses. Many of his best lines achieve their effect through traditional artifice, as with the chiasmus[4] in the third line of this passage:

> Noble Pryncis, in your prosperite,
> On sodeyn chaungis set your remembraunce,

[4] Inversion in the second phrase of the word order in the first.

Fresshnesse off floures, off braunchis the beute
Have ai on chaung a tremblyng attendaunce.

(*Fall*, III, 2199–2202)

Lydgate seems to have been struck by certain figured cadences in Chaucer, such as the "Who looketh lightly now but Palamoun" sequence in the *Knight's Tale* (1870), which he imitates several times, and the "Lo here" anaphora of the *Troilus* (V, 1849), echoes of which he tries to catch on at least five occasions, as here:

> Lo her the fyne[5] of loveres servise!
> Lo how that Love can his servantis quyte!
> Lo how he can his feythful men dispise,
> To sle[6] the trwe men, and fals to respite!
>
> (*Black Knight*, 400–403)

Again and again he returns to the opening lines of the *Parlement of Foules*, trying to capture that unforgettable cadence:[7]

> Our liff heer short, off wit the gret dulnesse,
> The hevy soule troublid with travaile,
> And off memorie the glacyng brotilnesse . . .[8]
>
> (*Fall*, III, 22–24)

Such imitation is Lydgate's sincerest tribute to Chaucer, more convincing than the many passages where he enlarges on his master's praise and laments the inadequacy of his followers:

> We may assay for to countrefete
> His gaye style, but it wyl not be;
> The welle is drie, with the lycoure swete,
> Bothe of Clye and of Caliope.[9]
>
> (*Flower of Courtesy*, 239–242)

The conventional affectation of modesty becomes here a genuine humility, and a recognition of the debt owed Chaucer:

> To God I pray, that he his soule have,
> After whos help of nede I moste crave,
> And seke his boke that is left behynde
> Som goodly worde therin for to fynde,

[5] end, result.   [6] slay.
[7] "The lyf so short, the craft so long to lerne."
[8] transient frailty.
[9] Clio and Calliope, muses of history and epic poetry, respectively.

To sett amonge the crokid lynys rude
Whiche I do write.

(*Troy*, II, 4701– 4706)

Lydgate knew Chaucer's work intimately, particularly the *Troilus*, the *Parlement* and the *Knight's Tale*; and these he echoes and quotes constantly. The other *Canterbury Tales* he knew less well, and his attempt to write a Canterbury link in the prologue to the *Siege of Thebes* (which he dramatizes as his own Canterbury tale) is rather clumsy; it shows, for instance, that he has the Miller, the Pardoner, and the Summoner hopelessly mixed up (32–35). However, the fact that he tried to lumber after his master is a sign of his devotion, for Lydgate would have found it difficult to justify or even to understand the *Tales* in the terms of the prevailing poetics of rhetorical sententiousness.

Lydgate's characteristic techniques can be illustrated only by extended quotation. The following is part of the nature description from the opening of the *Black Knight*:

I rose anon, and thoght I wolde goon
Unto the wode, to her the briddes sing,
When that the mysty vapour was agoon,
And clere and feyre was the morownyng,
And dewe also lyk sylver in shynyng
Upon the leves, as eny baume [10] suete,
Til firy Tytan with hys persaunt hete

Had dried up the lusty lycour nyw
Upon the herbes in the grene mede,
And that the floures of many dyvers hywe
Upon her stalkes gunne [11] for to sprede,
And for to splayen out her leves on brede [12]
Ageyn the sunne, golde-borned [13] in hys spere, [14]
That doun to hem cast hys bemes clere.

And by a ryver forth I gan costey, [15]
Of water clere as berel or cristal,
Til at the last I founde a lytil wey
Towarde a parke, enclosed with a wal
In compas rounde; and by a gate smal,
Who-so that wolde, frely myghte goon
Into this parke, walled with grene stoon.

And in I went to her the briddes songe,
Which on the braunches, bothe in pleyn and vale,
So loude songe that all the wode ronge,

Lyke as hyt sholde shever in pesis smale;
And as me thoghte that the nyghtyngale
Wyth so grete myght her voys gan out wrest, [16]
Ryght as her hert for love wolde brest. [17]

The soyle was pleyn, smothe, and wonder softe,
Al over-sprad wyth tapites [18] that Nature
Had made her-selfe, celured [19] eke alofte
With bowys grene, the floures for to cure, [20]
That in her beaute they may not longe endure
Fro al assaute of Phebus fervent fere, [21]
Which in his spere so hote shone, and clere.

(22–56)

The great achievement of this passage is one of literary synthesis, for it is essentially an interweaving of Chaucerian and other images, phrases, and ideas into a decorative pattern with a beauty of its own. It is the pattern that matters, for the tendency of the description is always away from physical concretion and toward abstract truth. The imagery, for instance, always relates the natural objects to human artifacts, to precious stones and jewels, or to decorative cloths; and the textures are not natural but artificial—the trees in the wood seem to be made of fragile china. Behind this "humanization" of nature lies the medieval view of nature as essentially meaningless except in a context of human ideas. The physical world is an image of order, decorum, and design, as we see in the account of the ordered functions of Titan and Nature herself. In the *Troy-book* this philosophical quality, the sense of ordered cyclic progression, is brought out very strongly in the many fine passages of nature description that punctuate the narrative, and provides an effective counterpoint to the fluctuations of human fortune.

The passage from the *Black Knight* is thus fundamentally nonrepresentational; and its truth is not one of physical quality or texture or movement, but inner and abstract. The world of sensuous reality is patterned out of existence; and in the pattern is established the stasis to which all Lydgate's poetry draws, and in which the uncomfortable contradictions of experience are eliminated. Lydgate may have seen the dawn many times; but when he describes it, he does not describe what he has seen:

[10] balm. [11] began. [12] abroad, openly.
[13] gold-burnished. [14] sphere. [15] skirt, follow.

[16] force, strain. [17] burst. [18] carpets. [19] canopied.
[20] protect. [21] fire.

The nyght ypassed, at springyng of the day,
Whan that the larke with a blissed lay
Gan to salue the lusty rowes[22] rede
Of Phebus char,[23] that so freschely sprede
Upon the bordure of the orient.

(Troy, I, 1197–1201)

The poet's job is not to describe "real" dawns, which you can see for yourself if you want to, but to draw out the metaphysical reality of dawn. This is done in terms of decorative art—the chariot of Phoebus with its stylized red rays, which would have been familiar to the medieval audience from their calendars and books of hours, and which would have reminded them of the ordered governance of the world:

That the world with stable feyth varieth accordable chaungynges; that the contrarious qualities of elementz holden among hemself allyaunce perdurable; that Phebus, the sonne, with his goldene chariet bryngeth forth the rosene day; that the moone hath comaundement over the nyghtes . . . al this accordaunce of thynges is bounde with love, that governeth erthe and see, and hath also comandement to the hevene.

(Boethius, book II, meter 8, Chaucer's translation)

Just as Lydgate's style is rhetorical, oriented toward conventional figural decoration, so his world is rhetorical, one in which the material of experience yields, through the filter of a purely literary and nonexperiential imagination, a series of conventional types and themes.

The futility of looking in Lydgate for the kind of transcript of real experience we habitually look for in poetry is illustrated by his description of persons, especially of women, as of the lady in the *Temple of Glass:*

 . . . which right as the sonne
Passeth the sterres and doth hir stremes donne,[24]
And Lucifer, to voide the nyghtes sorow,
In clerenes passeth erli bi the morow;
And so as Mai hath the sovereinte
Of evere moneth, of fairnes and beaute,
And as the rose in swetnes and odoure
Surmounteth floures, and bawme of al licour
Haveth the pris,[25] and as the rubie bright
Of al stones in beaute and in sight,

As it is know, hath the regalie:[26]
Right so this ladi with hir goodli eighe,[27]
And with the stremes of hir loke so bright,
Surmounteth all thurugh beaute in my sighte:
Forto tel hir gret semelines,
Hir womanhed, hir port,[28] and hir fairnes,
It was a mervaile, hou ever that nature
Coude in his werkis make a creature
So aungel like, so goodli on to se,
So femynyn or passing of beaute . . .

(251–270)

The description continues in the same vein for many lines, as if to demonstrate that Lydgate could go on forever without mentioning a single detail of the lady's appearance. Nearly all medieval description is rhetorically idealizing—even the pilgrims in the *General Prologue* are usually supreme in their chosen professions—but it is specially characteristic of Lydgate to move away so consistently and systematically from individuation and concretion and toward the metaphysical abstract of generalized truth. The description, the model for many similar descriptions, including one of more than 100 lines in the *Flower of Courtesy,* is not of a woman, but of womanliness.

The passage above demonstrates how closely the rhetorical ideal of amplification is wedded to Lydgate's characteristic ordering of reality in terms of nondescriptive abstraction. The technique is one of extended metaphorical analogy; but there are other techniques of idealization, and they are among Lydgate's most readily recognizable stylistic habits. One is to assert his own inadequacy to the task:

I am to rude her vertues everychone
Cunnyngly to discryve and write. . . .

(Flower of Courtesy, 176–177)

Lydgate's poetry is full of references to his never having gathered flowers in Tullius' garden, nor slept on Mount Cithaeron, nor drunk at the Well of Helicon, nor found favor with Calliope, having been born at Lydgate, "Wher Bachus liquor doth ful scarsli flete" *(Fall,* VIII, 194). Another technique is to declare that the full surpassing excellence of his theme would take too long to describe: "A large boke it wolde

---

[22] rays.   [23] chariot.   [24] make pale.   [25] prize.   [26] supremacy.   [27] eyes.   [28] bearing.

occupie" (*Troy*, III, 5565). Another is to assert the essential inexpressibility of the theme:

> O, who can write a lamentacioun
> Convenient,[29] O Troye, for thi sake?
> Or who can now wepe or sorwe make,
> Thi grete meschef to compleyne and crie?
> Certes, I trowe nat olde Jeremye.
>   . . .
> . . . nor thou Ezechiel . . . Nor Danyel. . . .
> Alle youre teris myghte nat suffise.
>   (*Troy*, IV, 7054–7082)

This passage goes on for fifty lines, and is one of many such where Lydgate expands his material in a typically "literary" way. A fourth technique is quotation of hitherto supreme exemplars of a particular virtue or passion that are now surpassed, as in the topos[30] for the overwhelming grief of Helen for the dead Paris:

> I trowe that never man before
> No woman sawe falle in swiche distresse,
> In swiche disjoint of dedly hevines,
> Nor for no wo so pitously rave:
> Nat Cleopatre goynge to hir grave,
> Nor woful Tesbe, that from the kave sterte,
> Whan she hir silfe smote unto the herte,
> Nor the feithful trewe Orestille . . .
>   (*Troy*, IV, 3654–3661)

And so for another twenty lines. All these techniques are conventional, and it would be true to say that it is in the elaboration of the conventional, whether in theme or in style, that Lydgate finds his truest home. He often has trouble organizing the intractable material of experience, and the things to be said so crowd upon him that his syntax bends and sinks beneath the pressure (Lydgate is one of the few writers who can produce sentences that lack not only a subject but also a predicate). But when he is secure in a familiar convention, Lydgate can often attain a richness of expression that, although it is a richness produced by accumulation of quantity rather than by density of quality, is one of his most characteristic achievements. The convention seems to release what is best in him, not to inhibit it. No better

illustrations could be given than his "Danse Macabre" or his handling of the *Ubi sunt* formula in the magnificent envoi on Rome at the end of book II of the *Fall*.

In the realm of action, Lydgate's technique, of systematically interpreting reality in terms of "ideal" stereotypes, involves the elimination of movement and development, and the substitution of static pictorial composition. One of Gower's gifts is to be able to catch the moment of significant action—Medea kissing her maid in her excitement—but Lydgate characteristically freezes the process of life into nonphysical abstraction. This, for instance, is how he describes Medea "falling in love":

> Al sodeinly hir fresche rosen hewe
> Ful ofte tyme gan chaunge and renewe,
> An hondrid sythe in a litel space.
> For now the blood from hir goodly face
> Unto hir hert unwarly gan avale,[31]
> And therewithal sche wexe ded and pale;
> And efte anoon, who that can take hed,
> Hir hewe chaungeth into a goodly red.
> But evere amonge[32] t'ennwen[33] hir colour,
> The rose was meynt[34] with the lillie flour;
> And though the rose stoundemele[35] gan pase,
> Yit the lillie abideth in his place
> Til nature made hem efte to mete.
> And thus with colde and with sodein hete
> Was Medea in hir silfe assailled.
> And passyngly vexed and travailed,
> For now sche brent, and now sche gan to colde.
>   (*Troy*, I, 1951–1967)

Chaucer spends a thousand lines of his most glowing art on this same movement of feeling in Criseyde, but for Lydgate all the complexities of human behavior are resolved into a remorselessly simple series of polarities. The familiar oxymoron of hot and cold is for him not merely a form of decoration, but actually takes the place of experiential material. Later the conflict in Medea's heart, when she debates on love with herself, is expressed in terms of a similar mechanical series of abstractions:

> For in hir breste ther was atwixe tweyne
> A gret debate, and a stronge bataille,
> So fervently eche other dide assaile;

---

[29] suitable.

[30] A term used to describe the conventional rhetorical form in which a conventional theme is expressed.

[31] flow.   [32] ever and again.   [33] blend, shade off.
[34] mixed.   [35] from time to time.

And this contek,[36] in ernest and no game,
Juparted[37] was betwixe Love and Schame.
(*Troy*, I, 2160–2164)

This simple psychomachy is elaborated through another eighty-four lines; but there is no progress, no further penetration to the heart of the matter, only decoration and amplification of the given pattern. Comparison with Criseyde's soliloquy (*Troilus*, II, 703–805) reveals the essential and profound difference between the poet responding imaginatively to the human situation and the rhetorician elaborating a thematic commonplace.

Perhaps of all Lydgate's "themes" the most frequently and elaborately developed is that of human duplicity, as in this account of Antenor's treachery:

> For undernethe he was with fraude fraught,
> This sleighti wolfe, til he his pray hath kaught;
> For he was clos and covert in his speche
> As a serpent, til he may do wreche,[38]
> Hydinge his venym under floures longe;
> And as a be, that stingeth with the tonge
> Whan he hath shad oute his hony sote,[39]
> —Sugre in the crop, venym in the rote—
> Right so, in soth, with tonge of scorpioun
> This Anthenor, rote of al tresoun,
> His tale tolde with a face pleyn,
> Liche the sonne that shyneth in the reyn,
> That faire sheweth though the weder be
> Wonder divers and troubly for to se.
> (*Troy*, IV, 5213–5226)

This same sequence of images is repeated, with variation and expansion, on at least twenty-five other occasions in Lydgate's poetry, and merges with another contrasting pattern of images expressive of universal mutability, the "sorrow after joy" theme. The economy of imagery is indicative of the way all reality is channeled into a number of literary stereotypes, and of the way in which every subtle shade of human experience, every subtle blend of moral black and white, is programmed in binary terms through Lydgate's literary computer.

The fascination of Lydgate's style is endless, and to some extent self-sufficient, for there is no other poet in whom "style" becomes so nearly an end in itself, a fixed entity of which the relation to "subject" is one of abstract congruence, not expressive embodiment. But the interest would be a superficial one if it were not part of a larger response to Lydgate's deeper patterns of meaning—not patterns of experience, for experience is essentially meaningless to Lydgate, but moral and philosophical patterns. We may conclude with a survey of these larger aspects of Lydgate's achievement.

Humor is not something we think of very readily in connection with Lydgate, but there is one field in which a set moralistic assumption releases irony of a kind that is all the more delightful for its being unexpected: the field of anti-feminist satire. Here Lydgate is in his element. In the *Troy-book*, whenever he comes to one of Guido's many diatribes against women, he prepares for it elaborately, with apologies and disclaimers of responsibility, then translates the offending passage with evident relish and skillful embellishment, ending with further excuses and disingenuous offers of defense, such as that, if women are by nature bad, then they can hardly be blamed for following their nature. The irony is never delicate; but it is sharp, and it hits home. Throughout the *Fall* too, the subject is one that arouses his keenest interest: he expands with great verve and brilliance Boccaccio's famous Juvenalian attack upon women (I, 6511) and makes a new interpretation of the Orpheus story as an allegory of the hell of marriage:

> But who hath onys infernal peynys seyn,
> Will never his thankis[40] come in the snare ageyn.
> (*Fall*, I, 5830–5831)

There is also elaborate ironical treatment of women in *Reason and Sensuality* and in the shorter poems (such as "Bycorne and Chichevache," "Beware of Doubleness," "Horns Away"), which have a pithy pungency and wit that we do not usually associate with Lydgate.

The irony here is clearly drawn from a moral commonplace, and it is in terms of the eloquent elucidation of moral commonplaces that we must see Lydgate's poetry. He has also, for instance, deep and enduring political concerns.

---

[36] strife. [37] put to the hazard. [38] vengeance.
[39] sweet.

[40] willingly.

The *Troy-book* is something of a "Mirour for Princes" in its analysis of political morality, and the *Fall* returns again and again to persistent themes: the evil of dissension among princes, the dangers of false succession, the reliance of lordship on the love of the people, and the necessity of personal integrity to good government. The themes are familiar; but they had a pressing relevance to the troubled and divided England of Lydgate's day, and they are handled with somber eloquence. Perhaps the most overtly political of his longer poems is the *Siege of Thebes*, which uses the classical story as a text for a debate on war and peace that must have seemed very pointed in the last years of Henry V's reign, when the continuance of the French wars was a burning issue.

In matters of love too, Lydgate's approach, as one might expect, is essentially moralistic. The portrait of the lover's service in the *Black Knight* and the *Temple of Glass* is one in which duty subsumes all passion and the exercise of virtue in love is made the precise analogue of virtue in general. The resemblance to Gower is close; but Lydgate's development of the doctrine is far more lofty and serious, as well as more attenuated, than Gower's. When he is writing within a strict formal tradition, as in the "Complaints" in the two poems, his imagination can produce, from the traditional apparatus of image, conceit, and classical allusion, a richness of order that is perfectly correspondent to his vision of life, a crystalline vision purged of the taint of earth. Lydgate's psychology of love is extremely simple, and is quite satisfied with arrows and wounds; but his expression of the perfectly refined ideal and doctrine of love has something that we might call moral fervor, though it is never transcendental.

It is, however, in the field of Boethian morality that Lydgate is most at home, and writes best. The *Troy-book* has many qualities—it is, indeed, the cornerstone of Lydgate's achievement—but its enduring effect upon the reader is in its solemn, moving, and deeply eloquent exposition of the great platitudes of human experience: the punishment of sin, the transitoriness of earthly happiness and the falseness of earthly fame, the mutability of Fortune, and the inevitablility of death. He may have begun the poem as a chivalric exemplar; but, as he wrote, his imagination was stirred to a contemplation of the story as a tragic text for the universal predicament. He rises to the theme with the full power of his rhetoric in such passages as the lament for Troy in book IV. The *Fall* too is like an enormous epilogue, or envoi on fame, and has moments, despite its central artistic incoherence, of even greater grandeur, when Lydgate is moved by something like tragic moral vision. The work as a whole is a dark panorama of universal history, held from chaos by the persistence and integrity of Lydgate's moral patterning.

Of Lydgate's religious poetry we have said little, though we might expect that it would be the heart of his achievement. For the most part he gives to it a different kind of attention, in which rhetoric is heightened beyond language into liturgical ritual. There are a number of religious poems, in particular the *Testament*, in which he speaks out of a simpler religious feeling, though it would be a mistake to treat this poem as autobiographical in any but the most conventionalized sense, since self-expression would be as foreign to Lydgate's idiom as self-consciousness would be. The last stanza is justly famous, though it is not in a manner that we can regard as characteristic of Lydgate:

> Tarye no lenger toward thyn herytage,
> Hast on thy weye and be of ryght good chere,
> Go eche day onward on thy pylgrymage,
> Thynke howe short tyme thou hast abyden here;
> Thy place is bygged[41] above the sterres clere,
> Noon erthly palys wrought in so statly wyse.
> Kome on, my frend, my brother most entere!
> For the I offered my blood in sacryfice.
>
> (*Testament*, 890–897)

Totally characteristic of Lydgate, however, is the *Life of Our Lady*, a rich anthology of Marian themes in which his devotional intensity achieves perfect poetic expression. The best writing is in the most formal passages such as that on the Conception, in which the exuberance of the Marian imagery is lavishly displayed, but above all in the Prologue, where the traditional images of *stella maris* and *flos campi* blend into a vision of the Virgin's birth as the dawning of day upon the world's night. Famil-

[41] built.

iar material is here exploited, through Lydgate's luminous rhetoric, with transfiguring effect, and it would not be too much to call this one of the finest passages of nonpersonal religious poetry in English.

SELECTED BIBLIOGRAPHY

I. Bibliography. G. Watson, ed., *The New Cambridge Bibliography of English Literature,* I (Cambridge, 1974).

II. Editions. Most of Lydgate's poems have been edited for the Early English Text Society. The major texts are as follows (OS, Original Series; ES, Extra Series): J. Schick, ed., *Temple of Glass,* ES 60 (London, 1891); R. Steele, ed., *Secrets of the Old Philosophers,* ES 66 (London, 1894); F. J. Furnivall and K. Locock, eds., *Pilgrimage of the Life of Man,* ES 77, 83, 92 (London, 1899–1904); E. Sieper, ed., *Reason and Sensuality,* ES 84, 89 (London, 1901–1903); H. Bergen, ed., *Troybook,* ES 97, 103, 106, 126 (London, 1906–1935); A. Erdmann and E. Erkwall, eds., *Siege of Thebes,* ES 108, 125 (London, 1911–1930); H. N. MacCracken, ed., *Minor Poems,* ES 107, religious poems (London, 1911), OS 192, secular poems (London, 1934); H. Bergen, ed., *Fall of Princes,* ES 121–124 (London, 1924–1927); F. Warren and B. White, eds., *The Dance of Death,* OS 181 (London, 1931).

III. Other Editions. C. Horstmann, ed., "St. Edmund and Fremund," in *Altenglische Legenden* (Heilbronn, 1881); C. Horstmann, ed., "The Life of St. Albon and St. Amphabel," in *Festschrift der Königstädtischen Realschule* (Berlin, 1882), also J. van der Westhuizen, ed. (Leiden, 1974); H. N. MacCracken ed., *The Serpent of Division,* prose (New Haven, 1911); E. P. Hammond, ed., *English Verse Between Chaucer and Surrey* (Durham, N. C., 1927), extensive selections from Lydgate, with excellent intro.; J. A. Lauritis, R. A. Klinefelter, and V. F. Gallagher, eds., *The Life of Our Lady,* Duquesne Studies, Philological Series no. 2 (Pittsburgh, 1961); J. Norton-Smith, ed., *John Lydgate: Poems,* Clarendon Medieval and Tudor Series (Oxford, 1966), valuable anthology, with full apparatus.

IV. Critical Studies. C. S. Lewis, *The Allegory of Love* (Oxford, 1936), valuable material on Lydgate (pp. 239–243); R. Weiss, *Humanism in England During the Fifteenth Century* (Oxford, 1947); W. F. Schirmer, *John Lydgate: A Study in the Culture of the XVth Century* (Tübingen, 1952), trans. by Ann E. Keep (London, 1961), a thorough and careful study of the whole range of Lydgate's work and its background; A. Renoir, *The Poetry of John Lydgate* (London, 1967); R. Woolf, *The English Religious Lyric in the Middle Ages* (Oxford, 1968), discussion of Lydgate's shorter religious poems; W. F. Bolton, ed., *The Middle Ages,* Sphere History of Literature in the English Language (London, 1970); D. Pearsall, *John Lydgate* (London, 1970); J. A. Burrow, *Ricardian Poetry* (London, 1971).

SIR THOMAS MALORY

(d. 1471)

M. C. Bradbrook

In his study W. B. Yeats kept a scrap of silk from a Japanese lady's dress, and a Samurai sword, as "things that are/Emblematic of love and war." These two themes are fundamental to the work of Sir Thomas Malory. Religion—the third of the great epic themes—is admittedly and nobly subordinated; only at the end, Guinevere, in expiation of her guilt in destroying the Round Table, becomes a nun; and Lancelot, for love of her and not for love of God, takes on himself the habit of perfection.

For nearly five hundred years, since its publication by William Caxton at Westminster on 31 July 1485, Malory's *Morte Darthur* has stood at the center of English literature. It has been read, and it has nourished the work of other writers; but it has been little discussed. This is one of the silent areas in English criticism, but such deceptively simple works, which offer little to be clever about, are the centers of high creative activity. Spenser's debt to Malory is clear; and throughout the nineteenth century he was used as a quarry. For the poetry of Tennyson and the Pre-Raphaelites he provided an essential basis; in our own day T. S. Eliot has described Malory as one of his favorite authors. Chaucer in the fourteenth century and Malory in the fifteenth together laid the foundations of modern English narrative; the scale of their work as well as its excellence, its breadth combined with its individuality, established and fortified the art of the imaginative story, in poetry and in prose. They are the only two English medieval writers who have been continuously and widely known from their own day to the present.

The differences between them are more obvious than the likeness. Chaucer, a diplomat and civil servant, writing for the elegant and sophisticated court of Richard II, with a cosmopolitan taste and a fine tact, a delicate malice and a most urbane wit, might have felt there was some rusticity about Malory, who did in fact begin his work by turning into prose an alliterative English poem of the fourteenth century, of the kind that Chaucer would certainly have thought exceedingly provincial. In *The Canterbury Tales,* it is the middle-class wife of Bath who tells an Arthurian fairy story, while Chaucer burlesques the whole tradition of romance in the delicious *Tale of Sir Thopas,* which he gives to himself to tell in his role of boring and incompetent simpleton. This is, of course, a burlesque of the popular and not of the courtly romance; but it suggests that in Chaucer's mind tales of wandering knights had already turned into old wives' tales.

Malory belonged to the next age, that turbulent fifteenth century whose disorder Shakespeare depicted in the trilogy of *Henry VI,* where the civil strife of the Wars of the Roses culminates with the scene of a lamenting king, set between a son who has killed his father and a father who has killed his son. Whether the Wars of the Roses were really disastrous for any but the small class of barons and knights is very problematic; but it was just this class, the remnants of an earlier society, from which Malory sprang, and which is idealized in the Round Table. Malory belonged to that older order of chivalry which finally went down on Bosworth Field in 1485, the year in which his work was published, 14 years after his own death.

Until 1966, Sir Thomas Malory was generally identified with a knight of Newbold Revell, in Warwickshire, who in his youth served with the great Richard Beauchamp, earl of Warwick. Later, however, he turned to a life of violence and died in Newgate Prison, 14 March 1471. Many scholars felt some embarrassment at thus identifying the author of "the noble and joyous book," and in 1966 William Matthews produced a rival candidate from the North. However, his case against the knight of Newbold Revell is much stronger than his case for any alternative figure.

Defenders of the Warwickshire knight have pointed out that in the fifteenth century it was too easy to frame a charge against political enemies. Thomas Malory was accused of breaking into an abbey and on two occasions of feloniously ravishing Joan, wife of Henry Smyth of Monks' Kirby—which need not mean more than abduction. As C. S. Lewis remarked, "He might, on the evidence, have been as good a knight as Tristram; for what should we think of Tristram himself if our knowledge of him were derived only from King Mark's solicitors?" Or indeed, what if we compare Malory with that pattern of chivalry, John Tiptoft, earl of Worcester? Otherwise known as the Butcher of England, in 1470 it was with great difficulty that he was brought to the scaffold through the London mob thirsting for his blood. His translation of *Controversia de nobilitate* was also published by Caxton.

Thus Malory's generally accepted identity as the knight of Newbold Revell should not merely be brushed aside.

Fortune's wheel whirled Malory continually lower and lower, in contrast to successful climbers like the Paston family, whose letters show them rising in the social scale throughout the fifteenth century by methods sometimes as violent as Malory's but more skillfully timed. The landless knight, the man-at-arms who followed his lord to foreign wars, often turned to violence when loosed upon his native soil, as the disbanded soldier took to begging or highway robbery. Though Malory himself was not landless, he behaved as one of this class, and some of his imprisonments were for debt. His story of violence, disaster, and stormy veerings to and fro may seem at variance with the modern notions of chivalry; but Malory seems to have retained the first chivalric virtue, that of loyalty to his lord. Here, however, his allegiance illustrates once more the decline of chivalry. Richard Beauchamp, earl of Warwick, whom he followed as a young man to Calais, was a pattern of courtesy as well as a great lord. Richard Neville, the Kingmaker, who succeeded to the title after his marriage to Beauchamp's grand-

daughter, and who made and unmade kings in Malory's later years, was the father of a queen, and himself greater than a king in possessions; but his rapid changes of party, his merciless slaughter of conquered enemies, above all his unnatural position of superiority and domination towards his lord the king seem to epitomize all that Malory and later even Shakespeare dreaded as the supreme evil of evil times—the dissolution of harmony, order, and degree which a divided rule may bring.

Malory wrote his work in prison. At the end of *The Tale of King Arthur*, standing first in the book, the Winchester MS has a note that it was written "by a knight prisoner, Sir Thomas Malleorré, that God send him good recover." At the end of the *Tales of Sir Gareth*, the writer appeals:

And I pray you all that readeth this tale to pray for him that this wrote, that God send him good deliverance soon and hastily.   Amen.

At the end of Caxton's printed version comes the paragraph entreating all gentlemen and gentlewomen "pray for me while I am on live that God send me good deliverance. And when I am dead, I pray you all pray for my soul." The writer himself adds such a prayer ". . . by Sir Thomas Maleoré knight as Jesu help him for His great might, as he is the servant of Jesu both day and night." This piteous little jingle suggests that by the ninth year of the reign of King Edward IV Malory had lost hope in an earthly deliverance.

Those who have seen works of art produced by prisoners during their confinement will not be surprised at the immense care and pains that are shown in *Le Morte Darthur* by the development of the style. Painfully and slowly Malory evolved his own prose, learned an eloquence, a craftsmanship, and a power of organization that could not have come easily to one who was not a clerk. He had all the time in the world in which to learn.

THE KNIGHTLY ROMANCE

STORYTELLING was the great art of the Middle Ages, and the romance was a special form of this art. It was a long-continuing and popular form; the stories that Malory told were also in substance many hundreds of years old. They were ennobled by long tradition; they were, too, believed to be true history. But they represented at the same time an enlarged picture of contemporary life. This seems one way of defining the romance. It gives an idealized version of the life of the knightly class; it is the warrior's daydream, designed for recreation (or "solace"), not instruction (or "doctrine"), and representing the average sensual man's point of view. Such stories might also reflect and celebrate contemporary events; Malory in *The Tale of the Noble King Arthur that was Emperor himself through Dignity of his Hands* seems to shadow the glorious campaigns of Henry V, as his source-poem had those of Edward III and the Black Prince. But it is quite exceptional for romances to carry religious overtones, as in the great fourteenth-century poem of *Sir Gawain and the Green Knight*. In Malory, the *Tale of the Sankgreal* is a separate story, in which the religious is simply a particular department of the marvellous. Miracles or legends of the saints are the religious equivalent of the knightly romance; the marvellous was allowed a very large share in both kinds.

Romance differs from epic in its readiness to include the fantastic, magical, and wishful elements largely within the action. In epic, though the world presented is enlarged and ennobled, it remains the world of everyday. It has been suggested that the epic material of one race or culture becomes romance when it is handed over to another race or culture and needs to be reinterpreted; when it has lost its social roots. Romance therefore presupposes epic; Malory recreated an epic story from romance.

The hero of a medieval romance, whatever the age in which he lived, always becomes a knight. In the romances of Troy, Hector is described as a knight, the "root and stock of chivalry"; Alexander becomes a medieval king. So, too, Arthur the Romano-British chieftain was seen as a contemporary ruler surrounded by his chivalry, the knights of the Round Table. The heroic early French epic of Charlemagne and the Twelve Peers of France underwent a similar transformation.

The medieval epic poem, such as *Beowulf* or the *Song of Roland*, dealt with the war leader and his band or *comitatus*; ultimately the structure of feudal society was based upon such bands, united by personal oaths of fidelity which bound vassal to lord and lord to vassal. The strong personal unity of a group of fighting men, in which unshakable loyalty and courage were essential for survival, developed into the feudal state in which the barons were bound to their lord the king, the lesser tenants to their own lords, and the whole structure depended upon a network of loyalties, all of a personal kind. The society depicted in the romances is the uppermost stratum of this social order. There is very little sense of the underlying and supporting levels of society. In Malory this is particularly noticeable. The churls who appear are churlishly treated, as when Lancelot strikes an uncooperative carter "a reremain," a blow over the back of his neck with a mailed fist, and summarily stretches him dead. Manners consist in giving each man his due; and the Lady Lionesse thinks a kitchen knave deserves nothing but insults.

The characters in romance are elected by age as well as class. They consist almost entirely of fighting men, their wives or mistresses, with an occasional clerk or an enchanter, a fairy or a fiend, a giant or a dwarf. Time does not work on the heroes of Malory; they may beget sons who grow up to manhood, without seeming to change in themselves: it is impossible to think of an old age, still less a late middle age, for Lancelot or Guinevere. There are very few old men or women, almost no infants or children. It is also a world in which family relationships, though they exist, are usually of comparatively little significance. Fathers are finally supplanted by sons (Lancelot by Galahad, Arthur by Mordred); the relation of husband to wife is a feudal and not a personal one. Brothers are related chiefly as brothers-in-arms; sisters and mothers hardly exist. The deep relationships in this world are those of knight and vassal, or its mirror image of lady and lover; and of these, the former is in Malory the most important, the last exhibiting the same virtue of fidelity which is more amply mirrored in the comradeship of arms. There is no doubt that even in the loves of Arthur, Lancelot, and Guinevere, the masculine loyalties triumph. When the strife between Gawain and Lancelot breaks out, Arthur cries:

Wit you well, my heart was never so heavy as it is now. And much more I am sorrier for my good knights' loss than for the loss of my fair queen; for queens I might have enow, but such a fellowship of good knights shall never be together in no company.

(Vinaver, p. 833[1])

It is the mature recognition of responsibility for their guilt toward society that keeps Lancelot and Guinevere apart in the end. After Arthur is dead, and she has betaken herself to the nunnery at Amesbury, the queen is sought out by Lancelot, and to her ladies she addresses herself before she speaks to him, and sends him away forever:

Through this same man and me hath all this war be wrought, and death of the most noblest knights of the world; for through our love that we have loved together is my most noble lord slain.

(p. 876)

So later still Sir Lancelot laments over the two he had loved. Guinevere dies and is buried beside Arthur.

For when I remember of her beauty and her noblesse, that was both with her king and with her, so when I saw his corpse and her corpse so lie together, truly mine heart would not serve to sustain my careful body. Also when I remember me how by my defaute and mine orgule and my pride that they were both laid full low, that were peerless ever was living of Cristen people, wit you well, said Sir Lancelot, this remembered, of their kindness and my unkindness, sank so to mine heart that I might not sustain myself.

(p. 880)

Even such lovers as Chaucer's Troilus and Criseyde, the delicacy and complexity of whose relationship is a matter of finest adjustment, are governed instinctively by the social demands that put marriage between a prince and the widowed daughter of the traitor Calchas quite out of court. Chaucer did not need to explain this; in Malory's day, when Edward IV married Elizabeth Woodville, Warwick the Kingmaker deserted him. For Malory, the story of Lancelot and Guinevere is one of divided loyalties; it is the social results of the love even more than the

[1] For convenience, the page references are to Vinaver's one-volume edition in the Oxford Standard Authors; but the spelling has been modernized throughout the quotations.

love itself which concern him, while the passionate story of Tristram and Isold fails to awaken his deeper interest, and remains episodic. Here the tragic end is missing, and the lovers are left happily together at Joyous Garde, Lancelot's castle, whither they have fled: their end is briefly mentioned by Lancelot, as the time of his own fall draws near (Vinaver, p. 828). This may be quite deliberate; the end of a well-known story could be suppressed to make a particular interpretation clearer, as Chaucer himself suppressed the death of Criseyde. Tristram and Isold are not faced by the same dilemma as Lancelot and Guinevere, since Mark cannot claim loyalty, being himself so treacherous; and the magic potion which they have drunk takes from their love the guilt and the glory of a voluntary choice. Theirs is a blind trancelike passion; Lancelot and Guinevere, though the queen's stormy rages and jealous outbursts may complicate the story and drive Lancelot like Tristram into madness, prove for each other a kind of fidelity that belongs not to the world of fancy but to the world of men.

In the great hymn in praise of fidelity in love, which opens Section IV of *Lancelot and Guinevere*, "The Knight of the Cart," Malory indulges in a rare lyric outburst. True love is likened unto summer; and in words which owe nothing to his "French book," though something perhaps to the joyous French songs that celebrate the coming of spring, he unites the love of man and woman with the great rhythms of the world and the seasons.

. . . For, like as winter rasure doth alway arace and deface green summer, so fareth it by unstable love in man and woman, for in many persons there is no stabylité; for we may see all day, for a little blast of winter's rasure, anon we shall deface and lay apart true love, for little or naught, that cost much thing. . . .

Wherefore I liken love nowadays unto summer and winter; for, like as the one is cold and the other is hot, so fareth love nowadays. And therefore all ye that be lovers, call unto your remembrance the month of May, like as did Queen Guinevere, for whom I make here a little mention, that while she lived she was a true lover, and therefore she had a good end.

(pp. 790–791)

The pathos of Malory's "dying fall," the cadence dropping to a minor chord, is his tribute to those inward feelings which in his masculine world receive so little direct expression. As always, the supreme virtue is truth.

The most famous and most magnificent passage in all Malory's work is the lament that closes it, the lament of Sir Ector de Maris over his brother, Sir Lancelot. Here the word "truest," sounds twice, like a tolling bell. It is the final picture of the perfect knight, the summary of all the paradoxical virtues of gentleness and sternness, all the defeated hopes that the knight prisoner had strengthened himself with in his prison.

Ah, Lancelot! he said, thou were head of all Cristen knights! And now I dare say, said Sir Ector, thou Sir Lancelot, there thou lyest, that thou were never matched of earthly knight's hand. And thou were the courteousest knight that ever bare shield! And thou were the truest friend to thy lover that ever bestrad horse, and thou were the truest lover of a sinful man that ever loved a woman, and thou were the kindest man that ever strake with sword. And thou were the goodliest person that ever came among press of knights, and thou was the meekest man and the gentlest that ever ate in hall among ladies, and thou were the sternest knight to thy mortal foe that ever put spear in the rest.

(p. 882)

THE ENGLISH ROUND TABLE

IF, then, the inner core of feeling which lies at the center of Malory's world is the masculine bond of fidelity, the old loyalty of the band of fighting men, we should expect him to encounter some difficulty in dealing with the French romances upon which his work is for the most part based, since in these the love of knight and lady was often the leading motif. The elaborate and fanciful code of manners which in theory governed the behavior of courtly lovers, involving the absolute subjection of the knight to the lady, with all the artifice of courtly etiquette, and all the exotic ritual of a mock religion, was never really acclimatized in England. The lovely dream of the garden of the rose, which Guillaume de Lorris wrote and Chaucer translated, had indeed inspired some of Chaucer's love poetry; and early in the fifteenth century also had inspired that of a nobler

prisoner than Malory, James I of Scotland, who, looking out of his prison tower, beheld a fair lady walking in a springtime garden, when

> suddenly my heart became her thrall
> For ever, of free will. . . .

But the courtly manners of royalty required a setting that most readers and writers of romance did not know; they remade the stories, so that the kings, queens, and knights became enlarged versions of themselves, with manners to correspond. Probably the most courtly poem in English about Arthur's knights is the fourteenth-century *Sir Gawain and the Green Knight*, in which a society as elegant as Chaucer's is depicted, and in which the maneuvering of the lady who tempts Gawain is as sophisticated as that of any heroine of Restoration comedy. A keen battle of wits between her and the knight (whom she takes at the greatest disadvantage by visiting him in bed) ends with the victory of the stronger sex; without discourtesy, Gawain repulses her, thus keeping his obligation as guest towards his host, the lady's husband.

This story was retold in rougher form as *Sir Gawain and the Carl of Carlisle*, and here the knight's adventures with his hostess take on a much cruder and more primitive form. In some cases, courtly romances ended as popular ballads, with all the fine-drawn sentiments, all the rich descriptions pared away, to leave the simple structure, the bare bones of some tragic story, told perhaps with noble simplicity, or perhaps only with confused, dull repetition and a plentiful use of well-worn phrases. Chaucer's *Tale if Sir Thopas*, though cruel, is not unjust to the popular romance which at its worst is unbearably boring.

Most of these English Arthurian romances deal with the adventures of some single knight. Sir Gawain, Sir Percival, Sir Launcefal and the rest are each shown as the center of a series of adventures. Some of the material belongs to the perennial world of the fairy tale; thus, tales of the fairy bride who rewards the knight with riches, with magic means to overcome his enemies, and sometimes with a fairy kingdom, are obviously popular subjects for a masculine daydream. Other tales tell of ordeals, the overcoming of magic obstacles, or war with giants, Saracens, devils. These are the two basic forms for the romantic adventures of a knightly hero.

In Malory, however, we meet a whole world of knights. Sir Lancelot is its undisputed champion, but Percival, Tristram, Galahad, Gawain, Gareth, and many others take for a while the center of the stage. Malory's great work, as it would appear from the Winchester MS, which came to light in 1934 in the library of Winchester College, is a collection or anthology of tales about the Round Table. It is not a single narrative, but a group of narratives, like the *Decameron* or the *Canterbury Tales;* based, however, on a different principle of selection, that of a common subject: all the tales are about Arthur's knights. To see the work in this way enables the reader to measure Malory's progress and his growing power in shaping his material.[2] Caxton, when he printed the work as if it were a single continuous narrative instead of an anthology, destroyed the perspective and blurred the outlines of Malory's work. By the recovery of their plan, the stories have acquired new shape and cohesion. First to be written was *The Tale of the Noble King Arthur that was Emperor himself through Dignity of his Hands.* This is a story of military triumph in which Arthur sets out to conquer Rome; which he does, and is crowned Emperor there, thus anticipating the glories of Charlemagne among epic heroes, and reflecting for Malory the triumphant conquests of Henry V. Professor Vinaver has shown how Malory modifies the course of Arthur's French campaign to correspond with the course of Henry's. This part of Malory's work is based on an English heroic poem, *Le Morte Arthur;* but here, as in the story of Tristram, Malory has cut out the tragic ending, and uses only the first part of the poem, which deals with Arthur's triumph. At the very end of his work he was to return to another English poem to help him in depicting *The Most Piteous Tale of the Morte Arthur Saunz Guerdon.* But in the interval he relied on various "French books," prose romances of great length, which he shaped and reorganized with increasing skill. Only for one or two stories, particularly *The Tale of Sir Gareth of Orkeney that was called Bewmaynes,* are the sources of his work unknown. To trace the history of the

stories of King Arthur is a lifetime's task; and the majority of scholars who give themselves to the study of Malory or of his originals are concerned mainly with constructing genealogical trees for the stories and disputing various theories of descent. This, though a fascinating game, is sometimes a way of evading the duty—at once more simple and more difficult—of seeing them as literature. But the idea of the Round Table is so central to Malory's work, and in itself so especially English a development of the story, that a brief sketch of it may be attempted.

MALORY AND THE HEROIC TRADITION

THREE hundred years before Malory, the poet Layamon gave an account of the founding of the Round Table. Arthur held a great feast at which his vassals from Britain, Scotland, Ireland, and Iceland assembled. A squabble about precedence developed. At first bread and cups were thrown and fists used. Then a young hostage of Arthur's household snatched up the carving knives from before the king, and the killing began. It took Arthur and a hundred armed men to quell the fight, under the most terrifying threats of instant death for men and mutilation for women related to those who began the brawl. If any sought revenge for what had happened, he would be torn in pieces by wild horses. The body of the man who began the fight was to be thrown out to rot unburied.

As a result of these measures, the dead were carried off and the feast went merrily on; but the cunning smith who offered to make Arthur a wondrous table at which sixteen hundred might sit without question of precedence seems to be catering less for the vassals of an overlord than for the members of some primitive horde. Arthur, however, appears as the dominant figure. In his words:

Sit down! sit down at once! or your lives will pay

is heard the authentic voice of command.

Precedence at feasts, and the order of service at the lord's table, was a matter of signifi-

[2] C. S. Lewis, *Essays on Malory* (Oxford, 1963), p. 23.

cance throughout the Middle Ages. The long narrow table on the dais in the opening scene of *Sir Gawain and the Green Knight* is set in customary fashion with the king in the middle, and his principal guests on each side. A round table would in fact have been a great curiosity and departure from custom, in one of those ceremonious occasions which the romances loved to depict; and in all stories, the feast which so frequently opens or closes them (the symbol of good fellowship and unity) is described in the usual sort of medieval hall with the usual high table on a dais. What generally happens is that the King is feasting his knights and declares that he will not eat till he sees a marvel. Instantly some damsel in distress or some strange apparition like the Green Knight appears and the adventure begins.

Although in most of the earlier romances the story is concerned with the adventures of a particular knight, there is a sense of the brotherhood of the Round Table given by these feasts at the beginning and end of the story; after a series of combats, it is usual for the valiant enemy of the hero to be accepted as a member of the Round Table. By the fourteenth century it was thought of as a fellowship akin to that of some knightly order, such as the Garter, or the Bath, and certain kinds of tournament became known as "round tables."

The Great Tournament is in Malory the last and supreme moment of unity and good fellowship for the Round Table; it is the expression of the bond which is about to be dissolved by the quarrel between Lancelot and Gawain, Arthur's champion and his nephew and heir. Tournaments, or mock battles, in which knightly qualities were displayed without the risk of real battle, had become something like a fifteenth-century Olympic Games; they were great pageants at which fortunes were spent upon equipment, and to which champions would travel from all over Europe. The last and most gorgeous occasion of this kind to be generally remembered is the encounter between Henry VIII and Francis I of France, known as the Field of the Cloth of Gold.

Such tournaments gave opportunity for the writer of romance to indulge in long descriptions of splendor, with detailed accounts of the dishes at the feasts, the armor of the knights,

and the order of combat. Here Malory departs from the habits of the age. He is not interested in descriptions but in action; and he does not do more than note the color of the knights' armor. Combat excites him, but his world lacks the stateliness and the ritual of Chaucer's and the Gawain poet's, the true courtly ceremoniousness.

He has, on the other hand, a very strong sense of the fellowship, which enables him to rise to the heights of the last books. This sense of the fellowship dominates one or two other works; such as the poem of *Lancelot du Laik* and the alliterative *Morte Arthur* on which Malory based the first of his tales. These poems imitate the literary form of the Chronicle History. Here there is an account of the king's challenge to lordship of a foreign land; then an invasion and a series of battles are described, very closely akin to the English wars in France. In each battle, a list of the eminent warriors taking part on both sides is given, and a list of those who fell. Such poems are no longer pure romance of adventure; they are histories. In Malory, too, there is this strong sense of history, implying the epic rather than the romantic style.

After his early tale of Arthur's conquest of Rome, Malory turned back for a time to the more primitive and wilder stories about Merlin. These belong to the oldest traditions of romance. In general, the more primitive the stories, the larger the part played by magic; thus, in the one Arthurian tale in the *Mabinogion* (a collection of Welsh tales in prose dealing with Celtic mythology), all the knights are possessed of superhuman powers, and are frankly figures of magical rather than human kind.

After his excursion into the realms of magic, Malory tells a number of tales about individual knights, in the same form roughly as the romances of adventure that have been described. These are tales of wanderings, in which the hero rides away on a quest. The quest for the Holy Grail includes five such tales of individual knights. The tragic tale of *The Knight with the Two Swords* and the tale of Gareth have each a strong and shapely coherence; others follow rather the interlacing and interweaving technique of the long French romances. The story of Tristram is of this kind, containing in itself several minor stories, such as the tale of Alexander le Orphelin.

The adventures of individual knights in their quests show them freed from all restrictions of ordinary life. Armor and tournaments may be realistic, but in a romance there is suppression of all the usual laws of cause and effect in action. The knightly champion has to meet giants, dragons, monsters, the king's enemies, sorcerers, and mysteries of all kinds. Heads that are cut off may be stuck on again; marvels and wonders are the rule and not the exception. The appearance and manners of the knight are familiar, merely an enlargement of the everyday, but he has no responsibilities, no followers. He rides through vast and shadowy landscapes and forests, where only the cities of Caerleon and Carlisle remind the listener that this is England. The modern reader may see a parallel in the world of science fiction, in which the admired technical apparatus which commands most prestige today is used to decorate the wildest fantasy. Romance indulges in the same mixture of the fanciful and the up-to-date. It allows the listener to identify himself with a hero of almost superhuman prowess, yet matches him against forces that stress his humanity and normality. Monsters from outer space are the modern equivalent of the fairy-tale giant.

Most romances of individual knights arrive at a happy ending; feasts and weddings wind them up. When the theme is the Round Table itself, however, the story ends with the great epic battle, the unsuccessful fight against odds. Whereas incidents of the individual romances defy cause and effect, in the epic of the Round Table morality is always felt behind the action; the ideal is a social and ethical one. It was to this graver subject that Malory finally turned at the end of his work, joining the tale of his great hero Lancelot with the fate of the whole fellowship.

The stories of Arthur and his knights can thus be seen to undergo a development not unrelated to the society that in an idealized form they reflect. In the earliest tales, magic and violence predominate; then the image of a society based on feudal ties of loyalty emerges; the adventures of individuals follow, with, in the more courtly versions, much stress on manners and on wooing, and in the popular versions, simply on adventure and marvels. In both, the ideal knight in quest of adventure undergoes a great variety of different trials, from which he usually emerges victorious. Finally, something akin to the older epic style reappears, reflecting also the form of contemporary chronicles and, in Malory, tinged with some shadowing from contemporary struggles. At his greatest, in the final passages dealing with the last battle and death of Arthur, he seems to reflect in an enlarged form all the troubles of his own society, the ruin that civil strife had brought upon him and his kind. This is imaginatively seen in the dissolution of the Round Table, the bond and fellowship of knighthood. Conquest, like true and faithful love, belongs to the past: the first and last campaigns of Arthur represent for Malory a youthful hope of the past contrasted with a tragic present.

The unity of "the hoole book" as Malory finally achieved it depends on unity of atmosphere and underlying concepts, leading finally to unification of statement and theme. In recent years, scholars have restressed the unity of Malory's work, and even the natural continuity of Caxton's additions as being like

a great cathedral where Saxon, Norman, Gothic, Renaissance and Georgian elements all co-exist and all grow together into something strange and admirable which none of its successive builders intended or foresaw. (*Essays on Malory*, p. 25)

TRAGIC THEMES IN MALORY

MALORY was, of course, not depicting the troubles of his time directly; he only was giving an imaginative form to them. Unlike the poets of the alliterative tradition, Langland and the rest, he has no counsel to give. The grace and beauty of the *Morte Darthur* spring largely from its freedom from any reflection, any complicated tangle of social or of emotional repercussions. It is a splendid holiday from all such teasing questions as our living in the daily world implies.

The fights are sheer trials of strength and skill; the love-making is free from sentimentality, complaint, or evasion—as the healthy union of animals. There is something extraordinarily clean about Malory's world. Nearly all the knights are good except Kay (who appears chiefly in the early books), Mark, Mordred, and a few characters like Breuntz sauns Pitié; but these are so clearly labelled, and their churlishness is so obvious, that the listener is quite untroubled by their fulfilling of their customary roles. Morgan le Fay, the wicked queen and Arthur's sister, is the villainess of the piece, a figure at once more remote and more powerful.

Blood flows very freely. Two strange knights meet, "and as soon as either saw other they made them ready to joust." When they had fought for half a day and nearly killed each other, they ask each other's name and discover that they are Sir Percival and Sir Ector de Maris, both in search of Sir Lancelot, who has run mad in the woods. Both feel themselves to be dying and are unable even to seek a priest for shriving. But Percival kneels and prays, and on a sudden appearance of the Holy Grail "forthwith they were as whole of hide and limb as ever they were in their life" (Vinaver, p. 603). An action that resembles nothing so much as the instinctive rushing together of two wild boars (Malory's favorite simile for his warriors) thus ends with a miracle that does not at all differ from the magic spells of the Lady Lionesse, who restored the heads of decapitated knights by enchantment. The knights are suitably chastened.

Then they gave thankings to God with great mildness

and gravely discuss what can have happened to them. Sir Ector explains to Sir Percival that they have seen the Holy Grail.

"So God me help," said Sir Percival, "I saw a damsel, as me thought, all in white, with a vessel in both her hands, and forthwith I was whole."
So then they took their horses and their harness, and mended it as well as they might that was broken; and so they mounted up and rode talking together. And there Sir Ector de Maris told Sir Percival how that he had sought his brother Sir Lancelot, long, and never could hear witting of him: "In many hard adventures have I been in this quest." And so either told other of their great adventures.
(pp. 603–604)

This condition of complete simplicity, a combination of violence and innocence, was presumably taken for granted by Malory himself and by his contemporaries. Vinaver points out how new is delight in the inarticulate assurance of the fighting man when King Arthur asks his knights for counsel. "They had no counsel, but said they were big enough." There is pathos in the loyalty of Sir Lancelot's kinsmen, when they warn him "insomuch as ye were taken with her, whether ye did right other wrong, it is now your part to hold with the queen," and he asks them "Wherefore, my fair lords, my kin and my friends, what will ye do?"

And anon they said with one voice:
"We will do as ye will do" (p. 827)

Taciturnity could go no further than the comment of the hermit when his salutary counsel to do penance is rejected by Gawain, on the plea that the life of a knight-errant is sufficiently hard in itself.

"Well," said the good man and then he held his peace. (p. 651)

Tacit et fecit might be the motto of any of Arthur's knights.

A knight finds his mother in bed with another knight. He strikes off her head. A lady whose knight is slain kills herself with his sword. Elaine gets Lancelot to her bed by enchantment, even within Arthur's court, and knowing that he thinks he is abed with Guinevere. Such a trick, which destroys all depth in the action when Shakespeare uses it in *All's Well that Ends Well* and *Measure for Measure,* does not jar in Malory. He comments:

And wit you well this lady was glad, and so was Sir Lancelot for he wende that he had had another in his arms. (p. 593)

After Lancelot has fled, being driven mad by the anger of Guinevere, the two ladies from mutual reproaches fall to common lament.

"As for that," said dame Elaine, "I dare undertake he is marred for ever and that have you made. For neither you nor I are like to rejoice him, for he made the most piteous groans when he leapt out at yonder bay window that I ever heard a man make. Alas!" said fair Elaine, and "Alas!" said the queen, "For now I wot well that we have lost him for ever."

(p. 595)

It is left to Sir Bors to rebuke both of them; he spares neither Elaine nor the queen, who proceeds to send out knights in quest for Lancelot, with "treasure enough" for their expenses—a fact that is duly recorded to Lancelot himself when he returns to his right mind.

"And therefore, brother," said Sir Ector, "make you ready to ride to the court with us. And I dare say, and make it good," said Sir Ector, "it hath cost my lady the Queen twenty thousand pounds the seeking of you."

(p. 616)

This, as Vinaver observes, is the only time an Arthurian quest is assessed in money terms. "There's beggary in the love that can be reckon'd," as Antony says, but perhaps it is not unfitting that one who knew the inside of a debtor's prison should use the hateful unfamiliar terms for once, to reckon the worth of Lancelot.

Set against Elaine the mother of Galahad, is Elaine the Maid of Astolat, whose story is perhaps the most inward and pathetic of all Malory's tales. Elaine of Astolat shares with her young brother Lavaine a kind of compulsive and enthralled devotion to Lancelot; it is at once completely innocent and frankly sensuous. She speaks to Lancelot in the voice of Miranda.

"Why, what would ye that I did?" said Sir Lancelot.
"Sir, I would have you to my husband," said Elaine.
"Fair damsel, I thank you heartily," said Sir Lancelot, "but truly," said he, "I cast me never to be wedded man."
"Then fair knight," said she, "will ye be my paramour?"
"Jesu defend me!" said Sir Lancelot, "For then I rewarded your father and your brother full evil for their great goodness."
"Alas then," said she, "I must die for your love."

Lancelot's attempt at consolation is a model of tactlessness. He informs her that he has had many other offers, and says that he would like to reward her for her kindness, which he will do

by settling up her a dowry of a thousand pounds a year.

And so he departs, attended by Lavaine:

"Father," said Sir Lavaine, "I dare make good she is a clean maiden as for my lord Sir Lancelot; but she doth as I do, for sithen I first saw my lord Sir Lancelot I could never depart from him, neither nought I will, and I may follow him."

(p. 778)

The death of Elaine, justifying her love against the counsel of her ghostly father, who bade her leave such thoughts ("Why should I leave such thoughts? am I not an earthly woman?") by submitting herself to God, is perhaps a more truly religious occasion than all the episodes of the Holy Grail. There is the clearest acceptance of bodily death; she asks her brother to write a letter "and while my body is hot let this letter be put in my right hand, and my hand bound fast to the letter until that I be cold." This letter containing her plaint to Lancelot and her last request that he would bury her and offer her mass-penny is delivered in the scene that is the most dramatically and picturesquely described in all Malory; the barge hung in black samite, hove to upon the Thames; the silent boatman; and the corpse on a fair bed, covered to her middle with cloth of gold.

And she lay as she had smiled.

(p. 780)

Death is the one fact that is emotionally charged in Malory. Again and again, when he records the deaths of Balin, of Gawain, of Arthur, and finally of Lancelot, he rises to heights of passion and of eloquence that are not matched elsewhere in the *Morte Darthur*. Although life is cheap and wounds are so frequent that the chief knights seem to be sorely wounded about an average of once a week, yet in the moment of death which is also the moment of truth, a life may be summed up, a judgment given, and a garland bestowed.

In the last tales, the emotionally charged fact of death and the imaginatively perceived disruption of the social order are combined, as Malory describes the mutual destruction of the Round Table and the death of his chief heroes. There is still nothing that could be called reflection, comment, or entanglement in daily living; there is, of course, the fully apprehended physical horror of battle.

> Then Sir Lucan took up the king the one party and Sir Bedwere the other party, and in the lifting up the king swooned and in the lifting Sir Lucan fell in a swoon, that parts of his guts fell out of his body. . . . And when the king awoke, he behold Sir Lucan how he lay foaming at the mouth and part of his guts lay at his feet. (p. 869)

But beyond this, there is the deeper pain that arises from remorse, from the failing of the Fellowship, and above all from the sense of mystery, which comes with the passing of Arthur in the black barge tended by the weeping queens. The good end of Lancelot and of Guinevere, and of the remnant of the knights, who took the cross and "died upon a Good Friday for God's sake"—the last words of the book—are in the nature of a *coda*. For the men and women of Malory are earthly men and women; and for them, the good life of earth, the active life of loving and fighting, and the unlimited horizons of Arthur's kingdoms are all.

THE DAY OF DESTINY

THE ancient heroic tradition of English poetry— the tradition of *Beowulf* and of *The Battle of Maldon*—descended to Malory through the English alliterative poetry of the fourteenth century upon which he based his earliest story, *The Tale of the Noble King Arthur that was Emperor himself through Dignity of his Hands*. His own shaping of the Arthurian tales, which had already undergone so many changes in the course of the three hundred years in which they had been the common property of writers all over Western Europe, was grave, masculine, and at its deepest levels concerned with personal relationships as part of the social structure and not as the private, secret joy and pain of man or woman. Elaine of Astolat, though a touching figure, is yet a minor one in his great tapestry. The French books had developed the subtlety and the fineness of courtly love, and had overlaid the primitive simplicities of the stories. The

author of *Sir Gawain and the Green Knight* had fused adventure and morality; at the center of his poem is a description of the emblem of the Five Wounds of Christ and the Five Joys of Mary which the good knight bears upon his shield. Malory's world is rougher and simpler than either of these. In the last two tales, *The Book of Sir Lancelot and Queen Guinevere* and *The Most Piteous Tale of the Morte Arthur Saunz Guerdon*, he attains to his full heroic theme.

In the intervening tales, his characters have a kind of depth and stability which the figures of English romances do not usually possess. Where interest is concentrated upon a marvellous succession of adventures, characters retain a fairy-tale flatness and remain simply types, upon which the fantasy of the listeners can be easily projected, and with whom they can readily identify themselves. The central figure in the warrior's daydream must be fairly indeterminate, if he is to act as an idealized self for all and sundry. Slowly, Arthur, Gawain, and Lancelot have become, if not characters in the full dramatic sense, at least figures defined by their existence in a mutual relationship to each other. They have social if not individual identities.

In *The Tale of the Noble King Arthur*, it is the king himself who is the hero. Here, instead of a quest, Malory depicts a whole campaign. There is nevertheless a magnificent preliminary description of Arthur's single-handed combat with the giant of St. Michael's Mount. A weird and terrifying scene first greets him as he climbs to the summit of the crag—a weeping woman by a new-made grave, two fires "flaming high" at which the bodies of little children, "broched in a manner like birds," are being roasted and tended by three captive damsels. In such a setting there is a tremendous hand-to-hand encounter. At the end of this, locked together, the king and the sorely wounded giant roll from the top to the bottom of the mountain.

> With that the warlow wrath Arthur under, and so they waltred and tumbled over the crags and bushes, and either cleght other full fast in their arms. And other whiles Arthur was above and other whiles under, and so weltering and wallowing they rolled down the hill, and they never left till they fell thereas the flood marked. But ever in the waltring Arthur

smites and hits him with a short dagger up to the hilts, and in his falling there brast of the giant's ribs three even at once. (p. 147)

The rough wit by which he is greeted by his comrades, "I have mickle wonder and Michael be of such making, that ever God would suffer him to abide in Heaven," is matched by Arthur's own, when in the fight with the Emperor he cuts off a giant by the knees: " 'Now art thou of a size,' said the king, 'like unto our fairies' and then he struck off his head swiftly" (Vinaver, p. 159). But the King's prowess having been established in his fight with the giant, others are permitted a large share in the victorious advance upon Rome.

In Arthur's campaign there is the first glimmering of a national pride, which was quite foreign to the knightly society of the Middle Ages, and to the medieval romance. It is manifest in the opening scenes, with the brilliant picture of an invading fleet setting out from England and making its way across to France. Only in the first and the last of the tales does geography become significant; and it does so because in both these parts of the story Malory is depicting the fate, not of individuals, but of a nation.

At the end there is a regression from the more civilized social bonds of the fellowship to the primitive ones of kinship. In the final books, rival brotherhoods to that of the Round Table appear. It is the five nephews of Arthur who in different ways oppose Lancelot—Aggravayne and Mordred by treachery, Gawain, Gaherys, and Gareth from mischance. These last dissociate themselves strongly from the plots of the other two, who lead a little band of twelve "and they were of Scotland, and other else of Sir Gawain's kin, other well-willers to his brother." On the other hand, Lancelot's danger draws togeher "all we ben of your blood and your well-willers," as Sir Bors tells him. Roused by a common sense of alarm, they had all wakened from sleep and come together at the moment when the treacherous assault upon the queen's chamber was made. The issue is clear to Lancelot.

"And therefore, my fellows," said Sir Lancelot, "I pray you all that ye will be of heart good, and help me in what need that ever I stand, for now is war comen to us all."

"Sir," said Sir Bors, "all is welcome that God sendeth us, and as we have taken much weal with you and much worship, we will take the woe with you as we have taken the weal."

And therefore they said, all the good knights.

"Look ye, take no discomfort! for there is no bond of knights under heaven but we shall be able to grieve them as much as they us, and therefore discomfort not yourself by no manner. And we shall gather together all that we love and that loveth us, and what that ye will have done shall be done. And therefore let us take the woe and the joy together." (p. 825)

The knightly virtue of loyalty has turned against itself. From this point all the efforts of Lancelot to avoid that which he knows is inevitable are doomed. Gawain refuses to oppose Lancelot; as a consequence his two younger brothers, sent as guards to the queen's trial, and going reluctantly and unarmed, are slain unawares by Lancelot in his rescue of the queen; and so the blood feud between himself and Gawain begins. Gawain denies what he well knows, that the deaths were sheer mischance; Lancelot will not defend himself at the cost of injury to Arthur or Gawain; he makes the most stupendous offers of penance for the deaths of Gaherys and Gareth, including a pilgrimage barefoot and in his shirt, from Sandwich to Carlisle, but Gawain will not be reconciled.

The pope finally intervenes and ends the war. The queen is returned to Arthur, and Lancelot is banished from the realm. To point the moral, here in his lament ancient examples of a tragic fall are evoked.

"Fortune is so variant, and the wheel so mutable, that there is no constant abiding. And that may be proved by many old chronicles, as of noble Ector of Troy and Alysaunder, the mighty conqueror, and many mo other. . . ." (p. 847)

So Sir Lancelot departs to Bayonne, and Arthur and his knights once again invade France, no longer as conquerors but in pursuit of vengeance. Then swiftly follows the treachery of Mordred, Arthur's nephew and bastard son, gotten upon his sister Morgawse, queen of Orkney. Mordred, left as regent in England, revolts against Arthur. The sin at the heart of Arthur's court is finally embodied in this dark figure. The fruitless attempt to destroy Lancelot fails, and Gawain dies repentant; the final battle, that between Arthur and the dark powers, draws on. Even here, at the last moment, a bid is made for peace; Arthur and Mordred hold a parley between their armies, but each in such mistrust that they warn their followers if any sword is drawn, they should advance and slay. Success seems imminent; but Fortune turns her wheel, and the Day of Destiny falls upon the chivalry of Britain.

> And so they met as their poyntement was, and were agreed and accorded throughly. And wine was fetched and they drank together. Right so came out an adder of a little heath bush, and it stung a knight in the foot. And so when the knight felt him so stung, he looked down and saw the adder; and anon he drew his sword to slay the adder, and thought none other harm. And when the host on both parties saw that sword drawn, then they blew beams, trumpets and horns, and shouted grimly, and so both hosts dressed them togethers. And King Arthur took his horse and said, "Alas, this unhappy day!" and so rode to his party, and Sir Mordred in like wise.
>
> (p. 867)

There is very little left of either army by the end of the day, when the father and son confront each other, afoot and weary, over the heaps of dead. Arthur drives his spear through Mordred's body, but Mordred thrusts himself forward to the butt end of the spear, to give Arthur his death's wound by the sword.

The growth of treachery and mistrust, and the vanity of all efforts by men to stay the course of fortune as it carries them to destruction give to these last books of the *Morte Darthur* an ironic unity and a singleness of action that are new to Malory, and far beyond the world of romance. He had achieved something of the same effect upon a smaller scale in his early tale of *Balin or the Knight with Two Swords.* Balin, a knight out of wild Northumberland, rough and uncouth, by his impulsive acts of vengeance brings down ruin upon himself and his house. Confronted by magic dangers, and invisible foes, he is a human figure imposed on a legendary background, whose very confusion and portentous horror enhances his rude and simple courage. Throughout the story the sense of doom is felt in the phrase so often applied to Balin, "he may not long endure"; in his last battle he rides forward at the challenging sound of the horn, with so ominous and savage a comparison that he seems like Roland riding to the Dark Tower.

> And so he heard an horn blow as it had been the death of a beast. "That blast," said Balyn, "is blowen for me, for I am the prize and yet am I not dead."
>
> (p. 67)

So he goes forward into combat, only to find, in the hour of death, that he has fought his own brother Balan, and that they have slain each other.

The slaying of the kinsman, here as in Arthur's last battle, is an act at once profoundly unnatural and yet felt to be inevitable; it marks the disruption of the last and deepest social bond. What symbolism might be seen in this act by more sophisticated ages is irrelevant to Malory, whose greatness lies in his literal significance, and in the boldness with which he faces the unshirkable mysteries of anger and fidelity, courage and grief, love and death. In Arthur's death scene there is a foreshadowing of Shakespeare's tableau in *Henry VI*: the civil strife, the lamenting king who is also the father killing the son, while the son also kills the father. Whether in the single story of Balin, or in the ruin of a kingdom, it is in depicting heroic tragic action that Malory attains his full stature. There are more purely romantic pleasures to be gained from his work, including, even for modern readers, the pleasures of the daydream; but there is no sickliness in his dreams, as there is no malice in his violence. His is a mirror of the active life, untouched by contemplation.

SELECTED BIBLIOGRAPHY

The bulk of the writing on Arthurian romance is to be found in learned journals, some of which are not readily accessible. Such articles have, therefore, not been listed here; anyone who wishes to do so will find a bibliography of periodical literature in the *Romantic Review* and in *Speculum*, the journal of the Medieval Academy of America (Cambridge, Mass.), together with reviews and notices. Much useful material will also be found in *Medium Aevum*, the journal of the Society for the Study of Medieval Language and Literature (Oxford).

I. Texts. H. O. Sommer, ed., *Le Morte Darthur*, 2 vols. (London, 1889–1891), a line by line reprint of the first edition (1485), with an introduction and glossary; E. Vinaver, ed., *The Works of Sir Thomas Malory*, 3 vols. (Oxford, 1947; 2nd ed. 1967; repr. with corrections, 1971), a critical and annotated ed. incorporating the readings of the Winchester MS. A one-volume ed., without the critical apparatus but with brief introduction and glossary, was published in 1954.

Only two copies are recorded of William Caxton's first edition of *The Noble and Ioyous Book Entytled Le Morte Darthur Notwythstondyng It Treateth of the Byrth Lyf and Actes of the Sayd Kyng Arthur of his Noble Knyghtes of the Rounde Table Theyr Mervayllous Enquestes and Adventures Thachyevyng of the Sankgreal and in Thende the Dolorous Deth and Departyng out of Thys World of Them Al Whiche Booke was Reduced in to Englysshe by Syr Thomas Malory Knyght* (Westminster, 1485) (John Rylands University Library of Manchester and the Pierpoint Morgan Library, New York). Only two copies exist (Rylands and Bodleian libraries) of the 2nd ed., printed by Wynkyn de Worde (Westminster, 1498).

Modernized texts include those by A. W. Pollard (London, 1902) and E. Rhys (London, 1910), each in two volumes. See also Derek Brewer, ed., *The Morte Darthur*, paperback, York Mediaeval Texts Series (1968, rev. ed., 1976). The valuable introduction, especially the treatment of Shame and Honour, has been highly influential; the notes and glossary make this the most useful compact edition of these great last books. *The Death of Arthur*, from Vinaver's work, has been published as a separate volume, *King Arthur and His Knights* (Oxford, 1975), also available in paperback.

II. Critical and Biographical Studies. G. H. Maynardier, *Arthur of the English Poets* (Boston, 1905), a study of the influence of Malory upon subsequent writers; V. D. Scudder, *The Morte Darthur and Its Sources* (London, 1917); J. D. Bruce, *Evolution of Arthurian Romance to 1300*, 2 vols. (Göttingen, 1923–1924), the most complete study of the early evolution of Arthurian legend; E. K. Chambers, *Arthur of Britain* (London, 1927), a more condensed study of Arthurian legend, which contains also a useful bibliographical note; E. Hicks, *Sir Thomas Malory, His Turbulent Career: A Biography* (Cambridge, Mass., 1928); E. Vinaver, *Sir Thomas Malory* (Oxford, 1929), a general study, written before the discovery of the Winchester MS in 1934; R. S. Loomis, ed., *Arthurian Literature in the Middle Ages* (Oxford, 1959), mainly on earlier work, but contains an essay on Malory by Vinaver; J. A. W. Bennett, ed., *Essays on Malory* (Oxford, 1963), a valuable collection of essays by W. Oakshott, C. S. Lewis, E. Vinaver, D. S. Brewer, P. E. Tucker, F. Whitehead, and S. Shaw, with biographical note by R. T. Davies, giving a reassessment in the light of the Winchester MS. The unity of "the hoole book" is defended by Lewis and Brewer; R. S. Loomis, *Development of Arthurian Romance* (London, 1963), defends the unity of Malory's work; W. Matthews, *The Ill-framed Knight* (Berkeley, Calif., 1966; London, 1967), a skeptical enquiry into the identity of Sir Thomas Malory, which on linguistic grounds suggests that the author of *Le Morte Darthur* may have been a Yorkshireman; R. T. Davies, ed., *King Arthur and His Knights of the Round Table* (London, 1967); P. J. C. Field, *Romance and Chronicle, A Study of Malory's Style* (London, 1967), a first attempt to deal with the prose style; Mark Lambert, *Malory, Style and Vision in The Morte Darthur* (New Haven, 1975), develops from Field, a valuable close reading of the text illustrated with comparisons from a wide field; Larry D. Benson, *Malory's Morte Darthur* (Cambridge, 1976), a well-documented, scholarly survey of Malory's relation to earlier romance, and also to the chivalry of his age.

JOHN SKELTON

(ca. 1460-1529)

Peter Green

My friend, sith ye are before us here presént,
To answer unto this noble audience,
Of that shall be reasoned ye must be content;
And, for as much as by the high pretence
That ye have now thorough pre-eminence
Of laureate triumph, your place is here reservèd,
We will understand how ye have it deservèd.

[*The Garland of Laurel*]

BETWEEN the death of Chaucer and the rise of Wyatt, English poetry, it is generally agreed, passed through a very dull phase indeed. "All smudge, blur, and scribble," C. S. Lewis calls it, "without a firm line or a clear colour anywhere." Somewhere the spark had failed; the great creative impulse of the Middle Ages was ebbing, the English Renaissance had not yet struggled to its birth. Literature lay in the hands of whimsical pedants such as Stephen Hawes or earnest translators like Barclay. Against this drably exhausted background the figure of John Skelton stands out with all the more striking clarity.

Energy, wit, originality, individualism; a mastery of vernacular idiom and rhythm; a capacity for direct observation which resembles that of a Dutch old master—every quality, in fact, most directly at variance with the general trend of his age, and remarkable at any period—these are what we associate with Skelton. He is, moreover, an eccentric in the great English tradition, a figure of prickly and paradoxical humors who would have appealed strongly to G. K. Chesterton. There are few characters from the early Tudor age of austerity who come across to us with more immediate impact. Skelton stalks through his own pages with egotistical panache, flaunting his laureate's robe (green and white, the Tudor colors, and picked out with "Calliope"[1] in letters of gold), quarreling, laughing, swearing, blasphemously devout, a master of polyglot abuse and political allegory, equally at home in an alehouse, a country rectory, or at court.

He was born about 1460, and was very probably a Northcountryman by origin, either from Cumberland or Yorkshire. He shows a good deal of local topographical knowledge, and has the borderer's characteristic dislike for the Scots, which he turned to good account in celebrating Flodden. ("Christ cense you with a frying-pan!" he devoutly apostrophizes the unfortunate King James.) Modern scholars have made it fairly clear that Skelton's antecedents lacked nobility; he may, indeed, have been that not uncommon phenomenon, a scholar-parson sprung from a family of tradesmen. This would do much to explain his self-conscious posturing assertiveness no less than his royalism, his conservatism, and his frantic attacks on any successful bourgeois parvenu—be he a knighted Flemish wooltrader or the great Cardinal Wolsey.

We know almost nothing of his early life. It seems fairly certain that he took his degree at Peterhouse, Cambridge, about 1478–1479; and in 1483 appeared his first known poem (if it is indeed by him: like several others in the Skeltonic canon, this one has had doubts cast on its authenticity), an elegy on the death of "the Noble Prince, King Edward the Fourth." This competent but unremarkable exercise in the twelve-line stanza does, however, emphasize one preoccupation of Skelton's that has for some reason been obscured behind the Jolly Jack Skel-

[1] The chief of the nine classical muses ("Regent is she of poets all") and associated with epic poetry in particular.

81

ton legend—his recurrent all-flesh-is-grass pessimism:

> For now am I gone, that late was in prosperity;
> To presume thereupon it is but a vanity,
> Not certain, but as a cherry-fair full of woe:
> Reignéd not I of late in great felicity?
> *Et, ecce, nunc in pulvere dormio!*
> [And lo! now in the dust I sleep!]

Skelton's Gothic graveyard humor and his rattling tavern bawdry, in fact, are two sides of the same coin; they are as closely interwoven as the love poet who wrote *Songs and Sonnets* is with the dean of St. Paul's preaching on *Death's Duel*.

Two years later the Battle of Bosworth Field was fought, and the first Tudor ascended the English throne. Henry VII, with some acumen, realized better than his predecessors had done the value of numbering learned men among his courtiers. To be sure, this was not a disinterested patronage of learning and the humanities. Latin was the international language of diplomacy; rhetoric and oratory were no less highly prized as instruments of political persuasion than they had been in Cicero's day; and scholarship was beginning to carry a certain amount of prestige. Besides, an articulate spokesman, particularly if he gave utterance in verse, was no bad acquisition for a dynasty anxious to establish its antecedents. It was not for nothing that Henry exploited a spurious connection with King Arthur by naming his son after the national hero.

It was this court to which Master John Skelton—turbulent, but not yet a priest—became attached, as "the Duc of Yorkes scolemaster," in 1494. The reputation he had by then acquired, and which doubtless helped to win him his position of trust, was as humanist rather than poet. He had, indeed, composed some religious poems, a series of love lyrics (some of them set to music by William Cornysshe of the Chapel Royal) and another pièce d'occasion on the death of the earl of Northumberland. But what weighed far heavier were his translations of Cicero and Diodorus Siculus—not to mention the fact that he had been made "laureate" of Oxford (1488/1489), Louvain (1492), and Cambridge (1493). This particular distinction must not be confused with our modern concept of a poet laureate; it was far more like a degree in rhetoric. Skelton's later office as king's orator was a different matter.

It was this side of Skelton's activities to which William Caxton was mainly referring when he paid the poet his tribute in *The Boke of Eneydos* (1490):

But I pray master John Skelton, late created poet laureate in the university of Oxenford, to oversee and correct this said book, and t'address and expoun' whereas shall be found fault to them that shall require it. For him I know for sufficient to expoun' and english every difficulty that is therein; for he hath late translated the epistles of Tully, and the book of Diodorus Siculus, and divers other works out of Latin into English—not in rude and old language but in polished and ornate terms, craftily, as he that hath read Vergil, Ovid, Tully, and all the other noble poets and orators, to me unknown. And also he hath read the nine Muses, and understands their musical sciences, and to whom of them each science is appropred: I suppose he hath drunken of Helicon's well. . . .

Now Skelton's translation of Diodorus Siculus survives; it is certainly ornate, if not polished. "Who readeth it once," Skelton modestly remarked of it, when composing the catalog of his works in *The Garland of Laurel*, "woulde read it again": a characteristic claim, but one not borne out by modern taste. For rank periphrastic prolixity, rhetorical curlicues, and expansion of its original text, this work must stand almost without rivals. It serves to remind us that much of Skelton's art was located squarely in the "aureate" tradition that led to Lyly's *Euphues*—and makes the originality of such pieces as *The Tunning of Elinour Rumming* all the more striking by contrast. Our old familiar Skelton, however, does peep out from time to time over Diodorus' shoulder, especially in matters of verbal innovation. F. M. Salter has listed no fewer than 816 neologisms in the *Diodorus* alone: an extraordinary number, and a fair guide to that rich verbal fantastication that forms one essential element of the "Skeltonic."

But while Master Skelton's official self was busy with rhetoric, court advancement, and the classics, his more private alter ego was strolling down Thames Street, whistling the latest air, head stuffed with old ballads, heart running on love. To this period, just before or just after 1490, belongs Skelton's early group of love lyrics: *Mannerly Margery Milk and Ale,* the lines *To Mistress Anne,* and (to the same recipient) the harshly disillusioned *Womanhood, Wanton, Ye Want;* the haunting rhythms of *My Darling Dear, My Daisy Flower:*

> My darling dear, my daisy flower,
> Let me, quod he, lie in your lap.
> Lie still, quod she, my paramour,
> Lie still hardely, and take a nap.
> His head was heavy, such was his hap,
> All drowsy dreaming, drowned in sleep,
> That of his love he took no keep.
> With, Hey, lullay, lullay, like a child,
> Thou sleepest too long, thou art beguiled.

Dame Edith Sitwell once described this as the drowsiest poem in the English language. True though this may be of the opening stanza, the conclusion is one of grim loss and deception. This theme, of sexual disappointment and emotional betrayal, recurs again and again. Skelton's loves are either beyond his reach, or turn common strumpets. The first is typified in the close-knit *Go, Piteous Heart:*

> One there is, and ever one shall be,
> For whose sake my heart is sore diseaséd;
> For whose love welcome disease to me!
> I am content so all parties be pleaséd:
> Yet, an God would, I would my pain were easéd!
> But Fortune enforceth me so carefully to endure
> That where I love best I dare not discure.

Contrast this with the bitterness of the following lines:

> Your key is meet for every lock,
> Your key is common and hangeth out;
> Your key is ready, we need not knock,
> Nor stand long wrestling there about;
> Of your door-gate ye have no doubt:
> But one thing is, that ye be lewd:
> Hold your tongue now, all beshrewd!

> To Mistress Anne, that farly sweet,
> That wones [lives] at The Key in Thamés Street.

This mood of emotional anxiety and suspicious pessimism permeates everything that Skelton wrote in his first London period. It forms a natural bridge from personal lyric to the almost paranoid fear of court intrigue that he displays in his first political satire, *The Bouge of Court;* and is well crystallized in a curious fragment written about the same time:

> Though ye suppose all jeopardies are passed,
> And all is done that ye looked for before,
> Ware yet, I rede you, of Fortune's double cast,
> For one false point she is wont to keep in store,
> And under the fell oft festered is the sore:
> That when ye think all danger for to pass
> Ware of the lizard lieth lurking in the grass.

Throughout his career, even in the most rambunctious and extrovert moments, the shadow of that lizard can always be glimpsed in the grass beside the bright tumbling cataract of his verse.

This is not, the reader may object, the Skelton we know. But then, the popular Skelton is at best only a partial truth, one element in a complex personality. The Rabelaisian, mud-slinging hedge-priest of legend was largely spawned from *The Merie Tales,* an anonymous, and often apocryphal, collection of anecdotes published soon after Skelton's death. Their main value is to show that Skelton was, in fact (like Dylan Thomas in our own day), the kind of person round whom legends tend to accumulate. They do, however, contain several quite credible episodes. This Skelton was latterly given a fresh lease on life by the modern enthusiasts who hoisted him into prominence again during the 1920's. They liked his slapdash vernacular immediacy, but ignored his complex and subtle prosodic variations. They appreciated his involvement with politics, and somehow managed to bypass the fact that he was a diehard reactionary. *Speak, Parrot*—with its recondite allusions, obscure symbolism, and multilingual quotations—perhaps reminded them of *The Waste Land;* much of its undeniable appeal to modern taste still lies in the fact that it is to a great extent incomprehensible. Lastly, and most important, they applauded his obvious blasphemies, without understanding the deep, all-pervasive religious faith that alone gave such blasphemies meaning or proportion.

The whole of Skelton's work, not merely those poems overtly religious in theme, must constantly be viewed in terms of the medieval spiritual framework that contains it. Skelton's Catholicism underlay many of his apparently irrational prejudices: his central animus against King James of Scotland was due to the fact that, for him, James was a *heretic*. And one form the lurking lizard took for Skelton was that of the rising flood of Lutheranism, the sectarian schism threatening Catholic Christendom. In *Colin Clout,* he says:

> And some have a smack
> Of Luther's sack . . .
> And some of them bark,
> Clatter and carp
> Of that heresiarch
> Called Wicliffista,
> The devilish dogmatista;
> And some be Hussians,
> And some be Arians,
> And some be Pelagians,
> And make much variance
> Between the clergy
> And the temporalty . . .

It is in such a context that we must consider his political satire and his devotional verse alike.

The main group of religious poems—*Vexilla Regis, Upon a Dead Man's Head,* and, above all, *Woefully Arrayed*—were probably composed either shortly before or shortly after 1498, when Skelton was consecrated priest: that event might well have stirred him to an active poetic assertion of faith such as he never afterward quite recaptured. *Woefully Arrayed,* indeed, with its sprung rhythms and incandescent intensity of feeling, cannot but remind us of Gerard Manley Hopkins:

Thus naked am I nailéd, O man, for thy sake!
I love thee, then love me; why sleepest thou? awake!
Remember my tender heart-root for thee brake,
With painés my veinés constrainéd to crake:
    Thus tuggéd to and fro,
    Thus wrappéd all in woe,
    Whereas never man was so,
Entreated thus in most cruel wise,
Was like a lamb offered in sacrifice,
    Woefully arrayed.

Of sharp thorn I have worn a crown on my head,
So painéd, so strainéd, so rueful, so red,
Thus bobbéd, thus robbéd, thus for thy love dead,
Unfeignéd I deignéd my blood for to shed:

My feet and handés sore
The sturdy nailés bore:
What might I suffer more
Than I have done, O man, for thee?
Come when thou list, welcome to me,
    Woefully arrayed.

If we forget this Skelton, and remember only the author of *Colin Clout* or *Philip Sparrow,* we not only lose a vital part of his creative impulse, but will, in all likelihood, be sadly at fault with our judgment of what remains.

The truth is that Skelton had no love for the new humanism that was sweeping over Europe. He abhorred the introduction of Greek into the universities; he was all for the old medieval trivium and quadrivium. A traditional Latinist to the core, he sniffed suspiciously at the winds of change and did not like what he smelled. This entrenched adherence to the old ways probably commended him to Henry VII, and earned him his post as dominie to the young prince. For the latter, in accordance with the fashion, Skelton composed a *Speculum Principis,* or Mirror for Princes: a stuffy little handbook of admonitions, one of which, in view of later events, deserves immortality: "Choose a wife for yourself," he advised the future Henry VIII. "Prize her always and uniquely."

Nothing could be more ludicrously wide of the truth than Agnes Strickland's comment on Skelton's tutorial efforts: "How probable it is," she wrote, "that the corruption imparted by this ribald and ill-living wretch laid the foundation for his royal pupil's grossest crimes." On the contrary, it seems abundantly clear that Skelton was scared half out of his wits by the ruthlessness of court intrigue, which fascinated and appalled him in about equal proportions. If he exerted any influence on Henry, it was in the direction of Polonius-like admonition and fuddy-duddy restraint. At any rate, this first taste of London life produced not a burst of drunken Skeltonics, but that sober, neurotic, horribly lifelike half-allegory, *The Bouge of Court* (*bouge* being a ration-allowance, and hence, here, the rewards or perquisites of court life).

In this poem Skelton displays, for the first but by no means the last time, his extraordinary gift for direct observation of life, both visual and auditory. He can catch the rhythms of natural speech just as he can select the significant descriptive detail. *The Bouge of Court* is narrated by a character called, appropriately, Drede (Modesty), who recounts a Ship-of-Fools dream that took place

> At Harwich port slumbering as I lay
> In mine hostés house, called Powers Key.

Though Drede, he says, has little money and no friends at court, the lady Danger tempts him with thoughts of adventure, and he embarks on the good ship Bouge of Court. Here he meets with such characters as Favell, the flatterer, Disdain, Riot, Dissimulation, Deceit, and the other eternal parasites that fawn around every ruler and whisper daggers below stairs. No poet has ever caught this horrible atmosphere with greater skill: the filed tongues, the soft gabble of scandal, the nods and hints and smooth insinuations, the sexual boasting, the social snobs, the hearty gallants with their dice and fashionable songs, the vulgar exhibitionists such as Riot, whose "hair was growen thorough out his hat," or slippery Dissimulation:

> Then in his hood I saw there faces twain:
> That one was lean and like a pinéd ghost,
> That other looked as he would me have slain;
> And to meward as he 'gan for to coast,
> When that he was even at me almost,
> I saw a knife hid in his one sleeve,
> Whereon was written this word, *Mischief.*

Dissimulation is all suggestiveness and half-finished sentences:

> Right now I spake with one, I trow, I see—
> But what—a straw! I may not tell all thing!
> By God, I say there is great heart-burning
> Between the person ye wot of and you . . .

and adds, characteristically:

> But I am loath for to raise a smoke,
> If ye could be otherwise agreed.

The poem ends with "lewd fellows" attempting Drede's murder; whereupon he woke from his nightmare, "caught pen and ink, and wrote this little book."

It seems almost certain that this strange, compulsive poem reflects some actual event in Skelton's life. Edwards (pp. 76–82) argues that Skelton was pensioned off as tutor to the duke of York in 1502, after Prince Arthur's premature death, and that his appointment to the benefice of Diss was due to Lady Margaret Beaufort, Henry VII's mother, who seems to have been Skelton's patron. But the evidence is slim, and there may have been other factors involved in Skelton's departure to the country a couple of years later. His imprisonment, for example (vouched for by a Court of Requests record, and datable to 10 June 1502), may have less trivial implications than Edwards chooses to assign to it. At any rate, in 1504, whether by choice or necessity, he retired from London to a country living in the heart of East Anglia. Here it was that the Skelton legend first developed; and here that Skelton's hitherto disciplined muse suddenly kicked up her heels and went skittering away in a mad gallop across the Norfolk countryside.

THE RECTOR OF DISS

THERE is some peculiar quality about East Anglia that seems to promote individualism and eccentricity; and to judge from the way the new rector of Diss carried on, this anarchic yeast was already fermenting busily at the beginning of the sixteenth century. The Reverend John Skelton certainly made his presence felt. He took a mistress, by whom he had a child; when his parishioners complained to the bishop of Norwich, he displayed his baby in the pulpit the next Sunday:

> If I had, sayde Skelton, broughte forthe thys chylde without armes or legges, or that it wer deformed, being a monstrous thyng, I woulde neuer haue blamed you to haue complayned to the bishop of me; but to complain without a cause, I say, as I said before in my antethem, *vos estis,* you be, and haue be, & wyll and shall be knaues, to complayne of me wythout a cause resonable.

The scandal seems to have blown over; at all events Skelton remained on excellent terms with his bishop—though to judge by the accusations of laxness among the clergy brought in *Colin Clout*, this is not altogether surprising.

Two in particular among his parishioners Skelton—no longer the hanger-on at court, but a sizable fish in this quiet country pond—found especially detestable. These were a wealthy old reprobate named John Clark and the rapacious bailiff of Diss, Adam Uddersall. When they were dead, Skelton (who, like Juvenal, was not by instinct a gentleman) decided to get his own back. He sat down in an inspired moment, his mind full of Goliardic fragments, popular ballads and lampoons, medieval *Reimprosa*, jingling leonine hexameters, and Anglo-Norman rhyming proverbial catalogs. All these disparate elements suddenly fused in his mind; and a new, unique verse form, the Skeltonic, was born. Much unprofitable time and vain scholarship have been expended on trying to trace the exact antecedents of this near-doggerel form; but poets of Skelton's kidney do not respond well to Teutonic source grubbing. In the last resort the Skeltonic, as we know it, is Skelton's own. Nothing quite like it had happened before, and all future use of the meter derived directly from Skelton's own practice. When Skelton wrote of Clark and Uddersall:

> Though these knaves be dead,
> Full of mischief and queed [evil],
> Yet, wheresoever they lie,
> Their names shall never die

he spoke truer than he knew. These two unfortunate Norfolk worthies have achieved a singular sort of immortality: they are enshrined—together with much splenetic objurgation in dog-Latin and somewhat vulgar English—in the first known example of Skeltonic verse.

As W. Nelson observed, with some moderation, "it is not easy to describe Skeltonics in the terms usual to prosody. One might almost say that the outstanding characteristic of the form is its formlessness." The line employed is, on average, short, though we find frequent exceptions: syllables range from three to eleven and more, and within any one sequence there tends to be great variety. The same rhyme may be held for line after line, till the writer's ingenuity gives out; in fact, the only firm prohibition seems to be against cross-rhyming. Latin may

be freely interspersed with English, sometimes in hexameters split at the caesura, sometimes in rhythmic rhyming jingles. The only way to grasp the pattern is by way of extended example. Here, then, is the galloping coda to Skelton's *Devout Trental for Old John Clarke*:

> *Jam jacet hic* stark dead,
> Never a tooth in his head.
> Adieu, Jayberd, adieu,
> In faith, deacon thou crew!
> *Frates, orate*
> For this knavate,
> By the holy rood,
> Did never man good:
> I pray you all,
> And pray shall,
> At this trental
> On knees to fall
> To the football;
> With, "Fill the black bowl
> For Jayberd's soul."
>   *Bibite multum:*
> *Ecce sepultum*
> *Sub pede stultum,*
> *Asinum, et mulum!*
> The devil kiss his *culum!*
> With, "Hey, ho, rumbelow!"
> *Rumpopulorum,*
> *Per omnia secula seculorum!*

Something, very clearly, has been happening to this staid dominie and would-be courtier. Rhyme royal and the aureate tradition have been thrown overboard. Not content with literary anarchy, Skelton is also parodying an office of the church, like some bawdy-devout thirteenth-century *jongleur*—a trick he is to repeat, at far greater length and in much more elaborate form, when he comes to write *Philip Sparrow*. What lies behind this sudden transformation? Perhaps it is no more than the simple, yet radical, fact of withdrawal from the metropolitan courtiers' merry-go-round: in the country, with leisure, Skelton's private self is allowed to emerge, to indulge in a little local horseplay, to observe the small tragedies and excitements of provincial life, to change its poetical scope and focus. It is an interesting and significant fact that no poem of this middle period is set outside East Anglia if, that is, we accept (as, following Edwards, I do; see Bibliography and note there) a late date for *The Tunning of Elinour*

Rumming, and place it with *Colin Clout* in 1522. Readers should be warned, however, that most scholars (e.g., Gordon and Nelson) would assimilate this poem to the East Anglian group. Carpenter (1967) regards it as virtually undatable but leans toward a date before 1512, though conceding that Edwards may nevertheless be right.

In *Philip Sparrow,* Skelton greatly extends and develops his newfound medium. The occasion of the poem was simple and touching. A young girl of Skelton's acquaintance, Jane Scrope, the daughter of a noble family, who was a pupil at Carrow Nunnery in the suburbs of Norwich, had a pet sparrow, which she loved dearly. (Till the importation of canaries and budgerigars the sparrow rated rather higher as a domestic luxury than might be gathered from the Biblical rate of exchange.) One day the inevitable happened; poor Philip fell a victim to Gib, the nunnery cat. Skelton undertook at Jane's behest to write a kind of requiem mass for the bird—he seems to have had a more than avuncular eye for young ladies—and the result got impressively and idiosyncratically out of hand. It is, as H. L. R. Edwards justly observes, his "most imitative, most original" poem. There are echoes in it of Catullus and Ovid, Martial and Statius, the medieval bird mass, and the death of Chanticleer's daughter in Caxton's *Reynard the Fox.* It is tenderly blasphemous and passionately devout; its grotesque yet splendid catalog of mourning birds seems to assimilate all created things into the harmonious pattern of the one true church—and does it by giving a fresh twist to the oldest rhetorical device employed by the Schoolmen. There are few more subtly haunting lines in Skelton than *Philip Sparrow*'s slow, spondaic opening, with its echoes from the Office for the Dead:

> *Pla ce bo!*
> Who is there, who?
> *Di le xi!*
> Dame Margery.
> *Fa, re, my, my.*
> Wherefore and why, why?
> For the soul of Philip Sparrow
> That was late slain at Carrow,
> Among the Nunés Black.
> For that sweet soulés sake,
> And for all sparrows' souls

> Set in our bead-rolls,
> *Pater noster qui,*
> With an *Ave Mari,*
> And with the corner of a Creed,
> The more shall be your meed.

Yet the odd thing is that *Philip Sparrow* succeeds in spite of itself. The faults it shows are glaringly obvious. It is far too long; it is an *olla podrida* of medieval snippets and tropes; and halfway through the Sparrow's mass is dropped altogether. Thereafter Skelton speaks in his own person (hitherto Jane had supposedly been the narrator) and turns the poem into a coyly stylized commendation of the young lady herself:

> Her lusty ruby ruddes [complexion]
> Resemble the rose buddés;
> Her lippés soft and merry
> Enblooméd like the cherry:
> It were an heavenly bliss
> Her sugared mouth to kiss.

But even while engaged upon such conventional conceits Skelton cannot wholly subdue that shrewd, realistic eye of his. Any other troubadour would have tactfully omitted Jane's wart; Skelton picks out the blemish and makes an added attraction of it. There is, too, a certain devastating emotional honesty about anyone who, after describing the bliss of embracing his beloved, adds in reassurance:

> And yet there was no vice,
> Nor yet no villany,
> But only fantasy.

Philip Sparrow remains tantalizingly uneven, however, exhibiting Skelton by turns at his best and worst. Indeed, it is remarkable that the tender, witty realist, the vernacular arch poet in him, triumphed over the aureate laureate and rhyming rhetorician as often as they did. Impenitent, indomitable, his individual genius survived all attempts to discipline it into a conventional mold; as often as not it was the mold that changed its shape.

If Skelton was at loggerheads with the East Anglian laity, he also had his share of trouble inside the church. He conducted a running feud with the Dominicans, and banned one of their friars from preaching in the church at Diss.

JOHN SKELTON

From 1505 to 1506 the young Thomas Wolsey (his cardinal's hat still a dream) was rector of the neighboring parish of Redgrave; and though this parvenu Ipswich cleric was often—indeed generally—absent, it is tempting to believe that it was here that Skelton's path and that of his formidable future adversary first crossed. (Skelton was certainly in touch with Wolsey's successor at Redgrave, William Dale, to arbitrate before an ecclesiastical court in Norwich.) But the nastiest episode with which Skelton had to deal during his incumbency at Diss was produced by a certain eccentric sporting parson (this very English species still survives in the area) who conceived the macabre and blasphemous idea of training his hawk inside the church itself. He ought to have known better than to meddle with the author of the *Devout Trental*.

Ware the Hawk describes the scene vividly: the shouting and flapping of wings, the locked door, Skelton's entry through a side passage, the fierce argument that ensued:

> This fond frantic falconer,
> With his polluted pawtener [wallet]
> As priest unreverent,
> Straight to the sacrament
> He made his hawk to fly,
> With hugeous shout and cry.
> The high altar he stripped naked;
> Thereon he stood and crakéd;
> He shook down all the clothés,
> And swore horrible oathés
> Before the face of God,
> By Moses and Aaron's rod,
> Ere that he hence yede
> His hawk should prey and feed
> Upon a pigeon's maw.
> The blood ran down raw
> Upon the altar-stone;
> The hawk tiréd on a bone;
> And in the holy place
> She dungéd there a chase
> Upon my corporas'[2] face . . .

The most important thing to realize about this poem is that it was written in deadly earnest: Skelton was shocked to the core by the blasphemy of the incident rather than by a mere personal intrusion on his official preserve. To

treat *Ware the Hawk* as an ordinary piece of abuse (as has so often been done) is to miss its point entirely. The central tirade is directed specifically against sacramental pollution:

> Then much more, by the rood,
> Where Christés precious blood
> Daily offeréd is,
> To be polluted thus;
> And that he wishéd withall
> That the dove's dung might fall
> Into my chalice at Mass,
> When consecrated was
> The blessed Sacrament.
> O priest unreverent!

From here it is an easy step to the poem's secondary theme: the general laxness of the clergy, of which this incident is only one example. Here we see in embryo the line of attack that was later to produce *Colin Clout* and—going yet further—the furious personal onslaughts against Cardinal Wolsey.

The incipient change of poetical tone—away from the private, personal theme toward matters of national importance—suggests that Skelton was beginning to find rural seclusion a little irksome; and the accession to the throne in 1509 of his old pupil, now metamorphosed into King Henry VIII, clinched matters. This was no time for witnessing wills, acting as arbiter in ecclesiastical courts, or exchanging small talk with the East Anglian gentry. There were better uses for Master Skelton's pen than composing a Latin *lamentatio* on the Great Fire of Norwich. In haste he sent off his loyal greetings, and attached a "Laud and Praise made for our Sovereign Lord the King," the opening stanza of which contained, as Edwards so rightly says, "an image from which was to spring the entire Tudor myth":

> The Rose both White and Red
> In one Rose now doth grow:
> Thus thorough every stead
> Thereof the fame doth blow.
> Grace the seed did sow:
> England, now gather floures,
> Exclude now all doloures.

This was fine poet laureate matter indeed; it exactly caught the national mood—relief that the bloody fratricidal struggle between York and

---

[2]*Corporas.* That is, the modern corporal, a piece of linen on which the elements of the eucharist are placed.

Lancaster was at last resolved; hope and expectation that the accomplished young prince would bring about a new Golden Age, restore past greatness and glory. To the end of his life Skelton never quite abandoned this vision; it makes his vehement onslaught against the rising bourgeois world of Wolsey and his successors all the more comprehensible. For nearly three years Skelton was kept waiting; then in 1512—perhaps on the recommendation of his good friend the prior of Westminster—he was brought back to court, with the resounding title of Orator Regius. Though he held his living till he died, East Anglia knew him no more. Yet it could truly be said of him, as in another sense he had said of old John Clark:

> *In parochia de Dis*
> *Non erat sibi similis*
> [In the parish of Diss
> There was no one like him.]

THE PARROT AND THE WOLF

WHEN Henry recalled his old tutor to the palace, he can have had no idea how potentially dangerous a man Skelton was. Something had happened to the rector of Diss during his years of exile. Spiritual anger had risen in his soul, a vast, all-embracing rage at the abuses and changes that he saw as threatening both his society and his faith; and now he had forged himself a weapon of real power with which to flay all adversaries alike—heretics, Protestants, self-indulgent priests, jumped-up politicos, drunken Flemish merchants, adherents of the new humanism, *arrivistes* of every sort. Fresh from the country, he took a look at the town; and the result was *The Manner of the World Nowadays*, a scarifying indictment of the contemporary social scene, all the more effective for its hammering repetitive framework:

> So many pointed caps
> Laced with double flaps,
> And so gay felted hats,
>   Saw I never:
> So many good lessons,
> So many good sermons,

> And so few devotions,
>   Saw I never.
>   . . .
> So many good workés,
> So few well-learnéd clerkés,
> And so few that goodness markés,
>   Saw I never:
> Such prankéd coats and sleevés,
> So few young men that prevés,[3]
> And such increase of thievés,
>   Saw I never.

And so on, in one all-embracing commination service over gallants, blasphemers, cuckold-makers, loose-living wives, chiseling lawyers, vagabondage, overspending, wrath, envy, gluttony, bribery, ridiculous fashions, foreign trade, and the emptying of the monasteries. But this was only a beginning, a preliminary broadside.

The king had other ideas about Skelton's duties. He tricked the poet out in his green-and-white official robe (of which Skelton was inordinately proud) and set him to compose an epitaph for Henry VII; after which, being fond of an evening's entertainment, he harnessed his former tutor's vituperativeness and powers of invective for a poetical slanging match—or "flyting" contest, to give it its more dignified Scottish title—with a gentleman of the court, Sir Christopher Garnesche. Skelton duly obliged; he also composed a couple of official pièces d'occasion on the defeat of the Scots at Flodden. (It is amusing that this anti-Hibernian borderer should be so poetically beholden to Scottish balladry himself. One has only to look at *Cowkelbie Sow* to realize the extent of his debt—though, as Lewis asserts, Skelton "would rise from the grave to bespatter us with new Skeltonics if we suggested that he had learnt his art from a Scotsman.") But Skelton's mind was on other matters—matters which led him to sail dangerously near the political wind.

By 1515 Thomas Wolsey was near the apogee of his career; in the same twelvemonth he was made cardinal and chancellor. To anyone at court the extent of his influence on Henry must have been obvious—and alarming. Skelton could not act directly; but he did the next best

[3]*Preves:* proves, equivalent perhaps to "turns out well" (Dyce, II, 203).

JOHN SKELTON

thing. He composed a vast secular morality play called *Magnificence* (1516) that was a close and instantly recognizable allegory of the contemporary political situation; as he later observed of this work in *The Garland of Laurel:* "who printeth it well in mind / Much doubleness of the worldé therein he may find." He timed his propaganda well; after Wolsey's meteoric rise, 1516 brought the chancellor some sharp setbacks and criticisms. Skelton, at any rate, took an old medieval form (as he had done in *The Bouge of Court*) and transformed it into a vehicle for court satire. His hero, Magnificence, is "an abstract Henry VIII, seen from the economic angle" (Edwards)—though he is real enough to throw one of that monarch's ungovernable tantrums onstage. There is the usual conflict over his soul between various virtues and vices—Felicity, Liberty, Measure, Redress, and Perseverance (among others) matched with Counterfeit Countenance, Crafty Conveyance, Cloaked Collusion, and Courtly Abusion: in other words, between Wolsey's extravagance and the restrained measures advocated by the duke of Norfolk's party.

As propaganda, *Magnificence* is daring, pointed, and superb. As a play it remains stupefyingly dull—apart, once again, from Skelton's uncanny ear for the nuances of dialogue and the delineation of character. As poetry it has moments of pure lyrical delight, such as the swooping, lilting rhythms of Courtly Abusion's song:

> What now, let see,
> Who looketh on me
> Well round about,
> How gay and how stout
> That I can wear
> Courtly my gear.
>
> My hair brusheth
> So pleasantly,
> My robe rusheth
> So ruttingly,
> Meseem I fly,
> I am so light
> To dance delight.

But such enchanting interludes have to be picked out from long slabs of lumbering iambics; in this *Magnificence* bears some resemblance to Tennyson's *The Princess.* For a modern reader, accustomed to post-Shakespearean theater, it suffers from being both abstract and static. Not even the subtle shifts of meter and rhythm introduced to differentiate each fresh character can keep the piece alive as drama.

Whether *Magnificence* was actually presented before Henry we do not know. It is not beyond the bounds of possibility; Latimer, it is said, could berate the king from his pulpit as soundly as he would his Wiltshire parishioners. But in any case no one could have failed to take the point; and ill-disposed persons doubtless made trouble for Skelton, as his poem *Against Venomous Tongues,* written later the same year, strongly suggests. But by now Skelton had, with understandable prudence, taken the lease of a house within the sanctuary at Westminster; and there Wolsey, with all his powers both spiritual and secular, could not touch him.

Yet for the next five years—years during which Luther's theses were nailed to the church door at Wittenburg, and the battle of "Trojans" and "Greeks" raged on among Oxford humanists—Skelton held his peace. Some way of silencing him, either by blackmail or friendly persuasion, must have been found: probably the former, because when he at last returned to the fray, in 1521, his meaning was hidden deep under a mass of symbolic allegory and obscure literary allusion. *Speak, Parrot* is an enigma, a nightmare, a nest of bewildering ambiguities. In its use of biblical names to conceal contemporary places and persons (e.g., "Esebon" = London, "Og" and "Sadok" both = Wolsey), *Speak, Parrot* anticipates later political satire, such as Dryden's *Absalom and Achitophel.* Parts of it read like the final section of *The Waste Land,* parts like the literary analogue of a Bosch triptych, verging on the edge of surrealism. The meter is close-knit rhyme royal, far from the loose, clattering, vernacular Skeltonic:

> Aaron was fired with Chaldee's fire called Ur,
> Jobab was brought up in the land of Hus,
> The lineage of Lot took support of Assúr,
> Jereboseth is Hebrew, who list the cause discuss—
> "Peace, Parrot, ye prate as ye were *ebrius:*
> Hist thee, *lieber Got von Himmelsreich, ich seg!*"
> In Popering grew pears when Parrot was an egg.

The following stanza opens with the rhetorical question "What is this to purpose?" and—

hardly surprisingly—instead of answering it, poses another cluster of vaguely apocalyptic images.

The curious thing about *Speak, Parrot* is that Skelton—like many poets who attempt this genre—put rather more into the poem than he intended. He may have set out simply to write a disguised attack on Wolsey, coupled with a slash at the new learning. He may have believed that his camouflage was merely protective, that

> *metaphora, allegoria* with all,
> Shall be his protection, his paves and his wall;

but in the very next stanza he gives himself away:

> Parrot is my own dear heart and my dear darling.
> Melpomene, that fair maid, she burnishéd his beak:
> I pray you, let Parrot have liberty to speak!

Most critics have simply assumed that Parrot could be equated with Skelton himself—a gross oversimplification. Edwards is much nearer the mark when he suggests that Parrot stands for the poetic faculty. Parrot has the gift of tongues, and works by means of irrational associations. Parrot loves women, and bright gewgaws, and the magic of incantatory words. Parrot stands, somehow, outside the political preoccupations of mankind, though he is not above criticizing them; he has a passion for mirrors, and will not putrefy when dead. Parrot, in short, is not Skelton so much as Skelton's poetical id: and the opening description of this spoiled, preening, exotic creature gleams sharp and lucid against the darkly obscure stanzas that follow:

> My name is Parrot, a bird of Paradise,
> By nature deviséd of a wonderous kind,
> Daintily dieted with divers delicate spice
> Till Euphrates, that flood, driveth me into Ind;
> Where men of that country by fortune me find
> And send me to greaté ladyés of estate:
> Then Parrot must have an almond or a date.

> A cage curiously carven, with a silver pin,
> Properly painted, to be my coverture;
> A mirror of glassé, that I may toot [gaze] therein:
> These, maidens full meekly with many a divers flower,
> Freshly they dress, and make sweet my bower,

> With "Speak, Parrot, I pray you!" full curtesly they say,
> "Parrot is a goodly bird, a pretty popinjay!"

> With my beaké bent, my little wonton eye,
> My feathers fresh as is the emerald green,
> About my neck a circulet like the rich rubý,
> My little leggés, my feet both feat and clean,
> I am a minion to wait upon a queen.
> "My proper Parrot, my little pretty fool!"
> With ladies I learn, and go with them to school.

The following year, 1522, came *Colin Clout*, a torrent of Skeltonics attacking the laxity of the church, and containing a final section that was a direct and open assault on Wolsey. The gloves were off now, and the tempo quickening. *Colin Clout* reads as though written for distribution as a pamphlet. Perhaps it was. The eponymous hero, of course, is the average, simple, English countryman, a kind of articulate hodge; and the poem consists largely of what Colin hears from "folk" as he goes to and fro in the land. These muttered, resentful rumors swell cumulatively to a tremendous crescendo of complaint against prelates, absentee parsons, ignorance of church doctrine, rapacious exploitation of church property, nonobservance of Lenten fasts, heresy, lascivious nuns—and the luxurious tapestries at Hampton Court. Indeed, the whole catalog, one realizes, has been leading up to the crowning diatribe against Wolsey himself. Skelton took care not to attack Catholicism or the clergy as institutions; to paraphrase George Orwell on Dickens as reformer, he wanted, not to abolish the Bumbles, but simply to improve them. Yet though his appeal to the bishops to set their own house in order might spring from religious zeal, his meddling in politics at times came perilously near treason:

> It is a busy thing
> For one man to rule a king
> Alone and make reckoning,
> To govern over all
> And rule a realm royall
> By one man's very wit.

"His wolf's head, wan, blo as lead, gapeth over the crown," he had written of Wolsey in *Speak, Parrot;* and the cardinal was soon—if we can believe the tradition—to take more direct action against so libelous a pamphleteer.

In that hectic year of 1522, between *Colin Clout* and its even more bitter—and undisguised—sequel, *Why Come Ye Not to Court?*, Skelton took time off from political satire to write a poem of a very different sort. It is safe to say that *The Tunning of Elinour Rumming* is his best-known work, and in many ways it deserves to be; but few people quite realize that it is unique, the only thing of its kind Skelton ever produced. Again, as in *Speak, Parrot*, we might be looking at a picture; but this time it is Brueghel or Rowlandson rather than Bosch. The scene is an alehouse in Leatherhead; the occasion, a drinking party of old crones, who come straggling in with goods or clothes to barter for ale:

> Instead of coin and money
> Some bringé her a coney,
> And some a pot with honey,
> Some a salt, and some a spoon,
> Some their hose, some their shoon;
> Some run a good trot
> With a skillet or a pot;
> Some fill their pot full
> Of good Lemster wool:
> An housewife of trust,
> When she is athirst,
> Such a web can spin,
> Her thrift is full thin.

Over them all presides the hostess, Dame Elinour herself. "The effect," as W. H. Auden well observed in his memorable essay on Skelton, "is like looking at the human skin through a magnifying glass":

> Maud Ruggy thither skippéd:
> She was ugly hippéd,
> And ugly thick lippéd,
> Like an onion sided,
> Like tan leather hided . . .
> One's head would have achéd
> To see her naked.
> She drank so of the dreggés,
> The dropsy was in her leggés;
> Her face glistering like glass,
> All foggy fat she was.
> She had also the gout
> In all her joints about;
> Her breath was sour and stale,
> And smelléd all of ale:
> Such a bedfellaw
> Would make one cast his craw.

This powerful, vivid, ugly, hilarious, compassionate poem has obvious antecedents in Langland's *Piers Plowman* and the more rambunctious descriptive passages of Chaucer's *Canterbury Tales*. In one sense it is a variation on Skelton's familiar all-flesh-is-grass theme, and these frowsty old beldames a deliberate contrast to Lydgate's more sensuous *Ballade on an Ale-Seller*, the central figure in which might be Elinour forty years back. Skelton has caught in these verses the whole essence of medieval peasant life—the dirt and poverty, the disfiguring, endless, hopeless physical toil, the proverbial humor and repetitive gossip, the frantic urge to shut out the world behind a curtain of drink and conviviality. When Pope raged against "beastly Skelton" he did not mean that Skelton is indecent in the sexual sense, which he is not; he was damning him for mentioning such taboo realities as vomiting and body odors; for writing poetry that exploded the polite pastoral myth of Phyllis and Corydon; for employing a vernacular, realistic, anti-"literary" idiom, with jolting prosody and rustic rhyme. Primitive poverty of the rural sort generates its own imagery; there was no place in the polite literary salon—at any rate till recently—for

> skin loose and slack
> Grainéd like a sack,

nor for the flapping withered breasts and crooked noses and hen dung and incontinent bladders and stinking breath and "whey-wormed" faces. Yet the poem as a whole is by no means the unthinking, uproarious jig that its heartier advocates would have us believe. Skelton's eye is too mercilessly exact for that, his crones carry too strong a flavor of old mortality about them. The picture is painted for us with Flemish precision: it is our task to extract the moral.

The chief interest of *Why Come Ye Not to Court?* (1522–1523) lies in its unsurpassed virulence of invective. Wolsey is accused of every crime from treachery to witchcraft; and as a final insult, Skelton attributes his loss of one eye to advanced syphilis, with scornful asides on

> his wretched original,
> And his base progeny,

And his greasy genealogy,
He came of the sang royall
That was cast out of a butcher's stall . . .

Yet the violence is of a badly frightened man; one gets the feeling that Skelton is piling on the insults to keep his own courage up—as well he might when facing a prelate who

> is set so high
> In his hierarchy
> Of frantic frenesy
> And foolish fantasy,
> That in the Chamber of Stars
> All matter there he mars.
> Clapping his rod on the board,
> No man dare speak a word,
> For he hath all the saying
> Without any renaying.

And, in fact, after this final effort, Skelton capitulated to authority. He never attacked Wolsey again; indeed, much to the embarrassment of modern editors, his last published work, the *Replication*, is prefaced by a positively fulsome dedication "to the most honourable, most mighty, and by far the most reverend father in Christ and in the Lord, Lord Thomas"—with all his titles appended.

There is a story, probably true, in *The Merie Tales*, which tells us that Skelton was brought before the cardinal, and knelt there while His Eminence delivered a lengthy reprimand. Tiring of this sport, Skelton begged a favor: "I pray your grace to let me lye doune and wallow, for I can kneele no longer." No one, to my knowledge, has suggested the obvious connection between this anecdote and that fulsome dedication, and deduced that Skelton, as so often, had his tongue in his cheek. How better could he hold this peacocking prelate up to ridicule than by such gross flattery after his previous invective?

But in any case Skelton's fighting days were over. He was an old man now, over sixty; it was time to sum up his poetic achievement. The result was that odd poem *The Garland of Laurel*, a prolonged exercise in self-advertisement—and a blessing to bibliographers, since Skelton enumerates all his works during the course of it, many of them lost. Again, like *The Bouge of Court*, we have a dream allegory: Pallas and the

Queen of Fame dispute over Skelton's merits. Shall he be admitted among the elect, or not? The answer, with Skelton himself conducting the debate, is never really in doubt.

There are some passages in *The Garland of Laurel* as powerful as anything Skelton ever wrote. Unlike most Tudor poets, he had a curious sense of local atmosphere, as here describing the Yorkshire woodland where his dream is set:

> Thus stood I in the frithy forest of Galtress,
> Ensoakéd with silt of the miry wose [ooze]
> Where hartés bellowing, emb
oséd with distress,
> Ran on the range so long, that I suppose
> Few men can tell now where the hind-calf goes . . .

And when he turns his hand again to lyrics, in honor of the various ladies assembled in Sheriff-Hutton Castle, he not only recaptures all the grace and ease of his youth, but adds something to them; a limpid tenderness, a vernal simplicity his verse had never before achieved:

> Merry Margaret,
>   As midsummer flower,
> Gentle as falcon
> Or hawk of the tower:
> With solace and gladness,
> Much mirth and no madness,
> All good and no badness;
>   So joyously,
>   So maidenly,
>   So womanly
>   Her demeaning
>   In every thing,
>   Far, far passing
>   That I can indite,
>   Or suffice to write
> Of Merry Margaret
>   As midsummer flower,
> Gentle as falcon
>   Or hawk of the tower.

That was his tribute to Margaret Hussey; and Margery Wentworth—to pick out one more—was no less well served:

> With marjoram gentle,
>   The flower of goodlihead,
> Embroidered the mantle
>   Is of your maidenhead.
> Plainly I cannot glose;
>   Ye be, as I devine,

JOHN SKELTON

The pretty primrose,
　The goodly columbine.
With marjoram gentle,
　The flower of goodlihead,
Embroidered the mantle
　Is of your maidenhead.

"With ladies I learn, and go with them to school": Parrot had spoken truly. Perhaps in the company of Isabel Knight, Margery Wentworth, Margaret Hussey, Lady Muriel Howard, and the rest, old Master Skelton found peace at last—as he had glimpsed it before, long ago, at the sign of The Key in Thames Street, or at the Black Nuns' Convent in Carrow-by-Norwich.

SKELTON LAUREATE

NOTHING is more curious—or, ultimately, more instructive—than the fluctuations of John Skelton's reputation through the ages. In his own lifetime he was esteemed a scholar and rhetorician, earning tributes from such critics as Caxton and Erasmus. Two decades after his death there was published the first collected edition, *The Pithy, Pleasant and Profitable Works* (1568), probably edited by John Stow (whose Chaucer had appeared seven years previously) and prefaced with a lengthy commendatory poem by Thomas Churchyard. But within twenty years it was a very different matter: the literary climate had undergone a radical transformation, and we find Puttenham attacking him, tooth and nail, in his *Art of English Poetry*. Skelton was, we are told:

a sharp satirist, but with more rayling and scoffery than became a Poet Lawreat, such among the Greeks were called Pantomimi, with us Buffons, altogether applying their wits to scurrilities and other ridiculous matters.

Puttenham goes on to contrast him, unfavorably, with Surrey and Wyatt, whose

conceits were loftie, their stiles stately, their conveyance cleanly, their terms proper, their meetre sweete and well-proportioned, in all imitating very naturally and studiously their Maister *Francis Petrarcha*.

Later, he rubs the point in, roundly condemning "small and popular musickes song . . . upon benches and barrels heads where they have none other audience than boys or countrey fellowes. . . . Such were the rimes of Skelton." Puttenham might have tagged Skelton with one of his own lines, and said of him (as Skelton said of the Comely Coistrown, whoever he may have been): "He lumb'reth on a lewd lute 'Roty bully joys.'" The portrait is one that, with minor variations, has survived to our own day.

Now these charges of Puttenham's place Skelton at once in the center of that perennial struggle that goes on in English literature—between the high literary conventions and vernacular realism; between "art for art's sake" and *la condition humaine;* between (to take a modern example) Henry James and H. G. Wells. Puttenham states roundly what many *littérateurs* merely imply: that poets have no business with low society or vulgar speech, and should avoid being rude to their betters and hanging about alehouses. When we remember just what Skelton's "scurrilities and other ridiculous matters" were—a sustained assault upon a powerful and dangerous politician, for the sake of justice and religious truth; a grim portrait of the lot of the Tudor peasantry; a well-justified onslaught against bigotry and oppression in church and state alike—then we understand better some of the elements that have once more brought Skelton into prominence, and earned him such glowing tributes from Auden and other modern writers. He is that very topical figure, a right-wing Christian radical, an anti-establishment Tory.

It is strange how his critics have always fastened on what constitutes a very small part of his work. Pope states that his poetry consists "almost wholly of Ribaldry, Obscenity, and Billingsgate language," which is so untrue as to make one wonder whether Pope had actually read him. Even Skelton's modern advocates present a similar picture, with the trifling difference that they approve it; taste has changed, but not (till very recently) the false picture of Skelton. Robert Graves, who did more than anyone to reintroduce him to modern readers, began his celebrated poem with the lines

JOHN SKELTON

What could be dafter
Than John Skelton's laughter?

And the answer, of course, is: almost anything. Skelton was very far from the Johnny-go-lightly of tradition. A serious man, you might say, if a man of wit; a passionately devout, if somewhat unorthodox, Catholic priest; a poet with a deep knowledge of music and hence an exquisite mastery in the subtler modulations of rhythm and meter; a scholar in love with language; perhaps, above all, that rarest of pre-Renaissance birds, a writer capable of *using his own eyes*, as Leonardo told his pupils to do, instead of "studiously imitating" Petrarch or whoever the fashionable man of the moment may have been. C. S. Lewis sums him up to perfection: "He has no real predecessors and no important disciples; he stands out of the streamy historical process, an unmistakable individual, a man we have met." Skelton embodies for us the last wholly authentic utterance of the Middle Ages, a voice soon to be drowned forever by the high tide of Renaissance and Reformation alike. It is a pleasant paradox—and one that he would have been the first to appreciate—that Skelton's rediscovery should have come between two world wars, and his peak of popularity have coincided with the crises of the atomic age.

Thus much Parrot hath openly expressed:
Let see who dare make up the rest.

SELECTED BIBLIOGRAPHY

I. BIBLIOGRAPHIES. No separate bibliography of Skelton exists, but there are detailed bibliographical descriptions of some of the early editions of the separate works (all extremely rare, fewer than half a dozen copies of each being recorded) in the Pforzheimer Catalogue, III. There are full and generally helpful bibliographical lists in Gordon (pp. 302–316) and Nelson (pp. 249–253), cited below, and a list of early manuscript sources in the *Cambridge Bibliography of English Literature*, I, 408–411, and *Supplement*, pp. 203–204.

II. COLLECTED WORKS. *Pithy, Pleasaunt and Profitable Workes of Maister Skelton, Poete Laureate, Nowe Collected and Newly Published by T. Marshe* (London, 1568); repr., 1736, and described as "Newly Collected by I. S." (John Stow?); A. Dyce, ed., *The Poetical Works*, 2 vols. (London, 1843), the first and only critical edition, superseded in some details (the *Speculum Principis* was unknown); *The Poetical Works* (Cambridge, Mass., 1855; repr. Boston, 1856, 1864, 1866, 1871, 1887) is largely a reprint of Dyce. P. Henderson, ed., *The Complete Poems* (London, 1931; 2nd ed. rev., 1948; 3rd ed., 1959), is the only complete text of Skelton's poems. It is based on Dyce, with minor modifications in the light of later research. There is a useful introduction, a very brief bibliography, notes, and glossary. This modernized text is used in the above essay.

III. SELECTIONS. E. Sandford, ed., *Select Poems* (London, 1819); W. H. Williams, ed., *A Selection From the Poetical Works* (London, 1902), contains a vigorous introduction, somewhat hampered by contemporary moral prejudices; R. Hughes, ed., *Poems* (London, 1924), earlier critical aberrations are treated with contempt but one or two solecisms are committed; beautifully produced but perhaps more for the bibliophile than the student; Robert Graves, ed., *John Skelton* (London, 1927), Augustan Books of English Poetry; R. Gant, ed., *Poems* (London, 1949); V. de Sola Pinto, ed., *John Skelton: A Selection From His Poems* (London, 1950), the most useful volume of selections, contains much beyond the usual anthology pieces and the introduction is shrewd and up-to-date.

IV. SEPARATE WORKS. *The Bibliotheca Historica of Diodorus Siculus, Translated by John Skelton: ca. 1485–1488*, edited from the unique MS in Corpus Christi College, Cambridge, by F. M. Salter and H. L. R. Edwards, 2 vols. (London, 1956–1957). *Agaynste a Comely Coystrowne: ca. 1525–1530*, 1st ed. by Richard Pynson (n.d.), never reprinted separately. *The Bowge of Court: ca. 1500*, two eds. published, before and after 1500, headed "Here begynneth a ly-tell treatyse named the Bowge of Court. (Anon.) west-myster. Wynken de worde." *Speculum Principis: 1501*, Modern Language Association Photo facs. XXVII (1925), edited with an introduction by F. M. Salter, in *Speculum*, 9 (1934), 25–37. *Phylllyp Sparowe: 1543?–1546*, early eds. include R. Kele (1545?), J. Wyghte (1552), A. Kitson (1565), A. Veale (n.d.), and J. Walley (n.d.); no modern separate reprints exist. *A Ballade of the Scottysshe Kynge: 1513.* 1st ed. by R. Faukes (1513). Edited by J. Ashton from Pynson's ed. (n.d.) in *A Century of Ballads* (Boston, 1882). *Magnyfycence: 1529–1532*, 1st ed. by J. Rastell. Modern eds. include Roxburghe Club ed. (1821) and R. L. Ramsay's ed. for the Early English Text Society (1908; repr. 1925, 1970); a separate ed. by J. S. Farmer appeared in 1910. *Collyn Clout:* 1532–1537, 1st ed. by R. Kele; other eds. include those of T. Godfrey (after 1532), J. Wyghte (1560?), A. Kyston (1565?), A. Veale (n.d.), J. Walley (n.d.). The author has accepted the date 1522 established by Nelson and Edwards. Gordon places it in 1519–1520, unconvincingly. *The Tunning of Elinour Rumming:* 1542–1548; most scholars date this poem *ca.* 1508. The author follows Edwards in placing it in the same year as *Colin Clout* (1522). 1st recorded ed. is J. Busbie and G. Loftis (1609). Published separately by S. Sand (1642), I. Dalton (1718), and the Fanfrolico Press (1928). *Why Come Ye Nat to Courte?:* 1542–1546; early eds. include R. Kele (1545?), R. Toy (1552), and A. Kytson (1565); edited by J. Zupitza, in *Archiv,* 85 (1890), 429–436. *A Garlande of Laurell:* 1523, 1st ed. by R. Faukes (1523); modern annotated text in E. P. Hammond, *English Verse Between Chaucer and Surrey* (Durham, N.C., 1927). *A Replycacion Agaynst Certayne Yong Scolers:* *ca.* 1528, 1st. ed. by R. Pynson.

V. CRITICAL AND BIOGRAPHICAL STUDIES. J. Bale, *Scriptorum Britanniae Catalogus* (London, 1557–1559); *Merie Tales of Skelton,* in Dyce, I, lvii–lxxiii; T. Fuller, *Worthies of England* (London, 1662); P. Bliss, ed., *Athenae Oxoniensis* (London, 1813); G. Schoeneberg, *Die Sprache John Skeltons in seinen kleineren Werken* (Marburg, 1888); A. Rey, *Skelton's Satirical Poems in Their Relation to Lydgate's "Order of Fools," "Cocke Lorell's Bote," and Barclay's "Ship of Fools"* (Berne, 1899), the first really valuable criticism of Skelton apart from Dyce. Rey took the useful material from Krumpholz and added much of great value concerning the whole tradition of the *Naarenschiff,* especially in relation to *The Bouge of Court.* A. Koelbing, *Zur Charakteristik John Skeltons* (Stuttgart, 1904), a preliminary study for

his later chapter in the *Cambridge History of English Literature* (1909), III, 56–79; A. Thuemmel, *Studien ueber John Skelton* (Leipzig, 1905), contains some valuable biographical work on Skelton's origins and career; E. Bischoffsberger, *Einfluss John Skeltons auf die englische Literatur* (Freiburg, 1914), a painstaking collection of *testimonia,* resting heavily on Dyce, tracing Skelton's influence on subsequent English poets; L. J. Lloyd, *John Skelton* (Oxford, 1938), a brief, general introduction to the poet, now superseded by the works of Nelson, Gordon, and Edwards; W. Nelson, *John Skelton, Laureate* (New York, 1939), the most complete and satisfying study of man and poetry alike, it stands supreme; I. A. Gordon, *John Skelton, Poet Laureate* (Melbourne, 1943), a thorough and perceptive study that suffers somewhat, presumably through wartime communications difficulties, from failure to assimilate important post-1937 materials; H. L. R. Edwards, *Skelton: The Life and Times of an Early Tudor Poet* (London, 1949), likely to remain the standard biography, although its aesthetic insight is less certain; E. M. Forster, *Two Cheers for Democracy* (London, 1951), contains a witty and just appraisal of Skelton delivered originally as a lecture—appropriately enough—at Aldeburgh. Despite minor inaccuracies, the brilliant quotations and general tone make this an excellent introduction to the poet. See also A. R. Heiserman, *Skelton and Satire* (Chicago, 1961); William O. Harris, *Skelton's* Magnifycence *and the Cardinal Virtue Tradition* (Chapel Hill, N.C., 1965); Eugene S. Fish, *John Skelton's Poetry* (New Haven, Conn., 1965); Nan Cooke Carpenter, *John Skelton* (New York, 1967); and Maurice Pollet, *John Skelton: Poet of Tudor England* (London, 1971), translated by John Warrington.

SIR THOMAS WYATT

(1503-1542)
Sergio Baldi
translated by *F. T. Prince*

THE STORY OF THE POEMS

ONLY a few of Sir Thomas Wyatt's poems were published during his lifetime. These appeared anonymously in two volumes of narrative and lyric poems entitled *The Courte of Venus* (ca. 1538) and *A Booke of Balettes* (ca. 1548), of which only fragments survive. For political reasons (unconnected with Wyatt's poems) they seem to have had a restricted circulation. In consequence, his poems were not available to English readers at large until fifteen years after his death, when they appeared in the famous *Songes and Sonettes, Written by the Ryght Honorable Lorde Henry Haward Late Earle of Surrey, and Other*. This volume, published by Richard Tottel in 1557, is now called *Tottel's Miscellany*, and is commonly described as the fountainhead of Elizabethan lyric verse. In it Wyatt's poems were given second place, after those of Surrey; but they were in fact the first English examples of the Italianate school of poetry that had sprung up at the court in the reign of Henry VIII.

This school of poetry was for the most part new. English medieval literature is indeed surprisingly poor in lyric poetry: Chaucer, John Lydgate, and John Skelton had composed only a few lyrics of an occasional kind, and the best English medieval lyrics (which are by no means remarkable) were confined to popular and comic poetry. But lyric poetry in Italy had an impressive tradition of cultivated writing going back to the thirteenth century, which had reached its greatest splendor in the work of Petrarch. France and Spain had already set out to emulate Italy; *Tottel's Miscellany* showed that England could now follow them.

Until 1579, when Edmund Spenser published his *Shepheardes Calendar, Tottel's Miscellany* remained almost the sole school of poetry for English writers. From it the poets of the first twenty years of Elizabeth's reign learned not only the seriousness of which the new lyric poetry was capable, but also many new means of expression, valid for all kinds of verse: the sonnet, the *ottava rima*, the iambic pentameter, poulter's measure, and countless rhetorical devices. They also found in it the Petrarchan poetic tradition that was to be one of the fundamental elements of all Elizabethan lyric verse, including that of Philip Sidney and Shakespeare.

Toward the end of the sixteenth century, when the lessons to be learned from *Tottel's Miscellany* had been left behind, and new preoccupations took hold of the minds of Englishmen, interest in the anthology died a natural death; and when it revived in the eighteenth century, this was due to the historical and critical studies characteristic of that period. The poetry of Wyatt and Surrey was then read, not as a pattern to be imitated or followed, but as valuable evidence of the beginnings of English literature. Taking this historical point of view, eighteenth- and nineteenth-century scholars passed a twofold judgment on *Tottel's Miscellany*. They granted it historical importance, since everyone could see its value as a pioneer experiment; but they did not recognize that it had any great poetic value, because the comparison with the lyrics of Sidney and Shakespeare was always in their minds, even if only half-consciously—and the taste of these learned readers was decidedly in favor of the later poets. Indeed, between the two foremost poets of *Tot-*

tel, Wyatt and Surrey, these critics decided explicitly in favor of Surrey. It is true that the eighteenth-century critics did so in ignorance of the chronology of the two poets, believing Surrey to be the elder, and Wyatt his disciple; but although the nineteenth-century scholars clarified the dates, they retained the earlier judgment on the relative achievements of the two poets. Even if some isolated critics recognized Wyatt's merits—George Gilfillan and Robert Bell in England, Bernard ten Brink in Germany, and Jean Jusserand in France—the reversal of the earlier judgment belongs wholly to the twentieth century, or rather, to be more precise, to the years between the two world wars.

Indeed, modern taste has completely rejected the nineteenth-century conclusions on Wyatt. Those qualities in him that were felt to show artificiality and lack of passion have come to be taken as proof of a praiseworthy absence of sentimentality. In his verse forms, both the "ballettes" and the sonnets, we now see not uncertain gropings toward regularity but the creations of a sense of rhythm not yet corrupted by the too easy smoothness of "correct" verse. The influence of Ezra Pound and T. S. Eliot in particular has led modern critics to look for dramatic compression and direct and living speech, rather than an outpouring of emotion, and to set less value on fixed patterns of prosody than on the emergence of an "organic" rhythm. The twentieth-century revaluation of John Donne led inevitably to a revaluation of Wyatt; and this inevitably led to a reversal of the accepted judgment. Wyatt is now considered a greater poet than Surrey.

Thus, in our day Wyatt is granted not only historic importance but also an individual poetic achievement. He is not only the poet who first brought Petrarchianism to England, and with it the Italian verse forms of the sonnet, the *ottava rima*, and the *terza rima*; he is also a poet inspired by his own profound awareness of unhappy love, which he seeks to express in vivid and dramatic images and language.

THE POET AND THE KING

HENRY WYATT, the poet's father, came of a good Yorkshire family. In the Wars of the Roses he had followed the fortunes of the Lancas-trians, and Henry VII had no sooner assumed power than he made Wyatt one of his Privy Council, as well as appointing him one of the executors of his will. Henry Wyatt's fortunes continued to prosper under Henry VIII. The new king created him Knight of the Bath at his coronation in 1509, and thenceforward he lived at court, holding various offices until his death in 1536.

His son Thomas was born in 1503, at Allington Castle in Kent, now the official residence of his family. The boy soon took his place at court. As early as 1516 he was a page at the christening of Princess Mary. It is not known with certainty whether he was the Wyatt who matriculated at St. John's College, Cambridge, in 1515, and left the university in 1520 as a master of arts. But it is certain that our Thomas Wyatt married Elizabeth Brooke, daughter of Lord Cobham, in 1520 or 1521; they had two children. This was, however, an unhappy marriage that ended in 1526 with Wyatt's repudiation of his wife on the ground of her adultery.

Of the emotions engaged in this marriage story (or indeed whether any emotions entered into it) we know nothing; and the same may be said of Wyatt's private life as a whole. But we can follow the poet in his gradual but steady rise at court. He first held minor appointments, as his father's son, and took part in tournaments with other young gentlemen of rank. Then, in 1526, when he was twenty-three, he began to achieve a certain political individuality and to make a career for himself in diplomacy. In that year he was a member of Sir Thomas Cheney's suite in a mission to Paris, and in 1527 he was attached to Sir John Russell on a similar journey to Rome.

In a letter from Paris, Cheney recommended Wyatt to Cardinal Wolsey as a young man who "hath as much wit to mark and remember everything he seeth as any young man hath in England"; and in Italy, Wyatt showed that he was capable of extricating himself from difficulties with some resourcefulness. Having been sent alone to Venice, although Italy was at the time overrun by the Spanish troops that were moving against Rome, he arrived without mishap; but on his return journey he was taken prisoner by the Spaniards, who demanded 3,000 ducats as his ransom. But the young man escaped before the ransom was paid, perhaps with the help of a messenger who had been sent with the money for his release.

Wyatt returned to England in May or June 1527; and at the following New Year he presented as a tribute to Queen Katharine his translation of the *De tranquillitate animi* of Plutarch, a humanist exercise that was published by Richard Pynson, probably in 1528, as *Tho. Wyatis Translatyon of Plutarckes Boke of the Quyete of Minde.* Soon after this he went abroad again, this time as high marshal of the town of Calais. This important post kept him away from court for nearly two years. He did not return to England until 1530, but he then remained there until 1537.

Documentary evidence is slight for this period of Wyatt's life. He is recorded as having represented his father as chief ewerer at the banquets celebrating Anne Boleyn's coronation in 1533, and we learn that in May 1534 he was imprisoned in the Fleet Prison for having had a brush with the guard in London and having killed one of them—a misdemeanor much less serious then than it would be now. A greater danger threatened Wyatt in May 1536, when he was again arrested and taken to the Tower of London. The reasons for his arrest and imprisonment have never been known with certainty, but rumor did not hesitate to link them with the disgrace of Anne Boleyn. What is certain is that he was released after six weeks, and was soon afterward nominated by the king as sheriff of Kent.

Marks of the king's favor toward Wyatt are noted throughout this period. Some almost contemporary anecdotes prove that Wyatt's personal friendship with the king was a matter of common report. He certainly had his share of the church lands confiscated by the king, and perhaps his rapid release from the Tower was also due to the king's personal intervention.

In the spring of 1537 Wyatt was knighted and sent as English ambassador to Spain; his mission was to seek to improve the relations between Henry VIII and Emperor Charles V, who was offended by Henry's divorce from Katharine of Aragon, his aunt. Wyatt's sojourn at the emperor's court lasted until June 1539. At the end of 1539, after a short stay in England, he was again sent abroad, to attend the emperor on his travels in France and Flanders. His specific task was to prevent too close an understanding between France and Spain, the two Catholic powers; and in this he seems to have achieved a measure of success.

Yet on his return in May 1540, Wyatt found himself again in danger. His most powerful patron, after the king, had been Thomas Cromwell. Cromwell fell, and was beheaded in July 1540; and at the beginning of 1541, Wyatt was sent to the Tower on a charge of treason. On this occasion he remained in captivity for two months. But the charge against him was flimsy, and he was easily able to prove his innocence. What was more important, his judges were left free to accept his evidence.

After Wyatt's release the king, as if to display his favor toward him, granted him a commission in the garrison of Calais, authorized profitable land transactions on his behalf, and appointed him to offices that were practically sinecures. Only his diplomatic career had suffered a check. But in October 1542 it seemed that he was also to resume his activities as a diplomat. An envoy from the emperor had arrived at Falmouth, and Wyatt was sent to meet him. The business was urgent, and Wyatt rode posthaste, day and night, without heeding the bad weather.

But he was no longer a young man, and the strain and exertion proved fatal. An attack of pneumonia forced Wyatt to halt at Sherborne, where he died on October 11. In Sherborne Abbey a modern inscription (1947) marks the vault where he was buried.

THE POET'S LOVE AFFAIRS

FROM this recital of bare facts little emerges that can really help us to interpret Wyatt's poetry. On the contrary, if we relied only on this evidence, we would conclude that, considering the circumstances of his time, Wyatt's life was not only fairly long but, on the whole, prosperous. For if, as we have seen, his thoughtlessness, or his personal or political enmities, sometimes placed him in danger, we have also seen that Wyatt always extricated himself, or was extricated, from those difficulties, and on each occasion at once resumed his successful career at court. And yet we find his apparent good fortune contradicted by his poetry, which is made up of endless complaints of unhappy love, growing more and more painful from page to page, until we reach the bitterness of the *Satires* and of some poetic "confessions" he left unfinished. If we are to believe the poems, Love itself is hostile to him, and responsible for all his misfortunes, even in public life, for these all befell him in the month consecrated to Love:

> You that in love find luck and abundance
>   And live in lust and joyful jollity,[1]
>   Arise, for shame! Do away sluggardy!
>   Arise, I say, do May some observance!
> Let me in bed lie dreaming in mischance;
>   Let me remember the haps[2] most unhappy
>   That me betid[3] in May most commonly,
>   As one whom Love list[4] little to advance.
> Sepham said true that my nativity
>   Mischanced[5] was with the ruler of the May;
>   He guessed, I prove, of that the verity.
> In May my wealth and eke[6] my life, I say,
>   Have stood so oft in such perplexity:
>   Rejoice! Let me dream of your felicity.
>
> (no. 92)[7]

We cannot consult the horoscope that the astrologer Edward Sepham cast for Thomas Wyatt; but we have seen that in May 1534, Wyatt was imprisoned in the Fleet, and that in May 1536 he found himself in the Tower. The reason for his imprisonment in the Tower was never revealed. However, it was widely rumored at the time that his arrest was linked with that of Anne Boleyn; and this story was repeated later by Nicholas Sanders in his *De origine ac progressu schismatis anglicani*, published in 1585. Sanders, a Catholic and a poet, was a bitter enemy of English Protestantism; and he is certainly not a reliable witness when he treats the story of Anne Boleyn. According to Sanders, Anne Boleyn had led a vicious life from her earliest youth, and had been Wyatt's mistress; and Wyatt tried to dissuade Henry VIII from marrying her by revealing the truth about his own love affair with the lady. Wyatt offered to give a practical demonstration of what he said; but

Henry, who was by this time infatuated, refused. Later, at the time of Anne's trial, the king protected the man who had sought to warn him of her unchasteness.

Even without a close knowledge of Henry VIII's mentality, we can say with some confidence that the king would have cut off Wyatt's head without more ado if, in 1533, when Henry was undoubtedly in love with Anne Boleyn, Wyatt had really offered to show him the lady in his own arms ("Annam in amplexus ipsius ruentem"). Indeed, a grandson of Thomas Wyatt, George Wyatt, writing toward the end of the sixteenth century, made this point before giving his own version of the story.

According to George Wyatt, his grandfather had fallen in love with Anne, and insistently paid court to her, in spite of her refusals; and one day he took from her a "tablet" that she wore at her girdle, and refused to give it back. In the meantime Henry wooed her, but was also refused, until he convinced her that he intended to marry her; she then gave him a ring as a token of their understanding. Soon afterward Henry, at a game of bowls with a group of courtiers, remarked to Wyatt, ostensibly referring to a cast in the game, but significantly showing the ring: "Wyatt, I tell thee, it is mine," whereupon Wyatt replied, "And if it may like your Majesty to give me leave to measure it, I hope it will be mine," and, taking the tablet from about his neck, he bent forward to measure the length of the cast with it. "It may be so," the king answered, having recognized the trinket, "but then I am deceived." And he immediately went to demand an explanation from Anne. Naturally she was able to explain everything, and Wyatt confirmed her story.

This was probably the truth of the matter. The love between Thomas Wyatt and Anne Boleyn was probably limited to an unsuccessful courtship on his part, though we cannot say to what extent his feelings might have been engaged. When Wyatt returned from Italy in 1527, he was probably ignorant of the relationship between the king and Anne Boleyn, and set about making love to her, but very soon made way for the king's passion. One of his earliest sonnets that may belong to this period is relevant here. We may notice that it is modeled in part on Petrarch's "Una candida cerva sopra l'erba," but

[1]pleasure.　[2]chances.　[3]happened.　[4]chose.
[5]unfortunate.　[6]also.
[7]References are to the numbers given the poems in Kenneth Muir and Patricia Thomson's edition of *The Collected Poems* (1969).

100

the diamond necklace (added by Wyatt) suggests a connection with Wyatt's story:

> Whoso list[8] to hunt I know where is an hind;
>   But as for me, alas I may no more:[9]
>   The vain travail[10] hath wearied me so sore,
>   I am of them that farthest cometh[11] behind;
> Yet may[12] I by no means my wearied mind
>   Draw from the Deer: but as she fleeth afore
>   Fainting I follow. I leave off therefore,
>   Since in a net I seek to hold the wind.
> Who list her hunt, I put him out of doubt,
>   As well as I may[13] spend his time in vain:
>   And, graven with diamonds, in letters plain
> There is written her fair neck round about:
>   *Noli me tangere,* for Ceasar's I am;
>   And wild for to hold, though I seem tame.
>
>   (no. 7)

Nineteenth-century scholars persuaded themselves that all Wyatt's love poems were written for Anne Boleyn, though there is no evidence at all for this belief, which is inspired only too obviously by Victorian romantic idealism. The intention was to make the poet almost into another Petrarch, with Anne Boleyn as his Laura—of course giving these figures the most refined interpretation, for in reality Petrarch's fidelity to Laura extended no further than his verse. But in Wyatt's poetry there is nowhere to be found even such a pretense of fidelity; and the last sonnet in his own manuscript (MS Egerton 2711) is clear on this point:

> If waker[14] care, if sudden pale colour,
>   If many sighs with little speech to plain,
>   Now joy, now woe, if they my cheer distain,
>   For hope of small, if much to fear therefore,
> To haste, to slack my pace less or more,
>   Be sign of love, then do I love again;
>   If thou ask whom, sure since I did refrain[15]
>   Her that did set our country in a roar,
> Th' unfeigned cheer[16] of Phillis hath the place
>   That Brunet had: she hath and ever shall.
>   She from myself now hath me in her grace:
> She hath in hand my wit, my will and all;
>   My heart alone well worthy she doth stay,[17]
>   Without whose help scant[18] do I live a day.
>
>   (no. 97)

[8]may like.   [9]am no longer able.   [10]labor.   [11]remain.
[12]can.   [13]he may.   [14]watchful.   [15]eschew.
[16]sincere countenance.   [17]sustain.   [18]hardly.

There can be no doubt about the identity of "her that did set our country in a roar"; indeed, Wyatt himself felt it to be so obvious that he prudently corrected the verse to "Brunet, that set my wealth in such a roar." On the other hand, we cannot identify Phillis any more than the Rachel and Leah whom Wyatt names elsewhere ("For Rachel have I served, for Leah cared I never"). The recorded facts of his life give us, in addition to the name of Anne Boleyn, those of at least two other women. The first was Elizabeth Brooke, whom he married in 1520 or 1521, and from whom he was separated in 1526. The second was Elizabeth Darrell, with whom he lived at least from the beginning of 1536 to 1541. But, with the exception of those few poems that can be said with certainty to have been written about Anne Boleyn, there is no evidence to assign to any of these three women this, that, or the other among his poems. Which of these three, for example, was the lady who loved him and whom he, in a unique poem, lamented that he could not love in return (no. 38)? Which of them could have been the lady of whom he always writes, who brought him so many sorrows and so little happiness? No name, not even that of Anne Boleyn, for all her queenship, can be said to account for so much suffering, a state of mind so out of harmony with his successful life in the world of affairs.

The sadness of Wyatt's poetry springs in fact from deeper sources; it is an innate melancholy of temperament often found in poets, many of whom give artistic expression only to the darker side of their nature or experience. And if in Wyatt's case this kind of temperamental sadness makes use of the terms of unhappy love, this is because he had in them found the best means of expressing his poetic self. Hence, when about 1536 the outlook grew dark, both for himself and for his country, even this gloom of outward circumstance found expression in imagery drawn from unhappy or disappointed love. Or rather, perhaps, the growing outward gloom turned inward and deepened those sufferings that love had always brought him.

The last pieces in Wyatt's own manuscript, written almost certainly after 1536, have a more bitter tone and an increased sadness, shared with the *Satires* and the *Penitential Psalms,* which belong to the same period. Yet this change of mood cannot be attributed solely to the execution of Anne Boleyn; one should bear in mind the other heads that rolled in swift succession during the reign of Henry VIII. These events could not fail to leave a mark on Wyatt's mind. The disgust with public life expressed in the *Satires*, the turning to God that appears in the version of Psalm 37, "Noli emulari" (no. 94), and in the *Penitential Psalms*, would be appropriate in a man who, unable to pass a clear and effective moral judgment on current events, takes refuge in a sweeping condemnation of worldly life and in a vague turning toward God. But since in Wyatt's poetic universe, love is the predominant form of emotion, any urgent and bitter feeling may take on an erotic content and can also give greater depth to his treatment of unhappy love.

We therefore should not be justified in attributing the change of tone in Wyatt's later poems to any special change or variation in the woman or women he loved. The natural development of his life certainly appears in Wyatt's poetry: outwardly in the manner of new metrical forms that he masters as he goes along, and inwardly in the quality of his emotion, which grows more mature. But these developments do not change his experience of passionate love, which remains constant throughout his poetry. He may have had numerous and various love affairs, but his personal experience of love remains the same. Hence, in order to discuss Wyatt's poetry, we can proceed as if in reality he never had more than one love affair and was never in love with more than one woman, not because we believe this to be literally true, but because Phillis, Rachel, and Leah are only passing incarnations or objectifications of a single poetic mood.

LOVE AND POETRY

IF we try to define the specific experience of love found in Wyatt's poetry, we must remark at once that although we can hardly doubt that at certain moments in his life Wyatt knew the sweetness of love fulfilled, as a poet he was never inspired by any such happiness. In the whole of his poetry there is not one hymn of triumphant love like, for example, Spenser's *Epithalamion*. Once only did Wyatt attempt to express the joy of mutual love, in "Once as me thought Fortune me kissed" (no. 65); but these verses are poetically a failure. The fact that he made only this one attempt, and that it did not succeed, shows clearly how alien to his poetic inspiration are the satisfactions or exultations of love. If he is to be moved to poetry, his happiness in love must be mingled with something less happy, such as doubt or jealousy; or, even if the two lovers love equally, their love must be unable to find complete expression. Thus it is in "I have loved and so doth she":

> Was ever heart so well agreed,
>   Since love was love, as I do trow,[19]
> That in their love so evil[20] did speed,
>   To love so well and live in woe?
>
> This mourn we both and hath done long
>   With woeful plaint and careful[21] voice;
> Alas! it is a grievous wrong
>   To love so well and not rejoice.
>
> (no. 180)

Happiness in love never enters into Wyatt's poetry unless it has been transformed into something bitter, either because it is not present happiness but a paradise that he has lost, or because it was never anything but a dream. One of his most famous lyrics, "They flee from me" (no. 37), may illustrate the lament for lost happiness:

> They flee from me that sometime did me seek
>   With naked foot stalking in[22] my chamber
> I have seen them gentle, tame, and meek
>   That now are wild and do not remember
>   That sometime they put themself in danger
> To take bread at my hand; and now they range
> Busily seeking with a continual change.
>
> Thanked be Fortune, it hath been otherwise
>   Twenty times better; but once in special,
> In thin array after a pleasant guise,
>   When her loose gown from her shoulders did fall,
>   And she me caught in her arms long and small;
> Therewithal sweetly did me kiss,
> And softly said, *Dear heart, how like you this?*

[19]believe.   [20]ill fare.   [21]full of care.   [22]into.

It was no dream: I lay broad waking.
  But all is turned thorough my gentleness
Into a strange fashion of forsaking;
  And I have leave to go of her goodness,
  And she also to use newfangleness.[23]
But since that I so kindly am served
I would fain know what she hath deserved.

The happiness that is recognized to be only a dream is very clearly seen in the sonnet "Unstable dream" (no. 79), which is less well known than "They flee from me" but is perhaps even more beautiful in its realism:

Unstable[24] dream according to the place,
  Be steadfast once, or at least be true:
  By tasted sweetness make me not to rue
  The sudden loss of thy false feigned grace.
By good respect in such a dangerous case
  Thou broughtes[25] not her into this tossing mew[26]
  But madest my sprite live my care to renew,
  My body in tempest her succour to embrace.
The body dead, the sprite had his desire;
  Painless was th' one, th' other in delight;
  Why then, alas, did it not keep it right,
Returning to leap into the fire,
  And where it was at wish could it not remain?
  Such mocks of dreams they turn to deadly pain.

Wyatt's poetry is, therefore, insofar as it succeeds as poetry, an expression of "the pains of love." Something in him makes it impossible for him, at least as a creative artist, to be happy in his love; and because he is moved to poetry only by the negative side of love, that is, by love checked or unvalued or lost, he is able to give vivid expression not only to the torments he has suffered for his lady but also, with equal intensity, to his own pain at not being able to return another's love. In the woman whose love is not returned, he recognizes a reflection of himself; the parts played by the lovers are different, but the experience is the same:

    There was never nothing more me pained,
      Nor nothing more me moved,
    As when my sweetheart her complained
      That ever she me loved.
      Alas the while!

    With piteous look she said and sighed:
      "Alas, what aileth me

To love and set my wealth so light
On him that loveth not me?"
  Alas the while!

      . . .

She wept and wrung her hands withal,
  The tears fell in my neck;
She turned her face and let it fall;
  Scarcely therewith could speak.
  Alas the while!

Her pains tormented me so sore
  That comfort had I none,
But cursed my fortune more and more
  To see her sob and groan.
  Alas the while!   (no. 38)

Moreover, since love always comes to him in the guise of suffering, Wyatt regards the state of not being in love as a freedom that he has wrested from Fate. He writes songs exulting in his liberation from Love's tyranny, and these may seem at first to be substitutes for those poems of happy love we have so far failed to find. But it would be difficult to point to any one of these pieces in which his rejoicing, which is somewhat unnatural, turns into poetry. Rather, these poems suggest exaggerated demonstrations of relief and triumph. The refrain of one of them, "Spite of thy hap hap hath well happed" (no. 23), has the ring of forced laughter, like that of another song, "But ha, ha, ha, full well is me / For I am now at liberty" (no. 224), which derives from Serafino Aquilano ("Ha, ha, ha, men rido tanto / Ch'io son vivo e son di fore"). And that his boasted liberty was illusory, and in any case unwelcome to him, is surely obvious, both from the many relapses that he admits and from the way in which he likes to recall his past sufferings, or even becomes absorbed in thoughts of revenge. His wounds still smart; and if some of these verses live as poetry, they live precisely because of that lingering pain. This appears when, in the "ballette" just mentioned (no. 224), he recalls "The woefull days so full of pain / The weary night all spent in vain," or when his newly won liberty is irksome to him and mingles with a bittersweet regret (no. 59):

Sometime I fled the fire that me brent,[27]
  By sea, by land, by water and by wind;

[23] inconstancy.   [24] unsteady.   [25] broughtest.   [26] cage.   [27] burnt.

And now I follow the coals that be quent[28]
  From Dover to Calais, against my mind,
Lo, how desire is both sprung and spent!
  And he may[29] see that whilom[30] was so blind;
And all his labour now he laugh to scorn
Meshed[31] in the briers that erst[32] was all to-torn[33]

In the world of Wyatt's poetry, to be in love and not to be in love are only two aspects of the lover's frustration, which remains constant. The poet interprets his whole life as one continued experience of unhappy love. The sonnet "You that in love find luck and abundance" (no. 92) has already been quoted as an illustration of this attitude, but Wyatt returns repeatedly to this theme of the fixed hostility of Fortune. Sometimes he writes "Fortune always I have thee found unjust" (no. 165); sometimes "The sun, the moon doth frown on thee / Thou hast darkness in daylight's stead" (no. 91). At other times he blames his lady for all the bitterness he has to bear (no. 83):

I lead a life unpleasant, nothing glad,
Cry and complaint offer, voids joyfulness,[34]
So changeth unrest that nought shall fade,
Pain and despite hath altered pleasantness:
Ago, long since, that she hath truly made
Disdain for troth, set light in steadfastness,[35]
I have good cause to sing this song:
Plain or rejoice who feeleth weal or wrong

And in a poem that may be unfinished, and is perhaps among the last he wrote, his bitterness takes on an almost cosmic quality:

If in the world there be more woe
  Than I have in my heart,
Whereso it is, it doth come fro,[36]
And in my breast there doth it grow
  For to encrease my smart
Alas! I am receipt[37] of every care,
And of my life each sorrow claims his part.
                          (no. 89)

Such bitterness was plainly a part of the poet himself: we can see that he too, before Charles Baudelaire, was both the wound and the knife,

"la plaie et le couteau." But Wyatt never became aware of this, so he fills his work with analyses of the symptoms and effects of love, and its true nature; and these discussions often constitute the psychological limits of his poetry. As in so many other love poets, these descriptions of love's symptoms and effects may sometimes be mere rhetoric, proving nothing but a desperate wish to convince the lady; they can be verses without inspiration, written only for a practical purpose. But in Wyatt these devices can also be suffused by a sense of wonder; and images that in themselves are worn and rhetorical take on the freshness of novelty, a freshness very rare indeed in Continental followers of Petrarch. Even the "ardours, flames, and innumerable deaths," which left Jusserand cold and which in almost all Petrarch's followers are only literary conventions, can take on simplicity and directness in Wyatt's poetry, and so become the basis of an astounding poetic art. It is difficult to grasp this at once, especially when Wyatt's following of some Italian original remains obvious. But we cannot fail to be convinced by the direct observation of personal experience and the vivid touches of realism that mingle with the literary devices. Consider the famous "What rage is this" (no. 101) and certain phrases of "What meaneth this?" (no. 183) that are still more direct, and even crude:

What meaneth this when I lie alone?
I toss, I turn, I sigh, I groan,
My bed me seems as hard as stone:
  What meaneth this?

I sigh, I plain continually;
The cloths that on my bed do lie
Always me thinks they lie awry:
  What meaneth this?

In slumber oft for fear I quake;
For heat and cold I burn and shake;
For lack of sleep my head doth ache:
  What meaneth this?

And yet, in spite of much analysis and discussion, Wyatt gives us no genuine meditation on the nature of love. When he is not interpreting it as the personification of a hostile Fate, or a torturing madness, he sets about making it, curiously enough, the basis of a theory of

---

[28] are quenched.   [29] can.   [30] once.   [31] entangled.
[32] formerly.   [33] torn.   [34] joyfulness avoids.
[35] taken constancy lightly.   [36] forth.   [37] receptacle.

rights. (There have been critics who have thought to find in this something characteristically Tudor, rather than medieval.)

Wyatt, for example, gained no new insight from translating Petrarch's *canzone* "Quell'antico mio dolce empio signore" ("Mine old dear enemy, my froward master," no. 8). For him the sufferings of love have no potential spiritual value; they are only a tax or penalty that he would be content to pay, however high, if he were sure of having the reward that should justly follow. Nor does he acknowledge the irrational nature of love; instead, he appears to be convinced that long service deserves to have "of right" its fitting recompense, the love of the lady:

> It is not now, but long and long ago
> I have you served as to my power and might
> As faithfully as any man might do,
> Claiming of you nothing of right, of right.
>   . . .
> If I had suffered this to you unware[38]
> Mine were the fault and you nothing to blame;
> But since you know my woe and all my care
> Why do I die? Alas for shame, for shame!
>
>   (no. 73)

In consequence, when the recompense or reward is not forthcoming, Wyatt follows Serafino Aquilano in calling on the woods, the mountains, the valleys, and the rivers to witness his wrongs. He throws the blame on the lady, hopes and believes that she will be punished by meeting with an equal unhappiness, and accuses Love of having a particular aversion for him. He does indeed plead with the lady at some length to grant him her favor; but he goes on to remind her of his "law of love," that is, his claim that he has a right over her, won by his sufferings and long service. Probably he had little practical success with these recriminations, which can only be described as legalistic. Their poetic value is certainly slight, based as they are solely on rational assumptions; they can deceive no one, even when supported by all the stylistic artifices Wyatt can bring to them. If poetry sometimes springs up in the midst of these arguments, it enters through some unexpected source of emotion, such as the contemplation of

his own sorrow, past or present, or the memory of some former happiness. Just as the characteristic fault of many of Wyatt's poems is a sudden lapse into abstract or practical considerations, so they are often correspondingly redeemed, by a bubbling up of poetry in the midst of a dry desert of arguments and recriminations. So, for example, in one of his many "complaints" on the injustice of his lot, he suddenly throws off a stanza like this:

> Hope is my hold,[39] yet in despair I speak;
> I drive[40] from time to time, and doth not reck[41]
> How long to love thus after Love's lust[42]
> In study still of that I dare not break:[43]
> Wherefore to serve and suffer still I must.
>
>   (no. 165)

At times one has the impression that his long servitude to love, always painful and apparently unrewarded, may have wearied Wyatt. But more often his weariness or impatience is merely incidental, a passing impulse, as when he urges the lady to make up her mind in the brusque lines:

> Madame, withouten many words
> Once I am sure ye will or no;
> And if you will, then leave your boards,[44]
> And use your wit, and show it so.
>
>   (no. 34)

Such a poem, like the short piece "To wet your eye withouten tear" (no. 170), is little more than a versified outburst of anger. Wyatt's poetry therefore seldom rises to a noble disdain; but, when it does so, it attains a fullness of lyrical emotion that he was never to surpass:

> My lute awake! perform the last
> Labour that thou and I shall waste,
>   And end that[45] I have now begun;
> For when this song is sung and past,
>   My lute be still, for I have done.
>
> As to be heard where ear is none,
> As lead to grave[46] in marble stone,
>   My song may pierce her heart as soon;
> Should we then sigh or sing or moan?
>   No, no, my lute, for I have done.

---

[38]unaware.

[39]stronghold.   [40]defer.   [41]care.   [42]Love's caprice.
[43]refer to.   [44]jests.   [45]what.   [46]engrave.

SIR THOMAS WYATT

The rocks do not so cruelly
Repulse the waves continually,
  As she my suit and affection,
So that I am past remedy;
  Whereby my lute and I have done.

Proud of the spoil that thou has got
Of simple hearts thorough love's shot,
  By whom, unkind, thou hast them won,
Think not he hath his bow forgot,
  Although my lute and I have done.

Vengeance shall fall on thy disdain,
That makest but game on earnest pain,
  Think not alone under the sun
Unquit to cause thy lovers plain,
  Although my lute and I have done.

Perhance thee lie withered and old
The winter nights that are so cold,
  Plaining in vain unto the moon;
Thy wishes then dare not be told;
  Care then who list, for I have done.

And then may chance thee to repent
The time that thou hast lost and spent
  To cause thy lovers sigh and swoon;
Then shalt thou know beauty but lent,
  And wish and want as I have done.

Now cease, my lute; this is the last
Labour that thou and I shall waste,
  And ended is that we begun;
Now is this song both sung and past:
  My lute, be still, for I have done.

(no. 66)

Here we have what is justly Wyatt's most famous poem; but such a proud disdain, giving birth to poetry and not merely competent verse, is not to be found again in anything he wrote. Generally he finds it difficult to overcome, on the one hand, the prosaic statement of practical experience and, on the other, his tendency to self-pity. "My pen take pain a little space" (no. 179) is a clear example of the latter, a variation in a minor key on "My lute awake."

However, though the tendency to self-pity sometimes weakens the force of "noble disdain," the mood of pathos can also, in its own right, rise to poetry. Certainly this theme recurs most often in Wyatt's poems, and is least dependent on literary fashions and models. Among the many variations on it the best-

known and most complete is undoubtedly "Forget not yet" (no. 203). Here pain and entreaty are fused in poetry that may be self-pitying, but is nonetheless intense and true:

Forget not yet the tried intent
Of such a truth[47] as I have meant,
My great travail[48] so gladly spent
  Forget not yet.

Forget not yet when first began
The weary life he know since when,
The suit, the service none tell can,
  Forget not yet.

Forget not yet the great assays,
The cruel wrong, the scornful ways,
The painful patience in denays,[49]
  Forget not yet.

Forget not yet, forget not this,
How long ago hath been and is
The mind that never meant amiss,
  Forget not yet.

Forget not then thine own approved,
The which[50] so long hath thee so loved,
Whose steadfast faith yet never moved:
  Forget not this.

THE FRENCH, ENGLISH, AND ITALIAN TRADITIONS

LOOKING at Wyatt's work in terms of technique, we find that three distinct traditions flow together to make his poetic manner: the tradition of the French *ballade*, that of the "ballette" (song set to music), and that of Italian Petrarchan poetry.

At the beginning of the sixteenth century in England, the French *ballade* had already established a fairly important tradition; yet Wyatt's poems offer us relatively few examples, even if those are of high quality, as we may see from "Though this the port and I thy servant true" (no. 78). "Ballettes," on the other hand, predominate over all the other forms of verse he wrote; and in these songs many readers have felt that Wyatt expressed his sense of life and love most finely.

[47] faithfulness. [48] toil. [49] refusals. [50] who.

106

The simplicity of style and meter in the "ballette" is usually explained by tracing it back to much earlier medieval verse forms, and rightly so. Yet until the first decade of the sixteenth century in England, this kind of poetry had been confined to popular tradition; from then on, it rose above this position as a result of Henry VIII's accession to the throne, and the new and powerful impetus this gave to music at court. To supply the king's chamber music with a repertory, Henry VIII's musicians, and Henry himself, drew upon the tradition of popular song. Thus they revived the short and simple metrical forms that went with the music, working them up in the form characteristic of the Tudor "ballette": short but varied lines falling generally into five stanzas. In this manner of writing Wyatt immediately stands out as the greatest poet of his time. In spite of the simplicity of the manner and style, he is able to convey a strong and deeply felt emotion; and within the brief compass of the lines, the words clearly suggest the music that will accompany them, falling into the languishing rhythms of *chanson triste.*

Here is one among the many possible examples (no. 174):

> With serving still
> This have I won,
> For my goodwill
> To be undone;
>
> And for redress
> Of all my pain,
> Disdainfulness
> I have again.
>
> And for reward
> Of all my smart
> Lo, thus unheard,
> I must depart!
>
> Wherefore all ye
> That after shall
> By fortune be,
> As I am, thrall,
>
> Example take
> What I have won,
> Thus for her sake
> To be undone!

But Wyatt's complex poetic sensibility could not find full expression in this simple style, however much he might refine it. Hence, in other instances, while he retains the sweet and smooth "ballette" rhythm, he replaces the simple syntax characteristic of the form with a syntax of his own, which is much more elaborate and difficult. We then have compositions that are intermediate in character between the "ballette" and the *ballade.* These are nevertheless wholly characteristic of Wyatt, for in them the complex and difficult unfolding of the sense is justified by the complexity of the emotion itself, while everything is finally fused in a harmony of both rhythm and syntax. We may see this in the following "ballette," where we also find (stanza 3) a slight trace of Petrarchianism:

> Such hap as I am happed in
> Had never man, of truth I ween;[51]
> At me fortune list[52] to begin,
> To show that[53] never had been seen,
> A new kind of unhappiness:
> Nor I cannot the thing I mean
> Myself express.
>
> Myself express my deadly pain,
> That can I well, if that might serve;
> But why I have[54] not help again
> That know I not,[55] unless I starve
> For hunger still amids my food:
> So granted is that I deserve
> To do me good.
>
> To do me good what may prevail?
> For I deserve and not desire,
> And still of cold I me bewail,
> And raked am in burning fire;
> For though I have (such is my lot)
> In hand to help that I require,
> It helpeth not.
>
> It helpeth not but to encrease
> That that by proof can be no more![56]
> That is the heat that cannot cease,
> And that I have to crave so sore.
> What wonder[57] is this greedy lust?
> To ask and have, and yet therefore
> Refrain I must.
>
> Refrain I must: what is the cause?
> Sure as they say: *so hawks be taught.*

[51] believe.   [52] liked.   [53] what.   [54] receive.
[55] I only know that.   [56] greater.   [57] caprice.

But in my case layth no such clause,
   For with such craft I am not caught.
Wherefore I say, and good cause why,
   With hapless hand no man hath raught[58]
      Such hap as I.   (no. 36)

Wyatt's debt to Petrarchianism is much more difficult to define than his debt to the English or French tradition. Petrarch and his followers chose to write their love poetry in the form of the sonnet, a composition of fourteen *endecasillabi* arranged in two quatrains and two tercets (the Shakespearian sonnet, made up of three quatrains and a couplet, is not found in Italian). Wyatt faithfully reproduces the Italian rhyme schemes; but he has not yet at his disposal the iambic pentameter, which can provide an English equivalent of the Italian *endecasillabo*. Chaucer's iambic pentameter, which had enabled him to reproduce both the Italian *endecasillabo* and the French *décasyllabe*, had deteriorated in the hands of his immediate followers, becoming predominantly accentual meter—the "broken-backed line" that remained the characteristic meter of English narrative verse throughout the fifteenth century and well into the sixteenth. For almost the whole of his poetic career, Wyatt seems to be satisfied with this meter, since he abandons it only in his later compositions (for example, in the *Penitential Psalms*, where he uses iambic pentameter, although with some variations from the norm).

For this reason the sonnets that Wyatt translated, and those he wrote himself, reproduce the Italian rhyme scheme, but not the Italian rhythms. They are almost all written in the "broken-backed line," which can leave modern readers with the impression that the verse does not scan. This was indeed the almost universal impression in the nineteenth century; but in our own time, since we have grown used to much more difficult poetic rhythms, the special rhythmic qualities of the "broken-backed line" have again been appreciated, and it has even been praised as more subtle than the iambic pentameter. Consequently we are now able to recognize in Wyatt's translations and sonnets the same feeling for rhythm and syntax that we have noted in his most characteristic *ballades* and "ballettes."

In the sonnets and translations this personal style may prove to be even more complex and difficult than elsewhere, but for that very reason we may also find it more beautiful. Here is an instance of how the Italian sonnet form has been adapted to Wyatt's individual sensibility:

I abide[59] and abide and better abide,[60]
   And after the old proverb, the happy day;
   And ever my lady to me doth say:
   "Let me alone and I will provide."
I abide and abide and tarry the tide,[61]
   And with abiding speed well ye may:[62]
   Thus do I abide, I wot,[63] always,
   Nother[64] obtaining nor yet denied.
Ay me! this long abiding
   Seemeth to me as who sayth[65]
   A prolonging of a dying death
Or refusing of a desired thing.
   Much were it better for to be plain
   Than to say "abide" and yet shall not obtain.
                (no. 227)

And yet, in spite of all this, or perhaps because of it, Wyatt's Petrarchianism does not go very deep. The inward significance of Petrarch's poetry eludes him; and even when he describes the same emotions in similar terms, his poem obstinately takes on a different meaning. Petrarch's experience of unsatisfied love points toward renunciation, a spiritual discipline; Wyatt's leads him to self-pity, pleading, and argument. Both poets describe their lady as "cruel," but by this word they mean very different things; Petrarch's lady is hard and immovable only because of her virtue, and in the cause of virtue, while Wyatt's is merely fickle, unfeeling, or ungrateful.

The two poets also differ from each other in their use of images. Unlike Petrarch, Wyatt never lingers tenderly over fine shades of emotion, or over the fragmentary stolen glimpses of his lady's beauty that rouse such emotions. Neither does he pause to fix moments of intense feeling by means of exquisitely illuminated miniatures. Hence there are no pictorial elements in his poems. When he adapts a sonnet of Petrarch to his own purpose, Wyatt chooses rather to cut away such visual beauties, and proceed without them. This is what he does in

---

[58] reached.

[59] endure.   [60] wait for.   [61] time.   [62] succeed.   [63] know.
[64] neither.   [65] what one might call.

the sonnet "Whoso list to hunt." Petrarch had written:

> Una candida cerva sopra l'erba
> Verde m'apparve con duo corna d'oro,
> Fra due riviere, all'ombra d'un alloro,
> Levando 'l sole, alla stagione acerba;

[A white deer with golden horns appeared to me on the green grass, between two rivers in the shade of a laurel tree, while the sun rose, in the fresh season (of spring).]

But Wyatt omits all the glowing beauty of the original image, and puts in its place a description of his own weariness and suffering:

> Whoso list to hunt I know where is an hind;
>   But as for me, alas I may no more:
>   The vain travail hath wearied me so sore,
>   I am of them that farthest cometh behind.
>
> (no. 7)

What Petrarch and Wyatt most obviously have in common is the importance in their poetry of the "pains of love." Wyatt's song "To cause accord or to agree" (no. 77) is an epitome of this aspect of Petrarchianism. In it he begins by stating the irreconcilable conflict in him between opposite forces, and then sets his own inexplicable state of feeling in opposition to reason: love makes him burn and freeze, he lives without a heart, he seeks life through death, and so on. To this example one can add a few other familiar Petrarchan themes, such as the idea that Love wounds him through his eyes, or that he hates himself and loves another; but these are unimportant, and Wyatt's Petrarchianism does not go beyond his use of such scattered conceits.

The truth is that the world of Petrarch's imagination remained closed to Wyatt. Its most subtle fancies are echoed only very rarely by the English poet; and then they are modified by his less pictorial and more musical style, and dwindle into fleeting touches that we might call grace notes. Thus the concluding tercet of Petrarch's sonnet "Io son sì stanco sotto il fascio antico," the gravely beautiful

> Qual' grazia, quale amore, o qual destino
> Mi darà penne in guisa di colomba,
> Ch'i' mi riposi e levimi da terra?

[What grace, or love, or destiny, will give me wings as of a dove, that I may find relief and raise myself above earth?]

becomes a fleeting fancy in Wyatt's "ballette" "All heavy minds" (no. 84):

> Who shall me give
> Feathered wings for to flee,
> The thing that doth me grieve
> That I may see?

Even the sonnets, in which we might expect that the verse form would keep the poet closer to his model, are Petrarchan only in the vaguest sense of the word. Wyatt's greatest sonnets, such as "I abide and abide and better abide" (no. 227) and "Unstable dream, according to the place" (no. 79), seem to be independent of any original. Others may be enriched by some image taken from Petrarch; but they are very unlike his work, and wholly characteristic of Wyatt's own. We might give as examples "The lively sparks that issue from those eyes" (no. 27; compare "Vive faville uscian da' duo bei lumi"), the *rondeau* (no. 1) "Behold, Love, thy power how she despiseth" (compare "Or vedi, Amor, che giovinetta donna"); there are many others.

There was deep divergence between the minds of the two poets, but this did not prevent Wyatt's study of Petrarch from leaving a deeper mark on his work than any we have yet mentioned: it gave him a discipline in poetic composition and style. His sonnet "The flaming sighs that boil within my breast" (no. 237) is Petrarchan in exactly the same way as a poem by one of Petrarch's best sixteenth-century imitators, which means that in it the writer has kept his individual sensibility while making use of the master's poetic apparatus to express it. It opens with imagery wholly within the tradition ("the flaming sighs," "the watered eyes") and ends with a theme characteristic of Wyatt (the presentation of himself as an example of the tormented lover). Yet one feels no sense of incoherence or incongruity. This is because Wyatt shows that he has now assimilated not just the use of certain imagery or phraseology, but also a calmness of tone, a serenity, that comes through mastery over difficult experience. We see here the poetic outcome of a passion finally brought under control:

The flaming sighs that boil within my breast
  Sometime break forth, and they can well declare
  The heart's unrest and how that it doth fare,
  The pain thereof, the grief, and all the rest.
The watered eyes from whence the tears do fall
  Do feel some force or else they would be dry;
  The wasted flesh of colour dead can try,[66]
  And something tell what sweetness is in gall.
And he that list[67] to see and to discern
  How care can force within a wearied mind,
  Come he to me! I am that place assigned.
But for all this no force, it doth no harm:[68]
  The wound, alas, hap in some other place,
  From whence no tool away the scar can rase.

This mastery of emotion in poetry was the lesson Wyatt learned from his translations of Petrarch. Perhaps he was led into translation by the practical exigencies of courtship; if so, the result went far beyond his original motives, and we cannot fail to perceive Wyatt's greatness as a translator. As the finest examples of his achievement we might choose "I find no peace and all my war is done" (no. 26: "Pace non trovo, e non ho da far guerra"), "My galley charged with forgetfulness" (no. 28: "Passa la nave mia colma di oblio"). Others could be added that are inferior only to the best; "Avising the bright beams of those fair eyes" (no. 29: "Mirando 'l sol de' begli occhi sereno") and "Ever mine hap is slack and slow in coming" (no. 30: "Mie venture al venir son tarde e pigre"). These are not only the product of technical skill; they show even more clearly an insight into a poetic world different from Wyatt's own, and an impulse to interpret in Petrarch's more spiritual manner his experience of passionate love.

Wyatt's other translations and adaptations from the Italian can also be included under the head of Petrarchianism if we choose to give the word a very wide interpretation. But the only other Italian poet who had as great an influence on Wyatt's verse was Serafino Aquilano (1466–1500), whose love poetry is not at all Petrarchan.

Wyatt certainly has greater temperamental affinity with Serafino than with Petrarch; and he follows him most often when he is furthest from Petrarch, in his use of wit and satire and his mocking familiar tone, which are found most clearly in the *strambotti* (short eight-line poems).

[66]prove by experience.   [67]may like.   [68]no matter.

Wyatt's interest was roused particularly by these little poems, several of which he translated. But Wyatt was by far the greater poet, and so it happens that he hits upon phrases that are great improvements on the Italian. Thus he sometimes reduces Serafino's too numerous "examples" or comparisons to a few essential images; and he translates

   La donna di natura mai si sazia
   Di dar effetto a ogni suo desiderio

[A woman is by nature never satisfied unless she puts all her desires into effect.]

with a single splendid line: "Unsatiate of my woe and thy desire" (no. 14). Therefore, in contrast with what happens when Wyatt translates Petrarch, he gives a deeper and richer meaning to the themes he takes from Serafino. The *strambotto* "L'aer che sente el mesto e gran clamore" becomes three beautiful stanzas in "Resound my voice, ye woods that hear me plain" (no. 22). The two octaves of "Donar non ti poss'io vago lavoro" are expanded into a new fullness of melody in "To seek eachwhere, where man doth live" (no. 85), one of the few of Wyatt's lyrics that in some degree anticipates Spenser's sonorous orchestration.

Serafino's influence on Wyatt is more psychological and technical than anything else. No doubt Wyatt read him with a respect we can no longer feel; and in his verse he found authority for some of the sarcastic witticisms to which he was himself inclined, but which had no precedent in English poetry, except in some folk songs that would have been considered beneath the notice of court poets. Serafino's invective and his abuse of women are echoed by Wyatt even when he does not directly translate from the Italian; and Wyatt gives us something more than a simple imitation. The relationship reveals a community of spirit in which Serafino is the more skillful, but Wyatt the more powerful, poet.

His following of Petrarch and Serafino helped Wyatt to find his own methods of writing. Among the other Italian poets he translated, the only other writer who made a similar, but lesser, contribution of this kind was Luigi Alamanni (1495–1556), whose first satire Wyatt adapted to his own situation. If Alamanni had any deeper influence on Wyatt, it was only in moderating the English poet's violent invective. Thus Wyatt's *First Satire* is calm in tone, almost good-humored, while in the *Second Satire* and *Third Satire* he gives full scope both to his own lively wit (which is well seen in his treatment of the Fable of the Country Mouse and the Town Mouse) and to his delight in strong language. Thus in the *Third Satire* he describes base courtiers as donkeys and swine:

> . . . for swine so groans
> In sty, and chaw the turds moulded on the ground,
> And drivel on pearls; the head still in the manger,
> Than of the harp the ass to hear the sound;

and so on.

His revulsion against the corruption of the court may be no less violent in the *First Satire*, but the studied calmness of Alamanni's tone has checked its expression. So it may be that we owe to the Italian's more detached point of view one of the most charming impressions Wyatt gives us of himself, as the nobleman out of favor enjoying the homely occupations of country life:

> This maketh me at home to hunt and hawk
> And in foul weather at my book to sit.
> In frost and snow then with my bow to stalk,
> No man doth mark where so I ride or go;
> In lusty lease at liberty I walk,
> And of these news I feel nor weal nor woe . . .
> But here I am in Kent and Christendom
> Among the muses where I read and rhyme:
> Where if thou list, my Poynz, for to come,
> Thou shalt be judge how I do spend my time.

Alamanni taught Wyatt the easy, yet controlled, movement of the *terza rima*, so often and so successfully used for epistolary poems in sixteenth-century Italy. Wyatt made the form his own in the *Second Satire* and *Third Satire*, and in his version of the *Penitential Psalms*; and this, merely as a lesson in technique, was certainly not to be despised.

The Italian tradition thus offered Wyatt a first-class school, in which he became a first-class pupil. Too often, even in Italy, Petrarchan poetry was merely conventional, a poetic exercise; but it was never this with Wyatt. His indi-

vidual feeling for love as a kind of passionate, sustained unhappiness gave life to all the literary conventions that he brought to it: it dominated his art and achieved full and exact expression in authentic poetry. His greatness goes beyond the place he occupies in textbooks of literary history. The fascination of his work has now been recognized, and it is not likely that it will again fall into neglect.

SELECTED BIBLIOGRAPHY

I. BIBLIOGRAPHIES. E. C. Hangen, *A Concordance to the Complete Poetical Works of Sir Thomas Wyatt* (Chicago, 1941; reiss. New York, 1969), based on Foxwell's ed.; M. C. O'Neel, "A Wyatt Bibliography," *Bulletin of Bibliography*, 37 (1970); B. Fishman, "Recent Studies in Wyatt and Surrey," *English Literary Renaissance*, 1 (1971); for the bibliography of the very rare eds. of *Songes and Sonettes* ("Tottel's Miscellany," 1557), see Rollins' ed. (below) and *Catalogue of the Library of Carl H. Pforzheimer* (New York, 1940).

II. COLLECTED EDITIONS. G. F. Nott, ed., *The Works of Henry Howard Earl of Surrey and of Sir Thomas Wyatt the Elder*, 2 vols. (London, 1815–1816); A. K. Foxwell, ed., *The Poems of Sir Thomas Wiat*, 2 vols. (London, 1913), text unreliable, but the notes still valuable; K. Muir, ed., *Collected Poems of Sir Thomas Wyatt* (London, 1948; reiss. with additions, 1963), in the Muses' Library, with full collation, valuable introduction, but without notes; K. Muir, ed., *Unpublished Poems by Sir Thomas Wyatt and His Circle* (Liverpool, 1961), includes new material of importance; K. Muir and P. Thomson, eds., *Collected Poems of Sir Thomas Wyatt* (Liverpool, 1969), the standard ed., with full collation and notes; J. Daalder, ed., *Wyatt's Collected Poems* (Oxford, 1975) with modern spelling and notes.

III. SEPARATE WORKS AND EARLY SELECTIONS. *Tho. Wyatis Translation of Plutarckes Booke of the Quyete of Mynde* (London, ca. 1528; facs. ed. by C. R. Baskervill, Cambridge, Mass., 1931); *The Court of Venus* (London (?), ca. 1538, ca. 1563), of which only fragments survive (see *A Boke of Balettes*, below); *A Boke of Balettes* (London (?), ca. 1548), of which only a fragment survives, edited, with the *Court of Venus*, by R. A. Fraser (Durham, N.C., 1955); *Certayne Psalmes Chosen out of the Psalter of David, Commonly Called the VII Penytentiall Psalmes, Drawen into Englyshe Meter by Sir Thomas Wyat Knight, Whereunto Is Added a Prologe of the Auctore Before Every Psalme Very Plesant and Profettable to the Godly Reader* (London, 1549); *Songes and Sonettes Written by the Ryght Honorable*

Lorde Henry Haward Late Earle of Surrey, and Other (London, 1557), the famous "Tottel's Miscellany," of which the standard ed. is H. E. Rollins, ed., Tottel's Miscellany (1557–1587), 2 vols. (Cambridge, Mass., 1928–1929; rev. 1965; facs. ed., 1970); R. Harrier, The Canon of Sir Thomas Wyatt's Poetry (Cambridge, Mass., 1975), description and history of the early printings, plus critical ed. of the poems in the Egerton (Wyatt's own) MS.

IV. GENERAL STUDIES. J. M. Berdan, Early Tudor Poetry, 1485–1547 (New York, 1920; reiss. 1929), the largest survey of the period; J. J. Scott, Les sonnets élisabéthains: La source et l'apport personnel (Paris, 1929); L. E. Pearson, Elizabethan Love Conventions (Berkeley, Calif., 1933; reiss. 1967); B. Pattison, Music and Poetry of the English Renaissance (London, 1948; reiss. 1970); H. A. Mason, Humanism and Poetry in the Early Tudor Period (London, 1959); J. Stevens, Music and Poetry in the Early Tudor Court (London, 1961); D. L. Peterson, The English Lyric from Wyatt to Donne (Princeton, 1967); G. Watson, The English Petrarchans: A Critical Bibliography of the "Canzoniere," Warburg Institute Surveys, no. 3 (London, 1969), lists all English translations and imitations of Petrarch's Italian short poems.

V. BIOGRAPHICAL AND CRITICAL STUDIES. W. E. Simonds, Sir Thomas Wyatt and His Poems (Boston, 1889); A. K. Foxwell, A Study of Sir Thomas Wyatt's Poems (London, 1911; reiss. New York, 1964); E. M. W. Tillyard, The Poetry of Sir Thomas Wyatt: A Selection and A Study (London, 1929; reiss. 1949), contains a very good selection of the poems; E. K. Chambers, Sir Thomas Wyatt and Some Collected Studies (London, 1933; reiss. 1965); S. Baldi, La poesia di Sir Thomas Wyatt, il primo petrarchista inglese (Florence, 1953), with full bibliography up to 1950; K. Muir, Life and Letters of Sir Thomas Wyatt (Liverpool, 1963), the standard scholarly life of Wyatt; R. Southall, The Courtly Maker: An Essay on the Poetry of Wyatt and His Contemporaries (Oxford, 1964); P. Thomson, Sir Thomas Wyatt and His Background (London, 1964); M. Domenichelli, Wyatt, il liuto infranto: Formalismo, convenzione e poesia alla corte Tudor (Ravenna, 1975).

VI. SPECIAL STUDIES ON WYATT'S TECHNIQUE. I. L. Mumford, "Musical Settings to the Poems of Sir Thomas Wyatt," Music and Letters, 37, no. 4 (1956); O. Hietsch, Die Petrarcaüebersetzungen Sir Thomas Wyatts: Eine sprachvergleichende Studie (Vienna, 1960), a very careful study, with full bibliography; I. L. Mumford, "The Canzone in Sixteenth-Century English Verse with Particular Reference to Wyatt's Renderings from Petrarch's "Canzoniere," English Miscellany, 11 (1960); J. Thompson, The Founding of English Metre (London, 1961), ch. 1, "Wyatt, Tottel, and Surrey"; I. L. Mumford, "Sir Thomas Wyatt's Verse and Italian Musical Sources," English Miscellany, 14 (1963); W. Maynard, "The Lyrics of Wyatt: Poems or Songs?" Review of English Studies, 16, no. 4 (1965); S. Baldi, "Una fonte petrarchesca di Sir Thomas Wyatt," in V. Gabrieli, ed., Friendship Garland: Essays Presented to Mario Praz (Rome, 1966), translated, with footnotes, as "Sir Thomas Wyatt and Vellutello," English Studies Today, 4th ser., 4 (1966); R. B. Ogle, "Wyatt and Petrarch, A Puzzle in Prosody," Journal for English and Germanic Philology, 73 (1974).

HENRY HOWARD, EARL OF SURREY

(1517-1547)

A. S. G. Edwards

HENRY HOWARD, earl of Surrey, traditionally has been linked to Thomas Wyatt. There are obvious reasons for connecting the two poets. After Wyatt's death Surrey was hailed by John Leland as his heir, and Surrey himself left several poems lamenting Wyatt's death. Elsewhere in his poetry there are a number of echoes and suggestions of Wyatt's influence. Most critics since Leland have tended to treat them as though their respective oeuvres can profitably be discussed together.

Yet at the same time there are striking differences that distinguish the two poets. The contours of their respective lives, for example, differ dramatically. Both were courtiers, and both experienced the uncertainties of royal favor under Henry VIII. But Wyatt was, in his public life, preeminently the servant of his king. His private personality remains elusive, masked by the discretion of the able courtier and diplomat. We are left to extrapolate a more complex and equivocal figure from his verse.

Surrey's career stands in stark contrast. It displays a movement toward an increasingly cavalier disregard for public appearance and private discretion that was ultimately to destroy him. He was born in 1517, heir to one of the most illustrious titles in England, the dukedom of Norfolk. He grew up as a favorite of Henry VIII. Part of his youth was spent as companion to Henry's illegitimate son Henry Fitzroy, duke of Richmond, whom he nostalgically recalls in his poem "So crewell prison howe could betyde, alas." In 1532, after a year at the French court, he married Lady Frances de Vere, daughter of the earl of Oxford. He probably saw his first military action in 1536, when he assisted his fa-

ther in suppressing the rising in the North of England called Pilgrimage of Grace.

Thus far Surrey's life and career had been notable only for their conventionality; they followed the orthodox pattern of the successful and accomplished courtier. In 1537, however, there appeared the first hint of a new Surrey, whose aggressive behavior contrasted strikingly with his earlier decorum, and there began a pattern of rebelliousness and defiance that led to his death. In July of that year he was arrested for offering violence to Edward Seymour within the precincts of the court, an offense punishable by death. The king was lenient, and Surrey suffered only a few months' confinement within Windsor Castle (celebrated in his sonnet "When Windsor walles sustained my wearied arm").

But Surrey's action was the harbinger of future instances of defiant assertion, which further evidence of the king's favor could not check. In early 1541 he was created knight and member of the Order of the Garter. But the execution of Katherine Howard, wife of Henry VIII, in 1542 and the consequent erosion of the Howards' influence at court seem to have provoked him to new excesses. He was sent to the Fleet Prison in July 1542 for issuing a challenge. By August he was free; but in January 1543 he was back in the Fleet, this time for several months on charges that included riotous conduct and eating meat during Lent (charges to which he responded in his poem "London hast thow accusèd me").

Henceforth conflict was at the forefront of Surrey's experience. In 1545 he joined the war against the French, was wounded at the siege of Montreuil, and subsequently was made commander at Boulogne. He held this position for some fifteen months, with indifferent success, until his recall in March 1546.

The last months of Surrey's life were inextricably involved with the balance of power at the court of the dying Henry VIII. It was apparent that the boy king Edward VI, Henry's successor, would be under the control of the Seymours, led by Surrey's old enemy Edward Seymour. The situation seems to have provoked Surrey beyond endurance. In December he tried to attack George Blage, a supporter of the Seymours. He was immediately arrested and subsequently charged with treason. In particular he was alleged to have quartered his arms with those of Edward the Confessor, thus claiming a personal right to the succession. Surrey was tried on January 13, 1547, and beheaded six days later, not yet thirty years of age. Henry VIII died nine days later.

That, in summary, was the public career of Surrey: courtier, then soldier, and ultimately adjudged traitor. And it was primarily in these public roles that his contemporaries were aware of him. Thus, in an admiring poem on Surrey written probably no more than five years after his death, George Cavendish makes no mention of Surrey's poetic achievements. Nor is this particularly surprising. Apart from his poems on Wyatt's death, none of his works were published during his lifetime. With the exception of three chapters from his Ecclesiastes translation and one of his Psalm translations, printed together about 1550, it was not until 1557, with the appearance of Tottel's *Miscellany*, that Surrey's verse was published. The same year also saw the publication of his translations from the *Aeneid*. It seems likely that until then knowledge of Surrey's poetic achievement was restricted to a very small circle of courtiers and friends among whom his works circulated in manuscript.

The point is important, since some portions of what were probably among Surrey's earliest poems are compositions characteristic of the kind of narrow courtly coterie to which he belonged and of the mannered artificiality of such a life. Surrey was one of a number of extremely competent versifiers whose inclination, as members of a tightly knit, educated, and clever group, was to produce verses not necessarily

"sincere" so much as distinguished by wit and facility of expression. Verbal adroitness and stylistic felicity took precedence over the expression of genuine feeling. George Puttenham's characterization of Wyatt and Surrey as "courtly makers" requires us to recover this world if we are to respond adequately to a number of Surrey's earlier poems.

An extreme instance of this need to appreciate the courtly context of Surrey's verse is provided by his sonnet to "Geraldine" ("From Tuscan cam my ladies worthi race"). This sonnet has helped to create one of the most durable, and most fanciful, legends about Surrey. Since Thomas Nashe first promulgated the story in *The Unfortunate Traveller* (1594), it was for centuries believed that the sonnet is a statement of Surrey's love for Lady Elizabeth Fitzgerald (the "Geraldine" of the sonnet). But in reality Surrey seems to have had only the most fleeting personal contact with a child who was probably only nine years old when the sonnet was written, and certainly no more than fourteen. Surrey's affirmation of his "love" is doubtless the compliment of an adroit courtier, possibly to a young lady who had recently joined the court circle.

This note of courtesy rather than sincerity characterizes a number of Surrey's other courtly poems. These works often draw upon or adapt preexisting conventions of amatory verse, at times reaching back to the Middle Ages. For example, his famous sonnet beginning

The soote[1] season, that bud and blome furth bringes,
With grene hath clad the hill and eke[2] the vale;
The nightingale with fethers new she singes;
The turtle to her make[3] hath tolde her tale;

evokes the position of the grieving lover in terms and techniques that would be wholly appropriate in a lyric of the fourteenth or fifteenth century. The seasonal motif, the end-stopped lines, the recurrent use of alliteration and assonance within the line, and the final differentiating of the lover from the world of vibrant nature surrounding him ("And thus I see among these pleasant thinges / Eche care decays, and yet my sorow springes") are all features of the love lyric that Surrey inherited from literary tradition. To

[1] sweet. [2] also. [3] mate.

mistake them for professions of genuine emotion is to misunderstand the convention in which Surrey was writing.

Many of Surrey's sonnets are concerned with love in this conventional rather than "sincere" sense. Such lyrics tend to have a relatively simple structure organized around some basic contrast: winter/summer, sickness/health, hot/cold, dichotomies that are applied to the situation of the lover vis-à-vis the object of his love. But the extremities of emotion that they assert rarely evoke any comparable response from the reader. Indeed, in some cases they probably were never intended to. A number of his sonnets are translations from the poems of Petrarch (1304–1374). Wyatt and Surrey were in fact the first poets to adapt the Petrarchan sonnet for English use. Surrey's role in this process was much smaller than Wyatt's: he translated or imitated only five of Petrarch's sonnets. But in the one sonnet that they both translated, Wyatt responds to the demands of the translation with a greater sense of its moral complexities than does Surrey. Surrey's version ("Love that doth raine and live within my thought") seems to engage in the conventions of courtly love without ever probing beneath them. And his other translations from the Italian, while often pleasing in their mellifluousness, never seem to validate poetically the intensity of emotion that they state.

Hence Surrey's Petrarchan sonnets occasionally appear to be variations on a theme, exercises in verse translation. Indeed, such artificiality has, at times, exposed them to criticism. But such criticism fails to perceive that conventionality of theme and expression was, in the fifteenth and sixteenth centuries, a poetic virtue, not a defect. Surrey's achievement in his Italian translations lies primarily in the realm of technique, of rendering Petrarch into English in a new and metrically rigorous verse form, the sonnet.

Elsewhere in his shorter poems Surrey contrives, in compositions less directly influenced by Petrarch, to evoke moods of great poignancy. It may be no coincidence that he often does this when he writes on themes or subjects drawn from personal experience. For example, he wrote several laments at his separation from his wife while he was on military service in France.

In two of these poems (those beginning "Gyrtt in my giltelesse gowne" and "O happy dames, that may embrace") his feelings are objictified by adopting the device of a female speaker. These poems are remarkably successful in their restrained but palpable evocation of endured loss. It seems relevant to note that Surrey unsuccessfully petitioned Henry VIII to have his wife and children join him at Boulogne.

Surrey's most famous "personal" poems are doubtless his several laments on the death of his fellow poet and courtier Thomas Wyatt. "Wyatt resteth here, that quick could never rest" is one of Surrey's finest works. Written in a simple, unadorned style, it nevertheless is a poem of considerable rhetorical skill and complexity. It has been shown to reflect a number of rhetorical commonplaces in the way in which it bewails Wyatt's loss and eulogizes the various aspects of his person (head, face, hands, tongue, and so on). But Surrey employs rhetoric unobtrusively; attention remains firmly focused on the figure being lamented, not on the manner of the lament itself. Indeed, the most distinctive feature of the poem is its air of restraint; sorrow is sublimated as elegiac praise. It is only in the last two lines that the poet concludes the formal catalog of virtues and expresses his own feelings directly.

Thus, for our gilte, this jewel have we lost.
The earth his bones, the heavens possesse his gost.

The contemplation of the figure of Wyatt is balanced against the reality of his loss and its meaning for those who remain to mourn him. The poem is one of Surrey's most remarkable pieces of compression. Its austere language evokes feelings that are both intensely experienced and precisely focused.

Surrey's touch was not always so sure. He left two other poems on Wyatt's death, both sonnets, that strain unsuccessfully to give effective form to feeling. The first ("Dyvers thy death doo dyverslye bemone") employs classical analogies to assert Surrey's grief without making the correspondences sufficiently apposite to be illuminating. The reader is left struggling to clarify his emotional response. The second sonnet ("In the rude age when science was not so rife") fails to compress expression into the discipline of its verse form; the result is that syntax and meaning often are largely impenetrable. And in one of Surrey's other poems reflecting direct personal experience, even his usually firm metrical control is insecure. "London, hast thow accusèd me" was written after he had been arrested for riot, perhaps even while he was confined to prison. It fluctuates between two distinct meters, neither of which is invariably regular. Indeed, uncertainty seems to inhere in the very meaning of the poem: it has been interpreted both as a satire and as a serious affirmation of the Protestant faith. Both possibilities are plausible and indicate the failure of the poem to impose coherence either of form or of structure on its subject matter.

Yet at other moments Surrey succeeds admirably in relating form and feeling. For example, his sonnet on the death of his squire Thomas Clere has a tautness of syntax and a deft balancing of contrasts and oppositions that compress genealogy, biography, and elegy into a very little space:

> Norfolk sprang[4] thee, Lambeth holds thee dead.
> Shelton for love, Surrey for Lord thou chase.[5]

It is clear that when he wrote without foreign models, Surrey did not invariably achieve artistic success. But at his best his poetic voice is original and unmistakable. His verses on the ages of man, for example, strike a note of reflective meditation:

> Laid in my quyett bedd, in study as I weare,[6]
> I saw within my troubled hed a heape of thoughtes
>   appeare;
>   And every thought did shew so lyvelye in myne
>   eyes,
> That now I sight,[7] and then I smylde, as cawse of
>   thought did ryse.

The verse remains relaxed and conversational, even as it recounts the horrors of encroaching age and decay. It is only in the final lines that there is any self-consciously rhetorical art:

> Wheare at I sight, and said, "Farewell, my wonted
>   joye;
> Trusse upp thie pack, and trudge from me to every
>   lytle boye,

And tell them thus from me, theire tyme moste
    happie is,
Yf, to their tyme, they reason had to know the truthe
    of this."

Here the use of word play, alliteration, and (in the last line) syntactical disjunction all serve to drive home the poem's "message." The poem combines rhetorical economy with delicately modulated personal feeling. Regrettably, Surrey never fully developed this vein of his talent.

But Surrey's genius finds its fullest expression not in his personal lyrics but in his translations from Virgil's *Aeneid*. When he undertook his versions of books II and IV is uncertain, but they probably can be placed some time after the bulk of his datable lyrics. There is some evidence to suggest a date about 1539–1540, but it is largely conjectural. Indeed, it is even possible that the translations of the two books were done at very different times.

It has been known for some time that Surrey, in preparing his translation, had access not only to the Latin text but also to the verse translation by the Scottish poet Gavin Douglas, bishop of Dunkeld (d. 1522). Nor is it surprising that Surrey should have been aware of this translation. Although it was not published until 1553, Douglas' work began circulating quite widely in manuscript in the 1520's. It is difficult to summarize Surrey's debt to Douglas. At a very rough count something under half the lines in his translation reflect some influence of Douglas; the proportions are about the same in both books. At times Surrey's borrowings take the form of appropriation of particular passages. At the other extreme he goes to Douglas for distinctive words (for example, "ugsome," meaning "ugly"). More typical is the borrowing of felicitous lines or phrases, which are reworked into passages of greater compression and poetic force. The poignant elegy on Priam's death is a case in point:

> Of Priamus this was the fatal fine,[8]
> The wofull end that was alotted him.
> When he had seen his palace all on flame,
> With ruine of his Troyan turrets eke,[9]
> That royal prince of Asie, which of late
> Reignd over so many peoples and realmes,

---

[4] bore.   [5] chose.   [6] were.   [7] sighed.   [8] death.   [9] also.

Like a great stock [10] now lieth on the shore;
His hed and shoulders parted ben in twaine,
A body now without renome [11] and fame.

Most of this passage is Surrey's own. But the opening line draws on Douglas' "Of Priamus thus was the finale fait"; the seventh and eighth lines are seemingly an expansion of Douglas' "Bot as a stok and of hakkit his hed"; and the final line compresses Douglas' "A corps but lyfe, renown or other fame." Such a passage suggests something of the flexibility in Surrey's approach to Douglas' text. Although he clearly knows Douglas very well, he is never slavish in his use of him but rewrites, expands, and compresses as his own sense of poetry, rhythm, and diction seems to require.

This must be stressed. Surrey's work is not merely a reworking of Douglas but an independent, and in some respects more successful, translation of the *Aeneid*. The most obvious expression of this independence is the greater economy and conciseness of Surrey's rendering. Putting it very roughly, Douglas' translation tends to be half as long again as Surrey's. Since both the books Surrey translates are swift-moving narratives, recounting the fall of Troy and Dido's tragic love for Aeneas, the result is a work that in tempo is much more faithful to the spirit of Virgil's original. The following passage, for example, from the beginning of book IV, owes nothing to Douglas:

. . . And when they were al gone
And the dimme mone doth eft [12] withold the light,
And sliding starres provoked unto sleepe,
Alone she mournes within her palace voide,
And sets her down on her forsaken bed.
And absent him she heares, when he is gone,
And seeth [13] eke. . . .

The lines are a quite faithful translation of the *Aeneid*, and they contrive to convey the essence of the original as well as the letter. The use of anaphora ("And . . . And . . . And") is calculatingly disrupted in the middle of the passage ("Alone she mournes within her palace voide") to emphasize Dido's solitude. This solitude is heightened by the use of sibilants to link words that stress the passage of time and her loneli-

ness ("sliding starres" . . . "sets" . . . "forsaken" . . . "absent"). At the break in the anaphora Dido ("she") is linked to this pattern of sound. The word "she" here is also related to another, initially subordinate pattern of assonance involving the long "e" sound that becomes stronger as the passage concludes ("she heares" . . . "he") and culminates in the final half line ("And seeth eke"), which unites the two patterns of alliteration and assonance to make sound dramatize the sense of the line. Analysis reveals an attention to the relationship of style, sound, and meaning that seeks to render the essence of the original as faithfully and economically as possible. Surrey can achieve some of his best effects when he is at his furthest remove from the more prolix Douglas.

Such a desire for fidelity does, of course, have its less happy aspects. C. S. Lewis has seized on the "coldness" of Surrey's rendering, which he sees as achieving an effect characterized as "Virgil in corsets." And indeed, Surrey's desire for fidelity to the original does on occasion have unfortunate consequences. At times it leads to syntactical weakness and ambiguity:

Like him that wandring in the bushes thick
Tredes on the adder with his rechlesse [14] foote
Rered for wrath, swelling her speckled neck,
Dismayd, geves back al sodenly for fere.

At other times it leads to unidiomatic dislocations of word order to reflect Latin constructions ("undertaken war," "crye greatest"). Elsewhere, Surrey's desire to translate literally produces phrases that are confused and inert (". . . he tendring my most humble sute / The right and faith . . ."). It is undeniable that, at times, Surrey as Virgilian translator can be curiously limp.

But against such intermittent failures must be set Surrey's consistent demonstration of his independence as translator. His choice of blank verse as the form of his translation was a historic one. He was the first English poet to employ it. The reasons that led Surrey to its use have never been satisfactorily identified. The most likely sources are either the *versi sciolti* ("unrhyming verse") of Italian translators of Virgil or Virgil's own unrhymed hexameters.

---

[10] trunk.   [11] renown.   [12] again.   [13] sighs.   [14] careless.

But whatever the influence or influences behind Surrey's choice of verse form, it can be fairly said that his manipulation of the form seems to reveal a rapidly growing grasp of its potentialities. If one were to venture a generalization, it might be said that his translation of book IV is a greater success than that of book II. Certainly the blank verse of book IV possesses a greater flexibility, a firmer technical mastery, than does the verse of book II. It is also the case that Surrey's blank verse techniques are better suited to the presentation of personal relationships (which predominate in book IV), particularly through the use of dialogue.

Some of Surrey's happiest renderings occur in speeches of book IV, where he employs blank verse to reflect the changing rhythm and cadence of fluctuating human emotion. These lines from Dido's opening speech in book IV are a case in point:

. . . "O sister Ann, what dreames
Be these, that me tormented thus afray? [15]
What new guest is this that to our realme is come?
  What one of chere! [16] how stout of hart in armies!
Truly I think (ne vain in my belefe)
Of goddish race some offspring shold he be:
Cowardry [17] notes hartes swarved out of kind.
He driven, Lord, with how hard destiny!
What battailes eke atchived [18] did he recount!
But that my mind is fixt unmoveably
Never with wight [19] in wedlock ay [20] to joyne
Sith my first love me left by death dissevered,
If geniall brands [21] and bed me lothed not,
To this one gilt [22] perchaunce yet might I yeld."

The passage meticulously mirrors the uncertainties and modulations of Dido's feelings, from her initial note of uncertainty and confusion, to the note of exclamatory admiration, to her syntactically elaborate attempts to qualify (unsuccessfully) the depths of feeling that she has unintentionally revealed. Surrey captures precisely the conflict of emotions that Dido's speech is intended to convey, and represents them in his sinewy blank verse.

Surrey's translation of Virgil is, then, uneven in quality. But for all its unevenness it is a work of some historical importance, for which serious poetic claims can be made. In the *Aeneid* he exposes the full range of his poetic resources. We observe his increasingly firm control over a wholly new verse form, as well as his related sense of the potentialities of syntax and assonance to achieve his effects. The work also has a role in the history of early English humanism. It is the first attempt in England to capture in the vernacular the feeling and meaning of Virgil's original. At times this attempt possibly leads to either superficiality or unidiomatic literalness, especially in contrast to Douglas' translation, which often reflects a more profound sense of the complexities of the original. But Surrey's perception of the style and technique of the *Aeneid* is possibly surer.

The contrast between Surrey's translations of Virgil and the final group of his works is a striking one. His translations from Ecclesiastes and the Psalms likely belong to the very end of his life. Indeed, it has been suggested, probably correctly, that his renderings of Psalms 8, 73, and 88 are in a very special sense occasional poems. That is to say, they were chosen because of their direct applicability to Surrey's own predicament: as he found himself facing disgrace, imprisonment, and death at the hands of his enemies. Without any strain, the argument can be extended to include his Ecclesiastes translations. The recognition of the autobiographical resonances gives a particular poignancy to many of the passages from these renderings. For example, Surrey's reference "To buylde my howses faier then sett I all my cure" may be intended to recall the classical structure that he built at Mount Surrey, near Norwich. More clearly pointed in its personal reference is his rueful reflection on the status of kings:

In better far estate stande children, poore any wyse
Then aged kyngs wedded to will that worke with out
  advice.

Or his *cri de coeur* at his personal isolation:

  Like to the roring waves the sunken shipp sur-
    rounde,
Great heaps of care did swallow me and I no succour
    found.
  For they whome no myschaunce could from my
    love devyde

---

[15] frighten. [16] bearing. [17] Cowardice.
[18] accomplished. [19] man. [20] ever.
[21] marital torches. [22] weakness.

Ar forced for my greater greif, from me their face to
hyde.

In making his translations, Surrey drew upon
the extremely popular Latin paraphrase of Ecclesiastes and the Psalms made by the sixteenth-
century scholar Joannes Campensis. His translations are less faithful to the original than is his
rendering of the *Aeneid,* for at times he expands
the Vulgate texts and also makes his own in-
terpolations. The result is a series of fluent and
cadenced renderings, generally without the intermittent infelicities that mar the *Aeneid* translation.

Nonetheless, it is difficult to know how to
respond to these translations. Even without any
awareness of the personal tragedy that probably
underlies them, they directly engage the emotions. But whether they are fully realized poems
is another matter. They have more the air of exercises undertaken for essentially private purposes—verses of reflection and admonition
through which Surrey is endeavoring to formal-
ize his own sense of his personal situation. At
one level they are perhaps too familiar, by virtue of the material they render; at another level
they are perhaps too inaccessible through our
inability to recover the impulses that underlie
the translations. They remain essentially elusive
works.

Indeed, Surrey's whole poetic achievement is
not easy to define. He has suffered from the
traditional comparison with Wyatt, a comparison that does him less than justice. Wyatt was a
master of the lyric form. Surrey's body of work
is both smaller and more diversified, extending
from lyric to classical and biblical translations.
His experimentation with form and subject matter created a substantial body of poetry that,
particularly in his innovative use of blank verse,
marks a significant development in the history
of English poetry. At his best, particularly in his
Aeneid translations and in some of his lyrics,
Surrey can claim a place as one of the finest styl-
ists of English Renaissance poetry. He manifests
a technical skill, a grasp of meter, diction, and
syntax that enabled him to create a style that
was elegant, effective, and unadorned. It is in
this sense that his name may be most appropriately linked with Wyatt's. For, in different

ways, they both justify Puttenham's summation
of their poetic careers:

. . . they greatly pollished our rude & homely maner
of vulgar Poesie, from that it had bene before, and for
that cause may iustly be sayd the first reformers of
our English meetre and stile.

SELECTED BIBLIOGRAPHY

I. BIBLIOGRAPHIES. There are useful bibliographies of Surrey in *New Cambridge Bibliography of English Literature,* I (Cambridge, 1974), cols. 1023–1024;
and by B. J. Fishman in *English Literary Renaissance,* 1
(1971), 188–191.

II. WORKS. F. M. Padelford, ed., *The Poems of
Henry Howard, Earl of Surrey* (London, 1920; repr.
1966), the standard ed.; Ruth Hughey, ed., *The Arundel Harington Manuscript of Tudor Poetry,* 2 vols. (Columbus, Ohio, 1960), contains a number of Surrey's
poems; F. H. Ridley, ed., *The Aeneid of Henry Howard, Earl of Surrey* (Berkeley, Calif., 1963), a useful ed.
of Surrey's *Aeneid* translations; Emrys Jones, ed.,
Henry Howard, Earl of Surrey, Poems (Oxford, 1964),
the best modern ed., virtually complete, with full and
illuminating annotation.

III. BIOGRAPHICAL AND TEXTUAL STUDIES. E. Cas-
ady, *Henry Howard, Earl of Surrey* (New York, 1938),
the standard biography; M. B. Davies, "Surrey at
Boulogne," *Huntington Library Quarterly,* 23
(1959–1960), 339–348, a useful account of Surrey's
military career at Boulogne; Hester W. Chapman,
Two Tudor Portraits (London, 1960); K. Muir, "Surrey
Poems in the Blage Manuscript," *Notes and Queries,*
n.s. 7 (1960), 368–370; C. Huttar, "Poems by Surrey
and Others in a Printed Miscellany Circa 1550," *English Miscellany,* 16 (1965), 9–18, an important article
that draws attention to the first publication of several
of Surrey's biblical paraphrases and suggests several
possible additions to the canon.

IV. CRITICAL STUDIES. A. Oras, "Surrey's Technique of Phonetic Echoes," *Journal of English and Germanic Philology,* 50 (1950), 289–308, a careful examination of an important aspect of Surrey's technique;
C. S. Lewis, *English Literature in the Sixteenth Century*
(London, 1954), pp. 230–235, a brief but suggestive
essay; H. A. Mason, "The Relation of Surrey to
Wyatt," in his *Humanism and Poetry in the Early Tudor
Period* (London, 1959), pp. 236–254; F. H. Ridley,
"Surrey's Debt to Gavin Douglas," *PMLA,* 75 (1961),
25–33; John Buxton, *A Tradition of Poetry* (London,
1967), pp. 18–35, a useful introductory essay; W. O.
Harris, " 'Love That Doth Raine': Surrey's Creative
Imitation," *Modern Philology,* 66 (1969), 298–305, an

examination of Surrey's translation of a Petrarch sonnet; C. W. Jentoft, "Surrey's Four 'Orations' and the Influence of Rhetoric on Dramatic Effect," *Papers on Language and Literature*, 9 (1973), 250–262, an examination of four of Surrey's poems characterized as "dramatic orations": "Good ladies ye that have," "O happy dames that my embrace," "Geve place ye lovers," and "London has thow accused me"; P. Bawcutt, "Douglas and Surrey: Translators of Virgil," *Essays and Studies*, 27 (1974), 52–67, an important examination of the relationship between the two translations; W. R. Davis, "Context in Surrey's Poetry," *English Literary Renaissance*, 4 (1974), 40–55, a useful survey of Surrey's lyric poetry.

EDMUND SPENSER

(ca. 1552-1599)

Alastair Fowler

I

"SAGE Homer, Virgil, Spenser laureate." Spenser is one of our few classics. For that very reason, although his status has never been very seriously threatened, ideas of him have changed. Different ages and critics have given very different accounts of his work. Up to the eighteenth century, his reputation depended far more than it would now on *The Shepherd's Calendar*. Spenser was consequently a pastoral and love poet: even in *The Faerie Queen* he was "Heroic Paramour of Faerie Land," to be compared with Ariosto or Petrarch. On the other hand he was also a learned poet, an English Virgil, edited, cited as a classical author, and widely imitated. This posed problems for neo-classically minded readers, who had a blindingly clear idea of exactly what a classic work ought to be. *The Faerie Queen* could easily seem a bit too "uncultivate" and Gothic. Their solution was to turn attention away from Spenser's design, which broke too many rules, to the serious moral content—or else to his descriptive pictorial art. *The Faerie Queen* became "an excellent piece of morality, policy, history"—or Mrs. Spence's "collection of pictures." The influential John Hughes completed this development by combining both approaches. He showed how Spenser could be valued both as an "imager of virtues and vices" and a "rough painter" ("The embellishments of description are rich and lavish . . . beyond comparison.") without looking to him for epic or romance coherence. Unfortunately Spenser's morality was largely embodied in allegory. If the neoclassical critics were prepared to accord this element a lowly but secure place, "allegories fulsome grow," and the romantic critics were inclined to jettison it altogether. For William Hazlitt the allegory was

something that would not bite so long as one left it alone. Even the perceptive critic James Russell Lowell followed this approach, recommending *The Faerie Queen* to those who wished "to be rid of thought." Spenser's sensuous vividness has always remained, together perhaps with the dazzling ease of transitions, and a deeper, more elusive imaginativeness, closer to dream. However variously described and subject to misunderstanding, he has occupied a special place in our literature as a nourisher of other poets' work. He was Cowley's first introduction to poetry; Pope's "mistress"; Wordsworth's "inspiration"; and a model to Milton, Dryden, Thomson, Yeats, and countless others. By almost common consent he is one of our most "poetic" poets, so that he serves as a sounding board even for those of a very different temper: his words run softly even through the lines of T. S. Eliot.

Twentieth-century criticism has been better equipped historically to interpret the poetry that Spenser wrote. Sharing a common view of him as a great and serious poet, it has mostly been taken up with explaining. The explanation tends to be detailed: the picture-gallery view has given way to iconographical studies. The best modern criticism is technically remarkable; but it usually lacks the proportion achieved in the eighteenth century by John Upton, still Spenser's best reader. Perhaps in consequence some judicious critics, who would not quite deny the greatness of Spenser, have nevertheless thought his poetry too much in need of difficult explanation to be worth the effort for modern readers. They have renewed and reinforced Ben Jonson's objections to his poetic diction and the Augustan charges of structural faults; or fallen back on the position that "the wittiest poets have been all short" (Owen Felltham).

Neocritical, in fact, is neoclassical writ small. Recently, however, critics have shown more interest in longer poems. At the same time, a better appreciation of Gothic interlace—interweaving of linear narratives—is allowing revaluation of Spenser's complex neo-Gothic form. Very early on, John Hughes and Richard Hurd guessed that Spenser's Gothic cathedral might have its own kind of unity. But the implications of that valuable analogy can only now be fully developed. Poetry such as Spenser's is too central to our literature to be really threatened by critical opinion; some of it is too profound even to need much conscious understanding. Still, it is as well, from time to time, to revise our notion of the achievement. Where are Spenser's excellences, for us? We are beginning to have more interest than our predecessors in his vision of the totality of human experience—a vision as wide, in its way, as Milton's, or Blake's, or Hugh MacDiarmid's. We should be more inclined to see him as pursuing the highest and most philosophical ends of poetry.

II

NOT much is known about Spenser's life. He was born in London, his "most kindly nurse," probably in 1552. Although related to the noble Spencers of Warwickshire and Northamptonshire, his immediate family circumstances seem to have been poor. He was educated at Merchant Taylors' School, an outstanding new grammar school, which he attended for eight years from its foundation in 1561. There the curriculum included a great deal of Latin, some Greek (certainly Homer), and the Hebrew psalter. As in other grammar schools, the Latin would be not only classical but Renaissance: Erasmus, Vives, perhaps Mantuanus' pastorals or Palingenius' *Zodiacus vitae*. Exceptionally, the curriculum extended to music and possibly even to English. For the headmaster was an advanced educationalist, the great Richard Mulcaster. No doctrinaire humanist, Mulcaster had a strong and original mind, which he expressed in a fine though sometimes obscure style. The ideas developed in *Positions* and *The Elementary* are sometimes ahead of any that have even yet been

realized; nevertheless, they are compatible with a deep sense of history. The latter gave Mulcaster a reverence for such fragile institutions as customs and languages. Thus, his classicism allowed for the possibility of different classical periods in modern literatures. He read Ariosto: he advocated regular teaching of the vernacular ("I honour Latin, but worship English"); he defended the education of women. Many of Mulcaster's ideas seem to find a later echo in Spenser's writing: not least the belief that literature and learning may form the character of the individual for the public good.

Together with Lancelot Andrewes, Spenser left school in 1569 for Pembroke Hall, Cambridge, where he was a sizar (an undergraduate receiving an allowance from the college to enable him to study), paying no fees but performing certain chores. The next four years were spent in completing the trivium begun at school—by reading rhetoric, logic, and philosophy; the three years after on the quadrivium—arithmetic, geometry, astronomy, and music. These studies centered on a small number of set authors, all classical. In 1573 Spenser proceeded B.A.; in 1576 M.A. At Cambridge an oral tradition then vigorously prevailed of lectures and public disputation. The level of learned eloquence was high, fitting an excessive number for the administrative offices available. (The size of the university was small by modern standards: about 1,800, of whom 250 were sizars.) Spenser's contemporaries included the much older Thomas Preston, author of *Cambyses*; the younger Abraham Fraunce, poet, rhetorician, literary theorist; and Gabriel Harvey.

Harvey, who was Spenser's senior by about three years, became a fellow of Pembroke Hall in 1570, praelector (or professor) of rhetoric in 1574. His *Ciceronianus* and *Rhetor* show him to have been a brilliant scholar and writer, surely possessing one of the sharpest minds of his time. And he was probably, as Virginia Woolf surmised, a brilliant talker. Yet his Cambridge career was erratic, and in the end unsuccessful. This may have been not altogether to his discredit: he had ideas progressive enough to provoke opposition—including Ramist reform in logic, and unsound "paradoxes" such as Copernicus' heliocentric hypothesis. But he was also arrogant, quarrelsome, tactless, vain, silly, and a misfit. The man who could write "Sometime my book is unto me a god / Sometime I throw it from me a rod" was too restless for mere scholarship. In another age he might have been a literary critic, or even a columnist. As it was, he went after preferment with the desperation of frustrated greatness, perpetually encouraging himself the while, in countless Machiavellian marginalia, to futile circumspections.

In spite (or perhaps because) of our knowing so many of his private thoughts, he remains a baffling figure. Most—like Nashe in their public quarrel, and perhaps Shakespeare, in Holofernes—have regarded him as a foolish pedant. He took himself seriously; so that others have tended not to. But it is not Harvey who seems pedantic when Spenser and he differ about quantity in English verse. His greater experience and wide reading enabled him to enlarge Spenser's tastes and perhaps to make him more contemporary, more European. Harvey came to recognize the quality of an early version of *The Faerie Queen*, although he preferred (rightly or wrongly) Spenser's lost "Comedies." But this advice was resisted. Spenser was well able to exert his own taste decisively, using a bet, for example, to press Harvey to read *Lazarillo de Tormes*. Their friendship, which mattered to both men, was reciprocal and not dependent.

How did Spenser regard Harvey? The sonnet he addressed to him from Dublin in 1586 seems comically inappropriate now: "happy above happiest men . . . sitting like a looker-on / Of this world's stage," wielding his "critic pen," careless of suspicion. But Harvey, who was not yet the failure of later years, nor demeaned by controversy with the unfair and clever Nashe, perhaps had still an outsider's early idealism. However that may be, this strange man also cherished ambitious hopes of following in the footsteps of Cheke and Smith, and of becoming great in the councils of the mighty. From 1576 he pursued the favor of Leicester and, from 1578, of Sidney. He was thus in a position to introduce Spenser to two of the greatest patrons of the age. And when Spenser's *Shepherd's Calendar* appeared anonymously in 1579, it bore a dedication to Sidney.

Although the Cambridge of Spenser's day was dominated by radical Puritans of Thomas Cartwright's stamp, Spenser emerged a moderate but fervent Protestant, with views comparable to those of Richard Hooker or gentle Archbishop Grindal (the Algrin of *The Shepherd's Calendar*). In 1578, after some time in the north, Spenser became secretary to Edward Young, the former master of Pembroke Hall. By October 5, 1579, however, he had entered the household of the earl of Leicester and was familiar with Leicester's nephew Sir Philip Sidney. Together with Sidney and Sir Edward Dyer he made the experiments in "artificial" or quantitative verse that are discussed and developed in the correspondence with Harvey, published in 1580 as *Three proper, and witty, familiar Letters*. (This spirited but unsuccessful attempt to capture in the vernacular the sophisticated obliquity of smart neo-Latin epistles got Gabriel Harvey into a great deal of trouble with the authorities.) Probably about the same time, Spenser was writing his "lost" works ("Epithalamion Thamesis," "The Court of Cupid," "Dreams," "Pageants," etc.), some of which may be early versions of parts of *The Faerie Queen*. Also in 1579 he married, almost certainly, Machabyas Childe, by whom he was to have two children, Sylvanus and Katherine.

Then, in 1580, Spenser went to Ireland as secretary to the new governor, Arthur Lord Grey. (The English were making another of their incoherent attempts to anglicize barbarous Ireland, partly by colonial settlement, partly by the sword.) Inexplicably this move has been represented as exile consequent on some disgrace (perhaps Spenser offended Leicester, as his *Virgil's Gnat* hints?). But humanistically trained men of letters expected and hoped to exercise their pens in administrative tasks. A career's success was gauged by the minor offices collected, and the estates. Spenser was clerk of faculties in the Court of Chancery (1581: a sinecure); commissioner for musters (1583); deputy to Lodowick Bryskett as clerk of the Council of Munster (1584); prebendary of Limerick Cathedral (1585: a sinecure); and justice of the County of Cork (1594). From 1582 he leased New Abbey near Dublin; in 1586 he was assigned, and in 1590 formally granted, the very large estate of Kilcolman (3,000 acres, or about 1,214 hectares). Kilcolman was Spenser's real and emotional home: its landscape finds reflection in many passages of his poetry. In fact, he should be regarded as one of our great Irish writers.

Even in Ireland, however, he still belonged to the literary milieu of the court. Lodowick Bryskett, whose dialogue *Discourse of Civil Life* (1583) has Spenser as one of its interlocutors, was a poet and former tutor of Sidney's. Ralegh visited his nearby estate in 1589. And manuscript circulation of Spenser's work is argued by Abraham Fraunce's ability to quote from *The Faerie Queen*, book 2, before its publication.

In 1589 and again in 1595 or 1596 Spenser made visits to London that occasioned flurries of publication, partly of old work revised: 1590, *The Faerie Queen*, part 1, and *Muiopotmos;* 1591, *Daphnaida* and *Complaints;* 1595, *Amoretti and Epithalamion* and *Colin Clout's Come Home Again;* 1596, *The Faerie Queen*, part 2 (books 4–6), *Prothalamion,* and *Four Hymns. The Faerie Queen* may never have been finished. Of the six missing books, only the Cantos of Mutability (published posthumously) remain.

The *Complaints* volume was suppressed, probably because Spenser had criticized William Cecil, lord Burghley, in *The Ruins of Time* and *Mother Hubberd's Tale.* Burghley was nevertheless included, although cautiously, among the sixteen nobles to whom *The Faerie Queen* was presented (it was dedicated to the queen herself). He seems not to have liked it. The queen, however, did. She paid Spenser the unique honor in 1591 of a life pension of £50 a year (a considerable sum—more than twice the rent for Kilcolman). In 1594 Spenser was remarried, to Elizabeth Boyle. He solemnized the wedding day, June 11, in *Amoretti and Epithalamion.* 1596 finds him celebrating with *Prothalamion* the spousals of the earl of Worcester's daughters at Essex House in London. The poem expresses "old woes," the loss of his patron Leicester, who had died in 1588, and his consequent friendlessness; but it also looks forward to the favor of a new patron, the earl of Essex. Spenser's successful career culminated with his nomination (as one "with good knowledge in learning and not unskilful or without experience in the service of the wars") to the post of high sheriff of Cork, on September 30, 1598. But within a month the rebels had overrun Munster and burned Kilcolman. Spenser returned to London with dispatches on Christmas Eve; and

on January 13, 1599, he died. He was buried in Westminster Abbey, near Chaucer, at the expense of Essex, "his hearse being carried by poets, and mournful verses and poems thrown into his tomb." There was an early tradition that Spenser died in want; but it seems to have been without basis.

III

The Shepherd's Calendar (1579) was Spenser's first considerable published work. This fact is a little misleading, in that he already had behind him the lost works, not to speak of the schoolboy translation of Van der Noodt's Protestant emblem book. Spenser was early drawn to poetry, yet had a slow development as a poet. Traditionally, pastoral offered an unassuming mode that might be attempted in prelude to more ambitious flights. *The Shepherd's Calendar,* however, is far from being apprentice work. It shows a high sense of control, and yet an astonishing freedom in the treatment of genre. It is far from mere imitation or combination of Theocritus, Virgil, Mantuan, and Marot. Indeed, considered historically, its achievement is so considerable as to make it a watershed on any map of English verse.

Spenser enlarged the pastoral tradition in several ways. The Renaissance eclogues by Mantuan and Barclay had already treated moral or religious matters: pastoral could be microcosmic and satiric rather than idyllic. Spenser took up this option and invested in it heavily. The landscape that he makes a mirror of his shepherd's plight is "barren ground, whom winter's wrath hath wasted": a land suffering from adverse weather, wolves, and disease. In fact, it is real country. And he introduces many fresh images from nature, such as the oak's top "bald and wasted with worms" and the bee "working her formal rooms in waxen frame," besides many country phrases not previously heard in serious poetry.

Most creative of all is his approach to the structure. Instead of the usual collection of independent "eclogues" (the term anciently implied separateness) Spenser has made a single work, unified by the structural principle of the natural year, and of seasons that symbolize stages in human life. As Pope noted, "the addition he has made of a calendar to his eclogues is very beautiful." The calendrical form not only holds the eclogues together, but contributes to their special character of endless variety combined with complex, elusive order. It works multifariously: in the changing weather; in seasonal customs (April's flower gathering was the occupation for that month by the conventions of visual art); explicitly astronomical imagery (Sol appears in July, the month of his own sign Leo, "making his way between the Cup,/ and golden Diadem"); and even in physical proportions (May is by far the longest eclogue, since the sun was known to stay longer in Gemini than in any other sign). Spenser also achieved controlled variety by varying the meter, all the way from rough alliterative lines to the gentle, grave stateliness of November's elegy for Dido:

> But now sike [such] happy cheer is turned to heavy chance,
> Such pleasance now displaced by dolour's dint:
> All music sleeps, where death doth lead the dance,
> And shepherds' wonted solace is extinct.
> The blue in black, the green in grey is tinct [tinged],
> The gaudy garlands deck her grave,
> The faded flowers her corse embrave.
> O heavy hearse,
> Mourn now my muse, now mourn with tears besprint [sprinkled].
> O careful verse.

(November 103–112)

Inset songs and fables introduce further variation. Then there is the alternation of three modes or categories—"plaintive," "moral," and "recreative"—and the interweaving of three large subjects: love, poetry, and religious politics. The command with which genres are deployed makes for admiration, even where this is not accompanied with understanding or enjoyment. Everything seems in scale, and orchestrated, giving a sense of various modes of life in harmony. January's love complaint gives way to February's *débat* between youth and age, which encloses (and perhaps underlies too) the fable of an episcopal oak and a Puritan briar. March offers an exploit of Cupid; April, an inset ode in praise of Elizabeth, with some delicately Skeltonic flower poetry; and May, a beast fable and more controversy.

The poetic statement made on this complex instrument is itself complex. For one thing, the shepherds enact a roman à clef, to which the key has been lost. Algrin is Archbishop Grindal and Hobbinol Gabriel Harvey; but others remain unidentified, even with the help of fashionably elaborate annotation by "E.K." (himself unknown). Moreover, some of the roles are multivalent. Thus, besides being a persona for Spenser, Colin Clout is a highly idealized laureate (combining poetic names from Skelton and Marot). Tityrus is both Virgil and Chaucer. And Pan figures severally as Henry VIII, as the pope, and as Christ. Nevertheless, the topical allegory is probably not intricate; Spenser seems to have tended to political simplicity as much as to intellectual subtlety.

Nowhere is there more subtlety than in the poem's structural pattern. To begin with, it sets out two calendars: the astronomical, running from March to February, and the Christian, from January to December. Circularity is suggested by the linking of the January and December eclogues, each of which has the single speaker Colin. They are "proportionable" in the octave ratio of perfect harmony, one being exactly twice as long as the other. Then, the plaintive (p), the moral (m), and the recreative (r) eclogues are arranged, with their speakers, in interlocking symmetries. For example, January to June (corresponding astrologically to the six "lunar" signs) form the sequence $p/m/r/r/m/p$. Moreover, Colin's concluding motto in June, as E.K. notes, answers that in January. Thus, the first half of the *Calendar* also forms a circle, a subsidiary "world," which may be interpreted as the mundane world of natural life. It begins with Colin's "wilfully" breaking his pipe and ends with his giving up false love and the unworthy Rosalind. Within this world are conflicts between the old and the new (February: oak versus briar), or between worldly pleasure and censorious morality (May: Palinode versus Piers). June, however, makes the challenges to an earthly paradise explicit, leading to July's myth of the Fall, and fatal disorders in nature. Here, at the poem's center, stands a mountain, the high place of God: there is mention of Sinai, Olivet, and "mighty Pan" or Christ.

The *Calendar*'s second half becomes increasingly dark, the secular idyll more and more plainly illusion. Art's solace now replaces that of nature. But the mirror of art, which itself mirrors nature, brings deeper disenchantments still. October questions the use of poetry and even the possibility of literary life. Its talk of war contradicts the olive coronal of April, the matching month (with sign in opposition) of the *Calendar*'s first half. To lighten this gloom there emerges the theme of grace. In September, Diggon Davie repents; in December, Colin himself. Indeed, one might see the whole *Calendar* as a confession of Colin's developing religious consciousness: as his palinode or retraction from earlier secularity. But the poem is more inclusive, more Chaucerian perhaps, than this would suggest. It finds room, after all, for natural beauty, for the worldly Palinode, for the retired Hobbinol. And it is the reformer Piers who overstates his case. The *Calendar* leaves us, in the end, with a sense of manifold fictive worlds, all comprehended in Spenser's detached vision of mutability.

This marvelous intellectual structure unfortunately no longer quite succeeds as poetry. This is not merely because of its coterie aspects—these are no insuperable obstacle with Shakespeare's poems. The reasons have to do with certain critical theories, fashionable in Spenser's day, about the language of literature. Following ideas of Joachim Du Bellay and others, he believed that a classical English style could be based on Chaucer's language. Hence his interweaving of rustic expressions appropriate to pastoral, Chaucerian archaisms, and ancient poetic words ("grieslie," "moe," "astert"), together with contrastingly easy conventional epithets ("riper age," "doleful verse"), to form a lexical tapestry of great, perhaps even excessive, richness. Especially desirable were dialectal or pseudodialectal words, parts, or mere spelling variants that preserved Chaucer's, Gavin Douglas', and earlier forms ("swincke," "sayne"). This diction was not quite so experimental then as it has since come to look; but intensified as it was by archaic syntax and combined with a style of plain pithy statement, its effect must always have been singular enough. Jonson says that Spenser "writ no language." Spenser might appeal to Theocritus' precedent—and to

the many poets who have followed his, rather than Jonson's, example. The smooth element of Spenser's diction has influenced poetic taste ever since. But some of his rougher innovations now seem as decisively wrongheaded as any in Wordsworth's *Lyrical Ballads*:

> My ragged ronts [bullocks] all shiver and shake,
> As doen high towers in an earthquake. . . .
> (February 5–6)

Another unfortunate theory concerned Chaucer's versification. At a time when the Chaucerian canon was uncertain, and accessible only in bad texts, his verse was universally held to be rough. It was imitated by such devices as the addition of final -*e*. Spenser's fashionably rough verse now seems almost as dated as that of his contemporaries. At best it is workmanlike. Above its shaggy lowliness, as above a rusticated ground story, rises the piano nobile of inset songs (April, August, November). Here, and in only a few other passages, the *Calendar* displays a liquid ease and subtlety of movement adequate to the brilliant rhetoric:

> Why do we longer live, (ah why live we so long)
> (November 73; cf. 81, 111)

Note how the *correctio*, or restatement, puts a different accent on "we" and "live," reinforcing the meaning yet also making a tenderly elegiac music. In such passages Spenser achieves a remarkably mellifluous flow. His special gift was for counterpointing a great many structures and textures: rhetorical, phonetic, metrical. So in

> The mantled meadows mourn,
> Their sundry colours turn.
> (November 128–129)

the lines are matched by their similar clause length, their words of equivalent syllables symmetrically distributed, their rhetorical parallelism, and their literal meaning; so that the switch from alliteration (monochromatic consonants) to assonance (monochromatic vowels) mimes the drab change of color. Spenser's later verse is full of such correspondences, in which form continuously accompanies sense in a ceremony of meaning. His smooth style, indeed,

126

has so dominated taste that we take it for granted and hardly notice the first beginnings. These should not be exaggerated either. The *Calendar* is high art, certainly; but only locally higher than that of Sidney. Overall, it is the *Calendar's* ambitious encyclopedic content that bodes well, not its poetic language. It already shows a very special combination of complicated medieval structure with Renaissance hyperconsciousness about consistency. But it has attracted too much attention for the good of Spenser's modern reputation.

Spenser continued to write pastoral throughout his life. In 1591 *Astrophel. A Pastoral Elegy* appeared as the framing introduction to a volume of elegies on Sidney. Certainly later than 1586, and probably later than 1590, it is a finer work than most of *The Shepherd's Calendar*, although it has not usually been valued so highly. The first part (lines 1–216) relates, under the allegory of a boar hunt, Sidney's death from a wound received at the battle of Zutphen (1586). Astrophel is gored by one of "the brutish nation" (the Spanish oppressors); mourned by his widow; and metamorphosed into a flower. This part, while always felicitous, preserves so impersonal a tone as to seem now a shade pallid, a little too consciously Bionesque. It is another matter with the Lay of Clorinda. This part, exactly half as long as the first—the proportions of harmony—purports to give the mourning song of Sidney's sister Mary, countess of Pembroke. It is a deeply serious expression of grief, from which Milton learned for *Lycidas*. Who is the mourner to address? She can hope for comfort neither from men nor from gods ("From them comes good, from them comes also ill"), so that she addresses her complaint to herself:

> The woods, the hills, the rivers shall resound
> The mournful accent of my sorrow's ground.
> (lines 23–24)

The resonance of "ground" ("ground bass," "basis") is characteristic of the Lay's self-referring style, which can be poignant—as in "The fairest flower . . . Was Astrophel; that *was*, we all may rue." The resolution in this second part is deeper and darker: Clorinda reflects that when we grieve we may be self-regarding, "Mourning in others, our own miseries". Sid-

ney is better where he is. If this part was by Mary herself, as some have suggested, she wrote a better poem than Spenser on this occasion.

In December 1591, from Kilcolman, Spenser dedicated to Sir Walter Ralegh *Colin Clout's Come Home Again*, a pastoral eclogue about a recent visit to court. This popular yet incompletely appreciated work is directly autobiographical, if not so literally as some have thought (it transports Gabriel Harvey, surely in wish-fulfillment, to Ireland). Its engaging method is that of general conversation, with no fewer than ten shepherds and shepherdesses interrupting and questioning Colin. These familiar exchanges establish a sense of Spenser's social and literary circle. They also, by their distancing or alienating effect, allow transitions through a wide range of tones, from the strangely exalted to the quietly humorous. The humor of Colin's account of his voyage is quite broad: the sea ("A world of waters heaped up on high"), ships ("Glued together with some subtle matter"), and mythologized admirals (Triton and Proteus) are consistently described as they might appear to an innocent, quite unironic shepherd's eye. Less obvious is the joke whereby the most extensive piece of alliteration—lines 25–26—comes in a speech of Hobbinol's. Harvey disliked this device.

Most good eclogues are deeper than they look; and this one, probably the longest and most complex in the language, is no exception. It has an elaborate symmetrical structure to reflect its various but carefully balanced moods. There is even an inset eclogue, an account of a previous conversation with Ralegh, "the Shepherd of the Ocean," in which the narrative's doubly reported status expresses the remoteness of a primitive river myth of sexual rivalry in the far past. The first half is divided between nature (the watery wilderness; wild Ireland) and art (epitomized by a catalogue of England's twelve chief poets). This passage, where Spenser authoritatively reviews his literary milieu and freely reveals his tastes, has an interest similar to that of, say, W. H. Auden's *Letter From Iceland*. Most praise goes to Daniel and Alabaster (both named), to Astrophel, Alcyon (Sir Arthur Gorges), and to the mysterious Aetion. The second half answers with a catalogue of twelve ladies, courteously praised, and a lofty encomium of the queen. Why then did Colin ever leave the court? His reply offsets the gallantry with a sharp attack on the court's incivility: "it is no sort of life," and all its glory is "but smoke, that fumeth soon away." Hobbinol speaks up for Leicester, giving a well-informed review of his patronage program; but Colin responds with renewed attacks, this time on the court's immorality.

All this has been seen as Spenser's ambivalence; and so in a way it may have been, in personal terms. But the poem's effect seems not so much ambiguous as poised. Peaceful England is excellent, by comparison with disordered Ireland: the court is frivolous, by comparison with true civility. More delicately poised still is Colin's balance of Rosalind's cruelty to him with the queen's to Ralegh (whose suffering carries conviction—"Ah my love's queen, and goddess of my life"). He even reconciles a near-blasphemous panegyric of Elizabeth with the elevation of another vassalage to a higher place within the poem's little world. Its sovereign center honors not the queen, but the courteous grace of an unnamed "maid" (probably Elizabeth Throckmorton, later Lady Ralegh), to whom Spenser pays ardent homage:

> And I hers ever only, ever one:
> One ever I all vowed hers to be,
> One ever I, and other's never none.
> (lines 477–479, of 955)

"Ever one . . . one ever . . . one ever" is no mere decorative rhetoric of chiasmus[1] or anaphora[2] but mimes the iconographic attitude of the three Graces, one facing forward, two turned in outgoing. For the rest, the poem glances at several of the main interests of Spenser's mature work: cosmogonic myth; a metaphysic of "Beauty the burning lamp of heaven's light"; and a passionate theology of love, with a myth of the androgynous Venus. He condemns the court's lewdness not from a puritanical standpoint, but because it profanes the "mighty mysteries" of love, "that dread lord." The

poem's range of feeling is immense; no work gives a better sense of the possibilities of eclogue.

IV

IN *Amoretti and Epithalamion* (1595) Spenser lays aside the pastoral weeds of Colin Clout to sing in his own person, as the lover of Elizabeth Boyle. Considering his early reputation as a love poet, it is strange how few now think him one of the great sonneteers. The *Amoretti* can easily seem low-pressure work, lacking the dramatic intensity of Sidney's *Astrophel and Stella*. However, interest grows when one appreciates how far Spenser's quieter virtues and more deeply poetic qualities have been missed. Take *Amoretti* 18, for example, in which the lover complains that whereas "The rolling wheel. . . . The hardest steel in tract of time doth tear" and raindrops wear the "firmest flint," yet he cannot move his lady. Stock images of obduracy; but how originally and deceptively they are put to work. Is the lady really discouraging? If tears are "but water," then the proverb holds and she will yield: only if tears are contrasted with rain would she be unmoved. Similarly when she "turns herself to laughter," who now is "the rolling wheel" and who "doth still remain"? Again, what association have flint and steel together, but kindled fire? The poetic indirection here is quite unlike anything in the other sonneteers of Spenser's time.

And in deeper ways too he is unlike them. Indeed, he came late enough in the vogue—after a dozen other English "sonnet sequences"—to have something different to offer. Shakespeare responded to a similar challenge by writing sonnets that seem to be about friendship and jealousy. But Spenser's are not about passion at all, in the ordinary sense, but about a love that ends happily, in marriage: the British romantic love, mingling friendship with sexual desire, in praise of which he wrote at greater length in *The Faerie Queen*. The lover of the *Amoretti* (partly followed by the reader) gets to know Elizabeth Boyle well, forming a full personal relation with her. And a keenly intelligent, witty person she is—an Elizabeth Bennett rather than a Penelope

---

[1] A figure of speech in which the word order in one clause is inverted in another phrase soon after.
[2] The repetition of a word or phrase at the beginning of successive clauses or verses.

Rich—with a firm, unmistakable character. Unlike the usual Petrarchist lady, who is a trigger of passion and little else, Elizabeth does not wound with Cupid's darts, but calms passion's storm (8), and, characterized herself by "goodly temperature" (13), frames and tempers her lover's feelings too. Even after they are mutually committed (84), we hear of her "too constant stiffness." This intense but tender courtship of a young girl by a middle-aged lover has the air of reality. (The general situation is probably autobiographical. In *Amoretti* 60, Spenser implies that he is forty; and Elizabeth in fact outlived him, to have children by a second marriage at dates that make it likely that she was at least fifteen years younger.) Their love is deep, but too serious, too responsible, for passion.

Nevertheless, Elizabeth must receive every tribute usually paid to a slavishly worshipped sonneteer's goddess. In performing this contract Spenser shows an astonishing capacity to fulfill the forms of love complaint, and yet all the time to be free from them, above them—not so much through irony or travesty (although these are sometimes not far away) as through the direct, open refusal of conventional literary attitudes. To the latter, he prefers the more complex human comedy. Sometimes, it is true, he carries the Petrarchist commonplaces far enough towards absurdity to expose their false logic, as in 32: "What then remains but I to ashes burn . . . ?" But more often the commonplaces—the fire and ice, the tyrant and captive, the storm and cruel tigress—are taken up with just a hint of distancing humor, a bantering tone or self-deprecating smile, to remind us that they belong to only one of the ways of wooing. The lover knows Elizabeth too well to think that she is really a tigress (in that way, at least). Not that the pains of love are merely acted, in a sense that would make them unreal. Indeed, where the idea of acting becomes most explicit, in the theatrical conceit of 54, the lady—who as unmoved spectator does not act—sits admonished; she is less than alive: "a senseless stone." Alternatively, the commonplaces may be taken up seriously but transformed. So it is with the erotic "blazon," or item-by-item portrait, which had generated much loose poetry, particularly in French and Italian. Spenser has extremely sensuous sonnets of this type, such as the complete blazon in 64. There are several on Elizabeth's eyes, hair, and breasts. In each case, however, the idea is elevated. In 76, her breasts are a "bower of bliss," *pome acerbe* ("unripe apples"), "like early fruit in May," between which the lover's frail thoughts dive "through amorous insight." But the very next sonnet shows the same apples in a dream, now ripe and "golden," laid out for a sacred feast. For they surpass even those that Hercules came by in the Hesperidean garden of chastity: "sweet fruit of pleasure brought from paradise / By love himself." It is the exalted desire of the *Song of Solomon.* Meanwhile, as he waits and woos, the lover is concerned to allay Elizabeth's anxiety about the loss of freedom that marriage would involve:

The doubt which ye misdeem, fair love, is vain,
That fondly fear to lose your liberty,
When losing one, two liberties ye gain,
And make him bond that bondage erst did fly.
Sweet be the bands, the which true love doth tie,
Without constraint or dread of any ill:
The gentle bird feels no captivity
Within her cage, but sings and feeds her fill.
There pride dare not approach, nor discord spill
  [destroy]
The league 'twixt them, that loyal love hath bound:
But simple truth and mutual good will,
Seeks with sweet peace to salve each other's wound:
There faith doth fearless dwell in brazen tower,
And spotless pleasure builds her sacred bower.
                                        (*Amoretti* 65)

There is a tenderness and reciprocity of feeling here that would be impossible to match anywhere else in the Renaissance sonnet.

Spenser could hardly have given such a love simple dramatic expression. Instead of Sidney's individually intense sonnets forming moments in a narrative, he has written what seems much more obviously a long stanzaic poem (as is expressed formally by linked rhyme schemes). This continuity between sonnets, allowing complex large-scale imagery and amplitude of thematic development, goes back beyond the Petrarchists to the prolonged meditations of Petrarch's *Rime* themselves. Like Petrarch (and like Shakespeare), Spenser uses a calendrical structure to suggest the variety and natural growth of emotion. Thus there are New Year and Easter sonnets, set in their appropriate numerological places. The contradictory feelings that some have seen as problematic or indicative of revision all belong to this "whole year's work," leading to the marriage day celebrated in *Epithalamion*. Like other Elizabethan "sonnet sequences," *Amoretti* is really part of a composite work, combining sonnets with other stanza forms. Linking it to *Epithalamion* are four "anacreontic odes," or sweet epigrams, which languish for the bliss of the wedding night. These serve as generic transition to the major ode that follows.

Amoretti may fascinate as an interesting departure from the usual sequence or as a shorter treatment of themes developed in *The Faerie Queen*. But *Epithalamion* is unique. Nothing shows Spenser's creativity better than this poem, which most agree to be the finest major ode in English, and to be surpassed in ancient literature—if at all—only by Pindar. Classical comparisons are inevitable, because Spenser here invented for English literature the humanist ceremonial mode that was to be so important for Michael Drayton, Robert Herrick, and others—and carried it at once to its greatest height. Like Catullus' *Carmina 61*, Spenser's poem moves in festal exaltation through the events of a wedding day. But its structure is very different, rising as it does through a crescendo of gathering voices and sounds and excitement to the roaring organs and public affirmation of the marriage service at the altar, in the central two stanzas or strophes; before the feasting, the public "bedding" of the bride, consummation, and soft recession into the silence and darkness of the night. Each stage is due and accepted:

Now welcome night, thou night so long expected,
That long day's labour dost at last defray,
And all my cares, which cruel love collected,
Hast summed in one, and cancelled for aye:
Spread thy broad wing over my love and me,
That no man may us see,
And in thy sable mantle us enwrap,
From fear of peril and foul horror free.
Let no false treason seek us to entrap,
Nor any dread disquiet once annoy
The safety of our joy:
But let the night be calm and quietsome,
Without tempestuous storms or sad affray:

Like as when Jove with fair Alcmena lay,
When he begot the great Tirynthian groom:
Or like as when he with thy self did lie,
And begot Majesty.
And let the maids and young men cease to sing:
Ne let the woods them answer nor their echo ring.

(stanza 18)

What audacity for a poet to dare to speak to the goddess Night about her lovemaking!—and yet how apt, at the juncture when he is about to become intimate with his own wife. Throughout, mythological imagery mingles with real, external with psychological. Indeed, the comprehensiveness takes in even negative feelings, such as dread of an "affray," and sexual fears of "Medusa's mazeful head." Spenser's robust yet sensitive personal address is unflinchingly inclusive, as he faces both day and unconscious night in the ritual of love. His ceremony remains reverent; yet it affirms nature and finds authenticity in the role of Jupiter, spouse of Night. These and other deep archetypes and powers are recognized and profoundly composed: the *Horae*, the *Gratiae*, the *amorini* of passion, Cynthia the chaste destroyer yet patroness of childbirth, and, in the one stanza, Juno foundress of marriage and female genius, together with Genius himself, god of pleasure and generation. As Spenser invokes them in turn, or turns from one wedding scene to another, he dwells on each in such a way that the stanzas acquire their own characters and modalities. They are like the dances of a suite. Now all is private communing with the "learned sisters"; now expectant bachelors wait for Hymen's torchlit masque to move off; now pristine garlanded "nymphs" make final arrangements. One stanza will be a blazon of Elizabeth's beauties admired by all ("lips like cherries charming men to bite"), the next a mysterious praise of her chaste inner character. The poem's movement through this variety is fluid but calm and firm and sure. It is as if everything had its inevitable place.

And so, in numerological terms, it had. The spatial disposition of *Epithalamion* mimes with extraordinary precision the astronomical events of the day that it celebrates. Thus the 24 stanzas represent its 24 hours, with night falling at the right point for Saint Barnabas' Day, the summer

130

solstice, "the longest day in all the year." Then, after stanza 16, the refrain changes from positive to negative: "The woods no more shall answer, nor your echo ring." And the *canzone*-like stanzas consist of pentameters and occasional trimeters, with the long lines numbering just 365 to represent the days of the year, during which the sun completes its journey round the 24 sidereal hours. The ceremony of time has never been realized so fully as in this most musical of Spenser's poems. It is indeed an "endless monument" to the poignantly short time of his day. Yet before the end it has carried the torches of its masque up to join the "thousand torches flaming bright" in the temple of the gods. It aspires to commemorate an anticipated cosmic event, addition to the communion of saints, eventual "stellification."

Prothalamion (1596), written for an aristocratic betrothal, has similar ceremonial qualities and a form almost as highly wrought. It too is a masterpiece of occasional art in the grand mannerist style. But, in spite of autobiographical references to "old woes," it is more public, more philosophical, and harder at first to warm to. Only after prolonged consideration and the effort of attending to its closely overdetermined images does its profundity emerge. It not only sums up the whole river-epithalamium genre, but sings the mutability of the height of life.

Spenser wrote other short works, notably the medievalizing satire *Mother Hubberd's Tale* and the lofty Christian-Platonic *Hymns*. The former is not dull; but neither does it show Spenser to have been a great satirist. As for the *Hymns*, they challenge more attention, as a vastly ambitious undertaking, a poetic theology of love and generation. Their extreme difficulty (and the correspondingly glorious opportunity they offer to the commentator) is not their only interest for Spenserians. They cast much cloudy light on Spenser's unexpected, syncretistic thinking. But this is not enough to make them great poems. Whether their metaphysical puzzles yield to solution or remain attributed to blunders, the *Hymns* must be counted noble failures. When all is said and done (and much has still to be said, for the love poems particularly), the work in which Spenser chiefly lives is *The Faerie Queen*.

V

The Faerie Queen occupies a very special place in English literature. Yet far more would acknowledge its classic status than would count themselves among its readers. There are doubtless several reasons for this, some of which I mention below. One may be a misconception about the kind of work *The Faerie Queen* is. Another, closely related, may be the disablement inflicted by much reading of "probable report" novels, which seems to produce insensitivity to less novelistic sorts of fictive realism. A third may be its length. For my own part, I was fortunate enough to come upon the poem during a convalescence: I could read without interruption. But there are other ways of reading such a work, which were not unknown to the Elizabethans themselves. In his translation of *Orlando Furioso*, Sir John Harington gives directions "for the several tales, where to begin and end, those that may conveniently be read single." Of course such a method will not give a very adequate idea of the work, unless it is complemented by reading *in extenso*. Much of the characteristic quality of *The Faerie Queen* depends on juxtaposition of stories and episodes of different kinds, on interrupted, interwoven narrative, on multiplication.

And this is perhaps the first point to take hold of: that it is a work of interlaced art. Suppose you are following the story of Belphoebe. You pick it up in book 2, canto 3, stanzas 21–42, a luscious ten-stanza description of the heroine, broken up by a comic encounter with Trompart and the upstart Braggadocchio. Belphoebe explains that true honor comes by hard work and is more likely to be found in the forest (or studying at home) than at court. But when she has fiercely rebuffed an improper advance, and fled, she makes no further appearance in book 2—nor in the next, until 3.5.57, where she cares for the wounded Timias. Her parentage and relation to Amoret are explained in the canto following, through the myth of Chrysogone. But then she disappears again until book 4, by which time several other stories have been woven into the fabric. If the reader loses track of these windings he should on no account despair: all is going according to plan; the sense of labyrinthine unsearchability is a desired effect.

Some degree of incomprehension is as deliberate a feature in Spenser's art as it is in certain types of medieval romance, or in the visual interlace of the *Book of Kells*. The reader may follow the pattern again and again, and have the experience, as in life, of gradual understanding.

To enjoy Spenser's *entrelacement*, feel free, first, to reread. Second, attend closely to the distant connections (whether of resemblance, variation, or contrast) between widely separate parts of the poem. As in most interlaced narratives, such internal allusions carry a great deal of the content. Third, notice the transitions between stories and between episodes. It is often at these points of juncture that Spenser indicates the fictive status of the various milieus that are brought into relation, and implies a deeper import. So the beautiful description of achieved true honor, Belphoebe alone, confronts the farcical pretensions of Braggadocchio (a thin character) and his sycophant. And this scene is in turn followed by Guyon's adventures on quite a different scale—far more minutely psychological—as he overcomes a series of difficulties in the pursuit of honor. The formal relation of interlaced narrative strands can offer a pleasure of its own, like that of abstract art. But with Spenser the interruptions of the story generally also give reminders of further reality. The breaks in his tapestry disclose glimpses of windows that look out on larger, more complex worlds. When Artegall returning victorious encounters the Blatant Beast (5.12.37), the juncture of stories shows how military success and administrative success are not enough: there is also a social world, with reputation to be won or lost. In this sense, polyphonic narrative serves the deeper purpose of comprehensiveness, of inclusiveness, of Renaissance epic's aspiration to complete unity. It is not quite the same as *entrelacement* in the older romances.

At one time, *The Faerie Queen* used to be thought of as the last great medieval work in English—although it was also supposed to have been written without much access to medieval literature. Now the manner of its medievalism is more problematic. Many would agree that Spenser knew Malory, together with other late romances. And there can be no doubt at all of his respect for old traditions: of his deep passion for "old records from ancient times derived," and of his avidity, as greedy as Guyon's, for romantic antiquities—chronicles and armor and heraldry and ruins and hermitages. *Ancient*—or, even older, *auncient*—is indeed one of his favorite words, which he is capable of using twice in the same line: "Ancient Ogyges, even the ancientest." There is some justice in C. S. Lewis' view that Spenser was "the first of the romantic medievalists." Certainly the retrospective Gothic taste in literature was identified from the start, in Pope and Thomas Warton for example, with a taste for *The Faerie Queen*. It should not be forgotten, however, that Spenser's own medieval enthusiasm was also coupled with a rather sharp stylishness. We miss a great deal of what he was about unless we appreciate his sophisticated modernity too. Not that Spenser was ever a merely fashionable writer. But he wrote in part to overgo Ariosto, who had established a vogue for Gothic costume narrative. It might be more accurate to characterize *The Faerie Queen* as mannerist neo-Gothic, rather than medieval. This stylistic character is reflected in the form, which is not romance but romantic epic.

Epic was supposed to give a sense of life's totality. And each Renaissance epicist in turn aimed at further, fuller inclusiveness, both by reaching out to a progressively more diverse or encyclopedic content, and by subsuming, whether through allusion or other means, contents already enclosed in the poetic domain of previous epics. Thus the commentators taught that Virgil's *Aeneid* combined an *Odyssey* (books 1–6) with an *Iliad* (7–12). Moreover, Julius Caesar Scaliger and other literary theorists had developed the doctrine that epic contains a wide variety of inset smaller forms. Spenser gave a creative turn to this idea: anticipating Milton's *Paradise Lost*, he included several different epic and romance forms in *The Faerie Queen*. Ariostan epic—all scramble and bravura and surprise—is probably his principal Italian ingredient. But he also uses Tasso's larger scale, especially for elaborate set pieces with luxuriant detail, such as the Bower of Bliss. Then there are passages of obscure Boiardan epic, burlesque, and puns like Pulci's, and even a few static hieroglyphs reminiscent of Trissino's *L'Italia Liberata dai Goti*. Ancient epic is represented not only in its Virgilian form—complete with descents into hell, games, extended similes, and stylistic formulas of the sort that Ford Madox Ford called "marmoreal Latinisms," but also in its Ovidian form (metamorphoses and loves of the gods). And it would risk Polonius's folly to enumerate the other types, such as pastoral epic, meandering through the world of the *Aethiopica* and the *Arcadia*; allegorical quests distantly resembling Deguilleville's or Hawes's; and (in the Cantos of Mutability) a procession like the ones in Du Bartas's Christian epic of creation.

All this should not be taken to mean that Spenser merely pillaged biblical, classical, medieval, and Renaissance epics for source material. (His sources are a separate topic, which hardly lends itself to brief treatment, being so poorly understood. Some of the poetical sources are beyond doubt. But the informational sources may have been fewer and more compendious, murkier and less literary, than scholars have assumed.) Allusion would be a better term than borrowing. Spenser is the first great allusive poet in English. And his mastery of generic variation goes further than I have suggested. With never a hint of pastiche, he deploys different kinds, almost as a composer scores for different instruments, to render life's various modes. Spenser is not always superior in handling a particular form. Ariosto's adventures, for example, run more easily; although Spenser's come very close in such an episode as Timias' skirmish with the foresters (3.5), and in any case are carrying more weight. But in shading such adventures into writing of other kinds, in using his far wider generic palette, in mixture, Spenser shows fictive genius of a different order altogether.

VI

THE detachment of *The Faerie Queen* from previous epics is reflected in its decisive formal individuation. Its meter, the "Spenserian stanza," that great legacy to Thomson and Shelley and Keats, contrives to be at once novel and traditional. By comparison with the brisk heroic stanza of Ariosto and Tasso, *ottava rima*—*a b a b a b c c*—the larger English stanza is spacious and unhurried; while its more intricately interlaced rhymes—*a b a b b c b c c*—further slow its pace (usually: exceptions include the sprightly cadence at 7.7.46) and knit it more closely together. The final alexandrine, which determines much of the effect of stateliness and weight, allows us to think not only of a nine-line stanza, but of an eight-line stanza rounded off: *a b a b b c b c C*—the ballade or *Monk's Tale* stanza, in fact, extended and transcended. Chaucer's stanza consists of two separate, symmetrical, couplet-linked halves: *a b a b / b c b c*. But the notional halves of the indivisible Spenserian stanza are united by its shared central line:

$$a\ b\ a\ b\ b$$
$$b\ c\ b\ c\ C.$$

An Elizabethan critic describing it—as Drayton described his own *Barons' Wars* stanza—might also have observed how it rests like a column on its hexameter base (six feet, a number of perfection), or how its rhymes occur two, three, and four times: the numbers grouped by Macrobius and others as forming the ratios of the fundamental musical concords.

Right in the midst the goddess' self did stand
Upon an altar of some costly mass,
Whose substance was uneath [difficult] to understand:
For neither precious stone, nor dureful brass,
Nor shining gold, nor mouldering clay it was;
But much more rare and precious to esteem,
Pure in aspéct, and like to crystal glass,
Yet glass was not, if one did rightly deem,
But being fair and brickle [brittle], likest glass did seem.

(4.10.39)

The Spenserian stanza has been well compared to a wave falling on a beach: breaking, it runs to implement the full alexandrine mark and to give, where needed, a meditative lull. It "closeth not but with a full satisfaction to the ear for so long detention." It is the greatest of all stanzas.

The Italianate division into cantos tends to be taken for granted, but it was an innovation in English. Spenser offset it against a different division, of antique association, into books. Within each book, the cantos may vary greatly in representational mode. This is indeed the poem's most copious source of variety. It relies on formal variegation more than on multiplication of narrative incident.

This point calls for enlargement. The stanza just quoted, describing a mysterious altar of Venus, comes from a canto about Scudamour's entry into the Temple of Venus, a fully realized allegorical place in the manner of medieval dream vision. Book 4 in general treats friendship; but this canto initiates us into the very sanctum of the virtue, its inner nature, foundation, ideals, meaning. In the same way, each book has some such medullary or "core" canto, in which, usually, the champion of a virtue visits a place that symbolizes its essential character. Saint George, the patron of Holiness, visits the House of Holiness in 1.10; Guyon, the patron of Temperance, the castle of Alma in 2.9; and Artegall Mercilla's Court in 5.9. In such cantos the virtue is developed visually through an orderly procession, a pageant tableau, or its descriptive equivalent. It is a special symbolic mode that goes back to medieval vision allegories. Valuations of it now differ sharply, usually according to the critic's familiarity with its subtle conventions. But few would question that in the fiction of a Chaucer or a Colonna or a Spenser it can be a profoundly eloquent, although very oblique, form. The expressionist mysteriousness of the Garden of Adonis or the Temple of Venus is quite unlike almost anything in Ariosto; it is more like Colonna's enigmatic *Hypnerotomachia,* that strange work of sexual mysticism, whose psychological intuitions fascinated many writers and artists of the Renaissance. To explain some features of Spenser's symbolic places it may help to compare the material of Venus' altar with the rich shining substance of the Fountain of Will in the Bower of Bliss (2.12.60), or to know that in erotic poetry, glass might figure the female pudendum (as, for example, in *Greek Anthology* 5.36). But schematic interpretation of the Temple of Venus would be unthinkable. Too much is deeply implicit or indirectly conveyed for that. How is the brittle glass related to Ptolomae's glass tower of marital fidelity at 3.2.20? And Phidias, whose Paphian idol is introduced to amplify the greater beauty of this living god: does his wretched love for a mere image belong with the many unhappy loves about the altar? Again, why do the lovers outside the Temple sport their pleasures, while those within, and closest to the strange hermaphroditic goddess, suffer and complain? If Spenser invites such questions, he does not encourage quick answers.

The strange symbolic places stand out prominently, each like a *temenos* or sanctuary or *arcanum* set in the deep forest of romance. But they form one kind of episode only, one component of the Spenserian book. Another sort, coming in an early position, serves to join the adventures and to show the relations between the virtues that the knights strive for. Thus Saint George, patron of holiness, and Guyon, patron of temperance, meet and almost fight at 2.1.26; and Britomart (chaste love) shows herself superior to Guyon in a trial of strength at 3.1.6. Then there are early passages that announce the book's subjects by developing emblems of the virtues in their abstract or common acceptation: Saint George's encounter with Error in 1.2, Guyon's visit to Medina's castle of moderation in 2.1, Cambina's reconciliation of combatants in 4.3. These passages pose the books' topics in broad terms. The subjects thus stated undergo modification as well as expansion, however, so that the virtues of the early emblems are by no means identical with those realized in the "core cantos." The latter present insights reached only after the experience (that is, adventures) of attempting the virtue. As for the intervening adventures themselves, they superficially appear like Ariosto's. But in reality they also contribute a medieval (or medievalizing) element. They have a far more continuous moral sense than the adventures of most romances—even of many medieval romances. The Spenserian hero encounters obstacles to his virtue, or aspects of the opposing vice, which are thus analyzed into branches or subdivisions like those familiar from older moral works such as Frère Lorens' *Somme le Roi.* (Sometimes the categories are surprising and thought-provoking, as when Sansloy, a brother of Sansfoy and Sansjoy—developed characters in book 1—makes a perfunctory appearance in book 2 on the quite different scale of an aberration from Medina's golden mean.) Certain of the vices are explored fully enough to call for "places" of their own, such as the Cave of Mammon (2.7) or the House of Busirane (3.11–12). Finally, there are "digressive" episodes, such as the inset chronicle histories at the Castle of Alma and the river-god spousals of Thames and Medway, or the subplot adventures of Florimell, Marinell, and Belphoebe.

If some such repertoire of forms gives variety within a book, each book has, nevertheless, its own individual character. And each seems so distinct in emotional key as to compose with the others a sequence of complementary movements. The apocalyptic book 1 runs a vast gamut of spiritual extremities, from dark to light. But in book 2 we move to a world at once more schematically controlled and more sensuously vivid, with a tendency to frequent confrontations between its single (almost single-minded) hero and his many, minutely problematic emotions. Book 3's ardors are in the ordinary proportion of romance. Its characters disperse in ramifying adventures; but they are regathered by the centripetal tendency of book 4, through which accumulating groups of four friends (true or false) join by aggregation in a movement towards the great nuptial feast of Thames and Medway. Book 5 is Draconian in its severity. But book 6 is unbraced and vulnerable, its knights disarmed or dressed in shepherds' clothes. Throughout, the atmosphere alters in the interests of variety, and alters again for a balanced view of the wholeness of human experience.

Perhaps for the same reason, the emotional colorations change without any hard-edged divisions. They shade into one another with a subtlety and delicacy that is one of the chief marks of Spenser's art. He seems to achieve the effect partly by running stories and themes over to blur the divisions, by arranging trailers or anticipations of any change of mood, and by suturing in the overlaps with an astonishing fineness and obliquity. (Metrically this finds reflection in a system of liaison of rhyme between stanzas.) Thus, although *The Faerie Queen* is manneristically composite and complicated outwardly, as a reading experience it is not like that at all. Inwardly it moves with an almost baroque fluidity. Its wonderful transitions, for example, have none of the alienating abruptness of Ariosto's, which, as scholars have noted, go back to medieval formulas such as "Mes a tant

laisse li contes a parler de . . . et retorne a . . ." ("Now I stop telling the story of . . . and return to . . ."). Instead we move by a smooth, imperceptible progression from episode to episode, mode to mode, with even the explicit junctures, where these occur, accomplishing more than a mere narrative cut-and-join.

Thus, 3.6 begins with the geniture of Belphoebe and her twinship with Amoret—an inset Ovidian tale of Chrysogone provides the canto's first mythological treatment of generation, inside an *occupatio* (a pretended refusal to discuss):

It were a goodly story, to declare,
By what strange accident fair Chrysogone
Conceived these infants, and how them she bare,
(3.6.5)

The work then slides into a lost Cupid myth. This naturally leads to a burlesque quarrel between the distraught Venus and the at first censorious then relenting Diana, until their accord brings discovery of the twin births of Belphoebe and Amoret and arrangements for their separate fostering: a separation that implies an emotional polarity corresponding to that which exists between the traditionally opposed goddesses (3.6.11–28). Cupid has been found, divided or "unfolded" into two forms. Then an apparently casual transition takes us into the famous Garden of Adonis: "She brought her to her joyous Paradise, / Where most she wonces [stays], when she on earth does dwell." Besides introducing a second mythological treatment of generation, however, this stanza adds a psychological, individually sexual strand, by its personal confession:

Whether in Paphos, or Cytheron hill,
Or it in Gnidus be, I wot not well;
But well I wot by trial, that this same
All other pleasant places doth excel, . . .

In the Garden itself (30–50), the metaphysical, physical, and mythic elements interweave with formidable ease yet without ever seeming clever—suggesting, rather, Virgil's profundity of feeling and suggestion.

There wont fair Venus often to enjoy
Her dear Adonis' joyous company,
And reap sweet pleasure of the wanton boy;

There yet, some say, in secret he does lie,
Lappèd in flowers and precious spicery,
By her hid from the world, and from the skill
Of Stygian gods, which do her love envy;
But she her self, when ever that she will,
Possesseth him, and of his sweetness takes her fill.

And sooth it seems they say: for he may not
For ever die, and ever buried be
In baleful night, where all things are forgot;
All be he subject to mortality,
Yet is etern in mutability,
And by succession made perpetual,
Transformèd oft, and changèd diversely:
For him the father of all forms they call;
Therefore needs mote [must] he live, that living
　　gives to all.

　　　　　　　　　　　　　　　　(3.6.46–47)

The Garden is where an individual partici-
pates, through the act of sex, in making new life;
and where the relation of form and matter, of
permanence and change, declares itself. It is a
Christian-Platonic-Pythagorean vision of the
soul's vocation in a world of accident. At the
same time, the canto is full of Spenser's own
characteristic bittersweet cheerful melancholy.
Wicked Time destroys the Garden's goodly
things; but the pity of that cannot make it other
than a gloriously creative place. Time's scythe
mows, but Venus can still "reap sweet pleasure." The canto began with explanation of
Belphoebe's inherited qualities, which led,
through the confrontation of Venus and Diana,
to the Garden of Adonis. But Spenser leaves the
Garden for the story of Belphoebe's vulnerable
twin, Amoret (52–53), and then (by a more distant modulation) for that of the still more fearful
Florimell. We have moved from Belphoebe almost to her opposite, with hardly a break.

VII

THE movement of *The Faerie Queen* seems
fluid and unpredictable, almost like human experience. To get this realistic effect it must
avoid obvious regularities of the composite
parts. Consequently order, although everywhere discoverable, is everywhere hidden.
Thus, placement of the so-called core cantos

varies from book to book: 1.10, 4.10, and 6.10,
but 2.9 and 5.9. Yet the variation is not random
either, since it follows a number symbolism (the
core cantos in ninth place enshrine cardinal virtues, Temperance and Justice). Similarly, the
contents of books broadly follow the sequence
of the planetary week, with book 1 as the book
of Sol, book 2 as Luna, and so forth. Truth
(troth, faith), the subject of book·1, was a usual
association or meaning of the sun; just as Una's
lion attendant—the terrible aspect of truth—
would have been recognized as Sol's astrological
house. The planetary series is interrupted, however, when book 3 proves to be not a book of
Mars but of his feminine and wiser counterpart
Minerva (a cult image of Queen Elizabeth). The
overall narrative pattern of yearly quests shows
a similarly regular irregularity. Saint George's
mission against the dragon and Guyon's against
Acrasia lead us to expect one adventure per
book. But books 3 and 4 have between them
only one, Scudamour's. Again, most of the
books feature the titular patron of a virtue, sent
out from Gloriana's court. In book 3, however,
it is Britomart, not Scudamour, who defeats Busirane and frees Amoret; while book 4 has two
other heroes, Cambel and Triamond, who do
not belong to Gloriana's order of knighthood.
These variations can easily seem random and
confused. But they turn out to be governed by a
structural logic, related to Christian-Platonic or
Neoplatonic concepts such as the Triad. The latter not only informs many groupings of characters—Sansfoy, Sansjoy, Sansloy, for example—
but also a division, confirmed by the order of
publication, into three-book parts.

Another structural pattern that runs throughout is the arrangement of thematic images in ascending sequence, from evil, through less evil
(or mixed), to good. In book 6 the series is of
human "garlands" ranging from the cannibals
gathered round Serena, through the lusty shepherds and lovely lasses round Pastorella, to the
"hundred naked maidens lily white, / All ranged
in a ring" round the three Graces—who themselves encircle "another damsel," Spenser's own
love. The theme makes connection through the
common figure of a garland, whose oblatory
meaning becomes explicit in the primitive ritual
(6.8.39, 6.9.8, 6.10.12, and 6.10.14). In the same
way bad Venuses taking pleasure at the Bower

of Bliss and the House of Malecasta precede the good Venus enjoying the Garden of Adonis. And the pains of a cruel Cupid triumphing at the House of Busirane (3.11–12) goes before the painful sentence pronounced by the "wise" Cupid at 6.8.22–25. It is a law of Fairyland. The quests are always making gradual labyrinthine approaches, or ascents in Platonic fashion, from perverse and dark images towards the reality of virtues themselves. The virtues have to be composed, step by step, in a process of integration. It is a remarkably inclusive vision. At the Temple of Venus are held in concord not only love and hate, "brethren both of half the blood" (4.10.32), but Venus and Cupid, potentially, and the pleasure and pain of love.

It is Spenser's Christian Platonism, his conception of things as images of reality, that makes sense of dwelling on symbolic objects rather than on probable action. Certainly *The Faerie Queen* is pictorial in the extreme. When Joseph Spence read it to his aged mother she said that he "had been showing her a collection of pictures;" and Pope appreciatively concurred. Not all post-Victorian critics have cared for this picturesque quality. Some have felt quite superior to the naïveté of speaking pictures. But we should remember that in the Renaissance—even partly in Ruskin's time—pictures spoke conceptually and articulately. Whether or not our ancestors were also in closer touch with the images of the unconscious, they demonstrably used a conscious and conventional iconographical language. The adventure of the champion of temperance is full of emblems of that virtue, such as the bridle or collar, which appears in the "gorgeous barbs" of Guyon's horse Brigador (*briglia d'oro*), in the bridle put on Occasion's tongue, and perhaps in the elaborately described "silken camus lily white" worn by Belphoebe (Latin *camus*, "bridle, collar"; English *camis*, "tunic"). Belphoebe also wore

> a golden baldric, which forelay
> Athwart her snowy breast, and did divide
> Her dainty paps; which like young fruit in May
> Now little gan to swell, and being tied
> Through her thin weed their places only signified.
> (2.3.29)

The half-exposed bosom regularly emblemized true honor, so that an Elizabethan reader was prepared in advance to recognize the values latent in Belphoebe's confrontation with Braggadocchio and Trompart.

Spenser does not always give explanatory labels to such relatively simple iconography. And even when he seems explicit, as with the cruel hag Occasion, the labeling abstraction by no means exhausts the image's meaning. Literature dominated iconography, rather than the reverse: Spenser was forming images not yet in any handbook. His figure was not Occasion in general (who would have been a young girl), but a very specific Occasion, incorporating such additional features as the lameness of Poena (slow retribution). Possibly Spenser himself could not have identified the composite figure much more fully, in other terms than he has actually used. He was exploring psychological depths: the springs of impatience, the penalties of guilt. His emblematic pictures and hieroglyphs were not, after all, merely quaint, but a means to self-discovery. Having only a smattering of the language of emblem, our best approach is to meditate on the scene as a whole and to take in details of mood and appearance. We need to feel Occasion's intemperate readiness to blame—perhaps to guess at the suggestion of self-punishing remorse in the cruelty of her son Furor—before we know how to bring iconography to bear.

In a fiction that uses images as its words in this way, language is apt to be of secondary importance, at least compared with an epic such as *Paradise Lost*. I do not mean that *The Faerie Queen* is carelessly or flatly written. Its style can reach intensity when a grand theme calls for it—as in the description of

> Death with most grim and grisly visage seen,
> Yet is he nought but parting of the breath;
> Ne ought to see, but like a shade to ween [suppose],
> Unbodièd, unsouled, unheard, unseen.
> (7.7.46)

And it varies with every change of mode— lyrical, narrative, descriptive. But much of the time it makes little conscious impression on the casual reader. Like the clean window glass that you do not notice so long as you focus on a distant object, the language of *The Faerie Queen* is usually transparent. Every now and them comes a more noticeable stanza, such as the intricately eloquent, densely patterned, much quoted description of the Cave of Sleep (1.1.41). But such "opaqueness" is unrepresentative of a narrative style that mostly effaces itself. This shaven manner of the narrative allegory contrasts with the richer sonority of description sustained in the "core" cantos. There, epiphanies stand out with the dense force of language of a major ode. The disparity is of course deliberate. For the discriminating reader, indeed, this balance of plane surfaces and enriched areas offers one of the main pleasures of the poem.

Not that the diction is neutral or colorless, even in the narrative allegory. It has too marked a medieval tinge for that. Still, the notorious archaisms are fewer and less frequent than critics suggest: many stanzas have none, and others have only the token *ne* or *eke* of the poem's soon-familiar idiolect. On the other hand, there is a good deal more sly wordplay than used to be recognized. Sometimes Spenser draws on proverbial lore, which may provide the basis of a whole episode, in the manner of Langland or Nashe or Brueghel. But more often the wit takes the form of what Hazlitt called "an allegorical play upon words": a punning ambiguity, that is, with one meaning in the story and the other in the allegory; as at 6.9.5, where Calidore, who brought the faults of the court with him in his courtly nature, inquires after the Blatant Beast, "If such a beast they saw, which he had thither brought." Altogether the language, which owes much in this to Gavin Douglas, brilliantly compounds the high-flown and the vernacular.

VIII

I have left until now the problems of the allegory, since these have been exaggerated into unnecessary stumbling blocks. Victorian and Georgian critics were predisposed against what they saw as didactic and mechanical "naïve allegory." But Spenser's poem would now be generally exonerated from these charges. If its moral seems in any sense too bare, it is not in the sense of being crude or obvious. Besides, there is now more feeling for what was a dominant form of literature in the Middle Ages, and at least one of the most prominent in the Renais-

sance. Spenser, however, wrote a special sort of allegory, whose characterics should be distinguished. He himself called *The Faerie Queen* "a continued allegory, or dark conceit" and noticed "how doubtfully all allegories may be construed" (Letter to Ralegh).

Like much Elizabethan criticism, this calls for sympathetic interpretation. When he calls the allegory "continued," Spenser probably means that it is not merely local, but kept up by the author all through. In this his poem differs from, say, *Orlando Furioso*. Ariosto has occasional allegories, such as that of Logistilla; and he was freely *allegorized*, by such anti-intentionalists *de ses jours* as Fornari and Bononome. But Spenser wrote throughout what was meant allegorically or symbolically. Unlike the strange places and marvels of medieval romance (and, to a large extent, those in Ariosto), Spenser's are interpreted. In consequence they are brought into unity with the rest of the work. Thus, the improbably numerous foundlings in book 6 are not left as a matter of surprise and delightful wonder. Spenser makes it plain that the marvel, anything but arbitrary, is designed to explore various relations between natural inheritance and "nurture" (environmental influences). To the various structures of the *Orlando*, therefore, *The Faerie Queen* adds another, quite distinct.

Moreover, this extra strand is itself manifold. Unlike Bunyan's allegory (which has only one sphere of reference, the religious), Spenser's may be religious or moral or psychological or philosophical or political. Most often, perhaps, it is moral, setting out virtues and vices, or distinctions within virtues and vices, in the narrative mode by which ethics used to be understood. Lucifera and the Giant Orgoglio present different kinds of pride; the six knights of Malecasta six steps into lechery. Other figures, however, such as Pyrochles and Cymochles, or Elissa and Perissa, treat polarities of a more psychological order. In Shamefastness and Praisedesire, indeed, Spenser explores the springs of moral behavior in two contrasting temperamental dispositions. It is often observed, and rightly, that his psychological insights seldom issue in character studies. But we should recall that each book really studies a single "supercharacter," its hero, whose traits are the individual allegorical characters. (And the Letter to

Ralegh hints that Arthur himself composes a superhero from the hero parts of individual books.) Regarded in this light, Spenser's poem is seen to analyze psychological experience in unusual depth. Even so, some of his greatest passages tend in another direction altogether, belonging to a philosophical allegory enacted either by abstract personifications (Mutability) or by mythological figures (Adonis).

There is also, particularly in book 5, a political allegory, which many have found repellent in its severity. The iron man Talus with his flail seems uncomfortably proleptic of the harshest modern riot police. What is one to think, in particular, of Spenser's attitude to Ireland? As a patriot, he worked for the English oppressors. Yet he hated violence and loved peace and justice. Such an attitude wins few friends now. It has even been asserted, by Yeats and others, that Spenser hated the Irish. The fact remains that in his prose *View of the Present State of Ireland* Spenser attempted what few British and American writers have emulated: to understand the Irish. It does not do to forget the magnitude of the disorders or the weakness of government in Spenser's time.

The allegory, of course, often has multiple implications. Indeed, the same character may have a political or topical, as well as a moral, meaning. Artegall, for example, combines Sovereign Power, Justice, and Maleness-in-generation (not portrayed as a superior role) with Leicester, Essex, Grey, and perhaps other historical figures. Similarly, Belphoebe represents Queen Elizabeth, but also Virginality. But in approaching these "antique praises unto present persons fit" we must not be tempted into looking for a key. Such figures represent insights into life; they should not be reduced to system, but responded to with a correspondingly personal intuition.

This is true of all Spenser's allegories. You cannot be too subtle in interpreting them; but you can easily be subtle in the wrong way. Alertness is everything. In the Cave of Mammon episode, Guyon's refraining from combat with golden Disdain (who resembles "an huge Giant") has attracted ingenious explanations: Guyon is learning that martial heroism is not enough, et cetera. But the alert reader will sense that the supercilious hero has blundered. Per-

haps what prompts him is a remembered law of Fairyland, that Giants are for fighting (as witness Orgoglio, Argante, Ollyphant, Corflambo, the Giant with the Scales, Geryoneo, and others). Or perhaps he reflects that Mammon's advice to "abstain from perilous fight" is unlikely to be dependable. (Another law: evil figures give bad advice.) In any event, by not fighting, Guyon has gone disastrously wrong. His moral heroism has degenerated into mere aristocratic *sdegno*: he is literally reconciled to disdain; and he rejects the world because he feels superior to it. He may be doing the right thing, but for the wrong reason. A really wakeful reader will also see Spenser's joke, that all the time golden Disdain is really not aristocratic but a "villain." Such a point is a matter for the attention of the third ear. The laws of Fairyland are not those of deductive logic.

IX

No sooner has one drawn attention to the complicated manifold character of *The Faerie Queen* than the balance must be righted by affirming its simplicity. Mere formal complication seems almost irrelevant to Spenser's serious purpose: his sophisticated detachment from forms serves other than formal values. He uses any means that will illustrate the deepest truth of the matter. Hence his easy freedom with sources. Since he is more concerned with truth than with elegance or poetic success, great predecessors never intimidate him. He has had his own glimpse of life; and in the end it is for his unified vision that we read *The Faerie Queen*.

Spenser's reliance on chivalric values may appear to contradict what I have just written, and to make any very high seriousness impossible. How can we take seriously a knighthood that was already outgrown in the poet's own time—that he himself presents, indeed, in anachronistic terms? Well, a reinterpreted knighthood, offering ideals for courtiers and administrators, may have formed a part of Spenser's purpose. But it would be a mistake to think of this as merely an aspiration to some Indian summer of English chivalry. At the very least, the adventures are moral psychomachies. And their content is quite as much private as public. They continually press behind virtues to the growth of "the fresh bud of virtue," to the "sacred nursery / Of virtue" "deep within the mind," and even to "the root" of all virtue, in love (4 Proem 2). In Spenser, virtues, and especially symbols of virtue, are "secret" or "hidden" (1.11.36, 3.1.10, 2.8.20). We may conclude that the heroes' approaches to the "sacred virtue(s)" pursue quests of self-discovery. Moreover, the virtues themselves, when discovered, are numinous mysteries that may even be described as "resembling God" (5 Proem 10). In fine, the adventures go to form a greater self: to fashion a person.

At the deepest level, therefore, the poem's narrative paradigm must be discovery: the discovery that characterizes romance, rather than the conflict of epic. Of course there are many battles, and the frequency of revenge is conspicuous. But *The Faerie Queen* usually avoids any simple *enantiodromia* or war of contraries. Indeed, its most striking moral feature is reconciliation or transcendence of opposites. It pursues wholeness. Is it more antipapist or more Catholic? More devoted to pleasure or to virtue? Traditional or innovative? Such questions have only to be formulated for us to see their inappropriateness. Spenser combines the great antipodes—reason and emotion, sovereignty and equity, male and female—into a single larger world of integrated identity. Not a bad emblem of *The Faerie Queen* would be Dame Concord's tempering of the fearful siblings Love and Hate (4.10.32). Unquestionably such *coincidentia oppositorum*, or union of opposites, runs the danger of limitless abysses. Perhaps in consequence, it arouses disagreeable apprehensions in some. Indeed, dislike of *The Faerie Queen*, when it arises, may have much to do with this feature. To lovers of the poem, distaste for it seems incomprehensibly perverse—like a distaste for life. But (again like life) *The Faerie Queen* can be difficult, dark with shades of half-thought meanings. The Victorian critics may not have been far wrong in calling it dreamlike. Only, its dream analysis is more worthwhile than they cared to admit—and already expressed by Spenser in what is more alert meditation than languid fantasy.

One of the pervasive antinomies that *The Faerie Queen* attempts to combine is the one between order and change. That Spenser shared Mulcaster's and Camden's reverence for ancient tradition needs no argument. His feeling for the sanctity of civilized order finds continued and varied expression, in metaphysical celebrations, in happy ceremonies, and in praises of Queen Elizabeth, not to mention execrations of savagery and disordered license. Nevertheless, Spenser may also be the first English poet to have written favorably of change, in any sense even remotely like what we should now call historical. In the Cantos of Mutability, Nature dismisses, it is true, Dame Mutability's claim to cosmic supremacy. But she does so for a strange and subtle reason: namely, that all things indeed change, "But by their change their being do dilate [implement]." Mutability, which generations of poets had taken as a subject of complaint, was for Spenser something quite different: a creative process, almost a subject of encomium. Her witnesses form the grand procession of the parts of time that has offered inspiration to many subsequent poets, and that all would now concede to be a high point of Spenser's oeuvre. Moreover, it sums up a vision informing the entire poem, of nature in multifarious transformation.

I well consider all that ye have said,
And find that all things steadfastness do hate
And changèd be: yet being rightly weighed
They are not changèd from their first estate;
But by their change their being do dilate:
And turning to themselves at length again,
Do work their own perfection so by fate:
Then over them change doth not rule and reign;
But they reign over change, and do their states maintain.

Cease therefore daughter further to aspire,
And thee content thus to be ruled by me:
For thy decay thou seek'st by thy desire;
But time shall come that all shall changèd be,
And from thenceforth, none no more change shall see.
So was the Titaness put down and whist [silenced],
And Jove confirmed in his imperial see.
Then was that whole assembly quite dismissed,
And Nature's self did vanish, whither no man wist [knew].   (Cantos of Mutability, 7.58–59)

140

The Faerie Queen as a whole could be said to hymn creation in process, rather than created nature. It aspires to unifying change; and, by exploring far back into historical origins, ancient myths, causes of wrath, and the deepest relations of "cousin passions," it searches, beneath outward and partial metamorphoses, for the changes of heart that could release life's fullness.

The world of *The Faerie Queen* is never vague. It may seem unsearchably vast and uncertain in measurement; but it is emotionally sure and distinctive in atmosphere. This has something to do with the long epic similes, which, like Homer's, introduce ordinary domesticities, but which have also a crisp, concentrated particularity that is Spenser's own ("The watery southwind from the seaboard coast"). From time to time, too, precise sensible details come into the story itself. These would be striking but for their immediate rightness: Arthur's savage squire shook his oaken plant so sternly "That like an hazel wand, it quiverèd and quook"; Glauce "the drunken lamp down in the oil did steep."

In general, of course, Spenser's poem needs the unfeatured continuum of romance. This is usually, with him, a fortuitous Brocéliande-like forest, "a forest wide, / Whose hideous horror and sad trembling sound / Full grisly seemed." This dark verdure serves as an unassertive background, from which marvels stand out in highlight: a Rich Strand, perhaps, heaped with "the wealth of the east," or a castle with magical flames guarding its porch. But the symbolic environments themselves are as distinct as places of the mind can well be. They are varied decisively, with a sharp discrimination that will be inherited (at whatever removes) by Dickens and Stevenson, Borges and de la Mare. One of Spenser's forests or caves is not like another. Here the "surges hoar, / . . . 'gainst the craggy clifts did loudly roar"; there dolphins drew the chariot of sad Cymoent so smoothly "that their broad flaggy fins no foam did rear, / Ne bubbling roundel they behind them sent." (Spenser is almost always specific about weather, being the first English, although not the first British, poet to notice it much.) The House of Busirane, with, its grandeurs and longueurs; Malecasta's fun house; and the difficult but desirable Temple of Venus: these are all places we should recognize instantly. As in dream, the presence of place is intense:

That house's form within was rude and strong,
Like an huge cave, hewn out of rocky clift,
From whose rough vault the rugged breaches [fractures] hung,
Embossed with massy gold of glorious gift,
And with rich metal loaded every rift,
That heavy ruin they did seem to threat;
And over them Arachne high did lift
Her cunning web, and spread her subtle net,
Enwrappèd in foul smoke and clouds more black than jet.
(2.7.28)

Unlike the world of common dreams, however, Spenser's Fairyland combines emotional precision with intense lucidity. We breathe in it a purer air that imparts not only excitement to the intellect but vigor to all the faculties. Its impression is fresh; yet it has been formed by thought, long brooded, deeply meditated. Its places and landscapes are symbolic rather than allegorical in a schematic way. And if it is pondered sufficiently, it is discovered to have a profundity that justifies the stress in early criticism on Spenser's "deep conceit."

Such poetry has never been easy to locate on the map of Parnassus. *The Faerie Queen* contrasts, in this respect, with the work of the more fashionable Sidney, who can quite readily be related to the mannerist literary movement of his time. Spenser fits in nowhere. Neither classical nor romantic, neither medieval nor merely neo-Gothic, neither historical nor wholly imaginary, neither fanciful nor rationally intelligible, his visionary work awaits the understanding and the judgment of ages. It has already shown an astonishing capacity to speak to our own century. How inadequate, we are bound to think, and yet how splendid too, was the inscription put on Spenser's monument in Westminster Abbey, naming him "the prince of poets in his time."

SELECTED BIBLIOGRAPHY

I. BIBLIOGRAPHIES, ETC. C. G. Osgood, *A Concordance to the Poems* (Washington, D.C., 1915; repr. Gloucester, Mass., 1963); C. H. Whitman, *A Subject Index to the Poems* (New Haven, 1918; repr. New York, 1966); Frederic I. Carpenter, *A Reference Guide to Edmund Spenser* (Chicago, 1923), with supplement by D. F. Atkinson (Baltimore, 1937; repr. New York, 1967); F. R. Johnson, *A Critical Bibliography of the Works Printed Before 1700* (Baltimore, 1933; repr. London, 1966; Folcroft, Pa., 1969); *Spenser Newsletter*, vols. 1–5, University of Western Ontario (1970–1974), vols. 5– , University of Massachusetts, Amherst and Holyoke Community College (1974–   ). R. M. Cummings, *Spenser: The Critical Heritage* (London, 1971); W. F. McNeir and F. Provost, *Edmund Spenser: An Annotated Bibliography 1937–1972* (Pittsburgh, 1975).

II. COLLECTED WORKS. *The Faerie Queen: The Shepherd's Calendar: Together With the Other Works of England's Arch-Poet, Edm. Spenser: Collected Into One Volume, and Carefully Corrected* (1611 or 1617), folio eds. of the collected poetry, consisting of seven separate sections independently printed at various dates, each with two main states, issued as single vol. bearing the date 1611 or 1617; *The Works of That Famous English Poet, Mr Edmond Spenser* (1679), the third folio but the first collected ed. of the poetry and prose, with glossary; J. Hughes, ed., *The Works of Mr. Edmund Spenser*, 6 vols. (1715), with glossary and essays; H. J. Todd, ed., *The Works*, 8 vols. (1805), a variorum ed., reviewed by Walter Scott, in *The Edinburgh Review*, 7 (1805); R. E. N. Dodge, ed., *The Poetical Works* (Boston, 1908), sparsely annotated; J. C. Smith and E. de Sélincourt, eds., *The Poetical Works*, 3 vols. (Oxford, 1909–1910), Oxford English Texts series, with textual and bibliographic notes; J. C. Smith and E. de Sélincourt, eds., *The Poetical Works* (London, 1912), Oxford Standard Authors ed., with textual notes, glossary, and critical intro. by E. de Sélincourt, contains the Spenser-Harvey letters, first printed as *Three proper, and witty, familiar Letters* (1580); W. L. Renwick, ed., *The Complete Works of Edmund Spenser*, 4 vols. (London, 1928–1934), omits *The Faerie Queen*, but includes all the other poems; E. Greenlaw *et al.*, eds., *The Works: A Variorum Edition*, 9 vols. (Baltimore, 1932–1949; repr. with index vol. by C. G. Osgood, 1957; and with A. C. Judson, *Life of Spenser*, in 11 vols., 1966).

III. SEPARATE WORKS IN VERSE. S. J. van der Noodt, *A Theatre for Worldlings* (1569), containing "Epigrams" and "Sonnets" trans. by Spenser, rev. in *Complaints* (1591); *The Shepherd's Calendar. Containing Twelve Eclogues Proportionable to the Twelve Months* (1579; repr. 1581, 1586, 1591, 1597; subsequently in the folio eds., and in 1653, with Latin trans.), includes preface and glosses by "E. K."; *The Faerie Queen* (1590), containing books 1–3 and Letter to Ralegh; 2nd ed., rev. (1596); *Daphnaida. An Elegy Upon the Death of . . . Douglas Howard . . . Wife of Arthur Gorges* (1591), repr. with the *Hymns* (1596); *Complaints. Containing Sundry Small Poems of the World's Vanity* (1591), including *The Ruins of Time, The Tears of the Muses, Virgil's Gnat, Prosopopoia: or Mother Hubberd's Tale, Ruins of Rome: by Bellay, Muiopotmos: Or the Fate of the Butterfly, Visions of the World's Vanity, The Visions of Bellay,* and *The Visions of Petrarch; Colin Clout's Come Home Again* (1595), containing the title poem, *Astrophel. A Pastoral Elegy Upon the Death of . . . Sidney* (including *The Doleful Lay of Clorinda* without a separate title), and other elegies, one by L[odovick] B[ryskett]; *Amoretti and Epithalamion* (1595); *Prothalamion: Or: A Spousal Verse* (1596); *Four Hymns* (1596), containing *An Hymn in Honour of Love, An Hymn in Honour of Beauty, An Hymn of Heavenly Love,* and *An Hymn of Heavenly Beauty; The Second Part of the Faerie Queen* (1596), containing books 4–6 (more copies printed than of the 1596 ed. of the first part), facs. of both parts of 1596 ed., G. Hough, ed., 2 vols. (London, 1976), folio ed. of *The Faerie Queen* (1609), first to include the Cantos of Mutability; J. Upton, ed., *The Faerie Queen. A New Edition With a Glossary, and Notes Explanatory and Critical*, 2 vols. (1758), a great and classic ed.; E. Welsford, ed., *Spenser: Four Hymns: Epithalamion* (Oxford, 1967); R. Beum, ed., *Epithalamion* (Columbus, Ohio, 1968); A. C. Hamilton, ed., *The Faerie Queen* (London, 1977), Longman Annotated Poets series; T. P. Roche, ed., *The Faerie Queen* (in press).

IV. SELECTED VERSE. C. S. Lewis, with essay "Edmund Spenser, 1552–1599," in G. B. Harrison, ed., *Major British Writers*, 2 vols. (New York, 1954), repr. in C. S. Lewis, *Studies in Medieval and Renaissance Literature* (Cambridge, 1966); P. C. Bayley, ed., *Spenser: "The Faerie Queen,"* book 2 (London, 1965); R. Kellogg and O. Steele, eds., *Books 1 and 2 of "The Faerie Queen": The Mutability Cantos and Selections From the Minor Poetry* (New York, 1965); P. C. Bayley, *Spenser: "The Faerie Queen,"* book 1 (London, 1966); A. C. Hamilton, ed., *Edmund Spenser: Selected Poetry* (New York, 1966); S. P. Zitner, *The Mutability Cantos* (London, 1968); A. K. Hieatt and C. Hieatt, eds., *Edmund Spenser: Selected Poetry* (New York, 1970); D. Brooks-Davies, ed., *Edmund Spenser: "The Faerie Queen": A Selection* (London, 1976).

V. CRITICAL AND BIOGRAPHICAL STUDIES. T. Warton, *Observations on "The Faerie Queen"* (London, 1754; enl., 1762; 2nd ed., repr. New York, 1968, 1969; Farnborough, 1969); R. Hurd, *Letters on Chivalry and Romance* (London, 1762), edited by E. J. Morley (1911); W. Hazlitt, *Lectures on the English Poets* (London, 1818); J. Ruskin, *The Stones of Venice*, vol. II (London, 1853), chs. 7, 8; J. Ruskin, *Modern Painters,* vol. III (London, 1856), ch. 8; James Russell Lowell, "Spenser," in *The Writings of James Russell Lowell*, IV (1892); E. Legouis, *Edmond Spenser* (Paris, 1923; rev. ed., Paris, 1956), English trans. (London, 1926); W. L. Renwick, *Edmund Spenser: An Essay on Renaissance Poetry* (London, 1925; repr. London, 1965); P. Henley, *Spenser in Ireland* (Cork, 1928; repr. New York, 1969); M. Y. Hughes, *Virgil and Spenser* (Berkeley, Calif., 1929; repr. Port Washington, N.Y., 1969); H. S. V. Jones, *A Spenser Handbook* (New York, 1930; repr. London, 1947); E. Greenlaw, *Studies in Spenser's Historical Allegory* (Baltimore, 1932; repr. New York, 1967); H. G. Lotspeich, *Classical Mythology in the Poetry of Edmund Spenser* (Princeton, 1932; repr. 1965); J. Spens, *Spenser's Faerie Queen: An Interpretation* (London, 1934; repr. New York, 1967); T. M. Raysor, ed., *Coleridge's Miscellaneous Criticism* (London, 1936); C. S. Lewis, *The Allegory of Love* (London, 1936); I. E. Rathborne, *The Meaning of Spenser's Fairyland* (New York, 1937; repr. New York, 1965); J. W. Bennett, *The Evolution of "The Faerie Queen"* (Chicago, 1942; repr. New York, 1960); V. K. Whitaker, *The Religious Basis of Spenser's Thought* (Stanford, Calif., 1950; repr. New York, 1966); H. Smith, *Elizabethan Poetry: A Study in Convention, Meaning and Expression* (Cambridge, Mass., 1952; repr. Ann Arbor, 1968); C. S. Lewis, *English Literature in the Sixteenth Century Excluding Drama* (Oxford, 1954); J. Arthos, *On the Poetry of Spenser and the Form of Romances* (London, 1956; repr. New York, 1970); H. Berger, *The Allegorical Temper. Vision and Reality in Book 2 of Spenser's "Faerie Queen"* (New Haven, 1957; repr. Hamden, Conn., 1967); W. R. Mueller, *Spenser's Critics: Changing Currents in Literary Taste* (Syracuse, N.Y., 1959), criticism of The Faerie Queen from 1715 to 1949, with intro.; S. T. Coleridge, *Shakespearian Criticism*, T. M. Raysor, ed., 2 vols. (London, 1960); A. K. Hieatt, *Short Time's Endless Monument. The Symbolism of the Numbers in Edmund Spenser's "Epithalamion"* (New York, 1960; repr. Port Washington, N.Y., 1972); R. Ellrodt, *Neoplatonism in the Poetry of Spenser* (Geneva, 1960), reviewed by C. S. Lewis, in *Études anglaises*, 14 (1961); A. W. Satterthwaite, *Spenser, Ronsard and Du Bellay* (Princeton, 1960); A. C. Hamilton, *The Structure of Allegory in "The Faerie Queen"* (Oxford, 1961); P. E. McLane, *Spenser's "Shepherd's Calendar": A Study in Elizabethan Allegory* (Notre Dame, Ind., 1961); G. Hough, *A Preface to "The Faerie Queen"* (London, 1962); T. Greene, *The Descent From Heaven: A Study in Epic Continuity* (New Haven, 1963); N. Frye, *Fables of Identity: Studies in Poetic Mythology* (New York, 1963); W. Nelson, *The Poetry of Edmund Spenser: A Study* (New York, 1963); T. P. Roche, *The Kindly Flame: A Study of the Third and Fourth Books of Spenser's "Faerie Queen"* (Princeton, 1964); A. Fowler, *Spenser and the Numbers of Time* (London–New York, 1964); A. B. Giamatti, *The Earthly Paradise and the Renaissance Epic* (Princeton, 1966); C. S. Lewis, *Spenser's Images of Life*, A. Fowler, ed. (Cambridge, 1967); E. A. F. Watson, *Spenser* (London, 1967); P. J. Alpers, *The Poetry of "The Faerie Queen"* (Princeton, 1967); T. K. Dunseath, *Spenser's Allegory of Justice in Book Five of "The Faerie Queen"* (Princeton, 1968); R. Sale, *Reading Spenser: An Introduction to "The Faerie Queen"* (New York, 1968); H. Maclean, ed., *Edmund Spenser's Poetry: Authoritative Texts; Criticism* (New York, 1968), texts and selections from 1590 to 1963; K. W. Grandsen, *A Critical Commentary on Spenser's "Faerie Queen"* (London, 1969); J. Aptekar, *Icons of Justice: Iconography and Thematic Imagery in Book 5 of "The Faerie Queen"* (New York, 1969); S. Meyer, *An Interpretation of Edmund Spenser's "Colin Clout"* (Notre Dame, Ind., 1969); M. Evans, *Spenser's Anatomy of Heroism: A Commentary on "The Faerie Queen"* (Cambridge, 1970); R. Freeman, *"The Faerie Queen": A Companion for Readers* (Berkeley, Calif., 1970); P. Bayley, *Edmund Spenser: Prince of Poets* (London, 1971); A. Fletcher, *The Prophetic Moment: An Essay on Spenser* (Chicago–London, 1971); J. E. Hankins, *Source and Meaning in Spenser's Allegory: A Study of "The Faerie Queen"* (Oxford, 1971); H. Tonkin, *Spenser's Courteous Pastoral: Book Six of "The Faerie Queen"* (Oxford, 1972); J. B. Bender, *Spenser and Literary Pictorialism* (Princeton, 1972); P. Cullen, *Infernal Triad: The Flesh, the World, and the Devil in Spenser and Milton* (Princeton, 1974); A. Fowler, *Conceitful Thought: The Interpretation of English Renaissance Poems* (Edinburgh, 1975); A. B. Giamatti, *Play of Double Senses: Spenser's "Faerie Queen"* (Englewood Cliffs, N.J., 1975); A. K. Hieatt, *Chaucer: Spenser: Milton: Mythopoeic Continuities and Transformations* (Montreal–London, 1975); M. Rose, *Spenser's Art. A Companion to Book 1 of "The Faerie Queen"* (Cambridge, Mass., 1975); I. G. MacCaffrey, *Spenser's Allegory: The Anatomy of Imagination* (Princeton, 1976); J. Nohrnberg, *The Analogy of "The Faerie Queen"* (Princeton, 1976).

VI. ARTICLES. W. R. Mueller and D. C. Allen, eds., *That Sovereign Light. Essays in Honor of Edmund Spenser, 1552–1952* (Baltimore, 1952; repr. New York, 1967); D. C. Allen, "The March Eclogue of *The Shepherd's Calendar*" and "*Muiopotmos*," in *Image and Meaning, Metaphoric Traditions in Renaissance Poetry* (Baltimore, 1960; rev. 1968); W. Nelson, ed., *Form and Convention in the Poetry of Edmund Spenser* (New York, 1961), Selected Papers From the English Institute; H. Berger, ed., *Spenser: A Collection of Critical Essays* (Englewood Cliffs, N.J., 1968); R. R. Elliott, ed., *The Prince of Poets: Essays on Edmund Spenser* (New York, 1968); A. Fowler, ed., *Silent Poetry: Essays in Numerological Analysis* (London–New

York, 1970), contains M. Baybak *et al.*, "Placement 'in the middest', in *The Faerie Queen*" and A. Dunlop, "The Unity of Spenser's *Amoretti*"; Editors of the *Journal of English Literary History, Critical Essays on Spenser From ELH* (Baltimore, 1970); J. F. Kermode, *Shakespeare, Spenser, Donne: Renaissance Essays* (London–New York, 1971); A. C. Hamilton, ed., *Es-sential Articles for the Study of Edmund Spenser* (Hamden, Conn., 1972); J. M. Kennedy and J. A. Reither, eds., *A Theatre for Spenserians: Papers of the International Spenser Colloquium, Fredericton, 1969* (Toronto, 1973); P. Bayley, ed., *Spenser: "The Faerie Queen"* (London, 1977).

SIR WALTER RALEGH

(ca.1554-1618)

Agnes M. C. Latham

SIR Walter Ralegh (or Raleigh) is valued above all as a man of action. His intellectual and literary gifts were an added ornament, proper to the Renaissance concept of a fully developed personality. Conversely, his many and varied occupations as soldier, seaman, courtier, and explorer seem to have increased his stature as a man of letters. His writings were almost always a by-product of his active life, designed to recommend his projects, to call attention to their success or to excuse their failure. He wrote because he had something he very urgently wanted to say, and this intimate personal urgency is one of the dominant characteristics of his work. It is reflected in the poignant, melancholy rhythms of *The History of the World,* in the passionate disarray of his verse, and equally in the direct, near-colloquial narrative of *The Last Fight of the Revenge* and *The Discovery of Guiana.* He never used fine writing for its own sake but he rose to meet what seemed to him a great occasion. Because he was living a full life in an expanding world he often met with great occasions. Some critics contend that he manufactured them—that he used his literary gifts to heighten any difficulties he encountered and to distort the truth in his own interest. Nobody denies him imagination, but it is perhaps true that he lacked judgment.

Walter Ralegh was born at Hayes Barton, Devonshire, in 1554, a younger son of a Devonshire gentleman, with his own way to make in the world, backed by a host of West Country kinsfolk who were doing the same thing. As a young man he fought on the Protestant side in the French wars of religion and in the Desmond rebellion in Ireland. When he was not fighting he spent some time in residence at Oriel College, Oxford, and at the Inns of Court, in London. All the time his eyes were fixed upon court favor, the highest prize that any fortune hunter could possibly hope to win, and by 1580 he had made it his. He became first favorite of the queen. That same vitality and vigor, charm and intelligence, that personal urgency which still survives in his written work, must have had twice the force when embodied in the man himself. Elizabeth could not resist it.

He flourished in her grace, but it was a full-time occupation, and personal adventure was for the moment in abeyance. In 1592 his fortunes took a spectacular turn for the worse. It was discovered that he had secretly married one of the queen's maids of honor, Elizabeth Throckmorton, a treachery his royal mistress could not forgive. The young earl of Essex, who had been disputing with him for the queen's affection, was there to fill his place. Ralegh was left to strive for distinction in the war at sea, taking part in maritime expeditions against Spain and leading a voyage of exploration to South America. He hoped to found an English colony in Guiana to be the nucleus of an overseas empire. As reigning favorite, arrogant and acquisitive (he had very expensive tastes, founding colonies being one of them), he had been far from popular. After his fall from favor he could be openly abused and derided. He was suspected of engineering the downfall of Essex, but that rash young nobleman suffered more from the encouragement of his friends than from the machinations of his rival.

When, in 1603, the old queen died and James VI of Scotland became James I of England, Ralegh was marked for destruction. The king was content to accept the popular estimate, enhanced by a deliberate whispering campaign in high circles. Before long Ralegh was charged with complicity in a plot to overthrow the king, make peace with Spain, and exact tolerance for

Roman Catholics. The nature and extent of his complicity in these ill-organized projects has never been made clear, but they do not seem such as would appeal to him. It was wholly to his advantage to be loyal and serviceable to the new king. Unhappily, he had by this time become alienated from his old friend and patron, Robert Cecil, who could still make or break him, and who chose the second. He may genuinely have feared him as a rival or simply used his disgrace as a stepping-stone to power. In spite of a superb defense, Ralegh was convicted upon the written evidence of one man. King James accorded him a last-minute reprieve and confined him for thirteen years in the Tower, while he made peace overtures to Spain in his own good time.

The new policy of appeasement was not too well liked. There were those who thought that Elizabeth's long struggle with Philip II of Spain should end in total victory rather than in a negotiated peace. Subjected to increasing pressure, James in 1616 agreed to release though not to pardon his prisoner, who for some time had been offering to open a gold mine in Guiana without provoking hostilities with Spain. No mine was found, and the English destroyed a Spanish outpost that lay in their way. Ralegh's young son was shot dead in the skirmish.

Ralegh himself had nearly died of a tropical fever during the voyage and had stayed at Trinidad. His lieutenant, Lawrence Keymis, led the prospectors inland. On his return, Ralegh denounced him for not finding the mine, whereupon Keymis retired to his cabin and killed himself. Ralegh returned empty-handed to an England that was deeply curious about the venture and not wholly unsympathetic. His defense of his proceedings was eagerly read. His letters recounting the disasters of the voyage were copied and passed from hand to hand, together with the verses he was said to have written on the fly-leaf of his Bible the night before he was beheaded. For James did not spare him, and his death took on the air of martyrdom, or at any rate of tragedy.

He appealed to the middle seventeenth century as a victim of Stuart tyranny. They saw him as anti-Spanish, anti-Catholic, and even anti-royalist, a witness in *The Discovery of Guiana* to England's colonial future and in *The History of* *the World* to a divine providence guiding events. Thus, in a way that would have amazed contemporaries, accustomed to hearing him called "damnable atheist" and "mischievous Machiavel," he became a hero. A small sheaf of minor works circulated as *The Remains of Sir Walter Raleigh*. Modern research has inevitably modified the picture. Sir Julian Corbett has queried his naval expertise. S. R. Gardiner is convinced of his guilt in 1618, and has some damaging documents to show relating to the last Guiana voyage. Mario Praz finds his policy Machiavellian, and Ralegh is credited with presiding over a club of freethinkers called the School of Night. Nothing has dimmed the vivid colors in which he is usually presented. The many biographies that attempt to unravel the riddle of his personality testify to its enduring fascination.

POET

RALEGH's poetry has survived only in stray pieces, sifted from the anthologies and commonplace books of the time, with subscriptions of dubious value. He preserved his anonymity more jealously than most Elizabethans, anxious as they were to appear gentlemen, with minds above money. He had more reason. The lady he adored was the greatest lady in the land. Much poetry was addressed to the queen in her public character. Ralegh addressed her personally and privately in the character of platonic mistress. This was not matter for the book stalls. His poetic reputation was confined to a select circle. It included George Puttenham, who had some firsthand knowledge of his verses, since he quotes from them in his *Art of English Poetry* (1589), describing Ralegh's vein as "most lofty, insolent and passionate." Spenser was also among the privileged few. In 1589 Ralegh visited him in Ireland and listened to readings from unpublished verse, after when he read in exchange some of his own, It was, says Spenser,

all a lamentable lay,
Of great unkindness, and of usage hard,
Of Cynthia the Ladie of the sea,
Which from her presence faultless him debarr'd . . .

146

Right well he sure did plain:
That could great Cynthia's sore displeasure break,
And move to take him to her grace again.
(*Colin Clouts Come Home Againe*, 1595)

The characters of Timias and Belphoebe, the maiden-huntress whom he loves but can never possess, are Spenser's idealized picture, in the third book of *The Faerie Queene*, of Ralegh and Elizabeth. He gives the story a happy ending, with Timias forgiven for having looked in the direction of another lady, and it would appear that in 1589 Ralegh, who had retired to Ireland in temporary disfavor, did indeed soothe the queen's vexation with some plaintive verses which have not survived outside Spenser's description of them. In 1592 there came the rift that verses could not heal—his marriage. It is possible to sympathize with both sides. He was a man approaching forty who wanted a home and children, the queen a woman of sixty, burdened with the crown of England, who felt that she had been fooled with sweet words. Ralegh tried to heal the wound, as he had before, with more words. Among the Cecil papers at Hatfield House, there is a manuscript fragment of some five hundred lines in his hand entitled "The Eleventh and Twelfth Books of the Ocean to Cynthia." Presumably he hoped that his friend Sir Robert Cecil might find occasion to show them to the queen and that he could perform again the feat of 1589. It was a far-fetched hope and it failed. If the verses seem inordinately passionate, it is worth reflecting how very much Ralegh lost when he lost the queen's regard.

The Hatfield fragments remain almost the only undoubted specimens of Ralegh's verse. The title suggests that they are a continuation of the "lamentable lay" known to Spenser, though it is difficult to imagine how ten earlier books could have been filled with matter so abstract. There is no narrative thread. The lines display only a perpetual flux and reflux of contrary feeling, as the poet remembers happier days and then recalls the painful present, only to deny the reality of present pain and grief in the contemplation of an eternity of beauty to which he must needs respond with an undying affection. Sensual love and sensual beauty, which are ephemeral, are strongly contrasted with their opposites:

And though strong reason hold before mine eyes
The images and forms of worlds past
Teaching the cause why all those flames that rise
From forms external, can no longer last

Than that those seeming beauties hold in prime,
Love's ground, his essence, and his empery,
All slaves to age, and vassals unto time,
Of which repentance writes the tragedy;

But this, my heart's desire could not conceive,
Whose love outflew the fastest flying time;
A beauty that can easily deceive
Th'arrest of years, and creeping age outclimb,

A spring of beauties which time ripeth not
Time that but works on frail mortality,
A sweetness which woe's wrongs outwipeth not,
Whom love hath chose for his divinity,

A vestal fire that burns but never wasteth,
That loseth naught by giving light to all,
That endless shines eachwhere, and endless lasteth,
Blossoms of pride that can nor fade nor fall.

In spite of its vague and transcendental manner the poem plainly relates to the current situation. It tells of "the tokens hung on breast and kindly worn," the showers of grace

Which now to others do their sweetness send . . .
Filling their barns with grain and towers with treasure,

and how, when the writer attempted

To seek new worlds, for gold, for praise, for glory,
To try desire, to try love severed far,
When I was gone she sent her memory
More strong than were ten thousand ships of war

To call me back, to leave great honour's thought,
To leave my friends, my fortune, my attempt
To leave the purpose I so long had sought . . .

The last book, "Entreating of Sorrow," breaks off in the middle of a line; and the fragment as a whole, though it is copied in a fair hand, is disorderly, reflecting what is perhaps an intentionally assumed desperation. The writer would like the reader to think that he is half-crazy and that his lines are something overheard rather than formally stated. They have a cloudy mag-

147

nificence and power but along with it a curious limpness. The poet seems to be inviting the emotion to take him where it will and attempts little control. C. S. Lewis speaks of "the monotony, the insanity, and the rich, dark colours of an obsessive despair." Metrically the verse is extremely fluent. There is a vaguely pastoral framework, perhaps continuing something in earlier books, much imagery of trees and fruit and corn and flowers, and some bold similes.

The lax construction and the absence of anything resembling climax are not characteristic of Ralegh's writing. His manner in lyrics tends to be terse, pointed, and epigrammatic. An instance is "Conceit Begotten by the Eyes," in which he treats his favorite theme of ephemeral passion:

> As ships in ports desired are drowned,
> As fruit once ripe, then falls to ground,
> As flies that seek for flames, are brought
> To cinders by the flames they sought:
> So fond Desire when it attains
> The life expires, the woe remains.

A poem that is notable for its abrupt, contemptuous rhythms is "The Lie," in which he savagely reveals the corruptions of society and forces upon it again and again the ultimate insult of "the lie."

> Go soul, the body's guest,
>   Upon a thankless errand,
> Fear not to touch the best,
>   The truth shall be thy warrant;
> Go, since I needs must die
> And give the world the lie.

The tradition that he was the author of this not very typical poem is possibly a tribute to his personality, his supposed disrespect for established sanctities. It is the kind of poem people could imagine him writing. A similar tradition assigns to him a much stranger poem, "The Passionate Man's Pilgrimage," in which the speaker is about to be beheaded and imagines his journey to a better land, where justice is not corrupt,

> For there Christ is the King's Atturney:
>   Who pleads for all without degrees
>   And he hath angels, but no fees.

If it is his, it must represent his feelings when in 1603 he awaited the headsman's ax and reflected upon the injustice and brutality of his trial. Where "The Lie" shocks with its matter, this poem shocks by its manner, the irregular verse form, the odd juxtaposition of legal terms and eschatology, the way the writer abandons himself in a kind of trance to chance rhythms and word associations:

> And by the happy blissful way
> More peaceful pilgrims I shall see,
> That have shook off their gowns of clay,
> And go apparelled fresh like me.
> I'll bring them first
> To slake their thirst,
> And then to taste those nectar suckets
> At the clear wells
> Where sweetness dwells,
> Drawn up by saints in crystal buckets.

It is hard to judge poetry written under stress, which may not be characteristic of the author's normal manner. One of the interesting things about Ralegh's verse is the number of times he seems to be writing under the pressure of strong emotion, with a rather strange abandon. An instance, close in both matter and manner to the last books of "Cynthia," is the little colloquy he devised upon the basis of the ballad of Walsingham:

> She hath left me here all alone,
>   All alone as unknown,
> Who sometimes did me lead with herself,
>   And me loved as her own.

The verses that he wrote in 1618, in expectation of death, are in another category, completely controlled. This time his sentence came as no surprise to him, and he met it with great gallantry. The verses were just one gesture among many. Sympathizers, who made endless copies of them, might not have been so much impressed had they realized that he was recalling a stanza of an earlier poem, to which he added a staid and devout couplet:

> Even such is time which takes in trust
> Our youth, our joys, and all we have,
> And pays us but with age and dust:
> Who in the dark and silent grave

When we have wandered all our ways
Shuts up the story of our days.
And from which earth and grave and dust
The Lord shall raise me up I trust.

The earlier piece lamented the passing of youth and beauty and sensuous delight and offered no comfort for it. It is a not uncommon mood with Ralegh, and is displayed perfectly in his answer to Marlowe's "Passionate Shepherd":

Time drives the flocks from field to fold,
When rivers rage, and rocks grow cold,
And Philomel becometh dumb,
The rest complain of cares to come.

The flowers do fade, and wanton fields
To wayward winter reckoning yields,
A honey tongue, a heart of gall,
Is fancy's spring, but sorrow's fall.

Too little of his poetry has survived for it to be easy to make any general assessment of it, to trace influences or suggest sources. It changes before the reader's eyes from the stilted angry couplets prefaced to Gascoigne's satire, *The Steel Glass*, in 1576, through the smoothness of "Nature That Washt Her Hands in Milk" and the terseness of "Conceit Begotten by the Eyes," to the turbulence of "The Books of the Ocean's Love to Cynthia" and the startling free associations of "The Passionate Man's Pilgrimage," to the grave serenity of "Even Such is Time." The one quality these pieces have in common is their disillusion. Contemporaries stress their sweetness. To Spenser, Ralegh's verse was "honied" and "with nectar sprinkled." It has in addition qualities of violence and of concentrated scorn, and a note of deep melancholy. Tucker Brooke has described it as "the froth that rises where unplumbed waters break on adamant."

SEAMAN

THE problem of establishing a reliable canon affects Ralegh's prose as well as his poetry. It has too long been taken for granted that all the pieces collected and published under his name

in the mid-seventeenth century were his. These doubts, however, do not arise in regard to his three best-known works, *The Last Fight of the Revenge, The Discovery of Guiana*, and *The History of the World*.

The first two are propaganda pieces. Ralegh was early convinced that England, threatened by the might of Catholic Spain, should not defend itself by sending reluctant recruits to fight land battles in France, Ireland, and the Low Countries, but should open a naval offensive concentrated upon cutting Spanish trade routes to the New World. It was not to be expected that the queen and her more conservative ministers would have much grasp of advanced naval strategy. Even today historians contend that England's first line of defense was the Continental coast, and that it would have been most ill-advised to exchange the European land theater for the experimental hazards of the Atlantic. Nonetheless Elizabeth was not averse to a supplementary policy of naval pressure, the more so because the seamen could pay themselves out of the profits of their privateering. Her Majesty, Ralegh complained long after, "did all by halves."

In 1591, Lord Thomas Howard was lying in wait at the Azores for the Spanish treasure fleet, which had been forced for fear of English commerce raiders to winter at Havana. He was watering and cleaning his ships when he was surprised by an armada from Spain, a predictable retort to English depredations. The largest ship in Howard's squadron, the *Revenge*, was commanded by Ralegh's Cornish cousin, Sir Richard Grenville. Grenville was the last to get away, and finding himself cut off from his commander he elected to sail through the middle of the Spanish fleet with all his guns blazing rather than to turn and run before the wind. To run would have been an entirely proper naval maneuver in no way parallel to "running" in a land battle. Grenville, always something of a fire-eater, preferred the other course and after a prolonged battle against spectacular odds lost the queen's best ship.

Ralegh's pamphlet, published anonymously, followed so promptly upon the action that he was still ignorant of the fact that Grenville had died of his wounds and had been buried at sea. The pamphlet was called *A Report of the Truth of the Fight About the Iles of Açores This Last Summer, Betwixt the Revenge One of Her Majesties Shippes and an Armada of the King of Spaine*, but is generally known as *The Last Fight of the Revenge at Sea*. Hakluyt reprinted it in his *Voyages* in 1598 and acknowledged Ralegh as the author. It would be natural to think that he was writing specifically in defense of his cousin but the text does not bear this out. Though Grenville, with great skill and plausibility, is transformed from a hothead into a hero, Ralegh's main concern is with the honor of England, the morale of its seamen, and the importance of the war at sea. Whoever commanded the *Revenge* (for a time he was hoping to command it himself), Ralegh would have made the same case with the same urgency.

In the pamphlet, he is not expert yet in the handling of prose. His sentences are often top-heavy and repetitive, but he is already a master of the telling phrase and gives a very strong sense of firsthand participation in the events he is describing. Through the incidents he selects and the emphasis he lays on them, he contrives to impose an epic pattern upon what might in hostile hands have been a sorry tale of the loss of a capital ship, elevating it, as Bacon puts it, "even to the height of an heroical fable." A plainness and directness in the writing, together with a convincing show of impartiality and fair-mindedness (except of course toward the enemy) give the narrative great power. All that can be objected against Grenville is in fact stated, but the reader responds in spite of it to the gallantry of the unequal encounter. Grenville need not have exposed his ship:

The other course had been the better, and might right well have answered in so great an impossibility of prevailing. Notwithstanding, out of the greatness of his mind, he could not be persuaded.

Thereafter the battle is described in a narrative calculated to make a "pure navy" man wince. Grenville had willfully exchanged the new strategy of long-range gunnery and maneuverable ships for a hand-to-hand encounter through the night—exactly the kind of fighting for which the Spaniards were equipped. Nonetheless, he held them off for an astonishingly long time, and Ralegh's rhetoric is equal to his theme. It is a piece of brilliant journalism:

But as the day increased, so our men decreased: and as the light grew more, by so much more grew our discomforts. For none appeared in sight but enemies, saving one small ship called the *Pilgrim*, commanded by Jacob Whiddon, who hovered all night to see the success; but in the morning bearing with the *Revenge*, was hunted like a hare among many ravenous hounds, but escaped. All the powder of the *Revenge* to the last barrel was now spent, all her pikes broken, forty of her best men slain, and the most part of the rest hurt. In the beginning of the fight she had but one hundred free from sickness, and four score and ten sick, laid in hold upon the ballast. A small troop to man such a ship, and a weak garrison to resist so mighty an army. By those hundred all was sustained, the volleys, boardings and enterings of fifteen ships of war besides those which beat her at large.

The statement that the ammunition was exhausted does not tally with the last phase of the story, in which the survivors successfully bargained for their lives in exchange for the ship, after locking the master gunner in his own gunroom lest he should obey Sir Richard's orders to sink the ship. Since he seemed only too ready to do so, he clearly had some powder at his disposal. Ralegh has no fault to find with the men, who had fought a good fight. Rehearsing their commonsense arguments, he tranquilly observes that these won the day, "it being no hard matter to dissuade men from death to life." This double vision is characteristic of him. He could see the practical necessities that coexist with heroic potentialities. His idealism is the stronger for being based in fact and shot with a faint astringent cynicism. He used his imagination as an instrument for discerning truth as well as for heightening and manipulating it. It is because of this paradoxical clearsightedness that he could make poetry out of disillusion.

A lively and very partisan account of the expedition against Cádiz, in which Ralegh served under Essex in 1596, exists in manuscript and was printed in 1700. Various manuscript fragments relate to the navy and naval affairs. Ralegh projected a full-scale naval history for Prince Henry, James's heir apparent, but it is doubtful if he advanced far with it.

SIR WALTER RALEGH

The Discovery of Guiana illustrates very plainly Ralegh's double mastery of fact and fiction. It gave him a bad name among contemporaries, as well as enchanting the world, then and ever since. It is a very much more substantial work than the pamphlet on the *Revenge*. It was published in 1596, with his name on the title page, and is based upon his own experience. It might appear at first sight to be purely personal propaganda, but the plan Ralegh recommended was well beyond the resources of any private individual. Quite simply, he proposed that England should take over South America, beginning with the only region not effectively colonized by Spain: the country drained by the Orinoco and its tributaries, then known as Guiana. The terrain that Ralegh actually traversed, from the mouth of the Orinoco to the Caroni river, is now part of Venezuela. It was a further step in the Spanish war, and required the support of queen and country. It was probably fortunate that no such support was forthcoming; it would have been a tremendous undertaking, and there is no doubt that here as elsewhere Ralegh's optimism leapt ahead of rational expectation. He was not ignorant of colonizing, having twice dispatched settlers to Virginia. Their fate—the first group came home and the second mysteriously disappeared in the wilderness—might have given him pause. Yet on his behalf it must be admitted that the Virginia venture was ultimately successful, though not before it had passed into the hands of a merchant syndicate.

Ralegh's policy in Guiana was more aggressive. He had come to realize that casual commerce raiding would never effectively stop the flow of gold and silver to Spain. What England needed was what Spain had in abundance, land bases from which to operate. He had reason to believe that behind the dense forests along the Orinoco lay a secret empire of the Inca. Its capital city, Manoa, situated on a vast inland sea, was known to the Spaniards as El Dorado. He had carefully studied Spanish chronicles, read Spanish letters seized at sea, and sifted the gossip of West Country ports. The exploits of Cortez and Pizarro provided encouraging parallels. Yet the great lake had no existence apart from

seasonal floods in the high valleys. Objects of wrought gold produced by obliging Indians were relics of the Chibcha civilization of Colombia, out of which the Spaniards had already carved the kingdom of New Granada. There was no truth in the story that some of the Inca princes had escaped and founded a new empire as rich as the old.

Ralegh's strategic plan was bold and brilliant. He intended to invade this new Inca empire with the help of the borderers, who claimed to have been dispossessed. Then, having established a benevolent rule, the English could lead all Guiana against the Spanish colonies to the west of it, mobilizing the deep resentment of the natives against the brutal conquistadors. This meant that Ralegh's own conduct, in contrast, had to be kindly and protective. He sang Elizabeth's praises—and who could do it better than he? She was stronger than the hated Spaniards and had freed many nations from their tyranny. "The like and a more large discourse I made to the rest of the nations both in my passing to Guiana, and to those of the borders, so as in that part of the world," he reports delightedly, "her majesty is very famous, whom they now call *Ezrabeta Cassipuna Aquerewana,* which is as much as Elizabeth, the great princess, or greatest commander."

One of the pleasantest aspects of the *Discovery* is Ralegh's sympathy with the native Indians, and his crusading fervor on their behalf. He emphasized their best qualities because they were to be enlisted as allies. In 1618, his argument that Guiana was English was based largely upon their power to enter into contracts and dispose of their own land by treaty with Europeans. He was genuinely charmed by their simple dignity. "The tawny women," he noted, were "excellently favoured, which came among us without deceit, stark naked." Old Chief Topiawari was touching in his grief for an only son lost in battle and he proved unexpectedly shrewd in council. His picturesque phraseology was worth reproducing:

He remembered in his father's time when he was very old, and himself a young man, that there came down into that large valley of Guiana a nation from so far off as the Sun slept (for such were his own words), with so great a multitude as they could not

151

be numbered nor resisted, and that they wore large coats and hats of crimson colour, which colour he expressed by showing a piece of red wood wherewith my tent was supported, and that they were . . . those that had slain and rooted out so many of the ancient people as there are leaves in the wood upon all the trees.

Significantly, Ralegh never reproaches the Indians for their religion nor congratulates himself upon the prospect of saving souls. He takes an intelligent interest in their customs and recounts them with tolerant understanding. It surprised him to find that they warred for women and not for gold, but he thought it over and saw that it made sense in a sparsely populated country.

The native chiefs, on their side, were captivated by his persuasive tongue. He could address them in their own heroic terms, and not without that necessary component of primitive heroism, much practical good sense. All the time, he carefully concealed the gold lust that was going to attract colonists, and freely distributed English coins as tokens from the queen. An attempt to recoup by sacking the Spanish settlement at Cumaná was beaten off with heavy losses. This was an uncomfortable incident that Ralegh touches on lightly. The expedition, in consequence, came home little the richer and was early discredited. Ralegh may have convinced himself too easily that he could preserve good relations with the Indians once Guiana was thrown open to English settlers, but it is plain, nonetheless, that he was thinking in terms larger than petty gain.

Part of *The Discovery of Guiana* is narrative, part descriptive (in terms that range from the geographical to the lyrical), part is a defense against charges of deliberate deceit and gross gullibility, and part is an eloquent statement of policy. By "discovery," Ralegh means the opening up and exploring of the country. He was not claiming to be the first to enter it. On the contrary, he rehearses the history of early Spanish expeditions with a strong sense of the drama inherent in them. He owed a good deal to current literature of the New World, with which he was very familiar. His personal narrative presumably originated in some kind of journal of the voyage.

Though it has often been challenged, the book is basically accurate. If there is deceit, the writer had first deceived himself. Ralegh believed in the "mighty, rich and beautiful empire of Guiana," and it is very hard for the reader not to share his delusion, as he confidently retails the information he had gathered from the border tribes, and from Antonio de Berrio, governor of Trinidad, who spent a lifetime seeking El Dorado and died still believing in it. Ralegh admits that his own party never entered the secret empire and he does not claim to have spoken face to face with anyone who had been in Manoa. He dallies pleasurably with stories of Amazons, remote sisters of *Ezrabeta Cassipuna Aquerewana*, which may well have had some foundation in tribal custom as well as in classical history. He gives details of the Ewaipanoma, "the men whose heads do grow beneath their shoulders," much in the spirit that modern explorers report on the Abominable Snowman. He was struck by the unanimity with which the Indians asserted their existence, and the odd way in which it corroborated Sir John Mandeville. But he goes no further than giving the reader his own reasons for crediting these wonders. He does not pose as an eyewitness.

In spite of the unfavorable climate and the rigors of the voyage the health of his party seems to have been excellent. They were a close-knit and efficient company, nearly all from the West Country. Ralegh praises the food available—fish, game, fruit, maize, cassava bread, and native wines. He finds hammocks comfortable and convenient. His interest in new drugs is excited by native balsams and by the lethal poison curare. Any hint that the rocks are metalliferous is exploited for rather more than it is worth, but he knows how gold occurs, in hard white spar or else in alluvial deposits.

The book went through many editions and was translated into Latin, Dutch, and French. It was read as an up-to-the-minute news item, as a story of adventure, as a description of a strange country, and as a practical prospectus for fortune hunters. But over and above all these it has an enduring charm, supplied by the same hand that shaped *The Last Fight of the Revenge* into a heroic paradigm. This time it was not epic but a kind of exotic pastoral. The land, the beauty of the land, and the promise of the land are what stay in the reader's mind, the brightness and newness of the brave New World. Every corner turned is in itself a small discovery:

I never saw a more beautiful country nor more lively prospects, hills so raised here and there over the valleys, the river winding into divers branches, the plains adjoining without bush or stubble, all fair green grass, the ground of hard sand easy to march on either for horses or foot, the deer crossing every path, the birds toward the evening singing on every tree with a thousand several tunes, cranes and herons of white, crimson, and carnation perching on the river's side, the air fresh with a gentle easterly wind, and every stone that we stooped to take up promised gold or silver by his complexion.

The unspoiled country, the courtesy of its inhabitants, the golden city always just behind the next mountain range entered into the English imagination, to be reflected in Prospero's enchanted island and in Milton's Eden.

In 1617 Ralegh set sail once more for Guiana, in a magnificently equipped vessel called the *Destiny.* This voyage ended in disaster. No mine was discovered and there was an affray with Spanish settlers. Ralegh came home to condemnation and the scaffold. The documents relative to the last Guiana expedition have been published in one volume by V. T. Harlow. They include the letters Ralegh wrote to his wife and sponsors, his famous *Apology for the Voyage to Guiana,* and the so-called *Short Apology,* which was addressed to his cousin Sir George Carew. All these circulated freely in manuscript at the time. The note of personal urgency and personal commitment is naturally at its strongest in them. The *Apology* was written in great haste, under cover of a simulated illness. The arguments, recast in 1889 and shorn of emotion, were used as part of the British answer to territorial claims by Venezuela, but the passage of years had made them less cogent. The territory Ralegh saw as ripe for colonization was never settled by English people, and the gold it yielded has had to await modern mining techniques.

HISTORIAN

RALEGH's *The History of the World* was composed during his thirteen years' imprisonment in the Tower. He was allowed to have his books and to employ secretaries and amanuenses. Inevitably there was some envious gossip, to which Ben Jonson contributed, suggesting that he had done little of the work himself or had not made his indebtedness sufficiently plain. Contemporaries, anxious only to have their own contributions recognized, did not criticize his reliance upon compendiums already published, which was considerable in places, and indeed is hardly surprising. He had no Hebrew and not much Greek, reading Greek authors as much as possible in Latin translations. His French was fluent. He read and presumably spoke Spanish and he cannot have been without Italian. He had time on his hands and we know from his friend Sir Robert Cecil that he could "toil terribly."

His plan was comprehensive, beginning with the Creation. He intended, after he had dealt with the ancient world, to concentrate chiefly upon his own country and to come as near as he dared to modern times. In the event, the work breaks off in the second century A.D. He was, he says in his Preface, uneasy about the reception of a modern history and disheartened by the death in 1612 of Prince Henry, whose interest in the project had supported and encouraged him.

The work, in its incomplete form, was published in 1614. It is carefully printed, with an engraved allegorical frontispiece and a number of maps and diagrams, and it fills nearly 800 pages in folio. It is one of the few works to which Ralegh put his name and he was promptly rebuked for his presumption. On the king's orders all copies were recalled some months after publication and not released until the title page had been removed. Ralegh, a prisoner under sentence of death, had no business to present himself as an author. Such at least is the common interpretation of the affair, based on a theory that there was a title page in the first edition, as well as the engraved frontispiece, on which no author's name appears. John Racin, Jr., has pointed out that an excision could not have been effected without leaving traces in surviving copies.

Nor would the suppression of the author's name, which in any case was an open secret, have satisfied King James, who is known to have condemned the book as "too saucy in censuring princes." It was an article of faith with James that kings were God's vice-regents. Therefore respect was their due from loyal subjects. Ralegh moved in another direction. The power of kings, he delighted to point out, however great they may look in the small theater of the world, is as nothing beside the power of God, who will exact satisfaction for all their sins. James is personally extolled as an admirable ruler, gentle of disposition and free of bloodguilt, but these comments are lost in the grand pattern of the book, which is designed so that "it may no less appear by evident proof than by asseveration, that ill-doing hath always been attended with ill success."

Ralegh traces this pattern very clearly in the summary history of the kings of England that he inserts in his Preface. He found it ready-made in the English chronicles, but whereas they are directed toward establishing a particular dynasty in divine favor and disestablishing rivals, Ralegh when he comes to deal with world history is more impartial. If it exasperated King James to be invited to look at himself through the wrong end of a telescope and see himself of no account, it must have been infinitely soothing to Ralegh, the prisoner in disgrace, to reduce the whole world to a scale where there was very little distinction between himself and his oppressors, except insofar as the very act of reduction, the detached clarity of vision, made him their superior. It is not for nothing that the Preface became known as *A Premonition to Princes*, and that the book ends with the famous apostrophe to Death, the Leveler:

It is therefore Death alone that can suddenly make man to know himself. He tells the proud and insolent that they are but abjects, and humbles them at the instant; makes them cry, complain and repent, yea even to hate their forepassed happiness. He takes the accounts of the rich and proves him a beggar—a naked beggar, which has interest in nothing but the gravel that fills his mouth. He holds a glass before the eyes of the most beautiful, and makes them see therein their deformity and rottenness; and they acknowledge it. O eloquent, just and mighty Death! Whom none could advise, thou hast persuaded; what none

hath dared, thou hast done; and whom all the world hath flattered, thou only hast cast out of the world and despised. Thou hast drawn together all the far-stretched greatness, all the pride, cruelty, and ambition of man, and covered it all over with these two words *Hic Jacet*.

While Ralegh belittles man and undermines worldly values, he sets all within the structure of God's providence. There is an order in this world, even if it is the sad one of sin and retribution. It is for this reason, and not from any idle pedantry, that he begins with the Creation and the Fall of Man. They are basic to his thesis. Thereafter he spends a long time on Bible history, since the Bible is revealed truth and makes a particularly plain demonstration of the working out of God's will. His strenuous efforts to clarify the chronology of the Old Testament and to relate it to what is otherwise known of the ancient world resulted in a series of intricate and impressive tables reproduced as an appendix to the book. From Jewish history he goes on to the Persians, the Greeks, and the Romans, always following the fortunes of kings and leaders of men, the people who inaugurate policy and whose deeds have been recorded. If these, the greatest, are found wanting, it is not suggested that there will be much for which to commend their inferiors. Man is judged by his rulers. He may suffer pitiably at their hands but he shares their nature and in a position of power would not behave much differently:

Only those few black swans I must except, who having the grace to value worldly vanities at no more than their own price, do by retaining the comfortable memory of a well-acted life, behold death without dread and the grave without fear; and embrace both as necessary guides towards endless glory.

Contemporaries were delighted by the comprehensiveness of the history and did not miss, as the modern reader must, the sense of intimate participation with which Ralegh could imbue a narrative of events that fell within his own experience. This is to some extent compensated for by his readiness to comment, generalize, and digress. He will analyze character and motive, assess policy, and expound upon the moral implication of events, giving not only a picture of the past but of the mind of the Renaissance judging the past. He retains his power to highlight the drama of events, and if he omits the small, revealing details, it is because they were not for the most part preserved by the earlier annalists he consulted. From time to time, though not so often as one might wish, he notes parallels in modern times and speaks of matters with which he is personally acquainted—of refugees smoked out of caves in the French wars, of the existence of Amazons in South America, of naval tactics, or of the fighting qualities of the English soldier. But the main purpose of his narrative is far from that of a modern historian. It gives a view of history that is theocentric and providential, and a pessimistic assessment of man. It has therefore been dismissed by critics as conventional, "rabbinical," and little better than medieval. This was not the opinion of contemporaries. Throughout the seventeenth century it was highly valued, because it presented a picture of life in consonance with the feeling of the times. Milton as well as Ralegh derived all history from the Creation and the Fall of Man.

In the eighteenth century it was beginning to lose ground as a historical work, though it was still valued for its piety and its excellent prose style. As a piece of writing it is the best thing Ralegh did. Ben Jonson, who was not easy to please, commended his prose, and Samuel Johnson, also a severe critic, found it acceptable a hundred and fifty years later, calling it "elegant." The *History* gave Ralegh considerable practice in summary narrative and terse comment. The vitality and robustness of the man are manifest in the style, together with a detachment, due in part to his isolation from the world and from his subject matter, and in part natural to him. His plainness has lost its initial awkwardness, but it derives much of its vigor from the fact that he never in his life had taken much count of formal propriety and correctness. He has no fear of sinking, and this in an age that tended to write uneasily and with excessive care.

The same absorption in direct communication ensures that when he rises it is not an empty tumescence. It is easy to select passages and label them "purple" but it is not fair to the writer. At its most magnificent, Ralegh's prose still echoes his own speaking voice. It changes because his subject has changed. His high style is at its most sustained in the Preface, its melancholy purged of excess sentiment by the note of cold disillusion. The rhythms of the long brooding sentences are extremely subtle—worthy to be set beside Donne, Browne, and Milton, yet demonstrably not quite like any one of them. Ralegh's music is Elizabethan rather than Jacobean. The mood, characteristic of its time, is a somber stoicism, intensified rather than lightened by a vision of divine order enforced by a remote and retributive deity.

"ATHEIST"

THE publication of *The History of the World*, with its pronounced if melancholy piety, removed the stigma of atheism from Ralegh's name to the satisfaction of contemporaries. Sentencing him in 1618, his judge observed: "Your faith hath heretofore been questioned, but I am resolved you are a good Christian, for your book, which is an admirable work, doth testify as much." One of the crowd that listened attentively to his speech from the scaffold reported afterward that he spoke "not one word of Christ, but of the great and incomprehensible God, with much zeal and adoration." The comment could be extended to *The History of the World*. Ralegh is there concerned with the source of ultimate power and ultimate order rather than with saving grace, but it is a question of emphasis, not of orthodoxy.

Even a cursory glance through his writings should absolve him of the charge of atheism, which so deeply shocked his own time. It was not, however, directed against a man of letters with published work to his credit but against a royal minion, an arrogant and extravagant upstart. Ralegh had a public image upon which mud of almost any kind would stick. The queen had given him positions of authority that he could not exercise without offense to somebody. A major cause of his unpopularity was the number of trade monopolies that had been assigned to him. He was known to be very rich. The jewels on his shoes alone were said to be worth more than £6,000. It was easy to claim that he lived in luxury at the expense of the poor and honest man. To the more obvious motives for envy and dislike, his enemies were able to add the sinister connotations of the word "atheist." It was used at the time as an indiscriminate term of reproach, often with no very exact theological implications. A bad man is manifestly no Christian. Atheism could be applied as simply as that. But there were sides to Ralegh's character that on a superficial level might appear to give better justification for it. It would not otherwise have hung about him for so many years, with its murky suggestions and brimstone odor, to be exploited relentlessly in the treason trial of 1603.

The first to use it was the Jesuit Robert Parsons, in an unflattering portrait of Elizabeth's court. His Latin pamphlet was widely read. A summary in English, published in 1592, speaks of "Sir Walter Ralegh's school of atheism and the conjuror who is master thereof and of the great diligence used to draw young gentlemen to this school." The writer seems to have been reflecting on Ralegh's interest in the physical sciences, in particular mathematics, as taught by a notable scholar, Thomas Harriot. Mathematical studies followed naturally from Ralegh's practical concern with navigation and cartography. Harriot, whom he maintained as a member of his household, can be plausibly identified as his "conjuror." He was one of the most advanced astronomers of his day and carried to his grave the odium that tended to accompany a man who probed God's mysteries in the physical universe.

As well as being a patron of Harriot, Ralegh was said to have been one of those to whom Marlowe "read the atheist lecture," and upon this slender foundation there has been built a supposition that he and Marlowe were closely acquainted. A theory with more substance is that both men were involved in a libertine circle known as the School of Night. This has become a critical commonplace. It is worth examining the foundation upon which it is built. Father Parsons, in a hostile pamphlet that circulated in the 1590's, spoke of Ralegh's "school of atheism." The commentators equate this with the phrase "school of night," which is used by Shakespeare in *Love's Labour's Lost* (1594), buried deep among some rather obvious pleasantries upon the hackneyed theme of fair and dark beauty. Biron is mocked because he has fallen in love with a Dark Lady. "Fie," cries the King of Navarre,

> black is the badge of Hell,
> The hue of dungeons, and the School of night.

This solitary, unemphatic, rather mysterious phrase has been used, with the help of much ingenious argument, to prove the play a satire upon Ralegh and his associates and their scientific studies. The argument, in fact, can stand without reference to "the school of night," though it is harder without it to bring in Ralegh. Shakespeare mocks pedants, who as plodders and killjoys have never found favor in comedy, and suggests that young men find their stars in women's eyes. The question may then be propounded whether he had any particular person or persons in mind, who they were, and what kind of audience would understand and enjoy sallies at their expense.

In 1594, rumors of atheism followed Ralegh to Dorset, where he had retired to his country house at Sherborne. An ecclesiastical commission was sent to investigate, perhaps to protect rather than to convict him. Anyhow, no prosecution followed, nor did the evidence warrant it. His offense seems to have been that at a dinner party he and his elder brother, Sir Carew Ralegh, baited a conventional parson, the Reverend William Ironside. Ralegh took up the position, theologically unexceptionable, that man cannot define the substance of the soul. The parson, unwilling to be put down by a layman, retorted with logic, and Ralegh proceeded to tie him in knots. Ernest Strathmann thinks that in essence the dispute was concerned with the validity of Aristotelian logic and hardly with theology at all, and that Ironside knew the local gossips had misinterpreted it. The consequences show that Ralegh was playing a dangerous game—and not for the first time. He enjoyed argument and had a gift for it. He would have done well to walk more circumspectly, but circumspection was never a characteristic of his. Infinitely plausible and warmly sympathetic when he was so disposed, he could on occasion be tactless and wantonly indiscreet. He had the intelligent man's confidence that truth speaks for itself and he was contemptuous of commonplace minds.

Ralegh was interested in the problems propounded by the nature of God, of creation, and of the image of God in man. They bulk large in *The History of the World*, especially in the second chapter. *A Treatise of the Soul*, said to be his work, was printed from a single manuscript copy in 1829. A minor piece called *Sceptick* was one of the first of his papers to be published and appeared regularly with his *Remains*. It is a collection of notes from Sextus Empiricus, and is confined to showing the imperfections of human knowledge. A philosophical position such as this can very easily be accompanied by faith in an inscrutable deity. Indeed it was regularly used by polemicists to throw man back upon God, all human props having been proved fallible. It is peculiarly liable to be misconstrued by narrow minds. Ralegh had a dangerous kind of disengagement, a tolerance when confronted with alien ideas, and an intellectual boldness. It is not hard to imagine him listening to Marlowe reading "the atheist lecture."

Over and above this, his own beliefs are marked by an austerity unlikely to recommend them to simpler minds and warmer hearts. He is constant, for instance, in his assertion that immortal souls are completely severed from all human concerns:

But hereof we are assured, that the long and dark night of death . . . shall cover us over till the world be no more. After which, and when we shall again receive organs glorified and incorruptible, the seats of angelical affections: in so great admiration shall the souls of the blessed be exercised as they cannot admit the mixture of any second or less joy, nor any return of foregone or mortal affection, towards friends, kindred, children. Of whom whether we shall retain any particular knowledge, or in any sort distinguish them, no man can assure us: and the wisest men doubt.

In his farewell letter to his wife, written while awaiting execution in 1603, this became "As for me, I am no more yours, nor you mine. Death hath cut us assunder: and God hath divided me from the world, and you from me." Gentle and practical, he begs her not to have scruples about marrying again, "For that will be best for you: both in respect of God and the world."

It is not always realized how profoundly unsentimental Ralegh was, even to hardness. This comes out very clearly in his brief *Instructions to His Son*, in which all readers find him too apt to recommend self-interest as a guiding principle in life. In politics he had a kind of Machiavellian realism, in which he differs from his fellow Elizabethans only in being more articulate. Many of his actions seem to contradict it. He was not a very shrewd politician and allowed himself to be outmaneuvered. He stood by the old queen, for instance, when self-interest should have sent him where the rest were going, to her probable heir. They quietly and industriously undermined him. In popular belief Machiavellian craft was as characteristic of him as atheism. He was the arch-plotter. Melodrama lit him luridly. At his trial he was addressed as "monster," "viper," and "spider of hell." Yet he had done much to advance his country and help his countrymen, notably the seamen and the West Country tinners. He was concerned with tin mining as lord warden of the stannaries. As vice-admiral of Devon and Cornwall he had charge of the Admiralty Courts. He had served his time as a member of parliament, where he spoke up for the underprivileged, against witch-hunts among nonconformists, and against taxing the poor. It was a matter of regret to him that he was never a member of the Privy Council.

During his imprisonment he wrote some able treatises upon current affairs. *The Prerogative of Parliaments* is an imaginary discussion in which a justice of the peace shows a rather haughty councilor that an English king must rule through his parliament or disregard it at his peril. As advice to a reigning Stuart, trying his best to bypass his parliaments, it was more timely than tactful. It appeared in 1628 under a foreign imprint. Prince Henry asked him to summarize the arguments against the pro-Spanish marriages that were proposed for the prince and his sister. These pamphlets are vigorous, orderly, and spare, not without the flash of anecdote or phrase with which Ralegh almost always lights up his arguments. It is he, for instance, who tells how Essex fatally alienated the queen by blurting out in a temper that "her conditions were as crooked as her carcase." Elsewhere he regrets that she had not "believed her men of war, as she did her scribes," for then they would have made the kings of Spain

"Kings of Figs and oranges, as in old times." A very Raleghan discourse, on a wider and more general subject, is *The Miseries of War*. It is typical of the disillusioned historian seeing through the pretenses of mankind. The Ralegh who nonetheless urged the exploitation of Guiana and pressed the war with Spain was, on his own admission, no more than human. "Of a long time my course was a course of vanity," he said in his speech from the scaffold. "I have been a seafaring man, a soldier, and a courtier, and in the temptations of the least of these there is enough to overthrow a good mind, and a good man."

His character was far from simple, and though much information is available about his life it is often too fragmentary to solve the contradictions. In his writing he combined cynicism with idealism, truth with fiction, and a somber pessimism with a contagious zest for life.

SELECTED BIBLIOGRAPHY

I. BIBLIOGRAPHIES. T. N. Brushfield, *The Bibliography of Sir Walter Ralegh* (Exeter, 1886), repr. from *The Western Antiquary*, 2nd ed. (1908). See also P. Lefranc (below), chs. 2–3, "Le canon raghlien."

II. COLLECTED WORKS. *Judicious and Select Essayes and Observations Upon the First Invention of Shipping, The Misery of Invasive Warre, The Navy Royall and the Sea-Service* [authorship of last questioned]; *With His Apologie for His Voyage to Guiana* (London, 1650). *Sir Walter Raleighs Sceptick, or Speculations* [a trans. from Sextus Empiricus, authorship questioned]; *and Observations of the Magnificency and Opulency of Cities* [a trans. from Italian, authorship questioned]; *His Seat of Government; and Letters to the King's Majestie, and Others of Qualitie* (also three poems: 1. "The Passionate Man's Pilgrimage," 2. "Even Such Is Time," 3. "On the Snuff of a Candle"); *Also His Demeanor Before His Execution* [i.e., his last speech] (London, 1651). *Remains of Sir Walter Raleigh* (London, 1651–1702). The editions between 1651 and 1702 contain in various combinations the items in the 1651 volume together with *His Instructions to His Sonne; and The Son's Advice to His Aged Father* (London, 1632), the second item almost certainly spurious. *Maxims of State* (London, 1642), authorship questioned. *Observations Touching Trade and Commerce With the Hollander* (London, 1653), authorship questioned. *The Prerogative of Parliaments in England* (Middleburg-Hamburg, 1628) [imprints probably false], facs. ed. (New York, 1969). *Three Discourses: I. Of a War With Spain, and Our Protecting the Netherlands; II. Of the Original and Fundamental Cause of Natural, Arbitrary, and Civil War; III. Of Ecclesiastical Power* (London, 1702), the last two discourses appeared in 1650 as *The Misery of Invasive Warre*. The section in Discourse II on *Civil or Unnatural War* is new. T. Birch, *The Works: Political, Commercial, and Philosophical, Together With His Letters and Poems . . . to Which Is Prefix'd a New Account of His Life*, 2 vols. (London, 1751), does not include *The History of the World* but adds to works previously collected some new poems and letters and *The Cabinet Council Containing the Chief Arts of Empire and Mysteries of State* (London, 1658), published as *Aphorisms of State* (London, 1661) and as *The Arts of Empire and Secrets of Government* (London, 1697) authorship questioned. *A Discourse Touching a Match Propounded by the Savoyan, Between the Lady Elizabeth and the Prince of Piedmont; A Discourse Touching a Marriage Between Prince Henry of England, and a Daughter of Savoy*, first published as *The Interest of England With Regard to Foreign Alliances* (London, 1750). *A Voyage for the Discovery of Guiana; An Introduction to a Breviary of the History of England With the Reign of King William I* (London, 1693), authorship questioned. William Oldys and Thomas Birch, *The Works of Sir Walter Ralegh, Kt. Now First Collected*, 8 vols. (Oxford, 1829): vol. I, *Lives*; vols. II–VII, *The History of the World*; vol. VIII contains the minor works in the 1751 ed. with some smaller pieces, including *A Relation of Cadiz Action*, first printed with the abridged *History of the World* (1700), and *A Treatise of the Soul*. The collection of poems is supplemented from Sir Egerton Brydges' unreliable ed. of 1813. *The Works* was reprinted in New York in 1965.

III. SELECTED WORKS. J. Hannah, ed., *The Courtly Poets From Ralegh to Montrose* (London, 1870); A. M. C. Latham, ed., *Poems* (London, 1929) and *Selected Prose and Poetry* (London, 1965).

IV. SEPARATE WORKS. *A Report of the Truth of the Fight About the Iles of Açores, This Last Summer, Betwixt the Revenge One of Her Majesties Shippes and an Armada of the King of Spaine* (London, 1591); repr. in Hakluyt's *Voyages*, II (London, 1599); not in Birch or the 1829 Oxford ed.; facs. eds. (Leeds, 1967; New York, 1969). *The Discovery of the Large, Rich, and Bewtiful Empire of Guiana*, three eds. (London, 1596); repr. in Hakluyt's *Voyages*, III; edited by R. H. Schomburgk, with topographical notes, a transcript of Ralegh's journal of his last voyage, and "Considerations on the Voyage to Guiana" [said to be by Ralegh but probably by Lawrence Keymis] (London, 1848); edited by V. T. Harlow, with transcripts of

Spanish documents and a reproduction of one of Ralegh's own maps (London, 1928); facs. eds. (Leeds, 1967; New York, 1968). *The History of the World. In Five Books* (London, 1614); nine eds. before 1700; repr. by W. Oldys, 2 vols. (London, 1736); edited by C. A. Patrides (London, 1971); early abridgments are *The Marrow of Historie* (London, 1650) and *An Abridgment of Sir Walter Ralegh's History* (London, 1698).

V. BIOGRAPHICAL AND CRITICAL STUDIES. W. Oldys, *The Life of Sir Walter Ralegh* (London, 1736); prefixed to *The History of the World;* repr. in *Works* (1829). A. Cayley, *The Life of Sir Walter Ralegh,* 2 vols. (London, 1805). S. R. Gardiner, "The Case Against Sir Walter Ralegh," in *Fortnightly Review,* n. s., 1 (1867). E. Edwards, *The Life of Sir Walter Ralegh . . . Together With His Letters,* 2 vols. (London, 1868), a standard and well-documented work and the only substantial collection of the letters. W. Stebbing, *Sir Walter Ralegh: A Biography* (Oxford, 1891; 2nd ed., 1899). J. S. Corbett, *Drake and the Tudor Navy,* 2 vols. (London, 1898). J. S. Corbett, *The Successors of Drake* (London, 1900). C. H. Firth, "Sir Walter Raleigh's History of the World," in *Proceedings of the British Academy, 1917–1918;* repr. in *Essays Historical and Literary* (Oxford, 1938). N. Kempner, *Raleghs staatstheoretische Schriften: Die Einführung des Machiavellismus in England* (Leipzig, 1928). M. Praz, "Un machiavellico Inglese: Sir Walter Raleigh," in *La cultura* (January 1929). V. T. Harlow, *Ralegh's Last Voyage* (London, 1932), reprints almost all available documents except the journal. E. Thompson, *Sir Walter Ralegh: The Last of the Elizabethans* (London, 1935). M. C. Bradbrook, *The School of Night: A Study*

in *the Literary Relationships of Sir Walter Ralegh* (Cambridge, 1936). C. F. Tucker Brooke, "Sir Walter Ralegh as Poet and Philosopher," in *English Literary History* (June 1938); repr. in *Essays on Shakespeare* (London, 1948). D. B. Quinn, *Ralegh and the British Empire* (London, 1947); for Ralegh's Virginia colony, see Quinn's *The Roanoke Voyages, 1584–1590,* 2 vols. (London, 1955). E. A. Strathmann, *Sir Walter Ralegh: A Study in Elizabethan Skepticism* (New York, 1951). P. Edwards, *Sir Walter Raleigh* (London, 1953), a general study of Ralegh as a literary figure. *The Oxford History of English Literature* (Oxford, 1945–   ): vol. III, *English Literature in the 16th Century,* by C. S. Lewis (1954); vol. V, *The Earlier Seventeenth Century, 1600–1660,* by Douglas Bush (1945; 2nd ed., 1962). Peter Ure, "The Poetry of Sir Walter Ralegh," in *Review of English Literature,* 1 (1960). W. F. Oakeshott, *The Queen and the Poet* (London, 1960), a highly speculative study of Ralegh's poetry against the background of his life, with some new poems. A. L. Rowse, *Ralegh and the Throckmortons* (London, 1962), contains decisive evidence of Ralegh's marriage. J. E. C. Hill, *Intellectual Origins of the English Revolution* (Oxford, 1965), esp. ch. 4, "Ralegh—Science, History, and Politics." P. Lefranc, *Sir Walter Ralegh Ecrivain: L'oeuvre et les idées* (Paris, 1968), the most thorough treatment yet accorded to Ralegh as a writer and thinker, with a very full bibliography. S. J. Greenblatt, *Sir Walter Ralegh. The Renaissance Man and His Roles* (New Haven, Conn., 1973). Robert Lacey, *Sir Walter Ralegh* (London, 1973). J. Racin, *Sir Walter Ralegh as Historian: An Analysis of "The History of the World"* (London, 1974).

SIR PHILIP SIDNEY

(1554-1586)

Kenneth Muir

WHEN the news of Sir Philip Sidney's death reached England, there was an extraordinary demonstration of grief. He was mourned by ordinary people as a soldier who had died fighting for the Protestant cause. He was mourned by his friends and relations as the "light of his family," a man who had seemed destined for greatness as a statesman. He was mourned by scholars and writers as a generous patron, and by his fellow poets as one of the best, and certainly one of the most influential, poets of his time. Oxford and Cambridge published collections of Latin elegies; and Edmund Spenser, Fulke Greville, and others contributed to *Astrophel*, a volume of English elegies. Years later, Greville regarded his friendship with Sidney as his chief title to fame; and when Percy Shelley wrote *Adonais*, he could speak of his great ancestor as one of the "inheritors of unfulfilled renown":

> Sidney, as he fought
> And as he fell, and as he lived and loved,
> Sublimely mild, a spirit without spot.

It is difficult to consider Sidney merely as a man of letters, since his writing was only a spare-time occupation. He is the best English example of the Renaissance ideal: he was Jack of all trades and master of them all. Not that he was simply a gifted amateur; although he sometimes spoke of his writings as toys, this (as K. O. Myrick has shown) "is but an example of *sprezzatura*, the courtly grace which conceals a sober purpose and is, indeed, the mark of consummate artistry"; or, as Greville put it, "men commonly (to keep above their works) seem to make toys of the utmost they can do."

The Sidney family became prominent in the middle of the fifteenth century. William Sidney was knighted after Flodden Field and became tutor to Edward VI. Henry Sidney, his son, was Edward's companion; and by his marriage to Mary Dudley he became connected with some of the most powerful families in England. Three years later, on November 30, 1554, Philip Sidney was born at Penshurst in Kent, an estate given to William Sidney by Edward VI. He was named, by what proved to be a singular irony, after his godfather, King Philip of Spain.

Philip Sidney was educated at Shrewsbury School and Christ Church, Oxford. He left Oxford in 1571, without taking a degree, when the colleges were closed on account of the plague. He spent a short time at Cambridge and then completed his education by traveling on the Continent. He was in Paris at the time of the massacre on St. Bartholemew's Eve, 1572, an event that left an indelible mark on his mind; he proceeded to Frankfurt, Heidelberg, Vienna, Hungary, Italy, Poland, and Holland, improving his knowledge of languages, acquiring insight into foreign affairs, and making many friends, of whom the most important was Hubert Languet, who hoped that Queen Elizabeth would become the champion of Protestantism.

Sidney visited Ireland, where his father was lord deputy, with the earl of Essex, who hoped to arrange a marriage between his daughter, Penelope, and Sidney; but it was not until Penelope had been married against her will to Lord Rich that Sidney fell in love with her. In 1577 he was sent on an embassy to congratulate Emperor Rudolph II on his succession, and he took the opportunity to travel widely, as he was still hoping for the formation of a Protestant League. On his return to court he wrote an appeal to the queen not to marry the duke of Anjou. Sidney never obtained an important post at court, and this may have been partly due to Elizabeth's resentment of his unsolicited advice. He became a member of Parliament in 1581, and he was knighted; but he was in debt and felt frustrated at not being allowed to exercise his talents as a statesman to the full. From the other frustration, of his unreturned love for Penelope, if we may assume that the frustration expressed in his sonnets had some basis in fact, he may have escaped by his marriage to Frances Walsingham in September 1583. He was involved in a scheme of colonization in the New World; and in 1585 the queen intervened to prevent him from sailing with Drake on an expedition to Spain. He left in November to take up the post of governor of Flushing. Nearly a year later, on October 2, 1586, he took part in a skirmish to prevent the relief of Zutphen. One horse was killed under him in the second charge. In the last charge he was struck in the thigh by a musketball, a wound he would have escaped if he had not thrown away his thighpieces on seeing that the lord marshal was not wearing his. As he was being carried off the field, he called for drink; but as he was putting the bottle to his lips, he noticed a dying soldier. "He delivered it to the poor man with these words, *Thy necessity is yet greater than mine*" (Greville). He was taken in a barge to Arnheim, where he was nursed by Lady Sidney; but it was soon obvious that his wound was fatal. He died on October 17, displaying singular courage and religious fortitude.

Some of Sidney's writings are of little importance. The metrical version of the Psalms, completed by his sister, the countess of Pembroke, perhaps with the help of other poets, is not worse than Milton's and was admired by Ruskin; but it is a work of piety rather than of poetry. The entertainment *The Lady of May*, performed before the queen, is a courtly trifle thought by some critics to have given Shakespeare a hint for the character of Holofernes in *Love's Labour's Lost*. His translation of part of Philippe de Mornay's *Vérité de la réligion chrétienne* is admirably straightforward and lucid (it has, however, recently been argued that the translation was by Arthur Golding). His masterpieces are *The Countess of Pembroke's Arcadia*, *Astrophel and Stella*, a few lyrical poems,

and *The Defence of Poesie* (or *Apologie for Poetry*, as one edition calls it).

The Defence was written in reply to Stephen Gosson's *School of Abuse* (1579), dedicated to Sidney, which attacked "poets, pipers, players, jesters, and such like caterpillars of a commonwealth." Poetry, Gosson argued, had been useful in the old days for celebrating "the notable exploits of worthy captains"; but modern poetry had a deplorable effect on the manners and morals of the age. The exact date of Sidney's reply is unknown. If the King James to whom Sidney refers was James VI of Scotland, four or five years must have elapsed before the *Defence* was completed; but it was, in any case, written before the first plays of Christopher Marlowe and Shakespeare were performed. Sidney could therefore say little in defense of the contemporary stage. The only modern play in which he could find anything to praise was *Gorboduc*, which had not been written for the popular stage; and even *Gorboduc*, "full of stately speeches and well-sounding phrases, climbing to the height of Seneca his style, and as full of notable morality which it doth most delightfully teach," violated the unities of time and place. Later readers have taken little delight in *Gorboduc*, but they have found plenty in Sidney's mocking description of plays written for the popular stage in which the unities were more grossly disregarded:

But if it be so in *Gorboduc*, how much more in all the rest, where you shall have Asia of the one side and Affricke of the other, and so many other under kingdoms, that the player when he comes in must ever begin with telling where he is, or else the tale will not be conceived. Now you shall have three ladies walk to gather flowers, and then we must believe the stage to be a garden. By and by we hear news of shipwreck in the same place: then we are to blame if we accept it not for a rock. Upon the back of that comes out a hideous monster with fire and smoke, and then the miserable beholders are bound to take it for a cave: while in the mean time two armies fly in, represented with four swords and bucklers, and then what hard heart will not receive it for a pitched field?

Now of time they are much more liberal. For ordinary it is that two young princes fall in love, after many traverses she is got with child, delivered of a fair boy; he is lost, groweth to a man, falleth in love, and is ready to get another child, and all this in two hours' space: which how absurd it is in sense, even sense may imagine, and art hath taught, and all ancient examples justified.

Shakespeare himself was to apologize for the representation of Agincourt by "four or five most vile and ragged foils"; and in *The Winter's Tale,* which might almost have been written to demonstrate how a great work of art could be made in defiance of the rules, he brings in Father Time to excuse just such a violation of the unities as Sidney satirizes.

Sidney's assumption that Seneca was the best model for tragedy was made by all Elizabethan critics, and the countess of Pembroke's circle of poets all attempted plays in the French Senecan manner. But, whatever the merits of Samuel Daniel's *Cleopatra* and Thomas Kyd's *Cornelia*— and poetically they are considerable—these plays were not intended for the stage. Sidney, we may be sure, would have delighted in *Hamlet* and *King Lear,* even though he objected to the mingling of kings and clowns.

Sidney was luckier with nondramatic poetry. He deplored the failure of the poets of his own age to equal the achievement of Chaucer in his *Troilus and Criseyde,* "of whom truly I know not whether to marvel more, either that he in that misty time could see so clearly, or that we in this clear age go so stumblingly after him." But he praises Henry Howard, earl of Surrey; and if he does not refer to Thomas Wyatt, we may suspect that he did not distinguish between the contributors to Tottel's *Songs and Sonnets,* in which Wyatt's and Surrey's lyrics had first appeared. He praises *The Mirror for Magistrates* and the book with which Spenser had just emerged as a fine poet, *The Shepheardes Calendar,* although, as he confesses, "that same framing of his style to an old rustic language, I dare not allow."

But the value of Sidney's essay, which was written before the golden age, does not depend on his criticism of his contemporaries. It depends, rather, on its tone and style, graceful, civilized, and urbane; on the fact that it contains the first real criticism in the language, unequaled before John Dryden; and on the easy mastery with which Sidney makes use of the ideas and methods of Julius Caesar Scaliger, Antonio Sebastiani Minturno, and Ludovico Castelvetro.

Like Horace, Sidney maintains that delightful teaching is the aim of poetry; and he argues that the poet is a more effective teacher than the philosopher because he is more concrete and gives pleasure as he teaches:

The philosopher showeth you the way, he informeth you of the particularities, as well of the tediousness of the way, as of the pleasant lodging you shall have when your journey is ended, as of the many by-turnings that may divert you from your way. But this is to no man but to him that will read him, and read him with attentive studious painfulness, which constant desire, whosoever hath in him hath already passed half the hardness of the way. . . . The philosopher teaches those who are already taught.

The poet, on the other hand, entices the reader to listen and makes him swallow the pill of morality by coating it with sugar:

For he doth not only show the way, but giveth so sweet a prospect into the way as will entice any man to enter into it. Nay, he doth, as if your journey should lie through a fair vineyard, at the very first give you a cluster of grapes that, full of that taste, you may long to pass further. He beginneth not with obscure definitions, which must blur the margent with interpretations and load the memory with doubtfulness, but he cometh to you with words set in delightful proportion.

The historian is likewise inferior to the poet because he is "better acquainted with a thousand years ago than with the present age," because he is "curious for antiquities and inquisitive of novelties," and because he is "so tied, not to what should be, but to what is, to the particular truth of things, and not to the general reason of things." Poets, untrammeled by the literal facts of history, are able, by representing virtue and vice, to encourage their readers to cultivate the one and shun the other.

Sidney distinguishes between verse and poetry, as Shelley was later to do; and he shows that poetry can be written in prose. "There have been many most excellent poets that never versified," he tells us; and, he adds characteristically, "now swarm many versifiers that need never answer to the name of poets." Heliodorus wrote in prose, so it is plainly "not rhyming and versing that maketh a poet."

SIR PHILIP SIDNEY

To the argument that Plato, the most poetical of philosophers, banished poets from his Republic, Sidney answers that "the poets of his time filled the world with wrong opinions of the Gods," that Plato was "banishing the abuse, not the thing," and that elsewhere he gave "divine commendation unto poetry." As for the charge that poetry is the mother of lies, Sidney shows that a poet is not lying, because he does not pretend that what he writes is literally true.

Although Sidney naturally stresses the didactic element in poetry, he was too fine a poet to believe that the inculcation of morality and virtue was its sole function. Nor, in spite of his justifiable strictures on his contemporaries, was his taste narrow. One of the most famous passages in the *Defence* is his shamefaced confession that he had enjoyed *Chevy Chase:*

Certainly I must confess mine own barbarousness, I never heard the old song of Percy and Douglas, that I found not my heart moved more than with a trumpet; and yet is it sung but by some blind crowder,[1] with no rougher voice than rude style: which being so evil apparelled in the dust and cobwebs of that uncivil age, what would it work, trimmed in the gorgeous eloquence of Pindar?

The whole essay is written in a singularly attractive style, witty and persuasive, and modeled, as Myrick has argued, on a classical oration. Gosson was scorned for dedicating his attack on poetry to Sidney; but the reply is quite without personalities, and even its invective is tempered with good humor and moderation, as in the concluding curse:

If you have so earth-creeping a mind that it cannot lift itself up to look to the sky of poetry, or rather, by a certain rustical disdain, will become such a Mome as to be a Momus of poetry; then, though I will not wish unto you the ass's ears of Midas, nor to be driven by a poet's verses as Bubonax was, to hang himself, not to be rhymed to death, as is said to be done in Ireland; yet thus much curse I must send you, in the behalf of all poets, that while you live, you live in love, and never get favour for lacking skill of a sonnet, and, when you die, your memory die from the earth for want of an epitaph.

The countess of Pembroke's *Arcadia* is the only English masterpiece that has been allowed to go out of print. It has never been included in

a popular series of classics, and one must conclude that it is read now only by scholars. It has, indeed, a reputation for tediousness. T. S. Eliot, though writing in defense of the countess of Pembroke's circle, dismissed *Arcadia* as "a monument of dullness"; F. L. Lucas called it "a rigmarole of affected coxcombry and china shepherdesses"; Virginia Woolf described her reactions as "half dreaming, half yawning." Dullness is the one fault that the general reader neither can nor should forgive. Yet for three generations the book was read by everyone interested in literature, and there were thirteen editions between 1590 and 1674. Its popularity was partly due, like that of Rupert Brooke's poetry, to the legend attaching to the author; but it was perused by dramatists in search of plots—with Shakespeare at their head—by those who loved romances, and by those who liked their moral lessons presented in a delightful form, by Charles I, and by John Milton, who spoke of it as a "vain, amatorious poem" while conceding its worth and wit.

If, therefore, the modern reader finds it tedious, it may be because he comes to it with the wrong expectations. The development of the novel since the early eighteenth century has conditioned our views of what prose fiction should be: we look for a plot embodying a theme, for subtle characterization, for criticism of society, and usually for realism. But Sidney was not attempting to write a novel; his book is set in an imaginary past, his characters are much less vital than those of the best Elizabethan and Jacobean dramatists, and his story is wildly improbable. We are bound to be disappointed if we ask of his masterpiece what it makes no attempt to provide.

Arcadia has been published in three versions. The short version, not published until 1926, was written first. Sidney described it in the dedication as "this idle work of mine," telling his sister, the countess, that it was not intended for publication:

being but a trifle, and that triflingly handled. Your dear self can best witness the manner, being done in loose sheets of paper, most of it in your presence, the rest, by sheets, sent unto you, as fast as they were done.

This version (the old *Arcadia,* as it is called) is in five books or acts. In his last years Sidney

[1] A fiddler.

began expanding and rewriting the work; and he had gotten halfway through the third book, without making any use of the original third book, when he died—or when he departed to take up his post as governor of Flushing. The first two books in the revised form are twice as long as those in the old *Arcadia*. This second version, divided into chapters probably by Fulke Greville, was published in 1590. Three years later the countess of Pembroke published the third version, which consists of the 1590 version without Greville's aids to the reader, but with the addition of the unexpanded concluding books. Some of the alterations in these books apparently were made by Sidney himself, or by his sister in accordance with his intentions; for others she may have been wholly responsible. Sidney had expressed a wish that the manuscript be destroyed, no doubt partly because the revision was incomplete.

The old *Arcadia* is a straightforward romance, with the events in approximately chronological order.[2] In the new *Arcadia*, Sidney remodeled the book under the influence of the *Æthiopian History* of Heliodorus and the *Diana* of Jorge de Montemayor. He deliberately upset the chronological sequence of events, interspersing the main plot with others. We know from *The Defence of Poesie* that Sidney regarded both Xenophon's *Cyropaedia* and Heliodorus' *Æthiopian History* as "absolute heroical poems," even though they were written in prose; and he rewrote *Arcadia* to convert it into a poem, mingling the heroic and the pastoral as Montemayor had done. Even in the old *Arcadia*, Sidney had followed Montemayor's example in interspersing verses in a predominantly prose narrative.

Some critics have argued that Sidney spoiled the original *Arcadia* by his attempt to improve it. They admit the extraordinary ingenuity of the revised version, the "marvellous involution and complexity" (as S. L. Wolff calls it), a kind of jigsaw puzzle in which every piece is essential to the grand design of the whole; but they suggest that the book is made impossibly difficult by its complicated structure, that no one at a first reading can follow the various strands in the pattern, and that, as William Hazlitt put it, it is "one of the greatest monuments of the abuse of intellectual power on record." It has even been maintained that the style of the first version, less highly wrought than that of the revision, is for that very reason without the excessive ornament and preciosity that makes Sidney's later prose so difficult to read and so unhappy a model.

Elizabethan reading habits were different from ours, and there is no evidence that Sidney's contemporaries found *Arcadia* unnecessarily complicated. That all would not be clear at first reading is surely irrelevant to an estimate of the book's success. It would be reread and discussed, digested and savored; and the complications would be a source of added pleasure. The modern reader, if he wishes to appreciate the book, cannot skim through it as he would through a best seller. He must be prepared to read it more as he would a narrative poem or James Joyce's *Ulysses*. Nor, I think, can it be seriously maintained that the style of the old *Arcadia* is superior to that of the new. Although as early as 1588 Abraham Fraunce had used a manuscript of the old *Arcadia* to provide examples of figures of speech for his *Arcadian Rhetorike*, its style is rough and unpolished compared with that of the new *Arcadia*. Many passages, it is true, Sidney used again with only slight modifications; but others he polished and

[2] For those who have not read the book, the following summary of the old *Arcadia* may be helpful: Basilius, terrified by an oracle prophesying disgrace and disaster to his family, abdicates for the year to which the prophecy refers. The two heroes, Pyrocles and Musidorus, fall in love with Philoclea and Pamela, the two daughters of Basilius. Pyrocles disguises himself as a woman, and Musidorus as a shepherd. Both Basilius and Gynecia, his wife, fall in love with Pyrocles, Gynecia having penetrated his disguise; but he tricks them both so that they share a bed with each other instead of with him, thus fulfilling part of the prophecy. Pyrocles and Musidorus are accused of seducing the princesses and of conspiring with Gynecia to murder Basilius, who, having taken a love potion intended for Pyrocles, appears to be dead. The heroes are about to be executed when Basilius revives; they are thus able to marry the princesses.

In the new *Arcadia* many other plots are interwoven with that of the original book: for instance, the story of Argalus and Parthenia, the story of the king of Paphlagonia and his two sons (used by Shakespeare for the subplot of *King Lear*), and the intrigues of Cecropia to obtain the throne for her son, Amphialus, and her cruel treatment of Philoclea and Pamela.

Sidney was confusing in his choice of names. Daiphantus is the name assumed by Pyrocles as well as a name given to Zelmane, the daughter of Plexirtus, and Zelmane is also a name used by Pyrocles.

refined, and many of the finest passages in the revised version are completely new.

A typical comparison may be made of the passages in the two versions describing Pyrocles after he has been lectured by Musidorus for falling in love with Philoclea:

These words spoken vehemently and proceeding from so dearly an esteemed friend as Musidorus did so pierce poor Pyrocles that his blushing cheeks did witness with him he rather could not help, than did not know his fault. Yet, desirous by degrees to bring his friend to a gentler consideration of him, and beginning with two or three broken sighs, answered to this purpose.

Pyrocles' mind was all this while so fixed upon another devotion, that he no more attentively marked his friend's discourse than the child that hath leave to play marks the last part of his lesson; or the diligent pilot in a dangerous tempest doth attend the unskillful words of a passenger; yet the very sound having imprinted the general point of his speech in his heart, pierced without any mislike of so dearly an esteemed friend, and desirous by degrees to bring him to a gentler consideration of him, with a shamefast look (witnessing he rather could not help, than did not know his fault) answered him to this purpose.

The revised version is superior in several ways. Sidney has obviously improved the structure of the prose; he has added two useful psychological touches to the character of Pyrocles; and he has inserted two similes and a metaphor. These might be regarded as supererogatory in prose fiction; but they are desirable ornaments in a heroic poem, which the new *Arcadia* was intended to be.

How much Sidney's style was admired by his contemporaries can be seen not merely from numerous references to it but also from the way it was imitated. Robert Greene, for example, who had written in a euphuistic style in the 1580s, adopted the Arcadian style for his two best romances, *Menaphon* and *Pandosto*. Sidney had complained of the artificiality and monotony of euphuism; his own style employs a much wider range of rhetorical figures and avoids the exaggerated use of antithesis and alliteration, as well as the absurd similes, that make *Euphues* so tedious. His own similes and metaphors, though frequently farfetched, are never mechanical. He speaks, for example, of blood mingling with the sea in these terms: "their blood had (as it were) filled the wrinkles of the sea's visage." He describes a tree reflected in a stream: "It seemed she looked into it and dressed her green locks by that running river." He writes of "beds of flowers, which being under the trees, the trees were to them a pavilion, and they to the trees a mosaical floor." He speaks of a storm as winter's child, "so extreme and foul a storm, that never any winter (I think) brought forth a fouler child." Instead of saying that Queen Helen spoke, he says: "But when her breath (aweary to be closed up in woe) broke the prison of her fair lips."

A longer passage, describing Pamela at her embroidery, has been condemned for absurdity:

For the flowers she had wrought carried such life in them that the cunningest painter might have learned of her needle: which with so pretty a manner made his careers to and fro through the cloth, as if the needle itself would have been loth to have gone fromward such a mistress, but that it hoped to return thenceward very quickly again: the cloth looking with many eyes upon her, and lovingly embracing the wounds she gave it: the sheers also were at hand to behead the silk that was grown too short. And if at any time she put her mouth to bite it off, it seemed, that where she had been long in making of a rose with her hand, she would in an instant make roses with her lips. . . .

The reader who does not enjoy this bravura piece is unlikely to appreciate *Arcadia* as a whole, for it is not only delightful in itself but also helps to create the total impression of one of the two heroines. G. K. Hunter has rightly observed that Sidney's similes are not, on the whole, concerned to make things more plain or even more vivid, but by comparing the less artificial to the more artificial, to stress the importance, the complexity, the significance of the world described. Each individual incident, every gesture, one might say, becomes universalized.

John Hoskins, in his *Directions for Speech and Style*, written in 1599, used *Arcadia* as his storehouse for figures of rhetoric; and, in commenting on the way Sidney "shunned usual phrases," he explained that "this of purpose did he write to keep his style from baseness." Virginia Woolf even suggested that "often the

SIR PHILIP SIDNEY

realism and vigour of the verse comes with a shock after the drowsy languor of the prose." But although Sidney was careful to keep his style from baseness in the heroic parts of *Arcadia*, he did this from a sense of literary decorum, as can be seen from the straightforward and direct prose he uses in passages of comic relief. In the heroic parts he was aiming at what Minturno advocated: "magnificent and sumptuous pomp of incidents and language."

This sumptuous pomp is not mainly a matter of vocabulary, though Sidney is fond of hyphenated epithets, but of using all the resources of rhetoric. Two of the commonest figures in *Arcadia* are antonomasia and periphrasis. Philoclea, for example, is called "the ornament of the Earth, the model of Heaven, the triumph of Nature, the light of Beauty, Queen of love"; and, instead of saying that the lambs bleated for their dams, Sidney tells us that "the pretty lambs with bleating oratory craved the dam's comfort." Hoskins gives several examples of this figure. Sidney calls a thresher "one of Ceres' servants"; and instead of "his name was known to high and low," he writes absurdly: "No prince could pretend height nor beggar lowness to bar him from the sounds thereof."

Many of the rhetorical figures consist of the repetition of words in different ways, the playing with them, and the departure from their natural order. Sometimes Sidney will end a sentence with a word taken from the beginning:

The thoughts are but overflowings of the mind, and the tongue is but a servant of the thoughts.
In shame there is no comfort, but to be beyond all bounds of shame.

At other times the word is repeated in the middle of the sentence, and in the following example the figure is underlined by alliteration:

That sight increased their compassion, and their compassion called up their care.

Sometimes Sidney interrupts a sentence with a parenthesis, reinforcing the meaning or correcting it (that is, epanorthosis):

In Thessalia I say there was (well I may say there was) a Prince.

Sometimes he uses oxymoron, as in the phrase "humane inhumanity"; and sometimes he plays with the meanings of words, as in the description of "a ship, or rather the carcass of the ship, or rather some few bones of the carcass."

These are only a few examples of the scores of different figures used by Sidney. The Arcadian style depends, not as euphuism does, on comparatively few overworked figures, but on the intensive use of a wide variety of figures; thus there is no danger of the reader's becoming tired of any particular one. It is a restless, brilliant, self-conscious prose, continually calling attention to itself as much as to the thing described and, it must be admitted, becoming intolerably affected in the hands of imitators without Sidney's comprehensive intelligence and high purpose.[3]

There are two qualities of Sidney's prose that have been appreciated by those who have been unable to enjoy its more obviously Elizabethan characteristics: its descriptive power and its rhythms. There had been great works of prose before the *Arcadia*, but Sidney was the first English writer to construct long and finely articulated sentences with a conscious but varied prose rhythm, the first, perhaps, to spend as much pains on the composition of prose as others spent on verse. On every page there are touches of beauty, visual and descriptive beauty and beauty of rhythm, often combined, as in the justly famous conclusion to a long sentence describing Arcadia:

Here a shepherd's boy piping, as though he should never be old: there a young shepherdess knitting, and withal singing, and it seemed that her voice comforted her hands to work, and her hands kept time to her voice's music.

[3] Shakespeare seems to have been influenced by Sidney's style in the prose of *King Lear*, I, ii (presumably because he had been reading *Arcadia* for the Gloucester scenes); but his most notable exercise in the Arcadian style, reading like a parody of it and put into the mouth of an anonymous courtier, is in *The Winter's Tale*, V, ii:

They seem'd almost, with staring on one another, to tear the cases of their eyes; there was speech in their dumbness, language in their very gesture; they looked as they had heard of a world ransom'd, or one destroy'd. A notable passion of wonder appeared in them; but the wisest beholder that knew no more but seeing could not say if th'importance were joy or sorrow—but in the extremity of the one it must needs be.

166

Another example, put into the mouth of the villainous Cecropia, has the same combination of qualities:

> Have you ever seen a pure rosewater kept in a crystal glass; how fine it looks, how sweet it smells, while that beautiful glass imprisons it? Break the prison, and let the water take his own course, doth it not embrace dust, and lose all his former sweetness and fairness? Truly so are we, if we have not the stay, rather than the restraint, of crystalline marriage.

Sidney's art, however, was a means to an end. We have seen how he maintained that the function of poetry was to teach delightfully. Although some critics have supposed that Sidney taught by means of allegory, it is clear that, apart from a few allegorical touches, he avoided the method of his friend Spenser. What he was seeking was to create an imaginary world in which human actions and passions could be displayed, freed from the accidentals of the real world. The golden world created by the poet was, moreover, more beautiful than the brazen world in which we live. Nature, Sidney tells us:

> never set forth the earth in so rich tapestry as diverse poets have done, neither with so pleasant rivers, fruitful trees, sweet-smelling flowers, nor whatsoever else may make the too much loved earth more lovely: her world is brazen, the poets only deliver a golden.

The poet's method is to teach indirectly, by means of his story:

> He cometh to you with words set in delightful proportion . . . and with a tale forsooth he cometh unto you, with a tale which holdeth children from play and old men from the chimney-corner; and pretending no more, doth intend the winning of the mind from wickedness to virtue.

Like the ideal actor of whom Hamlet speaks, Sidney's purpose was "to show virtue his own feature, scorn her own image, and the very age and body of the time his form and pressure."

In some ways the old *Arcadia* is more directly didactic than the new. Sidney cut out the narrator's moralizing, often transferring it to one of the characters in the story. The debates, as Myrick shows, "have been subordinated to the action, and the aphorisms have been half con-cealed in dramatic narration." The teaching is to be found mainly in the examples of human beings, good and bad, in their actions and words. As Hoskins points out, "Men are described excellently in *Arcadia*. . . . But he that will truly set down a man in a figured story must first learn truly to set down an humour, a passion, a virtue, a vice, and therein keeping decent proportion add but names and knit together the accidents and encounters." Hoskins adds that "the perfect expressing of all qualities is learned out of Aristotle's ten books of moral philosophy" and that "the understanding of Aristotle's *Rhetoric* is the directest means of skill to describe, to move, to appease, or to prevent any motion whatsoever; whereunto whosoever can fit his speech shall be truly eloquent." It is significant that Sidney had translated the first two books of *Rhetoric*, which are concerned with the tasks of persuasion, an analysis of human motives and emotions, and a list of the various lines of argument available to different kinds of speakers. Hoskins' views are supported by Greville, who tells us that Sidney's

> purpose was to limn out such exact pictures of every posture in the mind, that any man being forced, in the strains of this life, to pass through any straits or latitudes of good or ill fortune, might (as in a glass) see how to set a good countenance upon all the discountenances of adversity, and a stay upon the exorbitant smilings of chance.

Although it was natural for Hoskins, writing on rhetoric, and for Greville, who in his old age sought in Sidney's works the qualities he aimed at in his own and who in his account of Sidney was belaboring the decadence of a later age, to stress the moral purpose of *Arcadia*, they undoubtedly understood Sidney's intentions. It would be wrong, however, to suppose that the characters in *Arcadia* are mere exempla or that they are all plainly black or white. Cecropia has no redeeming characteristics, and Philanax and Pamela appear to be wholly admirable; but between these extremes there are many characters, weak and amiable, vain and brave, sinful but not vicious, who together provide a representative pageant of human nature. Basilius may be condemned for his foolishness, his credulity, and his attempted adultery; Gynecia may be held up as a bad example of passion usurping the place of reason; Amphialus may be a deluded egotist; but no one could pretend that these characters are wholly evil. The characters are revealed in their actions, and the reader is always guided in his response to what they do and say.

Even the heroes, Pyrocles and Musidorus, are not depicted as perfect; but it is interesting to notice that Sidney removed two flaws in their characters in the process of revision. In the old *Arcadia*, at the end of book III, the love of Pyrocles and Philoclea is consummated before matrimony. Sidney may well have felt, or have come to feel, that it was dangerous to depict Pyrocles succumbing to this temptation, especially since the author's comment is not disapproving:

He gives me occasion to leave him in so happy a plight, lest my pen might seem to grudge at the due bliss of these poor lovers, whose loyalty had but small respite of their fiery agonies.

Musidorus, with less excuse, is so overcome by the beauty of Pamela as she lies asleep that he determines to ravish her; but he is prevented by the timely arrival of some bandits. Musidorus is an unlikely ravisher, and Sidney may have felt that the incident would make Musidorus' final happiness undeserved. There is no reason to suppose that the countess of Pembroke was responsible for altering these two passages; but, if she did, the alterations were probably in accordance with Sidney's known wishes.

Sidney's teaching in *Arcadia* covers the whole range of private and public morality. We see the operations of lust, pride, ambition, anger, and egotism, no less than those of love, friendship, courtesy, and valor. We see the evils of superstition, tyranny, and anarchy, as well as the value of magnanimity, justice, and good counsel. We see how rebellion is caused by bad government, how courtesy and injustice, love and egotism, can be embodied in a single character. Sidney was providing, among other things, a lesson to his aristocratic readers on their duties to the state as well as on questions of private behavior. He demonstrates the dangers of a weak monarchy and of factious nobles; he shows the evils of "policy"; and, on a different plane, he exemplifies the workings of divine providence.

Nor does Sidney convey these lessons merely by the presentation of appropriate incidents and the depicting of different types of character: scattered through *Arcadia* there are orations, letters, and set speeches that further illustrate his points. Early in book I, for example, there is a letter written by Philanax to Basilius, urging him to follow wisdom and virtue and to ignore the oracle. Pyrocles, disguised as Zelmane, makes a "pacificatory oration" to the mutinous Arcadians. Pamela recites a prayer that Charles I borrowed for his private devotions. The evil Cecropia has three powerful speeches, one tempting Philoclea to marriage (III,5), one similarly addressed to Pamela (III,10), and one addressed to her son, urging him to rape Philoclea (III,17). It can be seen from the extract from the second of these that Sidney was quite prepared to give the devil his due, as Milton was to give some of his best poetry to Comus and Satan. Cecropia is endeavoring to combat Pamela's appeals to conscience by undermining her religion with Lucretian arguments:

Dear niece, or rather, dear daughter (if my affection and wish might prevail therein), how much doth it increase (trow you?) the earnest desire I have of this blessed match, to see these virtues of yours knit fast with such zeal of devotion, indeed the best bond, which the most politic wits have found, to hold man's wit in well doing? For, as children must first by fear be induced to know that, which after (when they do know) they are most glad of: so are these bugbears of opinions brought by great clerks into the world, to serve as shewels to keep them from those faults, whereto else the vanity of the world and weakness of senses might pull them. But in you (niece) whose excellency is such, as it need not to be held up by the staff of vulgar opinions, I would not you should love virtue servilely, for fear of I know not what, which you see not: but even for the good effects of virtue which you see. Fear, and indeed, foolish fear and fearful ignorance, was the first inventor of those conceits. . . . Be wise, and that wisdom shall be a God unto thee; be contented, and that is thy heaven: for else to think that those powers (if there be any such) above, are moved either by the eloquence of our prayers, or in a chafe by the folly of our actions, carries as much reason as if flies should think, that men take great care which of them hums sweetest, and which of them flies nimblest.

Such a speech displays not merely Sidney's usual eloquence but also his capacity to put

SIR PHILIP SIDNEY

himself in the place of characters with whom he could have had little sympathy. It could be said of him, to adapt John Keats's remark, that he had as much delight in depicting a Cecropia as a Pamela.

It is true, in a sense, as Virginia Woolf said, that "in the *Arcadia*, as in some luminous globe, all the seeds of English fiction lie latent." Although, as we have seen, *Arcadia* is essentially a heroic poem rather than a novel, we can find in it foreshadowings of later novels. It was not an accident that Richardson christened his first heroine Pamela, though Sidney's Pamela is closer in character to Clarissa. But we do Sidney an injustice if we treat him as a forerunner, an imperfect experimenter in a form of literature that was yet to be invented. *Arcadia* is, indeed, closer to Elizabethan drama than to any kind of novel and closer still, despite his avoidance of allegory, to *The Faerie Queene*. Unfinished though it is, *Arcadia* is incomparably the greatest Elizabethan prose work, precisely because it was conceived as a poem. Peter Heylyn called it:

a book which besides its excellent language, rare contrivances, and delectable stories, hath in it all the strains of Poesy, comprehendeth the universal art of speaking, and to them which can discern, and will observe, notable rules for demeanour both private and public.

We have seen that Sidney, in writing his *Defence of Poesie*, was somewhat embarrassed by the dearth of good poetry between the death of Chaucer and his own day. In spite of Wyatt, Surrey, and John Skelton in the first half of the century, there was a barren period between the death of Henry VIII (1547) and the accession of Elizabeth I (1558). Indeed, with the notable exception of Thomas Sackville's great "Induction," little memorable verse was written during the first twenty years of Elizabeth's reign. The transformation was brought about largely by Sidney, Spenser, and the poets associated with them. They determined to bring to English poetry the qualities of Pierre de Ronsard and Joachim Du Bellay, of Petrarch, of Ludovico Ariosto and Torquato Tasso, and to create a literature worthy to stand beside that of France and Italy.

At first both Spenser and Sidney wasted a great deal of time experimenting with classical meters. Almost all their work of this kind was lamentable, though Sidney did succeed in writing one poem in asclepiads that can still be read with pleasure:

O sweet woods, the delight of solitariness!
O how much I do like your solitariness!

Much more fruitful, however, were the verse experiments of other kinds scattered through *Arcadia*. They include examples of couplets, quatrains, six-line stanzas, madrigals, sonnets, double sestinas, canzone, and terza rima; and, although in some of these forms Sidney was a pioneer, they are all executed with remarkable skill. Some of the poems are suggested by the situations in *Arcadia*; others are detached eclogues; and in a few Sidney contrived to express more personal feeling (for instance, the lines beginning "The lad Philisides," written as a compliment to Penelope Devereux, and some stanzas about Hubert Languet). Their chief importance, however, lies in the fact that they are mostly poetic exercises, the means whereby Sidney taught himself to write. He and Spenser, by teaching themselves the craft of verse, not only made possible *Astrophel and Stella* and *The Faerie Queene* but also provided later poets with sure foundations on which to build.

The best poems in *Arcadia* are better than the worst sonnets in *Astrophel and Stella*. Sidney tells us in *The Defence of Poesie* that he had "slipped into the title of a poet," and here and there he displays the charm and mastery of his later work, as in the poem that begins "Lock up, fair lids, the treasure of my heart," or the famous "My true love hath my heart, and I have his."

Astrophel and Stella, Sidney's masterpiece, written while he was still in his twenties, was the first Elizabethan sonnet sequence interspersed with songs; it earned him the title English Petrarch. Some critics, indeed, have maintained that Sidney was not really in love with Penelope Devereux, that the sequence displays "detachment from the realities of ordinary passion," and that it was largely imitated from Continental models. But although we need not doubt that Sidney would not have written the sequence without the example of French and Italian sonneteers, none of the sonnets is merely a translation; the source hunters have been able to discover only a few examples of borrowing. There is, moreover, plenty of external evidence for identifying Stella with Penelope, besides the internal evidence of the sonnet in which Sidney puns on the name of her husband, Lord Rich. It may be mentioned, too, that this particular sonnet and stanzas from two of the interspersed songs were missing from the manuscripts that were first sent to the printing houses, possibly because they were regarded as too intimate for circulation, even among friends.

This does not mean, of course, that we can rely on the sonnets for biographical detail. Sidney was creating a work of art, even if he was also expressing his love. Although the poems doubtless reflect his real feelings, there is certainly an element of fiction, of dramatization. Some of the scenes may well be imaginary. The sonnet addressed to the River Thames may have been suggested by Petrarch's sonnets addressed to the Po and the Rhone (as Sir Sidney Lee believed) rather than by an actual incident. Even the feelings ascribed to Stella may have been invented. Stella was in love with Charles Blount before and after her forced marriage to Lord Rich; and it was this, rather than her "honor," that made her reject Sidney's advances. Sidney was not at liberty to tell the truth, even if the truth in this case had been as poetical as the fiction.

In *The Defence of Poesie* Sidney complains of the artificiality of much love poetry:

> But truly many of such writings, as come under the banner of unresistable love, if I were a mistress, would never persuade me they were in love: so coldly they apply fiery speeches, as men that had rather read lovers' writings, and so caught up certain swelling phrases.

It is clear that whatever the admixture of fiction in his own sonnets, he was determined at least to give the impression of a man deeply in love. In the very first sonnet—which probably was not written first—he makes the muse say to him: "Look in thy heart and write." In the third sonnet he dissociates himself from "dainty wits" and "Pindar's apes"—the imitators of Ronsard; and in Sonnet 28 he disclaims any allegorical intention. He writes, he tells us, "in

pure simplicity." Shakespeare, similarly, was to contrast his own "true plain words" with the ornate rhetoric of his rival. It is arguable that this kind of protest is itself a rhetorical device, and it has been pointed out that poets of the Pléiade had forestalled his attack on those who imitate "poor Petrarch's long-deceased woes"; but the important thing is that Sidney, unlike many Elizabethan sonneteers, does convince us by his art of the reality of his love. The beauty proceeding from art appears to be what Keats called "the true voice of feeling."

Not all the sonnets are equally serious. They range from conventional compliments and light-hearted conceits to the overflow of powerful feelings and bitter self-questionings. Some read almost like parodies, and in some of the best there is an undertone of irony. Those critics who have complained of the artificiality of the sonnets perhaps have failed to recognize the varying seriousness to be found in them. The variety of mood is one of the means by which Sidney convinces us of the reality of the experience.

As an example of Sidney's complex irony we may take Sonnet 74, which follows a conventional sonnet about Cupid and a song in which Astrophel describes how he stole a kiss from Stella while she was asleep—a stock subject for more than a thousand years. In the sonnet, however, Sidney pretends that he has never been visited by the muses, that he is a "poor layman":

> And this I swear by blackest brook of hell,
> I am no pick-purse of another's wit.

As Richard B. Young has shown, Sidney, "assuming the pose of ingenuousness and simplicity he finds in his models, makes fun of it by protesting too much." Even this does not exhaust the irony, for the first eight lines of the sonnet, in which he protests that he is not a plagiarist, are a close imitation of Persius.

Another example of irony is found in the famous sonnet on the moon (No. 31), which is not, as some critics have assumed, written in a mood of unqualified self-pity:

> With how sad steps, O Moon, thou climb'st the
> skies,
> How silently, and with how wan a face!

What, may it be, that even in heav'nly place
  That busy archer his sharp arrows tries?
Sure if that long-with-love-acquainted eyes
  Can judge of love, thou feel'st a lover's case:
  I read it in thy looks; thy languish'd grace,
  To me that feel the like, thy state descries.
Then ev'n of fellowship, O Moon, tell me
  Is constant love deem'd there but want of wit?
  Are beauties there as proud as here they be?
Do they above love to be lov'd, and yet
  Those lovers scorn whom that love doth pos-
    sess?
  Do they call virtue there ungratefulness?

The wan face and the languished grace of Diana in love with Endymion reflect on the half-pitiful and half-absurd figure of Astrophel; and in the sestet Sidney asks four questions. The first is aimed at those who regard his constancy as foolish; the next two are aimed at Stella, who, he implies, is the conventional proud beauty who despises the lover she deliberately attracts; and the last is aimed at himself for stigmatizing Stella's virtue, or chastity, as ingratitude.[4]

Thomas Nashe (in a preface to the first edition) described *Astrophel and Stella* as a "tragicomedy of love . . . performed by starlight . . . the argument cruel chastity; the prologue, Hope; the epilogue, Despair." This description is true as far as it goes, and the reference to starlight nicely hits off the climactic poem of the sequence; but the complexities and ironies that distinguish Sidney's sonnets from those of his many imitators are not brought out by Nashe's oversimplification.

The sequence exhibits three linked conflicts: that between reason and passion, between virtue and an adulterous love, in Astrophel's mind; the conflict in Stella's mind between sympathetic love and chastity; and the conflict between Astrophel and Stella, ending with his defeat. Many critics have contrasted the weakness and artificiality of the early sonnets with the impressiveness of the later ones; but it may well be that the sonnets were not composed in the order in which they were printed and that Sidney was varying his style to show the development of Astrophel's love, from the

[4] Charles Lamb, John Drinkwater, and others have taken the last line to mean "Do they call ungratefulness there a virtue?" But this interpretation would make the line intolerably clumsy, more difficult to read, and less subtle.

time when he "saw, and liked . . . liked, but loved not" to the later stages, when love had become an all-absorbing passion. The conventional description of Stella's eyes (No. 7), the equally conventional description of her face (No. 9), and the dragging in of Cupid and Venus for the paying of mythological compliments (Nos. 8, 11, 13, 19) do not so much show Sidney's immaturity as a poet as Astrophel's immaturity as a lover. Shakespeare, in the same way, showed the element of unreality in Romeo's love for Rosaline, Juliet's predecessor, by the conventional conceits he employs.

The attempt to reconcile love and virtue begins early in the sequence, when, in Sonnet 4, Astrophel protests that Stella

  shrines in flesh so true a Deity
That Virtue, thou thy self shalt be in love.

In the next sonnet (No. 5) he admits that the soul ought to govern the passions and that sexual love is a false idol, but he pleads that he cannot help loving Stella. He tells us (No. 16) that he has learned love right:

  As who by being poison'd doth poison know.

He laments the waste of his talents (No. 18) and admits the justice of a friend's criticism that his young mind is marred (No. 21), but he asks:

  Hath this world aught so fair as Stella is?

The conflict is intensified as the story comes to a climax. Sometimes Astrophel argues with himself, at other times he quotes what people say about him. When Stella confesses that she loves him platonically (No. 62), he prays:

  Dear, love me not, that ye may love me more.

His joy in her confession is soon changed to dissatisfaction with the platonic relationship she demands (Nos. 71, 72):

  But ah, Desire still cries: "Give me some food."

In the later sonnets the inner conflict is replaced by Astrophel's attempt to persuade Stella to surrender. He angers her by stealing a kiss (Second

Song), but is afterward permitted to kiss her. He rides to her house, confident of success (Nos. 84, 85), only to find her adamant in her chastity. He presses his suit at night, after everyone else has gone to bed, and is met by a tender but firm refusal in what is perhaps the most exquisite of the songs:

> No, no, no, no, my dear, let be.

This is followed by the bitter reproaches of the Fifth Song, which is close in spirit to the litany, oddly excluded from *Astrophel and Stella*, that has been thought, less plausibly, to have been written on the occasion of Penelope Devereux's marriage:

> Ring out your bells, let mourning shows be spread,
>   For Love is dead:
> All Love is dead, infected
> With plague of deep disdain:
> Worth, as nought worth rejected,
> And fair Faith scorn doth gain.
> From so ungrateful fancy,
> From such a female frenzie,
> From them that use men thus,
> Good Lord deliver us.

Astrophel recovers from his disappointment and again tries to persuade Stella to surrender, this time in a pastoral setting. Again she refuses him and makes explicit what had previously been implied:

> Tyrant Honour doth thus use thee,
> Stella's self might not refuse thee.

After this, Astrophel has to learn to live with his own despair, recognizing

> That in my woes for thee thou art my joy,
> And in my joys for thee my only annoy.

In two earlier sonnets, not included in *Astrophel and Stella* but providing a natural sequel, Sidney addresses Desire as

> Thou blind man's mark, thou fool's self-chosen snare,

and bids farewell to the "love, which reachest but to dust," so that he may embrace the love eternal.

This account of the central theme of *Astrophel and Stella* leaves out of consideration the extraordinary variety of mood in the sequence. Astrophel can be savage, as in his attack on Lord Rich (No. 24) or in his determination to cuckold him:

> Is it not evil that such a devil wants horns?

At other times he is able to smile at himself and to engage in conceits that are not meant to be taken seriously, as when, in reply to Stella's double "no," he professes to be delighted:

> For grammar says,—to grammar who says nay?
> That in one speech two negatives affirm!

The sonnets are firmly rooted in actuality, and we are given glimpses of the world outside—the designs of the Turks and the Poles, the campaign in Holland, intrigues in Scotland, the Irish question. There are no other Elizabethan sonnets—not even Shakespeare's—with such variety; and no others have such a coherent dramatic structure. The effect is obtained partly by the use of colloquial touches, the deliberate dissonances and the abrupt changes of mood that give the impression not of a poet with his singing robes about him, but of a man speaking to men or thinking aloud. "Sure, you say well," "O fools, or overwise," "What now, Sir Fool!"

> Guess we the cause? What, is it this? Fie, no.
> Or so? Much less. How then? Sure thus it is. . . .

> Come, let me write. And to what end? To ease
> A burthened heart.

> Let her go! Soft, but here she comes! Go to,
> Unkind, I love you not!

Sidney is using the sonnet form for dramatic monologue. These quotations are not taken from the best sonnets, but the effectiveness of the obvious masterpieces depends partly on their juxtaposition with the less "poetical" sonnets. That is why Sidney is a more important poet than he would seem to be from the anthologies. Even the great invocation to sleep gains from its context:

> Come Sleep, O Sleep, the certain knot of peace,
>   The baiting place of wit, the balm of woe,

The poor man's wealth, the prisoner's release,
The indifferent judge between the high and low,
With shield of proof, shield me from out the prease
Of those fierce darts Despair at me doth throw;
O make in me those civil wars to cease;
I will good tribute pay if thou do so.
Take thou of me smooth pillows, sweetest bed,
A chamber deaf to noise, and blind to light,
A rosy garland, and a weary head:
And if these things, as being thine by right,
Move not thy heavy grace, thou shalt in me
Livelier than elsewhere Stella's image see.

The images are not particularly original, but they are fitted into the form of the sonnet with exquisite skill, so that there is no padding and no forcing. From the point of view of poetic artistry, it is one of Sidney's finest achievements. The nice variation of vowel sounds; the subtle alliteration of *p, l,* and *s* in the octave, binding the lines and quatrains together, yet interrupted in the sixth line (because of its content) by the hard dentals; the cross alliteration in the second line (*bwbw*)—these are some of the indications of the poet's craftsmanship. Samuel Daniel, perhaps, among Sidney's followers equaled this sonnet from the point of view of sound, and Michael Drayton, once or twice, in perfection of phrasing; but Sidney has stamped the lines with his own individuality, and they are part of a larger whole, being sandwiched between two other sonnets on insomnia.

There are a number of shorter poems worthy to stand beside the best sonnets in *Astrophel and Stella*, several of which are familiar to the general reader from their appearance in every anthology of Elizabethan lyrics. The best of all, written to an Italian tune, exhibits Sidney's effortless mastery of a difficult stanza form:

The Nightingale, as soon as April bringeth
Unto her rested sense a perfect waking,
While late bare earth, proud of new clothing
    springeth,
Sings out her woes, a thorn her song-book making:
    And mournfully bewailing,
    Her throat in tunes expresseth
    What grief her breast oppresseth,
    For Tereus' force on her chaste will prevailing.
O Philomela fair, O take some gladness,
That here is juster cause of plaintful sadness:
Thine earth now springs, mine fadeth,
Thy thorn without, my thorn my heart invadeth.

There is no doubt of Sidney's greatness. The admiration felt for him as a man by those who knew him has been echoed, with justice, by successive biographers. Fulke Greville, looking back on the idol of his youth, could say truly that "the greatness which he affected was built upon true worth; esteeming fame more than riches, and noble actions far above nobility itself." But Sidney, as I have tried to show, was great not only as a man but also as a writer, partly because his writings reflect the singular beauty of his personality and partly because of his achievement in three diverse literary fields. His *Defence of Poesie* is the first real English criticism; his *Astrophel and Stella* is one of the seminal works of the sixteenth century, more influential, because more imitable, than *The Faerie Queene*; and *Arcadia* is the first great masterpiece of Elizabethan prose, which might be more generally acknowledged as such if it were more readily accessible to the general reader. Sidney achieved all this in the space of ten years, in the interstices of a life devoted to many other things: to politics, diplomacy, tournaments, travel, translation, love, and war. Sir William Temple, at the end of the seventeenth century, declared that he esteemed Sidney as "both the greatest poet and noblest genius of any that have left writings behind them, and published in ours or any other modern language." The praise is excessive, but it is a notable tribute from a man writing in an age so different from Sidney's.

SELECTED BIBLIOGRAPHY

I. BIBLIOGRAPHIES. S. A. Tannenbaum, *Sir Philip Sidney (Concise Bibliography)* (New York, 1941); M. Poirier, *Sir Philip Sidney, le chevalier poète élisabéthain* (Lille, 1948), with a list of relevant books.

II. COLLECTED EDITIONS. *The Countesse of Pembrokes Arcadia. Now the Third Time Published with Sundry New Additions* (London, 1598; repr. 10 times before 1700), including *Certaine Sonets, Defence of Poesie, Astrophel and Stella, Her Most Excellent Majestie Walking in Wansteet Garden* ("The Lady of May"), published presumably with the authority of Sidney's executors and providing good texts everywhere, including the first correct text of *Astrophel and Stella; The Works in Prose and Verse*, 14th ed., 3 vols. (London, 1724–1725); W. Gray, ed., *Miscellaneous Works and Letters* (Oxford, 1829; repr. Boston, 1860), with life and notes, omitting *Arcadia* and *Psalms* but including political pamphlets and some letters; A. B. Grosart, ed., *The Complete Poems*, 2 vols. (London, 1873), in Fuller Worthies' Library; G. E. Woodbury, ed., *The Defence of Poesie: A Letter to Queen Elizabeth; A Defence of Leicester* (Boston, 1908); J. Drinkwater, ed., *Poems* (London, 1909); A. Feuillerat, ed., *The Complete Works*, 4 vols. (Cambridge, 1912–1926), the standard ed., with full collations (except in the case of the "old" *Arcadia*) but without notes, and sometimes spoiled by a bad choice of text, and including the translation doubtfully attributed to Sidney (and finished by Arthur Golding) of Philip de Mornay's *A Woorke Concerning the Trewnesse of the Christian Religion* (1587); G. Bullett, ed., *Silver Poets of the Sixteenth Century* (London, 1947), including Wyatt, Surrey, Sidney, Walter Raleigh, and John Davies; W. A. Ringler, ed., *Poems* (Oxford, 1962), the standard ed., in Oxford English Texts Series; T. W. Craik, ed., *Selected Poetry and Prose* (London, 1965).

III. SEPARATE WORKS. *The Countesse of Pembrokes Arcadia* (London, 1590), facs. ed. by H. O. Sommer (London, 1891), Sidney's revision of the first three books of the "old" *Arcadia* (which remained in MS); *Syr P. S. His Astrophel and Stella . . . to the End of Which Are Added Sundry Other Rare Sonnets of Divers Noble Men and Gentlemen . . . for Thomas Newman* (London, 1591), with preface by Thomas Nashe, is an unauthorized and corrupt version, suppressed by Sidney's executors (the "Sundry Other Rare Sonnets" were stolen mainly from Samuel Daniel), repr. by Feuillerat, vol. II, without the "other rare sonnets," and in Sir Sidney Lee, ed., *Elizabethan Sonnets*, I (London, 1904); *Astrophel and Stella . . . for Mathew Lownes* (London, 1591), follows the above; *Syr P. S. His Astrophel and Stella . . . for Thomas Newman* (London, 1591), omits the preface and "other rare sonnets," and improves the text—modern eds. by A. W. Pollard (London, 1888) and M. Wilson (London, 1931), text compiled, translated, and prefaced by M. Poirier (Paris, 1957); *The Countesse of Pembrokes Arcadia . . . Now Since the First Edition Augmented and Ended* (London, 1593), the revised version of the first three books, with the last two books of the "old" *Arcadia*, slightly changed, also available in a modernized text, with seventeenth-century completion and continuation, E. A. Baker, ed. (London, 1907); *The Defence of Poesie . . . for William Ponsonby* (London, 1595), repr. by A. S. Cook (Boston, 1890), facs. ed. by Noel Douglas (London, 1928), the version authorized by Sidney's executors; *An Apologie for Poetry . . . for Henry Olney* (London, 1595), repr. by E. Arber (London, 1868), by E. S. Shuckburgh (Cambridge, 1891), by G. G. Smith in *Elizabethan Critical Essays*, I (London, 1904), by J. C. Collins (Oxford, 1907), by E. Rhys in *Prelude to Poetry* (London, 1927), and by G. Shep-

herd (Edinburgh, 1965); "A Discourse of Syr Ph. S. to the Queenes Majesty Touching Hir Mariage with Monsieur" (written 1580), in *Scrinia Ceciliana* (London, 1663) and in A. Collins, ed., *Letters and Memorials of State*, I (London, 1746); "Defence of Robert Dudley, Earl of Leicester" (written 1584), in A. Collins, ed., *Letters and Memorials of State*, I; *The Psalms of David, Begun by Sir P. Sidney and Finished by the Countess of Pembroke* (London, 1823), in *Select Early English Poets*, VIII (only the first forty-three sonnets are by Sidney), complete series repr. with comments in J. Ruskin, *Rock Honeycomb* (London, 1877), reiss. in Ruskin's *Works*, XXXI (London, 1907), and edited by J. C. A. Rathmell (New York, 1963); S. A. Pears, ed., *The Correspondence of Sir Philip Sidney and Hubert Languet* (London, 1845), also edited by W. A. Bradley (Boston, 1912).

IV. BIOGRAPHICAL AND CRITICAL STUDIES. G. Whetstone, *Sir Philip Sidney His Honorable Life, His Valiant Death, and True Virtues* (London, 1587), one of the many elegies on Sidney, containing valuable biographical material, especially about his death; F. Greville, *The Life of the Renowned Sir Philip Sidney* (London, 1652), repr. by N. Smith (Oxford, 1907), does not treat Sidney as a literary figure, but as a religious and political thinker; T. Zouch, *Memoirs of the Life and Writing of Sir Philip Sidney* (London, 1809); H. R. F. Bourne, *A Memoir of Sir Philip Sidney* (London, 1862), repr. as *Sir Philip Sidney, Type of English Chivalry* (London, 1891); J. A. Symonds, *Sir Philip Sidney* (London, 1886); B. Dobell, "New Light Upon Sir Philip Sidney's 'Arcadia,'" *Quarterly Review*, 211 (1909), 74–100; S. L. Wolff, *The Greek Romance in Elizabethan Prose Fiction* (New York, 1912); E. A. Greenlaw, "Sidney's *Arcadia* as an Example of Elizabethan Allegory," in *Anniversary Papers by Colleagues and Pupils of George Lyman Kittredge* (Boston, 1913), 327–337; M. W. Wallace, *The Life of Sir Philip Sidney* (Cambridge, 1915); J. G. Scott, *Les sonnets élisabéthains* (Paris, 1929), the most complete listing of sources and traditions for the sonnet sequences, including *Astrophel and Stella*; R. W. Zandvoort, *Sidney's Arcadia, a Comparison Between the Two Versions* (Amsterdam, 1929), the basic work on this subject; M. Wilson, *Sir Philip Sidney* (London, 1931); V. Woolf, *The Common Reader: Second Series* (London, 1932), contains the essay "The Countesse of Pembroke's Arcardia"; K. O. Myrick, *Sir Philip Sidney as a Literary Craftsman* (Cambridge, Mass., 1935), pioneer study of the art of Sidney's forms.

See also W. Ringler, "Master Drant's Rules," *Philological Quarterly*, 29 (1950), deleted passages from the "old" *Arcadia*, previously unprinted; and "Poems Attributed to Sir Philip Sidney," *Studies in Philology*, 47 (1950), 126–151; W. G. Crane, *Wit and Rhetoric in the*

Renaissance (New York, 1938); T. Moffet, *Nobilis, or A View of the Life and Death of a Sidney,* edited and translated from the Latin by V. B. Heltzel and H. H. Hudson (San Marino, Calif., 1940); C. M. Dowlin "Sidney and Other Men's Thought," *Review of English Studies,* 20 (1944), 257–271; T. Spencer, "The Poetry of Sidney," *Journal of English Literary History,* 12 (1945), brilliant treatment of Sidney's poetic "sincerity"; P. A. Duhamel, "Sidney's *Arcadia* and Elizabethan Rhetoric," *Studies in Philology,* 45 (1948), 134–150; J. F. Danby, *Poets on Fortune's Hill: Studies in Sidney, Shakespeare, Beaumont and Fletcher* (London, 1952), brilliant evocation of the moral ideals of the *Arcadia;* J. Buxton, *Sidney and the English Renaissance* (London, 1954), useful on Sidney's European connections; E. M. W. Tillyard, *The English Epic* (London, 1954); F. S. Boas, *Sir Philip Sidney, Representative Elizabethan* (London, 1955); D. P. Walker, "Ways of Dealing with Atheists: A Background to Pamela's Refutation of Cecropia," *Bibliothèque d'humanisme et renaissance,* 17 (1955), 252–277; J. L. Lever, *The Elizabethan Love Sonnet* (London, 1956); F. A. Yates, "Elizabethan Chivalry: The Romance of the Accession Day Tilts," *Journal of the Warburg and Courtauld Institutes,* 20 (1957), 4–25; R. B. Young et al., *Three Studies in the Renaissance: Sidney, Jonson, Milton* (New Haven, 1958), contains the essay "English Petrarke: A Study of Sidney's *Astrophel and Stella*"; R. L. Montgomery, *Symmetry and Sense: The Poetry of Sir Philip Sidney* (Austin, Tex., 1961); J. A. Van Dorsten, *Poets, Patrons and Professors* (London, 1962); W. R. Davis and R. A. Lanham, *Sidney's Arcadia* (New Haven, 1965); D. Kalstone, *Sidney's Poetry* (Cambridge, Mass., 1965).

RICHARD HOOKER

(ca. 1554-1600)

Arthur Pollard

THE writings of ecclesiastical controversy are usually more remarkable for their dullness and length than for any more admirable qualities. Occasionally, however, an exceptional work of lasting value has emerged from controversy of this kind. The greatest of such exceptions in English literature is Richard Hooker's *Of the Laws of Ecclesiastical Polity* (1593–1600), the work that established the position of the young Church of England at a time when it was surrounded by assailants, some of whom would have dragged it back to its allegiance to Rome and others who would have reformed it beyond all reason. The position that Hooker so carefully charted is one that has relevance to any understanding of the Church of England at every point between his time and ours. What John Dryden has to say about the church in *Religio laici*, the ways in which distinctions were made between Anglican and Methodist Evangelicals in the eighteenth century, and the whole relation of church and state that figures prominently in the Tractarian movement in the nineteenth century are all illuminated by an awareness of Hooker. But he is no mere ecclesiastical commentator. It is true that we cannot understand the church history of his time, the struggles of Anglican and Roman Catholic, Anglican and Puritan without him; but for this reason also the general political history of the age, tied so closely to matters of religion, makes no sense without Hooker.

Nor is it only an understanding of church affairs in the practical sense that is defective; Hooker's work is essential for a proper comprehension of both the theology and the philosophy of the period. He stands central in the tradition of Christian humanism, which means that he is an indispensable figure in relation to the literature of the period. He obviously affects the preachers, but we need to pay him due attention in our study of all the major writers of the late sixteenth and the seventeenth centuries. Edmund Spenser, William Shakespeare, John Donne, George Herbert, and John Milton can all at times be elucidated in the context of Hooker. Moreover, his own style, so appropriate a vehicle for a work so immense both in scope and in breadth of intellectual grasp and humane understanding, is itself a historic landmark in the development of English prose. The *Ecclesiastical Polity* might well be a landmark if only because it is a major scholastic work written not in Latin, the then-fashionable language of scholarship, but in English. Its importance, however, is greater than this, deriving from its intrinsic qualities. It is no exaggeration to say that its serene, majestic Ciceronian periods, involved but never obscure, lengthy but always preserving their momentum, and yet always under control, have never been surpassed in English literature. On several counts, therefore, Hooker will abundantly repay attention.

RELIGIOUS CONFLICT IN THE SIXTEENTH CENTURY

WE do not know exactly when Hooker was born at Exeter; but, whenever it was, it was an even more then normally troubled world into which he came. The date can be placed in the year 1553 or 1554. On July 6, 1553, the young Edward VI died and the new Protestant establishment was overthrown by the accession of his Roman Catholic sister, Mary. The religious turmoil in England had come to a head with Henry VIII's quarrel with the pope over his divorcing his first wife, Catharine of Aragon, in 1529–1530. The first phase of this turmoil may be said to stretch over the three decades that conclude with the Elizabethan Settlement in 1559. Henry's quarrel over his marriage was merely the occasion for the religious crisis, not its cause. Discontent with the Roman Catholic Church had been gathering strength over a long period and in many parts of Europe. At one level, the political, governments objected to the pope's pretensions to sovereignty over all their subjects. At another, the economic, ambitious eyes were cast upon the wealth of the church. At a third, the moral, men were quick to note the loose living of many churchmen. And at a fourth, the religious, they questioned some of the church's practices and beliefs, in particular its authoritarianism, which exalted its own authority over that of the Bible. Martin Luther first raised the standard of revolt in Germany in 1517, and the movement quickly spread. Henry, however, was no reformer in religion; indeed, he had written against Luther. His quarrel with Rome therefore brought about a schism, but did not establish a reformed church. In fact, England was left with a kind of hybrid national-Catholic church.

Under Henry's son and successor, Edward VI, the Church of England, guided by Thomas Cranmer, the archbishop of Canterbury, moved to a more definitely Protestant position. Cranmer was a reformer, not a revolutionary. He introduced the service of Holy Communion, but the Mass continued to be celebrated privately; the new General Confession coexisted alongside the practice of private confession; services were said in English, but some were still said in Latin. Cranmer's first prayer book (1549) was composed from the Roman Catholic breviary and from German Protestant books, chief among them Martin Bucer's *Simple and Religious Consultation;* but these were skillfully transformed by Cranmer's careful scholarship, beautiful style, and precise doctrinal views to express the Anglican position, and especially to support the view of the Eucharist as a commemoration of Christ's death rather than the Roman idea of a repeated sacrifice of Christ. With this latter change the function of the priest altered from that of a man divinely endowed to offer sacrifice to that of a minister appointed to teach and to preach. Some of the ceremonial and vestments associated with the old faith were done away with.

Most change provokes opposition, and not always from one side only. For some—the Roman Catholics—Cranmer had gone too far; for others—the Puritans—he had not gone anything like far enough. The Catholics were to rejoice at the succession of Mary in 1553. The new church of the Bible and the prayer book was destroyed, and with it perished many who had embraced the new faith. They came from all walks of life; but the chief among them was Cranmer himself, who was martyred at Oxford in 1556. Thousands saved their lives by fleeing to Frankfurt, Strasbourg, Basel, and Geneva, centers of extreme Protestantism. They returned at Mary's death in 1558, to strengthen the cause of the Puritans.

Mary was succeeded by her sister, Elizabeth, who established the religious settlement that bears her name. It would be wrong, however, to think that her long reign was one of tranquillity in religion. The Roman Catholic problem was still there, though it was now more political than religious, with hopes centered on the possible succession of Mary Queen of Scots to the throne of England. The crucial religious struggle lay between the Church of England and the Puritans, a struggle ultimately to end only after England had suffered civil war, regicide, and dictatorship. This happened in the two decades from 1640 to 1660, but in fact it was only political and military force that could constitute any danger to the church after 1600. The battle within, the controversy about religion, had been won before that date; and in that battle Richard Hooker played a not unworthy part. Indeed, a modern church historian has claimed that Hooker's *Ecclesiastical Polity* "marks the beginning of what we now call Anglicanism."[1]

LIFE OF HOOKER

IT is not only about Hooker's birth that we know so little. There is much in his life that we might like to learn, but the record is blank. He

[1] C. W. Dugmore, *The Mass and the English Reformers* (1958), p. 246.

was the subject of one of those quaint, attractive hagiographic sketches by which Izaak Walton has carved for himself an enduring niche in the temple of fame; and we still owe to Walton most of our knowledge of such details of Hooker's life as we possess. Even Walton did not know much about him; but he has left us some vivid details, such as the

. . . bad consequence [of] the kindness of Mrs *Churchmans* curing him of his late Distemper and Cold; for that was so gratefully apprehended by M. Hooker, that he thought himself bound in conscience to believe all that she said; so that the good man came to be perswaded by her, *that he was a man of a tender constitution,* and *that it was best for him to have a Wife that might prove a Nurse to him.* . . . And he . . . fearing no guile . . . trusted her to choose for him, promising upon a fair summons to return to *London,* and accept of her choice. . . . Now the Wife provided for him, was her daughter *Joan,* who brought him neither Beauty nor Portion; and for her conditions, they were too like that *Wife's* which is by *Solomon* compar'd to a *dripping house.* (Proverbs 19:13)[2]

Hooker's domestic trials are illustrated in the simultaneously amusing and pathetic account of what Sandys and George Cranmer (the archbishop's grandnephew) found on a visit to him, "where their best entertainment was his quiet company, which was presently denied them: for, Richard was call'd to rock the Cradle." Such details may or may not be true, but Walton's picture of the retired scholar dedicated to the task he had set himself is consistent with itself and is one that history has failed to alter.

Hooker went to school in his native Exeter and then, under the patronage of his uncle, John Hooker, chamberlain of the city, and of his uncle's friend, Bishop John Jewel of Salisbury, went at fifteen to Corpus Christi College, Oxford, in 1568. There he remained, first as student, then as fellow, until about 1580, when he moved to London and contracted the possibly mistaken marriage. In 1585 he was appointed master of the Temple, with the task of preaching

every Sunday morning to an influential congregation of London lawyers. A few of his sermons have survived. Hooker's appointment to the Temple was the most important single event in his life. It brought him into contact and conflict with the reader of the Temple and afternoon preacher, Walter Travers. As Thomas Fuller put it, "the pulpit spake pure Canterbury in the morning and Geneva in the afternoon" (*Worthies of England*). The controversy[3] grew; but to the credit of both Hooker and Travers, it was conducted with a seemliness rare at the time. At length, however, by reason of the passions it aroused, John Whitgift, the archbishop of Canterbury, intervened and inhibited Travers from further preaching. Walton quotes a letter to Whitgift in which we read that the controversy had led Hooker to begin "a Treatise, in which I intend a justification of the Law of our Ecclesiastical Polity; in which design God and his holy Angels shall at the last great day bear me witness which my conscience now does; that my meaning is not to provoke any, but rather to satisfy all tender consciences" (Keble's *Works of Hooker*, I, pp. 85–86). That task occupied him for the remaining fifteen years of his life. The first four books were published in 1593, the great fifth in 1597, and the remaining three were completed in a final fury of labor before his death in 1600.

ANGLICANS AND PURITANS

THE Elizabethan religious struggle was about authority in matters both of rule and of faith. For the Roman Catholics, authority resided in the church, in the pope at the head, and in the priest within each congregation. The church prescribed doctrine and practice. For the Puritans, authority derived from the Bible; and they claimed to draw all their doctrine and practice from that source. Most of them wished to espouse the presbyterian form of church government, in contrast with rule by bishops. This essentially meant independence for the local church, with power in the hands of lay elders

[2] C. J. Sisson argues cogently that Walton's stories of Hooker's marriage are untrue and were foisted upon the biographer by Edwin Sandys and George Cranmer, the first of whom had heard family stories to dispose him against Mrs. Hooker's family (*The Judicious Marriage of Mr. Hooker,* pp. 17–44).

[3] Walton gives a long account of the details (see Keble's edition of Hooker's *Works,* 1836, vol. 1, pp. 67–81).

and ordained pastors, free both of bishops and of state control. They also rejected ceremonial because it was unbiblical, outwardly symbolic of the sort of pretension they ascribed to the bishops, and a relic of Roman Catholicism.

The position of the Church of England lay between those of the Roman Catholics and the Puritans. It respected the authority of both church and Bible without deferring so exclusively to the one or the other as did its opponents. It claimed the need to use God-given reason as a means of interpretation. In this it left room for individual judgment, but at the same time it accepted the authority of the church in its government by bishops. In contrast with both its opponents, it linked its authority to that of the state by acknowledging the monarch as head of the church. The *via media* of Anglicanism is further demonstrated in its moderate use of ceremonial, neither so extravagant as Roman Catholic nor so austere as Puritan practice. The Elizabethan religious conflict was threefold in character; it was about government, about doctrine (and especially biblical authority and interpretation), and about ceremonial.

In strict chronological sense, the last came first. In the Convention of 1563 the Puritans launched an attack on the observance of saints' days, the practice of making the sign of the cross on a child's forehead at baptism, and the custom of kneeling to receive the bread and wine at Communion. All these they considered idolatrous and a relic of Catholicism. Over the years the attack moved to matters of doctrine, as, for instance, in the controversy between Thomas Cartwright and the future Archbishop Whitgift in 1572–1573, and ultimately to matters of authority. The pro-Puritan House of Commons made proposals at its sitting in 1584–1585 that were, in effect, an attack on the authority of the bishops. Elizabeth recognized, as did her successor James I, that no bishop meant no sovereign; and she refused to countenance the proposals. She and Whitgift formed a completely harmonious and irresistible partnership. His Articles of 1583—forbidding private preaching, requiring proper use of the liturgy and administration of the sacrament according to the Book of Common Prayer, demanding that ministers wear the prescribed dress and subscribe to the various oaths of obedience (to queen and bishop) and discipline—were designed to secure his purposes. To see that they did and to keep check on suspects, he set up the Ecclesiastical Commission in 1584. Two years later Whitgift was given powers of censorship over all publications through a Star Chamber decree. Despite this, controversy continued to rage, and indeed reached an unedifying climax in the notorious and abusive *Marprelate Tracts* of 1588–1589, a series of nine scurrilous, anonymous pamphlets, attacking and ridiculing the bishops, but at the same time in places arguing that "the externall gouernement of the Church of Christ be a thing so prescribed by the Lorde in the new testament, as it is not lawfull for any man to alter the same." The Puritans kicked hard, but Whitgift had won. He was the architect of the Elizabethan Settlement. Hooker was its apologist.

LAW, REASON, AND SCRIPTURE
(Ecclesiastical Polity I–IV)

HOOKER's greatness in this role is immediately made apparent in the *Ecclesiastical Polity* by the position that he takes at the beginning of his argument. Because the authority and interpretation of the Bible were so important a factor in the controversy, it might well be expected that he would begin with this question. It is the mark of his stature as a polemical writer that he does not. He sees that there is something more fundamental. He begins by considering the nature of law itself and the nature of man, which leads him to submit to law:

> Seeing that laws and ordinances in particular, whether such as we observe, or such as yourselves the Puritans would have established:—when the mind doth sift and examine them it must needs have often recourse to a number of doubts and questions about the nature, kinds, and qualities of laws in general; whereof unless it be thoroughly informed there will appear no certainty to stay our persuasion upon: I have for that cause set down an introduction on both sides needful to be considered: declaring therein what law is, how different kinds of law there are, and what force they are of according unto each kind.
>
> (Preface, C, VII, 2)

The first book is about law, and it begins with an appeal to the fundamental law of things, proceeding from God Himself. "The being of God is a kind of law to his working: for that perfection which God is, giveth perfection to that he doth" (Book I, II, 2). Here all law rests: "God therefore is a law both to himself, and to all other things besides" (I,II,3). Hooker then goes on to examine the law of nature (or reason), the law of nations, and the supernatural law of God. It is not sufficient, however, to justify the authority or to illustrate the variety of law. Hooker therefore examines its purpose, considering it in relation to man. Law is meant as man's guide. The argument must, in consequence, consider man's moral constitution. That is, it must take in questions of will, appetite, reason, and goodness. All goodness proceeds from God, and all goodness desired is therefore an aspiration toward God (I,v). Man may choose freely between will and appetite. "The object of Appetite is whatsoever sensible good may be wished for; the object of Will is that good which Reason doth lead us to seek" (I,VII,3). It is reason that makes the necessary distinction. Thus does Hooker begin by stating what law is and what man is. Thus does he lift the matter out of and beyond the bickering world of wrangling about ecclesiastical power and scriptural interpretation, and into the majestic realm of eternal verity. He is now ready to descend into the arena of detailed argument.

The second book considers the Puritan appeal to Scripture as "the only rule of all things" (Title). Here again Hooker's appeal is to fundamentals. He takes Cartwright's citation of Proverbs, 2, on the teaching of wisdom and disclaims that the first and ninth verses ("My son, if thou wilt receive my words, and hide my commandments with thee . . . then shalt thou understand righteousness and judgment") must refer exclusively to Scripture. There is a genial assurance about Hooker's reply: "The bounds of wisdom are large, and within them much is contained" (II,I,4). He continues: "Whatsoever either men on earth or the Angels of heaven do know, it is as a drop of that unemptiable fountain of wisdom" (*ibid.*). The inference is that wisdom is of God Himself and that He cannot be, and is not to be, confined to one way of teaching. Similarly, in relation to the credibility

of Scripture, Hooker shows that the Scriptures are not self-authenticating, that they require credence, and that they cannot themselves create that credence; it must be given to them.

We all believe that the Scriptures of God are sacred, and that they have proceeded from God; ourselves we assure that we do right well in so believing. We have for this point a demonstration sound and infallible. But it is not the word of God which doth or possibly can assure us, that we do well to think it his word. For if any one book of Scripture did give testimony to all, yet still that Scripture which giveth credit to the rest would require another Scripture to give credit unto it, neither could we ever come unto any pause whereon to rest our assurance this way; so that unless beside Scripture there was something which might assure us that we do well, we could not think we do well, no not in being assured that Scripture is a sacred and holy rule of well-doing. (II,IV,2)

We are back to the first book, to God and man in direct confrontation.

We are not to disqualify the faculties that God has given us. In our actions, conscience, and in our thinking, reason, must guide us. There *is* a place for human authority. Indeed, the appeal to, and choice of, passages from Scripture by the Puritans themselves is all done in the attempt to persuade; that is, it is directed by and to human authority. The result at best can only be, as Hooker puts it, "that *some things* which they maintain, as far as *some men* can *probably conjecture*, do *seem* to have been out of Scripture *not absurdly* gathered" (II,VII,9). The Puritan position, Hooker claims, is not only anti-intellectual; it is also rationally inconsistent. How else but by reason can the unbeliever be brought to conversion? (III,VIII,14).

Hooker does not ignore the necessity for intervention by the Holy Spirit; but "albeit the Spirit leads us into all truth and directs us in all goodness, yet because these workings of the Spirit in us are so privy and secret, we therefore stand on a plainer ground, when we gather by reason from the quality of things behaved or done, that the Spirit of God hath directed us in both, than if we settle ourselves to believe or to do any certain particular thing, as being moved thereto by the Spirit" (III,VIII,16). Reason must defend against that private interpretation or "enthusiasm" that for generations men were to see in every outburst of Scripture-centered revivalism, from the Puritans down to Ira David Sankey and Dwight Moody, and even to Billy Graham in our own day.

Hooker is careful to guard himself against the position into which it might appear that his attack on the Puritans was driving him. He defends himself against the possible accusation that he is denying the worth of Scripture. He is not doing that; he is merely attacking the wrong use of Scripture. He is quick to assure the reader:

Howbeit that here we swerve not in judgment, one thing especially we must observe, namely that the absolute perfection of Scripture is seen by relation unto that whereto it tendeth . . . that God did thereby intend to deliver, as in truth he doth, a full instruction in all things unto salvation necessary, the knowledge whereof man by nature could not otherwise in this attain unto. (II,VIII,5)

The Roman Catholics were mistaken in teaching that Scripture is insufficient, the Puritans in claiming that it is all-sufficient. As in other things, Hooker teaches that the *via Anglicana* pursues a middle course between these two extremes.

Absurd though he thought the Puritans' undiscriminating reliance on Scripture to be, Hooker goes on in the third book to consider their contention "That in Scripture there must be of necessity contained a form of church polity, the laws whereof may in nowise be altered" (Title). They cited Scripture to justify continued reform. Here was Hooker's difficulty, and the difficulty of all those who wished to follow the middle course. How could they claim that reform had gone far enough, and to what authority could they appeal to support a program of "So far and no farther"? Did they not lay themselves open to the charge of halfheartedness and of unwillingness to throw off the idolatries of Rome? Indeed they did; and along these lines the Puritan attack was marshaled. In reply Hooker, with an awareness of toleration unusual in his day, claims that church government need not be universally limited to one form alone (III,II.1). Moreover, it is sufficient that in things necessary, namely, "the articles of the Christian faith and the sacraments," a church

be in accord with Scripture; in things accessory or subsidiary, "because discretion may teach the Church what is convenient, we hold not the Church further tied herein unto Scripture, than that against Scripture nothing be admitted in the Church, lest that path which ought always to be kept even, do thereby come to be overgrown with brambles and thorns" (III,III,3).

Again, however, the argument must return to the question of authority. And again Hooker accuses the Puritans of misusing Scripture. First, they say that it must determine the mode of church government, then they quote it to suit themselves and derive general rules from it; "and so in effect they plainly grant that we ourselves may lawfully make laws for the Church, and are not bound out of Scripture only to take laws already made, as they meant who first alleged that principle whereof we speak" (III,VII,4). Thus Hooker can hold that "the government that is by Bishops" is "that which best agreeth with the sacred Scripture" (III,XI,14). From Scripture he derives the necessity for a hierarchy of the clergy and for a proper subordination; "as to the Apostles in the beginning, and to the Bishops always since, we find plainly both in Scripture and in all ecclesiastical records, other ministers of the word and sacraments have been" (III,XI,18). Order requires that this should be so.

LITURGY AND SACRAMENT
(*Ecclesiastical Polity V*)

WE are all but ready for the great fifth book with its comprehensive defense of the Church of England. The publication of 1593 was completed by a short apology in book IV for Anglican rites and ceremonies against the allegation that they were popish. Book V is the justification of what the Church of England does, of its polity and worship, its government and liturgy. The two could not be separated, for "the plot of discipline did not only bend itself to reform ceremonies, but seek farther to erect a popular authority of elders, and to take away episcopal jurisdiction, together with all other ornaments and means whereby any difference of inequality is upheld in the ecclesiastical order" (V, Dedication, 8).

As always, Hooker begins at the beginning by stating the grounds on which his argument is to be based. Where the Scriptures are not explicit, there are four propositions by which church polity must be guided. The first is that of intrinsic reasonableness, judged in the knowledge that the church proceeds from God and must therefore be both the most excellent form of human society and that which in each individual's estimation approaches nearest to God. "That which inwardly each man should be, the Church outwardly ought to testify" (V,vi,2). Second, Hooker appeals to the practice of antiquity (V,vii); third, to the authority of the church, which, "being a body which dieth not hath always power, as occasion requireth, no less to ordain that which never was, than to ratify what hath been before" (V,viii,1); and, last, to the church's power of dispensation to change when change is necessary (V,ix).

On this basis there follows an elaborate refutation of Puritan arguments about places of public worship, their arrangement and decoration (xi–xvii); about the Puritans' excessive stress on preaching (xviii–xxii); about prayer and especially the Book of Common Prayer (xxiii–xlix); about the sacraments (l–lvii), with a long section on baptism (lviii–lxv), catechizing (lxvi), the eucharistic controversy (lxvii–lxviii), observance of saints' days (lxix–lxxii), the marriage, churching, and burial services (lxxiii–lxxv); and, finally, the order and discipline of the clergy (lxxvi–lxxxi). Hooker's answer may be conveniently summarized under three heads: liturgy, sacrament, and establishment.

First, liturgy and the place in which it is enacted. Hooker argues for the special setting aside and dedication of the building in which God is to be worshipped and for its special decoration. The Puritans sought extreme simplicity. In reply Hooker asks: "Touching God himself, hath he anywhere revealed that it is his delight to dwell beggarly?" (V,xv,3). This is a shrewd thrust against those who insisted on the revelation of Scripture for doctrine and practice. Hooker with yet greater shrewdness goes on to quote Scripture, citing the regret of those who saw the second temple to be so inferior to that

of Solomon (Haggai 2:5, 9). This contrasts with Hooker's later ascription to the Puritans of such militant and destructively minded quotations in reference to church building as "Down with them, down with them, even to the very ground" (Psalms 137:7; V,xvii,1) and a whole series of others dealing with the overthrow of the high places by the Israelite princes (*ibid.*).

In the practice of worship the Puritans favored preaching as against simple reading of Scripture, and extempore prayer as against the ordered liturgy of the Book of Common Prayer. Hooker claims that God's Word can itself suffice for salvation (V,xxi,3). His polemic here seems to lead him, by positing an unnecessary opposition, to undervalue preaching. As always, of course, he protects himself with a caveat, taking care to speak of "sermons as keys to the kingdom of heaven, as wings to the soul, as spurs to the good affections of men, unto the sound and healthy as food, as physic unto diseased mind" (V,xxii,1). Nevertheless, he is misled by the Puritan emphasis on the unique importance of sermons into underestimating their worth (see V,xxii,17).

In the long section on prayer, Hooker meets and considers Puritan criticisms in detail: their allegation that the liturgy stemmed from unreformed medieval practice, their dislike of the surplice and of the use of gesture and ceremony, their criticism of the Book of Common Prayer's excessive length and miscellaneous composition, and of its redundant and unworthy petitions.[4] Hooker's chapters in this section of book V are more than ordinarily full of noble passages. Their nobility surely flows from the affection he had for the book about which he was writing. It must suffice to quote a single passage, his great eulogy of the psalter:

What is there for man to know which the Psalms are not able to teach? They are to beginners an easy and familiar introduction, a mighty augmentation of all virtue and knowledge in such as are entered before, a strong confirmation to the most perfect among others. Heroical magnanimity, exquisite justice,

---

[4] Cranmer's first prayer book (1549) had been modified in a Protestant direction in 1552, but the Elizabethan book of 1559 moved back to the position of the first book. The Puritans disliked its "vain repetitions," its pleas for temporal blessings, and its imitations of Roman Catholic prayers.

grave moderation, exact wisdom, repentance unfeigned, unwearied patience, the mysteries of God, the sufferings of Christ, the terrors of wrath, the comforts of grace, the works of Providence over this world, and the promised joys of that world which is to come, all good necessarily to be either known or done or had, this one celestial fountain yieldeth.

(V,XXXVII,2)

Turning to the sacraments, the first thing we must notice is the centering of Hooker's theology upon the Incarnation, there being no "way of saving man but by man himself . . . the love and mercy of God towards man, which this way are become such a spectacle as neither men nor angels can behold without a kind of heavenly astonishment" (V,LI,3). The sacraments serve to make us partakers of Christ; they are "heavenly Ceremonies, which God hath sanctified and ordained to be administered in his Church, first, as marks whereby to know when God doth impart the vital or saving grace of Christ unto all that are capable thereof, and secondly as means conditional which God requireth in them unto whom he imparteth grace" (V,LVII,3). They are moral instruments used by us, and their effects derive from Him. Thus, "at the time when He giveth His heavenly grace, He applieth by the hands of His ministers that which betokeneth the same: nor only betokeneth, but, being also accompanied for ever by such power as doth truly work, is in that respect termed God's instrument, a true efficient cause of grace" (VI,VI,11). The sacraments are a cause of grace; but the grace is from God, and the presence of our Lord in the sacrament is within the believer himself. Hooker's most explicit statement on the subject reads:

In the Eucharist we so receive the gift of God, that we know by grace what the grace is which God giveth us, the degrees of our own increase in holiness and virtue we see and can judge of them, we understand that the strength of our life begun in Christ is Christ, that his flesh is meat and his blood drink, not by surmised imagination but truly, even so truly that through faith we perceive in the body and blood sacramentally presented the very taste of eternal life, the grace of the sacrament is here as the food which we eat and drink. (V,LXVII,1)

He is therefore able to argue that "the real presence of Christ's most blessed body and blood is not therefore to be sought for in the sacrament, but in the worthy receiver of the sacrament" (V,LXVII,6).

ESTABLISHMENT
(Ecclesiastical Polity V–VIII)

IN the last chapters of book V, Hooker moves on to questions of establishment (the relation of church and state) and of the order and discipline of the clergy. Once again he starts at the beginning, with the belief that a man's religion, his relationship with God, is what he really most desires, and that all else derives from it.

Every man's religion is in him the wellspring of all other sound and sincere virtues, from whence both here in some sort and hereafter more abundantly their full joy and felicity ariseth, because while they live they are blessed of God and when they die their works follow them: so at this present we must call to mind how the very worldly peace and prosperity, the secular happiness, the temporal and natural good estate both of all men and of all dominions hangeth chiefly upon religion, and doth evermore give plain testimony that as well in this as in other considerations the priest is a pillar of that commonwealth wherein he faithfully serveth God. (V,LXXVI,1)

Not only does Hooker take the argument back to its origins but, as this passage shows, the logical grasp that achieves this is accompanied by a quality of vision that exalts the discussion and takes it out of those sterile and often abusive depths in which controversy in his time was customarily conducted.

The passage quoted also shows the importance that, for Hooker, attached to authority, to priesthood, to episcopacy and monarchy. Church and state were essentially interrelated and interdependent. The position of the king in respect of ecclesiastical law and the appointment of bishops, and indeed the whole question of his supremacy, is treated at length in book VIII, where Hooker approvingly quotes Ambrose: " 'Imperator bonus intra ecclesiam, non supra ecclesiam est': kings have dominion to exercise in ecclesiastical causes, but according to the laws of the Church" (VIII,II,17). The whole matter of authority is summed up in one of those passages in which Hooker's argument is carried forward by his fervent conviction. All authority derives from God; all who rule, rule from Him; all authority must therefore be properly given and properly revered.

The ministry of things divine is a function which as God did himself institute, so neither may men undertake the same but by authority and power given them in lawful manner. That God which is in no way deficient or wanting unto man in necessaries, and hath therefore given us the light of his heavenly truth, because without that inestimable benefit we must needs have wandered in darkness to our endless perdition and woe, hath in the like abundance of mercies ordained certain to attend upon the due execution of requisite parts and offices therein prescribed for the good of the whole world, which men thereunto assigned do hold their authority from him, whether they be such as himself immediately or as the Church in his name investeth, it being neither possible for all nor for every man without distinction convenient to take upon him a charge of so geat importance. They are therefore ministers of God, not only by way of subordination as princes and civil magistrates whose execution of judgment and justice the supreme hand of divine providence doth uphold, but ministers of God as from whom that authority is derived, and not from men. For in that they are Christ's ambassadors and his labourers, who should give them their commission but he whose most inward affairs they manage? Is not God alone the Father of spirits? Are not souls the purchase of Jesus Christ? What angel in Heaven could have said unto man as our Lord did unto Peter, "Feed my sheep: Preach: Baptize: Do this in remembrance of me: Whose sins ye retain they are retained: and their offences in heaven pardoned whose faults you shall on earth forgive?" What think we? Are these terrestrial sounds, or else are they voices uttered out of the clouds above? The power of the ministry of God translateth out of darkness into glory, it raiseth men from the earth and bringeth God himself down from heaven, by blessing visible elements it maketh them invisible grace, it giveth daily the Holy Ghost, it hath to dispose of that flesh which was given for the life of the world and that blood which was poured out to redeem souls, when it poureth malediction upon the heads of the wicked they perish, when it revoketh the same they revive. (V,LXXVII,1)

Again one notices the vision in this passage, the vision of the glory of Christian priesthood derived from God. Hooker sees it as a high calling with high responsibilities, and therefore deserving of a proper regard. This is the climax of the whole work. The last three books, which Hooker strove to finish before his death in 1600, deal with the Puritan claim for the necessity of lay elders (VI), with episcopacy (VII), and with the ecclesiastical jurisdiction of the monarch (VIII). Incidentally, Hooker ultimately argued for an apostolically determined episcopate, with "bishops invested above other pastors" (VII,XL,8). He believed, that is, that the order of bishops had been established by the apostles. He argues this, however, as a matter of history rather than of doctrine. He never appears to plead for an actual apostolic succession in the sense that the authority of the apostles had been physically handed down from bishop to bishop, from the first century through the ages. The last three books as a whole are really just an elaboration of the position about authority that Hooker so clearly and so passionately expresses in the statement quoted above.

HOOKER'S SERMONS

THE qualities of clarity and passion appear again in Hooker's sermons, seven of which have been preserved and may be found in Keble's edition. He appeals to reason, conscience, and refined feeling. He never condescends to his audience; but he does concede, at any rate by comparison with the demands he makes in the *Ecclesiastical Polity*. One feels that he has the same grasp of his subject in all its depth and breadth; he pursues it into all its subdivisions, not shirking any difficult issues; but his style is carefully adjusted to the different circumstances of his audience. His thought is still molded within the period and carried over several separate statements; but it is also more divided, more coordinate, more simply consecutive, less involved than in his main work. Sometimes it is as simple as the following: "In a Christian man there is first Nature; secondly Corruption, perverting Nature; thirdly Grace correcting, and amending Nature" (Sermon IV).

This is then expanded and illustrated. At another time it is a little more sophisticated, with variation of tone, of sentence order, and of rhetorical device:

Truth, they say, is the daughter of time: and in time who doubteth but God may discover that which, because we presently see not, must we needs therefore presently deny? Into the heart of Joseph, at what time his brethren made gain of his person by merchandise; into the heart of Daniel, at the hour wherein he left his native soil; hardly could it have struck what good so unpleasant accidents in the end would grow unto. (Sermon III)

Hooker's emotive comparisons are most often drawn from Scripture, but occasionally we come upon a vivid touch reminiscent of someone like Latimer with his racy style:

We forsake the Lord's inheritance and feed it not. What is the reason of this? Our own desires are settled where they should not be. We ourselves are like those [pregnant] women which have a longing to eat coals, and lime, and filth; we are fed, some with honour, some with ease, some with wealth; the gospel waxeth loathsome and unpleasant in our taste. (Sermon VI)

By contrast, however, Hooker can rise to a noble peroration such as this:

The earth may shake, the pillars of the world may tremble under us, the countenance of the heaven may be appalled, the sun may lose his light, the moon her beauty, the stars their glory; but concerning the man that trusteth in God. . . . what is there in the world that shall change his heart, overthrow his faith, alter his affection towards God, or the affection of God to him? . . . I am not ignorant whose precious blood hath been shed for me; I have a Shepherd full of kindness, full of care, and full of power: unto him I commit myself; his own finger hath engraven this sentence in the tables of my heart, "Satan hath desired to winnow thee as wheat, but I have prayed that thy faith fail not": therefore the assurance of my hope I will labour to keep as a jewel unto the end; and by labour, through the gracious mediation of his prayer, I shall keep it. (Sermon I)

HOOKER'S STYLE

CLARITY and passion are indeed the key qualities of Hooker's style. Where he is less than immediately clear, this is usually because of the difficulty and complexity of the statement he is making. I have already indicated indirectly something of his love of clarity in the repeated references to his insistence on examining any argument from its beginning. Yet he also realized that there must always be a point that we accept as the beginning, that is, that all arguments must proceed to some extent on assumptions from before the beginning, on necessary presuppositions. Speaking of those who demand "what Scripture can teach us the sacred authority of Scripture," he replies:

As though there were any kind of science in the world which leadeth men unto knowledge without presupposing a number of things already known. . . . The main principle whereupon our belief of all things therein contained dependeth is, that the Scriptures are the oracles of God himself. This in itself we cannot say is evident. . . . There must be therefore some former knowledge presupposed which doth herein assure the hearts of all believers. (III,VIII,13)

Just as Hooker takes care to indicate where he is starting, so also there is precision in the steps of his argument. None is missed, each is carefully indicated; there is a sure progression and a firm conclusion.

Where authority will support his case, it is quoted aptly and economically. Sometimes it is a single line, at others it may occupy a page or two. It is used both to confirm his own and to refute his opponents' arguments. It is employed copiously and sufficiently, but never superfluously. Hooker must have had an almost encyclopedic knowledge of the writings of the Christian Fathers. In his use of such authorities he fully lived up to the epithets that have been attached to his name. He was both learned and judicious. More than that, however, by his reliance on authorities he has demonstrated his regard for tradition, that historical sense of his that enabled him to argue for the continuity of the English church within the whole Catholic Church.

The clarity we have noted in his development of argument is seen again in his use of word and image. One never feels that Hooker is writing merely for effect. Logic always takes precedence over rhetoric. This is especially noticeable in a comparison of the first five books with the last three, which did not receive his final polishing. There one sees an occasional sharpness in his controversial tone that is rare in the earlier books. This does not mean that he refrains from hitting hard. Hooker addresses and attacks the Puritans directly. He deals at length, for instance, with the Anabaptists (a byword among the Elizabethans for licentiousness) and their moral and civil anarchic practices, then turns to the Puritans and, in effect, tells them that the end of their ways, though they may not realize it, is identical with that of the Anabaptists (Preface, C,vii,13). He is skillful in exposing and exploiting his adversaries' arguments. Occasionally, indeed, he deftly causes their own images to recoil upon themselves. Thus, taking Cartwright's example of the crooked stick and his view that it "is not straightened unless it be bent as far on the clear contrary side, that so it may settle itself at the length in a middle estate of evenness between both," he goes on to ask:

But how can these comparisons stand them in any stead? When they urge us to extreme opposition against the church of Rome, do they mean we should be drawn unto it only for a time, and afterwards return to a mediocrity? or was it the purpose of those reformed churches, which utterly abolished all popish ceremonies, to come in the end back again to the middle point of evenness and moderation?

(IV,viii,3)

Then, with beautifully modulated and restrained irony, he plays for the rest of the paragraph with the inconsistency between this statement and the Puritans' known intentions. Occasionally Hooker seems to extend his opponents' arguments unfairly, or perversely to refuse to see the point. When, for instance, he considers their view that "we are not so much to fear infection from Turks as from papists," he continues: "What of that? we must remember that by conforming rather ourselves in that respect to Turks, we should be spreaders of a worse infection into others than any we are likely to draw from papists by our conformity with them in ceremonies" (IV,vii,6). Hooker has, in fact, tried to conduct a sort of verbal sleight-of-hand. Not to "fear infection" from the Turks does not mean to "conform ourselves" to them. In general, however, he conducts the argument on a rare level of good manners and intellectual integrity; and, as Dean R. W. Church commented, he is rarer still among con-troversialists of his time in being "more intent on showing *why* [his] opponents are wrong than even the fact that they are so" (*Introduction to First Book of Hooker*, p. xvi).

In showing why his opponents are wrong, Hooker is presenting his own case; and it is in this positive direction that his true greatness lies. I have said that with him logic always takes precedence over rhetoric, but I have also said that clarity and passion are his characteristic qualities. These two statements are not contradictory. The conviction is in the logic; its power often flows from the passion. This can be illustrated even in his images. Speaking of the need to reform the corrupted church, he writes:

He which will perfectly recover a sick and restore a diseased body unto health, must not endeavour so much to bring it to a state of simple contrariety, as of fit proportion in contrariety unto those evils which are to be cured. He that will take away extreme heat by setting the body in extremity of cold, shall undoubtedly remove the disease, but together with it the diseased too.

(IV,viii,1)

One can feel the power in the argument of the first sentence; it is when we contemplate the image that we sense the feeling that becomes explicit and definite in the last phrase. This passage is apt also to illustrate three of Hooker's chief qualities: the observation that provides a rich store of exemplary material, the shrewdness of choice, and the quiet humor that is never far from his work.

Hooker's prose has been described as that of an "English Aristotle set to music" (D. C. Boughner, "Notes on Hooker's Prose," *Review of English Studies*, 15 [London, 1939], 194–200). His characteristic sentence is a long Ciceronian period, with an early indication of the subject, an elaborate development of it, and a matured conclusion. The logic is paralleled and supplemented by the rhythm. The sweep of the sentence matches the sweep of the thought. Nor is it only the sweep of the sentence; it is equally that of the paragraph:

A law therefore generally taken, is a directive rule unto goodness of operation. The rule of divine operations outward, is the definitive appointment of God's own wisdom set down within himself. The rule of natural agents that work by simple necessity, is the determination of the wisdom of God, known to God himself, the principal Director of them, but not unto them that are directed to execute the same. The rule of natural agents which work after a sort of their own accord, as the beasts do, is the judgment of common sense or fancy concerning the sensible goodness of those objects wherewith they are moved. The rule of ghostly or immaterial natures, as spirits and angels, is their intuitive intellectual judgment concerning the amiable beauty and high goodness of that object, which with unspeakable joy and delight doth set them on work. The rule of voluntary agents on earth is the sentence that Reason giveth concerning the goodness of those things which they are to do. And the sentences which Reason giveth are some more some less general, before it come to define in particular actions what is good.   (I,viii,4)

This paragraph opens with a short, precise assertion containing the two key words "rule" and "goodness," which will be repeated and dwelt upon in the following sentences. Each of the five sentences that follow illustrates the manner of operation of one of the rules; and there is an ascent, which Elizabethan readers would have recognized, from simple natural agents that work by necessity to the highest of created things, spirits and angels. Then, at the end, man's place, that of rational beings, is defined; and the paragraph closes with a statement about the way in which Reason, the guide to voluntary agents, determines goodness. The logic of Hooker's argument leads him in the next paragraph to consider the "main principles of Reason." In the paragraph I have quoted, we see Hooker using the rhetorical device of anaphora, or repetition of a word or phrase in successive sentences. His use of imagery as a device of argument has already been illustrated. In addition, a word may be given to the contribution that such devices as inversion and parenthesis make. Sometimes the inversion strengthens the connection with the previous sentence, as when a reference to Nature is continued in a sentence beginning "By her from Him we receive . . ." (I,viii,3). Principally, however, the inversion is emphatic, as in "infinite duties there are . . ." (ibid.).

Parenthesis is sufficiently illustrated in the passage below, one of the noblest in the whole of the *Ecclesiastical Polity*. It is the opening paragraph of the Preface, full of Hooker's sense of the nobility and solemnity of the task he was undertaking, and of the rancor of the conflict into which he was entering, pervaded by a foreboding as to what the end must be, yet fully resigned to whatever God would have come to pass:

Though for no other cause, yet for this; that posterity may know we have not loosely through silence permitted things to pass away as in a dream, there shall be for men's information extant thus much concerning the present state of the Church of God established among us, and their careful endeavour which would have upheld the same. At your hands, beloved in our Lord and Saviour Jesus Christ, (for in him the love which we bear unto all that would but seem to be born of him, it is not the sea of your gall and bitterness that shall ever drown,) I have no great cause to look for other than the selfsame portion and lot, which your manner hath been hitherto to lay on them that concur not in opinion and sentence with you. But our hope is, that the God of peace shall (notwithstanding man's nature too impatient of contumelious malediction) enable us quietly and even gladly to suffer all things, for that work's sake which we covet to perform.

Here and throughout Hooker's work is the realization of the Ciceronian ideal, *dicere ornate et copiose;* but it is more than this. Beneath the fullness and ornamentation of statement there is the informing passion of the whole.

HOOKER'S IDEAS
AND ENGLISH LITERATURE

"To follow completely the thought of Shakespeare and Milton and Richard Hooker is to have mastered a great system of intellectual and moral culture differing much from ours and now in large part forgotten, but not simpler than ours or from a logical point of view less adequate." These are the words of Hardin Craig (*The Enchanted Glass* [New York, 1936], p. 187). Students of literature may be more interested in following the thought of Shakespeare and Milton than that of Hooker, but they cannot do one without the other. As Craig points out elsewhere, "no such statement of the nature, scope, and function of law [as Hooker's] can perhaps elsewhere be found; but Hooker's analysis is none the less explicative of the thought of the age" (p. 28). This section can touch only briefly upon the parallels between Hooker and the major literary figures of his own and the succeeding generation. In doing so, reference will nevertheless be made to several important topics in Hooker's work: nature, law, order, reason, and the position of the Church of England.

"Obedience of creatures unto the law of nature is the stay of the whole world" (I,III,2). This is a key sentence in *The Ecclesiastical Polity*; it is also a key sentence in its time. The law was God-given; and in it was seen a hierarchy of creation, each creature filling its allotted place and fulfilling its allotted function.

The heavens themselves, the planets, and this centre
Observe degree, priority and place

. . .

How could communities,
Degrees in schools, and brotherhoods in cities,
Peaceful commerce from dividable shores,
The primogenitive and due of birth
But by degree stand in authentic place?
(*Troilus and Cressida*, I,III,85–86, 103–108)

The idea of order was the same, whether in nature or in society. In a similar manner Donne, in the *First Anniversary*, could argue:

'Tis all in pieces, all coherence gone,
All just supply, and all relation.
(213–214)

And Milton's Hell is above all else a denial of order, a refusal of obedience, an establishment of chaos:

To do aught good never will be our task,
But ever to do ill our sole delight,
As being the contrary to his high will
Whom we resist.
(*Paradise Lost*, I,159–161)

Donne more than once discoursed on the order of the world (as in *Sermons*, G. R. Potter and E. Simpson, eds., II, p. 170), and he used the argument from order to suggest that this was a way in which man's reason might be satisfied (*ibid.*, III, p. 359). Like Hooker, he believed that the intellectual faculty must cooperate with

faith. Indeed, he said as much in a quaint complimentary context in one of the epistles "To the Countess of Bedford": "Reason is our soul's left hand, faith her right."

Like Hooker, Donne held a high estimate of reason. Shakespeare displayed a similar attitude: "What a piece of work is a man! How noble in reason! how infinite in faculties" (*Hamlet*, II,II,305–307). Reason was not regarded merely as an intellectual faculty. "Right reason" meant more than this; it was an ethical guide as well. "Reason is the director of man's Will by discovering in action what is good" (*Ecclesiastical Polity*, I,VII,4). When reason fails, the undirected will becomes the victim of appetite. "Through neglect [of reason], abused we are with the show of that which is not; sometimes the subtilty of Satan inveigling us as it did Eve" (*ibid.*, I,VII,7). Satan is the personification of Reason denied, the embodiment of passionate disobedience, as God is the embodiment of Reason absolute. When he succeeds, Satan passes on his passionate disobedience to others.

Upstart Passions catch the Government
From Reason, and to servitude reduce
Man till then free.
(*Paradise Lost*, XII,88–90)

Adam and Eve, creatures

who not prone
And Brute as other Creatures, but endu'd
With Sanctitie of Reason, . . .
(*ibid.*, VII,505–507)

give way to passion, to a carnality that is "brute" in the same way that Gertrude did in *Hamlet*:

A beast that wants discourse of reason
Would have mourn'd longer.
(I,II,150–151)

Depraved man is always considered bestial by Shakespeare, because that condition represents a descent in the Chain of Being, or hierarchy of creation.

When man ascends, he becomes "in apprehension, how like a God"; and God is absolute Reason. Such absoluteness is free, rationally as well as by volition; that is, it is deliberate without being capricious. As Milton's God expresses it,

> . . . Necessitie and Chance
> Approach not mee, and what I will is Fate.
> *(Paradise Lost*, VII,172–173)

There is therefore no element of necessity, Milton claims, in God's foreknowledge of the Fall. Adam and Eve cannot object to their fate,

> As if Predestination over-rul'd
> Their will, dispos'd by absolute Decree
> Or high foreknowledge; they themselves decreed
> Their own revolt, not I: if I foreknew,
> Foreknowledge had no influence on their fault.
> *(ibid.,* III,114–118)

This is exactly Hooker's position: "Prescience, as prescience, hath in itself no causing efficiency" (V, Appx. no. I).

God is the source of all:

> One almightie is, from whom
> All things proceed and up to him return,
> If not deprav'd from good, . . .
> *(ibid.,* V,469–471)

And man, the highest of created things, has a soul that "Reason receives, and reason is her being" *(ibid.,* V,487). What is shown in the order of nature is an example for the order of society. Man by his reason has also to observe hierarchy therein. Hence the monarch is "the deputy elected by the Lord" *(Richard II,* III,II,57), and hence also the enormity of rebellion. Because the queen was head of the English church, the opposition of Catholics, loyal to the pope, himself a temporal ruler, and of Puritans, who wished to democratize her government, constituted an act against temporal, God-ordained authority. As a good Protestant and loyal subject, Spenser glorified Elizabeth; for him her rule embodied the sanctity of the individual state and the right of private judgment in spiritual matters. His anti-Catholicism appears in *The Shepherd's Calendar* (for instance, the July Eclogue), and with it there is praise for the shepherd Algrind (Archbishop Grindal); his anti-Puritanism is expressed, for example, in the figure of Kirkrapine in *The Faerie Queene,* book I. Donne's criticism of the two faiths, di-

verging in opposite directions from the Anglican *via media,* is in his third satire. Herbert also contrasts the two:

> She on the hills, which wantonly
> Allureth all in hope to be
> By her preferr'd,
> Hath kiss'd so long her painted shrines,
> That e'en her face by kissing shines,
> For her reward.

> She in the valley is so shy
> Of dressing, that her hair doth lie
> About her ears:
> While she avoids her neighbour's pride,
> She wholly goes on the other side,
> And nothing wears.
> ("The British Church")

This last image reminds us of what Jonathan Swift would do irreverently on the same subject in *A Tale of a Tub* (1704). Dryden also places the Church of England between the two extremes in his *Religio laici* (1682). Neither he nor Swift, however, had that deep affection for the Church of England that Herbert then goes on to express:

> But, dearest Mother, (what those miss)
> The mean thy praise and glory is,
> And long may be.

Hooker also seems to have had little of Herbert's lyrical enthusiasm; but he shared the sentiments here expressed, and by his massively rational exposition he has shown succeeding generations that for the Church of England the mean her praise and glory is.

CONCLUSION

THERE is a majestic quality about Hooker's work. It is seen in the breadth of his learning and the depth of his thinking. It is seen in his view of man and of God. From God issue law and authority, and to man is given the reason to understand the will of God and rightly to use the mediating agencies of Scripture and tradition that God in history has provided. The Puritans, Hooker felt, debased both God and man: God, by making Him arbitrary and even the slave of His own word; and man, by insisting on his depravity and intellectual helplessness. Both in what he believed and in what he opposed, Hooker was a Christian humanist.

The majesty of his thought is matched by the nobility of his style. He showed how the Ciceronian manner might be adapted to English. Others would follow him in this endeavor, but none would surpass his achievement. Milton's prose has a fine Latinate dignity, and of all Hooker's successors perhaps Jeremy Taylor approached nearest to him; but Taylor's rolling periods are not without a touch now and again of the flamboyance that, for instance, we find in Sir Thomas Browne. As a stylist Hooker is essentially unique.

The occasion from which the *Ecclesiastical Polity* took its birth has passed into the limbo of "old unhappy far-off things/And battles long ago"; but Hooker's work remains as one of those fortunate by-products that sometimes issue from such sad events. It gives formidable and memorable expression to subjects fundamental in man's experience in general, and indispensable to an understanding of English history and literature of the sixteenth and seventeenth centuries in particular. Sane, noble, sincere, supremely civilized, Hooker remains worth reading for himself; clear, comprehensive, profound, he is necessary reading properly and fully to elucidate his contemporaries.

SELECTED BIBLIOGRAPHY

I. BIBLIOGRAPHIES. E. Grislis and W. Speed Hill, "Richard Hooker: An Annotated Bibliography," in W. Speed Hill, ed., *Studies in Richard Hooker: Essays Preliminary to an Edition of His Works* (Cleveland–London, 1972), covers bibliography, biography, editions, MSS, and commentary.

II. COLLECTED EDITIONS. J. Gauden, ed., *Works of Richard Hooker* (London, 1662), also bound with Walton's *Life* (London, 1666); J. Keble, ed., *Works of Richard Hooker with an Account of His Life and Death by Isaac Walton*, 3 vols. (Oxford, 1836); rev. by R. W. Church and F. Paget, 3 vols. (Oxford, 1888).

III. INDIVIDUAL WORKS. *Of the Laws of Ecclesiastical Politie: Books I–V* ([1594]–1597; facs. of 1st ed., Menston, 1969); R. W. Church, ed., *Book I: Of the Laws of Ecclesiastical Polity* (Oxford, 1866), with a long and important intro.; R. Bayne, ed., *Of the Laws of Ecclesiastical Polity: Books I–V*, 2 vols. (London, 1907), also rev. by C. Morris (London, 1954).

IV. CRITICAL AND BIOGRAPHICAL STUDIES. Izaak Walton, *Lives* (London, 1665; rev. 1670, 1675), also edited by G. Saintsbury (London, 1927); F. Paget, *An Introduction to the Fifth Book of Hooker's Treatise of the Laws of Ecclesiastical Polity* (Oxford, 1899; rev. ed., 1907); C. J. Sisson, *The Judicious Marriage of Mr. Hooker and the Birth of "The Laws of Ecclesiastical Polity"* (Cambridge, 1940), which contains new material on Hooker's life; F. J. Shirley, Society for the Promotion of Christian Knowledge, *Richard Hooker and Contemporary Political Ideas* (London, 1949); P. Munz, *The Place of Hooker in the History of Thought* (London, 1952; repr. New York, 1970), which relates Hooker to ancient and medieval philosophy; N. Sykes, *Old Priest and New Presbyter: The Anglican Attitude to Episcopacy, Presbyterianism and Papacy Since the Reformation* (Cambridge, 1956); J. S. Marshall, *Hooker and the Anglican Tradition: An Historical and Theological Study of Hooker's Ecclesiastical Polities* (Sewanee, 1963); H. R. McAdoo, *The Spirit of Anglicanism: A Survey of Anglican Theological Method in the Seventeenth Century* (London–New York, 1965); W. Speed Hill, ed., *Studies in Richard Hooker: Essays Preliminary to an Edition of His Works* (Cleveland–London, 1972), essays covering evolution of the *Polity*, Hooker's politics, theology, churchmanship, and style.

JOHN LYLY AND GEORGE PEELE

(ca.1554-1606) / (ca.1556- ca.1597)

G. K. Hunter

LYLY AND PEELE are usually categorized by English literary historians (at least, since 1887) as "university wits." Nashe, Greene, Peele, Lodge, Lyly, Marlowe—the best-known names, but by no means the only members of the group—were not the first English writers to go to a university, nor were they the first or the last university men to live on their wits; but the phrase catches, nonetheless, the quality of their literary–historical importance well enough. These were the first writers to bring the full fruits of the new humanist education to the service of popular commercial entertainment; and so they provided foundations for a literature, and more especially a drama, which is one of the persisting glories of Europe. To see the importance of the university wits in this respect we need only compare the course of English Renaissance drama with that of the Continent. In Italy, the traditions of the popular commedia dell'arte remained obstinately separate from those of the commedia erudita, fostered in academies or courts. In France, the mixed audience of the refined and the popular seems hardly to have appeared. In Alexandre Hardy we have the beginnings of a dramaturgy that might have united the two sides; but the movement never got beyond a beginning. The emergence of the polite Hôtel de Rambouillet marked, in fact, an end to the potentialities of the Hôtel de Bourgogne.

The Valois courts in France, and the courts of the Italian princelings, had a tradition of lavish expenditure on culture and little or no truck with burgher entertainment. But the Tudor court was both more parsimonious and more parochial. Court artists, in the sense in which Ariosto or Tasso or Guarini were court artists, found little soil in London to support their exotic blooms. The intellectual movement associated with the Reformation had produced, in England, a new sense of the importance of education, a new respect for learning; but the graduates who came from the universities did not come into a world ringing with praises of Plautus and Terence; they came instead into a world suspicious of those that "smell too much of that writer Ovid and that writer Metamorphoses, and talk too much of Proserpina and Jupiter," as the hopeful graduates in the Parnassus plays[1] are warned when they try to get employment as actors.

The "university wits" were, intellectually, as their education had trained them to be, antidemocratic; their delight in the arcane, the remote, the exalted was coupled with a disdain for the local sweaty multitude and an irrational anger at the changing social situation in which "every mechanical mate abhors the English he was born to." Economically, however, the mechanical mates—the craftsmen–workers—had something (indeed, everything) to be said for them. They provided a real market for literary gifts, profane as well as pious; and outside the marketplace there were few buyers. The companies of actors (the "taffeta fools" of Nashe, the "rude grooms . . . apes . . . peasants . . . painted monsters" of Greene) provided the obvious executive arm of popular taste (as television companies do today); against them the intellectual snobbery of the age was concentrated, for what was the actor but a puppet:

. . . what sentence thou utterest on the stage, flows from the censure of our wits, and what sentence or conceit of the invention the people applaud for excellent, that comes from the secrets of our knowledge. I grant your action, though it be a kind of mechanical

[1] Three contemporary satirical plays about the tribulations of a scholarly career, performed at Cambridge as Christmas entertainments.

labour; yet, well done, 'tis worthy of praise; but you worthless, if, for so small a toy, you wax proud.

It is true that the shotgun marriage between the universities and the folk was blessed by the economic rather than the spiritual powers. Nonetheless, the literary children of the marriage easily united the gifts of both sides, for the gap between the two tastes was not as great as was sometimes supposed. The delight in the remote and the exalted was a popular as well as a learned taste. The Spanish romances of chivalry were popular in the least literate of circles. Moreover, the power to organize a story, to construct a speech, to excerpt and combine relevant material from out-of-the-way sources, to use encyclopedias, indexes, and summaries, is as much a basis for popular as for learned entertainment. Merely popular art tends to be imprisoned inside its own narrow traditions; unlearned authors can preserve, modify, or reestablish modes of writing, but they are unlikely to create new modes. The university wits revolutionized Elizabethan popular literature by bringing to its aid interests and expectations that had not previously been seen to be relevant, but which were close enough to the tradition to combine with it and create new wholes.

The position of the university wits, caught between a lively vernacular culture that could be despised intellectually but not disregarded economically, and a humanist ideal of literary excellence that remained obstinately an ideal rather than a reality—this position is reflected in their lives, humble in origin and straitened in circumstances, continuously involved in the vernacular realities of earning, and not earning, a living. But at the same time they remained caught intellectually by the dream of the poet as a god on earth, the dream of eloquence as the key to power, the dream of a civilization in which learning was the heart of kingship. In some ways, the position of these writers was recognizably equivalent to that of today's "scholarship boys"—poor but talented. And most of them quite literally needed scholarships before they could enter the university.

John Lyly was born in or about 1554. His father, Peter Lyly, was a minor ecclesiastical official—a notary—who settled in Canterbury for certain no later than 1562, when it is known that he was in the service of the archbishop. There is no evidence that Peter Lyly was a man of any substance or power; but, like Peele's father, he seems to have been a person of some culture, with cultured friends. Indeed it would have been surprising if he had not been cultured. His father, William Lily, was the famous grammarian, the friend of Erasmus and Sir Thomas More, the first high master of Saint Paul's School—that spearhead of the humanist educational advance. John Lyly was, in fact, born into what Feuillerat calls *une famille d'érudits*.

We do not know that Lyly went to the local grammar school—the King's School, Canterbury—but it is extremely improbable that he did not. From Canterbury, at any rate, he proceeded to Magdalen College, Oxford (*ca.* 1569), where, if we are to believe the remarks of his fictional alter ego, Euphues, he was not particularly contented:

Yet may I of all the rest most condemn Oxford of unkindness . . . who seemed to wean me before she brought me forth, and to give me bones to gnaw before I could get the teat to suck.

Anthony à Wood is probably drawing on this fictional self-portrait when he tells us that Lyly was "always averse to the crabbed studies of logic and philosophy" and "did in a manner neglect academical studies." Probably the most one can say is that Lyly, looking back to Oxford from his subsequent life, chose to regard the university as unprofitable. That he did not always think in these terms may be deduced from the letter he wrote to William Cecil, Lord Burghley, in May 1574 begging his Maecenas, with every conceivable flourish of flattery, to secure him a fellowship at Magdalen.

What is clearer and more relevant is that Oxford instruction seems to have formed Lyly's literary modes for the rest of his life. When he appeared in London (about 1576) to flourish his pen and find his fortune, the literary tools he had at his disposal were essentially those of his humanist education. When we turn to his first work, *Euphues*, discussed in the next section, this will become abundantly clear.

George Peele was born in 1556, a little later than John Lyly, into a not dissimilar household. As with Lyly, the family is recorded as having a permanent residence only a few years after the birth of the famous son—also in 1562, when James Peele was appointed clerk to Christ's Hospital, Newgate, London. His official duty seems to have been to regulate and record the philanthropic activities of the hospital, then newly set up as an asylum for orphans and the aged. James Peele had excellent qualifications for his post: he had already published one volume on double-entry bookkeeping and he shortly produced another; and he supervised collections for the poor in three London parishes. Moreover, he had literary talents which found vent not only in the verse that these books contain, but also (it seems likely) in verses for the civic pageants that were London's cultural expression of its bourgeois self-confidence.

He and his family lived in the hospital, where he found time not only to act as clerk, and to teach writing and arithmetic in the orphans' school, but also to conduct a private school in a room in his own house. George Peele clearly grew up in a household where learning and industry were a matter of daily example.

Like Lyly, George Peele had family connections that must have facilitated entry into a grammar school—the famous school of Christ's Hospital, then only in its infancy, but sufficiently developed to train boys for entry to the university. And in 1571 James Peele recorded in his accounts the hire of a horse to take his son to Oxford.

Peele has left us less definite statements of his views on Oxford than has Lyly. Of course, biographers have been anxious to prove that he neglected his studies in order to pursue poetry, but there is no evidence of such neglect. We know that he translated one of Euripides' *Iphigenia* plays into English verse, for William Gager, his contemporary at Christ Church and himself a celebrated academic playwright (in Latin), praises the work; but the play has not survived and there is no evidence that Peele followed Gager's advice and devoted himself to translation. Peele's literary future lay in fields for which Gager (and, presumably, Peele) had less admiration; about 1581 Peele appears to have left Oxford and (like Lyly before him) to have sought his literary fortune in London.

That the two men became acquainted in Lon-

don is made probable by their appearance together as authors of prefatory pieces commending Thomas Watson's Εκατομπαθία, or *Passionate Century of Love*, of 1582. The preface to this work, which is the first English sonnet sequence, appears to indicate the existence of a literary group, made up mainly of men who had been contemporaries at Oxford and had graduated, most of them now studying law in London, and perhaps under the general patronage of the seventeenth earl of Oxford. By this time Lyly had established his reputation by publishing *Euphues*, and Peele may well have thought of himself as set on the same course of courtly writing.

The road to fortune probably seemed clearer to both of them than it ever was to seem again, for it is clear that neither really achieved the recognition in society to which his early successes might have seemed to entitle him. Lyly's worldly success was greater, but no doubt he started off with the greater expectations. His disappointment is certainly more resonant, as appears in his famous petitionary letters to Elizabeth:

If your sacred Majesty think me unworthy, and that after ten years' tempest I must at the court suffer shipwreck of my time, my hopes, my wits, vouchsafe in your never-erring judgment some plank or rafter to waft me into a country, where, in my sad and settled devotion, I may in every corner of a thatched cottage write prayers instead of plays—prayers for your long and prosperous life and a repentance that I have played the fool so long, and yet live.   (1598)

Thirteen years your Highness' servant, but yet nothing; twenty friends that, though they say they will be sure, I find them sure to be slow; a thousand hopes, but all nothing; a hundred promises, but yet nothing. Thus casting up the inventory of my friends, hopes, promises and time, the *summa totalis* amounteth in all to just nothing. My last will is shorter than mine inventory—but three legacies: patience to my creditors, melancholy without measure to my friends, and beggary not without shame to my family.   (1601)

He seems to have given up literature before he took to begging letters. By Elizabethan standards he was a man of substance. His wife was an heiress; he was a member of parliament, an esquire of the body, a member of the Inns of Court. But none of this was satisfactory; it did

193

not give him either the security or power that he had sought. He died in 1606 in debt and in disappointment.

Peele's literary efforts also led to the begging letter. Greene, in 1592, described him as "driven, as myself, to extreme shifts"; but by "extreme shifts" Greene may have meant no more than dependence on the players, for he remarks in the next line, somewhat pettishly, "Thou art unworthy thy better hap, sith thou dependest on so mean a say." But in 1596 the evidence for his destitution is unambiguous. In this year he sent his daughter to Lord Burghley with a copy of his last work, *Anglorum Feriae,*

to present your wisdom with this small manual by this simple messenger, my eldest daughter and necessity's servant. Long sickness having so enfeebled me maketh bashfulness almost become impudency.

Peele died later the same year, leaving behind him (at the most) a reputation for wit and liveliness. Francis Meres indulged his passion for jingles by writing in 1598 that "as Anacreon died by the pot, so George Peele by the pox." The anonymous compiler of *The Merry Jests of George Peele* (1607) used Peele's name as a peg on which to hang a stale collection of old jokes, and the equally anonymous author of *The Puritan* (1607) made Peele a character in this comedy. Modern scholars have been reluctant to admit that the collection of anecdotes in *The Merry Jests* has little or nothing to do with the author of *David and Bethsabe.* But it is time to point out that the reputation of the university wits for full-blooded roistering is based on little more than a romantic and primitivist wish that it should have been so.

THE VISION OF EUPHUES

THE meaning of "wit" in the phrase "university wit" is the extended subject of the first literary work we have from either of these authors (or indeed, from any of the "university wits"). *Euphues, The Anatomy of Wit,* together with its distended sequel *Euphues and His England,* brought fame and a promise of prosperity to John Lyly to a degree that was not to be repeated in the literary annals of the period. *Euphues* became a fashion, a courtly craze. As the 1632 edition of Lyly's plays assures us, "All our ladies were then his scholars, and that Beauty in court which could not parley Euphuism was as little regarded as she which now there speaks not French." By 1581 five editions of *The Anatomy of Wit* had been published and four of the sequel; by 1640 there were twenty-five editions of the separate works and four editions of a double volume.

Euphues is often seen as a forerunner of the modern novel—a perspective that enables us to admire the development of the modern novel, but which is quite unfair to the assumptions and structure of the book as it was written. It is true that *Euphues* (especially the first part) tells a story; but not all storytelling belongs to the history of the novel.

The story tells how Euphues, "a young gentleman of great patrimony . . . of more wit than wealth, and yet of more wealth than wisdom," left the university town of Athens "disdaining counsel, leaving his country, loathing his old acquaintance" and sought "by wit to obtain some conquest" in the metropolis of Naples ("a place of more pleasure than profit, and yet of more profit than piety"). There he meets first with a father figure, Eubulus, whose sermon of good advice he refutes, using nature (rather than nurture) as his touchstone. Next he meets Philautus, a young gentleman, and swears "such an inviolable league of friendship with him, as neither time by piecemeal should impair, neither fancy utterly dissolve nor any suspicion infringe."

Philautus takes Euphues with him to the household of Don Ferrardo, "one of the chief governors of the city." Philautus is betrothed to Lucilla, Don Ferrardo's daughter, "heir to his whole revenues"; he had "won her by right of love, and would have worn her by rite of law, had not Euphues by strange destiny broken the bonds of marriage and forbidden the bans of matrimony." The main substance of the story appears in this sentence: with an extended display of wit, Euphues steals his friend's beloved. Many are the speeches and debates that surround the event, but the action is no more. In the end, however, all Euphues' wit gets him no further than he deserves. Having jilted one, Lucilla has learned to jilt another. Euphues finds himself the second victim, and so becomes reconciled with Philautus, the first. Ferrardo dies of grief and Lucilla is pushed offstage into a tantalizing limbo:

But what end came of her, seeing it is nothing incident to the history of Euphues, it were superfluous to insert it, and so incredible that all women would rather wonder at it than believe it; which event being so strange I had rather leave them in a muse what it should be than in a maze in telling what it was.

Euphues, having therefore "determined with himself never again to be entangled with such fond delights," retires to Athens, and there becomes a moral author. The book ends in a flurry of epistles giving good advice to all and sundry, and recording (among other events) the death of Lucilla.

I have given the narrative thread of this work; but the narrative is, as can be seen, a very slender thread. Lyly's real interest is in the moral debate that arises when "wit" ("Euphues" means a man of natural endowment, "he that is apt by goodness of wit") spurns good advice (Eu-bulus) and becomes involved with self-love (Phil-autus). Lyly sees that wit is a double-edged gift: on one side it raises the individual's sense of power; but it may do so to a point where wisdom becomes inaccessible. The road from wit to wisdom must lie through experience:

It is commonly said, yet do I think it a common lie, that experience is the mistress of fools; for in my opinion they be most fools that want it.

For Euphues, as for Lyly and the university wits in general, wit lay in Athens (Oxford) and experience lay in Naples (London?). For them, as for Euphues, the problem was to combine or to reconcile the two. Euphues seems best explained as an anatomy, a dissection or opening up, of this problem, together with a dream fulfillment in which Euphues–Lyly got the best of both worlds: both a conquest of experience by wit, and an arrival at wisdom:

Euphues having ended his discourse, and finished those precepts which he thought necessary for the instructing of youth, gave his mind to the continual study of Philosophy, insomuch as he became public Reader in the University, with such commendation as never any before him, in the which he continued for the space of ten years, only searching out the secrets of Nature and the hidden mysteries of philosophy, and having collected into three volumes his lectures, thought for the profit of young scholars to set them forth in print.

The great success of Euphues, The Anatomy of Wit bred the promise of a sequel. At the end of the last letter of the Anatomy Euphues promises:

I have occasion to go to Naples, that I may with more speed arrive in England, where I have heard of a woman that in all qualities excelleth any man. Which, if it be so, I shall think my labour as well bestowed as Saba did hers, when she travelled to see Salomon.

And subsequent additions enlarged the promise:

I have finished the first part of Euphues whom now I left ready to cross the seas to England . . . Euphues at his arrival I am assured will view Oxford . . . He is now on the seas . . . nothing can hinder his coming but death, neither anything hasten his departure but unkindness.

Unfortunately, after so much preparation, Euphues and His England is, in the fashion of sequels, rather a disappointment. It was a fairly obvious device, having established Euphues and Philautus as types of wit, and uncovered (or anatomized) the kind of problem they were best suited to expose, to bring them to England and allow them to repeat their operations on home ground. Euphues and His England is more than twice as long as its predecessor, and it is without the appendix of moral epistles that the first book contains. It is all narrative; but the narrative is now complex and involuted, very different from the terse and simple narrative line of The Anatomy of Wit. And one must admit that the terse form is better suited to Lyly's talents. The power to exploit the dilemmas and paradoxes of a simple social situation—the power to display wit, while anatomizing it—is less memorable in the sequel because the situations raise interests and expectations that are quite different from those that can be satisfied by euphuism.

I have said nothing, so far, about the famous style in which the *Euphues* books are written; a style whose name—euphuism—provides the only generally surviving part of the whole Lylian inheritance. "Euphuism" today is usually taken to mean any unnecessarily ornate or elaborate style: unnecessary, because good prose is now conceived not to require elaboration. This is not an entirely fair outlook on the true euphuism, which was justified historically to a greater extent than is usually allowed, and even today can be seen to be functional to the kind of "anatomy" that Lyly was writing.

To the Elizabethans, euphuism seemed to be characterized almost exclusively by its strings of similes drawn from the quainter reaches of classical natural history:

> Talking of stones, stars, plants, of fishes, flies,
> Playing with words and idle similes,

as Michael Drayton was later to describe it ("Epistle to Henry Reynolds"). Lyly was not the first to use these similes; they played a recognizable part in sermon styles of the Middle Ages and the Renaissance. What is remarkable in Lyly is not the materials he uses—after all, most of them came out of that storehouse of Renaissance commonplaces, Erasmus' *Similia*—but the degree of continuity and organization with which he uses them. The same is true of the elements of euphuism (in the strict sense) that are most obvious today: the patently balanced clauses, measured side by side and sharpened in their similarity by near rhyme and by alliteration: "not the carved visard of a lewd woman, but the incarnate visage of a lascivious wanton," "Ay, but Euphues gave the onset; ay, but Lucilla gave the occasion; ay, but Euphues first brake his mind; ay, but Lucilla bewrayed her meaning," "Philautus, thinking all to be gold that glistered, and all to be gospel that Euphues uttered, answered his forged gloze with this friendly close." Modern research has pointed out a whole history of verbal organization of this kind; but again the tightness of the organization is unique in Lyly.

This style is, I am suggesting, not only an elegant organization of Elizabethan material, but also a functional expression of the kind of world that, in *Euphues,* Lyly was trying to create. The *Euphues* style is functional to the "anatomy" procedure. An anatomy is an analysis, a breaking down into component parts. It exposes the relationships that are inherent in a static situation; it defines, it distinguishes, it relates, but it does not develop. The whole world of *Euphues* is a world of such static analogies, repetitions, and antitheses, in style no less than structure. Man at the center, witty but unwise, assured but ignorant, and his Ovidian mistress, hot though cold, desiring but dissembling—these are set into a whole framework of language and nature "methodized" (like an Elizabethan knot garden) to reflect their relationships and add fuel to their wit. Here is Lucilla simultaneously repulsing Euphues and encouraging him:

The spider weaveth a fine web to hang the fly, the wolf weareth a fair face to devour the lamb, the merlin striketh at the partridge, the eagle often snappeth at the fly, men are always laying baits for women, which are the weaker vessels: but as yet I could never hear man by such snares to entrap man: for true it is (that men themselves have by use observed) that it must be a hard winter when one wolf eateth another. I have read that the bull being tied to the fig tree loseth his strength, that the whole herd of deer stand at the gaze if they smell a sweet apple, that the dolphin by the sound of music is brought to the shore. And then no marvel it is that if the fierce bull be tamed with the fig tree, if that women (being as weak as sheep) be overcome with a fig, if the wild deer be caught with an apple, that the tame damsel is won with a blossom; if the fleet dolphin be allured with harmony, that women be entangled with the melody of men's speech, fair promises and solmn protestations. But folly it were for me to mark their mischiefs; sith I am neither able (neither they willing) to amend their manners, it becometh me rather to show what our sex should do, than to open what yours doth. And seeing I cannot by reason restrain your importunate suit, I will by rigour done on myself cause you to refrain the means. I would to God Ferrardo were in this point like to Lysander, which would not suffer his daughters to wear gorgeous apparel, saying it would rather make them common than comely. I would it were in Naples a law which was a custom in Egypt, that women should always go barefoot, to the intent they might keep themselves always at home, that they should be ever like to the snail, which hath ever his house on his head. I mean so to mortify myself that instead of silks I will wear sackcloth, for ouches [jewels] and bracelets, lear and caddis [coarse cloths]; for the lute, use the distaff, for the pen, the needle, for lovers' sonnets, David's psalms. But yet I am not so senseless altogether to reject your service: which if I were certainly assured to proceed of a simple mind, it should not receive so simple a reward. And what greater trial can I have of thy simplicity and truth than thine own request which desireth a trial? Ay, but in the coldest flint there is hot fire; the bee that hath honey in her mouth, hath a sting in her tail; the tree that beareth the sweetest fruit, hath a sour sap; yea the words of men, though they seem smooth as oil, yet their hearts are as crooked as the stalk of ivy. I would not, Euphues, that thou shouldst condemn me of rigour, in that I seek to assuage thy folly by reason; but take this by the way that although as yet I am disposed to like of none, yet whensoever I shall love any, I will not forget thee. In the mean season account me thy friend, for thy foe I will never be.

The vision of *Euphues* is of a world so beautifully organized that nothing is mislaid, nothing irrelevant. It can hardly move us; but it can hardly cease to fascinate us.

ENTERTAINMENTS AT COURT

THE London theatrical scene, in which Lyly and Peele made their first appearances about 1584, was by no means an inchoate or undeveloped one. The boy players (basically choristers) had been providing courtly dramatic entertainments for at least fifty years, and troupes of adult players were also well established. In 1576 the first public playhouse (The Theatre) was set up in Finsbury Fields, and in the same year Richard Farrant, master of the Children of the Chapel Royal, leased a "private" playhouse in the former monastery of the Blackfriars.

There was an obvious audience for drama (if we may judge by the noise of horror sounded by the preachers). By the beginning of the seventeenth century a London population of not much more than 150,000 was supporting four or five public playhouses, with audiences of twenty thousand or so per week.

Our concern, in this chapter, is not with these public theaters, however, but with court entertainments. Yet it is impossible to discuss court theatricals without noticing the extent to which these were parasitic upon the public perfor-

mances. The queen seems to have been fond of drama, but she was even fonder of her Privy Purse; and the declining situation of the English nobility in this period ensured that they did not set up self-sufficient household drama of any scale, but followed the queen's example and rested content with the nominal patronage of companies whose main source of income lay nearer to the marketplace.

The history of the boys' companies is a history of this fruitful compromise. I have mentioned above how Farrant leased a small theater in 1576. This Blackfriars theater (like the Saint Paul's boys' theater beside the cathedral) was called a "private" house. This meant that they charged more than the public ones (fourpence instead of a penny) and kept up a snobbish fiction that their performances were mere "exercises" to train the actors for their true fulfillment, the appearance before the queen.

The Blackfriars theater seems to have been quite a small building, probably forty-six by twenty-seven feet, if compared with the fifty-five feet square inner dimensions of the Fortune. But the real comparison should not be with the large public theaters, which had audiences of mixed social classes (at their best), but rather with the great halls of the royal palaces. The Great Chamber at Whitehall was only sixty-two by twenty-nine feet; and, considering that the queen's throne must have reduced the space available there, the Blackfriars can be seen to be of comparable dimensions.

Small, intimate, candle-lit, exclusive, the boys' theaters provided an ideal background for acting talents that could never have been robust or magnetic, but must have depended very largely on neatness and precision of ensemble delivery, with something of the "alienation effect," the cold virtuosity, that well-trained choristers still aspire to today. These gifts demand plays that are not too blatantly realistic or too emotionally immediate. To ask a boy to play Othello is like asking a modern chorister to sing Tosca.

The songs with which the plays for boy players seem to have abounded have, judging by those that have survived, the same cool self-consciousness of achieved artistic distance. Even when, as in Peele's *Arraignment of Paris*, "Colin the enamoured shepherd singeth his passion of love," the song is more delightful for its fanciful artifice than its passion:

> O gentle love, ungentle for thy deed,
>   Thou makest my heart,
>   A bloody mark,
> With piercing shot to bleed.
> Shoot soft, sweet love, for fear thou shoot amiss,
>   For fear too keen
>   Thy arrows been,
> And hit the heart where my beloved is.

The opening of Peele's *David and Bethsabe* is an excellent example of the dramatic use of song in the Elizabethan theater:

The Prologue-speaker draws a curtain and discovers Bethsabe, with her Maid, bathing over a spring: she sings, and David sits above viewing her.

SONG

> Hot sun, cool fire, tempered with sweet air,
> Black shade, fair nurse, shadow my white hair:
> Shine, sun; burn, fire; breathe, air, and ease me;
> Black shade, fair nurse, shroud me, and please
>   me:
> Shadow, my sweet nurse, keep me from burning,
> Make not my glad cause, cause of my mourning.
>   Let not my beauty's fire
>   Inflame unstaid desire,
>   Nor pierce any bright eye
>   That wandereth lightly.

The effect made here—of sensuous appeal, combined with chaste simplicity (we should imagine, I suppose, a lute accompaniment) —would be difficult to create in any terms less formal, more psychological or "realistic."

The songs printed in the collected edition of Lyly's plays (1632) are not certainly his, but they are certainly worthy of the settings which he provided. They sparkle with the assurance of complete simplicity, with a transparency that music (unless grossly inappropriate) will not muddy, but rather enhance:

> Sing to Apollo, god of day,
> Whose golden beams with morning play,
> And make her eyes so brightly shine,
> Aurora's face is called divine.
> Sing to Phoebus and that throne
> Of diamonds, which he sits upon.

> Io paeans let us sing
> To physic's and to poesy's king.
> Crown all his altars with bright fire,
> Laurels bind about his lyre,
> A Daphne's coronet for his head;
> The Muses dance about his bed,
> When on his ravishing lute he plays;
> Strew his temples round with bays.
> Io paeans let us sing
> To the glittering Delian king.

The conditions of courtly drama made the same general demands on the dramatist's power to "distance" his material. The queen, facing down the stage, was not only the principal spectator, but almost the principal performer ("the observed of all observers"). The play had to tone in with her regality, without infringing it. The play had to belong to the court, to enhance its self-admiration, but could not be allowed to be personal. The concept of regality must be vital but could not come too closely into personal focus.

Moreover, the court of the Virgin Queen was also a court of love: "At our exercises," says the Prologue to Lyly's *Midas*, "courtiers call for comedies, their subject is love." Love was the natural subject for courtly drama, but had to be brought into relationship with Queen Elizabeth's rejection of Eros, as a special aspect of that perpetual source of court entertainment— the debate between love and honor. Cupid appears regularly in Elizabethan court plays, but is never allowed to reign; the possibilities of the different modes of love are patterned against one another. In this patterning Lyly is the supreme artist.

Peele's *The Arraignment of Paris*, Lyly's *Campaspe* and his *Sapho and Phao* probably all appeared at court in the same "season": the Christmas Revels of 1583–1584. Although few spectators at the time are likely to have thought that they were witnessing the first fruits of a new literary era, and although today's view is no doubt conditioned by the disappearance of almost all preceding court drama, these three works are legitimately used by literary historians to mark the emergence of maturity in the Elizabethan drama. The three plays represent the first effective dramatic exercises of their authors. Peele's earlier *Iphigenia* (*ca.* 1579) seems to have been confined to his academic circle.

Nashe in 1589 spoke of Peele as "the chief supporter of pleasance now living, the *Atlas* of poetry, and *primus verborum Artifex*, whose first increase, *The Arraignment of Paris*, might plead to your opinions his pregnant dexterity of wit and manifold variety of invention, where (*me judice*) he goeth a step beyond all that write." *Campaspe* was not Lyly's "first increase" in any but the dramatic sphere, for he was already the famous author of two parts of *Euphues*; but in terms of theatrical history *Campaspe* and *Sapho* mark a new and decisive application of literary power to dramatic purposes.

All three plays should be seen as part of that crystallization of literary ability which is marked in poetry by the appearance of Spenser, the "new poet," with his *Shepherd's Calendar* of 1578–1579, and in prose by Lyly's *Euphues*. The dependence of *Campaspe* on *Euphues* is obvious enough, but is probably less vital than the dependence of Peele's *Arraignment of Paris* on Spenser's *The Shepherd's Calendar*. It is not simply that the main theme, the love of Oenone for the shepherd Paris, is mingled with the love of [Spenser's] Colin for the nymph Thestylis, his death and burial by [Spenser's] Hobbinol, Diggon, and Thenot. It is rather that Peele has used the whole poetic atmosphere of *The Shepherd's Calendar* to body forth the pastoral fiction that sustains his play. The violent and overemphatic rhetoric that wrecks our enjoyment of most ambitious Tudor dramaturgy is confined in *The Arraignment of Paris* to Até as Senecan prologue. Even in this rhetorical mode he manages to anticipate Marlowe's "mighty line":

> Condemned soul, Até from lowest hell
> And deadly rivers of the infernal Jove,
> Where bloodless ghosts in pains of endless date
> Fill ruthless ears with never-ceasing cries,
> Behold I come in place, and bring beside
> The bane of Troy: behold the fatal fruit
> Raught from the golden tree of Prosperpine.
> Proud Troy must fall, so bid the gods above
> And stately Ilium's lofty towers be raz'd
> By conquering hands of the victorious foe.

The goddesses' dispute is superimposed on a series of "scenes from the classical idylls," mediated by Spenser, and mellifluously handled by Peele:

> The watery flowers and lilies on the banks
> Like blazing comets burgeon all in ranks
> Under the hawthorn and the poplar tree,
> Where sacred Phoebe may delight to be
> The primrose and the purple hyacinth,
> The dainty violet and the wholesome mint,
> The double daisy and the cowslip, queen
> Of summer flowers, do over-peer the green;
> And round about the valley as ye pass
> Ye may ne see for peeping flowers the grass.

It is certainly a shock when, after the final dispute between the goddesses, Diana (being appointed arbitrator) turns to Queen Elizabeth and gives the apple to her. But the shock is to some extent absorbed by the pastoral mode in which this compliment, as well as the rest of the play, is couched:

> There wons within these pleasant shady woods
> Where neither storm nor sun's distemperature
> Have power to hurt by cruel heat or cold,
>
> . . .
>
> Amids the cypress springs, a gracious nymph
> That honours Dian for her chastity,
> And likes the labours well of Phoebe's groves.
> The place Elizium hight, and of the place
> Her name that governs there Eliza is
>
> . . .
>
> This peerless nymph whom heaven and earth
>   beloves,
> This paragon, this only this is she
> In whom do meet so many gifts in one,
> On whom our country gods so often gaze,
> In honour of whose name the muses sing,
>
> . . .

The shepherd is also the courtier (as in Spenser); the pastoral peace of England is threatened by the intervention of great affairs; only the queen can protect the shepherd world of this "second Troy" from the violent ruin that Até forecast.

The Arraignment of Paris and *Campaspe* have in common the characteristics shared by most early Elizabethan dramas: both are notable for the multifariousness of the material held within the dramatic framework—tumbling, singing, "an artificial charm of birds," spectacle of various kinds, philosophic disputes, dancing. This multifarious mode was one inherited from the Tudor interlude, and the main problem of early Elizabethan drama can be seen as the problem of how to unify this material. In this perspective *Campaspe* must be regarded as a more successful play than *The Arraignment of Paris*. Lyly's prose is a more obviously restricted medium than Peele's verse; but by this very restriction it imposes a greater unity than do Peele's fourteeners, decasyllabic couplets, blank verse, and songs in English, Latin, and Italian. The structure of *Campaspe* is also notable for its control of the separate episodes. The total cast is not much smaller (twenty-seven, as against thirty in Peele's play), but the central debate, between Alexander's love and his royalty, controls everything within the play in a way that does not find a counterpart in *The Arraignment of Paris*.

Alexander the Great captures a beautiful girl, Campaspe, who powerfully engages his amorous interests, but who has eventually to be rejected in favor of more regal matters, the love of commoners being an improper pursuit for princes. Campaspe is paired with a fellow commoner, Apelles, the court artist, and the irresolute and timid love between these two provides a charming vignette of the level at which the servitudes of love can be openly, even if fearfully, acknowledged:

Apel. Gentlewoman, the misfortune I had with your picture will put you to some pains to sit again to be painted.
Camp. It is small pains for me to sit still, but infinite for you to draw still.
Apel. No madam; to paint Venus was a pleasure, but to shadow the sweet face of Campaspe it is a heaven . . .

. . .

But will you give me leave to ask you a question without offence?
Camp. So that you will answer me another without excuse.
Apel. Whom do you love best in the world?
Camp. He that made me last in the world.
Apel. That was a god.
Camp. I had thought it had been a man. But whom do you honour most, Apelles?
Apel. The thing that is likest you, Campaspe.
Camp. My picture?
Apel. I dare not venture upon your person. But come, let us go in; for Alexander will think it long till we return. (IV.ii.18–45)

The prime instance of magnanimity (the central virtue of *The Faerie Queene*, of the court, and of

Campaspe) is Alexander's perception that Campaspe must belong to Apelles rather than Alexander:

Well, enjoy one another; I give her thee frankly, Apelles. Thou shalt see that Alexander maketh but a toy of love, and leadeth affection in fetters, using fancy as a fool to make him sport . . .
    Go, Apelles, take with you your Campaspe; Alexander is cloyed with looking on that which thou wonderest at. (V.iv.131–140)

But this has been led up to by other examples of the same virtue. Alexander in Apelles' studio tries to paint:

Alex. I had rather be setting of a battle than blotting of a board. But how have I done here?
Apel. Like a king.
Alex. I think so; but nothing more unlike a painter. (III.iv.109–113)

Alexander is worthy to rule, not because he knows everything, but because he recognizes what he does not know. Diogenes, whose role was thought important enough to justify his inclusion in one original title page ("A moste excellent comedie of Alexander, Campaspe and Diogenes") exists largely to make the same structural point: the famous

were I not Alexander, I would wish to be Diogenes

is used as the pivot of a relationship in which the king is unable to take over the role of the philosopher, but is justified in his kingship because he recognizes the limitation.

The Athens of *Campaspe* is, though as classical as the Mount Ida of Peele, obviously urban and intellectual. The pastoral mode of *The Arraignment of Paris* does not appear in Lyly's work until *Gallathea* (probably produced at court on 1 January 1588). *Gallathea* is a brilliant organization of modes of love (the principal interest of the courtier), so arranged that the delicacy, the civility, the pathos of doomed love is exposed without ever engaging violent or destructive identifications. The play is structurally a saraband of deceptions, slowly weaving together the nymphs whom their shepherd fathers have disguised as boys (to avoid sacrifice to Neptune), Cupid, who pretends to be a nymph (to defeat the chastity of Diana's nymphs), and Neptune, who disguises himself as a shepherd (to confound all the other deceivers).

Gallathea, perhaps more than any others by Lyly, serves to explain what he meant when he said (in the Blackfriars prologue to *Sapho and Phao*):

Our intent was at this time to move inward delight not outward lightness; and to breed (if it might be) soft smiling, not loud laughing . . .

We recognize ourselves in the capacity of the characters for self-deception, but the sense of pattern is so obvious that we recognize at the same time that what we have to deal with is an artifact, an organization of experience rather than a recording of it. In a charming scene (imitated by Shakespeare in *Twelfth Night*) the two disguised nymphs woo one another, each supposing the other to be a man, but fearful that "he" may turn out to be another woman:

Phillida. It is pity that Nature framed you not a woman, having a face so fair, so lovely a countenance, so modest a behaviour.
Gallathea. There is a tree in Tylos whose nuts have shells like fire, and being cracked, the kernel is but water.
Phil. What a toy is it to tell me of that tree, being nothing to the purpose. I say it is pity you are not a woman.
Galla. I would not wish to be a woman unless it were because thou art a man.
Phil. Nay, I do not wish to be a woman, for then I should not love thee, for I have sworn never to love a woman.
Galla. A strange humour in so pretty a youth, and according to mine, for myself will never love a woman.
Phil. It were a shame if a maiden should be a suitor (a thing hated in that sex) that thou shouldest deny to be her servant.
Galla. If it be a shame in me, it can be no commendation in you, for yourself is of that mind.
Phil. Suppose I were a virgin (I blush in supposing myself one) and that under the habit of a boy were the person of a maid; if I should utter my affection with signs, manifest my sweet love by my salt tears, and prove my loyalty unspotted, and my griefs intolerable, would not then that fair face pity this true heart?

Galla. Admit that I were as you would have me suppose that you are, and that I should with entreaties, prayers, oaths, bribes and whatever can be invented in love desire your favour, would you not yield?
Phil. Tush, you come in with "admit."
Galla. And you with "suppose."
Phil. What doubtful speeches be these? I fear me he is as I am, a maiden.
Galla. What dread riseth in my mind! I fear the boy to be as I am, a maiden.
Phil. Tush, it cannot be, his voice shows the contrary.
Galla. Yet I do not think it, for he would then have blushed.
Phil. Have you ever a sister?
Galla. If I had but one, my brother must needs have two; but I pray have you ever a one?
Phil. My father had but one daughter, and therefore I could have no sister.
Galla. Ay me, he is as I am, for his speeches be as mine are.
Phil. What shall I do? Either he is subtle or my sex simple.

. . .

Phil. Come let us into the grove, and make much one of another, that cannot tell what to think one of another. (III.ii.1–59)

The "soft smiling" depends on our capacity to avoid heavy involvement with the personal emotions of Phillida and Gallathea, while at the same time following (with delight) their general relevance to the less organized world of our emotions. Lyly offers us in this passage, as so often, the pleasure of a smiling superiority to and enjoyment of the accidents and misunderstandings that affect others in their lives and, even more, in their loves.

This smiling superiority to accidents and misfortunes lies close to the heart of a whole tradition in comedy, which is often thought of as first becoming self-conscious in Meredith's celebrated *Essay on the Idea of Comedy*. But Lyly's Blackfriars prologue to *Sapho and Phao* very effectively outlines its essential elements:

Our intent was at this time to move inward delight, not outward lightness: and to breed (if it might be) soft smiling, not loud laughing; knowing it to the wise to be as great pleasure to hear counsel mixed with wit, as to the foolish to have sport mingled with rudeness. They were banished the theatre of Athens, and from Rome hissed, that brought parasites on the stage with apish actions, or fools with uncivil habits, or courtesans with immodest words. We have endeavoured to be as far from unseemly speeches to make your ears glow as we hope you will be from unkind reports to make our cheeks blush.

Meredith saw the line of "high" comedy as characterized by the controlling wit of "brilliant, flippant, independent" women of the upper classes; and as far as Molière, Congreve, Wilde, and even Shakespeare are concerned, this is a fair enough account of the social milieu of high comedy. But Lyly's plays, although they have the same tone, lack the realism of social reference. The "crispness and cunning polish of the sentences" that Meredith remarks is not here the rhetoric of the great lady—Millamant or Célimène or Rosalind—but belongs very obviously to the author. Nonetheless, it sets up the same image of a world of delightfully artificial elegance that shames our stumbling realities into admiration. We laugh at the artifice of their world, but dare not show a trace of condescension, let alone contempt. For our delighted laughter at impossibility is accompanied all the time by a nostalgic desire that such elegance might be made possible. Unreal though the worlds of his plays may be, there can be little doubt that Lyly is the first dramatist in England to catch the amalgam of laughter and admiration that characterizes high comedy; and through his influence on Shakespeare he has no doubt affected later practitioners in the genre.

The differences between *Gallathea* and *The Importance of Being Ernest* should not, of course, be underestimated. Lyly's play rejoices in its self-conscious unreality. The play ends, as do several of Lyly's plays, in a metamorphosis, "a ready and puerile expedient," as Dr. Johnson called it:

Diana. Now things falling out as they do, you must leave these fond-found affections; nature will have it so, necessity must.

Galla. I will never love any but Phillida, her love is engraven in my heart with her eyes.

Phil. Nor I any but Gallathea, whose faith is imprinted in my thoughts by her words.

Nept. An idle choice, strange and foolish, for one virgin to dote on another; and to imagine a constant faith, where there can be no cause of affection. How like you this, Venus?

Venus. I like well and allow it; they shall both be possessed of their wishes, for never shall it be said that Nature or Fortune shall overthrow Love and Faith. Is your loves unspotted, begun with truth, continued with constancy, and not to be altered till death?

Galla. Die, Gallathea, if thy love be not so!

Phil. Accursed be thou, Phillida, if thy love be not so!

Diana. Suppose all this, Venus, what then?

Venus. Then shall it be seen, that I can turn one of them to be a man, and that I will!

Diana. Is it possible?

Venus. What is to Love or the Mistress of Love unpossible? Was it not Venus that did the like to Iphis and Ianthes; how say ye? are ye agreed? one to be a boy presently?

Phil. I am content, so I may embrace Gallathea.

Galla. I wish it, so I may enjoy Phillida.

(V.iii.122–146)

The point is not the artificiality of the device of metamorphosis, but its appositeness to the dance that precedes it, as a final figure designed to bring down the curtain and the house. Remember that the parts were played by boys, playing girls disguised as boys; the final metamorphosis is not an "expedient" that is imposed from outside the world of the play. It belongs entirely to the mode of artifice in which the play is constructed.

Restrictions of space prevent the pursuit of these themes into others of Lyly's plays (a task I have elsewhere essayed). I pass over *Love's Metamorphosis* (between 1589 and 1591), in many ways the purest of his plays: the least human, but the most sharply defined in terms of pattern.

I also forbear to explore *Endimion* (1588?) and *Midas* (1589?), the clearest examples of that thorny but inevitable court genre, the political allegory. The temptation of a court author to represent his sovereign, the source of his expectations, as a fountain of all virtues—a Deborah, a Semiramis, a Zenobia, a "Venus and Vesta"—was one that Lyly had given in to as early as *Euphues and His England*. Elizabeth is clearly glanced at in the Alexander of *Campaspe* and emerges sharply as the original of Sapho in *Sapho and Phao*, lovely but chaste, warmly human but never stooping to love, responsive but regal. In *Endimion*, Elizabeth is again bodied

202

forth, this time as Cynthia the moon goddess; and her loyal but hopeless lover, Endimion, is just as clearly the type of the courtier, condemned to adore from a fixed distance. That Endimion is any particular courtier (Leicester perhaps, or Oxford) is a much more doubtful proposition. Modern scholars have several times tried to discover the image of secret court intrigues in Lyly's plays, but there is no evidence that they were intended to be *drames à clef,* or indeed that such dramatizations would have been tolerated by the queen. They are effective enough as plays not to require this extra explanation.

Midas has some direct flattery of the queen, who appears, briefly mentioned (endowed with all the virtues) as the queen of Lesbos. The main topical effort of this play, written after the defeat of the Spanish Armada, is, however, to define her by contrast, building an elaborate picture of the "wicked" king, Midas, the gold-loving Philip II of Spain.

I pass over these plays in order to spend some time with *Mother Bombie,* the most Roman of Lyly's comedies. The title page does not tell us that *Mother Bombie,* "a pleasant conceited comedy," was performed at court, and it seems to be less inherently "courtly" than the others, being unconcerned with love and honor, with noble natures or even with virtue. Its setting is precise and local (Rochester); its characters are men of lowly station (merchants and servants); its mode of construction (intrigue) does not allow space for those characteristic Lylian moments of emotional self-debate and self-revelation (very often, the moment of falling in love).

Mother Bombie is, however, quite clearly Lylian. It picks up elements present in the plays from the beginning. The quick wit of the page or servant, with his disenchanted view of higher concerns, appears in the subplots of all the plays mentioned (except *Love's Metamorphosis*). But in *Mother Bombie* there is no main plot: the whole play is concerned with the parallel intrigues of servants, complementing one another and (in the manner of Plautine comedy) making the cause of the young to succeed, and that of the old to fail. The play moves forward with an almost mathematical precision of organization: four servants of four masters (two rich and two poor) intrigue together to promote the

matching of the foolish children of the rich masters (each of whom supposes the other's child to be wise) and (on the other hand) the wise children of the poor masters. In a manner to become widely current in Restoration comedy, the two wise children marry with the parents' blessing, while disguised as the idiots; but the idiots dressed in the wise children's clothes reveal their defects too plainly for that match to go forward. The intrigue is blocked in this four-square mode; but it is opened up by the addition of another pair of lovers, Maestius and Serena, impeded in their affections by the assumption that they are brother and sister. These turn out to be changelings for the idiots; the prohibition transfers to the idiots and Maestius and Serena can go ahead to marriage and wealth.

Mother Bombie is a play of matrimonial intrigue, but it is remarkably uninterested in what it feels like to be in love. Its predominant values are wit and good fellowship, and the goal toward which the action naturally moves is the tavern. The intrigue glances at the Roman slave's spur of manumission, but the stronger motive by far is the sheer love of witty intrigue for its own sake:

Dromio. Four makes a mess, and we have a mess of masters that must be cozened; let us lay our heads together; they are married and cannot.
Halfpenny. Let us consult at the tavern, where . . . we shall cast up our accounts, and discharge our stomachs, like men that can digest anything.
Lucio. I see not yet what you go about.
Dro. Lucio, that can pierce a mud wall of twenty foot thick, would make us believe he cannot see a candle through a paper lantern; his knavery is beyond Ela, and yet he says he knows not Gamut.
Lucio. I am ready; if any cozenage be ripe, I'll shake the tree.
Half. Nay, I hope to see thee so strong, to shake three trees at once.
Dro. We burn time, for I must give a reckoning of my days work; let us close to the bush, *ad deliberandum.*
Half. Indeed, *Inter pocula philosophandum,* it is good to plea among pots.
Riscio. Thine will be the worst; I fear we shall leave a halfpenny in hand.
Half. Why, sayest thou that? Thou hast left a print deeper in thy hand already, than a halfpenny can leave, unless it should sing[e] worse than an hot iron.

Lucio. All friends, and so let us sing; 'tis a pleasant thing to go into the tavern clearing the throat.

(II.i.122–128)

The play is ideally suited to the boys for whom it was written; for though it might seem in terms of subject matter to be low comedy, set against the high comedy of Lyly's other plays, it is in fact far more a graceful and witty descant on low life than a raw slice of it. Listening to a recent performance of *Mother Bombie* by the boys of Bristol Grammar School, I was struck afresh by the basic ironies involved in our response as adults to the acting of children. We are aware that these are children pretending to be grownups and that the children themselves are aware of this, and are themselves enjoying the disparity. We share with them their enjoyment of role-playing and dressing up, seen and accepted as part of that power to pattern experience that is the center of drama.

IN THE PUBLIC THEATER

Mother Bombie is a play set at some remove from the courtly center of Lyly's art. One other play by Lyly seems also to be on the edge of his natural milieu: *The Woman in the Moon*. Although the original text is printed "as it was presented before her Highness," the title page uniquely fails to name the actors, and the text strongly suggests that this play was not designed for the troupe of boy players at all. The troupe was prevented from acting in the decade 1590 to 1600; it is probable that this silence is connected with Lyly's one known attempt to break out of "entertainment" and into "significant statement." His involvement (on the side of the bishops) in the "Marprelate" controversy[2] seems to have involved the boys in some satirical activity; and this led to a wholesale suppression. Lyly may have been driven for the first time to the resource that the other university wits had had to face much earlier in their careers, the public theater. *The Woman in the Moon* may be regarded as an attempt to straddle the gap be-

[2] Martin Marprelate was a pseudonymous Puritan pamphleteer who attacked the Church of England and its clergy and provoked a cascade of pro and anti pamphlets.

tween the public theater, with its adult actors and its mixed audiences, and the court. The play is Lyly's one attempt at blank verse; this is presumably what the Prologue refers to when it says:

> Remember all is but a poet's dream;
> The first he had in Phoebus' holy bower;
> But not the last, unless the first displease.

The probability that this play was written for men, not for boys, is reinforced by the demands it makes for stage equipment (including a trapdoor) and its knockabout and collusive comedy involving the audience—especially that provided by Gunophilus, an interesting character halfway between Lyly's pages and Shakespeare's clowns. Here he is organizing a complex double deception:

Stesias. Where might I hide me to behold the same?
Gunophilus. O, in this cave, for over this they'll sit.

(*Pointing to a trap-door*)

Stes. But then I shall not see them when they kiss.
Gun. Yet you may hear what they say; if they kiss I'll hollow.
Stes. But do so then, my sweet Gunophilus;
And as a strong wind bursting from the earth,
So will I rise out of this hollow vault,
Making the woods shake with my furious words.
Gun. But if they come not at all, or when they come, do use themselves honestly, then come not out, lest you seeming jealous make her over-hate you.
Stes. Not for the world, unless I hear thee call,
Or else their wanton speech provoke me forth.
Gun. Well, in then. Wer't not a pretty jest to bury him quick? I warrant it would be a good while 'ere she would scratch him out of his grave with her nails, and yet she might too, for she hath digged such vaults in my face that ye may go from my chin to my eyebrows betwixt the skin and the flesh; wonder not at it, good people, I can prove there hath been two or three merchants with me to hire rooms to lay in wine, but that they do not stand so conveniently as they would wish (for indeed they are every one too near my mouth, and I am a great drinker), I had had a quarter's rent beforehand. Well, be it known unto all men, that I have done this to cornute my master, for yet I could never have opportunity. You would little think my neck is grown awry with looking back as I have been a-kissing, for fear he should come, and yet it is a fair example; beware of kissing, brethren.

What, doth the cave open? Ere she and he have done
he'll pick the lock with his horn.   (III.ii.189–218)

But in the main, *The Woman in the Moon* repeats the formulas that had fitted the boys and the court, and does so too well to gain much new vigor from the new milieu. The absence of any clearly developing narrative line, of any strong characterization or robust appeals to sentiment—these, coupled with a general stiffness in the handling of the poetic line, ensured that Lyly would not begin a second career in the public theater.

Where Lyly's skirmishings with the public theater are clearly marginal and written with his left hand, Peele's career is much more ambidextrous. Peele never made the stir in court that Lyly did; his manner was less polished, but it was more flexible. The spread of his interests was distributed across a great tract of taste, all the way from the dainty artifice of *The Arraignment of Paris* and its companionpiece, *The Hunting of Cupid* (now extant only in fragments), to the swashbuckling rhodomontade of *Alcazar* and (presumably) *Turkish Mahomet and Hiren the Fair Greek,* those favorites of the ancient Pistol (see 2 Henry IV, II.iv.173, for example).

Certain unifying factors in Peele's output can, of course, be seen; and of these the most obvious one is patriotism. There was a genuine bond between the courtly adoration of the Virgin Queen and popular chauvinism which saw England as the center of Christendom. Peele's occasional poems—his pageant-verses for the Lord Mayor's procession in 1585 and in 1591, his descriptions of knights jousting before Elizabeth, his Spenserian eclogue welcoming Essex back from the inglorious expedition to Portugal (1589)—were all, presumably, written for money or in the hope of money; we know that the earl of Northumberland paid him three pounds for *The Honour of the Garter*. But the emotion that sustains them seems to be Peele's genuine lyrical exaltation at finding himself a Londoner and an Englishman:

Lo, lovely London, rich and fortunate
Famed through the world for peace and happiness
                    . . .
O ten times treble happy men that fight
Under the cross of Christ and England's Queen

His sense of the present greatness of England is sustained by a magniloquent vision of the past, of the great families that have worn the garter, and of the Trojan ancestry that the Tudors claimed for themselves and for their realm.

In Peele's plays for the popular theater, Marlovian rhetoric seems the obvious means of projecting this lyrical enthusiasm:

Illustrious England, ancient seat of kings
                    . . .
What warlike nation trained in feats of arms,
What barbarous people, stubborn or untamed,
What climate under the meridian signs,
Or frozen zone under his brumal stage
Erst have not quaked and trembled at the name
Of Britain, and her mighty conquerors.
Her neighbour realms, as Scotland, Denmark, France,
Awed with their deeds and jealous of her arms,
Have begged defensive and offensive leagues.

The language that had been right for Tamburlaine "scourging kingdoms with his conquering sword" was right enough for Peele and for England. Indeed Marlowe's "high astounding terms" provided an effective breakthrough for all the university wits seeking to impose their poetic vision on a wide and generally uncultivated audience.

The material that Peele chose to poeticize (and so dramatize) in his first two public plays—*The Battle of Alcazar* (ca.1588) and *Edward I* (ca.1593)—must, I suppose, be called history. But the purpose of the plays is not to explain what happened, to open up a process of cause and effect. These "histories" or "chronicle plays" are concerned rather to collect a series of high-astounding events, suffered or perpetrated by persons of exceptional magnetism, vigor, or ferocity, and bearing well-known names. "How Queen Elinor fetched the King a box of the ear," "How Queen Elinor sunk into the ground at Charing Cross and rose again at Potters Hithe," "How Edward, the first Prince of Wales, was christened at Caernarvon," "How nine Scottish nobles asked the English King to choose which should be King of Scots"—such are the materials out of which Peele's *Edward I* is made. The heterogeneous elements are unified only by rhetoric and by patriotism. And patriotism, even when coupled with poetry, is not enough. Edward's virtues never become human; English

205

victories come too easily to create any feeling of tension. Only Elinor—Spanish and so (in 1588) proud, tyrannical, tempting, and perfidious—raises a flicker of continuing interest. Her death and deathbed confession of manifold wickednesses (like that of the queen in *Cymbeline*) gives the end of the play what little sense of finality it possesses.

Edward I (presumably) and *Alcazar* (certainly) were written for the Admiral's Men, the acting company financed by Philip Henslowe and having at its center the first great star actor on the English stage, Edward Alleyn (the founder of Dulwich College). Alleyn, the first actor to play Tamburlaine, Barabas, Faustus, and Greene's Orlando, was famous for his declamatory powers; and plays like Marlowe's made full use of these, centering their action on the passion of the one man. Peele's plays, however, fail to do this effectively. Edward I is a colorless paragon; but Muly Mahomet (in *The Battle of Alcazar*), though far from dominating the action, has something memorable in his rhetorical identity, something that declamation might have brought alive. Here he is at the end of his tether:

> Where shall I find some unfrequented place
> Some uncouth walk where I may curse my fill,
> My stars, my dam, my planets and my nurse,
> The fire, the air, the water and the earth,
> All causes that have thus conspired in one
> To nourish and preserve me to this shame.
> Thou that were at my birth predominate,
> Thou fatal star, what planet ere thou be,
> Spit out thy poison bad, and all the ill
> That fortune, fate or heaven may bode a man.
> Thou nurse infortunate, guilty of all,
> Thou mother of my life that broughtst me forth,
> Curst mayst thou be for such a cursed son,
> Curst by thy son with every curse thou hast.
> Ye elements of whom consists this clay,
> This mass of flesh, this cursed crazed corpse,
> Destroy, dissolve, disturb and dissipate
> What water, earth and air congealed.

The Battle of Alcazar is a strange example of the power of lurid rhetoric to exclude ordinary human sympathies. Historically speaking, there is little to be said in favor of any of the characters of the play. One Moorish dynast murders a host of others; the Turks take sides against him, and he is exiled and forced to turn for Christian aid to Sebastian of Portugal, who hopes to get Morocco for his pains, and Tom Stukeley, a renegade Englishman on his way to betray Ireland to the pope. Stukeley ought to be all that patriotic Englishmen abhor; but by presenting his history in a framework of ghosts crying "vindicta," Nemesis in her car, devils, "dead men's heads in dishes," and other aspects of infernal interest, Peele manages to suggest that Stukeley is the unfortunate victim of Heaven's quarrel with Muly Mahomet. The fact that, in the battle,

> Three bold Kings, confounded in their fight
> Fell to the earth, contending for a crown,

seems to have impressed Peele more than any sense of what the war was about. The category of the "spectacular" is one that should never be forgotten when we look at the work of the university wits, and *Alcazar* is more possible as a spectacular than as a tragedy. Indeed, it was the spectacular quality of the rhetoric (out-Tamburlaining Tamburlaine) that gave the play its fame and its infamy, as appears in Jonson's parody, in *Poetaster*:

> *2 Pyrgus.* Now you shall see me do the Moor.
> Master, lend my your scarf a little.
> *Tucca.* Here, 'tis at thy service, boy.
> · · ·
> *(The boy comes in on Minos' shoulders,
> who stalks as he acts.)*
> 2 Pyrgus. Where art thou, boy? where is Calipolis?
> > Fight earthquakes in the entrails of the earth,
> > And eastern whirlwinds in the hellish shades;
> > Some foul contagion of th' infected heavens
> > Blast all the trees, and in their cursed tops
> > The dismal night-raven and tragic owl
> > Breed and become forerunners of my fall.

Peele's later plays, probably written for the public stage (The Queen's Majesty's players), *David and Bethsabe* (*ca.* 1594) and *The Old Wife's Tale* (*ca.* 1594), show some retreat from the high point of public declamation that marked his individual muse as well as the general English mood in the years immediately following the Armada. Both of these later plays exemplify further the principle of "decorum" and the practice of "imitation," which serve to explain to some extent the apparent stylistic inconsistencies in

Peele's work. By decorum the Elizabethans meant varying the style to suit the subject matter and the audience. Peele's poetic gifts were not of a powerfully original or individualizing type, but he had the happy knack of being able to give poetic unity of tone to each of his productions, a tone which "imitated" or drew on an already well-known style. I have already mentioned the debt to Spenser in *The Arraignment of Paris* and to Marlowe in *Alcazar*. For *David and Bethsabe* he used the most popular book in English—the Bible—as his source, and this is reflected in style as well as in subject matter:

> Now comes my lover tripping like the roe,
> And brings my longings tangled in her hair.
> To joy her love I'll build a kingly bower
> Seated in hearing of a hundred streams,
> That, for their homage to her sovereign joys
> Shall, as the serpents fold into their nests,
> In oblique turnings wind the nimble waves
> About the circles of her curious walks,
> And with their murmur summon easeful sleep
> To lay his golden sceptre on her brows.
> Open the doors and entertain my love,
> Open I say and as you open, sing
> "Welcome fair Bethsabe, King David's darling."

This draws very effectively on the exotic imagery of the Song of Solomon, and on the characterization of David as the Psalmist, to create an idyll as charming as anything in *The Arraignment of Paris*, but accessible to a much wider public.

Unfortunately this stylistic unity within each of Peele's plays is not reflected, in this play or in others, by unity of action. This may be explained in part by the state of the texts that have come down to us (none of Peele's plays is free from a suspicion of textual corruption). *David and Bethsabe* draws on a great variety of incidents that appear in the second book of Samuel, not only the love of David for Bethsabe, but also the rape of Thamar, the revolt of Absalom and the succession of Solomon. One of the choruses naively admits to the procedure:

> Now since this story lends us other store
> To make a third discourse of David's life
> . . .

It does not seem that the play could ever have been a particularly coherent ordering of events.

"Unity" is, of course, a difficult criterion to apply to early Tudor drama, which had (like the interludes) self-sufficient standards quite unlike those of modern theater. In those didactic times, thematic unity seemed more important than unity of action; and from this point of view *David and Bethsabe* is a better play than most modern readers would be prepared to admit.

The Old Wife's Tale is the play by Peele which suffers least from his besetting sin of structural diffuseness, not because he reduced the wild variety of materials in the mixture, but rather because he made the variety and consequent incoherence a structural point of the play. The presenter is not here the ballad-monger of *Alcazar*:

> Now listen lordings, now begins the game,
> Sebastian's tragedy in this tragic war.

The presenter is Madge, the old wife of the title, who undertakes to tell "an old wife's winter's tale" to pass away the night for those who have no bed to go to, a tale "of the giant and the king's daughter" such as one might expect from such a speaker. The story is indeed bewildering in the variety of its elements and in the lack of connection between them: Sacrapant, a magician, keeps Delia captive, and effectively concealed from those who are questing for her, including her two brothers (as in *Comus*); Huanebango, a huffing braggart; and Booby (or Corebus), his servant. Also questing is Eumenides, a knight; and it is he who eventually rescues Delia, having intervened successfully in a parish burial dispute and obtained a dead man (Jack) as his helper. One should also mention a half-man-half-bear who utters prophecies to all the questers, and Lampriscus, a countryman with two daughters, one shrewish and one ugly, who have to resort to magic to get husbands.

For once, however, the poetic atmosphere holds all this in easy and obvious control. The quick transitions from rustic realities to romantic imaginings catch at the qualities which have given fairytales their universal appeal. The naïvety of the story is admitted, but is not seen as in need of apology. The symbolism implicit in the magic well, in the lamp under the earth, in the bargain with the dead man exerts its pressure, as in folklore, but is never made ponderous with explicit meaning. And it is so with the style as well. The homely similes of rustic prose are sometimes quite close to the gorgeous similes of Marlovian verse:

She it is that afflicts me with her continual clamours, and hangs on me like a bur. Poor she is, and proud she is, as poor as a sheep new shorn, and as proud of her hopes as a peacock of her tail well grown.

I had a daughter so hard favoured, so foul and ill-faced that I think a grove full of golden trees, and the leaves of rubies and diamonds would not be a dowry answerable to her deformity.

It is an interesting historical point that Victorian critics and their followers thought of Peele's play as a satire on primitive romantic drama. They supposed that the sophisticated literary mind that produced *The Arraignment of Paris* could only despise the folk elements that Madge's imagination conjures up. But the evidence points the other way. Maypoles, Morris dancing, lords of misrule, Whitsunales (fairs), disguisings and mummings, games of Saint George or Robin Hood were the generally accepted basis of courtly masquing and of the festivities that marked the queen's official progresses through the country. The queen and her ladies went maying like village wenches.

In the subplot of *Edward I,* Peele evokes the world of Robin Hood and his merry men, without giving any evidence of satire or condescension. In *The Old Wife's Tale* the virtues of humility and plain country ways are established right at the beginning, when the three courtly pages (Antic, Frolic, and Fantastic) are rescued by Clunch the smith, taken to his cottage, offered food and rest, and finally entertained by a story from the old wife, Madge:

Well since you be so importunate, my good man shall fill the pot and get him to bed; they that ply their work must keep good hours. One of you go lie with him. He is a clean-skinned man I tell you, without either spavin or windgall. So—I am content to drive away the time with an old wife's winter's tale.

Madge does not believe in the story any more than the pages do, or the modern audience; but she moves easily into its absurdities, and so do the sophisticated pages.

We misunderstand the English Renaissance if we forget how close to the soil was even the most sophisticated of lives. The nation was still basically a rural society. Plain fare, good housekeeping, and rustic hospitality were virtues accepted as the basis of English greatness, even in courtly circles. The university wits were able to reach and to affect a popular audience because they shared so high a proportion of that audience's assumptions.

SELECTED BIBLIOGRAPHY

ELIZABETHAN DRAMA

G. Saintsbury, *A History of Elizabethan Literature* (London, 1887); W. W. Greg, *Pastoral Poetry and Pastoral Drama: A Literary Inquiry, with Special Reference to the Pre-Restoration Stage in England* (London, 1906); F. S. Boas, *University Drama in the Tudor Age* (Oxford, 1914); W. Creizenach, *English Drama in the Age of Shakespeare* (London, 1916), translated from *Geschichte des neueren dramas,* Vol. IV; E. K. Chambers, *The Elizabethan Stage,* 4 vols. (Oxford, 1923); H. N. Hillebrand, *The Child Actors, A Chapter in Elizabethan Stage History* (London, 1964), first pub. in Vol. II of University of Illinois Studies in Language and Literature (Urbana, Ill., 1926); E. Welsford, *The Court Masque: A Study in the Relationship Between Poetry and the Revels* (Cambridge, 1927); M. C. Bradbrook, *Themes and Conventions of Elizabethan Tragedy* (London, 1935); E. C. Wilson, *England's Eliza. A Study of the Idealization of Queen Elizabeth in the Poetry of Her Age* (Cambridge, Mass., 1939); T. W. Baldwin, *William Shakspere's Five Act Structure* (Urbana, Ill., 1947); J. B. Leishman, ed., *The Three Parnassus Plays, 1598–1601* (London, 1949); M. C. Bradbrook, *The Growth and Structure of Elizabethan Comedy* (London, 1955); I. Ribner, *The English History Play in the Age of Shakespeare* (Princeton, 1957); F. A. Yates, "Elizabethan Chivalry. The Romance of the Accession Day Tilts," in *Journal of the Warburg and Courtauld Institutes,* 20 (1957), 4–25; G. Wickham, *Early English Stages,* 2 vols. (London, 1959–1963); M. C. Bradbrook, *The Rise of the Common Player* (London, 1962); D. M. Bevington, *From Mankind to Marlowe* (Cambridge, Mass., 1962); J. R. Brown and B. Harris, eds., *Elizabethan Theatre* (London, 1966).

JOHN LYLY AND GEORGE PEELE

JOHN LYLY

I. BIBLIOGRAPHY. W. W. Greg, *A Bibliography of the English Printed Drama to the Restoration*, 4 vols. (London, 1939–1959); S. A. Tannenbaum, *John Lyly: A Concise Bibliography* (New York, 1940); R. C. Johnson, ed., *Elizabethan Bibliographies Supplement V* (London, 1968).

II. COLLECTED WORKS. *Six Court Comedies* (London, 1632), contains *Campaspe, Sapho and Phao, Endimion, Gallathea, Midas, Mother Bombie*; F. W. Fairholt, ed., *The Dramatic Works of John Lyly*, 2 vols. (London, 1892); R. W. Bond, ed., *The Complete Works of John Lyly*, 3 vols. (Oxford, 1902), the standard ed. of the works, now out of print; L. Hotson, ed., *Queen Elizabeth's Entertainment at Mitcham. Attributed to John Lyly* (New Haven, 1953), reprints two Progress entertainments attributed to Lyly.

III. SEPARATE WORKS. *Euphues: The Anatomy of Wit* (1578), repr., "corrected and augmented," in 1579, and 17 times before 1640; *Euphues and His England* (1578), repr. 16 times before 1640; E. Arber, ed., *Euphues, the Anatomy of Wit, and Euphues and His England*, English Reprints (London, 1904); M. W. Croll and H. Clemons, eds., *Euphues, The Anatomy of Wit; Euphues and His England* (London, 1916), the standard ed. of *Euphues*; J. Winny, ed., *The Descent of Euphues: Three Elizabethan Romance Stories* (Cambridge, 1957), prints *Euphues the Anatomy of Wit*, 1578 state; *A Most Excellent Comedy of Alexander, Campaspe and Diogenes* (London, 1584), drama, repr. in 1591, in Dodsley's *Old Plays*, Malone Society Reprints (London, 1933), in J. M. Manly, ed., *Specimens of the Pre-Shakespearean Drama* (Boston, 1897–1898), in C. M. Gayley, ed., *Representative English Comedies* (New York, 1903), in J. Q. Adams, *Chief Pre-Shakespearean Dramas* (New York, 1924), in E. H. C. Oliphant, *Shakespeare and His Fellow Dramatists* (New York, 1929), and in A. K. McIlwraith, *Five Elizabethan Comedies* (London, 1935); *Sapho and Phao* (1584), repr. in 1591; *Pap with a Hatchet* (1589), a government-inspired contribution to the Marprelate controversy, usually attributed to Lyly; *Endimion, The Man in the Moon* (1591), drama, repr. in A. H. Thorndike, ed., *Minor Elizabethan Drama II* (London, 1910), in F. Schelling, *Typical Elizabethan Plays* (New York, 1926), in C. F. Tucker Brooke and N. B. Paradise, *English Drama 1580–1642* (Boston, 1933), in H. Spencer, *Elizabethan Plays* (Boston, 1933), in C. R. Baskervill, V. B. Heltzel, H. H. Nethercot, *Elizabethan and Stuart Plays* (New York, 1934), in E. W. Parks and R. C. Beatty, *The English Drama* (New York, 1935), and in W. A. Neilson, *Chief Elizabethan Dramatists* (New York, 1939); *Gallathea* (1588), drama, repr. A. B. Lancashire,

ed., in Regent's Renaissance Drama Series (Lincoln, Neb., 1969), also contains *Midas,* and in R. Fraser and N. Rabkin, eds., *Drama of the English Renaissance* (New York, 1976); *Midas* (1592), drama, repr. in C. W. Dilke's *Old English Plays* (London, 1814), and in J. Winny, ed., *Three Elizabethan Plays* (London, 1959); *Mother Bombie* (1594), drama, repr. 1598, in Dilke's *Old English Plays* (London, 1814), and Malone Society Reprints (London, 1939); *The Woman in the Moon* (1597), drama; *Love's Metamorphosis; A Witty and Courtly Pastoral* (1601), drama.

IV. SOME CRITICAL AND BIOGRAPHICAL STUDIES. J. D. Wilson, *John Lyly* (Cambridge, 1905), undergraduate prize essay; A. Feuillerat, *John Lyly. Contribution á l'histoire de la Renaissance en Angleterre* (Cambridge, 1910), a massive thesis, definitively documented; M. P. Tilley, *Elizabethan Proverb Love in Lyly's Euphues* (Ann Arbor, Mich., 1926); V. M. Jeffrey, *John Lyly and the Italian Renaissance* (Paris, 1929), shows Lyly's place in the mainstream of European courtly art; D. Jones, "John Lyly at St. Bartholomew's, or Much Ado About Washing," in C. J. Sisson, *Thomas Lodge and Other Elizabethans* (London, 1933), offers biographical detail on Lyly's last years; W. Ringler, "Immediate Source of Euphuism," in *PMLA*, 53 (1938), 678–686, on "Euphuism" in the works of Dr. Rainolds, notable university figure when Pettie and Lyly were at Oxford; G. Wilson Knight, "Lyly," in *Review of English Studies*, 15 (1939), 146–163; J. W. Bennett, "Oxford and Endimion," in *PMLA*, 57 (1942), 354–369, the play presented as an allegory of the earl of Oxford's court misadventures; B. F. Huppé, "Allegory of Love in Lyly's Court Comedies," in *English Literary History*, 14 (1947), 93–113; W. N. King, "John Lyly and Elizabethan Rhetoric," in *Studies in Philology*, 52 (1955), 149–161; J. A. Barish, "The Prose Style of John Lyly," in *English Literary History*, 23 (1956), 14–35; M. Mincoff, "Shakespeare and Lyly," in *Shakespeare Survey*, 14 (1961), 15–24; G. K. Hunter, *John Lyly: The Humanist as Courtier* (London, 1962); R. W. Zantvoort, "What Is Euphuism," in *Melanges . . . Mossé* (London, 1962); R. W. Turner, "Some Dialogues of Love in Lyly's Comedies," in *English Literary History*, 29 (1962), 276–288; J. Powell, "John Lyly and the Language of Play," in J. R. Brown and B. Harris, eds., *Elizabethan Theatre* (London, 1966); M. R. Best, "Lyly's Static Drama," in *Renaissance Drama*, n.s.1 (Evanston, Ill., 1968), 75–86; Peter Saccio, *The Court Comedies of John Lyly* (Princeton, 1969).

GEORGE PEELE

I. BIBLIOGRAPHY. W. W. Greg, *Two Elizabethan Stage Abridgements: The Battle of Alcazar and Orlando*

Furioso, Malone Society Reprints (London, 1922), the nature of "bad" quartos illustrated by comparison of the manuscript "plot" of *Alcazar* with the text of the 1594 quarto; T. Larsen, "A Bibliography of the Writings of George Peele," in *Modern Philology,* 32 (1934), 143–156, gives full biographical details; W. W. Greg, *A Bibliography of the English Printed Drama to the Restoration,* 4 vols. (London, 1939–1959); S. A. Tannenbaum, *George Peele: A Concise Bibliography* (New York, 1940).

II. COLLECTED WORKS. A. Dyce, ed., *The Works of George Peele,* 2 vols. (London, 1829; 2nd ed., 3 vols., 1829–1839), 3rd vol. of 1839 ed. contains supposititious works and the *Eclogue,* Dyce's text repr. in *Poetical and Dramatic Works of Robert Greene and George Peele* (London, 1861); H. Morley, ed., *Plays and Poems of George Peele,* Morley's Universal Library, no. 52 (London, 1887); A. H. Bullen, ed., *Works of George Peele,* 2 vols. (London, 1888); C. Prouty, ed., *The Life and Works of George Peele,* 3 vols. (New Haven, 1952–1970), I, D. H. Horne, ed., *Life and Minor Works* (1952), II, F. S. Hook, ed., *Edward I,* and J. Yoklavich, ed., *Alcazar* (1961), III, R. M. Benbow, ed., *The Arraignment of Paris,* E. Blistein, ed., *David and Bethsabe,* F. S. Hook, ed., *The Old Wives' Tale* (1970).

III. SEPARATE WORKS. *The Arraignment of Paris: A Pastoral* (1584), repr. in Malone Society Reprints (London, 1910), O. Smeaton, ed., Temple Dramatists (London, 1905), C. F. Tucker Brooke and N. B. Paradise, *English Drama 1580–1642* (Boston, 1933); *The Device of the Pageant Borne Before Woolstone Dixi, Lord Mayor of the City of London* (1585), repr. in Harleian Miscellany, 10 (1813), Nichols' *Progresses of Queen Elizabeth* (London, 1823), Percy Society (London, 1843); *A Farewell, Entitled to the Famous and Fortunate Generals of Our English Forces, Sir John Norris and Sir Francis Drake, Knights, With All Their Brave and Resolute Followers* (1589); *An Eclogue Gratulatory Entitled to the Right Honourable and Renowned Sheperd of Albion's Arcadia: Robert Earl of Essex and Ewe for His Welcome into England from Portugal* (1589); *Polyhymnia, Describing the Honourable Triumph at Tilt Before Her Majesty* (1590); *The Hunting of Cupid* (1591), the original ed. (entered in Stationers' Register 1591) is lost, but fragments remain among the mss of William Drummond of Hawthornden, E. W. Greg, ed., MSR, Collections I (London, 1911); *Descensus Astraeae. The Device of a Pageant Borne Before Master William Web, Lord Mayor of the City of London . . .* (1591), repr. in Harleian Miscellany, 10 (London, 1813), Percy Society (London, 1843); *The Famous Chronicle of King Edward the First, Surnamed Edward Longshanks, With His Return from the Holy Land. Also the Life of Llewellan, Rebel in Wales. Lastly the Sinking of Queen Elinor Who Sunk at Charingcross, and Rose Again at Pottershithe, Now*

Named Queenhithe (1593), drama, repr. in J. P. Collier, ed., Dodsley's *Old Plays,* 11 (1827), MSR (London, 1911); *The Honour of the Garter* (1593); *The Battle of Alcazar, Fought in Barbary, Between Sebastian King of Portugal, and Abdelmelec King of Morocco. With the Death of Captain Stukeley* (1594), drama, repr. in MSR (London, 1907); *Anglorum Feriae, England's Holidays Celebrated the 17th November Last, 1595, Beginning Happily the 38 Year of the Reign of Our Sovereign Lady Queen Elizabeth* (1595); *The Old Wife's Tale: A Pleasant Conceited Comedy* (1595), drama, repr. in MSR (London, 1908), in A. H. Thorndike, ed., *Minor Elizabethan Drama II* (London, 1910), and in C. F. Tucker Brooke and N. B. Paradise, *English Drama 1580–1642* (Boston, 1933); *The Love of King David and Fair Bethsabe: With the Tragedy of Absalon* (1599), drama, repr. in MSR (London, 1912), in J. M. Manly, ed., *Specimens of the Pre-Shakespearean Drama* (London, 1900), in A. H. Thorndike, ed., *Minor Elizabethan Drama I* (London, 1910), and in R. Fraser and N. Rabkin, eds., *Drama of the English Renaissance* (New York, 1976); *Merry and Conceited Jests of George Peele* (1607), repr. 1620 (?), 1627, and S. W. Singer and R. Triphook (London, 1809), and in W. C. Hazlitt, ed., *Shakespeare's Jest Books* (London, 1864).

IV. SOME CRITICAL AND BIOGRAPHICAL STUDIES. P. H. Cheffaud, *George Peele* (Paris, 1913), the standard, indeed the only, book; V. M. Jeffery, "The Source of Peele's *Arraignment of Paris,*" in *Modern Language Review,* 19 (1924), 175–187, establishes parallel with Paulilli's *Giuditio di Paride,* but no necessary connection; G. Jones, "The Intention of Peele's *Old Wives' Tale,*" in *Aberystwyth Studies,* 7 (1925), 79–83, *Old Wife's Tale* not a satire, but a "plain country story"; H. Jenkins, "Peele's *Old Wive's Tale,*" in *MLR,* 34 (1939), 177–185, we have only a "mutilated text" of the play; T. Larsen, "The Historical and Legendary Background of Peele's *Battle of Alcazar,*" in Royal Society of Canada *Proceedings and Transactions,* 33 (1939), 185–197; W. G. Rice, "A Principal Source of *The Battle of Alcazar,*" in *Modern Language Notes,* 58 (1943), 428–431; W. Clemen, *Die Tragödie vor Shakespeare: ihre Entwicklung im Spiegel der dramatischen Rede* (Heidelberg, 1955), tr. by T. S. Dorsch, *English Tragedy Before Shakespeare: The Development of Dramatic Speech* (London, 1961), chapter 2 on Peele's set speeches; I-S. Ekeblad (Ewbank), "The Love of King David and Fair Bethsabe," *English Studies,* 39 (1958), 57–62; L. B. Campbell, *Divine Poetry and Drama in Sixteenth-Century England* (Cambridge, 1959), *David and Bethsabe* and the tradition of divine poetry; C. De Stasio, "Il linguaggio drammatico di George Peele," in *English Miscellany,* 15 (1964), 61–87; I-S. Ewbank, "The House of David in Renaissance Drama," in *Renaissance Drama,* 8 (1965), 3–40; M. C. Bradbrook,

"Peele's Old Wive's Tale: A Play of Enchantment," in *English Studies,* 43 (1962), 323–330; S. Musgrove, "Peele's 'Old Wives Tale': An Afterpiece?," in *Journal of Australian Universities' Language and Lit. Association,* 23 (1965), 86–95; A. von Hendy, "The Triumph of Chastity: Form and Meaning in *The Arraignment of Paris,*" in *Renaissance Drama,* n.s. 1 (1968), 87–101; Leonard Ashley, *Authorship and Evidence . . . Illustrated by the Case of George Peele* (Geneva, 1968).

THOMAS KYD
and
EARLY ELIZABETHAN TRAGEDY

(*ca.* 1558-1594)

Philip Edwards

In 1586, England did not possess a single tragedy which anyone would now read for pleasure or witness on the stage except as a curiosity. By the end of 1592, English drama had Marlowe's *Tamburlaine*, *The Jew of Malta*, and *Dr. Faustus*, the early (lost) version of *Hamlet*, Kyd's *The Spanish Tragedy*, the Shakespearean *Henry VI* trilogy, Kyd's *Arden of Feversham*. The exact dates of these plays are uncertain, but it is clear enough that tragedy came suddenly. When we consider all the work that has been done on the sources and the heritage of Elizabethan tragedy, it seems unkind to say that it came not only suddenly but out of nowhere. Yet this is true. Elizabethan tragedy was really created, in a year or two, by two men of extraordinary originality, Christopher Marlowe and Thomas Kyd, who at one time were "wrytinge in one chamber." Of course, they built, as they had to, on what was available to them; their plays are shaped by tradition and convention. But what they themselves achieved, and what they were able to bequeath to Shakespeare, make what they inherited from the past seem almost unimportant.

Marlowe's originality and genius do not need to be established.

> From jigging veins of rhyming mother-wits,
> And such conceits as clownage keeps in pay,
> We'll lead you to the stately tent of war

So he opens *Tamburlaine*, and the insolence is excusable in the man who is going on to write *Dr. Faustus*. But to compare Kyd with him may seem rather comic. Marlowe towers over Kyd as a poet and as a mind, just as he towered over the cringing Kyd in life; after Marlowe's death, Kyd wrote: "That I should love or be familiar friend, with one so irreligious, were very rare. . . . He was intemperate and of a cruel heart, the very contraries to which, my greatest enemies will say by me." Kyd, even at his best, seems a little naïve and something of a plodder. All the same, when Francis Meres (in 1598) put Kyd among "our best for Tragedie" he was not wrong. In its conception, though obviously not in its execution, *The Spanish Tragedy* is more original, and greater, than *Richard III*. It is one of those rare works in which a minor writer, in a strange inspiration, shapes the future by producing something quite new.

TRAGEDY BEFORE KYD: THE 1560'S

The early period of Elizabethan tragedy in the late 1580's and very early 1590's had been preceded by a kind of false dawn a quarter of a century before, not long after Elizabeth's accession in 1558. The plays of the sixties are much more academic than the tragedies of the eighties. At that time there was no public theater in England: the first such building, The Theater, was erected in 1576. Plays written by educated men for educated audiences at court, in the universities, at the inns of court were much more likely to survive in manuscript or find their way into print than the stock-in-trade of the traveling companies of actors. Yet some of these plays, notably Thomas Preston's *Cambises* and John Pickering's *Horestes,* seem to belong to the popular stage, and if they have an academic or classical cast, they do so because tragedy at this time was something more than common fare. It took *The Spanish Tragedy* and *Arden of Feversham* to bring "the lofty measures of sententiously composed Tragedies" (as a contemporary put it) into the hurly-burly of action and passion that could excite ordinary spectators. Tragedy had to lose the stateliness it thought it lived by before it could achieve its true dignity.

There is no Senecan stiffness in William Wager's moral interlude, *Enough Is as Good as a Feast,* printed about 1565 and perhaps written some years earlier. It is a useful starting point, because it is so firmly in the morality tradition, a play built to incarnate an idea, the idea being almost the only conceivable one: the wages of sin are death and damnation. None of the characters has a personal name except Satan. Some names are of qualities or dispositions or passions—Ignorance, Precipitation, and Covetousness (for the Vice); some are of types of men—Heavenly Man and Worldly Man (for the hero); some are of calling or rank—Tenant, Physician. Worldly Man, who enters "stout and frolic," is a rich landlord. Persuaded by Heavenly Man and Contentation to renounce the world, he is quickly seduced back again by Covetousness (the Vice) and his gang. He sets his heart on his possessions, oppresses his tenants, and refuses to listen to their appeals. But God will not be mocked. Worldly Man makes plans to evict a tenant in order to use his cottage as a buttery. "Who the devil put that in your mind?" asks the Vice. And then:

> *Prophet* (without): O thou Earth, Earth, Earth!
>   hear the word of the Lord!
> Know thyself to be no better than clay or dust.
>   (*Let the Worldly Man look suddenly about him.*)
> See that thy life to God's truth do always accord:
> For from earth thou camest and to earth thou
>   must.
> *Covetousness:* What is the matter? what ails you?
>   why look you so about?
> *Worldly Man:* I heard a terrible noise, surely
>   without doubt,
> Which pronounced the words of the prophet
>   Jeremy:
> Saying Earth, Earth, turn thee speedily.

"God's plague" enters and the Worldly Man is smitten with a disease that no physician can cure. He tries to dictate his will.

> *Ignorance:* Here is ink and paper; what shall I
>   write?
> *Worldly Man:* 'In the name' first of all do thou
>   indite.
> *Ignorance:* 'In the name . . . in, in, in the name
>   . . .'—what more?
> *Worldly Man:* Of . . . of . . . of . . . of
>   . . .'—what more?
>
>   (*Falls down.*)

Satan enters, rubbing his hands, "Oh, oh, oh, oh, all is mine, all is mine." He hoists the dead hero on his back and carries him away to "everlasting fire."

Enough Is as Good as a Feast is a very harsh play. It is written as a warning, but its vision of life is of the weakness of man who turns always toward property and possessions as the needle of a compass turns toward the north, who repents too late and suffers in this world and the next on account of his frailty. There is no hesitancy in explaining suffering, and no qualm in accepting a stern God.

Although it is not always expounded with such confidence and pleasure, the retribution of an offended God provides the mechanism for tragedy for a generation or more to come. Thomas Preston's *Cambises,* a "lamentable tragedy," probably acted at court in 1561, gives the expected sequence on the title page: "many wicked deeds . . . and, last of all, his odious death by God's justice appointed." In the prologue, Preston uses an uncomfortable image for God's dealings with man—that of a fisherman snaring his prey. Cambises "oft had take the pleasant bait from hook," but in the end God caught him—"at last by subtle bait come to the fisher's hand."

The influence of the "morality" tradition on *Cambises* is very strong; many characters have no personal names: Commons Complaint, Small Hability, Cruelty, Shame. The Vice, clown-villain and the yeast of the play, is called Ambidexter. But *Cambises* is built round a story as well as round an idea, and there is more in the action than persuasion and yielding. The story is the familiar one of the deputy abusing his authority in the absence of the ruler, though when

Cambises has returned and Execution has done execution on the wicked deputy by flaying him on stage ("with a false skin"), the play gets a second wind as it displays the insolent brutality of the ruler himself. Ambidexter the tempter is not just an aspect of man, but an objectified mischiefmaker (as Bernard Spivack makes clear in his important book, *Shakespeare and the Allegory of Evil*). Ambidexter's malicious lies lead Cambises to murder his own brother. Ambidexter may seem too merry a fellow to be a very sinister incarnation of the devil, but *Cambises* nicely combines the two essential kinds of Elizabethan villainy: the malicious deceiver taking pleasure in destroying other men's happiness (Iago, Edmund), and the cruel tyrant-monster (Richard III).

Cambises runs through a series of vile crimes, and then, quite suddenly, "Enter the King, without a gown, a sword thrust up into his side, bleeding." His death has come upon him in a riding accident: a judgment of God upon a tyrant. Thus is the purpose of tragedy, as the age saw it, fulfilled; we have seen the deserved end of a proud and powerful man. William Farnham has traced the theme of *De casibus virorum illustrium* from Boccaccio through Chaucer to *The Mirror for Magistrates* and beyond in his *Medieval Heritage of Elizabethan Tragedy;* he quotes a statement about the nature of tragedy from one of those wonderful sociological accounts of the origins of literary genres to be found in Puttenham's *Arte of English Poesie* (1589 or earlier):

After their deaths, when the posterity stood no more in dread of them, their infamous life and tyrannies were laid open to all the world, their wickedness reproached, their follies and extreme insolencies derided, and their miserable ends painted out in plays and pageants, to show the mutability of fortune, and the just punishment of God in revenge of a vicious and evil life.

The death of Cambises may seem the least tragic thing in the world to us, conditioned to expect a closer relation between deed and suffering. But relatedness and responsibility are certainly present. Tragedy in that age begins and ends with the idea of retribution, the belief that every deed is a pendulum, that every crime has its punishment. If we are looking for the hero's share of responsibility in his own downfall, we shall not find an Elizabethan audience complaining that an accident to a wicked man in the hunting field is outside the proper range of consequence and tragic inevitability in a universe watched over by a jealous God. We may also recognize that there is more to a play like *Cambises* than the effect which the age believed in, that tragedy "maketh kings fear to be tyrants" (to use Sidney's words). There are too few monarchs in the average audience to keep tragedy alive, if that is its raison d'être. These tragedies of the rise and fall of tyrants have a different justification: the spectacle of careless brutality and outrageous indifference to law among the very powerful appeals as much as it appalls; the audience can both identify itself with lawlessness and find satisfaction in retribution. All this is surely proved by the success of *Tamburlaine* and *Richard III*. Marlowe's trouble is his reluctance—it is a matter of principle—to hand over his tyrant-monster to the devil.

Tragedies were indeed written in the 1560's for monarchs to watch as warnings to themselves. But *Gorboduc* (or *Ferrex and Porrex*) had no more success in altering Elizabeth's actions than it had as a drama. The play was written by the politically minded Thomas Norton and Thomas Sackville, and acted by "the Gentlemen of the Inner Temple," first of all at their own inn at Christmas 1561, and then before the queen at Whitehall on 18 January 1562. Sir Philip Sidney is one of the few people to have admired this play. It has merits for the historically minded: it is the first play to be written in blank verse; it reveals very closely the political bias which is so important an element in the tragedy of the time; it shows a use made of historical themes which Shakespeare and his fellows happily accepted; it shows clearly the fear of division and civil war that animated so many plays in a later generation; and it shows the influence of Seneca, which perhaps deserves a note before any discussion of *Gorboduc*.

The influence of Seneca (*ca.* 4 BC–AD 65) on Elizabethan drama was perhaps overstressed in the past, and then unnecessarily discredited. We are much more aware of the influence of moralities and popular conventions than were writers a half-century ago, but it must be allowed that Seneca did leave a deep mark on most tragedies of the Tudor period. The dramatists found him "damn'd good to steal from" while not, on the whole, accepting his general morality. They stole his sententious remarks, the ghosts, the chorus, the lip-licking vows of vengeance, the description of the gloomy underworld of Charon and Pluto; they stole the atrocious crimes of his brooding heroes and heroines; and—least defensibly—they stole his technique of stichomythia (dialogue in formal line-for-line exchange) and his long reports of offstage action. Seneca's tragedies, originally composed more for recitation than for acting, were all translated in the Elizabethan period. Perhaps the most influential of these, Jasper Heywood's translation of *Thyestes* (1560), may stand for all.

The ghost of Tantalus arises, groaning of the torments of hell, and the Fury, Megaera, urges him on to set discord between the brothers Atreus and Thyestes. (It is worth noting the fatal division of authority that obtains at Mycenae; Thyestes rules one year, Atreus the next.) In the second act, Atreus, a man of quite implacable malice, expresses his wrath toward his brother:

> not yet enough with fury great
> And rage doth burn my boiling breast; it ought to be
> replete
> With monster more.

He resolves to make his brother eat his own children, and, in Act IV, a messenger relates in great detail how the children were murdered and cooked:

> From bosoms yet alive outdrawn the trembling
> bowels shake,
> The veins yet breathe, the fearful heart doth yet both
> pant and quake,
> But he the strings doth turn in hand, and destinies
> behold,
> And of the guts the signs each one doth view not
> fully cold.
> When him the sacrifice had pleas'd, his diligence he
> puts
> To dress his brother's banquet now, and straight
> asunder cuts
> The bodies into quarters all, and by the stumps anon
> The shoulders wide, and brawns of arms, he strikes
> off every one.

In the fifth act, Atreus gloats over his triumphant revenge, and Thyestes learns what food it was he ate.

Gorboduc is Senecan in its general shape and scene structure and in its rhetorical abundance rather than in its attention to horror. The story and moral of *Gorboduc* are perhaps best told in the words of the original argument:

Gorboduc, king of Britain, divided his realm in his lifetime to his sons, Ferrex and Porrex. The sons fell to dissension. The younger killed the elder. The mother, that more dearly loved the elder, for revenge killed the younger. The people, moved with the cruelty of the fact, rose in rebellion and slew both father and mother. The nobility assembled and most terribly destroyed the rebels. And afterwards, for want of issue of the Prince, whereby the succession of the crown became uncertain, they fell to civil war, in which both they and many of their issue were slain, and the land for a long time almost desolate and miserably wasted.

By no means all of this energetic process is shown to the audience. The main dramatic fare is elaborate persuasion: proposition and response. In Act II, symmetrical scenes show Ferrex with his good and bad counselor, then Porrex with his, and a chorus sums up, confirming points that have already been very firmly made. The best part of the play is the final long speech of Eubulus, and its virtues are those of didactic expository verse. All the political platitudes of the age are assembled to make clear the cause for which the play was written. Kings must not be misled by flatterers; a kingdom without a known and acknowledged heir is open to anarchy; civil war is the worst of all evils; subjects must not take government into their own hands. One note (which perhaps Elizabeth did not sufficiently attend to) is not platitudinous:

> Parliament should have been holden
> And certain heirs appointed to the crown.

One wonders if the absorbing interest of the political situation which governs *Gorboduc*—that of two brothers warring for mastery—led George Gascoigne to produce his *Jocasta*, a version of Euripides' *Phoenissae*, at Gray's Inn in 1566. Polynices' bringing a foreign army from Argos to establish his right to Thebes, kept from him by Eteocles, seems just the situation to rouse the enthusiasm of an Elizabethan dramatist. It is heartening that Seneca was not the sole representative of classical tragedy on the Elizabethan stage; but this *Jocasta* is translated from the Italian of Lodovico Dolce's *Giocasta*, itself said to derive not directly from Euripides, but from a Latin version of the play. Euripides, fattened out with dumb shows, and given in a prosaically sententious verse, is rather heavy. The Euripidean *Jocasta* is little more than an oddity to remind us how innocent popular Elizabethan tragedy was of knowledge of its only real predecessor, the tragedy of ancient Greece.

Even as early as the 1560's, Elizabethan audiences knew the drama of passion. The boldness of the assignation scene between Horatio and Bel-imperia in *The Spanish Tragedy* might not seem so striking to one who knew the old Inner Temple play *Gismond of Salerne*, produced in 1566 or 1568 and revised and printed by one of its coauthors, R. Wilmot, in 1592 as *Tancred and Gismund*. A love tragedy taken from Boccaccio is interesting enough in this period of baleful tyrants and vengeful brothers. Because the father of the young widow Gismond will not let her remarry, she can enjoy only illicit relations with her lover Guishard, count Palurine; their place of meeting is through a trapdoor in Gismond's chamber. Seneca makes his appearance in Act IV; before the father discovers his daughter's disgrace, "Megaera ariseth out of hell":

> Vengeance and blood out of the deepest hells
> I bring the cursed house where Gismond dwells.

The inevitable sextet of Pluto, Proserpine, Charon, Minos, Aeacus, and Rhadamant must appear before we hear of Tancred's wrath. The count is brutally murdered (offstage) and the father sends Gismond (onstage) a cup containing her lover's heart. She pours poison in the goblet and takes her own life.

> To pass down to the paled ghosts of hell
> And there enjoy my love, whom thus my sire
> Would not permit in earth with me to dwell.

Gismond of Salerne, as a tragedy of the clash of powerful emotions—love and fatherly posses-

siveness—has something of an adult quality, and is refreshingly free from didacticism and moral reproof. It is a much better play than R.B.'s *Appius and Virginia* (printed 1575), a more popular kind of play which may have been acted by a boys' company about the year of Shakespeare's birth, 1564. *Appius and Virginia* is execrable; it is just about the level of the mechanicals' play of *Pyramus and Thisbe* in *A Midsummer Night's Dream*. The story is about the lust which the governor Appius conceives for the maiden Virginia and her preferring to die at her father's hands rather than stain her honor. ("Here tie a handkerchief about her eyes, and then strike off her head.") There are two moments of interest in the play: the sensuality of Appius' imagination as he sees himself at the center of an Ovidian scene with Virginia, and then the practical way in which the Vice, Haphazard, spurs on the dreamy Appius to encompass his ambition. The relationship between Haphazard and Appius is much like the relationship between the forthright Machiavellian, Lorenzo, and the sighing Balthazar in *The Spanish Tragedy*. Haphazard's bustling scheme is to get the girl's father out of the way by laying a false accusation against him that will get him into prison. Quite clearly the insolent disregard for all truth and honor in getting what one wants that we generally call, with the age, Machiavellian, emerged from the proclivities of the Vice. Spivack says of the Machiavellian villain:

The Elizabethans really understood him well enough, and indeed their traditional values within their transitional age taught them to apprehend the evil before they were actually aware of the man who later lent it his name. . . . It is a rare villain in the drama of that time, who is not in some degree a Machiavel. . . . The Florentine . . . contributed not so much an origin as an affirmation, not so much a manifesto as a guidebook.[1]

All the same, the most interesting Vice, in what is surely the most interesting of the tragedies of the sixties, *Horestes*, is not really of the Machiavellian kind at all. This play, by John Pickering, is the play where *Hamlet* starts, and it

[1] *Shakespeare and the Allegory of Evil*, pp. 375–376.

is not even mentioned in the standard work on Elizabethan revenge tragedy. Its full title is *A New Interlude of Vice, containing the History of Horestes, with the cruel revengement of his Father's death upon his own natural Mother.* It was printed in 1567; it obviously belongs to a popular stage. Horestes comes on the stage with one question: what shall he do about Clytemnestra? Being a pious man, he would not wish to act without divine sanction. Dame Nature tells him to pity, and to forgive—but his mother's offense stirs him too deeply.

O gods, therefore, sith you be just, unto whose
  power and will
All thing in heaven, and earth also, obey and serve
  until,
Declare to me your gracious mind—Shall I revenged
  be
Of good king Agamemnon's death? Ye gods, declare
  to me!
Or shall I let the adulterous dame still wallow in her
  sin?

Overhearing him, the Vice breaks in to say that he is the messenger of the gods sent to tell Horestes that their "wrathful doom" is that Horestes should take vengeance on Clytemnestra. The Vice further tells Horestes that his name is Courage. Horestes is buoyant, delighted to have divine sanction given to his own strong desire to punish his mother:

My hands do thirst her blood to have; naught can my
  mind content
Till that on her I have performed, O gods, your just
  judgement.

Twice in the play, Horestes rests his case on the lex talionis: "blood for blood my father's death doth crave."

Helped by Idumeus, Horestes brings an army and captures his mother in battle; his heart then does show some remorse, which pains the Vice. But, having hanged Egistus (onstage), he brings on Clytemnestra to see her lover's corpse; she is then led away by the Vice to be killed. This nameless Vice, who earlier called himself Courage, is finally referred to by his real name: Revenge. He reenters, singing a very interesting song, which ends:

And was it not ill
His mother to kill?
I pray you, how say you?

The resolution of the play, worked out with considerable subtlety, is most unexpected. Horestes proceeds to justify himself to Menelaus and Nestor; he says, of course, that he had no choice but to obey the will of the gods as it had been conveyed to him. Idumeus chimes in, and Nestor is convinced. Menelaus has qualms about matricide, but he goes along with the others, and is glad to give his daughter in marriage to Horestes. The Vice, regretting that Amity has got its place, leaves the play dressed like a pilgrim and confident that the malice of women will always find employment for him. Horestes is crowned by Truth and Duty, and the ending is a solemn triumph of political concord.

Even if some topical political comment is being made by Pickering, the complex moral attitude to revenge is still most interesting. The laborious arguments about the necessity of obeying the gods have an irony about them that makes Pickering seem generations ahead of his time: one man agrees with them out of piety, another out of policy, and the third out of a simple desire to be friendly. Yet the decree of the gods, which they are painfully trying to interpret and adjust themselves to, has been entirely invented by the Vice. The extraordinary feature of the play is that no one, except Egistus and Clytemnestra, is roundly condemned. Sympathy with Horestes never disappears; he is a man persuaded by a tempter to believe that a certain course of action is just. Although the cruelty and heartlessness are made clear, there is still understanding. Obviously Horestes is misled in supposing that the gods have made him their scourge and minister. The Vice really represents the spirit of self-justification in the vengeful heart of a wronged man; there are reminiscences of the feeling of divine support that comes to Hieronimo or to Hamlet, but in the case of Horestes the feeling has no basis in reality. Horestes escapes the retribution that is threatened at one point in the play and that the ethics of the time might seem to demand. His mistake is pardonable, his wrath is understandable, his remorse is genuine—and the deed is done. Pickering seems to insist that it is far more important for social peace to be established than for the remorseless process of blood demanding blood to continue. He is a Machiavellian himself.

Revenge flits in and out of the plays discussed above, but *Horestes* is the first play built around an examination of revenge as pleasure or duty or sin. Pickering is the pioneer of Elizabethan revenge tragedy; he begins not only the genre but also the great question of the avenger's justification—the question that is answered with confidence only in the pages of critics.

TRAGEDY IN THE PUBLIC THEATERS

CLASSICAL and academic tragedy did not die out at the end of the 1560's; it was kept alive in the 1590's by the countess of Pembroke and the diligent translators and imitators of Robert Garnier, the French Senecan, including Daniel and Kyd himself, and later by Sir William Alexander. A play presented before the queen by the gentlemen of Gray's Inn in early 1588 shows perfectly the strain of "classical" tragedy that Kyd was trying to blend into popular tragedy. This is *The Misfortunes of Arthur*, by Thomas Hughes with contributions from others. The ghost as prolocutor is exactly the Kydean variant of the clamorous shadows in Seneca's *Agamemnon* and *Thyestes*: the dead Gorlois rises from the underworld to enjoy the spectacle of revenge on the man who killed him. An alternative induction and epilogue provided by William Fulbecke are even nearer to Kyd in their underworld allusions and in the appearance of the dead man before Proserpine to be awarded his doom. We can also find Andrea's unholy delight at the end of the play at the carnage he has witnessed; elaborate processional dumbshows remind us of Hieronimo's pageant, and there are also long reports of battles. *The Misfortunes of Arthur* is a very dreary play, but it was an offering to the queen, and it reveals how certain features of *The Spanish Tragedy*, its close contemporary, were thought to provide elevation.

Scholars would give much to know more of the tradition of popular tragedy in the seventies and eighties, which presumably exerted a corresponding influence on Kyd. But its history is almost a blank. It is fairly clear that murder plays, domestic tragedies based on reports of actual murders, were popular. We can only guess the contents of two plays performed by the earl of Sussex's men in 1578 and 1579, *The Cruelty of a Stepmother* and *Murderous Michael*. Sussex's men also performed (perhaps in the late 1580's) *The History of Friar Francis*, which Heywood later described as a story of a woman who, "insatiately doting on a young gentleman," murdered her husband and was haunted by his ghost, "in most horrid and fearful shapes."

We cannot suppose that these plays were as good as the tragedy *Arden of Feversham* (printed in 1592, but possibly belonging to the late 1580's), but the excellence of *Arden* testifies to the strength of the genre. *Arden* has been attributed to Kyd, and it is certainly full of lines that remind us of him, but the play as a whole has little of the Seneca-Garnier cast of *The Spanish Tragedy;* it may well be that the Kydean moments are reminiscences.

If F. S. Boas[2] had been right in his original attribution to Kyd of the little prose work *The Murder of John Brewen*, Kyd's interest in the details of crimes of passion in ordinary life would have been proved, and we should be more inclined to allot *Arden of Feversham* to him. *The Murder of John Brewen* is in any case interesting in its own right as the sort of thing that dramatists fed on; it is a narrative of a sordid poisoning of a husband for which the wife was burned in Smithfield, and her lover hanged, in June 1592. The narrative of the murder is surrounded by sententious moralizings on a righteous God's insistence on vengeance for murder: "blood is an uncessant crier in the ears of the Lord, and he will not leave so vile a thing unpunished." The narrative itself gives an imaginative picture of the young woman: quite irresponsible and unprincipled, anxious only to get a tiresome new husband out of the way, readily planning and coolly carrying out a poisoning, dissembling affection with all the skill in the world, and callously leaving her husband alone in the house all night as he dies in extreme pain. One feels that once writers had got such monsters of their own society and neighborhood into their view and within the power of their

---

[2] See his Introduction to *The Works of Thomas Kyd* (1901).

pens, the translation of them into the scheming villains of tragedy was not difficult; the "Italianate" horrors of Jacobean tragedy have an ancestry much nearer home than Italy. Perhaps also the stock she-monsters of a far-off model drama—Medea, Phaedra, Clytemnestra—could be reduced to acceptable proportions for the Elizabethan stage (as, say, Goneril or Lady Macbeth) because of the audience's familiarity with the repulsive contrivances of Elizabethan adulterers.

Arden of Feversham was itself founded upon a narrative account of an actual murder that took place as far back as 1551 and was recorded in great detail in Holinshed's *Chronicle*. The story is of Alice's infatuation with the parvenu Mosbie, and her schemes to murder Arden, her husband, by one method after another until, all failing, she is at last forced to take a hand in stabbing him to death at his own table. The concept of the play as a single protracted effort to do murder is thoroughly interesting; the comedy of Will and Shakebag's repeated failures adds greatly to the sense of enormity, and the dramatist is able to make much of the growing tension between the lovers as their "freedom" is continually frustrated. The naturalness of the setting and the characters may seem at first a quaint and engaging familiarity. But the sense of everyday life is not achieved here, any more than elsewhere, by artlessness. The dramatist took great trouble to make even his minor characters credible members of the audience's own society; an example is in the excellent picture of the simpleminded servant, Michael. The protagonists are men with occupations as well as passions. Arden is not only a jealous husband; he is also a rather greedy landlord. Man is shown as an economic animal, who has to win his bread and is covetous of property, as well as an animal motivated by sexual drives. Much of Arden's fury at being cuckolded comes from his sense of humiliation that his rival is so much his social inferior, and an upstart. Greene is persuaded to become one of Alice's henchmen because of his bitterness toward Arden over what he considers the theft of abbey lands from him. The reality of bourgeois provincial society thus gives a fine wholeness to the characters.

The author does not encumber his realistic social setting with purely literary fashions of be-havior; the relations between the characters are convincingly real. Alice is a brilliant creation. Quite given over to her passion for Mosbie, she is recklessly impatient and unaffected by any sense of wrongdoing. Mosbie is a cautious man, ill at ease in his new wealth, and he does not at all enjoy the double relationship he must have with Arden. He is very much in the grip of the domineering Alice, but far too covetous of the possible fruits to break off the affair.

Perhaps the most interesting quality of *Arden of Feversham* is its freedom from the moral clichés of the tragedies of its time. Here is no ambitious king and his inevitable destruction. Of course, the murderers receive a fitting punishment, and there is an awkward attempt at the end of the play to show that Arden brought his suffering on himself. But the play's strength is in its power to present the passions of men and women at their extreme. The author is much too absorbed in his story of lust, malice, and intrigue to spend time apportioning praise and blame; in any case he is much too honest to simplify the matter of responsibility. Except for *Arden of Feversham* and *The Spanish Tragedy*, it is very rare to find a play written before *Romeo and Juliet* in which the complexity of life seems to interest the dramatist more than the facile proof that it is wicked to be wicked (the deadness of which I could demonstrate, if I lacked mercy, from the dogged tragedy *Locrine*).

LIFE AND ATTRIBUTABLE WORKS

THOMAS Kyd was born in London in 1558. His father, a very respectable citizen, was a scrivener. Kyd went to Merchant Taylors' school, but, like Shakespeare and unlike Nashe, Greene, and Marlowe, he did not enter a university; perhaps he was apprenticed to his father's trade. We know no more of his reasons for writing for the public stage than we do of his fellow dramatists'. In about 1587, he entered the service of a lord, and he remained with the lord until his own arrest in May 1593. We do not know who this lord was; he was the patron of a company of players, and the earl of Sussex, the earl of Pembroke, and Lord Strange have all been suggested. We learn about this patron from Kyd's long and pitiful letter to the lord keeper, Sir John Puckering, after his arrest and interrogation. The Privy Council had ordered rigorous measures to find and punish the author of attacks on London's foreign craftsmen. Kyd was under suspicion and his rooms were searched. Unfortunately, among some papers were found not the wanted "libels," but copies of a disputation held to be atheistic. Kyd insisted they were Marlowe's and had been shuffled in with his own papers when the two were sharing a room in 1591. Kyd's interrogation seems to have included the use of torture, but he was freed. (Marlowe was summoned to appear before the Privy Council, but it is assumed that he had not given his testimony before he was stabbed to death in the Deptford tavern.) Kyd's lord was apparently not convinced of the innocence of his servant, and would entertain him no further. Hence the rather desperate letter of appeal to Puckering, asking him to use his influence. It had no success; Kyd continued to live in disgrace and, no doubt, great poverty. He wrote his free translation of Garnier's *Cornélie* and dedicated it to the countess of Sussex, speaking of "those so bitter times and privy broken passions that I endured in the writing it." *Cornelia* was registered for publication in January 1594; before the year was out, Kyd was dead, at the age of thirty-six. In December, his mother, on behalf of her husband, formally refused to administer his estate. Her act is sometimes seen as a disavowal of her son, but is more likely to be simply a refusal to admit responsibility for his debts.

It is curious that the only work that can be definitely assigned to Kyd on evidence from his own day is the translation *Cornelia*. The many editions of *The Spanish Tragedy* never mentioned the author's name; indeed, not a single title page of this period boasts of Kyd as the author of the play that follows. We know that *The Spanish Tragedy* is Kyd's because of Heywood's ascription of it to him in 1612, and because of the palpable links between it and *Cornelia*. What hand he had in other plays remains a very dark question. It seems reasonable to assign the anonymous *Soliman and Perseda* to him. Kyd used a much abbreviated version of this for Hieronimo's cataclysmic playlet in *The Spanish Tragedy*. There was no necessity for him to use a

play written by himself, of course, and *Soliman and Perseda* is written in a more consistent style than *The Spanish Tragedy;* but there is a close kinship in phraseology and the handling of encounters between the characters. Also, *Soliman and Perseda* has a shell, or outer framework, that seems strongly Kydean. Love, Death, and Fortune act as a chorus to introduce, watch over, and comment on the action. The three argue about the share that each has in bringing about what has been witnessed on the stage, representing, as they do, three very different influences on human affairs: emotional life, the law of nature, the sway of chance. Their effect, as audience, is to emphasize that the affairs of mankind are like the actions of a play, and to emphasize the diminutive role of individual human plans in the patterning of events. The method by which, in *The Spanish Tragedy*, Revenge and the Ghost of Andrea convey the same sense that life resembles a play is altogether more subtle, but it is the same kind of method, and leaves the same question: Death may have the victory, but who does the work?

Soliman and Perseda is a play in the popular Turkish vein, Turkey providing as convenient an excuse for all sorts of barbaric excitements as Italy did for the next generation of dramatists. Violent murders on the stage are very frequent—stranglings and poisonings, and even death by precipitation from a tower. But it cannot compare in violence with its fellow *Selimus*, a very odd Turkish play of uncertain date and authorship (sometimes attributed to Robert Greene). *Selimus* seems to be deeply affected by *Tamburlaine* and *The Spanish Tragedy*, but its very primitive and formal dramatic method argues for its being an early play. Was it perhaps more of a forerunner than a pastiche? It is interesting for its textbook presentation of the Machiavellian atheist Selimus. Indeed, the whole play is a compendium of the conventional tragic requirements: political disunity, Machiavellianism, Senecan revenge with its underworld imagery, demonstration of the evils of ambition. But it is the violence we are speaking of, and let one incident serve. The stage directions for the short scene in which Acomat deals with the envoy from the emperor, his father, run: "Pulls out his eyes," "They cut off his hands and give them Acomat," "Opens his bosom and puts them in [the severed hands!]." The envoy may well call himself "The woefullest and sadd'st ambassador / That ever was dispatch'd to any king."

To the question, did Kyd write the early version of *Hamlet;* we can only answer that we do not know, but there is more evidence pointing to him than to any other dramatist. Thomas Nashe, in 1589, had attacked "a sort of shifting companions" who "leave the trade of *Noverint* [i.e., scrivener]" and have a go at literature. Though they do not have the necessary learning, he goes on, "yet English *Seneca* read by Candle-light yields many good sentences, as *Blood is a begger,* and so forth; and if you intreate him faire in a frostie morning, hee will affoord you whole Hamlets, I should say handfuls of Tragicall speeches." But Seneca is becoming exhausted. Nashe continues, "which makes his famished followers to imitate the Kid in *Æsop,* who, enamoured with the Foxes newfangles, forsooke all hopes of life to leape into a newe occupation; and these men, renouncing all possibilities of credite or estimation, to intermeddle with Italian Translations." Nashe seems to be referring to several dramatists, and there is no doubt that early scholars were a little too certain that Kyd was Nashe's main butt (the "Italian Translations" being taken to be Kyd's translation of Tasso's *Il Padre di Famiglia,* 1588). But while, as we have seen, there were Senecans aplenty, the coincidence in the quoted passage of Noverint, and Seneca, and "the Kid in Æsop," and the phrase "thrust *Elisium* into hell," which occurs after the portion quoted here, may seem a strong argument that Kyd was one of the dramatists in Nashe's mind, and therefore possibly the author of the early *Hamlet.* After all, it is not at all unlikely that Kyd should have accompanied *The Spanish Tragedy,* his play about a father's vengeance for a murdered son, with one about a son's vengeance for a murdered father.

THE SPANISH TRAGEDY

THE great variations in pace and dramatic method in *The Spanish Tragedy,* from the long expository speech and formal exchange of sentiments to rapid action accompanied by naturalistic dialogue, led the late Professor Schücking to argue that the play was the work of two authors, Thomas Watson and Thomas Kyd. Even if Schücking were right, one would have to confess that the blend of the two styles is most effective, and that the ease of movement from the stiffer to the more flexible rhetoric gives the play a range of tone quite beyond, shall we say, *Tamburlaine* on the one hand and *Arden of Feversham* on the other. But this very ease of movement argues for a single authorship; the control of the various levels of formality and informality is too secure for collaboration. One might instance the wide range of orchestral effect in Act III, scenes vi–x. The grotesque comedy of Pedringano's execution is mainly in prose, Hieronimo making his generalized reflections in verse (vi. 89–98). The effect of the completed act of justice on the distraught father-judge is then shown in Hieronimo's Garnier-like soliloquy:

> Where shall I run to breathe abroad my woes,
> My woes, whose weight hath wearied the earth?
> Or mine exclaims, that have surcharg'd the air
> With ceaseless plaints for my deceased son?

The formal lament is interrupted by the comic hangman, who brings with him the fatal letter of confession found on Pedringano; Hieronimo's triumph and bitterness find their voice in a sustained piece of rhetoric quite different in tone from that of the lament. A quick, stylized succession of scenes, formally presenting Isabella, insane, and Bel-imperia as prisoner, heightens the sense of general crisis; the formality then dissolves into the fine dialogue of the confrontation of Bel-imperia and her villainous brother, Lorenzo. The reason for employing the different styles may lie in Kyd's deliberate attempt to fuse the two worlds of tragedy—the classical and the popular—thus familiarizing the elevated, and elevating the familiar. Whatever the motive, the alternation gives a powerful dramatic effect. Kyd would have been a greater writer had he forged a single style capable of registering a wide range of levels of intensity, but the blend of voices that he produces is a very fine achievement.

The clinching evidence against the theory of composite authorship is the close weave of the design and the unity of effect of the whole play. The design of *The Spanish Tragedy* is most unusual. Although in Hieronimo the play obviously has a chief character, he is not a person of high position or great power, and he does not begin to dominate the play until the end of the second act. The turn of events suddenly thrusts the role of hero on a minor character a third of the way through the play. Those whom one might expect to be heroes, the kings and the viceroys, though they still lead armies and hold the keys of life and death, are in the background in this play; they are strangely ignorant, impotent, and variable creatures. An abstract diagram of *The Spanish Tragedy* would not resemble the diagram of a heroic play, a heavy black line to which all other lines refer, but a web or a net—the design of *Romeo and Juliet* rather than of *Richard III*.

The play opens with the ghost of Andrea, who has been killed in battle by Balthazar. Proserpine has sent him from the underworld, with Revenge as a companion and interpreter, to witness the death of the man who slew him. The two remain on the stage during the whole play, commenting on the actions at the end of each act. All this seems to have little to do with Hieronimo's revenge, which is certainly the main action of the play. But Kyd is immensely concerned with the web of consequence; for him, an action "complete in itself" means an action surrounded by layers of causation. Every event in the play looks a long way backward, or a long way forward. He must start his chain of causation somewhere, of course, and he chooses to bury his start in those long-winded early scenes about the war on the borders of Spain and Portugal. War is the beginning of Hieronimo's outcry over his dead son, and the war began with the ambition of that pale figure, the viceroy of Portugal:

> My late ambition hath distain'd my faith,
> My breach of faith occasion'd bloody wars,
> Those bloody wars have spent my treasure,
> And with my treasure my people's blood
> (I.iii.33–36)

(This is one of Kyd's favorite rhetorical figures, an ascent through consequences.) An insurgent Portugal has been defeated by Spain. The killing of Don Andrea by the viceroy's son is carefully presented as neither a base murder nor yet a chivalrous conquest; Balthazar took unfair advantage of Andrea's being outnumbered and thrown from his horse, and behaved in no way like a true knight. Balthazar is taken prisoner by young Horatio, Hieronimo's son, and by Lorenzo, nephew to the Spanish king.

Now, in happier days, Don Andrea had been the lover of Lorenzo's sister, Bel-imperia; he says that he possessed her in secret, but in fact the illicit affair was known. Andrea tells us about the affair at the very beginning of the play and the relationship is never forgotten. It stands with the ambition of the viceroy as the direct trigger of the play's action; war and sex drive the play forward. Bel-imperia hates Balthazar for killing Andrea and will do what she can to injure him. Her plan is wonderful: Balthazar has unluckily fallen in love with her; she needs a man and she woos Horatio (Andrea's friend), thus contriving at the same time a measured slight to Balthazar and a satisfaction of her own desires. So, in the train of motivation, vengefulness follows ambition and sexual desire. Her plan has the worst consequences: her preference for Horatio results in the smoldering hostility of Balthazar and Lorenzo, and vengefulness is repaid in kind. The two men break in on the secret garden assignation between the lovers, hang Horatio, and stab his dying body. So, at Act II, scene v, the "main action" of the play begins: Hieronimo's distress, his efforts to identify the murderers, and the grisly toll he eventually takes. The death of Balthazar, promised to Andrea, is accomplished. Hieronimo has his revenge, Bel-imperia has hers, Andrea his; but for each of them revenge has come in a grimly different manner from the way he or she wished or planned it.

When we look in this way at the layers of causation preceding Hieronimo's vengeance, we see a group of people who, with the exception of Lorenzo, are neither particularly bad nor particularly good, reacting impulsively and violently to the impulsive and violent reaction of others, and so on down the line. The dependence of Hieronimo's situation on a distant past is a most important element in Kyd's design, but the web or net is not yet really visible; it cannot be visible until our viewpoint has become more celestial, or infernal. But, before joining the gods, we need to look more closely at Lorenzo, one of the biggest strands in the web, and the one exception to the rule that the play shows average people being stung into action.

Lorenzo, begetter of Iago and a hundred dark villains, is himself the heir of the old Vice, whose occupation and delight it is to make mischief. The chain of consequences I have talked about would no doubt have lapsed into a series of bad-tempered quarrels if Lorenzo had not been a man who lives only to dominate others, to contrive and carry out evil. Sheer irresponsible villainy takes a high place in Kyd's scheme of locomotion. Lorenzo is not a wronged man, though he can find pretexts and excuses for his cruelty. True, he is proud, and the promotion of the socially inferior Horatio by the king and by Lorenzo's own sister is insufferable to Lorenzo. But he has no real cause for acting as he does. Bel-imperia's enraged question is not answered any more than is Othello's "Demand that demi-devil / Why he hath thus ensnared my soul and body."

> What madding fury did possess thy wits?
> Or wherein is't that I offended thee?
> (III.x.33–34)

Lorenzo's language is simple and direct, an index to his mind, just as the flaccid rhetoric of Balthazar, with which it is pointedly contrasted, is an index of his; see, for example, his curt reply to Balthazar's "ecstasies":

> Some cause there is that lets you not be lov'd:
> First that must needs be known and then remov'd.
> (II.i.31–32)

He moves with insolent ease to prize from Pedringano the secret of Bel-imperia's new lover:

> Where words prevail not, violence prevails:
> But gold doth more than either of them both.
> (II.i.108–109)

He helps with his own hands to murder Horatio, managing the sententious "these are the fruits of love" even as he drives his dagger home. He stands back to gaze at the swinging corpse, ignoring his sister's outcries:

> Although his life were still ambitious proud
> Yet is he at the highest now he is dead.
> (II.iv.60–61)

The work of hiding the murder and of pitting his wits against Hieronimo is dangerous and he exults in it. One accomplice is suborned to murder another, and he carefully arranges that the first will be arrested and hanged for that murder. A master of deception and cunning, of winning the confidence of those he proposes to use or to betray, he continues his plots for two reasons, the delight of it and self-preservation.

> I'll trust myself, myself shall be my friend,
> For die they shall: slaves are ordain'd to no other end.
> (III.ii.118–119)
> And thus experience bids the wise to deal.
> I lay the plot, he prosecutes the point,
> I set the trap, he breaks the worthless twigs
> And sees not that wherewith the bird was lim'd.
> Thus hopeful men, that mean to hold their own,
> Must look like fowlers to their dearest friends.
> (III.iv.39–44)

He overreaches, of course, by the complexity of his plans. He had intended to bribe the hangman, but decided against making a new accomplice; it is this unbribed hangman who brings to Hieronimo the all-important letter of Pedringano. Kyd has plotted this boomerang very carefully; he would not need the subtle irony of it if he wished just to demonstrate that a villain can become too clever and be hoist with his own petard. Lorenzo's miscalculation, by which the steps he takes to cover up his crime reveal his guilt to the knight-marshal, Hieronimo, is a focal point in the play's demonstration of the vanity of human plans. Even the mastermind Lorenzo is in control only to a certain point; he cannot measure the consequences of every action and is defeated by the unsuspected reactions of others, just as Bel-imperia was.

All drama trades heavily in defeated expectations; the ironic reversal by which measures to bring about a desired end move steadily to bring about its opposite is the stuff of tragedy from Aeschylus onward. Kyd does not make a reversal of this kind the center of his play as Marlowe does in *Faustus* or Shakespeare does in *Macbeth*. But he crowds his play with examples of dramatic irony, with the happy ignorance of people of the true trend of the events they are living in, of the true outcome of the plans they are making, of the true precedents of the situation they are dealing with. The best examples, after Lorenzo's unwitting self-betrayal, are the applause for the good acting of those who have really died in Hieronimo's play, and the scenes in Act II that have Bel-imperia's love life as their center. And how very interesting are Kyd's methods of presenting the mist of ignorance in which people move.

In her book *Shakespeare and the Idea of the Play*, Anne Righter describes how Kyd deliberately built his play on the idea of the world as a stage.[3] Andrea and Revenge hold a balance between the audience and the play-world:

> Here sit we down to see the mystery,
> And serve for chorus in this tragedy.

They are both spectators and a chorus, but "for Don Andrea . . . the events occurring on the stage below are painfully real, in no sense a rehearsal at second-hand." Andrea is in the play-world, and yet outside it, unable to communicate with his mistress. Righter notes how Hieronimo, right in the midst of the play-world's "reality," can think of what is going on in terms of a play:

> And actors in th' accursed tragedy
> Wast thou, Lorenzo, Balthazar and thou . . .?
> (III.vii.41–42)

She notes the complexity Kyd achieves, first in Hieronimo's mask and then in his culminating playlet, by having Andrea and Revenge as an audience for a stage audience watching Hieronimo's shows—yet Andrea and Revenge are themselves watched by the real theater audience. The real audience members are given a picture of themselves sitting on a stage. Their own life seems like that of a play-world.

The final play-within-the-play is worth looking at more closely in the light of Righter's discussion. The culmination of the drama, the completion of Hieronimo's efforts, is brought about by means of a play. Lorenzo and Balthazar play their parts to humor old Hieronimo. But they suddenly find, in their death wounds, the reality of what they act. For them, as for the court audience a moment later, a pretended reality suddenly veers into the plane of the reality of their own lives. Hieronimo addresses the dumbfounded stage audience:

> Haply you think, but bootless are your thoughts,
> That this is fabulously counterfeit

Suppose this was addressed to the real audience in the theater. When Hieronimo's pretended reality becomes real in the play-world, the pretended reality of the play-world becomes that much more real for the spectators. Life and play are wonderfully cemented.

However, Kyd's open and frequent use of the life/play identification is not meant to evoke tributes to the lifelikeness of his art, but to impress on us that human life *is* a play. The play becomes more real for the spectators because they are being drawn in to the stage reality, the reality of illusion. E. W. Talbert[4] has commented on the "three concentric circles of attention," not only in the play-within-the-play, but also in the scene in which Balthazar and Lorenzo overhear the profession of love between the unsuspecting Horatio and Bel-imperia, while watching them all are "the hovering ghost of Andrea and Revenge." To these three circles we must add Righter's fourth concentric circle, the audience standing and sitting around the stage in the Rose Theatre.

Each circle is unaware that it forms part of a different design seen by the circle around it. Horatio and Bel-imperia plan the fruition of their desires, but their future is in the hands of the concealed watchers; the fate of the concealed watchers is seen in a larger perspective by the spiritual chorus, and they again are known to be fictional creatures by the audience. Immediately following this great scene of the widening perspective of ignorance, the king, his brother, and the Portuguese ambassador enter, complacently discussing the marriage of Bel-imperia to Balthazar. As the king goes off, earnestly re-

---

[3] Pp. 77–81.

[4] In *Elizabethan Drama and Shakespeare's Early Plays*, p. 73.

questing his brother to persuade his daughter to the marriage, that same daughter enters with her lover for their fatal tryst. (Shakespeare surely had the effect of these scenes in his mind when he so brilliantly filled the interval during which the marriage of Romeo and Juliet is supposed to be consummated with Capulet's bland planning of Juliet's marriage to Paris.) For Andrea and Revenge, and for the theater audience, the oblivious royal matchmakers form a further circle of ignorance of larger perspectives.

The point is perhaps sufficiently clear. The technique of the play-within-the-play is only an accentuation of a dramatic method, including the use of watchers and the juxtaposition of scenes, by which Kyd shows people living in mere illusion as they busily arrange and manage their own lives: their future is being ordered by others even as they lay their plans. This use of dramatic irony intensifies the elaborate interaction of cause and effect that Kyd takes so much trouble to establish in his plot. We can look at the action of the play either along the line of interlocking events, from the viceroy's ambition onward, or in cross section, seeing the "concentric circles of attention"; and from both points of view we see men as puppets, placed in position by others and controlled by superior forces.

We have gone so far without considering what the ultimate "superior force" of the play-world may be because it is important to see how effectively the play goes forward by human locomotion alone, by the conflict of many emotions, reactions, plans, and deeds, whatever supernal forces are at work.

When we consider what Revenge and the ghost represent, we notice first the attention given to Andrea's bewilderment. He never understands the devious relationship of things, and perpetually complains to Revenge that the promised end is not in sight.

Andrea: Brought'st thou me hither to increase my pain?
   I look'd that Balthazar should have been slain:
   But 'tis my friend Horatio that is slain
   And they abuse fair Bel-imperia . . .
Revenge: Thou talk'st of harvest when the corn is green . . .
   Be still, and ere I lead thee from this place.
   I'll show thee Balthazar in heavy case.   (II.vi)

So Kyd calls attention to the intricacy of the plot in which he delights, and by which he conveys the complexity of life itself and the mystery of the way in which the universal tragedy moves forward.

How far are the actors fulfilling a future which has been arranged by the gods? Kyd uses a pre-Christian system of heaven and hell, though he awkwardly introduces more modern references at times. The foreign mythology gives him a certain freedom in treating of providence. Andrea is sent up to the living world by Proserpine in order that he should see the eventual death of Balthazar. References to the fulfilling of destiny are very frequent; Revenge is quite clearly an attendant of the gods and an agent of destiny: "I'll turn their friendship into fell despite" (I.v.6). To comfort the agitated Andrea in III.xv, he says,

> imagine thou
> What 'tis to be subject to destiny,

and brings on a dumb show prefiguring the events that are still to come. And yet these references to destiny, like the references to fate and the stars in *Romeo and Juliet,* are somehow peripheral or otiose. The action of the play seems self-explanatory on a human scale, without the intervention of divine decree. Revenge may be simply the personification of a bitterness in the heart of man—for there is no doubt at all that, if the role of predetermined fate is uncertain, the role of vengefulness is absolutely clear. Bel-imperia, Balthazar, Hieronimo, each initiates a course of action with revenge at its heart. Is it not this human spirit of revenge that turns friendship into fell despite? A good case can be made that the enigmatic and dreadful figure of Revenge is primarily a representation of human feelings. "Yet is my mood soliciting their souls," he says in III.xv. Men and women are subject to a destiny created by their own unforgiving wrath. In a world of relationships too involved for them to understand or control, their fates are hidden from them. But the gods see the whole design and they have foreknowledge of what men will bring upon themselves; Revenge knows what the passions he stands for will bring about.

Yet Hieronimo is a strong believer in the active intervention of the divine in these human toils. He appeals to the gods not to allow murder to go unpunished. It is his consistent belief that all information leading him toward the murderers and the accomplishment of his revenge is an offering from a just heaven. Andrea also gave thanks to "those infernal powers / That will not tolerate a lover's woe" (II.xv. 37–38).

The question of Hieronimo's relation with a divine plan is vexed, and has been much discussed. One way of solving the problem is to say that for the purposes of this play Kyd is a Manichean, a believer in dual realities—one pagan and one Christian. Revenge is of the Pagan netherworld, Justice is of the supernal Christian heaven. In *Titus Andronicus*, one character rather flippantly makes just this separation:

> Pluto sends you word
> If you will have Revenge from Hell, you shall.
> Marry, for Justice, she is so employed,
> He thinks, with Jove in Heaven, or somewhere else,
> So that perforce you needs must stay a time.
> (IV.iii.37–41)

The references to a Christian mythology seem so fitfully and arbitrarily interspersed with the pagan that I do not think one can separate them in *The Spanish Tragedy*. There is no difference between, "Till we do gain that Proserpine may grant / Revenge on them that murdered my son" (III.xiii.120–121), and

> heaven applies our drift,
> And all the saints do sit soliciting
> For vengeance on those cursed murderers.
> (IV.i.32–34)

Hieronimo's relation with the divine must be discussed in terms of a single providence, even though there are two different metaphors for this providence.

When Hieronimo finds the dead body of his son, he immediately vows to take revenge, as a satisfaction to his own grieving heart and as a duty he owes Horatio. And he imagines that heaven must be on his side in bringing murderers to punishment. He has no thought of exacting his revenge with his own hands. But he has to find the criminals before he can invoke the procedure of law. He moves stealthily and warily; he is the little man moving in the dangerous world of those who "will bear me down with their nobility." When he gets Bel-imperia's note, written in blood, he shows proper caution in not rushing off to accuse the royal family of murder. Kyd does excellent work with Hieronimo's movements toward discovery and legal atonement. For example, there is the great bitterness that he, an officer of the law, should have to sentence offenders but cannot bring to book those who have outraged him:

> This toils my body, this consumeth age,
> That only I to all men just must be,
> And neither gods nor men be just to me.
> (III.vi.8–10)

His feeling that he is a special case is the mistake of all humanity. During the play, Kyd shows two villains brought to justice *coram populo*—in public—apparently as a contrast to the frustrations of Hieronimo. But in fact these two examples of law in action only confirm the extremely capricious way in which justice works. In the Portuguese subplot, the sudden return of the ambassador saves Alexandro in the nick of time from being executed on the false charge of killing Balthazar, and Villuppo the calumniator takes his place. What might be interpreted as the intervention of God may also be regarded as a satirical account of the wheels of human justice. Pedringano is brought to the gallows for the murder of Serberine by the careful arrangement of the archmurderer, Lorenzo. Human justice is presented in a very ironic light.

These two examples of justice being brought about accidentally prepare us for Hieronimo's failure to awaken the king to the situation. The king is not even aware that Horatio is dead, though everyone else knows. Hieronimo's efforts to invoke justice are thwarted by Lorenzo's interference and by the exaggerated caution his now crazed mind leads him into.

Hier.: Justice, O justice to Hieronimo!
Lor.: Back! seest thou not the king is busy?
Hier.: Oh, is he so?
King: Who is he that interrupts our business?
Hier.: Not I. Hieronimo, beware: go by, go by.
(III.xii.27–31)

It is no surprise, from what the play has shown of the ways of judges and justice, that Hieronimo should give up the attempt to get at the king, and decide to be his own executioner. For a moment (III.xiii) he remembers the biblical *Vindicta mihi* ("Vengeance is mine, I will repay, saith the Lord"), and reminds himself that "mortal men may not appoint their time." But he makes up his mind all the same to strike, pretending mildness, patience, and courtesy, "Till to revenge thou know when, where and how." He is sure that he is not losing the support of heaven in punishing those who have offended heaven: "I see that heaven applies our drift" (IV.i.32), meaning that heaven is directing his course, or assisting him in his course.

There can be no doubt that the audience is on his side, whatever the Elizabethan preachers and moralists said about private revenge. We are in a different place from the preacher's auditory. But it is as gross a simplification to say that Hieronimo has, as he imagines, the blessing of heaven or is fulfilling its decrees as it is to say that he has become an enemy of heaven. We have at the same time to think of the certain sympathy of the audience for this man's lonely endeavor to punish evil men, and of the ironic way in which the sense of identification with heaven's will was handled in *Horestes*.

Hieronimo goes forward to work out his subtle vengeance: to perform a tragedy in which the actors will really die. He manages his vengeance and vindication superbly. As the court slowly realizes that the two princes are dead, Hieronimo draws a curtain with a flourish, shows the corpse of his son, and makes his explanation with passion and dignity.

See here my show, look on this spectacle:
Here lay my hope, and here my hope hath end:
Here lay my heart, and here my heart was slain:
Here lay my treasure, here my treasure lost:
Here lay my bliss, and here my bliss bereft:
But hope, heart, treasure, joy and bliss,
All fled, fail'd, died, yea, all decay'd with this.
From forth these wounds came breath that gave me
  life,
They murder'd me that made these fatal marks.
                                        (IV.iv.89–97)

But the ceremonial suicide that was to follow is frustrated, and Hieronimo's end is in a brawl and a flurry on the stage. With meaningless savagery, he bites out his own tongue and stabs the unoffending duke of Castile before he kills himself and falls to the ground to join Bel-imperia, Lorenzo, Balthazar, and the duke.

Has God brought all this about? Or is it the Devil's work? Should we not do what Kyd has done, and leave God and the Devil out of it? Suppose we accept what he has given us, a neutral pagan metaphor for the government of the universe with occasional lapses into Christian imagery. What then does the play present? We see a distressed man struggling for justice in this world. His sorrow has come on him out of a clear sky, no act of his having the least bearing on it. He is no prince, not even an attendant lord, but a commoner, and on his shoulders comes the burden of the world's justice. His promptings to seek for justice are not different from the promptings of his own human, vindictive heart. Sorrow for his dead son and the effort to find and to outwit the murderers put more of a strain on him than his mind can bear. Denied legal justice, he plans his own, supported (and how he needs support) by the conviction that he is an agent of avenging heaven. He brings off his revenge, but with a toll of deaths far beyond his own plans, in an ending of sordid savagery. He takes his own life, as his wife and Bel-imperia had taken theirs before.

In this closing disaster, there is a kind of triumph, a kind of victory, but no one feels it except the dead man who has been watching from the shadows, for whom the whole of Hieronimo's strivings have been only an inset within a larger story. Whether Hieronimo was right or whether he was wrong to imagine he had heaven's support is an open question in the play. On the human plane, on which essentially this play takes place, there is human pity for the human wanderer who tries to right a wrong and dies doing it in the best way he can, however clumsy and disastrous his individual efforts necessarily are. Kyd has left a blank where the moral dramatist would have set his seal of Christian approval or disapproval, or his presumptuous indication of the hand of heaven. And he has therefore written a tragedy and not a tract.

The moral world of *The Spanish Tragedy* is at the same time one of absurd artificiality and one of great reality. Sometimes we can only hear the croakings of the Senecan ravens, and we find the ideas of revenge and destiny so thickly and crudely plastered on the play that we long, not only for the voice of mercy and forgiveness to give forth even a whisper, but for a little more common sense among the strained reactions of the characters. But the Senecanism is a figure of speech, like the pastoral convention. It takes patience to translate it, for it seems to us to disguise and to distort rather than provide a language for reality. *The Spanish Tragedy* does in the end present a very powerful picture of the world as a group of blindfolded men bumping into each other as they strive to get even with those who have affronted them. We are shown men led by ambition, sexual desire, motiveless malignity, and general vindictiveness.

Against this heavily shaded picture, which we would scarcely take seriously if it were all that Kyd gave, we have to set Hieronimo. Hieronimo's voice is the voice of protest against criminal cruelty, the voice of real sorrow and love. He shares the vindictiveness of the rest, but in him the spirit of retribution (which Kyd seems determined to make us accept as the dominant human emotion) can be shown to rise to a not unrighteous passion for requiting an injury done to another. This is still not a world of tragedy. What does make the play a tragic one is its demonstration that each attempt at personal fulfillment interlocks with others in a way that defeats individual plans and makes a pattern that can only be seen by those looking on from above. For convenience, the play calls the pattern "destiny," but the pattern seems very much like the aggregation of individual deeds, too ironic to be anyone's design.

Our view of Hieronimo at the end of the play is many-sided. He may seem the man through whom the gods punish murder; an insane avenger; or a mere tool of destiny. What we are certain of is our own uncertainty, and that more important than our opinions about Hieronimo's relation with the divine will is our sense of his pain as he tries to clear a path through the unweeded garden of the world around him. The sense of uncertainty, the sense of pain, the sense of striving in a world too complex for any individual to begin to control or even to understand, the sense of life as a very grim play: these

are what, finally, the watchers from beyond Acheron, and the slow process up to the death of Hieronimo, are there to produce.

The date of *The Spanish Tragedy* is not known; it probably belongs to the last years of the 1580's. Since the dates of its contemporaries are also very difficult to fix with any accuracy, it is impossible to talk of influences that helped to shape the play, apart from the general traditions spoken of above. But even weighting the scales a bit will not suffice to show that *The Spanish Tragedy* is a derivative play. No source for it has ever been found. It is an original. If it seems crude in language, in sentiment, in its violence, one look at the other plays I have discussed dispels this impression. It enjoyed unusual popularity. Over a period of more than forty years, it remained in print in a series of new editions, eleven in all. The earliest record of its production is 1592; Philip Henslowe records twenty performances during the season at his theater, the Rose, at Bankside. It could be seen in London and the provinces for the rest of the century and beyond. The 1602 edition gives the play with large "additions," variously attributed at times to Shakespeare and to Ben Jonson (Jonson certainly received payment for some additions to the play). One of these additions is the famous Painter scene, an imaginative picture of Hieronimo's distress and madness. Unfortunately, the additions (which are really substitutions for certain sections of the old play) only hinder one's grasp of Kyd's purposes if one tries to read them with the original text. As time went on, *The Spanish Tragedy*, even with its new scenes, became an institution and not a play, a symbol of far-off, unsophisticated times, and the drama of the early seventeenth century is full of parodies and jests at its expense. Andrea's opening speech and Hieronimo's "O eyes, no eyes, but fountains fraught with tears" were two of the favorite butts. Jonson, as one may gather from the Induction to *Bartholomew Fair*, particularly resented the affection of the old theatergoers for the play he had helped to keep alive for the stage.

Uncertainty about dates prevents any useful discussion of the influence on each other of Kyd, Marlowe, and Shakespeare. *The Spanish Tragedy, Tamburlaine, Henry VI*, and *Titus An-*

dronicus are connected, and it is not enough to say that conventions of tragic writing at this time led to stereotypes of language and situation—though this is true. There are quite definite verbal borrowings, but it is risky to try to point out debtor and creditor. *The Spanish Tragedy* owes nothing in spirit to *Tamburlaine*, although it is arguable that Marlowe's was the earlier work. The splendid energy and imagination of Marlowe's restless heroes seem not to have affected Kyd at all. In the *Henry VI* plays, Shakespeare was working out an altogether different pattern from Kyd's: he was creating a new kind of tragic world, while not yet devoting himself to the tragic play. He is more effective than Kyd in creating images of the brutality of people, of the lust for power, of the uselessness of meaning well. It is his imaginative insight into the paths taken by the dangerous liquid, power, that gives these somewhat discursive plays their force. Their force is not really a tragic force. Nor is *Titus Andronicus* really a tragedy. As with *The Spanish Tragedy*, its dominant motive is an implacable resentment of affronts and injuries. It has a remarkably similar structure in that it is hinged in the middle: there is a turning point when the malice of others has led to a crime that the hero then has to avenge—Titus must take toll for Lavinia, as Hieronimo must for Horatio. Quite unlike Kyd, however, is the typical Shakespearean insistence that it is the folly of the hero, at the very beginning of the play, that triggers the action. The horrors of *Titus Andronicus*—murder, human sacrifice, rape, mutilation, enforced cannibalism—make *The Spanish Tragedy* seem, in comparison, a children's Christmas play. Unparalleled horrors are given grotesque Ovidian vestments of high poetry; it is not the Marlovian translation of the brutal act into a poetic act, because the brutality remains, garbed in rich verse. It is an exploration of its own kind, a virtuoso performance that seems to need little knowledge of the world, and to reflect little light. In *Dr. Faustus* and in *Richard III*, Marlowe and Shakespeare scale heights that Kyd could not have dreamed of attempting; yet *Richard III*, for all the brilliance of its conception of the hero's character, is much less subtle as tragedy than Kyd's play: the collapse of the hero seems to follow a stock pattern in contemporary moral-

ity. It is in *Romeo and Juliet* (1595?) that one feels that Shakespeare, less preoccupied with a hero and the fascination of the exchange of power, turned to embodying in tragedy Kyd's lessons on the irony of endeavor, actions that are self-canceling, the intricacy of the web of love, hate, and fortune. The temptation to compare *The Spanish Tragedy* with *Hamlet* has to be resisted. The earlier play is a more profound and lucid commentary on the later than any published piece of criticism; but the subject has been discussed endlessly, and all readers ought to remember the student who wrote, "A further point of similarity is that Hieronimo bites out his tongue and Hamlet says 'the rest is silence.' " I have, however, discussed *The Spanish Tragedy* in a way that will, I hope, make it clear that Shakespeare did not take the crude old revenge drama and make tragedy out of it. The tragic potentiality of the revenge play had already been established.

SELECTED BIBLIOGRAPHY

I. BIBLIOGRAPHIES. C. A. Crawford, *A Concordance to the Works of Thomas Kyd* (Louvain, 1906–1910), XV, Bang's *Materialien*; E. K. Chambers, *The Elizabethan Stage*, 4 vols. (Oxford, 1923); W. W. Greg, *A Bibliography of the English Printed Drama to the Restoration*, I, *Plays to 1616* (Oxford, 1939); A. Harbage, *Annals of English Drama, 975–1700* (Philadelphia, 1940; rev. by S. Schoenbaum, 1964); S. A. Tannenbaum, *Thomas Kyd (A Concise Bibliography)* (New York, 1941); F. P. Wilson, *The English Drama 1485–1585*, ed. with a bibliography by G. K. Hunter (Oxford, 1969).

II. ANTHOLOGIES AND COLLECTIONS. J. M. Manly, ed., *Specimens of Pre-Shakespearian Drama*, 2 vols. (Boston, 1897–1898), contains *Cambises, Gorboduc, The Spanish Tragedy*; F. S. Boas, ed., *The Works of Thomas Kyd* (Oxford, 1901), the standard ed., with a comprehensive biographical and critical introduction; C. F. Tucker Brooke, ed., *The Shakespeare Apocrypha* (Oxford, 1908; repr. 1967), contains *Arden of Feversham, Locrine*; J. W. Cunliffe, ed., *Early English Classical Tragedies* (Oxford, 1912), contains *Gorboduc, Jocasta, Gismond of Salerne, Misfortunes of Arthur*; J. Q. Adams, ed., *Chief Pre-Shakespearean Dramas* (Cambridge, Mass., 1924), contains *Gorboduc, Cambises*; A. K. McIlwraith, ed., *Five Elizabethan Tragedies* (Oxford, 1938; repr. 1971), contains *Thyestes, Gorboduc, The Spanish Tragedy, Arden of Feversham*; E. Creeth, ed., *Tudor Plays: An Anthology of Early English Drama*

(New York, 1966), contains *Gorboduc* and *Cambises*; R. Mark Benbow, ed., *W. Wager: The Longer Thou Livest and Enough Is as Good as a Feast* (London, 1967), Regent's Renaissance Drama Series, the only modern ed. of Wager; Peter Happé, ed., *Tudor Interludes* (Harmondsworth, 1972), contains *Appius and Virginia;* T. W. Craik, ed., *Minor Elizabethan Tragedies* (London, 1974), contains *Gorboduc, Cambises, The Spanish Tragedy, Arden of Feversham.*

III. INDIVIDUAL PLAYS. *The Seconde Tragedie of Seneca Entituled Thyestes Faithfully Englished by Iasper Heywood* (1560), in *Seneca His Tenne Tragedies,* Tudor Translations (London, 1927); *The Tragedie of Gorboduc . . . by Thomas Nortone, and . . . Thomas Sackvyle* (1565), Tudor Facsimile Texts (London, 1908); *A Comedy or Enterlude Intituled, Inough Is as Good as a Feast . . . by W. Wager* (undated: 1565?), Henry E. Huntington Facsimile Reprints (London, 1920); *A Newe Enterlude of Vice Conteyninge, The Historye of Horestes . . . by Iohn Pikeryng* (1567), Malone Society Reprint (London, 1962); *A Lamentable Tragedy Mixed Ful of Pleasant Mirth, Conteyning the Life of Cambises King of Percia . . . by Thomas Preston* (undated: 1569?), Tudor Facsimile Texts (London, 1910); *Iocasta: A Tragedie . . . by George Gascoygne and Francis Kinvvelmershe* (1573), in J. W. Cunliffe, ed., *Works* (Cambridge, 1907–1910); *A New Tragicall Comedie of Apius and Virginia . . . by R. B.* (1575), Malone Society Reprint (London, 1911); *Certain Devises and Shewes Presented to Her Maiestie . . . The Misfortunes of Arthur . . . by Thomas Hughes* (1587), Tudor Facsimile Texts (London, 1911); *The Tragedie of Tancred and Gismund. Compiled by the Gentlemen of the Inner Temple . . . Newly Revived and Polished . . . by R. W.* (1591), Malone Society Reprints (London, 1914); for the early version of *Gismond of Salerne,* see J. W. Cunliffe, ed., *Early English Classical Tragedies* (London, 1912); *The Lamentable and True Tragedie of M. Arden of Feversham in Kent* (1592), Malone Society Reprint (London, 1947); *The Spanish Tragedie, Containing the Lamentable End of Don Horatio, and Bel-Imperia: With the Pitiful Death of Olde Hieronimo* (undated: 1592?), Malone Society Reprint (London, 1948); *The Tragedye of Solyman and Perseda* (undated: 1592?), in F. S. Boas, ed., *Works of Kyd* (London, 1901); *The First Part of the Tragicall Raigne of Selimus, Sometime Emperour of the Turkes* (1594), Malone Society Reprint (London, 1908); *Cornelia* (1594) [alternative title page: *Pompey the Great, His Faire Corneliaes Tragedie . . . Written in French, by . . . Ro: Garnier; and Translated into English by Thomas Kyd* (1595)], in F. S. Boas, ed., *Works of Kyd* (London, 1901); *The Lamentable Tragedie of Locrine . . . by W. S.* (1595), Malone Society Reprint (London, 1908).

IV. SELECTED LATER EDITIONS OF "THE SPANISH TRAGEDY." *The Spanish Tragedie . . . with New Additions* (1602), Malone Society Reprint (London, 1925); R. Dodsley, ed., *Select Collection of Old Plays,* II (London, 1744); W. C. Hazlitt, ed., *Dodsley's Old Plays,* V (London, 1874); J. Schick, ed., *The Spanish Tragedy* The Temple Dramatists (London, 1898); P. Edwards, ed., *The Spanish Tragedy,* The Revels Plays (London, 1959); C. F. T. Brooke and N. B. Paradise, eds., *English Drama 1580–1642* (Lexington, Mass., 1962); A. S. Cairncross, ed., *The First Part of Hieronimo, and The Spanish Tragedy,* Regent's Renaissance Drama Series (London, 1967); T. W. Ross, ed., *The Spanish Tragedy,* The Fountainwell Drama Texts (Edinburgh, 1968), does not include additions of 1602; J. R. Mulryne, ed., *The Spanish Tragedy,* New Mermaids (London, 1970).

V. CRITICAL STUDIES. J. W. Cunliffe, *The Influence of Seneca on Elizabethan Tragedy* (1893); C. F. Tucker Brooke, *The Tudor Drama* (1912); L. E. Kastner and H. B. Charlton, *The Poetical Works of Sir William Alexander,* I (Manchester, England, 1921), introduction contains a valuable survey of Seneca and his influence on European drama; A. M. Witherspoon, *The Influence of Robert Garnier on Elizabethan Drama* (New Haven, 1924); P. W. Biesterfeldt, *Die Dramatische Technik Thomas Kyds* (Göttingen, 1935); M. C. Bradbrook, *Themes and Conventions of Elizabethan Tragedy* (Cambridge, 1935); W. Farnham, *The Medieval Heritage of Elizabethan Tragedy* (Berkeley, 1936); L. L. Schücking, *Die Zusatze Zur "Spanish Tragedy"* (Leipzig, 1938); H. Baker, *Induction to Tragedy* (Baton Rouge, 1939); F. T. Bowers, *Elizabethan Revenge Tragedy* (Princeton, 1940); H. H. Adams, *English Domestic or Homiletic Tragedy, 1575–1642* (New York, 1943); M. E. Prior, *The Language of Tragedy* (New York, 1947); A. P. Rossiter, *English Drama from Early Times to the Elizabethans* (London, 1950); F. Carrère, *Le Théâtre de Thomas Kyd* (Toulouse, 1951); M. Doran, *Endeavors of Art* (London, 1954); I. Ribner, *The English History Play in the Age of Shakespeare* (London, 1957); T. W. Craik, *The Tudor Interlude* (Leicester, 1958); William Empson, "The Spanish Tragedy," in D. Hudson, ed., *English Critical Essays: Twentieth Century* (Oxford, 1958); Bernard Spivack, *Shakespeare and the Allegory of Evil* (New York, 1958); W. Clemen, *English Tragedy Before Shakespeare* (London, 1961); D. M. Bevington, *From "Mankind" to Marlowe: Growth of Structure in the Popular Drama of Tudor England* (Cambridge, Mass., 1962); S. F. Johnson, "The Spanish Tragedy, or Babylon Revisited," in R. Hosley, ed., *Essays on Shakespeare and Elizabethan Drama in Honor of Hardin Craig* (New York, 1962); Anne Righter, *Shakespeare and the Idea of the Play* (London, 1962); L. L. Schücking, *Zur Verfasserschaft der "Spanish Tragedy,"* Bayerische Akademie der Wissenschaften, Sitzungsberichte (1963); E. W. Talbert, *Elizabethan Drama and Shakespeare's*

Early Plays (Chapel Hill, 1963); G. K. Hunter, "Ironies of Justice in *The Spanish Tragedy*," in *Renaissance Drama*, VIII (London, 1965); J. Barish, "*The Spanish Tragedy*, or the Pleasures and Perils of Rhetoric," in J. R. Brown and B. Harris, eds., *Elizabethan Theatre*, Stratford-upon-Avon Studies 9 (London, 1966); A. Freeman, *Thomas Kyd: Facts and Problems* (Oxford,

1967); J. M. R. Margeson, *The Origins of English Tragedy* (Oxford, 1967); G. K. Hunter, "Seneca and the Elizabethans: A Case-study in 'Influence,' " in *Shakespeare Survey*, 20 (Cambridge, 1967), pp. 17–26; D. M. Bevington, *Tudor Drama and Politics: A Critical Approach to Topical Meaning* (Cambridge, Mass., 1968).

GEORGE CHAPMAN

(ca. 1559-1634)

M. C. Bradbrook

LIFE

GEORGE CHAPMAN—poet, playwright, translator of Homer—has continued to command what in his lifetime he sought for, the attention of a judicious few. He was linked in literary friendship with Marlowe and Jonson, his name has been put forward as the "rival poet" of Shakespeare's *Sonnets;* he was hailed by one contemporary as "the father of English poetry." Keats's sonnet *On First Looking Into Chapman's Homer* records an enthusiasm shared by other romantics, while in the revival of Elizabethan drama that has marked the present century he was singled out by T. S. Eliot as "potentially the greatest artist of all these men; his was the mind that was the most classical; his was the drama that is the most independent in its tendency toward a dramatic form."[1] Eliot had already observed that "In Chapman especially there is a direct sensuous apprehension of thought, or a recreation of thought into feeling which is exactly what we find in Donne."[2]

Yet Chapman has not been restored to the living theater with Webster and Jonson; there is neither a complete edition of his whole works, nor a recent full-scale biography. Perhaps there is too much material for the first, too little for the second. For the range of Chapman's work, and its reliance on writings of classical, Italian, and French origin would present peculiar difficulties to an editor.

Publication extends from 1594 to 1616, after which he published little; it therefore covers the splendid decades of the final Elizabethan efflorescence and the earlier Jacobean period. Born in 1559, the year following Elizabeth's accession, and therefore five years older than Shakespeare and Marlowe, fourteen years older than Jonson, and seventeen years older than Donne, he did not venture into print until past the midpoint of life—thirty-five, corresponding to late middle age in those times; his venerable appearance and hoary head were commented on in the nineties. An Elizabethan who lived into another age, he survived most of his contemporaries, dying in 1634, the year when *Comus* was enacted, when Prynne had already mounted his attack on the stage, and while his former friend and collaborator Ben Jonson lay, like himself, old, ill, and out of favor.

It has been remarked by one of his critics that in his thought Chapman is nearer to Spenser than to Donne. As a poet he stands in the line from Spenser to Milton and Blake; his poetry is written, for the most part, for public occasions, especially marriages and funerals, although it seems the work of a lonely and isolated man seeking in general social relations to adjust himself to society. He seems to have shared with Spenser and even with Spenser's predecessors, Gascoigne and Turberville, the notion of poetry as an act of public service, in particular the ennobling of the English language by bringing in the fruits of other literatures. The establishment of the English tongue was part of the movement toward nationalism that marked the mid-sixteenth century.[3]

Chapman's coronet of sonnets is offered to "his Mistress, Philosophy"; of his private life little is known, but his comedies contain a number of men who go wooing on behalf of their friends. It would seem that, like Spenser's,

---

[1] See "Four Elizabethan Dramatists."
[2] See "The Metaphysical Poets." Both are published in *Selected Essays* (London, 1931).

[3] See my article "No Room at the Top," in B. Harris and J. R. Brown, eds., *Elizabethan Poetry,* Stratford-upon-Avon Studies in English, No. 2 (London, 1960).

232

his efforts were directed at securing friends and patrons.

The second son of a substantial yeoman and copyholder,[4] Chapman was born at Hitchin in Hertfordshire, about thirty miles from London. His mother, who died when George was seven, was the daughter of a royal huntsman, and granddaughter of John Grimeston of Uxborough—a strongly Protestant family. The grammar school at Hitchin, founded for the promotion of religion and good literature, was famous for plays. Chapman's service appears to have begun in the gentlemanly profession of servingman to Sir Ralph Sadler, a local magnate; there is no real evidence that he ever went to a university; his attacks on academic pedantry suggest the contrary.

Sir Ralph (1507–1587), one of the richest commoners in England, had been one of the three knights created on the field of the battle of Pinkie on 10 September 1547. He administered for the crown the royal manor of Hitchin, and when he went north in 1548 Thomas Chapman, George's elder brother, was in the train. Sir Ralph was twice, although then in his late seventies, given guardianship of the captive Mary Queen of Scots; the training his household provided for the young poet would therefore be likely to have been of a distinctly old-fashioned sort, although he was a man of letters as well as a soldier and diplomat. Forty years later Chapman was to dedicate one of his works to Sir Ralph Sadler's grandson. In order to serve Sir Ralph, he contracted debts for equipment; hence the record of his later career is furnished very largely on the one hand by dedications in hopes of patronage, and on the other hand by court proceedings by his creditors (or those who claimed to be so, for he sometimes fell into the hands of sharks). On the title page of his first work he writes himself: Gentleman.

After Sir Ralph's death, Chapman appears to have seen military service in the Low Countries. His cousin, Edward Grimeston the elder, had been the last governor of Calais; the younger Edward Grimeston was attached to the embassy in Paris and came back with Henry IV's ambassador to England. Their family tradition was strongly Protestant, and to his cousin, who wrote histories of France and the Netherlands, Chapman was indebted for much of the material in his French plays.

Chapman must have been back in England some time before the appearance of his first poem, where he describes in some detail Sir Francis Vere's ambush of Spanish troops at Nymaghan in 1591, from the point of view of a participant. One of his latest poems was an appeal on behalf of Sir Francis' brother, Sir Horace Vere, besieged in Mannheim in 1622, whom he describes as "pious and incomparable"; as late as 1624 he recalled a fighting retreat upon Ghent carried out by Sir John Norris in August 1582. These three were cited as England's greatest soldiers. Chapman's chief tragic heroes are soldiers: his translation of the great military epic of *The Iliad* was to be dedicated by him to Henry, Prince of Wales, the eldest son of James I and Anne of Denmark. Of him it was said "Arms had his love when love had scarce his heel," and his hero and model was Henry of Navarre. Chapman made this French king the center of the *Tragedy of Byron*. However, it is the martial character rather than acts of war that he celebrates; his soldiers for the most part go unrewarded, as too many did in real life. When the time came to turn from war to the arts and to seek a new patron, Chapman would have before him such models as the late earl of Leicester, who had supported useful works of a kind to further his own religiopolitical interests, such as translations of the classics, divinity, or history.[5]

Chapman seems to have fixed his hopes on the learned group clustered round Sir Walter Ralegh. The career of Spenser (as later of Lyly) might have warned him of the difficulties inherent in such an enterprise, yet one or two lucky poets such as Daniel and Drayton did find some security in a noble household. Never was anyone more unfortunate than Chapman in his choice of patrons. In Ralegh's circle, however, he met the mathematical scholars Roydon and Harriot; and possibly Christopher Marlowe. But Ralegh fell from royal favor in the spring of 1592 on account of his marriage (he had wedded one of the queen's maids of honor), and that sum-

---

[4] One whose estate is held by immemorial custom rather than by title deeds.

[5] See Eleanor Rosenberg's *Leicester, Patron of Letters* (New York, 1955).

mer he spent in the Tower of London. Chapman's poem *The Shadow of Night* laments obscurity and invokes Cynthia—Ralegh's special name for the queen. In 1596, *De Guiana Carmen Epicum* celebrates Ralegh's expedition to the New World, and is dedicated to one of his captains, Lawrence Keymis. We have evidence that Marlowe was also connected with Ralegh, but the closest tie between the two poets is supplied by Sir Thomas Walsingham, a cousin of the head of Elizabeth's intelligence service, Sir Francis Walsingham. Marlowe was staying with Walsingham in May 1593 when he was murdered. Chapman, who may have met the family through the Grimestons, long retained his connection; he not only dedicated his continuation of Marlowe's *Hero and Leander* to Lady Walsingham, describing her husband as "my honoured best friend," but his *Tragedy of Byron* (1608) was also dedicated to Walsingham and his young son, whom Chapman said he had "loved from birth."

When King James I succeeded to the throne in 1603, Lady Walsingham was put in charge of the royal children, and it may have been through her that Chapman received an appointment as server in ordinary to Prince Henry, an office he held for nine years. This placed him, as a royal servant, in the kind of position his grandfather had enjoyed; it was not a matter of wages, but rather of the royal livery, the prestige, and the chance to cultivate favor that also stood these household servants in good stead with the rest of the world. These nine years, 1603–1612, were Chapman's most productive period as a writer. In the late nineties, while writing his "dark" poems for the enlightened few, Chapman had also worked for Philip Henslowe, the impresario, writing plays for the Lord Admiral's Men at the Rose Theatre under the leadership of the great actor, Edward Alleyn. In this he was surprisingly successful: the first play of which a text survives, *The Blind Beggar of Alexandria* (1596), ran for a year. In *A Coronet for His Mistress Philosophy*, Chapman defends the stage as the noblest home of the Muses; by 1598 Francis Meres praised him for tragedy and comedy.

When the children's troupes reappeared in London in 1600, however, Chapman transferred to them: their intimate clublike atmosphere and the audience of courtiers, lawyers, and soldiers would be to his taste. In February 1603 he provided Paul's Boys with a scandalous play, *The Old Joiner of Aldgate*, on the latest City cause célèbre, at a time when the plot to get possession of a rich heiress, Agnes Howe, was still being investigated in the courts of law. Chapman succeeded in clearing himself from this impropriety, since the play had been licensed, but soon afterward he was imprisoned together with Jonson for libeling the Scots in *Eastward Ho!* (1605). This gay parody of the mid-Tudor prodigal son morality play, which did not spare the king himself, had been produced for the Children of the Chapel Royal at Blackfriars; the real culprit appears to have been a third collaborator, John Marston. Chapman was released, apparently through the good offices of the lord chamberlain, and the play, suitably amended, was later taken to court.

Before the turn of the century, Chapman had begun his translation of *The Iliad*, the first portion appearing in 1598, with a letter to Harriot, and a dedication to the earl of Essex, who was hailed as the reincarnation of Achilles. The earl was about to set off for Ireland, but when his miscalculation, and his ungovernable temper (too like that of Achilles) cost him his liberty and eventually his life, Chapman later transferred the patronage of this task to his royal master, Prince Henry.

Eastward Ho! was part of a "merry war" between the Children of the Chapel Royal and the Children of St. Paul's: the latter put on a sequel, *Northward Ho!* (1607), by Dekker and Webster, which contains a good-natured portrait of Chapman under the name of Bellamont. He is portrayed as an old, white-bearded man, "a poor unpreferred scholar" (IV.1.10), but friendly with the leading citizen Mayberry. In the opening scene he has come from Stourbridge Fair which "hath afforded me mirth beyond the length of five Latin comedies" (I.1.40–41), and he thinks he could make an excellent description of it for a comedy; but in act 4, scene 1, he appears in a nightcap, in deep composition of a tragedy, and dreaming of greatness. His foible in imagining himself the favorite of great men is depicted at some length. He thinks himself an "excellent statesman" who can be inspired with the spirit of Caesar or "have Pompey's soul within me." He confesses "I'm sometimes out of my wits," being "haunted with a Fury" (Furor Poeticus). His "Tragedy of Astyanax" he intends to have performed at the French court:

It shall be, sir, at the marriages of the Duke of Orleans and Chatillon the Admiral of France . . . the stage hung all with black velvet, and, while 'tis acted, myself will stand behind the Duke of Biron or some other chief minion or so—who shall, ay they shall take some occasion about the music of the fourth act, to step to the French King and say *Sire, voilà, il est votre très humble serviteur, le plus sage et divine esprit,* Monsieur Bellamont, all in French, thus pointing at me, or yon is the learned old English Gentleman Maister Bellamont, a very worthy man, to be one of your privy chamber or Poet Laureate.   (IV.i.48–60)

Chapman's plays, written and unwritten, are suggested here; the fate of Bellamont is to find himself amorously pursued by his son's whore, who in spite of his venerable appearance, comes as far as Ware in chase of him.

Chapman and Jonson had probably met as collaborators for Henslowe. *Eastward Ho!* is an admirably plotted play, and Chapman is the most likely collaborator for the stage version of Jonson's *Sejanus;* he wrote commendatory verses for this tragedy as well as for Jonson's *Volpone.* The next installment of *The Iliad* (1609), dedicated to Prince Henry, contained sonnets to many great nobles, especially the Howards and the Sidney–Pembroke circle. The audacious play on the duc de Biron (the erstwhile favorite of Henry IV, finally beheaded for treason in 1602) drew protests from the French ambassador, but was publicly offered by Chapman to Walsingham, to whom he had previously dedicated a comedy, *All Fools.*

Chapman seems to have followed the common habit of striking off special dedications for presentation—with, of course, the hope of a reward from each of the recipients. The master of the rolls, who appears more than once, was also of the household of Prince Henry; he received the public dedication of the *Memorable Masque of the Middle Temple and Lincoln's Inn,* one of the three great masques given at the marriage of the king's daughter, Princess Elizabeth, on Saint Valentine's Day, 1613, and which started from his house. Chapman appears to have satisfied Inigo Jones, who produced the setting, and

whose cause he espoused in the subsequent quarrel between Jones and Jonson. When the masque was produced, the death of Prince Henry in 1612 had already robbed Chapman of his best patron and destroyed any hope of a reward for the *Iliad,* which he protested had been promised. In the memorial verses that accompanied *The Whole Works of Homer* (1616) he laments

> Not thy thrice sacred will
> Signed with thy death, moves any to fulfil
> Thy just bequests to me; thou dead, then I
> Live dead, for giving thee eternity.
>   Ad Famam.
> To all times future, this time's mark extend:
> Homer no Patron found; nor Chapman, friend.
>   (*Poems,* pp. 388–389)[6]

He seems to have been imprisoned for debt again. His next patron, Robert Carr, earl of Somerset, proved the most unfortunate choice of all. The most stupid of King James's homosexual favorites, he had endeared himself to the monarch by falling off a horse—the king did this himself from time to time. After the death of Robert Cecil he succeeded to vast political power as secretary; then he married Lady Frances Howard, following her infamous divorce from the earl of Essex. The poem that Chapman wrote for the occasion, *Andromeda Liberata,* was totally misunderstood and failed to please. Before long, Carr, ousted by Buckingham, was implicated in the charge of murder brought against his wife. In May 1616 both were tried for poisoning Sir Thomas Overbury, with Bacon conducting the case for the crown; they were found guilty and imprisoned in the Tower for six years—although James, who was shattered and terrified, spared their lives. Chapman remained faithful to the tottering favorite and in 1614 dedicated to him *The Odyssey,* as a model tale of endurance under affliction; however, his *Hesiod* (1618) was dedicated to Bacon, who in his *Wisdom of the Ancients* had put forward views congenial to the poet.

In the previous year, 1617, Chapman was described in a law suit as "of mean or poor es-

---

[6] Quotations are taken from P. B. Bartlett's edition of *The Poems* and T. M. Parrott's edition of *The Comedies* and *The Tragedies.*

tate," and "doth now live in remote places and is hard to be found." He was being pursued for debt by the sons of a wealthy London merchant, to one of whom, Henry Jones, he had dedicated his funeral poem for Prince Henry. Chapman apparently took refuge with his brother Thomas, who had stood guarantor for his debt. Thomas was said to be worth about £300 a year in land (a fortune equaling that of Burbage or Shakespeare); since, in 1613, William Browne had described George Chapman as "the learned shepherd of fair Hitchin hill," and since he dedicated one copy of *The Crown of All Homer's Works* (1624) to Sir Ralph Sadler's grandson, the approach he made with his poem *Eugenia* (1614) to Lord Russell, whose estate was nearby, suggests that he kept up connections with his birthplace. This last poem was privately printed, and although he offered it as a "first anniversary," that is, the first of a series, it seems not to have secured him any favor. He therefore returned in the public dedication of *The Crown of All Homer's Works* to Somerset, who perhaps in his retirement took to the arts. However, when the poet died at seventy-five, it was Inigo Jones who erected a monument in St. Giles-in-the-Fields to "Georgius Chapmannus, poeta Homericus, Philosophus verus (etsi Christianus poeta)."

The authors of *Northward Ho!* endowed their fictional Chapman with skill in modern languages and music; in 1611 Chapman praised the Elizabethan virginal music of Bull, Byrd, and Gibbons, compared with "foreign novelty." In that year the poet and writing master, John Davies of Hereford, characterized him thus:

> To my highly valued friend, Mr George Chapman,
>   Father of our English Poets.
> I know thee not (good George) but by thy pen;
> For which I rank thee with the rarest men,
> And in that rank I put thee in the front
> Especially of poets of account,
> Who art the treasure of that company;
> But in thy hand too little coin doth lie;
> For of all men that now in London are,
> Poets get least in uttering their ware . . .

This sketch agrees with Chapman's own wry observation that a poet might be identified by his clothes.[7] Michael Drayton (also the subject

[7] In *A Justification of a Strange Action of Nero* (*Poems*, p. 346).

of commiseration for being "as poor as Job") saluted "reverend Chapman" for his translations of Greek poets, in an epistle addressed to their common friend and fellow poet, Henry Reynold. In his last collection of the *Homeric Hymns*, Chapman himself records his faith and his adversities:

> The work that I was born to do is done!
> Glory to him, that the conclusion
> Makes the beginning of my life; and never
> Let me be said to live, till I live ever . . .
>   (*Poems*, p. 416)

ending with a Latin prayer for the Trinity that formed his own daily and nightly offering.

LYRICAL POETRY

ALTHOUGH the three phases of Chapman's writing—lyric poet, dramatist, translator—can readily be distinguished, his development remained consistent. In his lyric works, the earliest and most doctrinal of his writings, his Stoicism was not yet fully developed, but he already shows himself both a Christian Platonist and a Stoic. He adhered passionately to poetry as the supreme form of revelation.

Nor is this all-comprising poesy, fantastic or mere fictive; but the most material and doctrinal illation of truth[8]   (Dedication of *The Odyssey, Poems*, p. 407)

For Chapman, however, although earlier champions of poetry had insisted on "perspicuity" or plainness, Truth dwelt at the bottom of a well. With Plato he maintained "Est enim ipsa Natura universa aenigmatum plena, nec quivis eam dignoscit" (*Poems*, p. 327).[9] Under a Hermetic or hieroglyphic form, allegorical or mythological poetry both concealed the occult wisdom of the ancients—and could best reveal it." Philosophy retired to darkest caves / She can discover" (*Poems*, p. 384). Scripture had long been interpreted in this fashion, whether in allegorical form for the *Song of Songs* or *Revelations*, or in

[8] Something which presents by inference, that is, a shadow or "inferring" of Platonic Truth.
[9] For universal Nature is herself full of riddles, nor does anyone comprehend it."

Christ's use of parable. The ancient Egyptians, the first repositories of wisdom, were thought to have transmitted their secrets through Hermes Trismegistus ("Thrice-Great Hermes," an honorific title of the Egyptian Hermes, or Thoth, the god of wisdom), and the Greeks through Orpheus. Orphic poets in each generation could renew and transmit this secret knowledge. They were not "makers," but divinely enraptured and inspired.

Chapman's poems have become much more intelligible in the last thirty years through a growing familiarity with the Neoplatonic doctrines of the Florentine philosophers Ficino and Pico della Mirandola. As part of the history of ideas they have been presented by such scholars as Kristaller, while their relevance to Florentine and other art has been expounded by Edgar Wind, Erwin Panofsky, Gombrich, and Roy Strong, and by various writers on the masques of Ben Jonson from D. J. Gordon to Stephen Orgel. It is hardly thinkable now that anyone should say, as did James Smith in 1934 (writing in *Scrutiny*), that he was unacquainted with Ficino. Numerology has been applied to poetry, especially to Spenser, by Alastair Fowler and Maren-Sofie Røstvig. The Hermeticists have been studied in relation to literature by Frances M. Yates, especially in relation to the cult of Queen Elizabeth and her iconography. Students of alchemy and early science have also studied them in their influence on figures such as Cornelius Agrippa.

The Shadow of Night is a good example of such a "dark" poem; it is directed toward Elizabeth, as she is Cynthia, the moon goddess. The virtues of the learned few will cause Chapman to "strike fire out of darkness" that "the brightest day might envy for beauty," as he assures the mathematician Roydon in his dedication (*Poems*, p. 19). In his second volume, addressing the the same learned friend, he becomes even more explicit:

The profane multitude I hate, and only consecrate my strange poems to those searching spirits, whom learning hath made noble, and nobility sacred. . . . But that poesy should be as pervial[10] as oratory, and plainness her special ornament were the plain way to barbarism. . . . That *Enargia*, or clearness of represen-

[10] clear.

tation, required in absolute poems is not the perspicuous delivery of a low invention; but high and hearty invention expressed in most significant and unaffected phrase. . . . Obscurity in affections of words and indigested conceits is pedantical and childish; but where it shroudeth itself in the heart of the subject, uttered with fitness of figures and expressive epithets; with that darkness will I labour still to be shadowed.   (*Poems*, p. 49)

Chapman is no Holofernes,[11] but he is convinced that poetry requires study and art; and that it must be difficult. He sounds very like the young T. S. Eliot. Chapman also compares his art with that of the painter, who aims not at likeness but at "lustre, shadow and heightening" to supply "motion, life and spirit." The "perspective" or point of view is all important.

In the next year (1595) Chapman's poem *Ovid's Banquet of Sense* presented an elaborate perspective on Ovidian erotic poetry and in particular on Marlowe's *Hero and Leander*, the verse narrative which Chapman was soon to provide with a sequel and corrective. *Ovid's Banquet* describes Ovid's encounter with Julia, the daughter of the Emperor Augustus, as she bathes in a garden bower, and her granting of various graces to the poet, who finally proclaims that he is inspired to write *The Art of Love*.

The "right perspective," in the sense that the word has been used above, has been the subject of much debate. In a brilliant study[12] Frank Kermode has traced the history of the theme; the Banquet of Sense is traditionally the antithesis of Plato's *Symposium*, in that it progresses downward through the five senses, from the finer to the grosser. In this poem there is also a downward progress through another series, the five stages of love—although the final stage, coitus, is not directly given, but adumbrated. Chapman's secret intention is therefore ironic; the arguments of Ovid are a misuse of reason, like that of Leander in his wooing of Hero. Kermode terms this "one of the most difficult poems in the language"; many have read it as a celebration of ideal beauty, in contradis-

[11] The pedantic schoolmaster satirized in Shakespeare's *Love's Labour's Lost*.

[12] Reprinted in Kermode's *Renaissance Essays* (London, 1971). The view has not gone unchallenged; see Waddington, *The Mind's Empire*, ch. 4 (London, 1974), and the introduction to Kermode's volume.

tinction to the earthly Venus of Shakespeare's *Venus and Adonis*. It would, however, be entirely in keeping for Chapman to present his meaning in an oblique way, perceptible only to initiates. John Marston was to defend his highly erotic *Metamorphosis of Pygmalion's Image* as a satire on eroticism; Donne's *Ecstasy* has been read both as Platonic trance and as prelude to seduction, while Ovid's *Art of Love* had itself been moralized in the manner of the *Song of Songs*. The difficulty of interpreting Chapman's poem lies not only in the difficulty of recovering the current meaning of a Banquet of Sense (for the Elizabethan, a "banquet" was a slight collation preparatory to a feast, and serving as a prologue or epilogue to it), but also in the conflict between any ironic intention and the rich baroque detail.

The icons of this poem, then, are presented in perspective, like those curious pictures to which Chapman refers more than once, which need to be looked at obliquely.[13] This topic is introduced by way of the statues of Niobe and her children at the beginning of the Banquet. This warning group decks the garden of delights. The poem may be meant to have two alternative readings:

> A cozening picture, which one way
> Shows like a crow, the other like a swan
> (*All Fools*, I. i. 47–48)

So the later tragic hero Chabot one way looks weak, unjust, bloody and monstrous, but "by the right laid line of truth" he is wise, just, and good. When Shakespeare's Cleopatra sees her Antony one way like a Gorgon and the other like a Mars, both are true.

Two voices can be heard, each with its own melody; but with all its intricacy and ingenuity—in a mode that was soon to become limpid and shallow, as it does in the Ovidian romances of Barksted and Heywood—*Ovid's Ban-*

---

[13] See *Hero and Leander, III*, 125–126; *Eugenia*, 173–180; *Chabot*, I. i. 68–72; also Inga-Stina Ewbank, "Webster's Realism, a Cunning Piece-Wrought Perspective," in *John Webster*, ed. Brian Morris (London, 1970); Waddington, *The Mind's Empire*, ch. 4, especially pp. 120–2. The most celebrated perspective pictures are Holbein's *The Ambassadors* in The National Gallery and William Scrots' *Edward VI* in The National Portrait Gallery, London. Compare M. C. Escher's modern puzzle painting.

quet of Sense lacks the passion that informs *The Shadow of Night*. The *Banquet of Sense* presents a beauty whose image is that of the sun, and a poet whose senses are inflamed to climax by sight. At its center Corinna sits naked and singing, a siren:

> And thus she sung, all naked as she sat,
> Laying her happy lute upon her thigh
> (st. 12; *Poems*, p. 56)

Ovid pleads for each sense in turn, but the poem ends with another cunning perspective picture, in which as a painter will draw only a part of a hand, but the rest can be imagined, the reader is to imagine the consummation:

> So in the compass of this curious frame,
> Ovid well knew there was much more intended,
> With whose omission, none must be offended.
> (st. 117; *Poems*, p. 82)

Chapman elsewhere uses double rhyme with mocking effect: if Ovid's verse is not heaven born

> blame me as his submitted debtor
> That never mistress had to make me better
> (st. 57; *Poems*, p. 67)

Marlowe had, of course, translated Ovid's *Art of Love*. His *Hero and Leander* was the first great Ovidian romance; he approved the strife out of which the world was made, and invokes it in simile for the consummation of the act of love, which he does not omit:

> She trembling strove; this strife of hers (like that
> Which made the world) another world begat
> Of unknown joy   (*Second Sestiad*, 291–293)

Hero radiates day in night:

> Then near the bed, she blushing stood upright,
> And from her countenance behold ye might
> A kind of twilight break, which through the hair,
> As from an orient cloud, glimpse here and there,
> And round about the chamber, this false morn
> Brought forth the day before the day was born.
> (*Second Sestiad*, 317–322)

Chapman's continuation of *Hero and Leander* (1598), which presents the obverse, the alterna-

GEORGE CHAPMAN

tive image to that of Marlowe, has in modern times evoked not only defense but enthusiasm. The presiding deity is Ceremony, and the nearest equivalent to this baroque and gorgeous icon is to be found in the figures of Jonson's masque, *Hymenaei*. Appearing to Leander with her magic pentacle, her mathematical crystal, and her rod of laurel to beat back Barbarism and Avarice, Ceremony presents herself ambiguously, for she has been outraged:

> Her face was changeable to every eye,
> One way looked ill, another graciously
> (*Third Sestiad*, 125–126; *Poems*, p. 137)

Leander at once prepares to abduct and wed Hero, but it is the girl's divided mind and distressed thoughts that occupy the main portion of Chapman's sequel. As priestess of Venus, she assumes a falsely ceremonious performance of her ritual duties, for which she is punished by her angry lady. The goddess breaks the priestess' crown of icicles that "figured chaste desires" and forces on her a funeral wreath of yew; from the smoke of Hero's sacrifice she creates a terrifying nymph (modeled on Dante's image of Fraud, *Inferno*, canto XVII). This is Dissimulation, "of lightning and of shreds begot"; her hair is knotted like a net, her arms dressed with golden pincers, knots, and pulleys, her body, girdled with snakes, ends in a scorpion's tail. The thing that Hero's mind created now stands before her, a nightmare form.

Hero's torn, divided mind gives dramatic depth to the baroque ornamentation, and supplies the true "corrective" to Marlowe. With extraordinary delicacy and intimacy Chapman renders the sense of physical privation, almost of bereavement of

> Sweet Hero, left upon her bed alone,
> Her maidenhead, her vows, Leander gone
> (*Third Sestiad*, 199–200; *Poems*, p. 138)

The instinctive fear that comes first to a despoiled girl—the fear of pregnancy—is conveyed obliquely by a simile:

> Strange thoughts possessed her, ransacking her breast
> For that that was not there, her wonted rest.

> She was a mother straight and bore with pain
> Thoughts that spake straight and wished their mother slain. (*Third Sestiad*, 225–228; *Poems*, p. 139)

No woman in Chapman's drama, not even Tamyra, is portrayed in greater depth, and the characterization contrasts very sharply with the purely physical intimacy of *Ovid's Banquet of Sense*, as when Corinna shrinks from Ovid's touch, starting like sparkles from a fire, her tender temper "proving her sharp, undulled with handling yet." As one critic observed, she is more like a filly than ideal beauty at this point.

Soon, however, in Leander's own sophisticated vein, Hero justifies herself, and proceeds to celebrate the marriage of another priestess, whom she exempts from her vow. At the marriage feast, the nymph Teras (meaning a portent, or comet) appears, and tells the ominous Tale of Hymen. In the event, not the gods but the fates destroy the lovers, Neptune finally turning them into two beautiful birds. This leaves them still within the realm of nature, if yet, as the Nature of Ovid's *Metamorphoses*, one permeated with the divine.

The splendid series of images that fills Chapman's part of the poem anticipates the images of the Jacobean masque; their emblematic force depends on the interpretation of stance and costume, gesture and insignia. The most substantial and learned explanation of the imagery has recently become more widely available in the essays of D. J. Gordon, collected by Stephen Orgel and published under the title *The Renaissance Imagination* (Berkeley, 1975). The work of Gordon on Chapman's poems and masque first established that iconological approach that has since been successfully applied to a number of writers, notably Jonson. In this poem, Chapman supplies a corrective not only to Marlowe (in irreverent mood, Hogarth's *Before* and *After* might be invoked) but to his own earlier "perspective picture" as well. More than any other poem of his, *Hero and Leander* justifies Eliot's praise of Chapman for "a direct sensuous apprehension of thought, or a recreation of thought into feeling."

If poetry is the vehicle for implementing truth, the process will appear in its style. Because truth dwells at the bottom of a well, or as

Donne puts it, on a steep hill, she can be found only when the listener (for this is still oral poetry) has wrought within himself vision and understanding. The final result might sound like some familiar proverb or platitude, but that platitude has been "proved upon the pulses." Chapman creates at first strange and grotesque icons that shock and stimulate; if visualized, they are monstrous. The poet by this means prompts a search for the soul through "sense" and "allegory"

which intends a more eminent expression of Virtue for her loveliness and Vice for her ugliness, in their several effects going beyond the life . . .
(Dedicatory letter to *The Odyssey; Poems*, p. 407)

This, for example, is Cynthia in her final metamorphosis as Hecate:

Then in thy clear and icy pentacle
Now execute a magic miracle . . .
Look with thy fierce aspect, be terror-strong;
Assume thy wondrous shape of half a furlong;
Put on thy feet of serpents, viperous hairs,
And act the fearful'st part of thy affairs.
(*Hymnus in Cynthiam*, 514–522; *Poems*, p. 42)

and here is Religion described some twenty years later:

. . . Her form, as if transform'd she were
Into a lean and lisping grasshopper,
As small and faintly spoke she; her strength's loss
Made her go lame, and leaning on the cross,
Stooping and crooked, and her joints did crack,
As all the weight of earth were on her back;
Her looks were like the pictures that are made
To th'optic reason; one way like a shade,
Another monster-like . . .
All hid in cobwebs came she forth, like these
Poor country churches, chapels call'd of ease . . .
All full of spiders was her homespun weed
Where souls like flies hung, of which some would
　strive
To break the net, their bodies yet alive,
Some (all their bodies eat) the spiders' thighs
Left hanging like the only wings of flies.
(*Eugenia*, 1614, 167–191; *Poems*, pp. 275–276)

In the metaphysical style of Donne, the intellectual agility behind some outrageous conceit may be aimed at stimulating the reader through the clash of opposites, or the rejection of accepted ideas, or the shock of paradox; it will use the direct reflection of sensuous experience. Chapman's method is nearer to that of Spenser, Milton, and Blake. However, the weight of his powerful rhythm and massive vocabulary is not Spenserian, but springs from his affinity to Marlowe, who is invoked in the third sestiad of *Hero and Leander*:

Then thou, most strangely intellectual fire,
That, proper to my soul, hast power t'inspire
Her burning faculties, and with the wings
Of thy unsphered flame, visit'st the springs
Of spirits immortal; now, (as swift as Time
Doth follow Motion), find th'eternal clime
Of his free soul, whose living subject stood
Up to the chin in the Pierean flood,
And drunk to me half this Musean story,
Inscribing it to deathless memory;
Tell it how much his late desires I tender. . . .
(183–195; *Poems*, p. 138)

Marlowe's crisp, detached, and often ironic couplets safeguard his rich hyperbole from any risks of cloying. Chapman does not share Marlowe's elegant brutality, but his terse and ringing "sentences" (generalizations) prove how the couplet form could curb his natural prolixity, and limit it within the similes or the reflected stories which, as C. S. Lewis remarked, are nested inside each other like a set of Chinese boxes.

The emblematic method of composition found its fullest expression in Chapman's masque for the wedding of Princess Elizabeth, the most costly and spectacular success of his career, in which he "digested" a "ground" (worked in a scenario) supplied by Inigo Jones. Jonson said that none but himself and Chapman could make a masque. In this masque of Virginians he was perhaps pleading for his old friend Ralegh, who had been befriended in his imprisonment by Chapman's new patron, Prince Henry.

To Prince Henry himself, in 1609, Chapman had dedicated his own Lachrimae, *The Tears of Peace*, an adaptation of Erasmus' *Querula Pacis* but a highly personal confession too. True inward Peace is seen in a vision burying Human Love, and attended by a procession of birds and beasts, more worthy than men. This concept is lifted straight from Angelo Poliziano's *Rusticus*.

The whole vision is introduced in the manner of a masque by the figure of Homer, who "rends down a cloud" that hides the vision. It is the presence of Homer as Induction that justifies the attack on "formal clerks, blown for profession," scholars who are "mere articulated clocks," broken limbs of true knowledge, that consists in knowledge of a man's self. We should remember that Prince Henry, then fifteen, was constantly lectured by his poets, who were all eager to take his education in hand; and the king himself had written a treatise for his son's edification.

If the conclusion of *The Tears of Peace* seems ingeniously to reconcile contempt of the world with hopes of royal favor, the "sickness" that delayed the translation of Homer may have been real. In a private dedication to Walsingham, Chapman speaks of his "shaken brain"; here he has talked of being "birth accurs'd". It could be that his deep sense of alienation sprang from some dissociation; he might have been epileptic or cataleptic. Such an affliction could explain that hatred of the body he so often expresses, as in these well-known lines, when, looking to the "life to come," he hopes to cast "the serpent's scale":

This load of life in life; this fleshly stone;
This bond and bundle of corruption;
This breathing sepulchre; this sponge of grief;
This smiling enemy; this household thief;
This glass of air, broken with less than breath;
This slave, bound face to face to death till death.[14]
(*The Tears of Peace*, 1015–20; *Poems*, p. 195)

Much earlier, in the letter to Harriot prefixed to his first translation from Homer (1598), he had given a powerful account of his own volcanic and fitful bursts of inspiration, alternating with Saturnian melancholy, and requiring for their detection some kind of spiritual telescope:

O had your perfect eye Organs to pierce
Into that chaos whence this stifled verse
By violence breaks; where glow-worm like doth shine
In nights of sorrow, this hid soul of mine;
And how her genuine forms struggle for birth
Under the claws of this foul panther, earth;

[14] These lines are adapted from *The Tragedy of Byron* (V. iv. 34–38) written in the previous year (1608).

Then under all these forms you should discern
My love to you, in my desire to learn
(*To Mr Harriot*, 41–47; *Poems*, p. 382)

The blindness of Homer, like that of Tiresias, is a condition of the seer. This paradox of Homer, poor, outcast, blind, seems to have given Chapman confidence to accept his own alienation; once he had identified with Homer, he had found "the work that I was born to do," and he spent the rest of his life following that vision which had come to him of the "grave and goodly person," whose bosom was transparent with fire, whose breath was flame.

Past and future things he saw
And was to both, and present times, their law
(*The Tears of Peace*, 37–38; *Poems*, p. 174)

The blind beggar's had been a holy role in his first comedy, although assumed in disguise; and he now reveals it was in those earlier days that the first vision of Homer came:

I am (said he) that spirit Elysian,
That in thy native air; and on the hill
Next Hitchin's left hand did thy bosom fill
With such a flood of soul; that thou wert fain
To vent it to the echoes of the vale;
When meditating of me, a sweet gale
Brought me upon thee; and thou didst inherit
My true sense (for the time then) in my spirit;
And I (invisible) went prompting thee
To those fair greens where thou didst English me.
(*The Tears of Peace*, 75–85; *Poems*, pp. 174–175)

The joy of this, "enough to break the twine / Of life and soul, so apt to break as mine," threw the poet into a new trance. Homer now tells the poet that he would be to him "Angel, Star and Fate" (92–93). This is perhaps the most direct claim to Furor Poeticus in all the poetry of the time.

Petrarch's Seven Penitential Psalms (1612), an adaptation rather than a translation, presents the poet laboring on "to my journey's end, a stranger"; but Chapman's own *Hymn to Christ on the Cross*, in the same volume, celebrates the redemptive power of His sufferings in the body "whose Vinegar thou nectar mak'st in me"; he hopes for such infusion of grace that he may say "Not I, but Christ in me":

Quiet so
My body's powers, that neither weal nor woe
May stir one thought up, 'gainst thy freest will
(*Petrarch's Seven Penitential Psalms*, 295–297;
Poems, pp. 226–227)

In this collection, which includes much from his commonplace book, Chapman prays, exhorts, counsels, but also includes some shrewd character sketches.

TRANSLATIONS

SINCE Homer occupied Chapman for nearly thirty years, it is not surprising that it is uneven. What Chapman did to Homer amounts to little, compared with what modern stage directors do to Shakespeare, what Brecht did also to Marlowe, Gay, and Kipling. Essex was hailed as the True Achilles, foreshadowed by Homer's; Odysseus' fortitude offers a model for Somerset. His scholarship, deficient by modern standards, was that of his time; knowledge of the Greeks came at second hand to almost everyone in England. Chapman used the parallel Greek text and Latin "crib" of Spondanus (Jean de Sponde), eked out with the *Lexicon* of Scapula.

Of course he is guilty of misreadings, as when he makes Odysseus' old nurse shriek for grief at the sight of the slaughtered suitors, instead of giving a cry of joy. In following "secret wisdom" Chapman, like the translators of Scripture, was prepared to accept apparent nonsense from time to time; on the other hand, when he reduces visions to proverbial "sentences" (platitudes), he can make Homer sound like a dreary Jacobean divine. Take, for example, the elaboration of a simile comparing a man's mind to his day—both gifts of Zeus:

The mind of man flies still out of his way
Unless God guide and prompt it every day
(*Odyssey*, xviii, 136–137)

Students of literature may measure the distance of Jacobean notions of early Greek poetry from our own by Chapman's translation. Homer here means something like the earlier English rough epic romances of Sir Bevis or Sir Guy. Students of language will find that Chapman, by using the old fourteener line in *The Iliad*, has reverted to an early Tudor style. Unlike King James's Bible, this translation is not for all time but of an age. Yet to his own age it constituted his chief instrument. One critic observes that "Chapman expands and contracts *The Iliad* like an accordion to play his own tune upon it." *The Odyssey* contains even more of Chapman— Coleridge declaring it to be as original a poem as *The Faerie Queen*. In reverting to heroic couplets, Chapman emphasized again that this was English Homer; this meter offers much more support than the lumbering hexameters of his *Iliad*. He attacked other scholars on behalf of "his" Homer, and never loses an opportunity to belabor Scaliger, the great Renaissance scholar and textual critic, for preferring Virgil; then he adds morals with the confidence of one in direct touch with Homer's spirit. Even Achilles becomes more deliberate, as when he talks to Hector like a sergeant-major on the soldier's need to cultivate hatred:

Therefore now, all worth that fits a man
Call to thee, all particular parts that fit a soldier,
And they all this include (beside the spirit and skill of
    war)
Hunger for slaughter and a hate that eats thy heart to
    eat
Thy foe's heart. This stirs, this supplies in death the
    killing heat;
And all this needest thou.   (*Iliad*, xxii, 230–235)

In the Penguin translation this appears as, "So summon any courage you have, this is the time to show your spearmanship and daring."

Jonson at first approved the translations; he quoted a passage to Drummond of Hawthornden that he thought "well done," and in commendatory verses for *Hesiod* (1618) he proclaims Chapman's monopoly of the rich and beautiful empire of Greek poetry (Chapman had used the same image in praising *Sejanus*):

Whose work could this be, Chapman, to refine
Old Hesiod's ore and give it us; but thine,
Who hadst before wrought in rich Homer's mine?
What treasure hast thou brought us! and what store
Still, still, dost thou arrive with at our shore,
To make thy honour and our wealth the more!
(*Ben Jonson*, ed. Herford and Simpson,
vol. 8, 1946, pp. 388–389)

GEORGE CHAPMAN

If in his private copy of Homer, Jonson criticized, his comments were not severe by the standards of the time. *The Invective against Jonson*, which Chapman left incomplete in manuscript and which accuses him of too much pride in his own learning, was not, it seems to me, connected with Homer but was rather part of the battle between Jonson and Inigo Jones, which took place in 1631–1633, at the end of Chapman's life. If he is brutal about the burning of Jonson's library, Jonson had been equally brutal in his *Expostulation* to Inigo Jones about the burning of his buildings, when his chief accusation was of crass ignorance.

Inigo's supplying a monument for Chapman witnesses to their continuing friendship; and Chapman's *Invective* fits into this public quarrel better than if the two old friends had fallen out between themselves. However it is taken, this example of "wrath in old age" is a sad conclusion to one of the two closest literary collaborations of Chapman's life.

COMEDIES

TODAY Chapman's comedy is the most neglected part of his work, but it was the earliest form in which he scored popular success—and succès de scandale—first in the Men's and then in the Choristers' theaters. *The Blind Beggar of Alexandria* (1596) developed the central role for a quick-change artist; elaborate doubling had been inevitable in the old days of four-men companies, but this form exploits multiple role-playing, and the ironies to be extracted from disguise. Here the banished Duke Cleanthes disguises himself as a blind hermit Irus (named from the beggar of the *Odyssey*), and also as Count Hermes, a swaggering soldier, and Leon, an elderly usurer. The whole play is a parody of Marlowe's tragedy; such lines as

Why, what is dalliance, says my servant then?
(sc. i. 160)

or

Come, gird this pistol closely to my side,
By which I make men fear my humour still,

And have slain two or three as 'twere my mood,
When I have done it most advisedly
(sc. i. 326–329)

indicate that both *Tamburlaine* and *The Jew of Malta* are contributory. In his various roles, Cleanthes woos two sisters, marries, cross-cuckolds himself, disguised, and gives evidence on his own behalf in a lawsuit (no doubt Chapman would have enjoyed doing the same). Other characters are his shadows: Bragadino ("I am Signior Bragadino, the martial Spaniardo . . .") and a foolish brother. As Count Hermes he kills a rival who is wooing his true love, the heiress of Egypt (Zenocrate was an Egyptian princess in *Tamburlaine*), but promptly launches into a Marlovian invitation:

But come, sweet love, if thou wilt come with me,
We two will live among the shadowy groves
And we will sit like shepherds on a hill . . .
Sometime I'll dive into the murmuring springs
And fetch thee stones to hang about thy neck,
Which by thy splendour will be turn'd to pearl . . .
(sc. ix. 24–33)

Count Hermes is disposed of by being swallowed alive in the earth. A courtier enters echoing old Hieronymo (the avenging father in Kyd's *The Spanish Tragedy*): "Who called out murther? Lady, was it you?"; but then, with an invasion of four mighty kings, we switch back to *Tamburlaine*. Staying only to collect the treasure owed to Leon, Duke Cleanthes easily defeats the kings, and after they have done homage, bestows two of them on two of his cast-off wives, now assumed widows. The expected end—his marriage with the princess—is missing, but a wedding procession and dance would suffice.

A Humourous Day's Mirth (1598), the earliest comedy of humors, stars the resourceful Lemot, and Florilla, a young Puritan wife, who, brought abroad to test her virtue, prepares to cuckold her elderly, uxorious husband. Her qualities are subsequently reflected not only in the last of Chapman's comedies, *The Widow's Tears*, but in Jonson's character Win-the-Fight Littlewit in *Bartholomew Fair*, and as late as Wycherley's Margery Pinchwife in *The Country Wife*. After she has been brought to a tavern, scolded, even bitten by her ruthless antagonist,

243

GEORGE CHAPMAN

Lemot, Florilla saves herself by reassuming the Puritan role. Gulls and fops provide a fast and farcical intrigue, with plenty of repartee for young gallants in the audience to memorize or copy down, and mockery of affected compliment and Puritan cant. This is how Lemot urges Florilla that her virtue must be put on trial:

Lemot: To live idle in this walk . . . is to make virtue an idle housewife and to hide herself in slothful cobwebs, that still should be adorned with actions of victory; no, madam, if you will worthily prove your constancy to your husband, you must put on rich apparel, fare daintily, hear music, read sonnets, be continually courted, kiss, dance, feast, revel all night among gallants . . .
Labervele: O vanity of vanities!
Florilla: O husband, this is perfect trial indeed!
Labervele: And you will try all this now, will you not?
Florilla: Yea, my good head; for it is written, we must pass to perfection through all temptation, Habakkuk the fourth.
Labervele: Habakkuk! cuck me no cucks! In a doors, I say! Thieves, Puritans, murderers! In a doors, I say. (sc. iv. 225–245)

The Puritan habit of scriptural quotation allows Labervele's obsessive mind to suppose the reference is to cuckoldry. The Book of Habakkuk has only three chapters in point of fact. Chapman puts himself into the play both as chief critic and plotter, and as the melancholy young scholar.

In *Northward Ho!*, which depicts Chapman, the neglected poet is invited by the citizen to "bring my wife upon the stage; would not her humour please the gentlemen?" Some of his City friends testified of Chapman that he was "a pleasant witty fellow," and the merry tricks that are the substance of *A Humourous Day's Mirth* are entirely English (although the scene is supposed to be France). The right perspective lies in a combination of witty caricature and good nature; the method is not satirical, as in Jonson's humor plays.

The next two plays were written for the Children's companies; both carry reveling titles from folk festivities—*All Fools*, and *May Day*—and are adapted freely from two plays by Terence, the classic Roman comic playwright

(*The Self-Tormentor* and *The Adelphi*), and from a commedia erudita (an Italian play composed on classical lines), respectively. Terentian comedy introduced to the English stage plots that were based on intrigue; for the lesson of classical art was the pleasure of contrivance. The clever servant or chief trickster, although sometimes outplayed at the end, is more often successful in defeating the older generation. It is a great pity that *The Old Joiner of Aldgate* is lost, since it might have shown how far Chapman could use this classical form for a modern news item.

Set in Florence, *All Fools* offers a Terentian quartet of lovers and a pair of fathers, one crusty, one benevolent; a younger brother supplies the trickery, only to be finally outwitted by the jealous man. It concludes with a tremendous oration on cuckoldry in praise of "the most fashionable and authentical horn"—in a prose vastly superior to the flat but competent verse of the main scenes.

May Day, set in Venice, reverts to the whirligig action of *A Humourous Day's Mirth*. Chapman altered the balance of his original; in the pursuit of love everyone disguises, as was the habit on May Day. Lodovico, the intriguer, ridicules his lovesick friend, who is found prostrate on the ground; others affect to think him drunk, mock his versifying ("Room for a passion"), but help him to a rope ladder. The classical stageset, with its twin housefronts, allows plenty of bedroom farce; the jests evolve out of each other at accelerating speed, as the unities of time and place concentrate them. The romantic lovers are purely conventional, all the action being manipulated by Angelo, a clever servant. *May Day* is of the stock from which was to come *The Alchemist*, and eventually *The Marriage of Figaro*; however, from this point onward, the speed of action in Chapman's plays begins to slow down, and he no longer relies upon a helter-skelter intrigue.

His Jacobean comedies, which were written at the same period as his more famous tragedies, are all concerned in some way with master–servant relationships, and no longer turn on disguise. The eponymous fools of *The Gentleman Usher* and *Monsieur d'Olive*—the first a gull, who is persuaded that the duke's son dotes on him, the second a gentleman affecting wit, who is dazzled by the prospect of being made an ambassador—occupy the center of attention, pushing the romantic love stories into the background, although these develop tragicomic potential. In common with other plays of the time, these are much more concerned with character than their Elizabethan forerunners, but they still revert at times to great set orations, such as that made by Monsieur d'Olive in praise of tobacco (one of the king's phobias). An affirmation of the complete freedom of the will and the inner rule of conscience sounds the same note as Chapman's great tragedies.

> A virtuous man is subject to no prince,
> But to his soul and honour; which are laws
> That carry fire and sword within themselves . . .
> (*The Gentleman Usher*, V. iv. 59–61)

The self-admiring and presumptuous fool who takes the lead in *Monsieur d'Olive* prides himself on his wit and eloquence; when he is promoted to ambassador, he behaves as if he were the very duke, and kisses his duchess. To her cry "How now, you fool? Out, you presumptuous gull!" his reply is in kind:

> How now, you baggage? 'Sfoot, are you so coy
> To the Duke's person, to his second self?
> Are you too good, dame, to enlarge yourself
> Unto your proper object? (II. ii. 304–307)

This satire extends into the romantic plot, which depicts the fantastic melancholy of a noble lady who fancies her reputation wronged, and lives only in darkness, waking at night time, balanced by the fantastic dotage of a noble earl who keeps the body of his dead wife embalmed in his chamber. Both are cured by trickery, based on character. The lady is drawn from retirement by exciting her jealousy; the earl is persuaded to marry a lady whom he is sent to woo on behalf of his friend. But this is subsidiary to the absurd inflation of Monsieur d'Olive, and the vast proliferation of plans and followers for his embassy, which is canceled before it sets out. Here was a topical subject, for James had appointed a number of ambassadors whose extravagance had been a jest in London; Chapman was risking censorship in ridiculing this form of ambition. The motto of the embassy is "discern and spy out!" but the bamboozled d'Olive becomes "a Christmas Lord . . . a laughter for the whole court." He is drawn back with a feigned love letter, which works on him as on Malvolio in *Twelfth Night*; but his final recompense is to be taken back into court, which offers a refuge from discharged followers and from duns.

The last comedy, *The Widow's Tears* (*ca.* 1611) combines a Marlovian force and energy with a satiric edge that is quite new in Chapman. Here, two stories are run consecutively, exposing the underlying impulses of ladies famous for chastity, and the triumph of Tharsalio (Confidence), both in direct attack and in devious plotting. A soldier, a younger brother, and trickster-in-chief, he first mends his fortune by carrying off the prize of the rich widow of his former master. He opens the play with an invocation to "Confidence" or audacity—"I will perform it in the conqueror's style"—and rushes upon his mistress in the spirit of an expedition to Guiana falling to loot. Repulsed by "this Saturnian peacock," as he terms her, he shrewdly assesses the situation in Freudian terms: "These angry heats that break out at the lips of these strait-laced ladies are but as symptoms of lustful fever that boils within them" (II. iii. 25–27). He bribes a bawd to warn the widow against his extraordinary virility. She has only to threaten him with an ambush against his life to lure him straight to her bedchamber. "This is the way on 't," he tells his brother, "boil their appetites to a full height of lust; and then take them down in the nick" (III. i. 99–100).

The second half of the play dramatizes Petronius' story of the Ephesian matron who, after entombing herself with her husband's corpse, was seduced by a young soldier and not only surrendered on his tomb, but offered her husband's body as substitute for a stolen corpse that the soldier had been sent to guard. Chapman gives a twist to the story by making it only a trick or test of chastity imposed by the disguised husband at the prompting of Tharsalio, his younger brother. Husband and wife have lived in complete harmony hitherto and she has protested undying constancy, as a result of which the husband bequeathed her all his estate. The sexual assumptions of this play issue from Tharsalio's frustrations and dreams of power: it is in his garb as a soldier that the disguised husband comes to the tomb. Tharsalio despises the grief of Cynthia: "To set open a shop of mourning. 'Tis palpable," and her waiting-maid admits "The wonder's over, and 'twas only for that I endured all this." Tharsalio's ostensible motive is partly that he has been mocked by the married pair, partly that he has laid a bet; but the implanting of tortuous doubts in his brother is done in the malicious style of an Iago. Tharsalio's tongue "leaves a slime" on whatever it touches; he greets the collapse of Cynthia's virtue with a jeering song and dance:

> She, she, she and only she
> She only, queen of love and chastity.

This is Dowland's song in praise of that earlier Cynthia, Queen Elizabeth.

The "right perspective" asks that his play be taken as exposing the unnatural role of the perfectly chaste and constant widow. Cynthia learns of the trick that has been played on her, and turns the tables by claiming that she had penetrated her husband's disguise. Her husband had idolized her, because her love and loyalty were so renowned (II. iii. 50–52); she too admits, "The praise I have had I would continue" (IV. iii. 80).

But such outrageous and insulting "tests" can work only if the woman's feelings are expunged, as here, and in Mozart's *Così fan tutte*. The play lacks the usual clutter of minor characters; from the destruction of the false image of Cynthia rises a creature as resourceful as any Chaucerian comic heroine and a worthy match for Tharsalio. All ends with a riotous speech from a totally imbecile "Governor," who is supposedly judging the "murder" of the husband and the "theft" of the corpse. It clashes against the mood of exposure referred to above and explodes the whole play:

I will do justice. If a court favourite write to me in a case of justice, I will pocket his letter and proceed. If a suitor in a case of justice thrusts a bribe into my hand, I will pocket his bribe and proceed . . . Shifters shall cheat and starve, and no man shall do good but where there is no need . . . It shall be the only note of love to the husband to love the wife; and none shall be more kindly welcome to him than he that cuckolds him . . . Fools shall have wealth and the learned shall live by their wits . . . To conclude, I will cart pride out of the town.   (V. iii. 261–320)

Each of Chapman's comedies has its own distinct flavor; the characters, like Ben Jonson's, do not really interact with each other, but fit in with each other to make a general pattern of relationships. The most successful are fools (Florilla, the Gentleman Usher, M. d'Olive) and of these, two are servants who do not know their place: the trickster who stage-manages the "game" turns into Tharsalio, a creation of the period when Chapman's imagination had been engaged in his tragedies of the aspiring man, Bussy or Byron. While in comedy Chapman had gaily reconciled himself with an "absurdist" world, the double aspect of this figure—jester and bravo, underminer and cynic—dislocates and wrenches the play so that it combines the elements of farce and saturnine exposure. The whole effect comes nearer to Jonson's middle comedies *Epicoene* and *The Alchemist* than anything Chapman had done before.

TRAGEDIES

IN TRAGEDY lay Chapman's most lasting achievement; preeminently in *Bussy D'Ambois* (1604), and the double play on Byron (1608). As these aspiring heroes launch into their great speeches, the power of the "mighty line" inherited from Marlowe rises with the force of a climbing rocket. Two plays are enough to put Chapman with Tourneur and Webster—Webster, who saluted Chapman as first among his fellows for his "full and heightened style" ("To the Reader," prefixed to *The White Devil*). *Bussy D'Ambois* enjoyed a long stage success; originally given at St. Paul's, the smallest and most intimate of the London theaters, it was played at Blackfriars with Nat Field, Chapman's "loved son" and a minor playwright, in the lead; later he revived it for the King's Men, and it reappeared on the Restoration stage, with Hart as Bussy.

Chapman's tragic heroes tower up as colossal, filled with divine afflatus, so that they seem to have descended into the world of time and space from some larger world, to which at death they return. Death is their apotheosis. At the very opening of *Bussy D'Ambois*, the grand style of a "secular oratorio" is established:

GEORGE CHAPMAN

Man is a torch borne in the wind; a dream
But of a shadow, summ'd with all his substance
(I. i. 18–19)

Beginning in poverty and obscurity, at the invitation of the king's brother, Monsieur, the noble Bussy comes to court in the splendor of the royal favor and royal costume. Monsieur has arranged this for his own ends; Bussy woos the duchess of Guise with a confidence beyond Tharsalio's, and next challenges three nobles to a duel, from which he emerges sole survivor. The messenger who describes it—for the children's troupes could not put fights on stage—terms it a heroic labor; Guise, a horrid murder. Adopted by the king as "my eagle," Bussy is given the further, Herculean task of cleansing the court from corruption by frank speech, and changes his allegiance to the king's party.

Tamyra, countess of Montsurry, famed for chastity and long vainly wooed by Monsieur, falls in love with Bussy, and with the aid of her confessor secretly summons him to her chamber. Betrayed to Monsieur, and by him to her husband, Bussy finds himself at enmity with both, and with the Guise. The friar by conjuration reveals the plotters, but although Bussy is given the clearest warning by spirits that he himself conjures up, he is trapped and assassinated in Tamyra's chamber; to which, after being tortured, she had summoned him by a letter written in blood and carried by Montsurry, disguised as the friar.

In the early part of the play, Bussy's aspiration relates him to Tamburlaine whose natural will, "lift upwards and divine," raised him to supreme power. But Bussy is placed in a modern court circle, and does not move with the freedom of Marlowe's heroes in their simpler, more archaic worlds. In the latter part of the play Bussy's self-will effects his ruin:

Should not my powers obey when she commands,
My motion must be rebel to my will;
My will to life.   (V. iii. 72–74)

In his essay "Royal Man" Edwin Muir observes that the mark of Chapman is excess:

His tragedies show us one great figure and a crowd of nobodies who destroy him . . . the conflict is be-

tween a man of flesh and blood, larger than life, and puppets of cardboard. Yet in spite of this, the hero's death is real; so that we involuntarily think of it as self-inflicted.

There is no consensus of critical opinion; one critic, Rees, takes Bussy for a ruffian, while another, Lever, sees in him an early champion of the Rights of Man. To the king he represents "man in his native noblesse," man as he was in the Golden Age; Bussy claims the right to "be King myself (as man was made)" and to "do a justice that exceeds the law."

Hercules, born of a god and a mortal woman, but called to godlike labors and eventually raised to divinity through the flames of his funeral pyre, represents the most favorable image of such humanity as Bussy's. But Bussy is not a naturalistic character; in the oceanic imagery that runs through the play, cosmic energy is constantly invoked and harnessed, as if by some act of conjuration. As spirits are raised by spells that invoke the powers latent in the universe, so the great epic similes present Bussy not so much as a man but rather as a great natural force.

His great heart will not down; 'tis like the sea
That partly by his own internal heat,
Partly the stars' daily and nightly motion,
Ardour and light, and partly of the place
The divers frames, but chiefly by the moon
Bristled with surges, never will be won
(No, not when th' hearts of all those powers are
    burst)
To make retreat into his settled home,
Till he be crown'd with his own quiet foam.
(I. ii. 157–165)

So Monsieur at first sees Bussy; later, in the scene where he and Bussy confront each other in insulting terms, heroic man becomes simply a courageous animal, like a wild horse or a tiger; his "cannibal valour" makes him ridiculous, impudent, and embittered, and will eventually lead to crime (III. ii. 423–458). Finally, the plot of Bussy's death being concluded, Monsieur presides over the scene from above, and acts as tragic chorus:

Now shall we see, that Nature hath no end
In her great works responsive to their worths,

That she, who makes so many eyes, and souls
To see and foresee, is stark blind herself.

(V. ii. 1– 4)

For Bussy is ruined by his own greatness, as gunpowder will destroy what it has been stored to protect. If his wrath is compared to a great natural tempest, Tamyra is compared with the treacherous sea, as the unknown forces within her transform her from a court lady to something like an elemental being:

O the unsounded sea of women's bloods,
That when 'tis calmest, 'tis most dangerous,
Not any wrinkle creaming in their faces,
When in their hearts are Scylla and Charybdis. . . .

(III. ii. 296–299)

Tamyra herself is appalled and alienated from what she discovers in herself—the fact that she makes use of the friar is an example of how religion itself may be turned to the service of "blood passion." When he learns of her infidelity her husband feels it as an earthquake or natural convulsion, and when she reveals the role played by the friar, Montsurry is driven to create images of obscenity, as by his physical attacks on her arms and breasts he makes Tamyra an emblem of adultery.

The later acts are filled with images of destruction, as the earlier ones had been with images of energy and natural power. Yet in conjuring up the spirits of darkness, Bussy invokes the powers of light, of the sun itself.

Terror of darkness, O thou king of flames. . . .

(V. iii. 41 ff.)

It was by harnessing cosmic force that the great magicians bound spirits to their will; Bussy himself is often called a "spirit" and a "devil," but in his death speech he once more asserts his will to aspire, and would die standing propped on his sword—a great duelist killed by a gang with a pistol shot.

It is obvious that Bussy is Achillean (as in the sequel, his brother was to resemble the patient Ulysses)[15] but the explicit comparison is with

---

[15] It is in the dedication to the *Odyssey* (1614) that Chapman contrasts Achilles and Ulysses as the active and the Senecal man, showing "the body's perturbation" and "the mind's empire." This contrast is applied by many critics to the plays: Bussy and Byron are Achillean; Clermont, Chabot and Cato, Ulyssean.

---

the dying Hercules of Seneca, who, suffering the torments of the poisoned shirt of Nessus, has himself consumed on a funeral pyre and so is taken up to the gods. The direct quotations from Seneca's *Hercules Oetaeus* include the lines so praised by Eliot:

. . . O my fame,
Live in despite of murther; take thy wings
And haste thee where the grey-eyed morn perfumes
Her rosy chariot with Sabaean spices:
Fly, where the evening from th'Iberian vales
Takes on her swarthy shoulders Hecate,
Crown'd with a grove of oaks; fly where men feel
The burning axletree, and those that suffer
Beneath the chariot of the snowy Bear. . . .

(V. iv. 98–106)

The incarnation of Achilles and Hercules belongs to a different world from that from which Tamyra and Montsurry feel themselves alienated in their final scenes of spectacular torments. Yet at the sight of his mistress' broken body, Bussy himself loses his heroic aspiration; he droops from his proud stance, and the verse droops with him:

O frail condition of strength, valour, virtue,
In me, like warning fire upon the top
Of some steep beacon, on a steeper hill;
Made to express it, like a falling star
Silently glanc'd—that like a thunderbolt
Look'd to have stuck, and shook the firmament

(V. iv. 141–146)

After his death, the epilogue, spoken by the friar's ghost, restores him to his proper sphere:

Farewell, brave relics of a complete man:
Look up, and see thy spirit made a star:
Join flames with Hercules . . .

. . . and th' aged sky
Cheer with new sparks of old humanity

(V. iv. 147–153)

Tamyra and her husband, who had in their passion been compared to volcanoes, are left extinguished; she seeks a desert but not for refuge; like "hunted tigers" she goes in search of her own death. They part their several ways.

It has been said that for Chapman the tragic flaw resided not in individuals but in the social order—meaning, at court. At the level of the intrigue this is true, but at the poetic level of the great natural images, and in the emblematic tableaux where action is arrested to offer an icon—the physical embodiment of a Platonic Idea—Chapman leaves the historical level behind. The paradoxical effort to join these two produces his strange perspectives where history is enlarged into myth. To Chapman's contemporaries, for example, the unknown Bussy would not have been destroyed by "nobodies." During the later years of Elizabeth, Monsieur had been the best-known and best-hated Frenchman in England. Pockmarked, deformed, and deplorably weak in character, he came to woo the queen; Sidney was banished from court, and a pamphlet writer had his right hand cut off, for daring to write against the French marriage. Monsieur had certainly betrayed many other men besides Bussy (whose actual death in 1579 happened during Monsieur's residence at the English court). The duke of Guise, instigator of the massacre of Saint Bartholomew's Day had already appeared on stage as the hero–villain of Marlowe's *Massacre at Paris*. This is as if figures like Marshal Pétain should appear in a play in which the central figure is Monsieur Un Tel, the French Joe Doakes.

Chapman, now himself on the fringes of the court, must have gathered the details of Bussy's death from his cousin Edward Grimeston, the diplomat and historian; for he relied on verbal reports. This was "history" as it was still in the making, waiting for its "form"—as distinct from the more strongly political approach that Jonson was at the same time practicing in *Sejanus*. Chapman greatly admired that play, and may have collaborated on the stage version, but submission to the facts of history would have been unacceptable to him. Thus, while taking his action from events within living memory, he freely modified it; in the sequel, he created for Bussy an entirely fictitious brother and reversed the role of the Guise.

Byron, the hero of Chapman's double tragedy, had been executed only six years before the date when it was written; the co-hero, or antagonist, Henry IV, was still on the throne of France, and the idol of Chapman's master, the martially minded Prince Henry. Chapman relied closely on his cousin Grimeston's *General Inventorie of the History of France* (1607), a translation from Mathieu. He was dealing with a much more famous story than that of the compara-

tively unknown Bussy; Byron had aspired to marry the niece of the emperor and to rule an independent kingdom.

The Conspiracy opens as the Machiavellian duke of Savoy seeks to trap Byron with royal honors. An agent provocateur, La Fin, undermines him; soon he is declaiming as his own the view that in political life virtues are merely imputed to kings, who are in reality no better than superstitious idols; and that "mere politic terms" of love, fame, loyalty are means of curbing by "ignorant conscience" all "the free-born powers of royal man." These views have been implanted in him by the same agent provocateur, whom he proceeds to introduce as a poor unknown—a deserving case—to the very man who had set La Fin on him in the first place.

Having thus been seduced and deluded in Italy, he is sent by the French king on a therapeutic embassy to England. These scenes have been cut by the censor; but enough remains to show how the fate of Essex was used as an example to Byron by the queen. Essex had been executed only a month or two before Byron landed; within a year the marshal of France and trodden the same path as the earl marshal of England; Henry's old comrade in arms had died the same death as Elizabeth's favorite.

Portrayals of the insinuating ways of spies and intelligence agents, of maneuvers for treaties and the control of a key fortress introduce the new world of *realpolitik*. Yet Byron is Achilles; he is Hercules, who has borne the weight of France on his shoulders; he is Ralegh, perhaps; he is Essex. In nothing is Chapman more original than in the manner in which here he combines a direct treatment of contemporary history in contemporary terms with the reflection of other native examples and with the gigantic images of the heroic past.

The sinister masked action of the play is implied in the first confrontation of Byron and the king, who when attacked for "foul ingratitude" as the only thing Byron fears, retorts coolly.

> No? not treason?
> Be circumspect, for to a credulous eye
> He comes invisible, veil'd with flattery,
> And flatterers look like friends, as wolves like dogs
> (III. ii. 243–245)

Byron realizes his vulnerability:

In my late projects I have cast myself
Into the arms of others and will see
If they will let me fall, or toss me up
Into th' affected compass of a throne
(III. iii. 35–36)

So he consults an astrologer who gives him the terrifying truth in the stars—that he is destined for execution. Immediately his blood flares; he cannot accept the truth and attacks the astrologer. Then the man who has been trapped by "intrigues" moves into another world, with his grandiloquent defiance of the stars; we are no longer speaking a political language or inhabiting a political world:

I'll wear those golden spurs upon my heels,
And kick at fate; be free, all worthy spirits
And stretch yourselves for greatness and for height;
Untruss your slaveries; you have height enough
Beneath this steep heaven to use all your reaches;
'Tis too far off to let you, or respect you
(III. iii. 129–134)

The magnificence of the challenge rises in a great image that surely brings to mind Ralegh, lying in the Tower under sentence of death, rather than Essex.

Give me a spirit that on this life's rough sea
Loves t' have his sails filled with a lusty wind,
Even till his sail yards tremble, his masts crack,
And his rapt ship runs on her side so low
That she drinks water, and her keel ploughs air.
There is no danger to a man that knows
What life and death is; there's not any law
Exceeds his knowledge; neither is it lawful
That he should stoop to any other law.
(III. iii. 135–143)

In the second play, we do not meet Byron's unfolding character but his situation, what Yeats would term "the body of fate."

Byron has simply lapsed; he sees himself as an old soldier put out of service by the peace he has won for France at the cost of thirty-five wounds; France is his and he will ruin her to re-create her.

We must reform and have a new creation
Of State and government, and on our Chaos
Will I sit brooding up another world.
(*Tragedy of Byron*, I. ii. 29–31)

Suddenly La Fin enters with the king; the agent provocateur has handed over all the papers that Byron had just told him to burn, and turned king's evidence. By the end of the first act we know that Byron is trapped. Again the censor has imposed cuts, following the protests of the French ambassador at the court of James—these were false images of reconciliation between the king's mistress and the queen, after a quarrel scene in which Marie de Medici was shown boxing the favorite's ears.

Byron leaves court, but after rejecting a summons from the king he returns, in complete credulity relying on the word of La Fin. Here Henry makes a last appeal for confession; Byron meets it with a last blank denial of any treason. The king, like his good angel, leaves him. The guard enter; one curt word marks his fall:

Resign your sword, my lord, the king commands it.
(IV. ii. 229)

From now onward his personality is gradually stripped of all superficies, in preparation for death. His shame is stressed at the end of this scene by a degrading simile:

Farewell for ever! so have I discern'd
An exhalation that would be a star
Fall, when the sun forsook it, in a sink.
(IV. ii. 291–293)

The long final act gradually separates out the strands of Byron's very being. At the trial, confronted by La Fin, he claims to have been bewitched by his betrayer; the judges object that witchcraft has no power to enforce the choice of a free soul. In spite of very lengthy pleas, which he thinks irresistible, and in spite of recognition that his crime springs from the negative aspect of the *virtú* that saved France, sentence is pronounced on him.

O of what contraries consists a man
Of what impossible mixtures; vice and virtue,
Corruption and eternesse at one time,
And in one subject, let together loose.
We have not any strength but weaken us,
No greatness but doth crush us into air,
Our knowledges do light us but to err,
Our ornaments are burthens, our delights
Are our tormentors. . . .   (V. iii. 189–197)

GEORGE CHAPMAN

Rage leads to a kind of metamorphosis; Byron dashes himself like a captive bird against its cage. Foaming like a wild boar at bay, he terrifies the executioner

I'll break my blood's high billows 'gainst my stars
(V. iv. 20)

recalls his defiance in the astronomer's house; but then he begins to crumble, sees the body as "a slave bound face to face to death till death." The fire in the blood dwindles as the sentence is read, his honors are stripped, and he kneels with the most eloquent death speech of the Jacobean stage. All the freedom that remains is that he should himself give the order to his headsman; and like a soldier, he does so.

Il dit au bourreau, *boute, boute, hé boute.*[16] C'était mourir en commandant et commander en mourant.

So the French historian.

Chapman gives him a speech of despair until the final lines; Byron still thinks of the earth, the seasons that will return and that he will not see; but in a sudden triumphal lifting of spirit, his soul rouses itself "like a falcon," and stretching "its silver wings" turns the separation of soul and body into a conquest.

The first acts of *Byron's Conspiracy,* the last acts of *Byron's Tragedy* magnificently unfold the hero's character and his fate. However, the speeches run to lengths that the modern theater would find and probably the Jacobean did find intolerable; Byron's speech of defense extends to 135 lines. Henry prays at length for peace with terrifying recollections of the havoc of war (*Tragedy,* I. i. 111–149). In this contest of virtue and fortune, the king is contrasted with Byron as the upright man (for this contrast Chapman drew heavily on Plutarch's *Life of Alexander*). Yet different levels of the play are allowed to operate distinctly; thus, as Peter Ure observed,[17] the ending is neither a display of sympathy for Byron's willful corruption of his virtues, nor a denial of the political moral of the play, as represented in the relations of Byron, the king, and La Fin. It is merely an admission that although fallen, Byron is still a complete

[16] "Strike, strike, O strike."
[17] See *Elizabethan and Jacobean Drama,* p. 143.

man, as Chapman and not as Machiavelli analyzed men.

He had seen at the beginning where the path might lead,

O 'tis a dangerous and a dreadful thing . . .
To trust our blood in others' veins and hang
'Twixt heaven and earth in vapours of their breaths
(*Conspiracy of Byron,* I. ii. 137–140)

a judgment that is not unfit to stand beside the statecraft of Bacon. "The greatest trust between man and man is the giving of counsel; for in other confidences men commit the parts of life . . . but to such as they make counsellors, they commit the whole."

Four years later the sententious *Revenge of Bussy D'Ambois* followed, giving the perfect Stoic hero a frame of moral observations. This play and its increasingly doctrinal successors have enticed critics to build symmetrical patterns out of Chapman's work, regardless of the varying quality and of the fact that these structures could not have been there at the beginning (Bussy and Byron, the types of Achilles, of the active life, of outer empire, are contrasted with Clermont D'Ambois, Chabot, Cato, types of Ulysses, of the mind's empire, of fortitude). But when he wrote *Bussy D'Ambois,* Chapman had barely started on *The Iliad*; the late plays exist only in revised forms.

The Revenge of Bussy D'Ambois centers on the imaginary brother of Bussy, and in the dedication Chapman protests that "the subject is not truth but things like truth." Therefore the "actual" history is not treated as "real" history. Clermont is the devoted servant and follower of the Guise, who had contrived Bussy's death, and in defense of his master Clermont, the admirable Stoic, justifies the massacre of Saint Bartholomew's Day. This again is not the metamorphosis of a nobody; everyone knew the reputation of the Guise. The actual name of the massacre is never actually used; its associations were too dreadful. In the final Dance of Death the figure of Admiral Coligny (killed in the same holocaust) appears, being otherwise unexplained.

Clermont is first of all a scholar, and given perhaps to paradox. Thus in one of the comedies, to quote a parallel, a scholar gives a defense of women's painting, usually considered a diabolic practice. For him the relation of master and servant takes precedence over his attachment to his mistress; a friendship "chaste and masculine" seems rather improbable at the corrupt court of the Valois, Henry III. In Clermont "the mind's empire," issuing in perfect self-control, makes the play almost devoid of action. His notion of a just revenge is to issue a challenge to Montsurry, which is not accepted. The central part of the play is given to a display of Clermont's valor, when he is taken in a treacherous ambush laid by the king; he "turn'd wild lightning in the lackeys' hands," proving that his resistance to taunts and outrage is not cowardice but mastery of his "blood." His sister, on the other hand, dresses herself in masculine attire in order to exact the vengeance that she feels due to Bussy.

The Guise speedily procures Clermont's release, but as speedily the king decides to assassinate the too-powerful subject; he falls, not without alarming warning of bloodshed to come, and a prophecy of the king's own assassination.

> that will make you feel
> How little safety lies in treacherous steel
> (V. iv. 59–60)

Clermont, having at last dispatched Montsurry in fair fight, commits suicide in order to rejoin the Guise; his death speech is almost a parody of Byron's self-stripping. As the archpreacher, Clermont before his death had indulged in many orations, and many virtuous digressions for edification: he recalls how the statues of Demedes were melted into chamber pots, how Homer made Achilles passionate to preach the necessity of restraint, or what the earl of Oxford said to Duke Casimir. Some of these set speeches are put into couplets to give added emphasis. His most famous self-definition and apology comes at the moment when he submits to the treachery of the ambush:

> . . . In this one thing, all the discipline
> Of manners and of manhood is contain'd;
> A man to join himself with the Universe,
> In his main sway, and make (in all things fit)
> One with that All, and go on, round as it . . .
> (IV. i. 137–141)

As a "refutation" of the very popular form of the revenge play, the whole structure of Chapman's play is as paradoxical as the detail; the idea is copied in Tourneur's *Atheist's Tragedy*, whose youthful hero, Charlemont, often speaks in the accents of Chapman, and whose motto is that "Patience is the honest man's revenge"—in which he is instructed by his father's ghost. A later hero, Charlerois of Massinger's *The Fatal Dowry* (1619), owes something to both models: these young men are Frenchmen, soldiers, and scholars, who can rouse even a cowardly enemy to valor, as Clermont in the end rouses Montsurry.

The Revenge of Bussy D'Ambois was begotten by despair upon impossibility. The need to preserve perfect calm in the face of betrayal, the need to give and exchange perfect devotion with a master, the blind and perpetually weeping lady offering her casket of treasure—these represent clamorous needs of Chapman's inner man, projected under a shell or carapace of "doctrine." It is a tragic confession if read between the lines—and the final need is the need for suicide.

Chapman's later tragedies, *Chabot, Admiral of France* and *Caesar and Pompey*, continue that "material instruction, elegant and sententious excitation to virtue and deflection from her contrary" that the dedication to *The Revenge of Bussy D'Ambois* had defined as the "soul, limbs and limits of an authentical tragedy." Both depict Stoics who face unjust condemnation; both are further removed from the living theater; both were specifically dedicated to victims of the political intrigues at the court of James; since both Somerset and Lionel Cranfield, earl of Middlesex, had been ruined by the king's favorite, the duke of Buckingham, the plays could have been dangerous to the author if this application had been made.

Chabot, the innocent servant accused of treachery by his king, refuses a pardon because to take it would be an admission of guilt, but dies of a broken heart; he has long been seen as an image of consolation for the earl of Somerset. The tragedy was not published until after Chapman's death, when it had been revised by James Shirley. *Caesar and Pompey* was said to have been "written long since but never to have touched the stage," when it was published in 1631 with a dedication to the earl of Middlesex.

Middlesex, born a citizen of London, who became a member of the Mercers' Company, was the ablest finance minister that James ever had. He succeeded in restoring the royal fortunes to some degree of solvency, and as lord treasurer became one of the two most powerful men in the government in the later years of King James.[18] But he antagonized Buckingham by opposing the war with Spain which, by 1624, Buckingham wanted, and the all-powerful favorite secured his impeachment and total political ruin. Chapman may well have felt that the fate of Cranfield mirrored yet once again that strife of fortune and virtue that had been the main subject of his tragedy, when he revised for publication a play in which there is no dialogue, only a series of public speeches; no slightest crack in the fortitude of the defeated Pompey and his wife; no lapse from the respect that greets Cato's lengthy sermons. Pompey assures his wife he treads the low earth as he trod on Caesar; Cato justifies suicide by the resurrection of the body (a most un-Stoic doctrine). The text for the whole is "Only a just man is a free man." The portrait of Caesar, young, confident, always superlatively lucky, might well be said to fit Buckingham; by 1631 Buckingham, fortunately for nearly everyone else, had met a violent death, at the hands of a desperate sailor.

This play does not show Chapman unpacking his heart so much as providing a set Consolation—almost as formal as a wedding masque—for the greatest fallen minister of the realm. There is one feature of *Caesar and Pompey* from which commentators shrink. A messenger enters at the beginning of act 2 to report the beginning of civil war. He has, however, been anticipated by an antimasque from an Elizabethan clown, Fronto, and a medieval devil, Ophioneus, clad in the old players' dress of skin, with speckled throat, and the face, wings, and tail of a dragon. The theatrical backchat of these two, about whether to commit suicide or go to hell some other and more exciting way, parodies Cato, and all the ensuing solemnity. The spirit of Kit Marlowe had evidently yet once

again returned maliciously to prompt his venerable friend, now a septuagenarian, with a scene out of the comic part of *Dr. Faustus*. Perhaps Cranfield, who was a London citizen and frequenter of plays, was amused at this false nose clapped on to the noble Roman pathos of the Dying Gladiator. It "explodes" the whole tragedy; what Ben Jonson would have written in the margin passes conjecture.

All Chapman's tragedies proclaim the emancipation of man from fortune's tyranny—his freedom even in the face of what is written into the stars, exerting on him the force of the whole universe. From the time of the great Italian humanists, man's freedom to make and unmake himself had challenged traditional submission to all sorts of authority, from Aristotle's to the pope's. Pico della Mirandola, *On the Dignity of Man*, appeared a hundred years before Chapman; in England, Marlowe had issued the challenge in dramatic form, with *Tamburlaine* and *Dr. Faustus*. In bringing this doctrine to the test of contemporary political history, Chapman aligns himself with the future, for in England during the seventeenth century the challenge was formulated in political terms. Inevitably, such a theme produced monodramas, with one great role; and so, Chapman has not regained a position in the living theater. Indeed, his later tragedies, where the doctrine is set out more philosophically, are closet plays, in the style of Fulke Greville, whose phrase he might well have adopted: "I know the world—and believe in God."

While the earlier plays keep reasonably close to history, the later ones make bold with facts, to the extent of showing the death of a man who was still alive; and this Chapman justifies on the grounds of edification in the dedication to *The Revenge of Bussy D'Ambois*.

CONCLUSION

TODAY Chapman's reputation rests on his finest lyrical poems and his two great tragedies. The minor works serve to illuminate the major poetry. He was not a craftsman in the same sense as Jonson, but the world of books was the world he inhabited. He appropriated the work of other

[18] See R. H. Tawney's *Business and Politics under James I: Lionel Cranfield as Merchant and Minister* (1958).

GEORGE CHAPMAN

poets in ways that almost prompt a comparison with Eliot, Pound, or Joyce—"Bad poets imitate; good poets steal." He would parody Spenser's funeral eclogue or Dowland's song; he wrote funeral poems—and a parody of a funeral oration. In poetry, although not presumably in life, he was prepared to defend Philip II of Spain, or the massacre of Saint Bartholomew's Day, for his interests remained political and international. He learned from fellow poets, Marlowe, Shakespeare, and Jonson in particular, but grafted new skills on his early training. He formulated his critical views in dedications and apologia, in a fashion very rare in England.

The bluff countenance, venerable but hearty, that appears in his portraits suggests the soldier. One meets such faces at Aldershot. His city friends spoke of him as "a pleasant witty fellow." His bawdy is infrequent, primitive, direct; if his comedies gaily accept an "absurdist" view of the world, his tragedies are based upon disjunctions at a variety of levels, from the cosmic to the stylist's.

His lyric poetry more often engages with the polarities of soldier and philosopher, action and contemplation, body and soul, fortune and virtue. Finally, as destiny and choice, he found a role in the ennobling of the language by translation as a form of public service; the Authorized Version of the Bible was being prepared as he labored at Homer, whom he probably thought of as second only to Holy Writ. Alas for the result; as Dr. Johnson said of women's preaching, it is not well done, but you are surprised to find it done at all.

If Chapman attained neither the intellectual stature of Donne nor the craftsmanship of Jonson, yet his character was solid English oak. He seems in later life to have taken upon himself the championship of fallen greatness and unpopular causes—nor did he lack a comforting conviction of his own oppressed worth. When imprisoned for his share in *Eastward Ho!*, he wrote to the lord chamberlain that the king's wrath is to his "most humble and zealous affection . . . so much the more stormy, by how much some of my obscure labours have strived to aspire instead of his illustre favour; and shall not be the least honour to his most Royal virtues." This, observes one critic, sounds almost too like Chapman to be true!

Disgraced once more for bringing the French queen and the king's mistress onstage, he appealed with equal intransigence. Yet again, when his poem in defense of the earl of Somerset and Lady Frances incensed all parties, he promptly published *A Free and Offenceless Justification of a Lately Published and Most Maliciously Misinterpreted Poem Entitled "Andromeda Liberata."* "Whilst I slept in my innocency, the envious man hath been here," he proclaimed, proposing to defend himself "from the better sort by a clear conscience and from the baser, by an eternal contempt."

A set of verses, *To Live with Little*, translated from his favorite Stoic, Epictetus, opens bravely, if inconsistently:

When thou seest any honour'd by the king,
Oppose thou this, thou thirsts for no such thing
(*Poems*, p. 243)

If "only within, thy help or ruin lies" there is hope, for "nought is so pliant as the human mind."

His achievement lay in the complex refracted rendering of that pliancy; the cloudy glowing visions that placed man in his cosmic setting, not in an intellectual system, but rather as a "dying animal" who, when his heart is "consumed away" may be gathered "into the artifice of eternity."[19]

An Elizabethan, writing in Jacobean times, he shows the temperament of the earlier writers, especially Marlowe, with whom his ties were closest, in attempting to face an age of growing internal tension, where his concern with political problems anticipated future conflicts. He spans the whole of this great period, and engages in a wide variety of literary work, so that he becomes a representative of tradition and a register of social change.

SELECTED BIBLIOGRAPHY

COLLECTED EDITIONS. *Chapman's Works,* 3 vols.: I, "The Plays," ed. with notes by R. H. Shepherd, II, "Poems and Minor Translations," with an essay by A. C. Swinburne, III, "Translations of the *Iliad* and *Odyssey*" (London, 1874–1875), this ed. is the only one to include all the works, textually it is not to be

[19] From W. B. Yeats, *Sailing to Byzantium.*

relied on; T. M. Parrott, ed., *The Tragedies of George Chapman* (London, 1910); T. M. Parrott, ed., *The Comedies of George Chapman* (London, 1914), the third vol. (Poems) did not appear, modernized text with full notes and intros., a very sound piece of work, the standard ed.; A. Holaday, *et al.*, eds., *The Comedies of George Chapman* (Urbana, Ill.–Chicago–London, 1970), the first of a projected series of vols., plays are individually edited with full textual variants, no general critical apparatus, old spelling; P. B. Bartlett, ed., *The Poems of George Chapman*, Modern Language Association of America (New York–Oxford, 1941), an old spelling text, with notes and intro., the standard ed.; A. Nicoll, ed., *Chapman's Homer*, 2 vols., Bollingen Series 41 (Princeton, 1956), a handsome ed., old spelling text, minimum annotation.

PLAYS. *The Blind Beggar of Alexandria* (1598), W. W. Greg, ed., Malone Society Reprints (London, 1928); *A Humourous Day's Mirth* (1599), W. W. Greg and D. N. Smith, eds., Malone Society Reprints (London, 1938); *Eastward Ho, made by Geo. Chapman, Ben Jonson, John Marston* (1605), appears in Parrott, in many eds. of Jonson's *Works* (Herford and Simpson, eds., Oxford, 1925–1952), in Marston's *Works* (H. Harvey Wood, ed., Edinburgh, 1934–1939), in Gayley, *Representative British Comedies*, vol. II (New York, 1903–1914), edited by J. W. Cunliffe, in J. H. Harris, ed. (New Haven, 1926), in C. F. T. Brooke and N. Paradise, eds., *Elizabethan Drama 1570–1642* (New Haven, 1930); *All Fools* (1605), repr. in Robert Dodsley's *Old English Plays*, 2nd ed., vol. IV (London, 1780), edited by Isaac Reed, 3rd ed., vol. IV (London, 1825), edited by John Payne Collier, W. N. Phelps, ed. (London, 1895), T. M. Parrott, ed. (Boston, 1907), F. Manley, ed., Regent's Renaissance Drama Series (London, 1968); *Monsieur d'Olive* (1606), repr. in C. W. Dilke, ed., *Old English Plays*, vol. III (London, 1814); *The Gentleman Usher* (1606), T. M. Parrott, ed. (Boston, 1907), J. H. Smith, ed., Regent's Renaissance Drama Series (London, 1970); *Bussy D'Ambois* (1607), repr. in 1608, 1641 (being much corrected and amended by the author before his death), 1646, 1657, C. W. Dilke, ed., *Old English Plays*, vol. III (London, 1814), F. S. Boas, ed. (Boston, 1905), A. Neilson, *Chief Elizabethan Dramatists* (London, 1911), Brooke and Paradise, Russell A. Fraser and N. Rabkin, *Drama of the English Renaissance*, vol. II (New York, 1976), also appears in modern English collectionism for which see *The Cambridge Bibliography of English Literature*, the most important single eds. are J. Jacquot (Paris, 1960), N. Brooke, Revels Plays Series (London, 1964), New Mermaids Series (London, 1965); *The Conspiracy and Tragedy of Charles, Duke of Byron, Marshal of France* (1608), W. N. Phelps, ed. (London, 1895); *May Day* (1611), repr. in C. W. Dilke, ed., *Old English Plays*, vol. IV (London, 1814); *The*

Widow's Tears (1612), repr. in Dodsley's *Old English Plays*, vol. VI (London, 1744; repr., 1780, 1825), Fraser and Rabkin, Revels Plays Series, vol. II (London, 1975), edited by A. Yamada, E. M. Smeak, ed., Regent's Renaissance Drama Series (London, 1967); *The Revenge of Bussy D'Ambois* (1613), F. S. Boas, ed. (Boston, 1905), repr., Scolar Press (London, 1968); *The Wars of Caesar and Pompey* (1631); *The Tragedy of Chabot, Admiral of France, written by George Chapman and James Shirley* (1639), apparently a revision by Shirley of a play written by Chapman *ca.* 1613, Ezra Lehman, ed. (Phila., 1916), with an intro. of tragedies drawn from French history.

DOUBTFUL PLAYS. *Sir Giles Goosecap.* Repr. in T. M. Parrott, ed., *Comedies* (London, 1914).

MASQUES. *The Memorable Masque of the Two Honourable Houses or Inns of Courts; The Middle Temple and Lincoln's Inn . . . Invented and fashioned with the ground and special structure of the whole work; by our kingdom's most artful and ingenious architect Inigo Jones. Supplied, applied, digested and written by George Chapman* (1613), repr. in J. Nichols, ed., *Progresses of James I*, vol. II (London, 1828).

TRANSLATIONS OF HOMER. *Seven Books of the Iliads of Homer. Prince of Poets* (1598), contains books I, II, VII–XI; *Achilles Shield* (1598), translated as the other seven books of Homer, out of his eighteenth book of Iliads; *Homer Prince of Poets, Translated according to the Greek in Twelve Books of His Iliads* (1610?, reiss., 1611), reprints the seven books of 1598 and adds books III–VI and XII; *The Iliads of Homer, Prince of Poets* (1611), R. Hooper, ed., 2 vols. (London, 1857), H. Morley, ed. (London, 1883), adds books XIII–XXIV and substitutes new versions of book I and part of II; *Homer's Odysseys* (1614?), contains books 1–XII; *Twenty-four Books of Homer's Odysseys* (1615?), R. Hooper, ed., 2 vols. (London, 1857; repr., 2 vols., 1897), adds books XIII–XXIV to a reissue of the previous item; *The Whole Works of Homer, Prince of Poets, in His Iliads and Odysseys* (1616), reissues of the eds. of 1611 and 1615? (repr., 1904; 2 vols., Oxford, 1930); *The Crown of All Homer's Works, Batrachomyomachia, or the Battle of Frogs and Mice. His Hymns and Epigrams* (1629[?]; repr., 1818), R. Hooper, ed. (London, 1858).

TRANSLATIONS OF OTHER WRITINGS. *Petrarch's Seven Penitential Psalms . . . with Other Philosophical Poems and a Hymn to Christ upon the Cross* (1612); *The Divine Poem of Musaeus: First of All Books Translated according to the Original* (1616), E. S. Donno, ed., Elizabethan Minor Epics Series (London, 1963); *The Georgics of Hesiod Translated Elaborately out of the Greek* (1618; repr., Amsterdam, 1971); *A Justification of a Strange Action of Nero . . . also a Just Reproof of a Roman Smell Feast, being the Fifth Satire of Juvenal Translated* (1629).

POEMS. *The Shadow of Night: Containing Two Poetical Hymns* (1594), repr. in A. Acheson, *Shakespeare and the Rival Poet* (London, 1903); *Ovid's Banquet of Sense. A Coronet for His Mistress Philosophy and His Amorous Zodiac* (1595), repr. in Acheson, the Scholar Press (London, 1970), E. S. Donno, ed., Elizabethan Minor Epics Series (London, 1963), the first poem only, in N. Alexander, ed., *Elizabethan Narrative Verse*, Stratford-upon-Avon Library Series, no. 3 (London, 1967), the first poem only; *Hero and Leander, Begun by Christopher Marlowe and Finished by George Chapman* (1958), repr. in both Chapman's and Marlowe's *Poems* in modern eds., e.g., Marlowe, L. C. Martin, ed. (London, 1931), Chapman, N. Alexander, ed. (London, 1967); *Euthymia Raptus: or the Tears of Peace* (1609), repr. in Acheson; *An Epicede or Funeral Song on the Death of Henry Prince of Wales* (1612), S. E. Brydges (London, 1818); *Andromeda Liberata, or the Nuptials of Perseus and Andromeda* (1614); *A Free and Offenceless Justification of a Lately Published and Most Maliciously Misinterpreted Poem: Entitled Andromeda Liberata* (1614); *Eugenia: or True Nobility's Trance, for the Death of the Thrice Noble and Religious: William, Lord Russell* (1614); *Pro Vere, Autumni Lachrymae. Inscribed to the Immortal Memory of the Pious and Incomparable Soldier, Sir Horatio Vere, Knight: Besieged and Distrest in Mannheim* (1622).

SOME BIOGRAPHICAL AND CRITICAL STUDIES. Janet Spens, "Chapman's Ethical Thought," in *Essays and Studies of the English Association*, XI (London, 1925), a pioneer study; F. L. Schoell, *Études sur l'humanisme continentale en Angleterre à la fin de la renaissance* (Paris, 1926), the first book to establish Chapman's borrowings from classical and modern authors and his "notebook" method of composition; T. S. Eliot, *Selected Essays* (London, 1932), contains the essays "Four Elizabethan Dramatists" and "Shakespeare and the Stoicism of Seneca," both influential in modern readings of the plays; George Chapman by James Smith: in "Revaluations" VII, *Scrutiny*, nos. 3 and 4 (London, 1935), deals mainly with "Bussy D'Ambois"; Hardin Craig, "Ethics in the Jacobean Drama: The Case of Chapman," in *Essays in Dramatic Literature; the Parrott Presentation Volume* (Princeton, 1935); Una Ellis Fermor, *The Jacobean Drama* (London, 1936), contains a chapter on Chapman; J. M. Higgins, "The Development of the Senecan Man: Chapman's Bussy D'Ambois and some precursors," in *Review of English Studies*, XXIII (London, 1947); J. M. Weiler, *George Chapman. The Effects of Stoicism upon His Tragedies* (New York, 1949), a useful work; E. Muir, *Essays on Literature and Society* (London, 1949), contains the essay on Chapman's tragedies, "Royal Man," one of the most penetrating brief studies; J. Jacquot, *George Chapman. Sa vie, sa poésie, son théâtre, sa pensée* (Paris, 1951), a fully documented and authoritative study, the standard work, with full bibliography; C. S. Lewis, "Hero and Leander," in *Proceedings of the British Academy*, XXXVIII (Oxford, 1952), the British Academy Warton Lecture for 1952; K. M. Burton, "The Political Tragedies of George Chapman and Ben Jonson," in *Essays in Criticism*, II, 4 (London, 1952); E. Rees, *The Tragedies of George Chapman* (Cambridge, Mass., 1954), initiates the highly moralistic approach in America, has been much disputed; R. Ornstein, *The Moral Vision of Jacobean Tragedy* (Madison, Wisc., 1960); I. Ribner, *Jacobean Tragedy* (London, 1962), contains a chapter dealing with "The Tragedy of Chabot" and Chapman's pessimism; E. M. Waith, *The Herculean Hero in Marlowe, Chapman, Shakespeare and Dryden* (London, 1962), a sensitive placing of Chapman in the tradition of "labouring Hercules"; M. McLure, *George Chapman, A Critical Study* (Toronto, 1966), a full study of the works and thought, very well supported, the best study in English; G. R. Hibbard, "George Chapman; Tragedy and the Providential View of History," in *Shakespeare Survey*, XX (London, 1967); J. Jacquot, "Bussy D'Ambois and Chapman in the tradition of "labouring Hercules"; M. McLure, *George Chapman, A Critical Study* (Toronto, wood Cliffs, N.J., 1970); J. F. Kermode, *Renaissance Essays* (London, 1971), contains a reprint of his lecture "Ovid's Banquet of Sense" originally in *John Rylands Library Bulletin*; J. W. Lever, *The Tragedy of State* (London, 1971), contains an essay on the Bussy plays, political tragedy in other Jacobean dramatists is also included; R. B. Waddington, *The Mind's Empire. Myth and Form in George Chapman's Narrative Poems* (Baltimore–London, 1974); R. Beament, *The Tragedies of George Chapman* (Salzburg, 1974), mainly on the background of thought; P. Ure, *Elizabethan and Jacobean Drama* (London, 1974), edited by J. C. Maxwell, a posthumous vol. containing four important essays on tragedies and comedies of Chapman.

FRANCIS BACON

(1561-1626)

Brian Vickers

For my name and memory, I leave it to men's charitable speeches, and to foreign nations, and the next ages. (Bacon's Will, XIV, 539)*

Francis Bacon, the glory of his age and nation, the adorner and ornament of learning, was born in York House, or York Place, in the Strand, on the two and twentieth day of January, in the year of our Lord 1561. His father was that famous counsellor to Queen Elizabeth, the second prop of the kingdom in his time, Sir Nicholas Bacon, knight, lord-keeper of the great seal of England; a lord of known prudence, sufficiency, moderation, and integrity. His mother was Anne, one of the daughters of Sir Anthony Cooke (unto whom the erudition of King Edward the Sixth had been committed); a choice lady, and eminent for piety, virtue, and learning; being exquisitely skilled, for a woman, in the Greek and Latin tongues. These being the parents, you may easily imagine what the issue was like to be; having had whatsoever nature or breeding could put into him. [I, 3]

So begins the first biography of Bacon, written in 1657 by William Rawley, his chaplain and editor of various posthumously published works. It is a good beginning, to the life as to the biography, yet the privileges of birth and place did not work out as gloriously as they promised. Educated at first at home (and evidently exceptionally well), Bacon went up to Trinity College, Cambridge, in April 1573, where he was under the special care of the master, John Whitgift, subsequently archbishop of Canterbury. Due to an outbreak of the plague Bacon had been in residence for only thirty-two months when he went down at Christmas 1575, just before his fifteenth birthday, but he had seen enough of the academic curriculum, he told

* All references are to James Spedding *et al., The Works of Francis Bacon*, 14 vols. (London, 1857–1874; repr. New York, 1968).

Rawley later, to conceive a strong dislike for Aristotle and his philosophy. After university, the next step in the training for a public career was to go to one of the Inns of Court, and Bacon was duly admitted to Gray's Inn in June 1576. But a better opportunity of gaining political experience arose, and in September he was sent by his father, the second most important statesman in England, to serve with Sir Amias Paulet, as ambassador to France. Bacon stayed in Paris from 1576 to 1579, presumably studying statecraft and performing routine diplomatic duties. The first setback to Bacon's career occurred on February 22, 1579, with the death of his father. Bacon was the second son of a second marriage, and thus the youngest of six sons. Nicholas Bacon had settled estates on the first five and was in the course of doing so for his youngest when he died. With no position, no land, and no income, Bacon returned to England and took up the law as a profession, advancing with remarkable speed, graduating in 1582, becoming bencher in 1586, reader (a lecturer entrusted with expounding the law) in 1588, and double reader in 1600, an extraordinary honor for one so young. At the same time he began a career in Parliament in 1584, as member for Melcombe Regis in Dorsetshire, and he was to sit in every Parliament from then until his disgrace in 1621. While Bacon is celebrated today as a writer and a scientist, we should not forget that for the main part of his life he was constantly occupied with the law (he lived in Gray's Inn and played a full part in its activities) and with public affairs at a high level. As the *Select Bibliography* shows, legal and political works came from his pen without interruption throughout this period. (If all his occasional works, and his many speeches in the House of Commons and [after 1618] the House of Lords were included,

257

the list would be twice as long. As it is, it comprises over seventy works, major and minor, of which fewer than twenty were published in his lifetime.)

Bacon's scientific, philosophical, and literary works were the product of his spare time—evenings, weekends, above all the vacations from the law terms—or when Parliament was not sitting. He was never a full-time philosopher or scientist, and while this fact makes his achievements the more remarkable, it also accounts for the frequently amateur nature of his work in these fields. He seems never to have had any contact with a major scientist or group of scientists, even though research groups of an ad hoc kind existed in London in the early seventeenth century, and some forms of public experiment were carried out at Gresham College. Bacon as a scientist was completely isolated, reading what books he could find, and at times employing a small army of scribes to make notes from them.

As a lawyer, parliamentarian, and politician Bacon was an expert in several fields, not surprisingly, perhaps, given his enormous industry and his family background. Bacon's father served both Henry VIII and Queen Elizabeth, who made him a knight, a privy councillor, and lord keeper of the great seal; his uncle, Sir William Cecil, later Lord Burghley, was the most powerful politician in England for many years. Through both sides of the family, Bacon was connected with influential figures in Tudor humanism (Sir John Cheke, Roger Ascham) and with many others who put their great learning to the service of the state as teachers and counselors. The ideology of the *vita activa*, the dedication of one's energies "pro bono publico," runs all the way through Bacon's career, with his strenuous pursuit of knowledge "for the glory of the Creator and the relief of man's estate" (III, 294). Yet in his life we also see the fundamental uncertainties of such a career. The theorists urged all able men to go to the court and serve the monarch, but neither Queen Elizabeth nor James I took much notice of their counselors. The political courtier was doomed to years of writing notes of advice, which the monarch might not even read, and to the practice of the baser arts of ingratiation and flattery. Many of Bacon's letters reveal the un-

avoidable but ignoble, and at times pathetic, attempt to catch the eye of people in power; and in those addressed to James I's favorite George Villiers, duke of Buckingham, it is impossible not to feel that Bacon is wasting his abilities on a man in every way his inferior. "The rising unto place is laborious," he wrote in one of his *Essays*, "and by pains men come to greater pains; and it is sometimes base; and by indignities men come to dignities" (VI, 399f.).

It was in his parliamentary career that Bacon suffered his second great setback. The queen may have ignored advice, but she certainly did not ignore criticism. In the Parliament of 1593 Bacon opposed what seemed to him, and to other members, an excessive tax raised over too short a period. The vote went against Bacon, the queen was furious, denying him access and reducing him to an abject suitor (VIII, 214–241). This piece of plain speaking cost him his hopes of advancement to the leading legal offices, attorney general and solicitor general; and his lifelong rival Sir Edward Coke moved up the ladder in front of him. Yet the queen employed Bacon in subordinate legal offices and accepted some of his writings that expounded or defended the government position. In the 1580's and 1590's Bacon had become attached to the earl of Essex, advising his patron on several political issues, and writing letters and speeches on his behalf. Bacon's advice was always sensible, yet it had little effect on Essex, who pursued a violent course and finally attempted to raise a rebellion against the crown. Easily defeated, he was formally prosecuted, and ironically enough, after years of neglect the queen made use of Bacon for the prosecution and in writing the official account (IX, 247–321). The affair inevitably damaged his reputation and led him to publish a self-defense (X, 139–160). While some critics will always regret that Bacon put his loyalty to England before his loyalty to his friend, they should also consider what the rule of Essex would have represented.

Under James I, Bacon's merits were recognized more quickly. Knighted in 1603, he became king's counsel in 1604, solicitor general in 1607, attorney general in 1613, a privy councillor in 1616, lord keeper in 1617, and lord chancellor in 1618. Having more than emulated his father in public office, he excelled him in rank, being elevated to the House of Lords as baron Verulam in 1618 and created viscount St. Albans in 1621. Although the promotion was remarkable, it was well earned, for Bacon was celebrated by his contemporaries for his forensic skills, his memory of cases and procedure, and his capacity to grasp all the complexities of the issue at stake. He was particularly in demand as a reporter of complicated parliamentary proceedings, where his clear thinking showed at its best. As the leading legal officer he took part in many state prosecutions for treason, including, alas, that of Sir Walter Ralegh (XIII, 379ff.), and he played a major part in the trials following the murder in 1613 of Sir Thomas Overbury. As one reads through the five volumes of Spedding's monumental *Letters and Life* devoted to this period, it is clear that Bacon was always in the thick of the most important public business. Yet he was still only a tool of James I, and the image that comes across is, rather like T. S. Eliot's Prufrock, of one "Deferential, glad to be of use": conscientious, yet always following the policies of others.

In only two areas could Bacon lead an independent existence. One was as a scientist, and even though the pressure of public work between 1612 and 1620 almost extinguished his scientific activities, the period between 1603 and 1610 had been tremendously productive, and he had assembled enough material and developed his ideas sufficiently to publish the beginnings of his *Great Instauration* in 1620. But even here the first part, he announced, was not yet written; and the second part, the *Novum organum*, although it is the work by which he became famous as a scientist, is itself only a fragment of what he had planned. As a "universal man" of the English Renaissance, Bacon was paying a high price for maintaining the *vita activa* on so many fronts.

The other area where Bacon was independent of crown policy was as a judge. As state prosecutor he necessarily expressed official attitudes, but in his own court he could administer the law according to his knowledge and beliefs. He did so with some authority, as we can see both from the tone of his official speeches and from the comments of his contemporaries. He was efficient as a judge in clearing off backlogs of business, and he gave fair judgments. Yet it

was here that the third and biggest setback of his career occurred: in 1621 he was accused of corruption, found guilty by the House of Lords, dismissed from Parliament and from all offices, temporarily imprisoned in the Tower, fined £40,000, and banned from coming within the verge (the twelve-mile radius around the court). Bacon had accepted presents from two men whose cases had been tried in his court; but his decision was not affected by the gifts—indeed it went against both suitors—so that he cannot be accused of perverting justice. Also, his offense has to be seen against the norms of his society, where men in power habitually sold offices to suitors and accepted lavish presents, indeed expected them. A scandal earlier that year had aroused a general wish to purge corruption in public places; Bacon was unfortunate in thus giving a weapon to his enemies, who encouraged the disgruntled suitors to denounce him; and he was unfortunate in that both James I and the duke of Buckingham coolly sacrificed him in order to improve their own images. He was careless, naïve, and foolish in accepting the gifts, and it was morally wrong to do so. No one would wish to deny that he was at fault, even though a comparable inquiry into the rest of the English ruling class would have removed many men from office.

Bacon's fall was an enormous physical and mental shock for him, and it blackened his name for centuries. Yet in removing him at one go from the ever increasing demands of public office it also liberated him for his own work. The remaining five years of life saw an enormous output in the most varied fields: history, poetry, the essay, a collection of apophthegms (witty sayings), and, above all, science. It is to this period that we owe the *Essays* in their final revision, the *New Atlantis*, and the *History of Henry the Seventh*, three works that no other seventeenth-century writer was capable of producing and that would alone guarantee his place in English literature. To this period also belong the major scientific works, written in Latin (the international scholarly language), which were intended to constitute the *Historia naturalis et experimentalis*; also the vast *Sylva sylvarum*, written in English, a curious compound of borrowings from the writings of others and of his own experiments and observation. It was in the pursuit of an experiment that he is said to have died, the amateur scientist being finally caught in a professional role. As John Aubrey recorded in *Brief Lives:*

Mr. Hobbes told me that the cause of his Lordship's death was trying an Experiment; viz. as he was taking the aire in a Coach with Dr. Witherborne . . . towards High-gate, snow lay on the ground, and it came into my Lord's thoughts, why flesh might not be preserved in snow, as in Salt. They were resolved they would try the Experiment presently. They alighted out of the Coach and went into a poore woman's house . . . and bought a Hen, and made the woman exenterate it, and then stuffed the body with Snow, and my Lord did help to doe it himselfe. The Snow so chilled him that he immediately fell so extremely ill that he could not return to his Lodging . . . but went to the Earl of Arundel's house at High-gate where they putt him into . . . a damp bed that had not been layn-in in about a yeare before; which gave him such a colde that in 2 or 3 dayes . . . he dyed of Suffocation.

He died on April 9, 1626, and was buried, as he had requested, in St. Michael's Church at St. Albans, where his mother lay.

In surveying Bacon's life and work one is struck by the range of his interests, the energy with which he pursued them, and their curious mixture of grandiose plan and incomplete execution. Bacon was constantly outlining ways of doing things better: his was an intensely practical mind, not much inclined to abstract speculation, but excelling at concrete schemes for improving study, or teaching, or practice. The English law, for instance, with all its proliferation of cases and statutes, seemed to him to cry out for reduction, for systematization. The principles at stake should be extracted, codified, preferably in the form of maxims or aphorisms; this would be a more practical form because of its greater applicability. As he wrote in 1596, "this delivering of knowledge in distinct and disjoined aphorisms doth leave the wit of man more free to turn and toss, and to make use of that which is delivered to more several purposes and applications" (VII, 321). For him the aphorism was concrete, not abstract, a kind of vessel to be "filled" with "good quantity of observation" (III, 405). That remark is from the

Advancement of Learning (1605); the persistence of Bacon's thinking in concrete terms is seen from the shape of the *Novum organum* (1620), which is made up of aphorisms, derived "from the senses and particulars" (IV, 50). The practicality of the aphorism is that it is the direct fruit of observation and experiment. If a number of these could be arranged into sequences of ascending generality then, Bacon thought, a scientific theory could emerge that would be true to life.

The association of the aphorism with concrete experience, and the concept of induction as a process of ascending from the particular to the general, and back again, are organizing ideas not only in Bacon's scientific works but in his writings about law (the maxim); about history (where Machiavelli is praised for discussing government in the form of *"discourse upon histories or examples.* For knowledge drawn freshly and in our view out of particulars, knoweth the best way to particulars again" [III, 453]); and about human life in general. The disciplines that we would describe today as psychology and sociology are represented in Bacon's work by his *Essays* and by the *Advancement of Learning,* especially in its Latin expansion, the *De augmentis scientiarum* (1623). The first version of the *Essays* (1597) consists of naked observations set down without ornament or padding; the ideas are marked off separately, and it is up to the reader to integrate them into his own life.

Some men's behaviour is like a verse, wherein every syllable is measured. [VI, 527]

Riches are for spending, and spending for honour and good actions. [VI, 530]

Discerne of the coming on of yeares, and think not to do the same things still. [VI, 531]

In dealing with cunning persons we must ever consider their ends to interpret their speeches, and it is good to say little to them, and that which they least looke for. [VI, 534]

Aphorisms are characteristically expressed in the present tense of the imperative; they are general laws to be taken "home to men's business and bosoms" (VI, 373), as Bacon said, accounting for the success of his efforts in this genre. For in Bacon's hands the essay was no whimsical effusion but was part of a psychological-sociological research program, as R. S. Crane has shown. In the *Advancement of Learning* Bacon called for more inquiry into both "moral knowledge," that is, the influence on men's mores and behavior of such factors as age, health and sickness, nobility, riches, prosperity and adversity, and "civil knowledge," such as conversation, negotiation, and government (III, 436); so he writes an essay on each of these topics and on other related ones. The *Essays* of 1597 are a fulfillment of the need, years before Bacon had in fact formulated it, showing once again the continuity in his thought, as ideas germinate and evolve. The *Essays* of 1612 and 1625 are richly observed analyses of man in his social setting, expressed in a fuller, more resonant language.

Like so many of the later works, *De augmentis* absorbs earlier fragments of Bacon's writing, becoming in the process a kind of intellectual autobiography; in it we find several miniature treatises organized in the form of aphorisms: "Articles of Inquiry Concerning Heavy and Light" (IV, 424ff.); "Examples of the Colours of Good and Evil" (IV, 459ff.); "Examples of Antitheses" (IV, 473ff.); "The Doctrine of Scattered Occasions," which is a commentary on some proverbs of Solomon as a treatise on statecraft (V, 37ff.); and "Example of a Treatise on Universal Justice or the Fountains of Equity" (V, 88 ff.). The range of subject matter—physics, rhetoric, moral philosophy, politics, jurisprudence—gives a good idea of the diversity yet unity of Bacon's thought.

Bacon valued the aphorism because it was concrete, practical not theoretical. In his distrust of theory he is part of the widespread movement throughout Renaissance Europe, beginning in Italy at the end of the fourteenth century, that propagated the *vita activa* and attacked the *vita contemplativa*, or religious life, outside the world. The nature of much of this writing is polemical, aggressive, taking a clear-cut, diametrically opposed view to that of its opponents, above all the Schoolmen, those medieval philosophers who worshipped the philosophy of Aristotle, extolling logic above rhetoric and venerating the syllogism as the main tool of knowledge. Of all the attacks on Scholasticism over a three-hundred-year period, few are as brilliant as that in Book I of the *Advancement of Learning*. Bacon's case is that knowledge, if isolated from criticism and growth, will wither and decay; and he makes his point not by neutral argument but by metaphor.

Surely, like as many substances in nature which are solid do putrefy and corrupt into worms, so it is the property of good and sound knowledge to putrefy and dissolve into a number of . . . vermiculate questions. [III, 285]

The rare word *vermiculate* ("wriggling like worms, tortuous") sums up one aspect of Bacon's critique of Scholastic method, its production of ever smaller, disputatious "questions," or problems derived from the text of Aristotle that could be solved, according to their system, only by internal logical argument, not by referring outward to reality.

The further consequence of this enclosure within a fixed corpus is described by Bacon in an even more pointed metaphor, drawing an analogy between their physical existence and their mental products. The Schoolmen,

. . . having sharp and strong wits, and abundance of leisure, and small variety of reading; but their wits being shut up in the cells of a few authors (chiefly Aristotle their dictator) as their persons were shut up in the cells of monasteries and colleges; and knowing little history, either of nature or time [that is, of the nature of the physical world or of human history] did out of no great quantity of matter, and infinite agitation of wit, spin out unto us those laborious webs of learning which are extant in their books.

That brilliant comparison, with the Schoolmen seen as spinning cobwebs of ingenuity out of a closed circle of knowledge—what an image for fruitless activity!—might seem to have clinched the matter. But Bacon has not finished yet; there are further levels of meaning, and feeling, to be drawn out:

For the wit and mind of man, if it work upon matter, which is the contemplation of the creatures of God, worketh according to the stuff, and is limited thereby; but if it work upon itself, as the spider worketh his web, then it is endless, and brings forth indeed cobwebs of learning, admirable for the fineness of thread and work, but of no substance or profit. [III, 285–286]

That is, thought processes that are anchored in the outside world can have some objective validity; those that are merely self-produced theories risk becoming insubstantial fantasies.

No one who has read that sequence ever forgets it. Bacon's images are memorable both for their striking force and for the imaginative fusion that takes place within them. Yet the *Advancement of Learning* is far more than a polemical work. It is in two books, of which the first is a defense of learning from all the attacks made on it in the Renaissance. Some of these were due to the weaknesses of learned men themselves; some were larger social prejudices (the scholar in his study was thought to be outside the *vita activa*, not contributing to society); some derived from the traditional opposition of the Church to men prying into the secrets of God—physics and astronomy, in particular, belonged to the realm of "forbidden knowledge" for the strictest ecclesiastics. Bacon answers all these charges brilliantly, refuting the prejudices and making a separation between science and religion that was to have great influence in the seventeenth century in legitimating scientific inquiry and removing it from the taint of atheism. These tasks completed, the second book is a survey of knowledge or, as Bacon put it with one of his characteristic organic metaphors, "a general and faithful perambulation of learning, with an enquiry what parts thereof lie fresh and waste," the map thus drawn serving to promote both public and private activities (III, 328). Although there are weaker sections (notably on mathematics)—Bacon was not omniscient—this survey of the range of knowledge is a *tour de force*, not least in the number of concrete proposals that Bacon makes for its improvement (he is the first to suggest the value of a history of literature, a history of science and knowledge in general). The whole work is animated by a great confidence and an almost religious belief in the eternal self-generating powers of human knowledge, as in the eloquent conclusion to Book I:

The images of men's wits and knowledges remain in books, exempted from the wrong of time and capable of perpetual renovation. Neither are they fitly to be called images, because they generate still, and cast their seeds in the minds of others, provoking and causing infinite actions and opinions in succeeding ages. So that if the invention of the ship was thought so noble, which carrieth riches and commodities from place to place, and consociateth the most remote regions in participation of their fruits, how much more are letters [literature, writing] to be magnified, which as ships pass through the vast seas of time, and make ages so distant to participate of the wisdom, illuminations, and inventions, the one of the other? [III, 318]

Human culture, history, science—all depend on communication and tradition. Seldom has that idea been more nobly expressed.

The *Advancement of Learning* is both negative and positive, then, both destructive and constructive. Indeed the two parts are integrated and together form a considered program for the renewal of science. Much medieval and Renaissance science had been philological: instead of observing and measuring physical, chemical, biological, and other processes at firsthand, writers compiled treatises from other writers' books. The fact that something was written down gave it a kind of innate authority, as if the act of writing or printing had guaranteed its truth. Consequently, all kinds of errors and fantasies were passed down for centuries, especially in the lore about animals or plants and herbs, as seen in some works attributed to Aristotle, and in Pliny's *Natural History*. Magical properties and mythical beasts (such as the unicorn) were all mingled with objective description. If science were to grow again, Bacon saw, two factors were crucial: observation, carried out by each scientist for himself and recorded in the simplest, least ambiguous language; and experiment, the controlled investigation of nature according to carefully programmed and repeatable patterns. Bacon's great prestige throughout Europe in the seventeenth and eighteenth centuries was due to his having formulated these essential points with clarity and force.

A major obstacle to progress was the reverence for classical antiquity. Bacon's education had been in Latin, as was customary, and he was steeped in a wide range of classical literature and philosophy. Yet he saw that respect for antique science would merely impede new developments, and he set out consciously to attack it. In the *Commentarius solutus*, a list of memoranda set down in two days during the summer vacation of 1608, he made a note of "Discoursing Skornfully of the Philosophy of the Graecians Wᵗʰ Some Better Respect to yᵉ Aegiptians, Persians, Caldes . . ." (XI, 64). He carried out this injunction in those remarkably violent works written between 1603 and 1608, "The Masculine Birth of Time," the "Goal of Valerius," and the "Refutation of Philosophies." This was the destructive part, the *pars destruens* as he called it, of his philosophy, with which he had "purged and swept and levelled the floor of the mind" (IV, 103) so that the new science would "no longer float in air, but rest on the solid foundations of experience of every kind, and the same well examined and weighed" (IV, 12).

This polemical activity was, historically speaking, the correct course for the early seventeenth century, but it may now seem to be of purely historical significance. We can all enjoy the imaginative energy with which Bacon attacked the past—time, as he said in a memorable metaphor, being a river on which the light and trivial matters have floated down to us but in which the substantial ones have sunk (III, 292)—but is that relevant today? Well, in any context where there is an exaggerated worship of tradition, the energy of rejection and revaluation is always needed. But Bacon's attack went beyond the immediate historical context into an exposure of fundamental processes in the human mind, what he called human "Idols." By "idol" he did not mean "an object of worship," in the Judaeo-Christian usage, but (in one of the original senses of the Greek *eidolon*) "an image in the mind, a mental fiction," what we might call today a misconception or fallacy. This idea had been present to him for a number of years, but reached its fullest exposition in the *Novum organum* (Book I, Aphorisms 38–58), where he distinguishes four categories, "Idols of the Tribe," "Idols of the Cave," "Idols of the Market-place," and "Idols of the Theatre."

The first class, those of the tribe, concern human perception, which is not an absolutely objective, reliable mechanism: "On the contrary, all perceptions as well of the sense as of the mind are according to the measure of the individual" (IV, 54). Recent work in psychology and the process of perception has shown just how true that observation is. If human understanding, in general, shapes what it sees, even more so do the "Idols of the Cave," the phantasms of each individual, who has "a cave or den of his own, which refracts and discolours the light of nature," owing to his personality, education, environment, or a number of other psychological factors (IV, 54). Human intercourse is by means of language, and in his third category, "Idols of the Market-place," Bacon makes an acute comment on the way in which not only "the ill and unfit choice of words wonderfully obstructs the understanding" but language itself can "throw all into confusion, and lead men away into numberless empty controversies and idle fancies" (IV, 55). Nor will more care with the definition of words solve this problem on its own; the causes lie deeper. Finally, the "Idols of the Theatre" are those received philosophical systems that are "but so many stage-plays, representing worlds of their own creation after an unreal and scenic fashion" (IV, 55). Science ought not to be the production of invention in that sense, the creation of an imaginary world, but the result of observation of the real world.

The reader who will follow Bacon's more detailed analysis of these phantasms and fallacies (IV, 56–69) will find it expounded clearly and convincingly. The later sections of the *Novum organum*, however, are considerably more technical, and one should begin with a modern outline of Bacon's whole system (see the works by Jones, Hesse, and Anderson). A general estimate of Bacon the scientist is inevitably mixed: he attacked the reliance on science from books, yet his "History of the Winds," for instance, draws heavily on Aristotle's *Problems*, Pliny's *Natural History*, and Acosta's *History of the Indies* (II, 4), while much of the *Sylva sylvarum* is drawn from a ragbag of utterly unscientific material (II, 327–329). Certainly the pressure under which Bacon worked in the last few years would partly account for this uncritical plagiarism, but he violates his own fundamental principles. Again, he was remarkably out of touch with many scientific achievements of his own day: the discoveries of Copernicus, Kepler, and Galileo; Gilbert's studies of magnetism; Napier's invention of logarithms, Harvey's discovery of the circulation of the blood—all of these he either ignored or dismissed. It is difficult not to feel that Bacon was an autodidact far outside the currents of thought of his day. His major weaknesses, viewing him from the perspective of Newton or Kepler, were his failure to realize the importance of mathematics in framing physical laws and his failure to see that quantification was essential to any development of the physical sciences.

In answer to Aristotle, Bacon called his scientific system the "new" organon, or instrument, to distinguish it from Aristotle's "old" one. Where Aristotelians had used the syllogism, which is a deductive method from a given principle, he used induction, which would proceed from concrete experience of individual phenomena to the cautious, but certain, formulation of universal physical laws. In both general and particular developments here, Bacon's polemical position against the ancients forced him into the opposite corner, so that his system is formed by opposition. Oddly enough, it is parasitic on the philosophers he opposes, determined by them rather than by the needs of the situation. His method of induction is laborious, and was not followed: later scientists showed how much quicker it is to propose a hypothesis and then verify or falsify it by experiment. Yet, as Mary Hesse has shown, in his concept of "anticipations" Bacon had a prototype of the hypothesis; he saw the importance of "negative instances," refuting experiments that would test confirmatory ones; and his concepts of scientific law, systematic analogy, and the mechanistic nature of matter were all important in the seventeenth-century context.

Bacon "wrote philosophy like a Lord Chancellor," William Harvey said, and the remark has usually been interpreted as a sign of scorn. That may have been the case, and certainly Harvey was the better experimental scientist. Yet the success of Bacon's propaganda in establishing a climate in which experimental science could flourish—he is quoted constantly as a pioneer and source of inspiration by all the scientists connected with the Royal Society—is due in part to his having been lord chancellor and to the prestige that the position gave. But it is due more to the faculties that brought him to eminence in that profession, intellectual penetration coupled with imagination and eloquence. Bacon's whole lifework was one of persuasion, whether as lawyer or parliamentarian, counsellor to the monarch, or advocate of the new science. He was the master rhetorician of his day in the sphere of public life. His work is remarkably geared to use. He collects proverbs, quotations, metaphors, pithy speeches—the ingredients of effective speaking, as it were—throughout his life, from the *Promus*, or storehouse, of formularies and elegancies, a collection of 1,655 proverbs and quotations set down, mostly from memory and for his own use, in the first days of the Christmas vacation of 1594, to the collection of *Apophthegms* which he assembled during his illness in 1624. Many of the proverbs in the *Promus* reappear in the *De augmentis* of 1623; that work also contains an expanded version of the collection of sophisms, "Colours of Good and Evil," which he had first published with the *Essays* of 1597. Such collections are the tools of the trade for the professional writer, as the published notebooks of many modern novelists and poets show. But in Bacon's case these are not isolated items. As his greatest scholar, James Spedding, first indicated (VII, 194f.), individual proverbs or quotations carried with them a whole web of association for Bacon, thought patterns that were not to emerge fully until years later.

The singlemindedness of Bacon's career as writer can be seen not only in method and style (where there is far more consistency than older accounts maintain), but in the preoccupation with the public good. There is no single work of Bacon that does not aim to be useful, either to the immediate political or legal situation, or to the world at large; there is no work that does not fit into his overall concern to help mankind. In a famous letter to his uncle, Lord Burghley, written in 1592, he claimed that his interest was less in civil than in "contemplative" affairs, that is, in study and learning:

. . . for I have taken all knowledge to be my province; and if I could purge it of two sorts of rovers [misleading, confusing trends], whereof the one with frivolous disputations, confutations, and verbosities, the other with blind experiments and auricular traditions and impostures, hath committed so many spoils, I hope I should bring in industrious observations, grounded conclusions, and profitable inventions and discoveries; the best state of that province. This, whether it be curiosity, or vain glory, or nature, or (if one take it favourably) *philanthropia,* is so fixed in my mind as it cannot be removed.   [VIII, 109]

That is a first sketch of the attack on Scholasticism in the *Advancement of Learning,* and it predicts his whole lifework. Contemplation should issue in action; enterprises that bear no fruit are valueless.

As we have seen, Bacon was formed by the traditions of the *vita activa,* according to which literature should not merely delight, but should also teach. His own literary works exemplify both demands admirably, for although they are as singleminded as everything else he wrote, they delight by their wit, playfulness, and imaginative empathy. The early "devices," protodramatic entertainments, partly masque and partly display orations (so important in the schools and universities of the Renaissance), while full of wit are prophetic of his later concerns. The *Conference of Pleasure* (1592) consists of four speeches: in praise of the worthiest virtue (fortitude); of the worthiest affection (love); of the worthiest power (knowledge); and of the worthiest person (Queen Elizabeth). Many of the ideas that emerged in the scientific work thirty years later are present here, but there is also a grace, a playfulness that is not always found, while the *laudatio* to the queen is of remarkable eloquence (VIII, 126–143). The same holiday high spirits permeate the six speeches that he wrote for the Gray's Inn masque at Christmas 1594 (VIII, 332–342). The speakers argue their cases, advising in turn "the Exercise of War," "the Study of Philosophy," "Eternizement and Fame by Buildings and Foundations," "Absoluteness of State and Treasure," "Virtue and a Gracious Government," and "Pastimes and Sports." The recipient of their advice, the Prince of Purpoole (the Lord of Misrule for the day) replies briefly, choosing the last as being the most appropriate at the moment, but promising to give the other topics his considered judgment—as well he might, since these are some of the major issues in the Renaissance "Advice to Princes" tradition. The topics link up with those recommended in Cas-

tiglione's tremendously influential treatise *Il cortegiano* (1528; English translation, 1561) and, on the other side, with Bacon's own *Essays.*

These holiday devices are relaxed and witty, but they are not far removed from reality. In the praise of the queen in 1592, Bacon spent most of his time justifying her actions since coming to power, producing an unsolicited piece of state propaganda; similarly, the fifth speaker in 1594 urges exactly the reforms that Bacon was himself to support in Parliament and elsewhere, such as the suppression of faction, reform of the laws, the encouragement of education, provision for the poor, and cultivation of underpopulated areas. The speech is, in effect, a manifesto for a complete political and social reform. Even more strikingly prophetic of Bacon's future concerns (and in particular of the *New Atlantis*) is the second speech, in praise of philosophy, which urges the ruler to make "the most innocent and meriting conquest, being the conquest of the works of nature," dedicating himself to "the searching out, inventing, and discovering of all whatsoever is hid and secret in the world" (VIII, 334). As ever, Bacon has practical proposals ready, four main institutions to be founded. The first is a library containing all notable books, in all languages; next, "a spacious, wonderful garden, wherein whatsoever plant" that exists in the world may be tended with care.

This garden to be built about with rooms to stable in all rare beasts and to cage in all rare birds; with two lakes adjoining, the one of fresh water the other of salt, for like variety of fishes. And so you may have in small compass a model of universal nature made private.

Then a museum to contain all the machines made by man, and all the "singularity" made by nature (presumably rocks, fossils, and such); finally, "such a still-house, so furnished with mills, instruments, furnaces, and vessels, as may be a palace fit for a philosopher's stone" (VIII, 335). These proposals show the width of Bacon's interests, ranging from chemistry and physics to the history of technology, and the biological sciences. He continued to urge them throughout his life, but without success; it was only fitting that when the Royal Society was founded in 1660 its official history should claim as joint patrons Charles II and Francis Bacon. At last the prince had listened to the counselor.

The third of these holiday devices, written for the queen's birthday in 1595, is the most brilliant and the most self-contained. That is, in addition to the speakers each representing some "course of life" (a Hermit, for contemplation or study; a Soldier, for fame and heroic exploits; a Counsellor of State, for experience), there is an overriding plot, the choice that the Squire has to make, between Erophilus and Philautia, love or self-love (VIII, 376–386). Bacon's skills in dialectic are seen in the way he allows each speaker to argue his case fully, each refuting the previous speaker, but then makes the Squire refute them all: "Wandering Hermit, storming Soldier, and hollow Statesman, the enchanting orators of Philautia, which have attempted by your high charms to turn resolved Erophilus into a statua deprived of action, or into a vulture attending about dead bodies, or into a monster with a double heart . . ." (VIII, 383), and so on, brilliantly exposing the blind side of each of their proposed ways of life. If the mark of the successful rhetorician is to be able to see both sides of a question, then Bacon had this ability in the highest degree. But of course there is a resolution: given his commitment to the active life and the service of others, it is inevitable that Philautia be defeated. So is she in Erasmus' *Praise of Folly,* so is she in Shakespeare ("Sin of self-love", Sonnet 62; ". . . Self-love, which is the most [pro]hibited sin in the canon," *All's Well That Ends Well,* I, i, 158). Bacon's belief that society is more important than the individual is shared by many Renaissance writers.

Discussions of Bacon naturally tend to position him toward the seventeenth century, which he did so much to influence. Yet a case can be made that he belonged, rather, to the late Renaissance, with its analogical way of thinking and its commitment to rhetoric, allegory, fable. If we consult the chronology of Bacon's writings, it is striking that many of his most important scientific works in the period 1603–1608, when his key ideas first become developed, were left unpublished, perhaps due to his realization that they were premature. All the same, when he decided in 1609 to publish something to indicate how his scientific ideas were devel-

oping, it is striking that he did not choose the form that he had been developing in the scientific works (the aphorism) or the general strategy of refutation of past philosophical systems followed by an outline of his own. Instead he chose to write a commentary on thirty-one classical myths and fables, such as the Cyclopes, Narcissus, Pan, Orpheus, and Proteus. The *De sapientia veterum,* or "Wisdom of the Ancients," is a unique mixture of mythography, political theory, and science. In the preface Bacon discusses the traditional, twofold function of parables: to obscure the truth (which he instantly rejects) and "to clear and throw light upon it," in other words "the employment of parables as a method of teaching." Such a method was much used in the infancy of civilization, he claims, "and even now if any one wish to let new light on any subject into men's minds . . . he must still go the same way and call in the aid of similitudes" (VI, 698). That is an important statement not only for Bacon's theory of communication but for the general process by which the imagination uses models in order to understand reality.

Each chapter of the *De sapientia veterum* consists of two parts: first, Bacon retells the fable, drawing on such popular Renaissance sources as the *De genealogia deorum* (1472) of Giovanni Boccaccio and the *Mythologiae sive explicationis fabularum* (1551) of Natale Conti. Often he goes into surprisingly full detail of iconography and symbolism, revealing a personal interest greater than the immediate needs warrant. Then in the second part he interprets the fable in political or scientific terms, with the free imaginative associations characteristic of allegory. Rebellion, for instance,

. . . because of the infinite calamities it inflicts both on kings and peoples is represented under the dreadful image of Typhon, with a hundred heads, denoting divided powers; flaming mouths, for devastations by fire; belts of snakes, for the pestilences which prevail, especially in sieges; iron hands, for slaughters; eagle's talons, for rapine; feathery body, for perpetual rumours, reports, trepidations, and the like. [VI, 703]

The coherence in method between that portrait and the allegorical beasts of Edmund Spenser's *The Faerie Queene* is apparent. The most striking of the scientific fables—"Pan, or Nature"; "Orpheus, or Philosophy"; "Coelum, or the Origin of Things"; "Proteus, or Matter"; "Cupid, or the Atom" (improbably enough!); "Daedalus, or the Mechanic"; "Sphinx, or Science"—show the same ability to draw striking significances out of apparently unrelated material. The element of surprise is strong in this work. The fable of Pan draws its interpretations from the realms of vision, magnetism, astronomy, astrology, meteorology, music, psychology, and physics, bringing in some of Bacon's key ideas (VI, 707–714). The *De sapientia veterum* used to be dismissed as farfetched or fantastic; today we can appreciate Bacon's ingenuity and the imaginative connections he makes between various levels of experience. To the student of his work there is also the added fascination of watching him weaving in his favorite themes, like a musical fantasia. Yet the work remains more mythography than science. Bacon's commitment is more to the analogy than to the scientific doctrine, and for that reason it is backward looking, unique but eccentric.

Another unique but much more successful scientific-literary work is the *New Atlantis*, written in 1624 but first published in 1627, following, as Bacon had intended, the *Sylva sylvarum*. His chaplain Rawley records that "This fable my Lord devised, to the end that he might exhibit therein a model or description of a college instituted for the interpreting of nature and the producing of great and marvellous works for the benefit of men, under the name of Salomon's House, or the College of the Six Days' Works" (III, 127). So far these are orthodox Baconian interests, familiar to us since the holiday devices written thirty years earlier. The reader who approaches this work for the first time, knowing something of Bacon's scientific program, will receive a surprise when he turns the page:

We sailed from Peru, (where we had continued by the space of one whole year,) for China and Japan, by the South Sea; taking with us victuals for twelve months; and had good winds from the east, though soft and weak, for five months' space and more. But then . . . there arose strong and great winds from the south, with a point east; which carried us up (for all that we could do) towards the north: by which time our victuals failed us, though we had made good spare of them. So that finding ourselves in the midst of the greatest wilderness of waters in the world, without victual, we gave ourselves for lost men, and prepared for death.   [III, 128]

That opening has a plainness and directness of language that reminds us of Hakluyt's *Voyages* or one of the travel books of the day. The fable begins with an imaginary voyage, as do several Utopias, from that of Sir Thomas More to Swift's *Gulliver's Travels*. Bacon will give us an account of an ideal scientific institute, sure enough, but he first creates a full narrative and dramatic framework. Like so many of his works it is unfinished, but of what remains the proportion of fiction to fact, of narrative to scientific planning, is more than two to one; so far did his imagination expand here.

The lost mariners pray to God and are rewarded by sighting a remote island, from which a boat puts out, partly to see if they need help but also to prevent them from landing if they are carrying any infectious diseases. The inhabitants of the island, which is called Bensalem, are Christians and welcome the crew to the "Strangers' House," where the philanthropy that characterizes this whole society is made manifest. They are given medicines against sickness (including a modern-sounding "box of small grey or whitish pills"), and the Governor of the House visits them regularly to answer their questions about the origin of the community. Bacon draws on Plato's *Timaeus* and the legends of Atlantis (III, 141), interweaving some of his own ideas about early civilizations to make a leisurely and smooth narrative, switching between the fully rendered experiences of the sailors in the present and the Governor's more wide-ranging account of the island's history. If all Utopias exist to criticize the deficiencies of the societies in which they are written, the qualities that emerge so favorably from the way of life on Bensalem are its humanity, harmony, and grace. The Platonic strand is in fact less important than a kind of Old Testament atmosphere, created by direct quotations and imitations but seen also in the patriarchal structure of the Feast of the Family, for instance, where the Father presides with dignity and respect (III, 148–151). All of these events are described in the fullest and richest detail without any narrow concern for narrative "function." Allowing his imagination freedom, Bacon creates a world that is both harmonious and sumptuous. As we know from his private life, or the essay "Of Masques," for example, Bacon had a great interest in rich fabrics and colors, and the *New Atlantis* is full of gorgeous stuffs and ornament. The officer who meets them on their arrival wears "a gown with wide sleeves, of a kind of water chamolet, of an excellent azure colour, far more glossy than ours; his under apparel was green; and so was his hat, being in the form of a turban" (III, 131). The *"Tirsan,"* or Father of the Family, sits in a chair the "state" or canopy of which is an intricate pattern of interwoven ivy, "an ivy somewhat whiter than ours, like the leaf of a silver asp, but more shining," the canopy being "curiously [ornately] wrought with silver and silk of divers colours, broiding or binding in the ivy . . ." (III, 148). The children of the Father are symbolized by a cluster of "daintily enamelled grapes," purple or greenish yellow according to their sex, which is carried in front of the Father "as an ensign of honour when he goeth in public" (III, 149f.). All descriptions are excelled, however, by that of the Fathers of Salomon's House, whose apparel and attendants reach a level of splendor rarely seen even in Jacobean England (III, 154–156).

The words that best sum up this section of the *New Atlantis* are *solemnity* and *ceremony,* as the peak of a rich social hierarchy is described in admiring detail. Yet Bacon's mind is at work as well as his fantasy. A conversation with one of the inhabitants turns suddenly into a vigorous criticism of the debasement of marriage in our society, attacking the Pauline notion of marriage as merely a remedy for lust, and the corruptions of adultery, fornication, and prostitution that have come to destroy "the faithful nuptial union of man and wife, that was first instituted" (III, 152–154). The passage is so outspoken that in the Pitt Press edition of 1900 the editor, G. C. Moore Smith, noted that "It has unfortunately seemed necessary to omit one passage of Bacon's work as unsuitable for an edition which may be read in schools."

Once the Father of Salomon's House appears, the didactic section announced by Rawley finally begins. The purposes of this College of Six Days' Works (it is dedicated to studying the works of God in the six days of Creation) are "the finding out of the true nature of all things" (III, 146) and "the Knowledge of Causes . . . and the enlarging of the bounds of Human Empire, to the effecting of all things possible" (III, 156). To that end they have built underground laboratories for coagulation, refrigeration, and conservation (III, 156), to study that valid connection between cold and the preservation of food that Bacon was pursuing on that wintry day in Highgate. They have also built observatories, lakes for the study of marine life, machines driven by water and wind, chambers for altering the air to treat certain illnesses, experimental institutes for the preparation of food and drink, dispensaries, furnaces, perspective houses where optical illusions can be produced, and acoustic laboratories to create and transform sounds by mechanical means, to represent the human voice synthetically, to make hearing aids, and to "convey sounds in trunks and pipes, in strange lines and distances." They can create and imitate smells, make a waterproof fire bomb, and build airplanes, submarines (first shown by Cornelius Drebbel in 1620), clocks that do not need winding, and so on. The world of the *New Atlantis* is no fantasy, but the world of modern science and technology. Far from being a dry technical treatise, this sequence shows Bacon's ingenuity and practicality at their imaginative best. Few have had his range of curiosity.

Perhaps the last point to be stressed about the *New Atlantis* is its humanitarianism. Throughout the fable, men help each other willingly, and at every stage they are thanked. All "principal inventors" who have benefited mankind are remembered through their statues, while every day the people give thanks to God for his works, asking his aid to turn their labors "into good and holy uses." They publish "profitable inventions" and give counsel to people to remedy diseases. All is done to make human life easier to bear and to enjoy. The work concludes with a list of thirty-three more processes, which, if pursued, would further benefit mankind, such as "the retardation of age," "the curing of diseases counted incurable," and "the mitigation of pain" (III, 167–168). One of the most pregnant details in the work, then, is the description of Bacon's ideal, the humane scientist: "He was a man of middle stature and age, comely of person, and had an aspect as if he pitied men" (III, 154).

The *New Atlantis* is a fable that constructs an ideal society. In the writing of history, ideals have a more ambivalent place. While some medieval and Renaissance historians produced works that justified an ideal moral order by the patterns of victory or defeat which, they claimed, attended on human good or evil, Bacon wrote that "we are much beholden to Machiavel and others, that write what men do and not what they ought to do" (III, 430). Bacon's views on the writing of history, expressed at some length in the *Advancement of Learning* (III, 333–344; expanded, IV, 292–314), make an interesting comparison with his own practice of it in *The History of Henry the Seventh*, as L. F. Dean and G. H. Nadel have shown. For Bacon history should be objective, distorted neither by the historian's feelings nor by his "favourite political doctrines"; it should not be prolix, or verbose; it should have a unified "continuance or contexture of the thread of the narration"; it should reveal "the true and inward" motions of business, which are often more discernible in little events than in great; and "above all things (for this is the ornament and life of Civil History), I wish events to be coupled with their causes" (IV, 301ff.; compare the scientists in the *New Atlantis* on their procedures for "finding out the true nature of all things," especially "the knowledge of causes"). *Henry the Seventh* fulfills all of these requirements: it is cool, dispassionate, building up an objective and indeed critical portrait of the king. Out of the turgid mass of the chronicle sources it constructs a clear and coherent narrative, an achievement that Anne Righter has not unjustly compared to that of Shakespeare in his history plays—both writers show a grasp of motive, an eye for the telling incident, an economy in selection and presentation.

Bacon's interest in the reign of Henry VII can be dated to a fragment written while Queen Elizabeth was alive (VI, 17–22), in which he proposed writing a history of England from the time of Henry VII to the present, and to a letter written in 1605 (X, 249–252); ideas from both sources were repeated in the *Advancement* (III, 336ff.). The attraction of the early sixteenth century to Bacon was that "profitable and instructing history" is best derived, he thought, not from the periods of "great wars and conquests," which are often "the works of fortune and fall out in barbarous times," but rather from "times refined in policies and industries" (VI, 19)—that is, from periods when the general cultural level is high enough to afford scope for Bacon's interests in political maneuvering, the development of law, the management of institutions, and so on. Henry VII came to the throne in a time of troubles, all of which he overcame by his own efforts, for "in his government he was led by none" (VI, 21), in effect performing the offices of both king and prime minister. The particular interest that Henry had for Bacon was that he ruled alone, rather like one of Machiavelli's princes, and thus the practice of "policy" or statecraft could be studied in a pure form. As Bacon wrote in a passage added to the Latin translation of the *Advancement*, Henry VII "was the most conspicuous for policy of all the kings who preceded him" (IV, 306).

The structure of the work is chronological, although not in the dogged manner of an annal; Bacon does not treat all the events of the reign at the same tempo or with the same degree of detail. His personal interests emerge, too, in the importance he attaches to the king's creation and administration of laws (VI, 85–88, 95–97, etc.). In the imaginary speeches that he writes for the characters, continuing the practice of classical and Renaissance historians, one can find traces of Bacon's own opinions, but he does not force his own political views onto them. His freedom from a mechanically chronological account is seen by the space he gives to two episodes in which the king's enemies tried to disguise one of their number as a nobleman in order to embarrass the government: first, the masquerade of Lambert Simnell as the Lord Plantagenet (VI, 45–59); second, the much better-known plot to present Perkin Warbeck as one of the princes said to have been murdered in the Tower by Richard III (Richard, duke of York), second son to Edward IV, who, if alive, would be the legitimate king (VI, 132–172, 186–195, 201–203). Bacon gives over a quarter of the book to these two episodes, seemingly fascinated by the arts of dissimulation that they reveal. As elsewhere, I have shown the use of theatrical imagery, frequent and positive throughout his work, takes on here thematic importance, in response to the element of disguise and false presentation. The organizer of the first plot is chosen because "none could hold the book so well to prompt and instruct this stage-play" (VI, 46); the plotters shift their actor to Ireland so that there should not be "too near looking, and too much perspective into his disguise," thinking it good "after the manner of scenes in stage plays and masks, to show it afar off" (VI, 47). The developments of the metaphor are detailed and ingenious, revealing a wide acquaintance with the theater.

Throughout the work Bacon's style is economical but effective. It has the narrative clarity of the opening of the *New Atlantis,* as in the account of the Cornish rebellion (VI, 175–182); it abounds in metaphor, as in the analysis of the effects of civil disturbance (VI, 60–61); and it can use syntactical patterning for many precise effects. Thus in dealing with the rebellion the king first rewards his own soldiers for their victory, then deals with the rebel leader: "After matter of honour and liberality, followed matter of severity and execution. The Lord Audley was led from Newgate to Tower-Hill, in a paper coat painted with his own arms; the arms reversed, the coat torn; and he at Tower-Hill beheaded" (VI, 182). There the inversion in word order (coat-arms; arms-coat) is the hinge around which the sentence turns, moving to a relentless "severity" by the awful violence of the three verbs arranged in parallel: "reversed, torn, beheaded."

The most impressive sequence is the concluding analysis of the king's character (VI, 237–245), where Bacon fulfills his own injunction of coupling events with their causes. Historians have rightly pointed out that Bacon drew on printed sources, inevitably so since he wrote the book in the amazingly short space of five months, immediately after his fall in 1621, when he was denied access to London, where the important manuscript materials were. (He did use the *Historia regis Henrici Septimi* of Bernard André, in the famous collection of Sir Robert Colton.) Yet those who will read the main sources, the chronicles of John Hall and John Speed, will have to concede that what sets Bacon's account above theirs are the same quali-

ties that brought him to eminence in so many fields: intellectual penetration, insight into human behavior, clarity of organization, vividness of imagination, and enormous and flexible powers of expression. In one of those curious revolutions in taste that literary history affords us, in 1786 an anonymous writer published *Henry VII,* "Now first *new written,*" his design being to "smooth the old language, and render it rather more pleasant to the ear." The reviewer in the *Monthly Review* (vol. 77 [1787], pp. 308–310) angrily rejected the efforts of this "Moderniser," who not only "mangled, and injured" the language but "perverted the sense," saying in defense of Bacon that although his style sometimes has the "quaintness" of Jacobean English, his *History of the Reign of Henry the Seventh* has nevertheless been looked upon as a pattern for historical composition; the true sublimity of which consists more in the greatness of thinking than in the pomp of expression;—in tracing circumstances with judgment,—in relating them with clearness and connexion, and in making every part of the story instructive." In addition to these excellences, he wrote, the work gives us "that native simplicity and genuine dignity, which are the greatest ornaments of Bacon's writings."

Bacon's works will always repay study, whatever we feel about his political disgrace or his uneven achievement as a scientist. For one thing he was fortunate to have been born in a great period for the English language and English literature. As Ben Jonson wrote about 1618 in his notebook, *Discoveries,* "Sir Francis Bacon, Lord Chancellor, is he who hath fill'd up all numbers; and perform'd that in our tongue which may be compared, or preferred, either to insolent Greece, or haughty Rome. In short, within his view, and about his times, were all the wits born that could honour a language, or help study. Now things daily fall, wits grow downward, and eloquence grows backward; so that he may be named, and stand, as the mark and *akme* of our language." Yet language is but the surface manifestation of mental processes: the example of Bacon will always be an inspiration to those who wish to observe the energies and resources of the human mind.

FRANCIS BACON

SELECTED BIBLIOGRAPHY

I. Bibliographies. R. W. Gibson, *Francis Bacon. A Bibliography of His Works and of Baconiana to the Year 1750* (Oxford, 1950), and *Supplement* (1959); J. K. Houck, *Francis Bacon*, which is *Elizabethan Bibliographies Supplements*, 15 (1968).

II. Collected Works. James Spedding, R. L. Ellis, and D. D. Heath, eds., *The Works of Francis Bacon*, 14 vols. (London, 1857–1874; repr. New York, 1968), which comprises vols. I–V: "Philosophical Works" (English translations of the Latin works in vols. IV and V); vols. VI–VII: "Literary and Professional Works"; and vols. VIII–XIV: "The Letters and the Life of Francis Bacon, Including All His Occasional Works" (chronologically arranged, with biographical commentary; indispensable).

III. Separate Works. Volume and page references are to James Spedding *et al.*, eds., *The Works of Francis Bacon* (1857–1874). Items marked with an asterisk were published during Bacon's lifetime.

1589: *An Advertisement Touching the Controversies of the Church of England* (London, 1640), VIII, 74–95.

1592: *A Conference of Pleasure* (two speeches from a "device" written for the queen's birthday, November 17; presented as if by Essex (London, 1734), VIII, 123–143; edited by Spedding from a better MS, containing four speeches (London, 1870).

1592: *Certain Observations Made Upon a Libel Published This Present Year, 1592* (London, 1657), VIII, 146–208.

1594: *A True Report of the Detestable Treason, Intended by Dr. Roderigo Lopez*, VIII, 274–288.

1594: *Argument in Chudleigh's Case*, trans. from Law French, VII, 617–636.

1594: *A Promus of Formularies and Elegancies*, a notebook of quotations and ideas; excerpts, VII, 197–211; complete edition by Mrs. Henry Pott (London, 1883).

1594: *Gesta Grayorum* (London, 1685), Gray's Inn Christmas masque, for which Bacon wrote six speeches; VIII, 332–342; D. S. Bland, ed. (Liverpool, 1968).

1595: *Of Love and Self-love*, a device for the queen's birthday, presented by Essex; VIII, 376–386.

1596: *Advice to the Earl of Rutland on His Travels*, IX, 6–20.

1596: *Advice to Fulke Greville on His Studies*, IX, 21–26; ascribed to Bacon by Spedding; confirmed by V. F. Snow's discovery of the MS in the Public Record Office; see *Huntington Library Quarterly*, 23 (1960), pp. 369–378.

*1597: *Essays* (first version: 10 essays; VI, 523–534; parallel-column version in E. Arber, ed., *A Harmony of the Essays of Francis Bacon* (London, 1871, 1895). Originally published with *Meditationes sacrae*, VII, 233–242; trans. as "Religious Meditations," VII, 243–254, and with *Of the Colours of Good and Evil, a Fragment*, VII, 75–92.

1597: *Maxims of the Law* (London, 1630), VII, 313–387.

*1599: *Letter Written out of England to an English Gentleman in Padua*, IX, 110–119; a quasi-official account of the conspiracy of Edward Squire and the Jesuit Walpole against the queen. Spedding ascribed it to Bacon; this was confirmed by Corinna Rickert, *Modern Language Review*, 51 (1956), pp. 71–72.

1600: *Reading on the Statute of Uses* (London, 1642), VII, 395–445.

*1601: *A Declaration of the Practices and Treasons . . . Committed by Robert, Late Earl of Essex*, IX, 247–321.

ca. 1602: *Letter and Discourse to Sir Henry Savill, Touching Helps for the Intellectual Powers* (London, 1657), VII, 97–103.

ca. 1602: *A Confession of Faith* (London, 1648), VII, 219–226.

ca. 1602: *The History of the Reign of K. Henry the Eighth, K. Edward, Q. Mary, and Part of the Reign of Q. Elizabeth* (London, 1663), VI, 17–22; first sketch for *Henry VII*.

ca. 1603: *De interpretatione naturae prooemium* (London, 1653), III, 518–520; trans. "On the Interpretation of Nature. Proem," X, 84–87.

ca. 1603: *Valerius Terminus of the Interpretation of Nature* (London, 1734), III, 215–252.

ca. 1603: *Temporis partus masculus* (London, 1653), III, 527–539; trans. "The Masculine Birth of Time; or the Great Instauration of the Dominion of Man Over the Universe," by B. Farrington, in *The Philosophy of Francis Bacon* (Liverpool, 1964), pp. 59–72.

*1603: *A Brief Discourse Touching the Happy Union of the Kingdoms of England and Scotland*, X, 90–99.

*1604: *Certain Considerations Touching the Better Pacification and Edification of the Church of England*, X, 103–127.

*1604: *Apology in Certain Imputations Concerning the Late Earl of Essex*, X, 139–160.

ca. 1604: *Cogitationes de natura rerum* (London, 1653), III, 15–35; trans. "Thoughts on the Nature of Things," V, 419–439.

271

ca. 1604: *Cogitationes de scientia humana,* III, 183–198.

*1605: *The Twoo Bookes of Francis Bacon. Of the Proficience and Advancement of Learning, Divine and Humane,* III, 261–491; W. A. Wright, ed. (Oxford, 1868); F. G. Selby, ed. (London, 1892); A. Johnston, ed. (Oxford, 1974), with *New Atlantis;* Bk. 1, W. A. Armstrong, ed. (London, 1975).

1606: *Partis instaurationis secundae delineatio et argumentum* (London, 1653), III, 547–557.

1607: *Cogitata et visa de interpretatione naturae* (London, 1653), III, 591–620; trans. "Thoughts and Conclusions on the Interpretation of Nature or a Science Productive of Works," in B. Farrington, *The Philosophy of Francis Bacon,* 73–102.

1608: *Argument in the Case of the Post-nati of Scotland* (London, 1641), VII, 641–679.

1608: *Commentarius Solutus,* a private notebook of ideas and plans, XI, 39–95.

1608: *In felicem memoriam Elizabethae, Angliae Reginae* (London, 1658), VI, 291–303; trans. "On the Fortunate Memory of Elizabeth, Queen of England," VI, 305–318.

1608: *Of the True Greatness of the Kingdom of Britain* (London, 1734), VII, 45–64.

1608: *Redargutio philosophiarum* (London, in part, 1653), III, 557–585; trans. "The Refutation of Philosophies," in B. Farrington, *The Philosophy of Francis Bacon,* 103–133.

1609: *Discourse on the Plantation in Ireland* (London, 1657), XI, 116–126.

*1609: *De sapientia veterum,* VI, 617–686; trans. "Of the Wisdom of the Ancients," VI, 687–764; English trans. by Sir Arthur Gorges (1619).

ca. 1610: *The Beginning of the History of Great Britain* (London, 1657), VI, 275–279.

ca. 1610: *De principiis atque originibus* (London, 1653), III, 79–118; trans. "On Principles and Origins, According to the Fables of Cupid and Coelum," V, 459–500.

1611: *Charge on Opening the Court of the Verge* (London, 1662), XI, 265–275.

before
1612: *Essays* (MS version, differing from the published second edition; some variants in Spedding, VI, 541–591; complete parallel-text edition by E. Arber, *A Harmony of the Essays* (London, 1871, 1895).

*1612: *Essays* (second edition, much enlarged; 40 essays; VI, 541–591; for the original dedication to Prince Henry, see XI, 340–341).

1612: *In Henricum principem Walliae elogium* (London, 1763), VI, 323–325; trans. "Memorial of Henry Prince of Wales," VI, 327–329.

1612: *Descriptio globi intellectualis* and *Thema coeli* (London, 1653), III, 727–780; trans. "Description of the Heavenly Globe" and "Theory of the Heaven," V, 501–559.

*1614: *The Charge of Sir Francis Bacon, Knight, His Majesty's Attorney-General, Touching Duels,* XI, 399–416.

1615: *The Charge Against Oliver St. John* (London, 1657), XII, 136–146.

ca. 1615: *De fluxu et refluxu maris* (London, 1653), III, 47–61; trans. "On the Ebb and Flow of the Sea," V, 441–458.

1616: *The Argument of Sir Francis Bacon in the Case of De rege inconsulto,* VII, 687–725.

1616: *The Arguments of Law of Sir Francis Bacon, Knight, the King's Solicitor-General, in Certain Great and Difficult Cases* (London, 1730), VII, 521–566.

1616: *The Charge Against the Countess and Earl of Somerset, Concerning the Poisoning of Sir Thomas Overbury* (London, 1679), XII, 297–320.

1616: *Letter of Advice to the Duke of Buckingham* (London, 1661; fuller text, 1663), XIII, 13–56.

1616: *Proposition Touching Amendment of Laws* (London, 1657), XIII, 61–71.

1617: *Speech on Taking His Seat in Chancery as Lord Keeper of the Great Seal* (London, 1651), XIII, 182–193.

1617: *Speech to the Judges Before the Circuit* (London, 1657), XIII, 211–214.

*1620: *Instauratio magna,* I, 119–147; trans. "The Great Instauration," IV, 3–35; the "Prooemium," Dedicatory Letter, Preface, and "Plan of the Work" only. Part 1 was to be partially represented by Book II of the *Advancement of Learning;* Part 2 was the *Novum organum.*

*1620: *Novum organum* (the first two books only, of a projected eight (?); I, 149–365; trans. "The New Organon," IV, 37–248; T. Fowler, ed. (Oxford, 1878; rev. ed., 1889). For the presentation letter to James I, see XIV, 119f.

*1620: *Parasceve aa historiam naturalem et experimentalem* (published in the same volume as the *Novum organum*), I, 391–411; trans. "Preparative Towards a Natural and Experimental History," IV, 249–271.

1622: *Advertisement Touching a Holy War* (London, 1629), VII, 9–36.

*1622: *The History of the Reign of King Henry the Seventh,* VII, 23–245; J. R. Lumby, ed.

(Cambridge, 1876; rev. ed., 1892); V. Gabrieli, ed. (Bari, 1964); R. Lockyer, ed. (London, 1971); F. J. Levy, ed. (Indianapolis, 1972).

*1622: *Historia naturalis et experimentalis:* (i) *Historia ventorum,* II, 7–78; trans. "Natural and Experimental History": (i) "History of the Winds," V, 125–200. Bacon proposed to issue this, the third part of the *Instauratio magna,* in monthly installments. The remaining titles were to be the histories (ii) *Densi et rari;* (iii) *Gravis et levis;* (iv) *Sympathiae et antipathiae rerum;* (v) *Sulphuris, mercurii, et salis;* and (vi) *Vitae et mortis.* The prefaces to these, together with the fragment, *Abecedarium naturae,* follow (II, 79–88); trans., V, 201–211.

*1623: *Historia vitae et mortis,* II, 101–226; trans. "The History of Life and Death," IV, 213–335.

1623: *Historia densi et rari* (London, 1658), II, 241–305; trans. "The History of Dense and Rare," IV, 337–400.

1623: *The Beginning of the History of the Reign of King Henry the Eighth* (London, 1629), VI, 269–270.

*1623: *De dignitate & augmentis scientiarum, libros IX* (much expanded Latin version of *The Advancement of Learning*), I, 423–837; trans., IV, 273–498, and V, 3–119; trans. *Of the Advancement and Proficience of Learning,* by Gilbert Wats (Oxford, 1640).

*1623: *Novis orbis scientiarum, sive desiderata* (appended to preceding item), I, 838–840; trans. "The New World of Sciences, or Desiderata," V, 121–123.

1624: *Considerations Touching a War With Spain* (London, 1629), XIV, 469–505.

1624: *New Atlantis* (London, 1626), at the end of the *Sylva sylvarum* volume, III, 125–166; G. C. Moore Smith, ed. (Cambridge, 1900); A. Johnston, ed., with *The Advancement of Learning* (Oxford, 1974).

1624: *Magnalia naturae, praecipue quoad usus humanos* (in English, III, 167–168; published at end of *New Atlantis*).

*1624: *Apophthegms New and Old. Collected by the Right Honourable Francis Lo. Verulam, Viscount St. Alban,* VII, 121–165; other *Apophthegms* from later collections, VII, 166–184.

*1624: *Translation of Certain Psalms Into English Verse,* VII, 273–286.

*1625: *Essays or Counsels, Civil and Moral* (third version, expanded further, to 58 essays, VI, 371–520; W. A. Wright, ed. (London,

1862); S. F. Reynolds, ed. (Oxford, 1890); also in Arber, *A Harmony of the Essays.*

1626: *Sylva Sylvarum: or a Natural History. In Ten Centuries,* II, 331–680.

IV. COLLECTED EDITIONS (BEFORE SPEDDING):

1629: *Certaine Miscellany Works,* W. Rawley, ed.

1638: *Operum moralium et civilium,* W. Rawley, ed. (Latin translations; 2nd ed. of that year added *Novum organum*).

1648: *The Remains of the Right Honourable Francis Lord Verulam . . .* (repr., 1656, under the title *The Mirrour of State and Eloquence*).

1653: *Scripta in naturali et universali philosophia* (Amsterdam), Isaac Gruter, ed.; first printing of many of Bacon's scientific fragments and sketches.

1657: *Resuscitatio, or, Bringing Into Publick Light Several Pieces of the Works, Civil, Historical, Philosophical, & Theological, Hitherto Sleeping; of the Right Honourable Francis Bacon . . . Together With His Lordship's Life,* W. Rawley, ed. (repr., 1661).

1658: *Opuscula varia posthuma,* W. Rawley, ed. (repr., 1663).

1670: *The Second Part of the Resuscitatio,* W. Rawley, ed. (both parts repr., 1671).

1679: *Baconiana, or Certain Genuine Remains of Sr. Francis Bacon . . . in Arguments Civil and Moral, Theological and Bibliographical,* Archbishop T. Tenison, ed.

1702: *Letters of Sir Francis Bacon,* Robert Stephens, ed. (repr., 1736).

1730: *Opera omnia,* J. Blackbourne, ed., 4 vols.

1733: *The Philosophical Works of Francis Bacon . . . Methodized and Made English,* Peter Shaw, ed., 4 vols.

1734: *Letters and Remains,* Robert Stephens, ed.

1740: *Works:* 4 vols., life by D. Mallet.

1765: *Works,* Thomas Birch, ed., 5 vols.

1825–1834: *Works,* Basil Montagu, ed., 15 vols.

V. BOOKS ON BACON AND HIS WORK. C. D. Broad, *The Philosophy of Francis Bacon* (Cambridge, 1926), repr. in his *Ethics and the History of Philosophy* (London, 1952), 117–143; C. W. Lemmi, *The Classic Deities in Bacon: A Study in Mythological Symbolism* (Baltimore, 1933); excerpts in Vickers, *Essential Articles on Francis Bacon* (see below); C. Williams, *Bacon* (London, 1933); R. F. Jones, *Ancients and Moderns. A Study of the Rise of the Scientific Movement in Seventeenth-Century England* (St. Louis, 1936; rev. ed., 1961), excerpted in Vickers, *Essential Articles* (see below); H. Craig, *The Enchanted Glass. The Elizabethan Mind in Literature* (Oxford, 1936, 1960); K. Wallace, *Francis Bacon on Communication and Rhetoric* (Chapel Hill, N.C., 1943); F. H. Anderson, *The Philosophy of Francis Bacon* (Chicago, 1948); B. Farrington, *Francis Bacon:*

Philosopher of Industrial Science (New York, 1949; London, 1951); H. Haydn, *The Counter-Renaissance* (New York, 1950); D. G. James, *The Dream of Learning* (Oxford, 1951); A. W. Green, *Sir Francis Bacon: His Life and Works* (Denver, Colo., 1952); P. Rossi, *Francesco Bacone, dalla magia alla scienza* (Bari, 1958); rev. ed., trans. by S. Rabinovitch, *Francis Bacon: From Magic to Science* (London, 1968); N. W. Gilbert, *Renaissance Concepts of Method* (New York, 1960); E. Sewell, *The Orphic Voice: Poetry and Natural History* (London, 1961); F. H. Anderson, *Francis Bacon, His Career and Thought* (Berkeley, Calif., 1962); L. Eiseley, *Francis Bacon and the Modern Dilemma* (Lincoln, Nebr., 1962); C. D. Bowen, *Francis Bacon: The Temper of a Man* (London, 1963); H. van Leeuwen, *The Problem of Certainty in English Thought, 1630–1690* (The Hague, 1963); B. Farrington, *The Philosophy of Francis Bacon. An Essay on Its Development From 1603 to 1609, With New Translations of Fundamental Texts* (Liverpool, 1964); H. Fisch, *Jerusalem and Albion* (London, 1964); C. Hill, *Intellectual Origins of the English Revolution* (London, 1965); K. R. Wallace, *Francis Bacon on the Nature of Man* (Urbana, Ill., 1967); F. J. Levy, *Tudor Historical Thought* (San Marino, Calif., 1967); B. Vickers, *Francis Bacon and Renaissance Prose* (Cambridge, 1968); B. Vickers, ed., *Essential Articles for the Study of Francis Bacon* (Hamden, Conn., 1968; London, 1972), which includes excerpts from C. W. Lemmi and R. F. Jones (previously cited) and also the following articles: V. K. Whitaker, "Francis Bacon's Intellectual Milieu"; G. Bullough, "Bacon and the Defence of Learning"; M. Hesse, "Francis Bacon's Philosophy of Science"; M. E. Prior, "Bacon's Man of Science"; P. H. Kocher, "Francis Bacon on the Science of Jurisprudence"; K. R. Wallace, "Discussion in Parliament and Francis Bacon"; L. F. Dean, "Sir Francis Bacon's Theory of Civil History-Writing"; G. H. Nadel, "History as Psychology in Francis Bacon's Theory of History"; J. L. Harrison, "Bacon's View of Rhetoric, Poetry, and the Imagination"; R. S. Crane, "The Relation of Bacon's *Essays* to His Program for the Advancement of Learning"; R. Tarselius, " 'All Colours Will Agree in the Dark': A Note on a Feature in the Style of Francis Bacon"; and A. Righter, "Francis Bacon." See also R. M. Adolph, *The Rise of Modern Prose Style* (Cambridge, Mass., 1968); H. B. White, *Peace Among the Willows. The Political Philosophy of Francis Bacon* (The Hague, 1968); W. A. Sessions, ed., "The Legacy of Francis Bacon," a special issue of *Studies in the Literary Imagination*, 4, no. 1 (April 1971), which includes J. M. Steadman, "Beyond Hercules: Bacon and the Scientist as Hero"; B. Vickers, "Bacon's Use of Theatrical Imagery"; and eight other new essays; L. Jardine, *Francis Bacon. Discovery and the Art of Discourse* (Cambridge, 1974); J. Stephens, *Francis Bacon and the Style of Science* (Chicago, 1975); and J. L. Marwil, *The Trials of Counsel. Francis Bacon in 1621* (Detroit, 1976).

CHRISTOPHER MARLOWE

(1564-1593)

Philip Henderson

A GOOD deal more is known about Christopher Marlowe, for good or ill, than about any other dramatist of the Elizabethan Age. Since the discovery in 1925 of the inquest proceedings after his death, described in Leslie Hotson's *The Death of Christopher Marlowe*, followed in 1929 by Professor F. S. Boas's *Marlowe and His Circle*, the balance of interest tended for some time to shift from his work to his life. More is known about Marlowe than about others chiefly because his name occurs fairly frequently in academic, secret service, and police records—or their equivalent in his day. But we do not know enough to form a complete picture of him, though the psychological criticism of our own time has inferred much. Evidently, in his brief, tragic, and passionate life, Marlowe was the kind of man who could not help making enemies and letting off squibs *pour épater le bourgeois*. He seems to have lived, as he thought, dangerously.

In a now famous phrase, T. S. Eliot described Marlowe in his essay "Shakespeare and the Stoicism of Seneca" as "the most thoughtful, the most blasphemous (and, therefore, probably the most Christian) of his contemporaries." To his contemporaries, however, he appeared in a different light. His fellow playwright Robert Greene attacks him, in *A Groatsworth of Wit*, as an epicure, an atheist, and a Machiavellian. Nevertheless, it was Marlowe, with his intellectual passion and his overreaching Machiavellian hero-villains, who indicated the direction of subsequent Elizabethan tragedy. Chapman, Marston, Webster, Tourneur, Jonson, and, at first, even Shakespeare, followed the course he had mapped out.

The eldest son of John Marlowe of the Shoemakers Guild and Katherine Arthur, a Dover girl of yeoman stock, Christopher Marlowe was baptized at St. George's Church, Canterbury, on 26 February 1564, exactly two months before the baptism of William Shakespeare at Stratford-upon-Avon. Both poets came from the same stratum of society—the rising middle class. Marlowe was entitled to call himself a gentleman by virtue of his Cambridge degree, Shakespeare by virtue of a newly established coat of arms. Both poets, by their genius, won the patronage of the great. Shakespeare managed his affairs so well that he was able to buy the finest house in his native town, and on his death he was commemorated by a bust in his parish church; Marlowe lies in an unmarked grave at Deptford. In contemporary records Marlowe's name is spelled variously: Marley, Morley, Marlin, Merlin, Merling. Both he and his father signed themselves Marley, although the baptismal register reads "Christofer the sonne of John Marlow."[1] From King's School, Canterbury, Marlowe went to Corpus Christi College, Cambridge, in December 1580, on a scholarship founded by Matthew Parker, master of the college from 1544 to 1553 and later archbishop of Canterbury. The scholarship was for six years and was granted more or less on the understanding that those holding it should study for the church. "Merling," however, first appears in the college records as a student of dialectics.

Outwardly Marlowe's academic career was uneventful, except for mysterious and increasingly long absences after his second year. During his last year, in 1587, it needed the intervention of the Privy Council before the university would allow him to take his M.A. degree. For it appeared that not only had Christopher Mar-

---

[1] Marlowe's signature of 1585 as a witness to the will of Katherine Benchkyn was discovered in 1939 by F. W. Tyler, former sublibrarian, Canterbury Cathedral.

lowe given up all idea of going into the church, but it was rumored that he intended to join Dr. Allen's Catholic seminary at Rheims. As it was, the Privy Council assured the worried university authorities that "in all his actions Christopher Morley had behaved himself orderly and discreetly whereby he had done Her Majesty good service." The dispatch, which Leslie Hotson established as referring to Marlowe, concluded, "Because it was not her Majesty's pleasure that any one employed as he had been in matters touching the benefit of his country should be defamed by those that are ignorant in th'affairs he went about." The dispatch is dated June 1587, and in October of the same year "Morley" is mentioned again in a letter from Utrecht to William Cecil, Lord Burghley, as among the secretary of state's messengers. This, however, may refer to Thomas Morley, the musician, who was working as a secret agent in the Lowlands at this time. It is not known whether Marlowe's government service was confined to carrying dispatches to and from ambassadors and courts abroad or whether he was one of Sir Francis Walsingham's regular spies. The likelihood is (taking into consideration his friends and associates) that he did work as a spy. Such work would have given him ample opportunity to practice "Machiavellian" policy. The rumor that he "was determined to have gone beyond the seas to Rheims" was in all probability only too well founded. As a secret agent seeking information about the more treasonable activities of English Catholics abroad, this is just where he would have gone. There is, in fact, a reference in *The Massacre at Paris* to a "sort of English priests" who "hatch forth treason 'gainst their natural Queen" at the seminary at Rheims.

With such powerful backing, Marlowe took his M.A. degree, in July 1587, and before the end of the year both parts of *Tamburlaine the Great* had been performed on the London stages. He was twenty-three. He had had six years at the university and was to have another five years in which to complete his work. During that time he wrote at least five more plays, *Hero and Leander*, and translations of Ovid's *Amores* and of Book I of Lucan's *Pharsalia*. During the remaining five years of his life he lived chiefly in London, in the theatrical district of Shoreditch, though he may have traveled a good deal on government commissions. In September

1589 he was imprisoned in Newgate for his part in a street fight in which the son of a Holborn publican was killed, and appeared for trial, together with Thomas Watson, the poet and playwright, at the Old Bailey on 3 December. He was discharged with a warning to keep the peace. This he failed to do, for three years later he was summoned to appear at the Middlesex Sessions for assaulting two Shoreditch constables in Holywell Street. The constables said that they went in fear of their lives because of him. But there is no evidence that Marlowe ever answered this particular charge. He was doubtless "otherwise employed" at the time. In the early part of 1592 he appears to have been at the siege of Rouen, where English troops had been sent to uphold the Protestant cause against the Catholic League, for on 12 March a "Mr. Marlin" arrived at Dieppe with a letter from the English garrison at Rouen to Sir Henry Unton. From Dieppe, Unton sent him back to England with a letter to Lord Burghley. *The Massacre at Paris*, Marlowe's most topical play, shows such an intimate knowledge of French politics that it was probably written soon after these events. Its hero-villain, the duke of Guise, was the same Guise whom the chivalrous Unton challenged three times to single combat to answer his insulting references to Queen Elizabeth I.

In the autumn of 1592 appeared Robert Greene's *A Groatsworth of Wit*, attacking both Marlowe, as the "Famous Gracer of Tragedians," and Shakespeare, as "the Upstart Crow beautified in our feathers." Some of Greene's most scandalous charges against Marlowe were cut out by Henry Chettle. These, said Chettle, "at the perusing of Greene's book . . . I thought he in some displeasure writ; or had it been true, yet to publish it was intolerable. With neither of them that take offence was I acquainted, and with one of them I care not if I never be." This was evidently intended for Marlowe, for Chettle makes handsome amends to Shakespeare.

In September 1592, in or near the Chequers Inn, Canterbury, Marlowe was engaged in another fight, this time with William Corkine, musician and tailor, the father, presumably, of the William Corkine[2] who in 1612 published the

---

[2] See William Urry, "Marlowe and Canterbury," *Times Literary Supplement*, 13 February 1964.

Second Book of Airs, containing a setting of Marlowe's poem "Come live with me and be my love."

In May 1593 Thomas Kyd, the dramatist, was arrested and interrogated for having in his possession heretical papers "denying the deity of Jesus Christ," which he said belonged to Marlowe and had been accidentally shuffled among his own "waste and idle papers" when he and Marlowe were "writing together in the same room two years since." As a result of this, on 18 May Marlowe himself was summoned before the Privy Council and on 20 May he was "commanded to give his daily attendance on their Lordships until he shall be licensed to the contrary." It is noticeable that Marlowe was neither imprisoned nor examined under torture, like Kyd, but given the usual courtesies afforded to a gentleman on such occasions. In the warrant he is referred to as "Christopher Marley of London, gentleman," who was at that time understood to be living in Kent at the house of Thomas Walsingham of Scadbury, a second cousin of Sir Francis Walsingham, the secretary of state. There is no evidence of Marlowe's examination by the Privy Council. Twelve days later he was stabbed to death in a tavern on Deptford Strand in the company of three men, one of whom was the notorious spy and agent provocateur Robert Poley.

Marlowe's death has given rise to more speculations than almost any other event in his life. But the various theories advanced to account for it raise more problems than they settle. More recently they have reached fantastic proportions in Calvin Hoffman's contention that Marlowe was not killed at all, but lived on in exile and wrote all the plays and poems attributed to the actor Shakespeare.[3] Returning to established fact, we know that either just before or just after Marlowe was killed at Deptford by Ingram Frizer, a swindler in the employment of Thomas Walsingham, an informer, Richard Baines, laid before the Privy Council a "Note containing the opinion of one Christopher Marly concerning his damnable judgement of religion and scorn of God's word." The evidently horrified informer concluded his long list of Marlowe's

blasphemies with a demand that "the mouth of so dangerous a member may be stopped."

Marlowe's reported table talk is of two kinds, one consisting of blasphemies that Christians in any age will find horrible—such as "that Christ deserved better to die than Barabbas" and "that if the Jews among whom He was born did crucify Him they best knew Him and whence He came"—and, on the other hand, a rationalistic criticism of the Scriptures of the sort now known as the Higher Criticism. The most dangerous indictment was that he was in the habit of saying that "the first beginning of religion was only to keep men in awe" (which he seems to have got from Machiavelli) and that "almost into every company he cometh he persuadeth men to atheism, willing them not be afeard of bugbears and hobgoblins." There are also references to such subjects as the age of Adam ("That the Indians and many authors of antiquity have assuredly written above sixteen thousand years agone, whereas Adam is proved to have lived within six thousand years"), the poor literary style of the New Testament (that he could have written it much better), and that Moses made the Jews travel for forty years in the wilderness, "a journey which might have been done in less than one year," in order that those "who were privy to his subtleties might perish, and so an everlasting superstition remain in the hearts of the people." To these dangerous speculations Marlowe is said to have added a plea for homosexuality and smoking—"that all they that love not tobacco and boys were fools"—smoking being at that time a practice more or less confined to Ralegh and his immediate circle. In fact Ralegh is directly involved in Marlowe's reported sayings—that "Moses was but a jugler, and that one Heriots [Thomas Harriot], being Sir Walter Ralegh's man, can do more than he." Some of Baines's charges are repeated in Kyd's letters to Sir John Puckering, written after Marlowe's death, and in *Remembrances of Words and Matter Against Richard Cholmeley,* which names Ralegh as having heard "the atheist lecture." Though Marlowe evidently took a delight in shocking his contemporaries, one can still see behind the Baines note a keenly humorous and scientific mind at work.

There is no space here to discuss the vexed question of whether Marlowe was killed ac-

[3] *The Murder of the Man Who Was Shakespeare* (New York, 1955).

CHRISTOPHER MARLOWE

cidentally, or deliberately murdered, as some think; still less the cloudy subject of the School of Night, which Shakespeare jokingly referred to in *Love's Labour's Lost* and which is supposed to have been a "little Academe" of science and comparative religion whose members, including Marlowe, Ralegh, Chapman, Harriot, Royden, and the "wizard" earl of Northumberland, took "night" as their symbol for the deep knowledge hidden from the vulgar. Whether this existed or not, there can be no doubt about the range and depth of Marlowe's speculation, which becomes apparent the more his plays are studied. It is very doubtful, however, whether he was what is now known as an atheist. The dilemma in *Doctor Faustus* is presented quite objectively, but there are signs in the passionate conviction, in the anguish of the writing, that it was at least a dilemma with which the poet himself was quite familiar. Ralegh's writings, on the other hand, show him as far from being an atheist, though the charge was flung at him at his trial. Thomas Harriot, the most distinguished English astronomer and mathematician before Newton, we are told, "did not like (or valued not) the old story of the Creation of the World. He could not believe the old position; he would say *ex nihilo nihil fit. . . .* He was a Deist." The probability is that Marlowe was also a deist, however terrifying his opinions might have appeared to his more simpleminded contemporaries.

Marlowe's death was hailed triumphantly by the Puritan pamphleteers as a manifest instance of God's judgment upon "a filthy playmaker," an atheist and a blasphemer. Shakespeare seems to be referring to it in *As You Like It* in Touchstone's rather flippant remark that "when a man's verses cannot be understood nor a man's good wit seconded with the forward child Understanding, it strikes a man more dead than a great reckoning in a little room." According to the inquest after his death, Marlowe was killed after supper during a quarrel about the bill—"le recknyng"—in a private room of Mistress Bull's house at Deptford. This inquest was reexamined by G. Thurston, secretary of the Coroners' Society of England and Wales.[4] His conclu-

sion is that "the very oddity of Frizer's evidence is the best argument for its truth," that "there is nothing to suggest that the inquisition was not regularly executed, and that the probable mechanism of Marlowe's death was so unusual and unexpected that fabrication is unlikely." In *As You Like It*, Touchstone's lines are followed almost immediately by a direct quotation from *Hero and Leander*, when Phoebe says:

Dead Shepherd, now I find thy saw of might:
"Who ever lov'd, that lov'd not at first sight?"

The dead shepherd's other friends delivered themselves of equally brief and affectionate remarks. Peele wrote of "Marley the Muses' Darling"; Chapman said that he stood up to the chin in the Pierian flood; Nashe—who also wrote an "Elegy on Marlowe's Untimely Death," which appeared in some copies of the first edition of *Dido*, none of which now survives—spoke of "poor deceased Kit Marlowe." Only Kyd, who had gotten into trouble because of him, said that he "was intemperate and of a cruel heart" and in the habit of "attempting sudden privy injuries to men." The best epitaph was written by Michael Drayton in the next century:

. . . Marlowe, bathèd in the Thespian springs,
Had in him those brave translunary things
That your first poets had; his raptures were
All fire and air, which made his verses clear,
For that fine madness still he did retain
Which rightly should possess a poet's brain.

In truth, Marlowe differed from his contemporaries not so much in degree as in kind. He was, said Swinburne, "the most daring and inspired pioneer in all our poetic literature, the first English poet whose powers may be called sublime."

PLAYS AND POEMS

ONLY one of Marlowe's plays, the first and second parts of *Tamburlaine the Great*, was published in his lifetime. This appeared anonymously in 1590. Next to appear, in 1594, the year after his death, were *Edward II* and *Dido*,

[4] "Christopher Marlowe's Death," *Contemporary Review* (March–April 1964).

CHRISTOPHER MARLOWE

Queen of Carthage, which carries Nashe's name as well as Marlowe's on the title page. No collected edition of the plays appeared, and the result is that the texts vary from the comparatively good *Tamburlaine* and *Edward II* to the varying degrees of corruption of *The Massacre at Paris* and *Doctor Faustus*, of which two widely different versions survive, the 1616 text being almost twice as long as that of 1604. Nothing in the Marlowe canon has given rise to more disagreement among scholars than the relative value of these two basic texts—unless it be the date of the play itself. Probably more of Marlowe's original drafts survive in the so-called B text of 1616; the 1604 Quarto (A text) evidently represents an abridged version adapted to the needs of a touring company.[5] Marlowe's texts suffered the fate of all very popular plays in that age, mauled and maltreated by the players and periodically polished up by some theatrical hack. But fragmentary as they mostly are, it is by no means certain that this is not something very like the state in which he left them. We cannot, that is, blame everything upon inferior collaborators and the corruption of texts, and the temper of the man himself may survive in the spasmodic brilliance of his work.

Marlowe's plays held the stage right into the middle of the next century, until the Puritans closed the theaters. Edward Gayton in his *Pleasant Notes Upon Don Quixote* (1651) tells us that on holiday afternoons, and especially at Shrovetide, an audience composed largely of sailors, watermen, shoemakers, butchers, and apprentices would force the players to act their favorite pieces—"sometimes *Tamerlane*, sometimes *Jugurth*, sometimes *The Jew of Malta*, and sometimes parts of all these. . . . And unless these were done . . . the benches, the tiles, the laths, the stones, the oranges, apples and nuts flew about most liberally."[6] From then on *Tamburlaine* was regarded as unactable until Donald Wolfit and Tyrone Guthrie produced a shortened version of both parts at the Old Vic, London, in 1951. Sickening as the experience was, it left no doubt at all of Marlowe's mastery of theatrical effect.

After all, the Elizabethan stage had to compete in interest with the adjacent bear- and bull-baiting rings, to say nothing of the ever-popular public executions for high treason, which, in these years of the Jesuit mission to England, were fairly numerous. *Doctor Faustus* also owed its popularity largely to the provision made for scenic effects: the thunder and lightning, the hellfire, the shaggy-haired devils who were said to run roaring across the stage with fireworks in their mouths—a difficult operation, surely, even for hardened Elizabethan players. Similarly, *The Massacre at Paris*, in addition to its topicality, provided a perfect orgy of killings. Marlowe correctly gauged the taste of the public. Few scenes in drama are more horrifying than the entrance of Tamburlaine, lashing the conquered kings harnessed to his coach, and no lines more famous than his

> Holla, ye pampered jades of Asia:
> What, can ye draw but twenty miles a day?
> (Part 2. IV. iii. 3980–3981)[7]

But we no longer find it amusing when the starving Bajazeth in his cage is advised to eat his wife before she gets too thin. It is significant that it has been left to our own age to produce a play that had not been staged for over three hundred and fifty years on account of its barbarity.

But, in spite of the parade of horrors—Shakespeare's early *Titus Andronicus* in Marlowe's manner outdoes even his master in this respect—Elizabethan audiences were very appreciative of both acting and poetry. Indeed, had they not been such keen critics of both, there could hardly have been a poetic drama at all. The important thing in the theater of Marlowe and Shakespeare was the spoken word, which was then a far more living thing than it is to the modern filmgoer or television viewer. Acting in the earlier days of the drama may have been of the more loudmouthed and flamboyant kind popularized by Edward Alleyn—for whom Marlowe, it seems, wrote his title roles—but it developed with such rapidity that the conventions of 1587, the date of *Tamburlaine*, were outmoded by 1597, the date of *Henry IV*, in

[5] See W. W. Greg, ed., *Marlowe's Doctor Faustus, 1604–1616: Parallel Texts* (Oxford, 1950).
[6] Quoted by Percy Simpson in *Studies in Elizabethan Drama*, "Marlowe's Tragical History of Doctor Faustus."
[7] Line references are to the C. F. Tucker Brooke edition (Oxford, 1910).

which Tamburlaine's tirades were already being parodied by Ancient Pistol. By that time Alleyn's "great and thundering speech" had given place to the more restrained and subtle art of Richard Burbage.

Marlowe's own verse developed with even more rapidity during the five years of his life as a working dramatist, from the rhetorical lyricism of *Tamburlaine* to the flexible and subtle instrument it becomes in *Edward II* and *Doctor Faustus*. Thus he prepared the way for the later Elizabethan blank verse, which expresses a greater variety of emotion than any other medium. In *Hero and Leander* and *All Ovids Elegies* he also shows himself a master of the polished, witty heroic couplet, a tradition that he may be said to have established. That the same man should, in the short space of five years, have written works so different as *Tamburlaine* and *Edward II*, *Doctor Faustus* and *Hero and Leander*, is nothing less than astonishing. It used to be said that Marlowe lacked a sense of humor. Nowadays the tendency is to see comic touches everywhere in his work. His comedy can be savage, as in *The Jew of Malta* and *Tamburlaine;* it can also be subtly ironic, as in *Doctor Faustus* and *Hero and Leander*. Indeed, in all Marlowe's work there is an ambivalence of tone which is only now beginning to be appreciated, so that he may be seen as anticipating both the modern Theater of Cruelty and the Theater of the Absurd.

DIDO, QUEEN OF CARTHAGE

DIDO is usually judged to be Marlowe's earliest play, though he may have taken it up again and revised it later for production at court by the Children of the Chapel Royal. It appears to have been much admired by Shakespeare, and may be the play instanced by Hamlet in his conversation with the players at Elsinore. "An excellent play," says the Prince of Denmark, "well digested in the scenes, set down with as much modesty as cunning. But it was never acted; or, if it was, not above once, for it pleased not the million. One speech chiefly I loved, 'twas Aeneas' tale to Dido, and thereabout of it especially where he speaks of Priam's slaughter" (*Hamlet*, II.2). Indeed it is a remarkable passage:

> At last came Pyrrhus fell and full of ire,
> His harness dropping blood, and on his spear
> The mangled head of Priam's youngest son,
> And after him his band of myrmidons,
> With balls of wildfire in their murdering paws
> (II. i. 508–512)

It is a style that achieved its effect, as T. S. Eliot was the first to point out, by stopping just short of caricature,[8] a nightmare horror heightened by sadistic relish of the grotesqueness of horror, which comes out again in such lines as:

> We saw Cassandra sprawling in the streets
> (II. i. 569)

and, of Hecuba:

> At last the soldiers pull'd her by the heels,
> And swung her howling in the empty air
> (II. i. 542–543)

In its use of calculated hyperbole it is a tone very characteristic of Marlowe. A great deal of *Dido* is taken straight from the *Aeneid*, though Marlowe fills out Virgil's account of the sack of Troy with gory details and imagery that Ethel Seaton has recently shown he got from the medieval romances, especially from Lydgate's *Troy Book*.[9] Characteristically, an amorous scene between Jove and Ganymede, "that female wanton boy," is added by way of prologue, suggested by half a line in the *Aeneid*, and Marlowe's temperamental ardor reveals itself unmistakably in Dido's cry

> And I must perish in his burning arms
> (III. iv. 1017)

and

> For in his looks I see eternity,
> And he'll make me immortal with a kiss
> (IV. iv. 1328–1329)

lines echoed in Faustus' address to the shade of Helen of Troy, though with terrifying undertones.

On the whole, *Dido* has (for Marlowe) a

[8] *The Sacred Wood* (London, 1920).
[9] "Marlowe's Light Reading," in *Elizabethan and Jacobean Studies Presented to Frank Percy Wilson* (London, 1959).

greater preponderance of rather monotonous end-stopped lines, though in other places may be detected the strength and radiance of his maturity, as in the magnificent description of the Greeks tumbling out of the wooden horse:

In whose stern faces shin'd the quenchless fire
That after burnt the pride of Asia
(II. i. 481–482)

which in *Doctor Faustus* is transmuted to

And burnt the topless towers of Ilium
(1329)

For all through Marlowe's work there is this habit of improving on his best lines and outdoing his best theatrical effects.

What Nashe did to this play is not known, though Havelock Ellis conjectures that it was "elaborated and considerably enlarged by Nashe in a manner that is sometimes a caricature, perhaps not quite consciously of Marlowe's manner." In *The Unfortunate Traveller* (1594), Nashe certainly showed himself to be a satirical connoisseur of literary modes, though now the satirical touches in *Dido* appear to be as much Marlowe's as Nashe's. The most recent and best treatment of *Dido* is, however, to be found in H. J. Oliver's excellent introduction to his edition of 1968, and in Brian Gibbons' chapter, "Unstable Proteus" (*Christopher Marlowe*, Mermaid Critical Commentaries). "The power and depth of Dido's emotion," writes Dr. Gibbons, "are dramatically realised in what we are accustomed to think of as a uniquely Shakespearean manner: and in fact it is essentially the *dramatic* power of Dido which influences Shakespeare in *Antony and Cleopatra*."

TAMBURLAINE THE GREAT

FOR *Tamburlaine*, the play by which he won his first and most resounding success, Marlowe took the career of the Tartar conqueror Timur the Lame, or Tamerlane, as he found it reported in the Renaissance historians. The first part was so successful that a sequel was called for at once. On the publication of both parts in 1590

they were described as "two tragical discourses," which suggests rhetoric rather than drama. But in spite of the undeniable monotony of this high-pitched rhetoric, a design is perceptible in both parts. Part 1 recounts Tamburlaine's rise to power by a clever manipulation of the rivalries at the decadent Persian court; he achieves the summit of his power by his conquest of Bajazeth, the Great Turk whom he uses, literally, as his footstool and carries about in an iron cage. This, and Bajazeth's suicide by dashing out his brains against the bars of the cage, was evidently regarded as the high spot of the first part. There is also a flyting match—or abusive contest—between the two queens, Zenocrate and Zabina. After a remarkable passage of hysterical prose, Zabina also brains herself against her husband's cage. Tamburlaine's love for Zenocrate, however, exerts a certain moderating influence upon him and he spares the life of her father, the soldan of Egypt, instead of adding his to the pile of corpses by which he mounts to overlordship of the Near and Middle East. At the conclusion of Part 1, Tamburlaine entombs "the Great Turk and his fair empress," marries Zenocrate and, having no further territorial demands to make for the moment, "takes truce with all the world."

By the time he came to write *The Second Part of the Bloody Conquests of Mighty Tamburlaine* Marlowe had exhausted most of his material. Part 2 is therefore devoted to showing the degeneration of Tamburlaine's character as an enemy of both gods and men and the madness which overtakes him after Zenocrate's death, when he plans to make war against heaven and to

. . . set black streamers in the firmament,
To signify the slaughter of the gods.
(Part 2. V. iii. 4441–4442)

He burns down the town where Zenocrate has died, murders his own son (who has no taste for war), harnesses the conquered kings to his coach, shoots the governor of Babylon to death as he hangs in chains, burns the Koran, and challenges Mahomet to "come down" and avenge it. What is most notable is that in spite of the enormity of his material, Marlowe shows a cool control throughout, combining the richness and melody of Spenser with the driving power of his own peculiarly masculine line. The arrogant prologue tells us how far this was an innovation:

From jigging veins of rhyming mother wits,
And such conceits as clownage keeps in pay,
We'll lead you to the stately tent of war,
Where you shall hear the Scythian Tamburlaine
Threatening the world with high astounding terms,
And scourging kingdoms with his conquering sword.
View but his picture in this tragic glass,
And then applaud his fortunes as you please.

There has been much discussion, notably in Roy Battenhouse's *Marlowe's Tamburlaine* (1941), as to whether Marlowe admired his hero and identified with him. The answer is surely contained in the last two lines of the prologue. The dramatist's attitude is apparently objective and noncommittal. His aim, he says in effect, is to hold the mirror up to nature. Whether we approve of what we see in "this tragic glass" does not concern him. But, in spite of that, it is quite clear that Marlowe was not writing a morality on the lines of a medieval fall of princes. He did not, that is, conceive *Tamburlaine* as a play in ten acts. The second part was written in response to popular demand.

Though he announces from time to time that he is the Scourge of God, and must therefore fulfill this character by being a terror to the world, Tamburlaine is only repeating the Renaissance view of himself, which Marlowe found in George Whetstone's *The English Mirror* (1586), his principal source. What really interested him was Tamburlaine as an example of the heroic will—the man who rose from humble origins (like himself) to become master of the world. Both the radiant beauty and the structure of the verse reflect this, as William Empson has so well defined it in his *Seven Types of Ambiguity*. "Marlowe's idea of the heroic soul," writes Empson, "has extreme simplicity and unbounded appetite, so that . . . after one subordinate clause has opened out of another with inalterable energy, it can still roar at the close with the same directness as in the opening line. . . . That a conditional clause should have been held back through all these successive lightnings of poetry, and that after their achievement, it should still be present with the same conviction *and resolution,* is itself a statement of the heroic character."

Tamburlaine moves and lives in an element of fire, for fire is an element that not only aspires but consumes everything in its way. He is repeatedly compared to the sun in glory, from whom the meaner planets take their light. His consort, Zenocrate, is invested with the cold contemplative light of the moon, and together they form the active and passive principles of all life. The whole of the first part of the play is transfigured by the golden light of the conqueror's divine being, and when he dies we are told that his flesh "is not of force enough to hold the fiery spirit it contains." His life passes before us in a dream of passion, filled with visions of far lands and vast multitudinous armies, delirious with blood and slaughter and a metaphysical thirst for the infinite. His vision, we are told, is "lift upward and divine"; at first he conquers by the power of rhetoric and the splendor of his being, and to the last he is

Still climbing after knowledge infinite
(Part 1. II. vi. 875)

Indeed, in *Tamburlaine* Marlowe achieved a height of idealism he never reached again, for in it he embodied the free poetic imagination of the Renaissance. It is also his most sustained performance. If perversity, too, may be found in the all-too-obvious delight in bloodshed and cruelty, there is also a more pleasing naiveté in the roll of resounding place names, as though the poet had fallen in love with his atlas—the great *Theatrum Orbis Terrarum* (1570) of Abraham Ortelius, which he first discovered in the library of his Cambridge college.

THE JEW OF MALTA

THOUGH described on the title page of the 1633 edition as a tragedy, *The Jew of Malta* is, in spirit at least, a savage satirical comedy. As a play of Machiavellian policy, it is of quite a different "kind" from *Tamburlaine*. Its first recorded performance was on 26 February 1592 by Lord Strange's players at the Rose Theatre, Bankside, with Edward Alleyn in the title role.

It recounts how Barabas, a rich Jew, is despoiled of his wealth by Farnese, the Christian governor of Malta, in order that the long-overdue Turkish tribute money may be paid. Farnese justifies this extortion by saying that Malta is accursed for harboring Jews at all, and he gives Barabas the choice of becoming a Christian and giving up only half his wealth, or remaining a Jew and losing it all. Barabas, unlike the other Jews, proudly chooses the latter alternative, accusing the Knights of Malta of hypocrisy. The rest of the play is devoted to the Jew's revenge, in which he plays off Turk against Christian. The plot is a complicated one and reaches such melodramatic heights as to become almost farcical. From the grand Marlovian creation of the opening scenes, Barabas degenerates into a skinny figure of maniacal hatred. His revenge is so complete that at the end he becomes governor of Malta himself. At this point, however, he makes his first false move and encompasses his own destruction. When his old enemy Farnese is delivered up to him as a prisoner, instead of putting him to death, he makes a deal with him and plans to deliver the Turks into his hands. Farnese proves the more ruthless and the more cunning of the two, and it is Barabas, and not Calymath, the Turk, who falls through the trapdoor into the boiling cauldron. His greed overreached his policy.

In the prologue, Machiavelli appears in person and declares:

> I count religion but a childish toy,
> And hold there is no sin but ignorance.
> (14–15)

He then treats the audience to a short discourse on political realism:

> Many will talk of title to a crown.
> What right had Caesar to the empery?
> Might first made kings, and laws were then most sure
> When like the Draco's they were writ in blood.
> Hence comes it, that a strong built citadel
> Commands much more than letters can import.
> (18–23)

In other words, armaments are more important than culture. Marlowe was interested in fortification, and in *Tamburlaine*, Part 2, "the Scourge of God" delivers a lecture to his sons on the subject. Here, however, Marlowe is being self-consciously tough. The doctrine expressed is, of course, a travesty of Machiavelli's subtle statecraft, though it probably comes from Gentillet's *Contre-Machiavel*. To the popular Elizabethan imagination the "Machiavel" was only another word for the devil. Even so, it is not unlikely that Marlowe felt an affinity with him. Blake said that Milton was of the devil's party without knowing it. Marlowe seems to have known it.

Throughout *The Jew of Malta*, in which he regards the society of his time with cynicism and contempt, Marlowe constantly underlines the contrast between what men profess to believe and what they actually do. It pleases him, as in *Tamburlaine*, Part 2, to expose the hypocrisy of the Christians, as when Farnese tells Barabas:

> Excess of wealth is cause of covetousness:
> And covetousness, O 'tis a monstrous sin!
> (I. 356–357)

and Barabas cries:

> What? bring you Scripture to confirm your wrongs?
> Preach me not out of my possessions. (I. 343–344)

He has already told us his opinion of the Christians:

> Rather had I, a Jew, be hated thus,
> Than pitied in a Christian poverty.
> For I can see no fruits in all their faith,
> But malice, falsehood, and excessive pride,
> Which methinks fits not their profession.
> Haply some hapless man hath conscience,
> And for his conscience lives in beggary.
> (I. 152–158)

But nowhere does Barabas become a great tragic figure like Shylock. Though he too has a daughter whom he loves more than anything except his gold—his cry "O girl, O gold, O beauty, O my bliss!" is echoed by Shylock's "O my ducats, O my daughter!"—the assuaging element of humanity is quite absent from the play, which is nearer in spirit to Jonson's *Volpone* than Shakespeare's *The Merchant of Venice*. Marlowe's conception of Barabas is summed up in the lines:

I am not of the tribe of Levy, I,
That can so soon forget an injury.
We Jews can fawn like spaniels when we please,
And when we grin we bite   (II. 779–782)

For like Kyd's *The Spanish Tragedy*, *The Jew of Malta* is an early example of the revenge play, so characteristic of later Elizabethan or Jacobean tragedy. In it we exchange brilliant light for darkness, heroic exploit for cunning intrigue, vaulting rhetoric for the sly aside. Everyone breaks faith with everyone else on the grounds of self-interest and expediency. Farnese breaks his promise to the Turks, because he is not bound to keep faith with infidels, though the Turks treat him with consideration and courtesy; Barabas justifies his deception of both Turks and Christians, "for all are heretics that are not Jews." Religion, far from being a childish toy, is shown for what Machiavelli said it was—an instrument of policy. And the monster Ithamore exclaims in fiendish delight:

Why, was there ever seen such villainy,
So neatly plotted, and so well perform'd?
                    (III. 1220–1221)

The radical change in the quality of the verse after the second act has often been commented upon and a variety of reasons has been given for it, none of them convincing. It has been supposed that Marlowe lost interest in his play halfway through and left it to someone else to finish. But throughout there are flashes of a mordant wit that can only be Marlowe's, especially in the scene between Barabas and the friars who come to convert him, but with one eye on his gold, in the fourth act. This act begins ominously enough with:

There is no music to a Christian's knell.
How sweet the bells ring now the nuns are dead
That sound at other times like tinkers' pans!
I was afraid the poison had not wrought,
Or though it wrought, it would have done no good,
For every year they swell, and yet they live
                    (IV. 1509–1514)

Because such verse is deficient in the lyricism of *Tamburlaine* or *Doctor Faustus*, or even in the hard splendor of the first act of this play, it has been too hastily assumed that such a passage cannot be Marlowe's. But since each of his plays is of a different kind, he employed in each a different kind of verse. In *The Jew of Malta* he developed a tone suitable to the spirit of the play—a savage farce—which Eliot thinks is perhaps "his most powerful and mature tone."

It is evident from this play that Marlowe used the drama as a vehicle for mocking the orthodoxies of his time. Marlowe even mocks himself, when Ithamore serenades the whore Belamira with a parody of *The Passionate Shepherd to His Love*. As Ellis-Fermor writes:

For in Marlowe we find, earlier than in any of his contemporaries, the significant schism between the ideal or spiritual world and the world pragmatically estimated by everyday observation, which seems, in one form or another, to be an essential part of any tragic conception of the universe. The cleavage is anticipated in *Tamburlaine* and presented in its full operation in *Faustus,* where the possibility of reconciling the course of man's life with the aspiration of his spiritual instincts is rejected.[10]

The success of *The Jew of Malta* was greatly augmented when in 1594 the Jewish Doctor Lopez was executed on the absurd charge of trying to poison the queen. The play was one of the most popular pieces in Henslowe's repertory and came to be known simply as *The Jew*. We do not know its source, nor exactly when it was written. But the original of Barabas may have been David Passi, a wealthy Jewish merchant of Constantinople, who was involved in the Turkish designs against Malta, cleverly playing off Turk against Christian. Passi was also concerned with English diplomacy in the Mediterranean and his career came to an end in 1591. It is possible that Marlowe knew of his activities firsthand through his secret-service work. On the other hand, several families of wealthy Jews were living in London at this time, among them Alvarez Mendes, a kinsman of Joao Miques, counsellor of the sultan and governor of Naxos. A fierce quarrel, well known in diplomatic circles, developed between these two men in 1591–1592. When the Turkish besiegers enter Malta in the last act by way of the city sewers, Marlowe is evidently recalling an account of the siege of Tripoli that follows a chapter on

[10] *The Jacobean Drama* (London, 1936).

284

Malta in Washington's *Navigations, Peregrinations and Voyages made into Turkey by Nicholas Nicholay* (1585). As usual, wide reading and considerable experience went into the making of this play.

THE MASSACRE AT PARIS

POLITICS is also the center of *The Massacre at Paris*, which presents the general massacre of the Huguenots on St. Bartholomew's Eve, 1572. The play, another very popular piece, came to be known as *The Guise*, since the action is dominated by the duke of Guise, who is shown as a pure type of Machiavellian hero-villain, with his somberly powerful opening soliloquy (which, incidentally, follows the pattern of Gloucester's long soliloquy at the opening of *Richard III*):

> Oft have I levell'd, and at last have learn'd,
> That peril is the chiefest way to happiness,
> And resolution honour's fairest aim.
> What glory is there in a common good
> That hangs for every peasant to achieve?
> That like I best that flies beyond my reach . . .
> Although my downfall be the deepest hell.
> (94–99; 104)

Here is a remarkable piece of self-criticism on Marlowe's part. But, as usual with him in scenes of carnage, the writing in this play betrays an almost breathless sense of exhilaration, though it has come down to us in a far worse state textually than any of his others. From the existence of a manuscript draft of the scene of Mugeron's murder, which was discovered among Alleyn's papers by J. P. Collier and is now at the Folger Shakespeare Library, Washington, D.C., we can see that the published text is a drastically cut acting version of an original that must have been at least twice as long.[11] There are only hints of what the complete work may have been like. The Guise was evidently one of Alleyn's great roles. At a performance in January 1593, during a short season interrupted

---

[11] This draft, once thought to be in Marlowe's hand, has been shown by R. E. Alton ("Marlowe Authenticated," *Times Literary Supplement*, 25 April 1964) to be quite unlike the general character of Marlowe's signature of 1585.

by the plague, the takings at the Rose Theatre were unusually high. Indeed, the play, as we have it, is all killing. It is noteworthy, however, that the duke of Guise can pause to argue with Ramus about Aristotle before contemptuously ordering him to be stabbed. Nevertheless, as the leader of the Catholic party, he uses religion purely as an instrument of policy, exclaiming:

> Religion! *O Diabole!*
> Fie, I am ashamed, however that I seem,
> To think a word of such a simple sound
> Of so great matter should be made the ground.
> (123–126)

At the height of the villainy a note of parody creeps in. After murdering the king, her son, who has inconvenient scruples about killing so many of his Huguenot subjects, Catharine de Medici cries: "Tush, all shall die unless I have my will"—her will being to rule France through her other son, Henry III. "His mind, you see," she explains, "runs on his minions." But Henry III is by no means so enfeebled as not to be aware of the queen mother's designs and, after the murder of the duke of Guise, the tide of massacre begins to run in the other direction. Spurning the duke's body with his foot, Henry cries:

> Ah this sweet sight is physic to my soul.
> Go fetch his son for to behold his death.
> Surcharg'd with guilt of thousand massacres,
> Mounser of Lorraine sink away to hell
> This is the traitor that has spent my gold
> In making foreign wars and civil broils.
> Did he not draw a sort of English priests
> From Douai to the seminary at Rheims,
> To hatch forth treason 'gainst their natural Queen?
> Did he not cause the King of Spain's huge fleet
> To threaten England and to menace me?
> (1032–1035; 1040–1046)

He is then stabbed by a Jacobin friar and with his dying breath calls for the English ambassador to convey loving messages to the queen of England, "whom God has blessed for hating papistry." And he bids the weeping Epernon to dry his eyes and

> whet thy sword on Sixtus' bones,
> That it may keenly slice the Catholics.
> (1250–1251)

Normally there was a ban on political and religious subjects in the Elizabethan theater, but this play must have been regarded as such good anti-Catholic propaganda that the master of the revels was glad to pass it. Apart from anything else, it is interesting as showing the intensity of Marlowe's feelings as an anti-Catholic government agent, for he evidently knew the political background pretty well.

EDWARD II

THE Prologue to *Doctor Faustus* mentions a play dealing with "dalliance of love / In courts of kings where state is overturn'd." This is usually taken to refer to *Edward II*. Indeed in his chronicle play Marlowe is chiefly interested in the king's passion for his favorite, Piers Gaveston. His sources are Holinshed and Stow, but he gives far more importance to Gaveston than Holinshed does. Gaveston on his first appearance tells the audience how he intends to entertain the king, now that he has been recalled from exile in defiance of the barons and the bishops:

Sweet prince, I come; these, these thy amorous lines
Might have enforc'd me to have swum from France
And like Leander, gasp'd upon the sand . . .
I must have wanton poets, pleasant wits,
Musicians, that with touching of a string
May draw the pliant king which way I please.
Music and poetry is his delight,
Therefore I'll have Italian masques by night,
Sweet speeches, comedies, and pleasing shows,
And in the day, when he shall walk abroad,
Like sylvan nymphs my pages shall be clad,
My men like satyrs grazing on the lawns,
Shall with their goat feet dance an antic hay.

(6–8; 51–60)

Some years later, in the masque of *Actaeon and Diana*, Ben Jonson faithfully followed the prescription contained in the last part of this speech for the delight of James I. But to Holinshed it appears that Gaveston furnished the court with "companies of jesters, ruffians, flattering parasites, musicians and other vile and naughty ribauds, that the king might spend both days and nights in jesting, playing, banqueting, and in such other filthy and dishonourable exercises"—which is a far cry from the fine voluptuousness of Marlowe's lines.

Marlowe makes the five years during which Gaveston was the king's favorite (1307–1312) virtually the center of the play. After the murder of Gaveston halfway through, and the introduction of the new favorites, the Spensers and Baldock, the interest rather dwindles until the king's prolonged martyrdom at the hands of the revengeful queen and of Mortimer, a Machiavellian figure who has become the queen's lover in a bid for supreme power. It has recently been argued that Mortimer, with his mock humility when offered the protectorship, derives from Shakespeare's Richard III, thus making Marlowe indebted to Shakespeare rather than Shakespeare to Marlowe, as had previously been supposed.

Much of *Edward II* consists of the barons' and bishops' fulminations against the king for "frolicking with his minion." This wordy quarreling breaks out occasionally into civil war when the king says that he is prepared to make all England's towns huge heaps of stone, so long as he has a corner left in which to frolic with his Gaveston. But Edward is no match for his military barons and embattled clerics, nor for that matter for Queen Isabel with her "eyes of steel," and there is a deposition scene that foreshadows the similar scene in *Richard II*. But, as always with Shakespeare, who, we are sometimes told, was influenced by this play, there is in *Richard II* a sense of tragic destiny and a concern for the condition of England that are nowhere to be found in Marlowe. It is likely that Marlowe learned much more from the *Henry VI* trilogy, though there are those who believe that he collaborated with Shakespeare on these plays, together with Greene and Peele. The chronology of the history plays is discussed in F. P. Wilson's *Marlowe and the Early Shakespeare*, where it is suggested that *King John* may have been written in 1590. When, however, the three parts of *Henry VI* are performed together, little doubt remains that they are almost entirely the work of Shakespeare, however much he may have been indebted at the beginning of his career to the current theatrical language of the time—a language whose accents were largely determined by Marlowe and Kyd.

CHRISTOPHER MARLOWE

In *Edward II* Marlowe makes a step in the direction of the Shakespearean type of history play—and, outside Shakespeare, it is by far the best history play written in the 1590's, altogether remarkable for its economy, dramatic tension, and skillful use of its source. In it Marlowe is handling social groups and is not concerned so much with one dominating individual. In the complementary figures of Edward and Mortimer he contrasts weakness with strength. Irving Ribner has noted how Shakespeare took up this idea from Marlowe and continued to use it in some of the greatest of his later plays.[12]

Evidently Alleyn judged that there was no part for him in the play, for it was performed by Pembroke's men probably for the first time during the brief winter season of 1592–1593. Like *Doctor Faustus*, *Edward II* is a study in weakness and failure and the king himself, gentle, poetic creature that he is, though driven to outbursts of desperate cruelty by the pack of jackals who surround him, is Marlowe's most human creation. But equally skillful is the delineation of the cold and cynical time-server Gaveston—a perfect foil to the king, who is at the mercy of every mood and for whom the world is hardly more than a show. The Spensers and Baldock are also clever portraits of the type of social climber with which every Renaissance court was infested—the scholar Baldock especially, with his boast that "my gentry/I fetched from Oxford, not from heraldry." His creator could say the same, though in his case it was Cambridge. And how characteristic of the same mind is the Younger Spenser's prescriptions for self-advancement:

> Then Baldock, you must cast the scholar off,
> And learn to court it like a gentleman . . .
> You must be proud, bold, pleasant, resolute,
> And now and then, stab as occasion serves.
> (751–752, 762–763)

And Baldock's reply that though he may be curatelike in his attire he is

> . . . inwardly licentious enough,
> And apt for any kind of villany.
> (770–771)

Gaveston, in the view of Charlton and Waller, "bears the mark of his creator both in his sensual and luxuriant imagination and in his devil-may-care insolence, his ironical recklessness. This . . . indeed may be very much what Marlowe himself actually was."[13]

In *Tamburlaine* Marlowe tells us that "A god is not so glorious as a king." But in *Edward II* the poor king is overruled at every point. In the second half of the play he is subjected to every sort of foul indignity until, at last, shut up in the castle sewer, he is murdered revoltingly with a red-hot spit—a savage comment on his homosexual habits. Particularly sinister is the figure of Lightborn, the murderer, with his professional pride in his calling. As he tells Mortimer:

> 'Tis not the first time I have killed a man.
> I learn'd in Naples how to poison flowers,
> To strangle with a lawn thrust through the throat,
> To pierce the windpipe with a needle's point,
> Or whilst one is asleep, to take a quill
> And blow a little powder in his ears,
> Or open his mouth, and pour quicksilver down.
> But yet I have a braver way than these.
> (2362–2369)

He is careful to win the king's confidence before killing him—a scene, considered purely technically, of considerable dramatic skill, but by any human standard quite appalling. The horror of the conclusion is somewhat mitigated by the mournful nobility of Mortimer's last words as he is led out to execution, anticipating Hamlet's soliloquy on death:

> Farewell fair Queen, weep not for Mortimer,
> That scorns the world, and, as a traveller,
> Goes to discover countries yet unknown.
> (2632–2634)

DOCTOR FAUSTUS

IN this great play Marlowe turns from politics and intrigue to principalities and powers. Once more a prologue defines its scope:

> Not marching now in fields of Thrasimene,
> Where Mars did mate the Carthaginians,

---

[12] Irving Ribner, *The English History Play in the Age of Shakespeare* (London, rev. ed., 1965).

[13] See their Introduction to *Edward II*, vol. V of R. H. Case, ed., *The Works and Life*.

Nor sporting in the dalliance of love,
In courts of kings where state is overturn'd,
Nor in the pomp of proud audacious deeds,
Intends our Muse to vaunt his heavenly verse:
Only this, Gentlemen, we must perform,
The form of Faustus' fortunes good or bad.

(1–8)

Although all the most important action of this play is confined to a little room (it is another "great reckoning in a little room"), outside that room lies infinite space and all eternity.

After tracing his early career as a doctor of divinity at Wittenburg, Marlowe tells us that Faustus, "glutted now with learning's golden gifts," turns to magic and necromancy, "the metaphysics of magicians"—

Till swoll'n with cunning of self-conceit,
His waxen wings did mount above his reach,
And melting, heavens conspir'd his overthrow.

(20–22)

As Harry Levin has pointed out, Marlowe himself belonged to the intellectual type known in his own time as an overreacher, one given to hyperbole and, in his use of the image of Icarus, he unconsciously showed that he was aware of it.[14] For Faustus is self-damned. "Give none the blame but thine own self-will, thy proud and aspiring mind, which brought thee into the wrath of God and utter damnation" reads Marlowe's source, which is closely followed throughout the play.[15]

Everyone coming to *Doctor Faustus* for the first time is at a loss before its combination of "heavenly verse" and flat, colorless, frequently foolish writing in the central scenes. To us it is broken-backed and stands like the ruin of a cathedral. An Elizabethan audience, however, familiar as it was with tragedy relieved by farce, would not in all likelihood have seen the play in those terms. After all, the scenes of foolery are taken straight from the "Faustbook"—which, in spite of its serious subject, is like many of the jest books of the period—and, in a sense, the foolery reinforces the bitter irony of the play as a whole. For this—trifling conjuring tricks, horseplay with caps of invisibility which enable him to snatch dishes away from the pope at a Vatican banquet—is really all that Faustus gets in his pact with the devil in exchange for his soul. The whole point is that Faustus is tricked. The omnipotence that, in the opening scenes of the play, he believes he will achieve through witchcraft turns out to be illusory, and in fact he exchanges knowledge for shadows, felicity for eternal torment. How far Marlowe was responsible for the foolish scenes in the Vatican and the dull, lifeless scenes at the emperor's court it is impossible to say. It seems clear, however, that he worked with a collaborator who no doubt knocked together the farcical prose scenes. In 1602, Bird and Rowley were paid four pounds for "additions." These must have been fairly considerable, as authors were seldom paid more than six to eight pounds for a whole play. But *Doctor Faustus* was not published until 1604, more than a decade after Marlowe's death, and he may have left it in a fragmentary form that necessitated its being filled out by other hands, as *Hero and Leander* was completed by Chapman and (perhaps) *Dido* by Nashe.

After signing the bond with Lucifer giving his soul in exchange for twenty-four years in which he may "live in all voluptuousness," Faustus blasphemously exclaims "Consummatum est!"—the last words of Christ on the cross—adding, with desperate bravado:

This word "damnation" terrifies not him,
For he confounds hell in Elysium.
His ghost be with the old philosophers! . . .
Tell me what is that Lucifer thy lord?
   Meph.: Arch-regent and commander of all spirits.
   Faust.: Was not that Lucifer an angel once?
   Meph.: Yes, Faustus, and most dearly lov'd of God.
   Faust.: How comes it then that he is prince of devils?
   Meph.: O by aspiring pride and insolence,
For which God threw him from the face of heaven.
   Faust.: And what are you that live with Lucifer?
   Meph.: Unhappy spirits that fell with Lucifer,
Conspir'd against our God with Lucifer,
And are for ever damn'd with Lucifer.
   Faust.: Where are you damn'd?

---

[14] See Levin's *The Overreacher: A Study of Christopher Marlowe.*

[15] *The History of the Damnable Life and and Deserved Death of Doctor John Faust,* tr. from the German "Faustbook" by "P.F." in 1592. This pamphlet is the only evidence we have for dating Marlowe's *Faustus.* The 1592 edition is described as "newly imprinted," suggesting that there may have been an earlier edition.

CHRISTOPHER MARLOWE

Meph.: In hell.
  Faust.: How comes it then that thou art out of hell?
  Meph.: Why this is hell, nor am I out of it.
Think'st thou that I who saw the face of God,
And tasted the eternal joys of heaven,
Am not tormented with ten thousand hells
In being depriv'd of everlasting bliss?
O Faustus, leave these frivolous demands,
Which strike a terror to my fainting soul.
  Faust.: What, is great Mephostophilis so passionate,
For being deprived of the joys of heaven?
Learn thou of Faustus manly fortitude
And scorn those joys thou never shalt possess.
(294–296, 298–322)

The irony of the situation is that Faustus is by no means so "resolute" as he likes to think. His defiance is only a mask for his agonized uncertainty; the reverse of his intellectual pride is despair, and it is for his despair that he is damned. Marlowe's theology is impeccable. He knows all the arguments. Like a clever debater with his "how comes it, then?" Faustus tries to catch out Mephostophilis in some inconsistency, at one point exclaiming, in his university phraseology, "Tush, these are freshmen's suppositions!" Although Faustus dismisses hell as an old wives' tale, he is obsessed by the idea of it, and continually questions Mephostophilis as to its nature and whereabouts. The terrible reply comes:

Hell hath no limits, nor is circumscrib'd
In one self place, for where we are is hell,
And where hell is, must we ever be.
(553–555)

But in reality Mephostophilis tells him nothing that he does not know already, and having achieved so little by his bond with Lucifer, in the second half of the play Faustus begins to repent of it. He is tormented by the thought that he has sold eternity for a toy, and bitterly accuses Mephostophilis of depriving him of the everlasting joys of heaven. " 'Twas thine own seeking, Faustus," replies the fiend, "Thank thyself." And he throws the scholar's humanism back at him with the argument that as heaven was made for man, "Therefore is man more excellent." "If it were made for man," cries Faustus, "'twas made for me. I will renounce this magic and repent." But the evil angel reminds him that since his bond with Lucifer he is a spirit—that is, a devil—and that God cannot pity him. The powers of evil, having reduced him to despair, now tempt him to suicide. If he takes his own life, they will have his soul in any case.

His ruin is completed by a request to have Helen of Troy as his paramour. She is thereupon conjured up by Mephostophilis to turn his mind from all thoughts of salvation, and Faustus, embracing her, exclaims:

Sweet Helen, make me immortal with a kiss.
Her lips suck forth my soul . . .
(1330–1331)

But this vision of Helen is no more substantial than that which he himself had conjured up earlier in the play for the delectation of the scholars and as proof of his magical powers. Whether or not she is now, on her second appearance, to be seen as a succuba (to have bodily connection with whom is damnation), to Faustus she is

fairer than the evening air,
Clad in the beauty of a thousand stars,
Brighter art thou than flaming Jupiter,
When he appeared to hapless Semele,
More lovely than the monarch of the sky
In wanton Arethusa's azur'd arms . . .
(1341–1346)

Faustus is, in reality, invoking his muse, the embodiment of his lyrical impulse. To be damned for this would seem to be more than a little hard, and after the fading of his splendid vision, the devils of the medieval church enter and claim their victim. Faustus' heart is now so hardened with intellectual pride, we are told, that he cannot repent of his bargain with Lucifer. As a matter of fact, he is continually attempting to repent in the second half of the play, and the final scene is one long agonized repentance.

See, see where Christ's blood streams in the firmament!
One drop would save my soul   (1432–1433)

he cries. But it is too late. He has signed his bond with Lucifer and asked for Helen as his paramour (though he compares her to Jupiter, just as earlier Mephostophilis had promised to get him women "as beautiful as was bright Lucifer before his fall") and his term is up. Longing to transcend human nature, to be a demigod, Faustus at last desperately seeks to be far less than a man, to turn to air, to be "transmogrified" into an animal, to be sucked up like a mist into the clouds, to be changed to little water drops and fall into the ocean and "ne'er be found."

Just before the end there is a moving scene in prose—the earliest example in English drama of tragic prose—which is sufficient answer to those who say that Marlowe lacked humanity. "Ah my sweet chamber-fellow," cries Faustus to one of the scholars, "had I lived with thee, then had I lived still but now must die eternally . . . and must remain in hell for ever. Hell, ah hell for ever! Sweet friends, what shall become of Faustus being in hell for ever?" "Yet Faustus," replies one of the scholars, "call on God." "On God, whom Faustus hath abjured?" cries the distracted man. "On God, whom Faustus hath blasphemed? Ah my God, I would weep, but the devil draws in my tears. Gush forth blood instead of tears, yea life and soul! Oh he stays my tongue. I would lift up my hands, but see they hold them, they hold them!" It was a stroke of genius to place this short poignant scene, in which Faustus is thoroughly humanized, just before the terrible loneliness on the edge of eternity. In the last soliloquy, which reaches an intensity equaled only by Shakespeare, the regular five-foot iambic line is broken up under the stress of passion in a way that is not found again until Jacobean drama, just as in the dialogues with Mephostophilis, Marlowe reaches a point of grave sublimity not reached again in English poetry until Milton. It took a great dramatist to put this tremendous conception on the stage.

HERO AND LEANDER AND THE POEMS

NEVERTHELESS, both *Edward II* and *Doctor Faustus* virtually end with an agonized shriek—curiously prophetic of their author's "untimely end." Marlowe also left behind him a spirited translation of Ovid's *Amores* in heroic couplets and a mock-heroic narrative poem in the same measure, *Hero and Leander*. Nowhere else does he appear in so sunny a frame of mind. Without these poems we should never have known the other side of his genius, the side beloved of his friends.

Hero, in Marlowe's poem, recalls no figure so much as Botticelli's girlish Venus riding in her scallop shell among the crisped sea waves—a figure which combines the tenderness of the Christian ethos with the hard clarity and grace of the classic world. She is described to perfection in one line:

> So young, so gentle, and so debonair.
> (I. 288)

Yet a mischievous spirit of burlesque breaks out in the lines describing her ceremonial robes, just as it does in the description of the Temple of Venus, where she officiates as a temple virgin, or "Venus' nun" (Elizabethan slang for prostitute). Here, through the crystal pavement, might be seen

> the gods in sundry shapes,
> Committing heady riots, incest, rapes . . .
> Jove slyly stealing from his sister's bed,
> To dally with Idalian Ganymed,
> And for his love Europa bellowing loud,
> And tumbling with the rainbow in a cloud.
> (I. 143–150)

Such lines are an indication of the spirit in which Marlowe approached his subject. Again, when Leander is swimming the Hellespont, he is lustfully waylaid by Neptune and exclaims

> You are deceiv'd; I am no woman, I
> (II. 192)

an episode of which it has been pointed out that Marlowe may be intending to suggest no more than that Leander is here embraced by the sea waves, personified by Neptune. However that may be, one can understand better what his contemporaries meant when they called him an epicure when he writes of Leander

> Even as delicious meat is to the taste,
> So was his neck in touching, and surpast

The white of Pelops' shoulder. I could tell ye
How smooth his breast was, and how white his belly.
(I. 63–66)

Throughout the poem a detached cynical wit, aimed at the conventions of the love poetry of his age, alternates with the "inveigling harmony" of the verse. But there is also a new and surprising tenderness, at once grave and gay, in the treatment of Hero's virginal fears, which reminds one of the Haidée episode in Byron's *Don Juan*. And surely the first meeting of the lovers in the Temple of Venus anticipates the meeting of Romeo and Juliet at Capulet's feast:

These lovers parlèd by the touch of hands:
True love is mute, and oft amazèd stands.
(I. 185–186)

The poem is, in fact, as J. B. Steane has shown, a complex of contradictory moods, and the often vigorous colloquial language of the love scenes looks forward to the metaphysical wit of Donne rather than back to the entranced tapestry world of Spenser. The same fusion of romance and humor appears in Shakespeare's more sensual *Venus and Adonis*, which was written about the same time. Together, the two poems established a tradition continued through Donne's *Elegies* into the verse of Jonson, Herrick, and other Caroline poets.

Hero and Leander was published in 1598 by Edward Blount, stationer in St. Paul's churchyard and one of Marlowe's friends. He dedicated it to the dead poet's patron, Sir Thomas Walsingham. In the same year another edition appeared as "Begun by Christopher Marloe, and finished by George Chapman," dedicated to Lady Audrey Walsingham. Chapman hastens to pay those dues to ceremony and marriage which had not entered the heads of Marlowe's lovers. He points out that their tragic end is the just reward of their "loose and secret" loves; but, in one of the most charming passages in his otherwise rather heavy-handed though not unworthy continuation, he changes the dead lovers into a pair of goldfinches:

Like two sweet birds, surnam'd th' Acanthides,
Which we call thistle-wasps, that near no seas
Dare ever come, but still in couples fly,
And feed on thistle-tops . . . (VI. 276–279)

Chapman's contribution has been in general severely handled. But, as Millar Maclure points out in his 1968 edition of the poem, he does manage to recapture, "with his own difference, the irony and elegance of Marlowe's asides. . . . No one else could have done it so well."

Another poem, *The Passionate Shepherd to His Love*, to which Ralegh wrote an ironic sequel, appeared in *The Passionate Pilgrim*, a popular anthology of 1599, and in a slightly different version in *England's Helicon* in 1600. It is a far more conventional poem than *Hero and Leander* and has the glassy artificiality typical of the Elizabethan lyric. Meanwhile, *All Ovid's Elegies*, an underrated work closely related to *Hero and Leander* in both tone and subject matter, was issued surreptitiously in an undated edition purporting to be printed in Holland. It was bound with Sir John Davies' bawdy epigrams by the printer who evidently relied on its scandalous appeal. It was burnt, in default of its author, by order of the ecclesiastical censors at Stationers' Hall in June 1599. The next year the translation of the First Book of Lucan's *Pharsalia* appeared under the imprint of Thomas Thorpe, the promoter and printer of Shakespeare's *Sonnets*. This translation reveals such mastery that it can no longer be regarded as an undergraduate work, though it has many affinities with *Tamburlaine*.

CONCLUSION

FRAGMENTARY as his texts often are, Marlowe emerges, the closer he is studied, as a master of stagecraft in the earlier days of the English drama—the pioneer from whose example those who followed profited most. He shares with Kyd the distinction of having introduced tragic blank verse and the drama of revenge to the stage, but he developed both far beyond Kyd's capacities. His life was as dangerous as his thought and, as much as he dared, he used the drama as a vehicle for his revolutionary conceptions, though the conclusions of all his plays were necessarily orthodox. His verse developed, during his five years as a working dramatist, from the "high astounding terms" of *Tamburlaine* to a much quieter and more flexible instrument, progressively nearer to the rhythm of ordinary speech. Nevertheless, in each of his plays he experiments with a different kind of verse suitable to the subject. His raptures were by no means all air and fire; for, in spite of the splendor of the verse, which invests the images of cruelty with a certain crystalline remoteness, *Tamburlaine* is still nauseating—both in its savage humor and in its sadism. Marlowe, in fact, had his full share of what Swinburne calls "the hideous lust of pain," and his perception of evil seems to have been unusually keen. In this respect his true successors are Webster, Marston, Tourneur, and Chapman, whose *Bussy d'Ambois* and *The Conspiracie*, with their heroic scorn of the world and ultimate defeatism, are like a continuation and extension of Marlowe's work.

If *Dido* be taken as the beginning and *Hero and Leander* as the end, Marlowe's work presents a singular unity, for both are Renaissance-classic in conception, the one inspired by Virgil, the other by "witty" Ovid. Tamburlaine and Faustus, with their longing for infinite knowledge, infinite power, and infinite loveliness, are typical Renaissance figures. Faustus, "the insatiable speculator," instead of being burnt by the church like Giordano Bruno, went to the everlasting bonfire; but Tamburlaine, with his heroic frenzy, his feeling for immanence, and his impiety, would seem to derive as much from Bruno as Barabas and the Guise ultimately derive from Machiavelli. No other poet has quite the same uninhibited delight in physical beauty and ability to paint it in such clear, cool colors. If Spenser's exquisite sensibility was flawed by a Puritanical sense of sin, *Hero and Leander* is perfect as "an anti-Spenserian manifesto . . . an Epithalamion without benefit of clergy,"[16] with its wicked parody of scholastic reasoning in Leander's sophistic attack on Hero's virginity.

Marlow was quite aware of the peril of the course he followed, but with his passion for extremes, peril was ever the chiefest way to happiness. He may, as Mario Praz and Harry Levin contend, have suffered from both a Ganymede and an Icarus complex. But an analysis of his imagery shows that the pattern of his thought is determined by a preoccupation with fire, the

stars, the heavens, the flight of birds, and all things clear, brilliant, swiftly moving, and aspiring. Like Icarus, he flew for a short while toward the sun—then, his waxen wings melting, he fell as melodramatically as any of his aspiring heroes, providing his age, as Levin remarks, with the perfect example of the atheist's tragedy.

SELECTED BIBLIOGRAPHY

I. BIBLIOGRAPHY. C. Crawford, *The Marlowe Concordance*, 3 vols. (Louvain, 1911–1932; repr. 1963); C. F. Tucker Brooke, *The Marlowe Canon* (London, 1922); S. A. Tannenbaum, *Christopher Marlowe: A Concise Bibliography* (New York, 1937; 1st supp., 1947); R. C. Johnson, comp., *Elizabethan Bibliographies Supplement No. 6* (London, 1968), covers 1946–1965. See also appropriate volumes of *The Cambridge Bibliography of English Literature* and *The Oxford History of English Literature*.

II. COLLECTED EDITIONS. A. Dyce, ed., *The Works*, 3 vols. (London, 1850; 1-vol. ed., rev. and corrected, 1858); A. H. Bullen, ed., *The Works*, 3 vols. (London, 1885); Havelock Ellis, ed., *Christopher Marlowe* (London, 1903; new ed., 1951), with a general intro. on the Elizabethan drama by J. A. Symonds; C. F. Tucker Brooke, ed., *The Works* (Oxford, 1910), the standard 1-vol. ed.; R. H. Case, gen. ed., *The Works and Life*, 6 vols. (London, 1930–1933); C. F. Tucker Brooke, ed., *The Life of Marlowe and Dido* (London, 1930); U. M. Ellis-Fermor, ed., *Tamburlaine the Great* (London, 1930; 2nd ed., 1951); H. S. Bennett, ed., *The Jew of Malta and The Massacre at Paris* (1931); F. S. Boas, ed., *Doctor Faustus* (London, 1932; 2nd ed., 1949); H. B. Charlton and R. D. Waller, eds., *Edward II* (1933); 2nd ed. rev. by F. N. Lees (1955); L. C. Martin, ed., *Poems* (1931); M. Maclure, ed., *The Poems*, The Revels Plays (London, 1968); J. B. Steane, ed., *The Complete Plays* (Harmondsworth, 1969); R. Gill, ed., *The Plays*, World's Classics (Oxford, 1971); S. Orgel, ed., *The Complete Poems and Translations* (Harmondsworth, 1971).

III. PLAYS. *Tamburlaine the Great* (London, 1590); acting version prepared by Tyrone Guthrie and Donald Wolfit (London, 1951); J. D. Jump, ed., Regents Renaissance Drama Series (London, 1967); J. W. Harper, ed., New Mermaids (London, 1971).

The Troublesome Reigne and Lamentable Death of Edward the Second (London, 1594): W. M. Merchant, ed., New Mermaids (London, 1967).

The Tragedie of Dido Queene of Carthage, by Christopher Marloe and Thomas Nash, Gent. (London, 1594): H. J. Oliver, ed., The Revels Plays (London, 1968), contains an excellent introduction.

---

[16] M. C. Bradbrook, *Shakespeare and Elizabethan Poetry*.

The Massacre at Paris (1602?): H. J. Oliver, ed., The Revels Plays (London, 1968).

The Tragical History of Dr Faustus (A text, London, 1604; B. text, 1616): W. W. Greg, ed., *Marlowe's Doctor Faustus, 1604–1616: Parallel Texts* (Oxford, 1950); W. W. Greg, *The Tragical History of the Life and Death of Doctor Faustus; A "Conjectural Reconstruction"* (Oxford, 1950); J. D. Jump, ed., The Revels Plays (London, 1962); R. Gill, ed., New Mermaids (London, 1965); Scolar Press facs. (London, 1970).

The Famous Tragedy of the Rich Jew of Malta (1633): T. W. Craik, ed., New Mermaids (London, 1966); Scolar Press facs. (London, 1970).

IV. POEMS. *All Ovid's Elegies* (Middleburg, 1595?), trans.; *Hero and Leander* (London, 1598), begun by Marlowe and finished by George Chapman; Scolar Press facs. (London, 1968); *Lucan's First Booke Translated Line for Line* (London, 1600); *The Passionate Shepherd to His Love* (London, 1600), in *England's Helicon*.

V. BIOGRAPHICAL AND CRITICAL STUDIES. W. Rose, ed., *The History of the Damnable Life and Deserved Death of Doctor John Faustus*, tr. into English by P. F. Gent, London, 1592 (London, 1925); T. Beard, *The Theatre of God's Judgements* (London, 1597), a Puritan attack; W. Vaughn, *The Golden Grove* (London, 1600); J. A. Symonds, *Shakespeare's Predecessors in the English Drama* (London, 1884; new ed., 1900); A. W. Verity, *The Influence of Christopher Marlowe on Shakespeare's Earlier Style* (Cambridge, 1886); J. G. Lewis, *Christopher Marlowe: His Life and Works* (Canterbury, 1890); J. H. Ingram, *Christopher Marlowe and His Associates* (London, 1904), contains useful material, but now rather out of date; A. C. Swinburne, *The Age of Shakespeare* (London, 1908); T. S. Eliot, *The Sacred Wood* (London, 1920), includes "Notes on the Blank Verse of Christopher Marlowe"; C. F. Tucker Brooke, *The Reputation of Christopher Marlowe* (New Haven, 1922); J. L. Hotson, *The Death of Christopher Marlowe* (Cambridge, Mass., 1925); U. M. Ellis-Fermor, *Christopher Marlowe* (London, 1927); S. A. Tannenbaum, *The Assassination of Christopher Marlowe* (New York, 1928), argues that Ralegh was directly responsible for Marlowe's death; F. S. Boas, *Marlowe and His Circle: A Biographical Survey* (Oxford, 1929; 2nd ed., 1931), the fullest discussion of this subject, with facsimiles of documents; M. Praz, "Christopher Marlowe," in *English Studies*, 13 (December 1931); M. Eccles, *Christopher Marlowe in London* (Cambridge, Mass., 1934); M. C. Bradbrook, *Themes and Conventions of Elizabethan Tragedy* (Cambridge, 1935); M. C. Bradbrook, *The School of Night* (Cambridge, 1936), contains a chapter on Marlowe and his association with Ralegh; U. M. Ellis-Fermor, *The Jacobean Drama* (London, 1936; rev. eds., 1947, 1953, 1958), for Marlowe's influence; J. Bakeless, *Christopher Marlowe* (London, 1938);

F. S. Boas, *Christopher Marlowe; A Biographical and Critical Study* (Oxford, 1940; repr. with suppl. note, 1953); M. B. Smith, *Marlowe's Imagery and the Marlowe Canon* (Philadelphia, 1940).

R. Battenhouse, *Marlowe's Tamburlaine* (Nashville, 1941); E. G. Clark, *Ralegh and Marlowe: A Study in Elizabethan Fustian* (New York, 1941); J. Bakeless, *The Tragical History of Christopher Marlowe*, 2 vols. (Cambridge, Mass., 1942), contains an exhaustive bibliography; L. Kirschbaum, "Marlowe's Faustus: A Reconsideration," in *Review of English Studies*, 19 (1943); P. H. Kocher, *Christopher Marlowe: A Study of His Thought, Learning and Character* (Chapel Hill, N.C., 1946); W. W. Greg, "The Damnation of Faustus," in *Modern Language Review*, 12 (April 1946); C. Norman, *The Muses' Darling: The Life of Christopher Marlowe* (New York, 1946), includes facsimiles; G. I. Duthie, "The Dramatic Structure of Marlowe's 'Tamburlaine the Great,' Parts I and II," in *Essays and Studies*, n.s. (1948); H. Gardner, "Milton's Satan and the Theme of Damnation in Elizabethan Tragedy," in *Essays and Studies*, n.s. (1948); M. M. Mahood, "Marlowe's Heroes," in his *Poetry and Humanism* (London, 1950); M. Poirier, *Christopher Marlowe* (London, 1951); M. C. Bradbrook, *Shakespeare and Elizabethan Poetry* (London, 1951); P. Henderson, *Christopher Marlowe*, Men and Books Series (London, 1952; 2nd ed., 1974), contains Baines's charges in full and other material; F. P. Wilson, *Marlowe and the Early Shakespeare* (Oxford, 1953), the Clark lectures, Trinity College, Cambridge; Harry Levin, *The Overreacher: A Study of Christopher Marlowe* (London, 1954); C. S. Lewis, "Hero and Leander," in *Proceedings of the British Academy* (1954); J. C. Maxwell, "Marlowe," in B. Ford, ed., *A Guide to English Literature*, II, *The Age of Shakespeare* (Harmondsworth, 1955); P. Simpson, *Studies in Elizabethan Drama* (Oxford, 1955), contains a chapter, "Marlowe's Tragical History of Doctor Faustus," that first appeared in *Essays and Studies*, 19 (1929); W. Clemen, *Die Tragödie vor Shakespeare* (Heidelberg, 1955), trans. by T. S. Dorsch as *English Tragedy Before Shakespeare* (1961), contains three chapters on Marlowe's development; I. Ribner, *The English History Play in the Age of Shakespeare* (London, 1957); E. Seaton, "Marlowe's Light Reading," in *Elizabethan and Jacobean Studies, Presented to F. P. Wilson* (Oxford, 1959), shows Marlowe's indebtedness to the medieval romances; C. Leech, "Marlowe's Edward II: Power and Suffering," in *Critical Quarterly*, I, 3 (1959); J. P. Brockbank, *Marlowe: Dr Faustus* (London, 1962); D. Cole, *Suffering and Evil in the Plays of Christopher Marlowe* (Princeton, 1962); E. M. Waith, *The Herculean Hero* (Englewood Cliffs, N.J., 1962); A. L. Rowse, *Christopher Marlowe* (London, 1964), argues that Marlowe is the rival poet of Shakespeare's sonnets; J. B. Steane, *Marlowe: A Critical Study* (Cambridge, 1964), the best recent study; L. C. Knight, "The Strange Case of Christopher Marlowe," in his *Further Explorations* (London, 1965); A. D. Wraight and V. F. Stern, *In Search of Christopher Marlowe* (London, 1965), a pictorial biography; W. A. Armstrong, *Marlowe's Tamburlaine: The Image and the Stage* (Hull, 1966); N. Brooke, "Marlowe's Humour," in *Elizabethan Theatre*, Stratford-upon-Avon Studies Series, No. 9 (London, 1966); W. Sanders, *The Dramatist and the Received Idea* (Cambridge, 1968), studies in the plays of Marlowe and Shakespeare; B. Morris, ed., *Christopher Marlowe*, Mermaid Critical Commentaries (London, 1968); W. Farnham, ed., *Twentieth Century Interpretations of "Doctor Faustus": A Collection of Critical Essays* (Englewood Cliffs, N.J., 1969); J. D. Jump, ed., *Marlowe: "Doctor Faustus": A Casebook* (London, 1969).

WILLIAM SHAKESPEARE
(1564-1616)

Stanley Wells

WILLIAM SHAKESPEARE was baptized in the great church of Holy Trinity, Stratford-upon-Avon, on 26 April 1564. Probably he was born no more than two or three days previously; 23 April, St. George's Day, traditionally celebrated as the date of his birth, is as likely to be correct as any. At the time, his father was an up-and-coming young man who took a prominent part in administering the town's affairs. He had married Mary Arden, who came from a family of higher social standing, about 1552, the year in which he was fined 12d. for failing to remove a dung-hill from outside his house. For years after this, as his children were born and as some of them grew up, his position among his fellow townsmen improved. He was a member of the glovers' guild, and also dealt in wool and probably other commodities. In 1556 he was appointed an ale taster, with responsibility for the price and quality of the bread and ale offered to the town's two thousand or so inhabitants. He moved upward in the hierarchy: as constable (1558), principal burgess (about 1559), chamberlain (1561), alderman (1565), and, in 1568, bailiff, or mayor, and justice of the peace.

At this high point in his career he was the father of two sons, William and Gilbert (1566–1612). Two daughters, Joan and Margaret, had died in infancy. Another Joan was born in 1569; a Richard born in 1574 lived, apparently in Stratford and as a bachelor, until 1613. A late child, Edmund, came in 1580; he became an actor in London and died early, aged twenty-seven.

When young William was four years old, he could have had the excitement of seeing his father, dressed in furred scarlet robes and wearing the aldermanic thumb ring, regularly attended by two mace-bearing sergeants in buff, presiding at fairs and markets. Perhaps a little later, he would have begun to attend a "petty school" to acquire the rudiments of an education that would be furthered at the King's New School. We have no lists of the pupils at this time, but his father's position would have qualified him to attend, and the education offered was such as lies behind the plays and poems. The school had a well-qualified master, with the relatively good salary of £20 a year, from which he had to spare £4 to pay an usher, or assistant, to teach the younger boys. At the age of about eight Shakespeare would have begun a regime that might well have sent him "unwillingly" on the quarter-of-a-mile walk from his father's Henley Street house to the schoolroom above the Guildhall and next to the Guild Chapel. Classes began in the early morning, and hours were long. The basic medium of instruction was Latin. A charming scene in *The Merry Wives of Windsor* (IV.i), hardly required by the plot, shows a schoolmaster instructing young boys in their grammar, and must be an amused recollection of the dramatist's own schooldays. From grammar the pupils progressed to rhetoric and logic, and to works of classical literature. They might read Aesop's *Fables* and the fairly easy plays of Terence and Plautus, on one of which Shakespeare was to base an early comedy. They might even act scenes from them. They would go on to Caesar, Cicero, Virgil, Horace, and Ovid, who was clearly a favorite with Shakespeare in both the original and Arthur Golding's translation published in 1567.

But there was a life beyond school. Shakespeare lived in a beautiful and fertile part of the country; the river and fields were at hand; he could enjoy country pursuits. He had younger brothers and sisters to play with. Each Sunday the family would go to church, where his father as bailiff and, later, deputy bailiff, sat in the

295

front pew as his rank required. There he would hear the sonorous phrases of the Bible, in either the Bishops' or the Geneva version, the Homilies, and the Book of Common Prayer, all of which made a lasting impression on him, as well as lengthy sermons that may have been less memorable. Sometimes groups of traveling players came to Stratford. Shakespeare's father would have the duty of licensing them to perform, and probably the boy saw his first plays in the Guildhall immediately below his schoolroom.

As he grew into adolescence, his father's fortunes waned. John Shakespeare fell into debt, and after 1576 stopped attending council meetings. His fellows treated him leniently, but in 1586 felt obliged to replace him as alderman. In 1592 he was listed among those persistently failing to go to church, perhaps for fear of arrest for debt.

But by this time William was in London, already displaying the genius that would enable him to recoup the family fortune. How he kept himself after leaving school we do not know. In 1582, at the age of eighteen, he married Anne Hathaway of Shottery, a mile or so from his home. The marriage was hasty, the bride, eight years older than her husband, pregnant. The clerk of the Worcester court, to which application for a special license was made on 27 November, wrote her name, mistakenly, it seems, as Anne Whateley of Temple Grafton. A daughter, Susanna, was baptized in Holy Trinity on 26 May 1583, and twins, Hamnet and Judith, on 2 February 1585.

The seven years that follow are a blank in our knowledge. Shakespeare may, as Aubrey reported a century later, have become a "schoolmaster in the country." He may have followed one or more of the innumerable other avocations—lawyer, soldier, sailor, actor, printer—that have been foisted upon him. He may have traveled overseas. All we know is that at some point he left Stratford, joined a theatrical company, went to London, and began to write—not necessarily in that order. The first certain printed allusion to him shows that, as actor turned playwright, he had aroused the envy of the dying Robert Greene who, in 1592, wrote scornfully of an "upstart crow" who thought himself "the only Shakescene in a country."

Parodying a line from *3 Henry VI*, Greene conveniently helps to establish a date by which that play was written. His malice provoked a defense of Shakespeare by a minor playwright, Henry Chettle, who wrote of him as one whose "demeanor" was "no less civil than he excellent in the quality he professes. Besides, divers of worship have reported his uprightness of dealing, which argues his honesty, and his facetious grace in writing, which approves his art." Evidently he was well established in London by this time. But apparently he lived always in lodgings there, setting up no household. He seems to have felt that his roots were in Stratford. His family stayed there. How often he visited them we cannot tell. He had no more children. Perhaps he was gradually able to help his father who, in 1596, applied successfully for a grant of arms, and so became a gentleman. In August of the same year, William's son, Hamnet, died. In October, William was lodging in Bishopsgate, London, but in the next year he showed that he looked on Stratford as his permanent home by buying a large house, New Place, next to the Guild Chapel and the grammar school.

Over the following years, his growing worldly success can be followed in both Stratford and London records. In 1598 a minor writer, Francis Meres, published a book called *Palladis Tamia: Wit's Treasury*, which includes the passage:

As Plautus and Seneca are accounted the best for comedy and tragedy among the Latins, so Shakespeare among the English is the most excellent in both kinds for the stage; for comedy, witness his *Gentlemen of Verona*, his *Errors*, his *Love Labour's Lost*, his *Love Labour's Won*, his *Midsummer's Night Dream* and his *Merchant of Venice*: for tragedy, his *Richard II*, *Richard III*, *Henry IV*, *King John*, *Titus Andronicus* and his *Romeo and Juliet*.

We do not know what he meant by *Love Labour's Won*. It may be a lost play or an alternative title for a surviving one. The main importance of the list is that it gives us a date by which all these plays had been written. Add to it the two narrative poems, the three parts of *Henry VI*, *The Taming of the Shrew*, and (perhaps) the sonnets, and it is a remarkable output for a man of thirty-four, especially one who is usually regarded as a late starter.

WILLIAM SHAKESPEARE

In October 1598 Richard Quiney, whose son was to marry Shakespeare's daughter Judith, went to London to plead with the Privy Council on behalf of Stratford Corporation, in difficulties because of fires and bad weather. He wrote a letter, never delivered, to Shakespeare asking for the loan of £30, a sum large enough to suggest confidence in his friend's prosperity. In 1601 Shakespeare's father died. In May of the following year he paid £327 for 127 acres of land in Old Stratford. In 1604 he was lodging in London with a Huguenot family called Mountjoy, and became mildly involved with their daughter's marital problems. In the same year, through a lawyer, he sued for recovery of a small debt in Stratford. In 1605 he paid £440 for an interest in the Stratford tithes. In June 1607 his daughter Susanna married a distinguished physician, John Hall, in Stratford; his only grandchild, Elizabeth, was christened the following February. In 1609 his mother died there.

About 1610, Shakespeare's increasing involvement with Stratford suggests that he was withdrawing from his London responsibilities and retiring to New Place. He was only forty-six years old, an age at which a healthy man was no more likely to retire then than now. Possibly he had a physical breakdown. If so, it was not totally disabling. He was in London in 1612 for the lawsuit from which we know of his involvement with the Mountjoys. In March 1613 he bought a house in the Blackfriars for £140; he seems to have regarded it rather as an investment than as a domicile. In the same year the last of his three brothers died. In late 1614 and 1615 he was involved in disputes about the enclosure of the land whose tithes he owned. In February 1616 his second daughter, Judith, married Thomas Quiney, causing William to make alterations to the draft of his will, which was signed on 25 March. By now, surely, he knew that he was mortally ill. He died, according to his monument, on 23 April, and was buried in a prominent position in the chancel of Holy Trinity Church.

This selection of historical records shows clearly that Shakespeare's life is at least as well documented as those of most of his contemporaries who did not belong to great families. The identification of the Stratford worthy with the world's playwright is confirmed, if any confir-

mation is necessary, by the inscription on the memorial in the parish church, erected by 1623, which links him with Socrates and Virgil, and by much in the far greater memorial of that year, the First Folio edition of his plays, in which his great contemporary and rival, Ben Jonson, calls him "Sweet Swan of Avon."

SHAKESPEARE'S INTELLECTUAL AND THEATRICAL BACKGROUND

FOR a poetic dramatist, Shakespeare was born at the right time. He grew up during a period of increasing stability and prosperity in England. Queen Elizabeth was unifying the nation. Patriotic sentiment was increasing. Continental influences were helping in the transmission of classical knowledge which we call the Renaissance. The arts in general were flourishing; those of literature and drama bounded forward far more rapidly than in the earlier part of the century. The years between Shakespeare's birth and his emergence in London saw the appearance of the first major translations of Ovid, Apuleius, Horace, Heliodorus, Plutarch, Homer, Seneca, and Virgil; Shakespeare seems to have known most of these, and those of Ovid and Plutarch, at least, had a profound influence on him. During the same period appeared William Painter's *Palace of Pleasure*, an important collection of tales including some by Boccaccio that Shakespeare used; Holinshed's *Chronicles*; Lyly's *Euphues*; Sidney's *Arcadia* and *Astrophil and Stella*; early books of Spenser's *Faerie Queene*; Lodge's *Rosalynde*; prose romances and other pamphlets of Robert Greene; the early writings of Thomas Nashe; and other books that Shakespeare either used or must have known. Indeed, it is no exaggeration to say that almost all Shakespeare's major sources are in books written or first translated into English during the first thirty years of his life, though of course he could have read the Latin works, and, probably, those in French and Italian, even if they had not been translated. The greatest earlier English author known to him was Chaucer, and he was considerably influenced by the publication in 1603 of Florio's translation of Montaigne's *Essays*.

English dramatic literature developed greatly in Shakespeare's early years. Four years before his birth, blank verse was introduced as a dramatic medium in Sackville and Norton's *Gorboduc*. When he was two years old, George Gascoigne's *Supposes*, a translation from Ariosto and the first play written entirely in English prose, was acted; he was to draw on it in *The Taming of the Shrew*. These are early landmarks. He was already a young man before the pace of development really accelerated. John Lyly's courtly comedies, mostly in prose, began to appear in 1584, the year in which George Peele's *The Arraignment of Paris* was presented to the queen. The pace increased in the later 1580's, with Kyd's *The Spanish Tragedy*, Greene's *James IV*, and, above all, the emergence of Christopher Marlowe. Shakespeare was finding his feet in the theater. Our knowledge of the exact ordering of events in this period is so uncertain that we cannot always say whether he was influenced by the writers of these plays or himself exerted influence on them. What is undeniable is that English drama was rapidly increasing in range, scope, and power. Prose was for the first time becoming a rich dramatic medium—all the more so for its intermingling with verse styles that were immeasurably enriched by the ever more flexible uses that writers were making of blank verse. Growth in the size of acting companies and in the popularity of theatrical entertainment encouraged the writing of more ambitious plays, interweaving plot with subplot, tragedy with comedy, diversified with songs, dances, masques, and spectacular effects in ways that were unknown only a few years before.

The rapid progress of dramatic literature was thus inextricably linked with equally important developments in the theatrical arts. Shakespeare was twelve when James Burbage, already the father of the boy who was to become the greatest actor of Shakespeare's company, erected the Theatre, the first building in England designed primarily for theatrical performances. Before this, acting companies had roamed the land, the better ones under noble protection, playing where they could—in halls of great houses, at the Inns of Court, in guildhalls, and in innyards. Now one company, at least, had a permanent building; it was followed by others. The companies grew in size. They had the facilities to perform increasingly ambitious plays. They were encouraged by enthusiastic audiences and by the pleasure taken in drama by the queen and her court, even though they had also to resist the opposition of Puritan forces. They were, at the least, highly competent. Some gained international reputations. Boy actors, progressing through a system of apprenticeship, played female roles in a fully professional manner.

The Elizabethan theater, with its open roof, thrust, uncurtained stage, absence of representational scenery, rear opening, and upper level, was a sophisticated, if fundamentally simple, instrument. Modern theater designers are returning with excitement to its basic principles. It could accommodate spectacle and machinery, yet many plays written for it could be performed also in the unequipped halls that companies had to use on tour. It was a nonrepresentational, emblematic medium, shaped by and shaping the poetic dramas that prevailed on its stages.

We do not know when Shakespeare joined a company of players. In 1587 the Queen's Men lost one of their actors through manslaughter in Oxfordshire. They visited Stratford soon afterward. That they there enlisted Shakespeare is no more than an intriguing speculation. Some evidence suggests that he may have belonged to Pembroke's Men, first heard of in 1592. Certainly he was one of the Lord Chamberlain's Men shortly after they were founded, in 1594, and remained with them throughout his career. Rapidly this became London's leading company, outshining its main rival, the Lord Admiral's Men, led by Edward Alleyn. With the Chamberlain's Men, Shakespeare became a complete man of the theater: actor, businessman, and dramatic poet. He is the only leading playwright of his time to have had so stable a relationship with a single company. He wrote with their actors specifically in mind, and the conditions in which they performed helped also to shape his plays. They flourished; built the Globe as their London base from 1599; survived the competition of the successful children's companies in the early years of the new century; acquired King James I as their patron in 1603, soon after his accession; increased in size while remaining relatively stable in membership; and by 1609 were using the Blackfriars as a winter house—a "private" theater, enclosed, smaller, more exclusive in its patronage than the Globe. Perhaps it affected Shakespeare's playwriting style; yet his plays continued to be performed at the Globe and elsewhere.

EARLY SHAKESPEARE

THE beginnings of Shakespeare's career as a writer are obscure. We have no juvenilia, sketches, or drafts. Yet beginnings there must have been. Even his earliest plays demonstrate a verbal power that suggests a practiced writer. Problems of chronology bedevil attempts to study his development. Regrettably, the editors of the First Folio did not print the plays in order of composition but imposed on them an arrangement into kinds: comedies, histories, and tragedies. The divisions are imperfect. Some of the tragedies are historical; some of the histories are tragical; and Shakespeare's greatest comic character appears in one of the histories. Shakespeare was no neoclassical respecter of the limits of dramatic genres. By reference to external evidence, such as contemporary allusions, and internal evidence, mainly stylistic development, scholars have attempted to determine the order of the plays' composition. The chronology proposed by E. K. Chambers is still accepted, with slight modification, as orthodox; but it remains partially conjectural. To treat the works in the assumed order of their composition would suggest more certainty about this order than is justified. To adopt the Folio's grouping would risk losing all sense of Shakespeare's development. In these pages the works will be divided into four groups: those written by about 1594, then those written between about 1594 and 1600, 1600 and 1607, and 1607 and 1612. Within these divisions the plays will be grouped by genre.

EARLY HISTORIES

ONE of the earliest theatrical projects in which Shakespeare was engaged was also one of the most ambitious: to transfer to the stage Edward Hall's narrative, in the last part of *The Union of the Two Noble and Illustre Families of Lancaster and York* (1548), of events, spanning over fifty years, that led to the founding of the Tudor dynasty in the marriage of Henry VII to Elizabeth of York. The resulting plays were printed in the First Folio as *1, 2,* and *3 Henry VI* and *Richard III.* The first three seem to have been written by 1592, when Greene alluded to a line from the third. Bad texts of the second and third appeared in 1594 and 1595 respectively, as *The First Part of the Contention Betwixt the Two Famous Houses of York and Lancaster* and *The True Tragedy of Richard, Duke of York.* It has often been doubted whether *1 Henry VI* is entirely by Shakespeare. He may have revised someone else's work in order to form a dramatic sequence, but the plays are so closely related to one another that they are easily conceived of as the product of a single mind.

The enormous cast lists of the *Henry VI* plays reflect the difficulty of concentrating and focusing the mass of historical material. Some of the exposition of dynastic issues is labored, some of the action sketchily represented. Shakespeare's powers of individual characterization through language were not yet fully developed, and in *Henry VI* he was saddled with the liability of a passive hero. Perhaps in deference to decorum, Parts One and Three are composed entirely in verse; it does not avoid monotony. And some of the theatrical conventions employed are very much of their time, as the direction "Enter the KING with a supplication, and the QUEEN with Suffolk's head" (Part Two, IV.iv) is enough to show.

Nevertheless, these plays have many merits. They examine England's past in the light of its present at a time of national self-consciousness, of pride in national unity, and of fear that it might be dissipated, as Henry V's had been. On the way, they entertain and teach. They also display a deeply serious concern with political problems: the responsibilities of a king, his relationship with his people, the need for national unity, the relationship between national welfare and self-interest, the suffering caused by dissension, whether between nations or opposing factions within a nation, often mirrored in the image of a family, royal or not.

These concerns are bodied forth with much artistic success in the dramatic form and style. Part One, for example, opens with masterly thematic appropriateness in its portrayal of the ritual of national and personal mourning over the body of Henry V, nobly expressed, but rapidly degenerating into a family squabble. The scene ends with Winchester's declaration of personal ambition, just as the play ends with similar sentiments from Suffolk:

> Margaret shall now be Queen, and rule the King;
> But I will rule both her, the King, and realm.

Though the poetic style of these plays is often formal and declamatory, with extended similes and frequent classical allusions, there are also vivid, deflationary moments of colloquialism, as when Joan of Arc answers the enumeration of Talbot's honors with:

> Him that thou magnifi'st with all these titles,
> Stinking and fly-blown lies here at our feet.
> (Part One, IV.vii. 75–76)*

Part Two has some excellent prose. The scenes of Cade's rebellion show at an early stage Shakespeare's capacity for serious comedy. The horrifying episode in which Cade comments on the severed heads of Say and Cromer (IV.iii) justifies this Senecan device, because it combines with situation and language to provide an entirely convincing representation of the savagery of mob rule.

At times Shakespeare withdraws from the hurly-burly of violent action into reflective scenes of great beauty. The pastoral idea is expressed as well as anywhere in the remarkable scene of the Battle of Towton (Part Three, II.v), which, for all its stylization, forms a perfect dramatic emblem of the personal consequences of war. Henry, dismissed from the battle as useless, envies the shepherd's life. To one side of him appears a son carrying the body of a man he has killed, whom he discovers to be his father; to the other, a father carrying the body of a man he has killed, whom he discovers to be his son. Henry joins in their grief, and adds his own:

> Was ever King so griev'd for subjects' woe?
> Much is your sorrow; mine ten times so much.

*All quotations are from Peter Alexander, ed., *The Complete Works* (London–Glasgow, 1951).

Many of the most powerful scenes in these plays are of mourning, especially of children and parents. Yet the plays are memorable also for their portrayal of energetic evil, sometimes in figures of amoral wit, even charm. Especially remarkable are the duke of York's sons: Edward, later King Edward IV; George, duke of Clarence; and Richard, duke of Gloucester. Richard grows rapidly in menace in Part Three, emerging as the complete antihero in the splendid soliloquy in which he declares his ambitions:

> I'll drown more sailors than the mermaid shall;
> I'll slay more gazers than the basilisk;
> I'll play the orator as well as Nestor,
> Deceive more slily than Ulysses could,
> And, like a Sinon, take another Troy.
> I can add colours to the chameleon,
> Change shapes with Protheus for advantages,
> And set the murderous Machiavel to school.
> Can I do this, and cannot get a crown?
> Tut, were it farther off, I'll pluck it down.
> (III.ii. 186–195)

The rhetorical patterning, the end-stopped lines, the classical allusions, often regarded as limitations of Shakespeare's early style, contribute to a wonderfully energetic portrayal of the flights of Richard's imagination, which leads naturally to his dominance in *Richard III*. This play, of which a bad quarto appeared in 1597, cannot have been written much later than its precursors; but in it Shakespeare creates from his chronicle sources an aesthetically and morally satisfying pattern that shows him as the complete master of his material, able to subdue the world of fact to that of art.

Again, family relationships are important. Richard's engineering of Clarence's murder is ironically contrasted with their elder brother Edward's deathbed efforts to reunite the family. Richard bustles his way to the throne, overcoming all obstacles in a gloriously entertaining display of cynical hypocrisy, intelligence, and wit. But the forces of retribution grow in strength and are especially associated with women's mourning for the victims of past crimes. Murders of innocent children are seen in these plays as ultimate crimes against humanity. Richard's downfall begins when he alienates his chief supporter, Buckingham, by asking him to arrange the murder of his young nephews, the princes in the Tower. Tyrrel's description of their deaths (IV.iii) is an emotional climax. Opposition to Richard is focused in the idealized figure of Richmond, and the grand climax to the ritual of this and all these plays comes as the ghosts of Richard's victims appear to him and to Richmond. Richard's waking soliloquy shows that his self-sufficiency has defeated itself:

> I shall despair. There is no creature loves me;
> And if I die no soul will pity me:
> And wherefore should they, since that I myself
> Find in myself no pity to myself?
> (V.iii. 200–203)

He dies fighting, and Richmond's closing speech restates the image of England as a family:

> England hath long been mad, and scarr'd herself;
> The brother blindly shed the brother's blood,
> The father rashly slaughter'd his own son,
> The son, compell'd, been butcher to the sire.

Now he, as Henry VII, and Elizabeth, heirs of the houses of Lancaster and York, will bring unity to the kingdom. This patriotic climax, spoken by Elizabeth's grandfather, must have been peculiarly satisfying to the plays' first audiences.

Shakespeare is also concerned with dynastic issues in *King John*, a play about an earlier period of English history, first printed in 1623 but apparently written in the early 1590's. It is based in part on *The Troublesome Reign of John, King of England*, printed anonymously in 1591. As in the *Henry VI* plays, there is a strong sense of the futility and wastefulness of war. Shakespeare portrays a conflict in which neither side is right. King John knows that his claim to the English throne is weak. The French king, Philip, withdraws his support of the rival claimant, Prince Arthur, when John offers to make an advantageous match between his niece and the French dauphin. On both sides, selfishness, scheming, and personal greed put "commodity"—self-interest—before the common good. Shakespeare treats the situation ironically in, for instance, the scene before Angiers (II.i). The French Herald calls on the citizens to admit Arthur,

> Who by the hand of France this day hath made
> Much work for tears in many an English mother,
> Whose sons lie scattered on the bleeding ground.
> (II.i. 302–304)

The English Herald immediately calls on them to admit John and his soldiers,

> all with purpled hands,
> Dy'd in the dying slaughter of their foes.
> (II.i. 322–323)

The blood of both sides is wasted, for neither has won. There is a farcical element in the impasse and in John's acquiescence in the suggestion that the opposing armies should unite to

> lay this Angiers even with the ground;
> Then after fight who shall be king of it.
> (II.i. 399–400)

The ironical attitude finds personal embodiment in the figure of the Bastard, Philip Faulconbridge, who serves for the first half of the play as an ironic commentator. But grief is important here, too. Prince Arthur's mother, Constance, gives powerful expression to suffering and loss, and Arthur's threatened blinding and his death form an emotional focus. The discovery of his body turns the Bastard from a commentator into a participant, committed to humanity and England's welfare; and he ends the play as his country's spokesman:

> This England never did, nor never shall,
> Lie at the proud foot of a conqueror,
> But when it first did help to wound itself. . . .
> Come the three corners of the world in arms,
> And we shall shock them. Nought shall make us rue,
> If England to itself do rest but true.

EARLY COMEDIES

THE mode of the history play was new when Shakespeare began to work in it; he may even have originated it. Comedy, however, had a long ancestry; and his early plays in this kind draw heavily on traditional modes and conventions, as if he were consciously experimenting, learning his craft by a process that included both imitation and innovation.

The Two Gentlemen of Verona, not printed until 1623, is clearly an early play. It derives partly from the prose romances popular in the late sixteenth century. The simple plot comes, perhaps indirectly, from a Portuguese romance, *Diana,* by Jorge de Montemayor. Shakespeare's craftsmanship in shaping it for the stage often falters. The play reveals his limited capacity at this period to orchestrate dialogue. Thirteen of its twenty scenes rely exclusively upon soliloquy, duologue, and the aside as comment. Scenes requiring the ability to show a number of characters talking together are generally unsuccessful. Most of the characters are only two-dimensional; some are laughably unrealized.

But *The Two Gentlemen of Verona* is full of charm and promise. It uses many motifs that Shakespeare was to develop in later plays. Those episodes in which he works within his limitations are often entirely successful. An example is the delightful scene (IV.ii) in which Proteus serenades his new love with "Who is Silvia?", while his old love looks on in disguise. The ironic wordplay of Julia's dialogue with the Host suggests real depth of character. Valentine and Proteus, too, have some human substance; and Proteus' servant, Launce, is the first in the great line of Shakespearian clowns. His monologues are masterpieces of comic dramatic prose, constructed with an artistry consummate enough to give the impression of artlessness. Some of the verse, too, is masterly; witness the astonishing matching of sound to sense in Proteus' tribute to the power of poetry:

For Orpheus' lute was strung with poets' sinews,
Whose golden touch could soften steel and stones,
Make tigers tame, and huge leviathans
Forsake unsounded deeps to dance on sands.
(III.ii. 78–81)

The Two Gentlemen of Verona shows Shakespeare as already a great writer, though not a great playwright.

The Comedy of Errors, also printed in 1623, was written by Christmas 1594, when it was played at Gray's Inn. Its dramatic economy is much superior to that of *The Two Gentlemen of Verona.* Here, Shakespeare draws heavily on the traditions of Roman comedy. The action takes place in Ephesus within a single day and is based on Plautus' farce *Menaechmi,* which tells of a man accompanied by his slave and in search of his long-lost twin brother. Shakespeare turns the slave into a servant, Dromio, and gives him, too, a twin, who serves his master Antipholus' brother. The identical twins have identical names, and the result is a great increase in the possible errors of identification. Shakespeare frames the classically derived main action within an episode based on the romantic story of the wanderings of Apollonius of Tyre, which he was to use again in *Pericles.* This gives the Antipholuses a father, Egeon, and the comic complexities of the main action are overshadowed by his being condemned to die at five o'clock unless he can find someone to redeem him. By this and other means Shakespeare interfuses what might have been a merely mechanical farce with pointers to the potentially serious consequences of the misunderstandings. The untying of the comic knot is preceded by a moving lament from Egeon, about to be executed, who is not recognized by the man he believes to be the son he has brought up from birth. The resolution is effected by an Abbess who turns out to be Egeon's wife, a surprise to the audience paralleled in Shakespeare's work only by the apparent resurrection of Hermione in *The Winter's Tale.*

The ending of *The Comedy of Errors* is not just a solution of an intellectual puzzle, it is charged with emotional power. This play is a kind of diploma piece. In it Shakespeare outdoes his classical progenitors. He adapts his style admirably to his material. He modifies the intellectual complexity of his plot by infusing romantic motifs into it, and by relaxing the pace of the action from time to time to allow for the inclusion of discursive set pieces such as Dromio of Syracuse's marvelous prose description of the kitchen wench who was "spherical, like a globe." There is no faltering here.

The Taming of the Shrew, printed in the Folio, has a problematic relative, a play printed in 1594 as *The Taming of a Shrew,* once looked on as Shakespeare's source, now more generally regarded as a corrupt text of his play. It includes a rounding off of the Christopher Sly framework, which corresponds with nothing in the Folio. Perhaps that text is damaged too. Editors and directors sometimes, justifiably, add these episodes to the Folio text on the grounds that they may derive from lost Shakespearian originals.

In *The Comedy of Errors* Shakespeare shows people losing their sense of identity when recognition is withheld from them and acquiring a sense of reaffirmed identity when normality returns. In the Induction to *The Taming of the Shrew* he suggests how changes in external circumstances may join with the power of rhetoric to create a sense of changed identity. This play draws partly on conventions of Roman comedy, partly on English folk tale and drama. It owes a distinct debt to *Supposes*, George Gascoigne's prose translation of Ariosto's *I Suppositi*. "Supposes" is as much a key word in *The Taming of the Shrew* as is "errors" in *The Comedy of Errors*. The Induction displays the trick by which Sly is made to suppose that he is not a tinker but "a mighty lord." In the play performed for Sly's amusement, Lucentio, wooing Bianca, employs various "counterfeit supposes," but they are superficial. He, the shallowly romantic lover, is opposed to the unromantic Petruchio, who comes

> to wive it wealthily in Padua;
> If wealthily, then happily in Padua.
> (I.ii.73–74)

Petruchio is offered Kate, the shrew, apparently a far less attractive match than Bianca. And the most vital part of the play demonstrates the "suppose" by which he transforms the shrew into the ideal wife. The process is partly physical, partly mental. But its effect is not to reduce Kate to a state of subjection. Rather it teaches her the importance in human relationships of the ability to participate imaginatively in other people's lives. The play's final scene derives warmth and joy from the fact that Kate, in her new relationship with Petruchio, feels a freedom and wholeness that were previously outside her grasp. The achievement of Petruchio the realist is a romantic one: he creates an illusion and turns it into reality.

The Taming of the Shrew is a robust play that acts splendidly. It shows Shakespeare experimenting with techniques of structure and language in order to integrate a variety of diverse materials. It is interesting in the critical attitude that it adopts to romantic conventions. It contains much fine verse and prose; but, in the surviving text, it lacks the subordination of all the parts to the whole, which causes a less ambitious play, such as *The Comedy of Errors*, to seem a more rounded work of art.

Love's Labour's Lost is so different as to remind us forcibly of the uncertainties in the chronology of the early plays. Here Shakespeare seems to be writing for a more sophisticated, even courtly audience. The influences of earlier comedy appear to have been filtered through the plays of John Lyly, the leading court dramatist. The play contains topical allusions, some no longer explicable, which may also suggest that it originally had a coterie audience. It was first published in 1598, "as it was presented before her Highness this last Christmas," when it was said to be "newly corrected and augmented." But it was also acted in the public theaters—according to the title page of the second quarto, of 1631, "at the Blackfriars and the Globe"—and a court performance of 1605 suggests that it was not purely topical in its appeal.

In this play Shakespeare employs an exceptionally wide range of verse and prose styles, demonstrating his command of verbal artifice. This is appropriate, for the play is much concerned with artificiality. The king and his three lords have imposed unnatural restrictions on themselves. Beside them Shakespeare places Holofernes, the pedant who stands as an awful warning of what they may become if they persist in their denial of nature, and Costard and Jaquenetta, unspoiled children of nature. The arrival of the Princess of France and her three ladies offers an immediate challenge to the lords' resolutions, and the play's patterned, dancelike progress charts their slow acceptance of their own natures, their acknowledgments of the demands of society, and of the need for a proper and courteous use of the intelligence. Artificial behavior is reflected in artificial language. Significantly, the most important communication in the play does not need to be put into words:

> *Marcade* . . . the news I bring
> Is heavy in my tongue. The King your father—
> *Princess*

Dead, for my life!
Marcade   Even so; my tale is told.

(V.ii.706–709)

Artifice gives way before the ultimate reality of death. The lovers are forced into new relationships with one another, and Shakespeare shows that the adjustment is not easy.

The subdued ending of *Love's Labour's Lost* represents one of Shakespeare's most daring experiments with comic form. Usually the comic climax brings happiness; this one brings grief. After it there comes a slow movement toward resignation and hope, but the happy ending lies in the future, at least twelve months away; and that, says Berowne, is "too long for a play." *Love's Labour's Lost* offers its audience full enjoyment of artifice but also invites a critical attitude toward it. The play grows from intellectual playfulness to a warm humanity that comes to full, disturbing flood at the close. It is a play of ideas, a brilliantly dramatized debate; though in some senses it is of its age, it can still reach out vividly to us.

Shakespeare's early experiments in comedy have their perfect outcome in *A Midsummer Night's Dream*, printed in 1600 but probably written by 1595. No single influence is dominant. The design of the play came from Shakespeare's imagination, as it had for *Love's Labour's Lost*, with which it has much in common. It too has a patterned structure, a wide range of prose and verse styles, comedy springing from the follies of young love, a play-within-the-play. It has a similar grace of language, less intricacy and self-conscious brilliance. The theory that it was written for an aristocratic marriage is unsupported by external evidence; but marriage is central to the play's design, linking each of the distinct groups of characters. Theseus is to be married; the lovers wish to be, and finally are; the fairies, who have marital problems, are to intervene in the human plans for marriage and to deliver the concluding epithalamium; the laborers are to provide the entertainment for the multiple marriages, and one of them is bemusedly to receive the amorous attention of the Fairy Queen.

Though marriages form the natural conclusion to the action, there are, in the usual way of comedy, obstacles to be overcome. Misunderstandings among the young lovers are exacerbated by Puck's mischief; dissension between the Fairy King and Queen must be settled before human happiness can be achieved. The supernatural world is lightly suggestive of inexplicable influences upon human behavior, especially in love—"reason and love keep little company together now-a-days." And Shakespeare is led to explore the relationship between reason and the imagination in a way that suggests an affinity between love and artistic responsiveness. The inexperienced lovers are bewildered by their own emotions. The laborers are hopelessly confused by the problem of distinguishing between appearance and reality. But the lovers, temporarily released from the bands of society, come out of the dream world of the wood wiser than they had gone into it. Bottom is taken out of himself by his encounter with the Fairy Queen and, though he regards it as a dream, acknowledges it as "a most rare vision." Theseus looks with the eye of reason, but Hippolyta knows that

all the story of the night told over,
And all their minds transfigur'd so together,
More witnesseth than fancy's images,
And grows to something of great constancy.

(V.i. 23–26)

The last act is a glorious celebration, a dance in which the shifting relationships between the performers of the interlude, the images they try to present, and their audience mirror the conflicting claims of illusion and reality, the world of the imagination—in which openness to experience can lead to wisdom—and the need to acknowledge the hard facts of life. The performance ends in goodwill and courtesy, on which the fairies bestow their blessing; and Puck, in his closing lines, reminds us that we are at liberty to take what we have seen as either truth or illusion:

If we shadows have offended,
Think but this, and all is mended,
That you have but slumb'red here
While these visions did appear.

The goodwill of the audience can help the players to "mend." As Holofernes had shown, imaginative detachment is "not generous, not gentle, not humble"; and, as we had witnessed in *The Taming of the Shrew*, imagination can turn illusion into reality.

EARLY TRAGEDIES

SHAKESPEARE was more tentative in his early explorations of tragic than of comic form. Tragedies were conventionally based on history, and *Titus Andronicus* is set in the fourth century A.D., but the story, like that of his other early tragedy, *Romeo and Juliet*, is fictitious. Shakespeare may have adapted it from an earlier version of *The History of Titus Andronicus*, which survives only as an eighteenth-century chapbook. Ovid, whose *Metamorphoses* appears on stage (IV.i), is an important influence, as is Seneca. Except for Act Three, Scene Two, which first appeared in print in 1623, the play was printed in 1594; and it may have been written several years earlier, perhaps in collaboration with George Peele, perhaps merely under his influence. Popular in its time, it can now be enjoyed only with an exercise of the historical imagination, for its presentation of physical horror can easily seem ludicrous. The disjunction between action and language can bewilder, as when Marcus, seeing his niece with "her hands cut off, and her tongue cut out, and ravish'd" (II.iv), delivers nearly fifty lines of beautifully modulated blank verse; or, still more surprisingly, when Titus, having persuaded Aaron to cut off his hand, betrays no more emotion in what he says than if he had taken off a glove. Nevertheless, it is in the portrayal of suffering that the play justifies itself, and more than one production has shown that, given the right kind of stylized presentation, its ritualistic tableaux of suffering and woe can be profoundly moving. As in the early histories, Shakespeare is most successful in the expression of grief and the portrayal of energetic evil. Titus' lament over his mutilated daughter is elemental in a way that looks forward to Lear:

> I am the sea; hark how her sighs do blow.
> She is the weeping welkin, I the earth;
> Then must my sea be moved with her sighs;
> Then must my earth with her continual tears
> Become a deluge, overflow'd and drown'd.
> (III.i. 226–230)

Aaron, the Moorish villain, displays an enjoyment of evil and a cynical intelligence that relate him to Richard III and Iago; he develops into the play's most complex character. The final horrifying bloodbath, in which Titus serves Tamora with her two sons' heads baked in a pie, kills his own daughter and Tamora, and is himself killed by the emperor, who is then killed by Titus' son, is skillfully engineered; but the events are efficiently rather than imaginatively presented, and tragic emotions are not stirred.

Shakespeare took the well-known story of Romeo and Juliet from Arthur Brooke's long poem *The Tragical History of Romeus and Juliet*, published in 1562 and reprinted in 1587. The play is more markedly experimental than *Titus Andronicus*. It is not set in antiquity but in the sixteenth century. It has affinities with romantic comedy, telling of wooing and marriage. Its poetical center is the balcony scene, perhaps the most celebrated expression of romantic love in our literature; the romance is offset by much witty and bawdy comedy. The tragic outcome of the lovers' passion is the result of external circumstances: the still timelessness of Romeo and Juliet's inward experience, perfectly conveyed at the end of the balcony scene, is threatened and finally destroyed by the time-tied processes of the public feud between their families. The play, first printed in 1597, seems from its verbal styles to have been written several years after *Titus Andronicus*. For the first time among the plays discussed so far, we feel, not merely that the design is ambitious, but that Shakespeare's fecundity overflows the measure. Every rift is laden with ore, and the finished work delights and astonishes by its inventiveness, variety, complexity, and generosity. But it is not undisciplined. Indeed, this play is "early" in the sense that it still relies partly on formal verse structures—the lovers' first conversation, a moment of private communion in the public bustle of the ball, is cast in the form of a sonnet—and on clearly patterned action. Public strife is counterbalanced by private communion; the Prince, the civic governor, has his counterpart in Friar Lawrence, the personal confessor; Romeo's confidant, Mercutio, is matched by Juliet's, her Nurse. Characterization is both brilliant and functional. Shakespeare's verbal virtuosity makes marvelous individuals out of Mercutio and the Nurse, but they too are part of the pattern, each failing one of the lovers in understanding, pushing them still further into isolation. In their bawdy physicality, too, they act as foils to the lovers, whose passion includes but transcends the physical. Romeo and Juliet are gradually destroyed by the world of external reality: the world of uncomprehending relatives and friends, in which the senseless family feud—a symbol of misunderstanding, of the failures in human communication—destroys the most precious representatives of the families. Romeo and Juliet had achieved understanding and union; they had risked—and, in a sense, lost—all for the values of personal love. In this sense comedy is banished from the end of the play. The Prince calls together the heads of the opposing families and speaks of general woe. But out of the suffering comes a hard-won reconciliation. As in some of Shakespeare's later comedies, the union of lovers accompanies the healing of breaches among members of the older generation; but here the lovers are dead.

THE POEMS

BECAUSE of plague, London's theaters were closed for almost two years between June 1592 and June 1594. Shakespeare turned to nondramatic writing, perhaps because he feared that he might need an alternative career. A new kind of narrative poem was coming into vogue: tales of love based on Ovidian stories and techniques. Thomas Lodge's *Scilla's Metamorphosis* (1589) is an early example. Another, perhaps the finest, is Christopher Marlowe's *Hero and Leander*. Marlowe died in 1593, but the poem was not published until 1598. *Venus and Adonis* was printed in 1593, with the author's dedication to Henry Wriothesley, earl of Southampton, calling the poem "the first heir of my invention"— presumably meaning either his first poem or his first work to be printed. It was extraordinarily popular; at least eleven editions appeared before 1620, and five more by 1640. Partly it had a

succès de scandale; Shakespeare makes Venus the suitor, Adonis her reluctant victim, which adds a piquant eroticism to Ovid's story.

The poem's success has not been maintained. Like *Love's Labour's Lost*, it is a sophisticated work, drawing attention to its craftsmanship, demanding admiration rather than submission. It will not be enjoyed if it is read for its story alone: Shakespeare takes nearly 1,200 lines where Ovid took about 75. Yet the narrative is unfolded with such order, clarity, and ease of versification that the general impression is one of speed. The style, though artificial, is varied, ranging from metaphysical elaboration to pared simplicity. Adonis provides the main psychological interest. His innocence and idealism contrast with Venus' experience and paradoxically physical, materialist outlook. It is the goddess who represents lust, the human boy who stands up for love. The tension between his youthful withdrawal from sexual experience and her overmature anxiety to rush into it provides the poem's dramatic impetus. Adonis' immaturity, amusing and touching, is appropriate to the essentially nontragic nature of a story with a quasi-tragic ending.

The Rape of Lucrece, printed the following year and also dedicated, more warmly, to Southampton, is a contrasting companion piece. The earlier poem is mythological. *Lucrece*, composed in the seven-line rhyme royal, is historical, based not on the *Metamorphoses* but on the *Fasti* ("Chronicles"). It is about people in society; its tone is not that of high comedy, but of tragedy. Like *Venus and Adonis*, it opens with speed in a stanza that carries concentrated suggestions of the power of Tarquin's lust. A long poem could not be sustained at this pitch, nor would the slender story support it. Shakespeare ekes out his material with meditative soliloquies, discursive episodes, and long moralizing passages. The amplificatory technique is less successful here than in *Venus and Adonis*. There we could remain detached enough to enjoy the poet's verbal flights, his decorative ingenuity, his digressive skill. *Lucrece* seems to demand more engagement with the emotions of the characters. Even the least relevant passages are often fine in their own right, but the parts are greater than the whole. Most important from the point of view of Shakespeare's later development seem to be those passages describing how Tarquin against his better nature is drawn inexorably on toward the crime that will destroy him. Just as a basic theme of Shakespearian comedy, the search for and final achievement of self-knowledge, is adumbrated in *Venus and Adonis*, so a basic motif of his tragedies, the problem caused by an absence of self-knowledge so disastrous that it is finally destructive of self, emerges in *Lucrece*. Tarquin, we are told, as he moves toward Lucrece's chamber, "still pursues his fear" (l. 308). Macbeth, before he kills Duncan, imagines Murder moving "With Tarquin's ravishing strides, towards his design" (II.i.55).

It may have been about the time that Shakespeare was writing the essentially public narrative poems that he also wrote his most seemingly private compositions, his sonnets. When they were written is only one of the mysteries about them. In 1598 Francis Meres referred to Shakespeare's "sugared sonnets among his private friends." In 1599 William Jaggard published corrupt versions of two of them in *The Passionate Pilgrim*, a volume of poems that he attributed to Shakespeare and that also includes three extracts from *Love's Labour's Lost*, four poems known to be by other poets, and eleven of unknown authorship that few have ascribed to Shakespeare. The complete 154 sonnets did not appear until 1609, though the title-page declaration "Never before imprinted" implies that they were not new. The publication appears to be unauthorized. It has a dedication by the publisher, Thomas Thorpe: "To the only begetter of these ensuing sonnets Mr W.H. all happiness and that eternity promised by our ever-living poet wisheth the well-wishing adventurer in setting forth." This sentence has been endlessly discussed, but we still do not know who Mr W.H. is, nor in what sense he was the sonnets' "only begetter." The volume also includes "A Lover's Complaint," a narrative poem of doubtful authenticity.

Sonnet sequences were popular in the 1590's, and Shakespeare's interest in the sonnet form is reflected in some of his early plays, especially *Romeo and Juliet* and *Love's Labour's Lost*. The fact that he did not publish his sonnets may imply that he thought of them as personal poems, but this is not altogether borne out by

their content. Some are generalized meditations; some are comparatively formal utterances, like the first seventeen, in which he urges a young man to marry and beget children. Some proclaim a public design in the attempt to eternize their addressee. Some hint at a personal drama. The relationship between the poet and his friend is so close that it is sometimes interpreted as homosexual, though this is explicitly denied (20). It is threatened by another poet who seeks to replace the author in his friend's affections; the poet's mistress, a "black" woman (as he calls her), or Dark Lady, seduces the friend: the poet is more concerned for the friend than for his own relationship with the woman, which he frequently deplores. Sonnets 127–152 are mainly about the woman. They include some of the most tortured and introverted of the poems; it is difficult to imagine the poet wishing to show them even to the woman, let alone make them public. This personal drama might be fictional; if so, it is inefficiently projected. The sonnets are partly "dramatic" in the sense that some of them are written as if from within a particular situation, like speeches from a lost play. Some can be related to classical poetry; some draw on poetic conventions of the time; some represent a deliberate reaction against convention: few if any other sonnets of the time are as bawdy or as insulting to their addressees as some of Shakespeare's. A dramatic poet as great as Shakespeare may have written sonnets on imaginary themes that sound personal, but we know of no reason why he should have done so without intending to publish them. Yet as an autobiographical document, the sonnets are most unsatisfactory. Innumerable attempts have been made to rearrange them into a more coherent sequence, to identify the persons involved, and to elucidate topical allusions. None has succeeded.

To read all the sonnets consecutively is difficult. Though almost all of them have, superficially, the same form, this obscures the fact that their wide range of modes, of tone, of variations within the basic form, of intensity, and of interrelationship imposes disparate demands upon the attention. Some, including many of the most popular, are lyrical, confident outpourings of love, conveyed largely through natural imagery; some express the lover's humility and abasement. Some are well-ordered meditations on eternal poetic themes of time, the transience of beauty and of love; on the power of art, the inevitability of death; some are more narrowly, even enigmatically, related to a particular situation. Some are intellectual, witty workings out of poetic conceits; some, no less intellectual, are tortured, introspective self-communings. Though some seem to belong to the world of *The Two Gentlemen of Verona* or *Romeo and Juliet*, others are closer to *Measure for Measure* or *Troilus and Cressida*. Shakespeare the man remains as fascinatingly enigmatic in the sonnets as in the plays.

LATER HISTORIES AND
MAJOR COMEDIES

AFTER his wide-ranging earlier experiments, Shakespeare narrowed his scope and, during several prolific years after about 1594, wrote only comedies and history plays, of which *Richard II* alone is in tragic form. Here Shakespeare steps backward in his dramatization of history to begin a tetralogy, which, by carrying the story up to the reign of Henry V, will complete an eight-play sequence. The plays are strongly linked, yet each has its own individuality. *Richard II*, written about 1595, was printed in 1597. It was of topical interest. Queen Elizabeth was aging. Anxiety about the succession was growing. The queen's indulgence of her favorites caused unrest; comparisons were drawn between her and Richard II. The absence from the play of the deposition scene (IV.i) in the three editions printed during her lifetime must be attributed to censorship, official or not; and the commissioning by Essex's supporters of a special performance on the eve of his rebellion, in 1601, shows that many drew the parallel.

Nevertheless, Shakespeare's play has no obvious topical allusions. He emphasizes the universal rather than the particular elements of Bolingbroke's usurpation. The play is full of moral ambiguity. Richard, a faulty human being and a weak king, has the unquestioned right to the throne. Bolingbroke has no hereditary right but is wronged by Richard and better fitted for kingship. Shakespeare skillfully manipulates the audience's sympathies. In the early scenes we can only condemn Richard's frivolity and irresponsibility, which culminate in his callous and unconstitutional treatment of his dying uncle, John of Gaunt, whose noble speech on England (II.i. 31–68) laments the lapsing values of the old order. But after Bolingbroke becomes king, and also abuses power in the executions of Bushy and Bagot and the arrest of the Bishop of Carlisle—another spokesman for traditional values—and as Richard's expression of his sufferings grows in eloquence, Richard takes on the stature of a tragic hero. Through him Shakespeare orchestrates, in wonderfully melodious verse, all the resonances of the situation; and the play expands from a political drama into an exploration of the sources of power, of the hold that symbols, including words, can have over men's imaginations, of the tensions between the demands of office and the qualities of those who hold office, of private and public values, of the differences and similarities between a "large kingdom" and a "little grave."

Bolingbroke's guilt haunts him throughout the next two plays of the sequence. Carlisle's prophecy that civil war will follow usurpation is fulfilled. *1 Henry IV* (printed twice in 1598 and reprinted five times before 1623) shows the king, wishing to expiate his guilt by a pilgrimage to Jerusalem, anguished by both national and filial rebellion. Just as, in *A Midsummer Night's Dream*, Oberon and Titania must be reconciled before the mortals' course of love can run smooth, so the dissolute Hal must reform and be reconciled with his father before rebellion can be put down. The issue resolves into a personal conflict between Hotspur, the rebel leader, and Hal, who defeats expectation and becomes the victor. Shakespeare has adjusted the facts, chronicled by Holinshed, to create a basically simple foundation on which he builds a history play with a greater social and emotional range than he had so far attempted. Here his genius for character portrayal, achieved largely through an astonishing capacity to deploy and extend the full resources of the English language, is at its greatest. Dominant is Falstaff, Shakespeare's invention, though distantly related to the historical Sir John Oldcastle as portrayed in *The Famous Victories of Henry V*, a minor source play printed in 1598. The character is rich, as the soliloquies particularly demonstrate; but the profundity of the role derives also from its integration into the total design, most subtly in the first tavern scene (II.iv) when Falstaff and Hal in turn take on the role of the king. Behind the game lurks reality, a subconscious and premonitory acknowledgment on Falstaff's part that the "son of England" should not "prove a thief and take purses," and on Hal's that he is bound eventually to "banish plump Jack." The tavern world provides more fully realized representatives of the ordinary folk of England than we have seen before. It is part of Hal's achievement to link this world with the court and the battlefield.

At the beginning of *2 Henry IV*, Hal seems to have returned to his former ways. There is an uncharacteristic element of repetition in the pattern of paternal reproach, filial repentance, and reconciliation. This may result from an initial uncertainty about whether to treat Henry IV's reign in one play or two. But Part Two has its individual tone, darker and more disturbing than its predecessor's. It brings to the surface moral issues only latent in the earlier play. Even there Falstaff at his most contemptible, stabbing Hotspur's corpse, was juxtaposed with Hal at his most heroic. Here, though we may temporarily condone Falstaff's misuse of his powers of conscription and his exploitation of Shallow and his companions, his self-exculpations are less disarming. In the great tavern scene (II.iv) his amorous exchanges with the deplorable Doll Tearsheet are poignant rather than funny, overshadowed by impotence and the fear of death. But Shakespeare does not encourage us to be morally complacent. Mistress Quickly and even Doll are presented in ways that show his delight in normal human instincts, as well as an awareness that they may be dangerous when out of control. Prince John may have right on his side, but the trick by which he betrays the rebels is distasteful; we can warm to Falstaff's condemnation of "the sober-blooded boy." The darker side of tavern life is savagely evident in the tiny scene (V.iv) of Doll's carting—"the man is dead that you and Pistol beat amongst you." The scene is strategically placed just before Hal's entrance as king; we can see the need for his rejection of Falstaff, though we can see the sadness of it, too.

2 Henry IV was written about 1598. First printed in 1600, it was, unlike Part One, not reprinted until 1623. At this stage in his career, Shakespeare was using a higher proportion of prose over verse than at any other period and was achieving with it some of his most complex and truly poetical effects. The political scenes of this play use verse, much of it very fine. But the quintessentially Shakespearian parts are the tavern scene and the Justice Shallow episodes, in which prose is handled with a subtlety matched only in Chekhov for the dramatic expression of emotional complexity.

Shakespeare rounded off his second historical sequence with *Henry V*. An apparent allusion to Essex in the Chorus to Act V suggests that it was written in 1599. A corrupt text of the following year omits the Choruses, first printed in 1623. *Henry V,* composed at the zenith of Shakespeare's career as a comic dramatist, brings history close to comic form. It has a wooing scene and ends, as comedies conventionally do, with a marriage, one that will unite realms as well as hearts (V.ii. 351). Our reactions are guided by the Chorus—Shakespeare's most extended use of this device except in *Pericles*—who speaks some of the play's finest poetry. From the "civil broils" of the earlier plays Shakespeare turns to portray a country united in war against France. There is more glory in such a war, and the play is famous—or notorious—as an expression of patriotism. It has less inwardness than its predecessors. But the horrors of war are strongly presented; the goal of war is peace, and the play suggests that inward peace of conscience is necessary in one who would win national peace. Henry shows concern about the justification for his course of action. More than once, and from both sides of the Channel, we are reminded of his "wilder days." The transition from "madcap prince" to the "mirror of all Christian kings" involves loss. Falstaff is dying; "the king has killed his heart." But Henry has accepted the responsibilities of kingship and talks of them, and its hollow rewards, in a speech that recalls one by his father (*2 Henry IV*, III.i. 1–31) and anticipates (historically) one by his son (*3 Henry VI*, II.v. 1–54). "The King is but a man" (IV.i. 103), and this one moves among his men with an honesty unimaginable in Richard II and quite different from his father's "courtship to the common people" (*Richard II*, I.iv. 24). His success in battle removes the guilt of his inheritance. He has become the "star of England" (final Chorus, 6). If in the process he has made difficult decisions with harsh consequences, that, Shakespeare implies, is the price of political success.

MAJOR COMEDIES

SHAKESPEARE wrote his later histories over the same period as his greatest comedies. *The Merchant of Venice*, dating from about 1596, was entered in the Stationers' Register in 1598 and printed in 1600. Much of the plot material is implausible, deriving from folktale and legend. The wooing story comes from a collection published in Italian in 1558 as *Il Pecorone*, by Ser Giovanni Fiorentino. The pound-of-flesh story was well known. A lost play, *The Jew*, mentioned in 1579, may have been a source, and Shakespeare must have known Marlowe's *The Jew of Malta*.

The plot's sharp conflict between romantic and antiromantic values leads Shakespeare to define, partly by contrast, his first great romantic heroine and his first great comic antagonist. The opposition of Portia and Shylock provides the chief dramatic impetus, culminating in the controlled excitement of the trial (IV.i). It is easy to think of the play in terms of contrasts: between the beautiful, generous, merciful Portia and the scheming, miserly, legalistic Shylock; between their religions, Christianity and Judaism; between their settings, the idealized Belmont and the money markets of Venice; between the heights of lyrical poetry to which Portia can rise and Shylock's harsh prose. There are other tensions, too: the familiar conflict, in Bassanio, between love and friendship; the opposition, in the episodes of the caskets, between attractive but hollow superficiality and the rewards given to those "that choose not by the view" (III.ii. 131).

The oppositions in the play, though strong, are not entirely simple. The world of Belmont is idealized but flawed. The generous Bassanio has been prodigal. Antonio, noble in friendship, admits to treating Shylock with contempt.

Gratiano, though ebullient, is vindictive. Even Portia has to adopt Shylock's legalism to achieve her good ends. Shylock, though villainous, has dignity, eloquence, and pathos. We may deplore his values yet respect his tenacity. Despite its lyricism, grace, drama, and high comedy, many people find *The Merchant of Venice* disturbing and express unease with it. Shakespeare portrays here a clash of values rather like that between Henry V and Falstaff. We know which side is right. We have no doubt that Portia should defeat Shylock as King Henry has to reject Falstaff. But in both plays there is pain in the defeat as well as joy in the victory.

Much Ado About Nothing, usually dated about 1598—it is not mentioned by Meres and was published in quarto in 1600—is also based on a traditional tale. It places less emphasis on poetry and romance, more on prose and wit. The young lovers of the main plot, Claudio and Hero, are unconvincing advocates for romantic values. Admittedly, Claudio expresses his love for Hero eloquently in the play's first verse passage, but only after he has assured himself that she is an heiress. We never see him alone with her, and their relationship seems as insubstantial as that of Lucentio and Bianca in *The Taming of the Shrew*. Claudio falls remarkably easily into the deception that Don John engineers, and gives Hero no opportunity to defend herself before launching into his bitter denunciations at the altar where they were to have been married. Her apparent death leads him to no real soul searchings, and her forgiveness and their subsequent reconciliation are sketchily presented. Questions are raised that might have been answered if we had more knowledge of Shakespeare's intentions. If Claudio is played as a callow adolescent, we may pity his succumbing to Don John's evil trickery. If he is more maturely presented, we may look on him rather as an illustration of the hollowness of attitudes to love that are based on illusion instead of knowledge and understanding.

Certainly the lovers of the main plot are less convincing than those of the subplot. There is more true poetry in single prose sentences of Beatrice's—"There was a star danc'd, and under that was I born"—than in many lines of Claudio's verse. This overturning of expectations is one of the ways in which romantic values are questioned. Beatrice and Benedick's "merry war," for all its wrangling, suggests a true engagement of personalities. The brief passage in which they declare their love (IV.i. 255-end) is perhaps the best prose love scene in the language, and we believe in them as complex and developing individuals.

In *Much Ado About Nothing* recurrent overhearings become a structural principle. "Nothing" in the title has been taken as a pun on "noting," and certainly the "misprisions" arising from the overhearings create the complications of the action. Almost all are tricked. Yet a fruitful counterpoint arises from the relationships of the different sets of characters. Dogberry and his companions of the watch have already overheard Borachio's confession when Claudio denounces Hero. The presence of Beatrice and Benedick during the scene of the thwarted wedding is an additional reassurance to the audience. Dogberry and his fellows are the most naturally befuddled characters, yet it is their basic goodwill that, in spite of almost insuperable barriers to communication, resolves the action. The play's interpretative problems are not essentially different from those of most stage works for which we have limited knowledge of the author's intentions. And they enhance rather than diminish its theatrical robustness. It withstands varied treatments and is a constant source of pleasure.

There is a legend that Shakespeare wrote *The Merry Wives of Windsor* rapidly, because Queen Elizabeth wanted to see "Sir John in love." A passage in Act Five alluding to the ceremony of the Feast of the Knights of the Garter clearly has topical reference, and the play almost certainly has some connection with special Garter ceremonies, but we cannot be sure in what year. 1597 has been suggested, but the play's relationship with the other Falstaff plays seems to require a later date. It was first published, in a bad text, in 1602; a better text appeared in the Folio. In spite of its superficial naturalism it has a strongly literary background. Several of the characters derive from Shakespeare's own plays about Henry IV; and though no clear source of the plot has been identified, it is closely related to the ribald tales of tricked lovers and husbands included in many contemporary collections.

Legends about the play's origin, and the fact that its central character is called Falstaff, have damaged its critical reputation. It might be more profitably approached as another of Shakespeare's experiments. It is untypical in various ways. It includes proportionally more prose than any other of his plays. It is his only comedy to have an English setting and to be closely related to contemporary life. In Master Ford, Shakespeare comes closer than anywhere else to writing "humours" comedy in the Jonsonian style. But Shakespeare could never commit himself to Jonson's antiromantic view of life. Ford is shamed out of his jealous humor and kneels to his wife for pardon. Falstaff also undergoes a corrective process of castigation leading to penitence. Shakespeare's essential romanticism shows itself too in the subplot of Anne Page and her suitors. The climax of the love plot comes in the verse passage in which Fenton, safely married, not merely defends his deception of Anne's parents but rebukes them for their previous opposition to the match and their willingness to have her married for money (V.v. 207–217).

The Merry Wives of Windsor does not belong to the mainstream of Shakespearian comedy but is recognizably Shakespearian. It is a neat, ingenious, witty comedy of situation. It has attributes of the corrective, satirical comedy that Jonson was making popular at the close of the century, but it also displays a strong moral bent and a romantic attitude to love and marriage. The style suits the matter, and much of the writing is delightful, even if it would not be at home in *Henry IV*. The characterization is partly by types, but the major roles offer excellent opportunities to their performers, and there are passages of subtly manipulated dialogue. Critics have patronized the play. Audiences never fail to enjoy it.

Pastoralism, derived from classical models, exerted an important influence on sixteenth-century literature. We have seen how some of Shakespeare's kings envied the shepherd his life attuned to the seasons and the natural processes. Elsewhere, too, Shakespeare plays with pastoral conventions. In *The Two Gentlemen of Verona* and *A Midsummer Night's Dream*, for example, the movement of lovers from their accustomed environment to a place apart assists their self-discovery. But it is in *As You Like It* that Shakespeare conducts his most searching examination of the pastoral ideal. The play, first published in 1623, is based on Thomas Lodge's *Rosalynde*, a prose romance printed in 1590 and reprinted in 1592, 1596, and 1598. Shakespeare's play of the book, written about 1600, is exceptionally literary in its origins, and he does not attempt to conceal its artificiality. He manipulates the relationship between story and dialogue, between the enactment of events and reflection upon the events, between characters as agents of the action and characters as talkers, to permit the introduction of many of the commonplace debating topics of his times: the relationship for instance between nature and fortune, nature and nurture, court and country. These topics are all associated with the pastoral tradition. Related to them is an idea that fascinated Shakespeare: that wisdom is a kind of folly, folly a potential source of wisdom. He seems to have felt that the effort to attain wisdom may result in an overearnestness that can lead to folly, and that the unguardedness of the subconscious, relaxed mind may, for all its dangers, bring the rewards of unsought illumination. He betrays a concern with the proper use of man's time on earth; and in this comedy in which the central character plays so elaborate, extended, and ultimately important a game, the idea of time, of its uses and abuses, is also, appropriately, pervasive.

Rosalind's game is directed toward the attainment of love, and attitudes to love are dominant among the play's concepts. The forest of Arden is inhabited by lovers, actual and potential. Silvius and Phebe are straight out of the Renaissance pastoral convention, unreal but touching, because in them Shakespeare isolates one aspect of love. Opposed to it is the earthy love affair of Touchstone and Audrey. Touchstone's attitude is partly a criticism of Silvius' but is itself criticized: being purely physical, it is, as he perceives himself, temporary. Subsuming both of these attitudes is that of Orlando and Rosalind. Orlando has attributes of the conventional lover. He hangs verses on trees, sighs out his soul in praise of his beloved. Yet his idealism is robust enough to withstand the mockery of Jaques, the professed cynic, whose criticism is seen to be destructive, joyless, self-absorbed, and without love.

The fullest character of the play, the one who embraces most attitudes within herself and resolves them into a rich synthesis of personality, is Rosalind. Aware of the humorous aspects of love, she knows its potency, too. Her awareness of the danger of folly becomes a self-awareness born of experience, her boyish disguise a means of simultaneously revealing and controlling her emotion. She bears secrets; her revelation that she is a woman is an inward as well as an outward resolution of the play's action. In an early scene Amiens congratulates Duke Senior on being able to "translate the stubbornness of fortune / Into so quiet and so sweet a style" (II.i. 19–20). The quality of human experience is determined partly by the character of the experiencer; Jaques will always be melancholy, but Rosalind and Orlando can win quietness and sweetness from adversity by an exercise of the imagination. To this extent, life can be as we like it.

As You Like It gains its impetus rather from the juxtaposition of opposed attitudes than from plot tension. In *Twelfth Night*, also written about 1600 and not published until 1623, Shakespeare returns to a tighter structure. Part of the plot is based on a story from Barnaby Rich's *Farewell to Military Profession* (1581), but Shakespeare idealizes its characters and heightens its romantic tone. The romance framework of separation, search, and reunion that he had already used in *The Comedy of Errors* is here more closely integrated into the action, and there is only one pair of twins to cause comic complications. As in *As You Like It*, love is a unifying motif, but it is often a wistful, frustrated, and sometimes nonsexual emotion. The play opens with Orsino's richly romantic expression of thwarted passion. Death overhangs the early scenes: the death of Olivia's brother, to whose memory she is dedicated, and the supposed death of Viola's brother. Olivia is jested out of her mourning, and Viola is more resilient, but passion continues to be thwarted, sometimes because those who declare it are lost in the fantasies of self-love. Olivia, wooed by Orsino, Sir Andrew, and Malvolio, responds to none of them. She also is thwarted, loving Viola in the belief that she is a man. Viola in her disguise can express her love for Orsino only obliquely. The lovers' folly generates comedy, of which Olivia's fool, Feste, makes much capital. From their first appearance together, an opposition is set up between Malvolio, the professed wise man, and Feste, the professional fool. The exposure of Malvolio is engineered by Maria and Sir Toby Belch, the upholder of the festive virtues of cakes and ale. Feste joins in, and the comedy deepens disturbingly as Malvolio remains incapable of seeing the truth. The play's most positive values are embodied in the enchanting Viola, and it is her reunion with her brother, celebrated in a moving antiphon (V.i. 218–249), that resolves the action. Now there are no obstacles to the union of Viola and Orsino, Olivia and Sebastian. For them, the shadows are dispelled; but Malvolio remains unregenerate, and Sir Toby's harshness to Sir Andrew sours our view of him. After the lovers' happiness, we are left with the wise but lonely Feste's song of the wind and the rain.

UNROMANTIC COMEDIES AND LATER TRAGEDIES

ABOUT 1600, Shakespeare's imagination turned in new directions. Two tragedies, *Julius Caesar* and *Hamlet*, may even have been written before *Twelfth Night*. An isolated elegy, "The Phoenix and the Turtle," dense, plangent, and probably of irrecoverable allegorical significance, appeared in Robert Chester's *Love's Martyr* in 1601. After that, there appears to be a period of uncertainty and experimentation before the full, confident achievement of the later tragedies.

All's Well That Ends Well, first printed in 1623, is usually dated 1602–1603 because of its links with *Measure for Measure*, which can more confidently be assigned to 1604. Since about 1900, these plays, along with *Troilus and Cressida*, have frequently been classed as "problem plays." Shakespeare based the main plot of *All's Well That Ends Well* on a story from Boccaccio's *Decameron*, which he probably read in the English translation in William Painter's *Palace of Pleasure* (1566–1567). He added important characters, notably the Countess; invented the subplot of Parolles; and elaborated both the story and the manner of its telling. In his hands the tale of a physician's daughter who healed a king and demanded as a reward the hand of a handsome, rich, and reluctant young nobleman be-

comes the vehicle for a discussion of many ideas about human life, especially the extent to which human virtue is innate or acquired. The subplot of the cowardly Parolles illumines the ideas cast up by the main plot, and the comedy of his exposure reflects upon the disgraceful behavior of the nobleman, Bertram. Boccaccio's story employs motifs of fairy tale and folk legend. In some ways Shakespeare enhances its romantic nature, adding, for example, the motif of apparent resurrection that recurs frequently in his work. But his treatment of the story is generally unromantic, producing a tension between the conventionality of some of its elements and the reality of the terms in which he presents them. The play's intellectual qualities, the unromantic nature of its despicable hero, and the fact that the heroine is obliged to behave in an unladylike manner to win him, have counted against its popularity; but it fascinates by its comic brilliance, its passages of tender and delicate emotional writing, and its deeply serious concern with the events and characters that it portrays.

Measure for Measure, too, betrays a tension between conventional plot elements and psychological verisimilitude. First printed in 1623, it is based on a two-part play, *Promos and Cassandra* (1578), by George Whetstone. In his first three acts Shakespeare involves us intimately in his characters' moral dilemmas. Claudio's sin of fornication is hardly more than a technical offense. It seems monstrous that he is condemned by Duke Vincentio's "outward-sainted" deputy, Angelo. Isabella's scenes of pleading with Angelo are both personally and intellectually involving, and his internal crisis as he discovers his susceptibility to sexual emotion moves us even while we deplore his duplicity. The scene (III.i) in which the Duke advises Claudio to be "absolute for death" and Claudio expresses his fear of death is a masterly demonstration of what Keats called Shakespeare's "negative capability" in its convincing expression of opposed attitudes.

After this point Shakespeare changes the focus. The duke, in his manipulations, becomes a surrogate playwright. Claudio's fate interests us, yet he appears once only and has a single, brief speech. Angelo becomes a subject of argument rather than an object of psychological exploration. In the final scene much is left to the interpreters. Isabella and the brother she had believed dead are given no words to speak on their reunion, nor does she make any verbal response to the Duke's two unexpected proposals of marriage. Yet the scene works up to an exciting climax as the Duke tests Isabella's capacity to exercise mercy, and, as in *All's Well That Ends Well*, a silent moment of kneeling has great theatrical power. *Measure for Measure* is passionately and explicitly concerned with moral issues. Each of the "good" characters fails in some respect; none of the evil ones lacks some redeeming quality. Even Barnardine, the drunken, convicted murderer, is finally forgiven his "earthly faults." We are all, in the last analysis, "desperately mortal."

The problems of *Troilus and Cressida* differ from those of *All's Well That Ends Well* and *Measure for Measure*. We do not know how long it had been written before its entry in the Stationers' Register on 7 February 1603. The statement made then that it had been played at the Globe was repeated on the original title page of the 1609 quarto, but this page was withdrawn and an added, anonymous epistle described it as "a new play, never staled with the stage, never clapper-clawed with the palms of the vulgar, and passing full of the palm comical." In the Folio it was originally to have appeared among the tragedies, but, perhaps because of copyright difficulties, printing was delayed and it was finally placed between the histories and the tragedies.

This draws attention to problems about the play's genre. Its inspiration is partly classical, partly medieval. Shakespeare went to the first installment of Chapman's translation of Homer, published in 1598, and to Caxton, Lydgate, and Ovid, for the material relating to the siege of Troy; but the love story, which is a late accretion, derives largely from Chaucer's *Troilus and Criseyde*, and the underlying assumptions about the Greeks and Trojans are also generally medieval. The plot is partly historical: it deals with what was regarded as the first important event in the world's history. There is some comedy, largely satirical, in Shakespeare's handling of the story. The tone is in many ways tragic, yet no character achieves tragic stature. *Troilus and Cressida* stands alone, a uniquely exploratory work. It is in every way uncompromising. The language is difficult, the action frequently slow,

the dialogue philosophical. Great characters of antiquity—Agamemnon, Achilles, Ajax, Hector—are portrayed as all too fallibly human. Helen, the cause of the Trojan War, is shown on her only appearance (III.i) as a silly sensualist. The most poignant figure is Troilus. Shakespeare makes us feel the intensity of his obsession with Cressida as keenly as his bitter disillusionment at her treachery. Yet we also see him, and the other characters, from outside, as through the wrong end of a telescope, distanced, diminished. Then "Love, friendship, charity" are seen as "subjects all / To envious and calumniating Time" (III.iii. 173–174). Agamemnon epitomizes part of the play's effect in his contrast between the "extant moment" and "what's past and what's to come," which is, he says, "strewed with husks / And formless ruin of oblivion" (IV.v. 166). Thersites, the professional fool, is deflating, reductive, savagely bitter, a railer rather than a jester. As he reduces war to its lowest level, so Pandarus reduces love. Pandarus' final, exhausted meditation breaks across the time barrier of the play, linking the past with the present and suggesting a vision of all between as a "formless ruin of oblivion." All that is left of the great events of Troy is a dying old pander, bequeathing his diseases to the audience.

LATER TRAGEDIES

A Swiss visitor to London, Thomas Platter, saw a play about Julius Caesar on 21 September 1599. Probably this was an early performance of Shakespeare's play, in which he turns again to politics. Drawing heavily on Thomas North's fine translation of Plutarch's *Lives of the Noble Grecians and Romans* (1579), he turns history into drama, unerringly finding the right style for the subject; the language is classical in its lucidity and eloquence. And he succeeds once again in relating the particular to the general. Characteristically, the first scene sounds a basic theme: the citizens "make holiday to see Caesar, and to rejoice in his triumph," yet the Tribunes denigrate him, and their comments on Pompey, the last popular hero, suggest both the transitoriness of human glory and the fickleness of the mob, which will be much exploited later in the play. Caesar dominates the action even after his death, yet Cassius, Brutus, and Mark Antony are of no less interest. Brutus is one of Shakespeare's most problematic characters. He is "with himself at war" (I.ii. 46), and is easily seen as an adumbration of the later tragic heroes. Self-doubt, perhaps subconscious, is suggested by the rhetoric with which he dresses up the inglorious deed in noble but hollow words: "Let's be sacrificers, but not butchers, Caius" (II.i. 166). Soothing self-delusion contrasts with brutal reality as he talks of "waving our red weapons o'er our heads" crying " 'Peace, freedom, and liberty!' " (III.i. 110–111). What this leads to is the senseless and ferocious murder of Cinna the poet (III.iii).

The Romans were especially associated with rhetoric; it is also one of the dramatist's instruments. In this play Shakespeare examines its uses and abuses. With it Cassius seduces Brutus, and Brutus deceives himself and hopes to justify his actions. Caesar creates glory for himself by a rhetoric of action as well as words; and the Forum scene (III.ii) magnificently demonstrates the power of emotive speech to sway men, to lower a crowd into a mob, to overwhelm reason by passion. At its climax we take aesthetic pleasure in the rhetorical virtuosity with which Shakespeare's artistry endows Antony as he calmly, intellectually, manipulates the crowd, finally standing at the still center of the storm of his own creation. Words continue to be important: in the quarrel of Brutus and Cassius (IV.iii), in Antony's taunt that Brutus has tried to disguise his guilt with "good words" (V.i. 30), in the fact that false words cause Cassius' death (V.iii). Antony ends the play with fine words about Brutus, but are they true? Do we know Brutus better than Antony did? Does Shakespeare end with a totally affirmative statement, or an implied question?—with an endorsement of the verdict of history, or a hint that history has its own rhetoric, no more to be trusted than any other of the words of men?

With *Hamlet*, we may feel, Shakespeare's return to tragic territory is complete, yet some critics have classed this work, written and acted by 26 July 1602 (when it was entered on the Stationers' Register), as a problem play. Its rapid popularity is attested by the publication of a pirated, seriously corrupt text—the bad quarto—in 1603. A much better text, apparently based on Shakespeare's manuscript, appeared in the following year. This "good" quarto has about 230 lines that are not in the theatrically influenced First Folio text (1623), which however adds about 80 lines. Editors print a composite version. Shakespeare's source may have been a play, now lost and referred to as the Ur-*Hamlet*, known to have existed by 1589.

Hamlet is exceptionally long and ambitious. It is far-ranging in linguistic effect. Shakespeare's virtuosity enables him to create distinctive styles with which to individualize characters such as Claudius, Polonius, the Gravediggers, and Osric. The play offers a wide variety of theatrical entertainment, including such well-tried pleasures as a ghost, a play-within-the-play, a mad scene, a duel, and several deaths. Emotionally, too, the range is wide. This is Shakespeare's most humorous tragedy. Yet the comedy is never incidental. Polonius' verbal deviousness and Osric's affected circumlocutions, comic in themselves, are among the many barriers to honest communication that intensify Hamlet's tragic dilemma. The Gravediggers' phlegmatic humor is an essential element in Hamlet's contemplation of death. And Hamlet's own wit has both a princely elegance that adds to the sense of waste evoked by his destruction, and a savage intellectuality that defines his isolation from those around him and serves him as a weapon against hypocrisy and deception.

Hamlet's appeal derives from his youth, intelligence, charm, vulnerability, and, above all, his intellectual and emotional honesty. He is a raw nerve in the Danish court, disconcertingly liable to make the instinctive rather than the conditioned response. Though this cuts him off from those around him, it puts him into a position of peculiar intimacy with the audience. And in his soliloquies, Shakespeare shows us Hamlet's own raw nerves. Hamlet lacks a distinctive style, at least until the play's closing stages. This is a symptom of his inability to identify himself, to voice his emotions from within a defined personality. But it enables him to speak in a wonderful range of styles, reflecting the openness to experience that is an essential feature of his honesty. The language of his soliloquies presents us not with conclusions,

315

but with the very processes of his mind. Never before had dramatic language so vividly revealed "the quick forge and working-house of thought" (*Henry V*, V Chorus. 23).

Hamlet's progress through the play is a dual exploration of outer and inner worlds. The ghost's command requires that he discover the truth about those who surround him; it leads also to intense self-questioning about his own attitudes to life and, especially, death. During this process he both undergoes and inflicts torments. He causes mental suffering to his mother and to Ophelia, for whose death he is indirectly responsible. He kills Polonius and engineers the deaths of Rosencrantz and Guildenstern. He arrives finally at the truth about the world around him. Whether he ultimately reaches a state of self-knowledge and acceptance is less certain. The new quietude that he demonstrates after his return from England suggests to some critics a fatalistic submission to worldly values; for others, it indicates rather a state of spiritual grace reflecting a full integration of his own personality along with an acknowledgment of human responsibility. Generations of readers and spectators share in Hamlet's self-questionings; it is partly because of his openness to disparate interpretation that he continues to fascinate.

Othello, given at court on 1 November 1604 and first published in 1622, must have been written in 1602 or 1603. Like *Romeo and Juliet*, it is based, not on history or legend, but on a contemporary fiction. Shakespeare here transforms a rather sordid tale from Giraldo Cinthio's *Hecatommitthi* (1565), which he seems to have read in Italian. Whereas *Hamlet* is discursive and amplificatory, *Othello* is swift, concise, and tautly constructed. Most of Shakespeare's tragic heroes are royal figures whose fate is inextricably bound up with their nations and whose suffering has a metaphysical dimension. Othello is a servant of the state, not a ruler. His play is in some senses a domestic tragedy, in which we are invited to concentrate on individual human beings rather than to see a connection between their fates and universal, elemental forces. All Shakespeare's tragedies show evil at work. Only in *Othello* is it concentrated in one, centrally placed intriguer. Iago is the playwright within the play. He controls the plot, makes it up as he goes along with improvisatory genius; and, also

like the playwright, he retreats ultimately into silence. He is several times called a devil, and historians have seen him as a development of the stereotype of the Vice, an allegorical presentation of an abstract concept. On stage he is as much of a human being as any of the other characters.

In some of Shakespeare's plays we are frequently invited to see the stage action as emblematic of a larger dramatic conflict being played out on a universal stage. The significance of *Othello* resides more purely in the passions and fates of the human beings whom we see before us. But Shakespeare does not present the tale as a documentary imitation of reality. We are made conscious of paradox. Iago, who reveals his villainy to the audience, is "honest" to everyone in the play except Roderigo. Othello's physical blackness joins with the traditional symbolism of black and white as a fruitful source of irony and ambiguity. The language draws our attention to general concepts, and causes us to reflect on the varieties of human behavior. Iago is a rationalist. His characteristic language is a cynically reductive prose; he speaks of the act of love as a bestial coupling: "An old black ram / Is tupping your white ewe" (I.i. 89–90). Othello is a nobly credulous idealist. His "free and open nature" makes him think "men honest that but seem to be so" (I.iii. 393–394). His susceptibility to Iago's corruptive power is a concomitant of his virtue. For him, Shakespeare created a magniloquent verse style suggestive rather of imagination than of intellectuality. The contrast between these two, the way that Iago drags Othello down to his own level, and that Othello, too late, shakes himself clear of him, forms the central dramatic action. The universality of the play lies in our consciousness of Iago's plausibility and our sympathy with Othello's insecurities. Inside the most loving human relationship lie seeds that, once germinated, may destroy it. In Claudius' words:

> There lies within the very flame of love
> A kind of wick or snuff that will abate it.
> (*Hamlet*, IV.vii. 114–115)

In *King Lear*, Shakespeare compounded a story from legendary history with one from prose fiction. Holinshed tells briefly the tale of King Lear. Other versions (all ending happily) include a play, *King Leir*, written by 1594, which is one of Shakespeare's sources. Its publication in 1605 may have given him the impetus to write his play, first recorded in a court performance on 26 December 1606 and printed in 1608. His subplot of the earl of Gloucester derives from Sir Philip Sidney's *Arcadia* (1590). His interweaving of the two stories is crucial to his design. Lear and Gloucester are both faulty but not wicked. Lear has two evil daughters and a good one, Gloucester has an evil son and a good one. Each misjudges his offspring, favors but is turned against by the evil ones, wrongs the good one, suffers as a consequence, learns the truth, and dies. Gloucester's error and suffering are mainly physical. His evil son, Edmund, is a bastard, begotten in adultery. The climax of Gloucester's suffering comes when Lear's daughters, Goneril and Regan, put out his eyes. Lear's fault lies in his warped judgment, and his suffering is primarily mental; its climax is his madness after his daughters have cast him out into the storm. Other characters relate to this patterning. The Fool, physically frail, "labours to out-jest" Lear's "heart-struck injuries" (III.i. 16–17) and to bring him to an understanding of his situation by way of his mind, in snatches of song, witticisms, paradoxes, and parables. Kent, the other servant who remains faithful to Lear through the storm, is more practical, ministering rather to his physical needs. Edmund's sexuality, which in his adulterous relationship with both Goneril and Regan brings about his downfall, recalls his father's. Edgar, Gloucester's virtuous son, metamorphosed into Poor Tom, is of both physical and mental help to his father. The callous, skeptical rationality of Edmund, Goneril, and Regan is opposed to the imagination and sympathy of Edgar, the Fool, and Cordelia.

The employment of the two basic components of human life, the body and the mind, as a structural principle reflects the depth of Shakespeare's concern with fundamentals in this play. In his examination of the values by which men live, he stresses the pre-Christian setting of his story, avoiding any suggestion of religious dogma. His play explores the paradoxes of value. Those who are committed to the world

and the flesh destroy themselves. They are deceived by false appearances; so, initially, are Gloucester and Lear. But these two come to "see better" (I.i. 157) when they trust the mind rather than the body. Nowhere is this more apparent than in Shakespeare's causing Gloucester's apprehension of the truth about his sons to follow immediately upon his blinding: "A man may see how this world goes with no eyes" (IV.vi. 150–151). Lear and Gloucester go through purgatory and commune with one another in the amazing scene on Dover cliff. Lear's cynical and disillusioned statements here are only one facet of the play. After this comes his return to sanity and his reconciliation with Cordelia, which is also a reconciliation with life. Nor is this negated by Cordelia's death. This relentlessly unsentimental play puts Lear through the greatest mental torment, but ultimately the man who had vowed never again to see Cordelia's face seeks desperately in her eyes for signs of life. He has learned that she is indeed "most rich, being poor; / Most choice, forsaken; and most lov'd, despis'd" (I.i. 250–251). His final outpouring of love is unselfish; she can do nothing for him now. Her body is dead and useless, but the values for which she stood are those that endure.

Macbeth, written probably in 1606, is easily Shakespeare's shortest tragedy. Its topic was particularly relevant to the patron of his company, James I, and the only surviving text, of 1623, may have been specially written or adapted for court performance. Holinshed again provided the basic narrative, but, as in *King Lear*, Shakespeare treated it with much more freedom than in the English histories. To a greater extent even than in *King Lear*, he seems more interested in general ideas than in historical accuracy or particularity of characterization. Many of the characters are purely functional. Duncan is primarily a symbol of the values that Macbeth is to overthrow. He is counterbalanced by the equally generalized Weird Sisters. Even Banquo figures mainly as a measure of the norm from which Macbeth deviates. The witches, with their incantations, spells, and grotesque rituals, suggest evil as a universal force that can be tapped and channeled through human agents.

Like her counterparts in *King Lear*, Lady Macbeth, the play's principal human embodiment of evil, attempts to deny the powers of the imagination. A speech from *All's Well That Ends Well* epitomizes this aspect of *Macbeth*. "They say miracles are past," says Lafeu, "and we have our philosophical persons to make modern and familiar things supernatural and causeless. Hence is it that we make trifles of terrors, ensconcing ourselves into seeming knowledge when we should submit ourselves to an unknown fear" (II.iii. 1–6). Lady Macbeth seeks to reduce "supernatural and causeless"—inexplicable—things to the level of the "modern"—commonplace—"and familiar": "The sleeping and the dead/Are but as pictures. . . . A little water clears us of this deed" (II.ii. 53–54, 67). This is the "seeming knowledge" that turns "terrors" into "trifles," and refuses to acknowledge the "unknown fear" of which Macbeth is so vividly conscious. His imaginative visions almost overwhelm his reason. Better for him if they had, for the play acts out the truth of Lafeu's statement. Lady Macbeth's rationalistic urgings of her husband are at odds with her own incantation "Come you spirits. . . ." (I.v. 37ff.), and when her reason breaks down, her self-assurance is seen to be only a "seeming knowledge" that gives way, too late, to the "unknown fear." Her sleepwalking scene, a soliloquy unheard even by its speaker, is a technically brilliant device to reveal the subconscious acknowledgment in her divided being of "things supernatural and causeless."

In his last three tragedies Shakespeare returns to more fully documented periods of history and, in two of them, to a more particularized presentation of it. The exception is *Timon of Athens*, a problematic play. Thematic resemblances to *King Lear* and *Coriolanus* along with stylistic evidence cause it generally to be dated 1606–1608, but the state of the text, first printed in 1623, is such that study of it can be only provisional. As it appears to have been printed from an uncompleted manuscript, it is exceptionally interesting to the student of Shakespeare's working methods. There are signs of the rapidity of composition with which he was credited by his contemporaries. He seems to have been anxious to lay down the groundwork, to evolve a shape and structure that could later have been filled in. He concentrates on the cen-

tral role, which is long and taxing. Minor characters might have been developed later; there is uncertainty about some of their names, and there are many anomalies in the action. While some of the language, both verse and prose, is polished, other passages are obviously in draft, veering between verse and prose. There are strong lines of recurrent imagery that might later have been more subtly worked into the structure. The acts of eating and drinking, for instance, and the opposition between roots and gold take on heavily symbolic associations. As in *King Lear*, Shakespeare is concerned with the difference between "true need," which can be satisfied by roots, and superfluity, represented by banquets and gold.

We usually read the play in an edited version, in which some of the imperfections have been smoothed away. Much more tinkering is needed to create a performable text. The result is that this play is peculiarly open to interpretation, raising more questions than it answers. Its strongly schematic quality allies it more closely with *King Lear* and *Macbeth* than with *Coriolanus* and *Antony and Cleopatra*. It is based on Plutarch and treats Timon's story as a two-part structure: Timon in prosperity, followed by Timon in adversity. In the first part, the rich, lavish, magnanimous lord is contrasted with Apemantus, the cynic philosopher. As Timon learns that he has spent all he owned, his flatterers are revealed, in skillfully satirical episodes, as a "knot of mouth-friends" (III.vi. 89), and Apemantus is partly justified. An awkwardly unrelated scene, which might well have become the climax of a subplot, shows the Athenians' ingratitude to Alcibiades. The second part, as it stands, is virtually an interrupted soliloquy by Timon, in which he encounters those he had known in his former way of life. In his misanthropy induced by disillusionment he is as extravagant as he had previously been in his generosity. Now he resembles Apemantus, as a fine scene (IV.iii) between them shows, but Apemantus is a contented cynic, whereas Timon needs to give full emotional vent to his rejection of mankind. The appearance of his steward, Flavius, comes as a reminder of the possibility of love, loyalty, and friendship; and Timon himself accepts, though with difficulty, that he is mistaken in his wholesale denunciation of mankind. The final scenes, showing Timon's death and Alcibiades' successful campaign against Athens, are sketchy.

Timon of Athens is underdeveloped and inconclusive. Its tone is harsh and bitter, though other attitudes are present in Flavius and other servants, in Alcibiades, even in Timon's tirades, which suggest a desire to be reconciled with humanity by the very force with which he rejects it. The play has pungent invective, clever satire, a few passages of noble poetry, a clear if crude structure, and some profound revelations of humanity. We can only guess what it might have become if Shakespeare had completed it.

His remaining tragedies, *Coriolanus* and *Antony and Cleopatra*, both first published in 1623, are based closely on Plutarch and reflect Plutarch's concern with the idiosyncrasies and oddities of human character and with the way such characteristics shape national as well as human destinies. *Coriolanus* (probably written 1607–1608) tells a story of war and peace, love and hate. The broad framework is one of national warfare, epitomized in a personal conflict between Caius Marcius, later Coriolanus, and the Volscian leader, Tullus Aufidius. Their relationship is ambiguous; after Coriolanus has been banished from Rome, Aufidius welcomes him with "I . . . do contest/As hotly and as nobly with thy love/As ever in ambitious strength I did/Contend against thy valour" (IV.v. 109–113). Strife within Rome also resolves itself into a largely personal conflict, between Coriolanus and the two unscrupulous Tribunes. His arrogance, inseparable from his valor, brings about his banishment, so that from being the enemy within the state he becomes identified with the enemy outside it. He is at conflict, too, within his own family. His mother, Volumnia, eager for his fame, expresses her love for him in terms that might rather betoken hatred: "O, he is wounded, I thank the gods for't" (II.i. 114). Sharing his hatred of the commons, she yet advises him to dissemble with his nature to catch their votes, and so forces a conflict within Coriolanus himself. His efforts to play the part for which she casts him produce some comedy, but the issues of integrity and honor with which the play is concerned are focused in his ultimate refusal to do so, "Lest I surcease to honour mine own truth,/And

by my body's action teach my mind/A most inherent baseness" (III.ii. 121–122). In his consequent banishment he has to pretend hatred of those he loves. When his family come to plead with him, he is forced into self-recognition: "I melt, and am not/Of stronger earth than others" (V.iii. 28–29). His mother insists again on the need for compromise, for, if he conquers Rome, he conquers her. He "holds her by the hand, silent" in a moment of submission that is also a moment of self-examination.

O mother, mother!
What have you done? Behold, the heavens do ope,
The gods look down, and this unnatural scene
They laugh at. O my mother, mother! O!
You have won a happy victory to Rome;
But for your son—believe it, O believe it!—
Most dangerously you have with him prevail'd,
If not most mortal to him. But let it come.
(V.iv. 182–189)

Acknowledging that he can no longer maintain a godlike aloofness from natural emotion, he accepts the full burden of his humanity and also the inevitability of his death. "But let it come" is the equivalent in this play to Hamlet's "The readiness is all," and to "Ripeness is all" in *King Lear*. But it is the final paradox of the mother-son relationship in *Coriolanus* that Volumnia, in calling forth a full expression of her son's love, brings about his death. Thus closely are love and hate allied.

Coriolanus is a great achievement of the intellect and the historical imagination. Its characteristic style seems to be carved out of granite. *Antony and Cleopatra*, written about the same time (it was entered in the Stationers' Register on 20 May 1608), is less intellectual and even more imaginative. Few of Shakespeare's plays derive their greatness less from their design, more from their characterization and language. Its style is supple, relaxed, and sensuous. Cleopatra rivals Falstaff as Shakespeare's greatest feat of characterization, and her "infinite variety" is created largely by the flexibility and range of the language with which Shakespeare endows her. The scope of *Antony and Cleopatra* is vast. The action takes place over an area that seems particularly large because characters move so easily from one part of it to another, far distant. Empires are at stake; the play is peopled by their leaders. Nevertheless, much of the play's setting is domestic. Many scenes portray the home life of Egypt's queen, and Shakespeare's greatness as a dramatic writer shows itself particularly in a dialogue of nuance, which gives great significance to oblique statements, exclamations, pauses, and silences. So when Cleopatra is brought to comfort Antony after his "doting" withdrawal from battle:

Eros	Nay, gentle madam, to him! Comfort him.
Iras	Do, most dear Queen.
Charmian	Do? Why, what else?
Cleopatra	Let me sit down. O Juno!
Antony	No, no, no, no, no.
Eros	See you here, sir?
Antony	O, fie, fie, fie!
Charmian	Madam!
Iras	Madam, O good Empress!
Eros	Sir, sir! (III.ix. 25–34)

Or, in one of Shakespeare's most pregnant monosyllables:

Thyreus	He [Caesar] knows that you embrace not Antony As you did love, but as you fear'd him.
Cleopatra	O!
	(III.xiii. 56–57)

But when necessary Shakespeare writes to the very height of his eloquence. Language is intimately related to form, and so a double tragedy presents special problems. In Shakespeare's only other one, *Romeo and Juliet,* the hero and heroine at least die in the same scene; here, their deaths are necessarily separated, and Shakespeare averts anticlimax in the second, Cleopatra's, partly by introducing a new character—the Clown who carries the instrument of her death—partly by the richly symbolic nature of her conversation with him, and, above all, by the transcendent poetry of her closing speeches.

The tension between Egyptian and Roman values in *Antony and Cleopatra* is an aspect of Shakespeare's recurrent portrayal of the opposing claims of festivity and austerity, license and discipline, in plays such as *Twelfth Night* and *1* and *2 Henry IV.* Style and imagery cause us to relate this conflict to the divergent claims of the

imagination and the reason, and to man's sense of the potential glory of human achievement along with his awareness of the limitations imposed by mortality. So, as in *Julius Caesar* and *Troilus and Cressida,* we can both live in the moment and see it in relation to eternity. Antony is "the triple pillar of the world" and a "strumpet's fool" (I.i. 12–13); "Kingdoms are clay" (I.i. 35); "Royal Egypt" is "No more but e'en a woman . . ." (IV.xv. 71–73); and the instrument of Cleopatra's death is a worm. These extremes are shown not simply in opposition, but sometimes in double perspective, at other times, movingly, in dissolution from one to the other: Antony, dying, "cannot hold this visible shape" (IV.xiv. 14), "The crown o' th' earth doth melt" (IV.xv. 63). Ultimately Shakespeare seems to support the values of sensitivity and the imagination. In Falstaff he had done so covertly; here, he does so openly. Enobarbus learns the limitations of reason and regrets that he has followed its dictates; and Cleopatra's ultimate celebration of the flesh in the spirit creates a vision that may lack substance but is glorious while it lasts. No other tragic character except, perhaps, Wagner's Isolde, dies with such exaltation.

LATE SHAKESPEARE

WE saw that Shakespeare's return to tragedy overlapped with his later experiments in comedy. Similarly, while he was writing his last tragedies his thoughts seem to have been turning again to comedy, though only, as we should expect, because he saw new possibilities in the form. Four of his late plays make up perhaps the most closely interrelated group among his output. All employ motifs of romance literature. Their plots include highly improbable and supernatural elements. They tell of highborn families and lovers separated by catastrophe, sometimes natural, sometimes humanly contrived. They span large areas of space and time, and involve leading characters in great suffering. Settings are remote. The presentation of character tends to the general and the ideal. Suffering is overcome, obstacles to reunion and reconciliation are removed, sometimes as a result of supernatural intervention, and harmony is restored.

WILLIAM SHAKESPEARE

All these characteristics can be found in Shakespeare's earlier comedies, but they are present in greater concentration in what are variously known as the Last Plays, the Romances, or the Late Romances. And these plays have more than superficial resemblances. Shakespeare was never one-track minded. Even plays that employ a relatively narrow focus, such as *Richard II* and *King Lear*, have a range of emotional impact. *Timon of Athens* shows the extremes of a man's experience but, as Apemantus says, little between them: "The middle of humanity thou never knewest, but the extremity of both ends" (IV.iii. 299–301). In his late plays Shakespeare shows a wish to encompass the extremes in a yoking of opposites that will confine a full range of human experience within the local and temporal limitations of a play, and will synthesize the disparate elements so as to allow each to exert its energy.

External influences have sometimes been adduced as an explanation of Shakespeare's change of direction. The increased use of spectacle in the late plays has been attributed both to the growing popularity of masques at court and to the acquisition by the King's Men of an indoor theater, the Blackfriars, which would offer increased opportunities for spectacular staging. Yet the company continued to use the Globe, and the late plays were performed there as well. The first, *Pericles*, presents almost as many problems as *Timon of Athens*. It may have been written before both the purchase of the Blackfriars and the composition of the last of the tragedies. It is based on the old story of Apollonius of Tyre, told by John Gower in his *Confessio Amantis* (1385–1393), and on the version of it in Laurence Twine's *The Pattern of Painful Adventures* (1576?). Shakespeare had already used the tale, in *The Comedy of Errors*, and his attention may have been drawn to it again by the reissue of Twine's book in 1607. Like *Antony and Cleopatra*, *Pericles* was entered in the Stationers' Register on 20 May 1608 by Edward Blount, who, however, published neither. A prose romance by George Wilkins, *The Painful Adventures of Pericles, Prince of Tyre*, published in 1608, refers to the play on the title page and borrows from both it and Twine. *Pericles* was very popular on the stage, but the text published in 1609 is corrupt. It was reprinted five times by 1635, but Heminges and Condell omitted it from the First Folio, presumably because they knew how defective this text was and could not find a better. It is so badly garbled, especially in the first two acts, as to have raised doubts about its title-page ascription to Shakespeare, and some scholars believe that it was either his revision of another dramatist's work or a collaboration.

Editors of *Pericles*, as of *Timon of Athens*, smooth away some of its defects. If we read it with sympathy, we can imagine that the authentic play stood high among Shakespeare's achievements. The device of a presenter, the poet Gower, is used to frame and control the far-flung narrative; and the archaic style and naive tone of his choruses induce the proper mood for the reception of a tale of wonder. The initial stages of the action, in which Pericles gains a wife, Thaisa, are episodic; but it gains in concentration with the birth at sea of their daughter, Marina, and Thaisa's apparent death. Even in its damaged state, some of the verse associated with these events has a unique magic. Marina is a mystically ideal portrayal of the power of chastity, and her presence in a brothel, the inmates of which are sketched with truly Shakespearian immediacy, is one illustration of the play's use of extremes. As in all the romances, there is a strong sense that life is controlled by inscrutable, if ultimately beneficent, powers, symbolized by sea and storm. Thus, Marina laments:

> Ay me! poor maid,
> Born in a tempest, when my mother died,
> This world to me is like a lasting storm,
> Whirring me from my friends.
> (IV.i. 18–21)

Out of the tempest comes a calm of which music is the apt symbol. Thaisa, believed dead and committed to the waves, is revived to the sound of instruments, and Marina sings to her father to try to restore him from the coma into which grief has driven him. Their protracted reunion scene, masterly in its control, draws from Pericles' lines in which he expresses two recurrent ideas of these plays: the close relationship between the apparent extremes of pain and joy, and the capacity of the young to renew their parents' lives:

321

O Helicanus, strike me, honour'd sir;
Give me a gash, put me to present pain,
Lest this great sea of joys rushing upon me
O'erbear the shores of my mortality,
And drown me with their sweetness. O, come hither,
Thou that beget'st him that did thee beget;
Thou that wast born at sea, buried at Tharsus,
And found at sea again!   (V.i. 189–196)

When Marina's identity is established, the music of the spheres induces in Pericles a vision of Diana leading to the revelation that Thaisa is alive and to the miraculously joyful outcome of the action.

Shakespeare appears to have followed *Pericles* with *Cymbeline*, composed probably 1609–1610 and first published in 1623, in which he implausibly yokes together Roman Britain and Renaissance Italy. The historical background is freely based on Holinshed, and the intrigue tale derives from Boccaccio. The play is peopled by antithetical characters: some, such as Imogen, Pisanio, Belarius, and those children of nature, Arviragus and Guiderius, are paragons of virtue; others, such as Cloten and the Queen, are "Too bad for bad report" (I.i. 17). Iachimo moves from outright villainy to penitence; Posthumus from virtue to debasement brought about by Iachimo's deception, and back to virtue again. Some of the characters seem the reverse of their true selves: the Queen conceals her villainy from most of those around her, Posthumus is made to believe that Imogen is false to him; some—Imogen, Cloten, Posthumus—are disguised for part of the action; others—Arviragus and Guiderius—are unaware of their own true identity. The plot is based on both national and personal opposition: Britain and Rome are at war; many of the characters are at enmity with one another. The design of some of the scenes stresses the falsity of appearance, as when Cloten's attendant lords comment upon him in ironical asides (I.ii), or the Queen's villainous plotting is framed by her instructions to her ladies about gathering flowers (I.v). The language, too, is frequently antithetical. The play's oppositions reach their climax in the scene (IV.ii) in which Imogen, disguised as a boy and believed to be dead as the result of the Queen's drugs, is mourned by the two young men who, unknown to any of them, are her brothers, and

lain to rest beside the headless body of Cloten. She has said she values him less than the "meanest garment" of her husband, Posthumus; now he is dressed in Posthumus' clothes. The beauty of the verse in which Imogen is mourned and of the flowers with which the bodies are strewn is juxtaposed with the hideous spectacle of the headless corpse; and her waking speech, in which she identifies Cloten with Posthumus, is perhaps the most bizarre and daring in the whole of Shakespeare.

If this scene gives us both heaven and hell simultaneously, the final one gives us heaven alone. It is prepared for by the appearance of Jupiter to the sleeping Posthumus, which raises the action on to a plane of the ideal. The multiple denouements of the final scene, in which all disguises are removed, all identities made known, and all misunderstandings removed, strike with the wonder—and, unless tactfully performed, the implausibility—of the miraculous achievement of the impossible. In the play's closing lines, Cymbeline celebrates the resolution of discord into harmony:

> . . . Let
> A Roman and a British ensign wave
> Friendly together . . .
> . . . Never was a war did cease,
> Ere bloody hands were wash'd, with such a peace.

Cymbeline is a fantasy, an exercise in virtuosity, intricate in style and self-conscious in its artifice. In *The Winter's Tale*, which Simon Forman saw at the Globe on 15 May 1611 and which was probably written later than *Cymbeline*, Shakespeare engages more closely with reality. The story, based on a prose romance of the 1580's, Robert Greene's *Pandosto*, covers sixteen years and moves in space from the Sicilian court to the Bohemian countryside, and back to the court again. The central character, Leontes, king of Sicily, passes through extremes of emotion, from the near tragedy of his suffering, culminating in the death of his son and the apparent deaths of his wife and daughter, through the "saint-like sorrow" (V.i. 2) of his penitence to the rapture of the ending, in which he is reunited with those he had believed dead.

Shakespeare fully exploits the variety of theatrical entertainment inherent in this material.

But whereas *Cymbeline* works largely through the juxtaposition of opposed elements, *The Winter's Tale* is notable rather for the transitions by which the movement between extremes is controlled. Leontes' obsessive sexual jealousy is vividly experienced, but the audience is partly distanced from it by Paulina's ironical attitude and by the grotesqueness of Leontes' language. The first movement of the play reaches a powerful climax in the trial of his queen, Hermione (III.ii). Shakespeare skillfully guides us into the idealized pastoralism of the middle section by presenting the terrible (and improbable) subsequent events—the abandonment of Leontes' infant daughter, Perdita, on the shore of Bohemia along with the deaths of Antigonus and the entire crew of the ship on which they traveled—through the eyes of the comically uninvolved Clown and with the assistance of the notorious bear (III.iii).

Long gaps of time are inconvenient to dramatists. Shakespeare solves the problem in *The Winter's Tale* by giving Time a prominent place in the play's structure of ideas. The opening scene includes a poetic evocation of childhood illusions of timelessness (I.i. 62–74); Time makes a personal appearance, as the Chorus (IV.i); Florizel's love speech magically suggests that Perdita's beauty and his love for her can suspend the passage of time (IV.iv. 134–143); the concluding episodes show time offering opportunities for repentance and redemption; and a sense of renewal is created by the fact that the son and daughter of the estranged kings bring about their parents' reconciliation by their marriage. Also prominent among the play's ideas is the antithesis, commonplace in the thought of the period, between art and nature. Their relationship is explicitly discussed in IV.iv, and a kind of art is apparent in the exercise of the will by which Leontes expresses his penitence and the lovers control their ardor.

These ideas merge in the final scene. Shakespeare departs from his source in keeping Hermione alive, and the daring stroke of making her pose as her own statue is symbolically appropriate as well as theatrically effective. Hermione's resurrection is a conquest over time. Self-control brings its rewards as art melts into nature and the stone becomes flesh. The play ends in the joy and wonder characteristic of romance, but they are counterpointed by our consciousness of the suffering out of which the miracle has emerged.

Shakespeare's last independently written play, *The Tempest*, published in 1623, was performed at court on 1 November 1611; probably he wrote it during that year. In its composition he drew on his reading of Ovid, Montaigne, and contemporary travel literature; but he wove the plot out of his own imagination, creating a fantasy that is his most overtly symbolic drama. We have no reason to believe that he knew he was coming to the end of his career, but it is easy to see this as an exceptionally personal play. In it he disciplines the sprawling material of romance by confining it within the limits of the neoclassical unities that he had employed only once before, in the early *Comedy of Errors*. Instead of following the events of the tale from beginning to end and place to place, he concentrates the action into a few hours and the locale into a few acres. We see only the end of the story; the earlier stages are recapitulated in Prospero's narration. This creates a tension between form and content that finds many correspondences in the action. Like Oberon, Duke Vincentio, and Iago before him, Prospero is a playwright within the play. He seeks to discipline his erring fellows and needs self-discipline to do so. His power, though magical, is limited. He can create visions, but they are easily destroyed: the masque vanishes into air at his recollection of Caliban's malice. Prospero can exercise moral influence, but only over those who are predisposed to receive it. Alonso and Ferdinand are better for their experiences, but Antonio and Sebastian remain unregenerate.

It is easy to see this as an allegory of the artist and his work. The masque can only fulfill its purpose of pleasing and instructing if it is received with sympathy. The artist needs a fit audience. *The Tempest* itself may be regarded as one of the glories of mankind or a load of wastepaper. To this extent it may properly be considered as an autobiographical document. But it is very much more. The compression of the plot necessitates a high degree of stylization. The resultant symbolic action and generalized characterization open the play to a wide range of interpretation. Though Prospero can be seen as an artist, he can be seen also as a father, a teacher, a scholar, a scientist, a magistrate, an explorer, a ruler, even a god. We can discuss the play in terms of the artist and his public; but it relates also to many of the concepts that we have found recurring in Shakespeare's work: art and nature, nature and fortune, the imagination and reason, justice and mercy, sin and retribution, guilt and repentance, right rule and rebellion, illusion and reality, self-deception and self-knowledge.

The Tempest resists clear-cut allegorical readings; this is a measure of its success. It is a supremely poetic drama, not just because it includes some of Shakespeare's greatest poetry, but because it speaks, as the greatest poetry does, on many levels, universally relevant and—if we can hear Ariel's music—universally effective.

SHAKESPEARE AND FLETCHER

SHAKESPEARE'S successor as leading dramatist for the King's Men was John Fletcher (1579–1625), known for his collaboration with Francis Beaumont (*ca.* 1584–1616), who gave up writing for the stage about 1613. At about this time, Fletcher appears to have begun to collaborate with Shakespeare. *Henry VIII*, published as the last of the Histories in the First Folio (1623), was in performance, possibly for the first time, at the Globe when the theater burned down on 29 June 1613. For a long time its attribution to Shakespeare was unquestioned, but in 1850 James Spedding propounded the theory that parts of it are by Fletcher, and many other scholars have followed him in this belief. Certainly in its overall layout it is unlike the history plays that Shakespeare had written during the 1590's, though in its elegiac tone, its generalized characterization, and the sense that it conveys of destiny working itself out through human life, it has something in common with his romances. It has less variety than most of Shakespeare's plays and presents a series of tableaux showing, as the Prologue says, "How . . . mightiness meets misery." We see the falls successively of Buckingham, Wolsey, and Queen Katherine, each of them eloquent in resignation. But the play works toward the birth of Anne Boleyn's child, and the last scene fulsomely celebrates not only the future Queen Elizabeth I, but also her successor, the patron of the King's Men.

So shall she leave her blessedness to one—
When heaven shall call her from this cloud of darkness—
Who from the sacred ashes of her honour
Shall star-like rise, as great in fame as she was,
And so stand fix'd. (V.v. 43–47)

This speech is not generally attributed to Shakespeare.

Henry VIII has been successful in the theater. It offers several strong acting roles and great opportunities for spectacle, which have caused it to be performed particularly at times of national rejoicing, such as coronations. Some of its most effective passages, including Wolsey's well-known "Farewell, a long farewell, to all my greatness!" (III.ii. 351), are attributed to Fletcher. According to a Stationers' Register entry of 9 September 1653, Shakespeare and Fletcher collaborated on a play called *Cardenio*, now lost, which was given twice at court by the King's Men in the season 1613–1614. A manuscript of it may have lain beyond a play called *The Double Falsehood* by Lewis Theobald, one of Shakespeare's editors, which was acted at Drury Lane in 1727 and printed the following year. The last surviving play in which Shakespeare is believed to have had a hand is *The Two Noble Kinsmen,* a tragicomedy written at some time between February 1613 (the date of the performance of a masque by Francis Beaumont from which it borrows a dance) and 31 October 1614 (when Jonson's *Bartholomew Fair,* which contains an allusion to it, was first performed). It was omitted from the First Folio but appeared in 1634 as "written by the memorable worthies of their time, Mr John Fletcher, and Mr William Shakespeare, Gent." The passages generally attributed to Shakespeare make up about one-third of the play and are characteristic of his late verse style.

The works surveyed in the preceding pages have given Shakespeare his status as the greatest writer in English, perhaps in any language. Like most great artists, he built on foundations laid by other men. His genius was not primarily innovative, though, as we have seen, he constantly experimented with dramatic forms and techniques. The theatrical medium appears to have provided a necessary challenge that sometimes constrained him. In plays such as *The Comedy of Errors, As You Like It, Othello,* and *The Tempest* we feel an absolute matching of content and form. In others, such as *The Merchant of Venice, Hamlet, King Lear,* and *Cymbeline,* signs of struggle may be discerned. The teeming fullness of Shakespeare's creativity results sometimes in writing of convoluted, even bizarre, density and in structures that make exceptional demands in both complexity and length on theater audiences.

Yet his powers as an entertainer were such that his plays can appeal on many levels. The best of them are dramatic and linguistic structures of infinite complexity, which explore mankind's most fundamental concerns. Even in so brief a study as this we have seen something of his interest in government of both the individual and the state, in the moral pressures of society upon the individual, in the part played by reason and the imagination in human affairs, in the need for self-knowledge, in the relation between the past and present, and in the power of language. These are philosophical questions. Shakespeare uses the emblematic and metaphorical techniques of the poetic dramatist to body them forth with a wholly human particularity that is as recognizable today as it was to his first audiences.

THE PUBLICATION OF SHAKESPEARE'S WORKS

SHAKESPEARE seems to have concerned himself with the printing of only two of his works, the poems *Venus and Adonis* (1593) and *The Rape of Lucrece* (1594). These volumes bear his only dedications, both to the earl of Southampton, and are carefully printed. As for the plays, Shakespeare apparently regarded performance as publication. The scripts belonged to the company, which in general was not anxious to release them for performance. But there was a market for printed plays, and several of Shakespeare's appeared first in corrupt texts that seem to have been assembled from memory by some of the actors who appeared in them. These are known as the "bad" quartos. Sometimes, however, printers were able to work from Shakespeare's own manuscripts, or transcripts of them. Texts produced from such authoritative sources are known, even when they are poorly printed, as "good" quartos. Altogether, nineteen of Shakespeare's plays appeared in separately printed editions in his own lifetime, and *Othello* followed in 1622. Some appeared only in bad texts, some only in good ones, and some in both. The Sonnets were printed in 1609 in a good text.

After Shakespeare died, his colleagues John Heminges and Henry Condell undertook a collected edition of his plays. They had at their disposal the printed quartos and a number of manuscripts, some of which had been annotated for theatrical use. They brought them together in the First Folio, which appeared in 1623, with the Droeshout engraving of Shakespeare, their dedication to the brother earls of Pembroke and Montgomery, their epistle "To the Great Variety of Readers," several commendatory poems including the well-known one by Ben Jonson, and a list of the "Principal Actors" in the plays. The Folio included eighteen plays not previously printed but omitted *Pericles* and *The Two Noble Kinsmen.*

No literary manuscript by Shakespeare survives, unless we accept the attribution to him of three pages of a collaborative play, *Sir Thomas More,* of uncertain date. Otherwise the early printed editions give us our only evidence of what Shakespeare wrote. Unfortunately, this evidence is often unreliable and conflicting. There are many misprints both in the quartos and in the Folio, some obvious, some only suspected. When a play survives in both quarto and Folio, there are often divergences that may be attributed to a variety of causes, including errors of transcription; printing errors; theatrical alterations, omissions, and additions; censorship; authorial revision; and so on. Even the Folio-only plays sometimes show signs of departing from the author's manuscript from which they must ultimately derive.

For a long time no systematic attempts were made to correct Shakespeare's texts. In reprints of the quartos, which went on appearing during the seventeenth century, sporadic corrections of obvious misprints were made, but these texts have no independent authority. Nor do the reprints of the Folio of 1632, 1663, and 1685. The second issue (1664) of the third Folio was the first to include *Pericles;* it also added six apocryphal plays.

Only in the eighteenth century was a start made on the process of correcting the early texts and presenting them in newly attractive and helpful ways. In 1709 the playwright Nicholas Rowe issued an edition, in six volumes, which was prefaced by the first formal biography and illustrated with engravings. It was based on the fourth Folio, with some consultation of quartos; but Rowe, like almost all subsequent editors, introduced modernizations of spelling and punctuation. His is the first edition to divide the plays systematically into acts and scenes, and to indicate locations for the scenes. He also made many necessary textual corrections. The process that Rowe began was continued and developed by many later editors with varying degrees of thoroughness and scholarship. For modern readers, editions from Rowe's to those of the mid-nineteenth century are of mainly historical interest; but it is worth remembering that during this period most of the standard emendations were made, and many explanatory annotations that are still current were first offered. Equally, many conventions of presentation were established, some of which continued to be adopted, often unthinkingly, by later editors. Rowe's successors included Alexander Pope (1723–1725); Lewis Theobald (1733); Sir Thomas Hanmer (1743–1744); William Warburton (1747); Samuel Johnson (1765), whose preface and notes put him among the great Shakespeare critics; Edward Capell (1767–1768); George Steevens (1773, 1778, 1785, 1793); and Edmond Malone (1790). Much of the scholarship of these editors was brought together in the second edition of Malone, completed by James Boswell the younger, published in 1823, and sometimes called the Third Variorum. (The First Variorum [1803] was Isaac Reed's, based on Steevens; the Second Variorum was an 1813 reprint of this.)

Of the many complete editions that appeared during the nineteenth century, the most important is the nine-volume Cambridge Shakespeare (1863–1866, revised 1891–1893), edited by W. G. Clark, J. Glover, and W. A. Wright. For many years this edition was the standard text, especially in the single-volume, Globe version of 1864. In 1871 appeared the first volume of the American New Variorum, a play-by-play edition edited originally by H. H. Furness, which is still in progress. W. J. Craig's Oxford edition dates from 1891, and the thirty-seven volumes of the original Arden edition were published from 1899 to 1924.

At the beginning of the twentieth century a revolution in textual studies greatly advanced understanding of the bases of Shakespeare's text and transformed attitudes to the editing of his works. A number of important editions have resulted. *The New Shakespeare* (1921–1966), edited by J. Dover Wilson and others, has valuable notes and other material but is textually eccentric. G. L. Kittredge's (1936, revised in 1970) has a reliable text and excellent notes. Peter Alexander's unannotated, collected edition (1951) is often used for reference, though it follows the line numbering of the Globe. Hardin Craig's annotated text (1951) has been popular in the United States. In 1951 a new Arden began to appear, a one-play-per-volume series with detailed annotation, which in general is now regarded as the standard edition for scholarly purposes. It is still incomplete. C. J. Sisson's one-volume edition (1954) has useful introductions and appendices. The Pelican (1956–1967) and Signet (1963–1968) lightly annotated paperback editions have been reprinted as hardback single volumes; the New Penguin (1967–   ) offers fuller annotation and more extended introductions. The Riverside edition (1974), under the general editorship of G. Blakemore Evans, has an overconservative text, but otherwise its wealth of ancillary material makes it the ideal desert-island Shakespeare.

There is no end to the editing of Shakespeare, partly because an infinite number of solutions can be offered to the problems posed by his text, partly because different methods of presentation and annotation are required for an ever-changing readership, and a little because of advances in scholarship. No satisfactory old-spelling edition has appeared, but those wishing to read the texts as they were originally printed are well served by *The Norton Facsimile* of the First Folio of Shakespeare, prepared by Charlton Hinman (1968), and by the Shakespeare Quarto Facsimiles, edited by W. W. Greg and, later, Charlton Hinman (1939–   ).

SHAKESPEARE IN PERFORMANCE

WE know little about performances of Shakespeare's plays during the years immediately following his death. Court performances are recorded, and it is clear that some, at least, of the plays remained in the regular repertory of the King's Men. The closing of the theaters in 1642, when Cromwell came to power, is the most decisive break in the history of the English stage. When they reopened, in 1660, conditions changed greatly. The new buildings resembled the closed, private theaters of the earlier period rather than the open, public ones. Women took over the boys' roles. Some of Shakespeare's plays, especially the romantic comedies, were not revived. Patents were given to only two companies, and the plays were distributed between them. Some, such as Hamlet, Othello, and Julius Caesar, continued to be performed in versions which, if abbreviated, were not substantially altered. Others were radically adapted both to suit the new conditions and to conform to changes in taste. Sir William Davenant (1606–1668), who boasted of being Shakespeare's natural son and who had written for the Caroline stage, led one of the new companies, for which he adapted Macbeth (1663) and combined parts of Measure for Measure and Much Ado About Nothing to make The Law Against Lovers (1662). He collaborated with the young John Dryden on an adaptation of The Tempest as The Enchanted Isle (1667; further revised as an opera by Thomas Shadwell, in 1673). Dryden himself adapted Troilus and Cressida (1679); Nahum Tate, King Lear (1681); and Colley Cibber, Richard III (1699). The Macbeth had singing, dancing, and flying witches; additional scenes for the women characters; and a moralistic dying speech for Macbeth. The Enchanted Isle added sisters for both Miranda and Caliban; balanced Ferdinand with Hippolito, who has never seen a woman; added a female sprite; and greatly increased the play's spectacular appeal.

Tate introduced into King Lear a love affair between Edgar and Cordelia; omitted the Fool; and sent Lear, Gloucester, and Kent into peaceful retirement. Cibber greatly shortened Richard III, altered its structure, added passages from other plays, omitted important characters, and increased the relative length of Richard's role. All these authors rewrote and added speeches. Their adaptations, and others like them, are important because they kept the original plays off the stage, some of them well into the nineteenth century. Cibber's influence extends even as far as Sir Laurence Olivier's film (1955).

The greatest actor on the Restoration stage was Thomas Betterton (ca. 1635–1710), who played many of the principal Shakespearian roles, most notably Hamlet. No one of comparable stature emerged until David Garrick (1717–1778) made his sensational London debut in Cibber's Richard III in 1741. He excelled in roles as varied as Benedick, Richard III, Hamlet, Romeo, King Lear, and Macbeth. Though he restored Shakespeare's language in some passages of the adaptations, he made new versions of The Taming of the Shrew (as Catharine and Petruchio, 1756), The Winter's Tale (as Florizel and Perdita, 1756), and Hamlet (1772). His great admiration was largely instrumental in establishing the reverential attitude to Shakespeare as England's major classic author, and the Jubilee that Garrick organized at Stratford-upon-Avon in 1769 was the first large-scale celebration.

This attitude intensified during the Romantic period. Like Garrick, John Philip Kemble (1757–1823) was important as actor, manager, and, to a lesser extent, play reviser. He and his sister, Sarah Siddons (1755–1831), were classical performers: he, impressive as Hamlet, Brutus, and Coriolanus; she, as Volumnia, Constance, and, supremely, Lady Macbeth. Far different was Edmund Kean (1787–1833), volatile and electrifying as Shylock, Richard III, Hamlet, and Othello.

Objections to the standard adaptations were increasingly voiced, and among the earliest to put them into practice was William Charles Macready (1793–1873), who in 1838 restored Shakespeare's King Lear. But the performances of the greatest integrity since the early seventeenth century seem to be those of Samuel Phelps (1804–1878), the actor-manager who presented all but six of Shakespeare's plays at Sadler's Wells from 1844 to 1862. Increasingly during the nineteenth century attention was paid to visual effect. With Macready and Phelps it was controlled with discretion and taste, but Charles Kean (1811–1868), whose major productions were given at the Princess's from 1850 to 1859, sacrificed textual integrity and even theatrical excitement to pictorialism and archaeological verisimilitude. Sir Henry Irving (1838–1905) was a far finer actor as well as the successful manager of the Lyceum.

Reaction against the spectacular tradition began effectively with the work of William Poel (1852–1934), whose productions with the Elizabethan Stage Society (founded in 1894), though textually impure, attempted with some success to return to Elizabethan staging methods and so opened the way for performances in which better texts could be played without rearrangements necessitated by scene changing. He worked with Harley Granville Barker (1877–1946), whose productions at the Savoy from 1912 to 1914 showed that it was possible to combine textual integrity with scenic appeal.

The period between the two world wars included much experimentation, as in the modern-dress productions of Sir Barry Jackson (1879–1961), Sir Tyrone Guthrie (1900–1971), and others, though disciples of William Poel such as Robert Atkins (1886–1972), W. Bridges-Adams (1889–1965), and B. Iden-Payne (1881–1976) directed performances in a more traditional style. Gradually directors increased in importance, though Sir Donald Wolfit (1902–1968) continued the tradition of the actor-manager, and major players, including Dame Sybil Thorndike (1882–1976), Dame Edith Evans (1888–1976), Sir John Gielgud, and Sir Laurence (later Lord) Olivier, distinguished themselves in Shakespearian roles at the Old Vic, the Stratford Memorial Theatre, and elsewhere.

The dominance of the director increased still further after World War II, with the work of Peter Brook, Peter Hall, John Barton, and Trevor Nunn, all of whom have worked at what is now the Royal Shakespeare Theatre, Stratford-upon-Avon, which, since the closure of the Old Vic in 1963, has become the main center of Shakespearian production in England, although important performances have been given at the National Theatre and by many other companies.

Shakespeare belongs, of course, to far more than the English stage. Books by Charles Shattuck and Robert Speaight listed in the bibliography tell something of the story of his popularity in American and continental theaters. Annual festivals at Ashland, Oregon; Stratford, Connecticut; Stratford, Ontario; and in Central Park, New York City, present his work to the great American public. All over the world the plays are enjoyed in many languages, and through the media of radio, television, cinema, and the phonograph as well as the stage. Shakespeare's wooden O has become the great globe itself.

SHAKESPEARE'S CRITICS

CRITICAL comment on Shakespeare by his contemporaries is limited to scattered remarks such as Francis Meres's empty eulogy, William Drummond of Hawthornden's reports of Ben Jonson's informal conversation, and the tributes printed in the First Folio. For a century or more after this, most comment is of a general nature, and much of it tells us more about the taste of the time than about Shakespeare. John Dryden wrote the first important criticism, mainly in the *Essay on the Dramatic Poetry of the Last Age* (1672), the preface to *Troilus and Cressida* (1679), his adaptation of Shakespeare's play, and the *Essay of Dramatic Poesy* (1688). Though he found that "the fury of his fancy often transported him beyond the bounds of judgement, either in coining of new words and phrases, or racking words which were in use, into the violence of a catachresis," he praised Shakespeare nobly as "the man who of all modern and, perhaps, ancient poets had the largest and most comprehensive soul." Thomas Rymer's notoriously destructive criticism of *Othello* comes in his *Short View of Tragedy* (1693).

During the eighteenth century, editions of the plays provided an outlet for opinion. Dryden's view that Shakespeare's greatness lies in his successful imitation of nature persisted. Alexander Pope, in his preface (1725), wrote, "His characters are so much nature herself that 'tis a sort of injury to call them by so distant a name as copies of her." Dr. Johnson, in his magisterial preface and in the pithy notes to his edition (1765), enumerated both Shakespeare's faults and his merits. He found Shakespeare's morality unsatisfying: "He sacrifices virtue to convenience, and is so much more careful to please than to instruct, that he seems to write without any moral purpose." But he also praised Shakespeare as "the poet that holds up to his readers a faithful mirror of manners and of life."

During the later part of the century there developed a fascination with Shakespeare's characters as independent creations, evinced in William Richardson's *Philosophical Analysis of Some of Shakespeare's Remarkable Characters* (1774) and Maurice Morgann's fine *Essay on the Dramatic Character of Sir John Falstaff* (1794), which is romantic in its imaginative identification with the character. Walter Whiter's *Specimen of a Commentary on Shakespeare* (1777) anticipates some of the imagery criticism of the twentieth century.

German interest developed early, and August Wilhelm Schlegel probably influenced Samuel Taylor Coleridge, whose detailed appreciations, seminal in their effect, have to be retrieved from a multitude of sources, including notebooks, marginalia, and other people's reports of his lectures. Coleridge encouraged a reverential submission to Shakespeare, finding that the plays have their own organic unity. William Hazlitt's eulogistic *Characters of Shakespear's Plays* (1817), based in part on his theater reviews, reveals a preoccupation with dramatic character that reflects the nature of performances in an age of great acting. Keen theatergoer though he was, Hazlitt shared some of the sentiments that Charles Lamb expressed in his essay "On the Tragedies of Shakespeare Considered With Reference to Their Fitness for Stage Representation" (1811), in which he argued that the plays suffer in performance. The mid-nineteenth century produced little distinguished Shakespeare criticism, but its later decades saw an increase in scholarly interest, which, along with the establishment of English studies as a university discipline, greatly increased the amount of serious writing on Shakespeare. Edward Dowden's *Shakspere: His Mind and Art* (1875) is a thoughtful study of Shakespeare's development that has had deserved popularity. Much of Bernard Shaw's brilliant, sometimes iconoclastic, criticism is found in the reviews of performances written for the *Saturday Review* from 1895 to 1898. Far different is A. C. Bradley's sensitive, scrupulous, philosophical study, *Shakespearean Tragedy* (1904), limited to *Hamlet, Othello, King Lear,* and *Macbeth,* which is in some respects a culmination of earlier interest in character portrayal.

A reaction against this is found in the work of E. E. Stoll and L. L. Schücking, both of whom sought a more objective approach, insisting that Shakespeare should be considered in the context of his life and the literary conventions of his age. Stoll, in his many writings, asserted the importance of poetry, and the primacy of plot over character. Harley Granville-Barker, in his series of prefaces to individual plays, published from 1927 to 1947, usefully discussed them in terms of the problems and opportunities with which they confront their performers.

In the 1930's the dominance of a school of criticism concerned with close verbal analysis precipitated language-based studies such as Caroline Spurgeon's pioneering *Shakespeare's Imagery and What It Tells Us* (1935), Wolfgang H. Clemen's *The Development of Shakespeare's Imagery* (1936, translated 1951), and the many books of G. Wilson Knight, a verbal critic of great subtlety who has added to our understanding of Shakespeare's symbolism and, more generally, of his imaginative processes. From among the critics of more recent years it is difficult to distinguish equally dominant figures. This may be because we lack historical perspective, but it also reflects the increasing fragmentation of critical approaches to Shakespeare. The bibliography appended to this essay lists important studies of the sources and of the literary and dramatic background by, among others, W. W. Lawrence, M. C. Bradbrook, Geoffrey Bullough, Kenneth Muir, Anne Righter, and Emrys Jones; of the historical background by Hardin Craig, Lily B. Campbell, and E. M. W. Tillyard; writings showing a particular concern with Shakespeare's social environment, by S. L. Bethell and Alfred Harbage; theatrically based studies by Arthur Colby Sprague, Nevill Coghill, John Russell Brown, Marvin Rosenberg, and Joseph G. Price; ones based on psychoanalytical procedures, by J. I. M. Stewart and Ernest Jones;

others grounded in moral preoccupations, by Derek Traversi, L. C. Knights, and Arthur Sewell; some with an anthropological basis, by Northrop Frye, C. L. Barber, and John Holloway; and examples of close stylistic analysis by M. M. Mahood, Harry Levin, and Maurice Charney. Most of these critics, and others, are, to a greater or lesser degree, eclectic in their methods. Shakespeare continues to stimulate not merely professional diploma pieces but challenging criticism, because his works remain alive as an intellectual and imaginative force, constantly creating newly fruitful relationships between themselves and those who experience them whether in the theater or on the page. So long as they are enjoyed, there will be something new to be said about them.

SELECTED BIBLIOGRAPHY

This bibliography is, necessarily, highly selective. Individual essays, which often contain good criticism, are omitted; they, along with other items, may be traced through the bibliographies listed in the opening section and through the annual bibliographies, critical surveys, and reviews in the Shakespeare periodicals. Reprints are not listed.

I. BIBLIOGRAPHIES. William Jaggard, *Shakespeare Bibliography: A Dictionary of Every Known Issue of the Writings of Our National Poet and of Recorded Opinion Thereon in the English Language* (Stratford-upon-Avon, 1911); W. Ebisch and L. L. Schücking, *A Shakespeare Bibliography* (Oxford, 1931), and *Supplement for the Years 1930–35* (Oxford, 1937); Gordon Ross Smith, *A Classified Shakespeare Bibliography, 1936–1958* (University Park, Pa., 1963); Ronald S. Berman, *A Reader's Guide to Shakespeare's Plays* (Chicago, 1965; rev. 1973); Stanley Wells, ed., *Shakespeare: Select Bibliographical Guides* (Oxford, 1973); and James G. McManaway and Jeanne Addison Roberts, *A Selective Bibliography of Shakespeare* (Charlottesville, Va., 1975).

II. COLLECTED EDITIONS. W. G. Clark, W. A. Wright, and J. Glover, eds., 9 vols. (London, 1863–1866; 2nd ed., 1867; 3rd ed., revised by Wright, 1891–1893), the Cambridge Shakespeare, on which the Globe (1864) was based; H. H. Furness, Jr., *et al.*, eds. (Philadelphia, 1871–1928; New York, 1929–1955), the New Variorum; C. F. Tucker Brooke, ed., *The Shakespeare Apocrypha* (Oxford, 1918); J. Dover Wilson, Sir A. T. Quiller-Couch, *et al.*, eds. (Cambridge, 1921–1966), the New Shakespeare; G. L. Kittredge, ed.

(Boston, 1936); W. W. Greg and Charlton Hinman, eds., *Shakespeare Quarto Facsimiles* (London, 1939–1952; Oxford, 1957–); Peter Alexander, ed. (London–Glasgow, 1951); Hardin Craig, ed. (Chicago, 1951); U. Ellis-Fermor, Harold F. Brooks, Harold Jenkins, and Brian Morris, eds. (London, 1951–), the new Arden; C. J. Sisson, ed. (London, 1954); Alfred Harbage, general ed. (Baltimore, 1956–1967; one-volume ed. [the Pelican], 1969); Sylvan Barnet, general ed. (New York, 1963–1968; one-volume ed. [the Signet], 1972); *Shakespeare's Poems . . . a Facsimile of the Earliest Editions* (New Haven, 1964), with a preface by Louis M. Martz and Eugene M. Waith; T. J. B. Spencer, general ed. (Harmondsworth, 1967–), the New Penguin; Charlton Hinman, ed., *The First Folio of Shakespeare* (New York, 1968), a facsimile; and G. Blakemore Evans, ed. (Boston, 1974, the Riverside).

III. TEXTUAL STUDIES. A. W. Pollard, *Shakespeare Folios and Quartos: A Study in the Bibliography of Shakespeare's Plays 1594–1685* (London, 1909); A. W. Pollard, *Shakespeare's Fight With the Pirates and the Problems of the Transmission of His Text* (London, 1917; 2nd ed., Cambridge, 1920); W. W. Greg, *The Editorial Problem in Shakespeare: A Survey of the Foundations of the Text* (Oxford, 1943; rev., 1951–1954); Alice Walker, *Textual Problems of the First Folio: "Richard III," "King Lear," "Troilus and Cressida," "2 Henry IV," "Othello"* (Cambridge, 1933); W. W. Greg, *The Shakespeare First Folio: Its Bibliographical and Textual History* (Oxford, 1955); C. J. Sisson, *New Readings in Shakespeare*, 2 vols. (Cambridge, 1956); Charlton Hinman, *The Printing and Proof-Reading of the First Folio of Shakespeare*, 2 vols. (Oxford, 1963); E. A. J. Honigmann, *The Stability of Shakespeare's Text* (London, 1965); and Fredson Bowers, *On Editing Shakespeare and the Elizabethan Dramatists* (Philadelphia, 1955; 2nd ed., Charlottesville, Va., 1966).

IV. REFERENCE WORKS AND PERIODICALS. *Shakespeare Jahrbuch*, West, vols. 1–99 (Berlin, 1865–1963), vols. 100– (Heidelberg, 1964–); E. A. Abbott, *A Shakespearian Grammar* (London, 1869; rev. 1871); Alexander Schmidt, *Shakespeare–Lexicon*, 2 vols. (Berlin, 1874–1875; rev. by G. Sarrazin, 4th ed., Berlin, 1923); C. T. Onions, *A Shakespeare Glossary* (Oxford, 1911); F. G. Stokes, *A Dictionary of the Characters and Proper Names in the Works of Shakespeare* (London, 1924); E. H. Sugden, *A Topographical Dictionary to the Works of Shakespeare and His Fellow Dramatists* (Manchester, 1925); Eric Partridge, *Shakespeare's Bawdy: A Literary and Psychological Essay and a Comprehensive Glossary* (London, 1947; rev., 1968); *Shakespeare Survey* (Cambridge, 1948–); *Shakespeare Quarterly* (New York, 1950–1972; Washington, D.C., 1972–); W. H. Thomson, *Shakespeare's Characters: A Historical Dictionary* (Altrincham, 1951); F. E. Halliday, *A Shakespeare Companion 1550–1950* (London, 1952), rev. as *A Shakespeare Companion 1564–1964* (Harmondsworth, 1964); Helge Kökeritz, *Shakespeare's Names: A Pronouncing Dictionary* (New Haven, 1959); *Shakespeare Jahrbuch*, East (Weimar, 1965–); *Shakespeare Studies*, vols. 1–3 (Cincinnati, 1965–1967), vols. 4–7 (Dubuque, Iowa, 1968–1971), vol. 8– (Columbia, S.C., 1972–); Oscar James Campbell and Edward G. Quinn, *The Reader's Encyclopaedia of Shakespeare* (New York, 1966); Peter J. Seng, *The Vocal Songs in the Plays of Shakespeare* (Cambridge, Mass., 1967); Marvin Spevack, *A Complete and Systematic Concordance to the Works of Shakespeare* (Hildesheim, 1968–1970); Marvin Spevack, *The Harvard Concordance to Shakespeare* (Cambridge, Mass., 1973); Kenneth Muir and S. Schoenbaum, eds., *A New Companion to Shakespeare Studies* (Cambridge, 1971); and Stanley Wells, *Shakespeare: An Illustrated Dictionary* (London–New York, 1978).

V. BIOGRAPHICAL STUDIES. Sir Edmund K. Chambers, *William Shakespeare: A Study of Facts and Problems*, 2 vols. (Oxford, 1930), abridged by Charles Williams as *A Short Life of Shakespeare With the Sources* (Oxford, 1933); Leslie Hotson, *Shakespeare Versus Shallow* (Boston, 1931); J. Dover Wilson, *The Essential Shakespeare: A Biographical Adventure* (Cambridge, 1932); Leslie Hotson, *I, William Shakespeare* (London, 1937); Edgar I. Fripp, *Shakespeare, Man and Artist*, 2 vols. (Oxford, 1938); T. W. Baldwin, *William Shakespere's Petty School* (Urbana, Ill., 1943); T. W. Baldwin, *William Shakespere's Small Latine and Lesse Greeke*, 2 vols. (Urbana, Ill., 1944); Leslie Hotson, *Shakespeare's Sonnets Dated: and Other Essays* (Oxford, 1949); M. M. Reese, *Shakespeare: His World and His Work* (London, 1953); Kenneth Muir, *Shakespeare as Collaborator* (London, 1960); Gerald Eades Bentley, *Shakespeare: A Biographical Handbook* (New Haven, 1961); Mark Eccles, *Shakespeare in Warwickshire* (Madison, Wis., 1961); Peter Quennell, *Shakespeare* (London, 1963); Peter Alexander, *Shakespeare* (Oxford, 1964); S. Schoenbaum, *Shakespeare's Lives* (Oxford, 1970); S. Schoenbaum, *Shakespeare: A Documentary Life* (Oxford, 1975; compact ed., 1977); and Robert Speaight, *Shakespeare: The Man and His Achievement* (London, 1977).

VI. REPUTATION AND HISTORY OF CRITICISM. D. Nichol Smith, *Shakespeare in the Eighteenth Century* (Oxford, 1928); A. Ralli, *A History of Shakespearian Criticism*, 2 vols. (Oxford, 1932); J. Munro, *The Shakespeare Allusion-Book*, 2 vols. (Oxford, 1932), rev. by Sir Edmund K. Chambers; Gerald Eades Bentley, *Shakespeare and Jonson: Their Reputations in the Seventeenth Century Compared*, 2 vols. (Chicago, 1945); Louis Marder, *His Exits and His Entrances: The Story of Shakespeare's Reputation* (Philadelphia, 1963); Oswald Le Winter, ed., *Shakespeare in Europe* (Cleveland, 1963); Alfred Harbage, *Conceptions of Shakespeare* (Cambridge, Mass., 1966); Arthur M. Eastman, *A Short History of Shakespearean Criticism* (New York, 1968); and Brian Vickers, ed., *Shakespeare: The Critical Heritage*, vol. 1, 1623–1692 (London, 1974), vol. 2, 1693–1733 (London, 1974), vol. 3, 1733–1752 (London, 1975), vol. 4, 1753–1765 (London, 1976), in progress.

VII. SOURCES, INFLUENCES, AND BACKGROUND STUDIES. Edward W. Naylor, *Shakespeare and Music* (London, 1896; rev., 1931); D. H. Madden, *The Diary of Master William Silence: A Study of Shakespeare and of Elizabethan Sport* (London, 1897; rev., 1907); Sir Sidney Lee and C. T. Onions, eds., *Shakespeare's England: An Account of the Life and Manners of His Age*, 2 vols. (Oxford, 1916); Richmond Noble, *Shakespeare's Use of Song* (London, 1923; rev., 1931); Richmond Noble, *Shakespeare's Biblical Knowledge and Use of the Book of Common Prayer* (London, 1935); M. C. Linthicum, *Costume in the Drama of Shakespeure and His Contemporaries* (Oxford, 1936); Hardin Craig, *The Enchanted Glass: The Elizabethan Mind in Literature* (Oxford, 1936); W. C. Curry, *Shakespeare's Philosophical Patterns* (Baton Rouge, La., 1937); E. M. W. Tillyard, *The Elizabethan World Picture* (London, 1943); E. C. Pettet, *Shakespeare and the Romance Tradition* (London, 1949); C. W. Scott-Giles, *Shakespeare's Heraldry* (London, 1950); J. B. Bamborough, *The Little World of Man* (London, 1952); J. A. K. Thomson, *Shakespeare and the Classics* (London, 1952); F. P. Wilson, *Marlowe and the Early Shakespeare* (Oxford, 1953); Virgil K. Whitaker, *Shakespeare's Use of Learning* (San Marino, Calif., 1953); Paul A. Jorgensen, *Shakespeare's Military World* (Berkeley, Calif., 1956); Geoffrey Bullough, ed., *Narrative and Dramatic Sources of Shakespeare* (London, 1957–1975); K. M. Briggs, *The Anatomy of Puck* (London, 1959); W. Moelwyn Merchant, *Shakespeare and the Artist* (Oxford, 1959); K. M. Briggs, *Pale Hecate's Team* (London, 1962); F. W. Sternfeld, *Music in Shakespearian Tragedy* (London, 1963); R. M. Frye, *Shakespeare and Christian Doctrine* (Princeton, N.J., 1963); T. J. B. Spencer, *Shakespeare's Plutarch* (Harmondsworth, 1964); Phyllis Hartnoll, *Shakespeare in Music* (London, 1964); A. F. Falconer, *Shakespeare and the Sea* (London, 1964); George W. Keeton, *Shakespeare's Legal and Political Background* (London, 1967); John W. Velz, *Shakespeare and the Classical Tradition: A Critical Guide to Commentary* (Minneapolis, 1968); T. J. B. Spencer, ed., *Elizabethan Love Stories* (Harmondsworth, 1968); Richard Hosley, ed., *Shakespeare's Holinshed* (New York, 1968); Carol Gesner, *Shakespeare and the Greek Romance* (Lexington, Ky., 1970); Peter C. Milward, *Shakespeare's Religious Background* (London, 1973); E. A. C. Colman, *The Dramatic Use of Bawdy in Shakespeare* (London, 1974); Kenneth Muir, *Shakespeare's Sources* (London, 1977); and Emrys Jones, *The Origins of Shakespeare* (Oxford, 1977).

VIII. LANGUAGE AND STYLE. Walter Whiter, *A Specimen of a Commentary on Shakespeare* (1794), edited by Alan Over and Mary Bell (London, 1967); Caroline F. E. Spurgeon, *Shakespeare's Imagery and What It Tells Us* (Cambridge, 1935); Sister Miriam Joseph, *Shakespeare and the Arts of Language* (New York, 1947); Wolfgang H. Clemen, *The Development of Shakespeare's Imagery* (London, 1951); B. Ifor Evans, *The Language of Shakespeare's Plays* (London, 1952); Hilda M. Hulme, *Explorations in Shakespeare's Language: Some Problems of Lexical Meaning in the Dramatic Text* (London, 1962); Brian Vickers, *The Artistry of Shakespeare's Prose* (London, 1968); and G. L. Brook, *The Language of Shakespeare* (London, 1976).

IX. SHAKESPEARE'S THEATER. Sir Edmund K. Chambers, *The Elizabethan Stage*, 4 vols. (Oxford, 1923); Alfred Harbage, *Shakespeare's Audience* (New York, 1941); Irwin Smith, *Shakespeare's Globe Playhouse: A Modern Reconstruction* (New York, 1956); Leslie Hotson, *Shakespeare's Wooden O* (London, 1959); Bertram Joseph, *Acting Shakespeare* (London, 1960); Bernard Beckerman, *Shakespeare at the Globe: 1599–1609* (New York, 1962); Irwin Smith, *Shakespeare's Blackfriars Playhouse: Its History and Design* (New York, 1964); J. L. Styan, *Shakespeare's Stagecraft* (Cambridge, 1967); C. Walter Hodges, *The Globe Restored* (London, 1953; 2nd ed., Oxford, 1968); and Andrew Gurr, *The Shakespearian Stage, 1571–1642* (Cambridge, 1970).

X. SHAKESPEARE IN THE POST-RESTORATION THEATER. George C. D. Odell, *Shakespeare—From Betterton to Irving*, 2 vols. (New York, 1920); Hazelton Spencer, *Shakespeare Improved: The Restoration Versions in Quarto and on the Stage* (Cambridge, Mass., 1927); Arthur Colby Sprague, *Shakespeare and the Actors: The Stage Business in His Plays, 1660–1905* (Cambridge, Mass., 1944); C. B. Hogan, *Shakespeare in the Theatre 1701–1800*, 2 vols. (Oxford, 1952–1957); Arthur Colby Sprague, *Shakespearian Players and Performances* (Cambridge, Mass., 1953); J. C. Trewin, *Shakespeare on the English Stage 1900–1964* (London, 1964); G. Wilson Knight, *Shakespearian Production: With Especial Reference to the Tragedies* (London, 1964); Christopher Spencer, ed., *Five Restoration Adaptations of Shakespeare* (Urbana, Ill., 1965); Charles H. Shattuck, *The Shakespeare Promptbooks: A Descriptive Catalogue* (Urbana, Ill., 1965); John Russell Brown, *Shakespeare's Plays in Performance* (London, 1966); Gámini Salgádo, ed., *Eyewitnesses of Shakespeare: First-Hand Accounts of Performances, 1590–1890* (London, 1975); Charles H. Shattuck, *Shakespeare on the American Stage, From the Hallams to Edwin Booth* (Washington, D.C., 1976); Robert Speaight, *Shakespeare on the Stage: An Illustrated History of Shakespearian Performance* (London, 1973); J. L. Styan, *The Shakespeare Revolution* (Cambridge, 1977); and Stanley Wells, *Royal Shakespeare: Four Major Productions at Stratford-upon-Avon* (Manchester, 1977).

XI. GENERAL CRITICAL STUDIES. William Hazlitt, *The Characters of Shakespear's Plays* (London, 1817); Edward Dowden, *Shakspere: A Critical Study of His Mind and Art* (London, 1875); D. Nichol Smith, ed., *Eighteenth-Century Essays on Shakespeare* (Glasgow, 1903; rev., Oxford, 1963); A. C. Bradley, *Oxford Lectures on Poetry* (London, 1909); L. L. Schücking, *Character Problems in Shakespeare's Plays* (London, 1922); Elmer Edgar Stoll, *Shakespeare Studies, Historical and Comparative in Method* (New York, 1927); Harley Granville-Barker, *Prefaces to Shakespeare*, 5 vols. (London, 1927–1947); T. M. Raysor, ed., *Coleridge's Shakespearian Criticism*, 2 vols. (London, 1930; rev., London, 1960); G. Wilson Knight, *The Wheel of Fire* (Oxford, 1930; rev., London, 1949); G. Wilson Knight, *The Imperial Theme* (Oxford, 1931); G. Wilson Knight, *The Shakespearian Tempest* (Oxford, 1932); Elmer Edgar Stoll, *Art and Artifice in Shakespeare: A Study in Dramatic Contrast and Illusion* (Cambridge, 1933); J. Middleton Murry, *Shakespeare* (London, 1936); Elmer Edgar Stoll, *Shakespeare's Young Lovers* (Oxford, 1937); Mark van Doren, *Shakespeare* (London, 1939); Elmer Edgar Stoll, *Shakespeare and Other Masters* (Cambridge, Mass., 1940); Oscar James Campbell, *Shakespeare's Satire* (London, 1943); S. L. Bethell, *Shakespeare and the Popular Dramatic Tradition* (London, 1944); F. P. Wilson, *Elizabethan and Jacobean* (Oxford, 1945); E. A. Armstrong, *Shakespeare's Imagination: A Study of the Psychology of Association and Inspiration* (London, 1946; rev., Gloucester, Mass., 1963); Alfred Harbage, *As They Liked It: An Essay on Shakespeare and Morality* (New York, 1947); Dame Edith Sitwell, *A Notebook on William Shakespeare* (London, 1948); J. I. M. Stewart, *Character and Motive in Shakespeare: Some Recent Appraisals Examined* (London, 1949); Arthur Sewell, *Character and Society in Shakespeare* (Oxford, 1951); Harold C. Goddard, *The Meaning of Shakespeare*, 2 vols. (Chicago, 1951); M. C. Bradbrook, *Shakespeare and Elizabethan Poetry* (London, 1951); Alfred Harbage, *Shakespeare and the Rival Traditions* (New York, 1952); Patrick Cruttwell, *The Shakespearean Moment and Its Place in the Poetry of the Seventeenth Century* (London, 1954); G. Wilson Knight, *The Sovereign Flower* (London, 1958); L. C. Knights, *Some Shakespearian Themes* (London, 1959); Samuel Taylor Coleridge, *Writings on Shakespeare*, edited by Terence Hawkes (New York, 1959), repr. as *Coleridge on Shakespeare* (Harmondsworth, 1969); W. K. Wimsatt, ed., *Samuel Johnson on Shakespeare* (New York, 1960), repr. as *Dr. Johnson on Shakespeare* (Harmondsworth, 1969); A. P. Rossiter, *Angel With Horns: and Other Shakespeare Lectures* (London, 1961); J. R. Brown and Bernard Harris, eds., *Early Shakespeare*, Stratford-upon-Avon Studies 3 (London, 1961); Anne Righter, *Shakespeare and the Idea of the Play* (London, 1962); Theodore Spencer, *Shakespeare and the Nature of Man* (Cambridge, Mass., 1962); Edwin Wilson, ed., *Shaw on Shakespeare* (London, 1962); Ernest Schanzer, *The Problem Plays of Shakespeare: A Study of "Julius Caesar," "Measure for Measure," "Antony and Cleopatra"* (London, 1963); Jan Kott, *Shakespeare Our Contemporary* (London, 1964; rev., 1967); Nevill Coghill, *Shakespeare's Professional Skills* (London, 1964); Marion B. North, *Dualities in Shakespeare* (Toronto, 1966); J. R. Brown and Bernard Harris, eds., *Later Shakespeare*, Stratford-upon-Avon Studies 8 (London, 1966); A. C. Hamilton, *The Early Shakespeare* (San Marino, Calif., 1967); Norman Rabkin, *Shakespeare and the Common Understanding* (New York, 1967); Arthur Sherbo, ed., *Johnson on Shakespeare*, 2 vols. (New Haven, 1968), which are vols. VII and VIII of the Yale edition of Samuel Johnson; Philip Edwards, *Shakespeare and the Confines of Art* (London, 1968); M. C. Bradbrook, *Shakespeare the Craftsman* (London, 1969); F. P. Wilson, *Shakespearian and Other Studies*, ed. Helen Gardner (Oxford, 1969); Emrys Jones, *Scenic Form in Shakespeare* (Oxford, 1971); J. L. Calderwood, *Shakespeare's Metadrama* (Minneapolis, 1971); Michael Goldman, *Shakespeare and the Energies of Drama* (Princeton, 1972); Wolfgang H. Clemen, *Shakespeare's Dramatic Art* (London, 1972); Kenneth Muir, *Shakespeare the Professional and Related Studies* (London, 1973); Theodore Weiss, *The Breath of Clowns and Kings: Shakespeare's Early Comedies and Histories* (New York, 1971); and David P. Young, *The Heart's Forest: A Study of Shakespeare's Pastoral Plays* (New Haven, 1972).

XII. CRITICAL STUDIES OF THE COMEDIES. W. W. Lawrence, *Shakespeare's Problem Comedies* (New York, 1931); Frances Yates, *A Study of "Love's Labour's Lost"* (Cambridge, 1936); Oscar James Campbell, *Comicall Satyre and Shakespeare's "Troilus and Cressida"* (San Marino, Calif., 1938); H. B. Charlton, *Shakespearian Comedy* (London, 1938); George Gordon, *Shakespearian Comedy and Other Studies* (London, 1944); David Lloyd Stevenson, *The Love-Game Comedy* (New York, 1946); Ronald Watkins, *Moonlight at the Globe: An Essay in Shakespeare Production Based on Performance of "A Midsummer Night's Dream" at Harrow School* (London, 1946); G. Wilson Knight, *The Crown of Life: Essays in Interpretation of Shakespeare's Final Plays* (Oxford, 1947); S. L. Bethell, *"The Winter's Tale": A Study* (London, 1947); E. M. W. Tillyard, *Shakespeare's Last Plays* (London, 1948); E. M. W. Tillyard, *Shakespeare's Problem Plays* (London, 1950); S. C. Sen Gupta, *Shakespearian Comedy* (London, 1950); Leslie Hotson, *Shakespeare's Motley* (London, 1952); Enid Welsford, *The Fool: His Social and Literary*

History (London, 1953); Mary Lascelles, *Shakespeare's "Measure for Measure"* (London, 1953); Leslie Hotson, *The First Night of "Twelfth Night"* (New York, 1954); Derek Traversi, *Shakespeare: The Last Phase* (London, 1954); R. H. Goldsmith, *Wise Fools in Shakespeare* (East Lansing, Mich., 1955; Liverpool, 1958); John Russell Brown, *Shakespeare and His Comedies* (London, 1957; rev., 1962); C. L. Barber, *Shakespeare's Festive Comedy: A Study of Dramatic Form and Its Relation to Social Custom* (Princeton, 1959); Bertrand Evans, *Shakespeare's Comedies* (Oxford, 1960); Kenneth Muir, *Last Periods of Shakespeare, Racine, and Ibsen* (Liverpool, 1961); William Green, *Shakespeare's "Merry Wives of Windsor"* (Princeton, 1962); Bernard Grebanier, *The Truth About Shylock* (New York, 1962); D. R. C. Marsh, *The Recurring Miracle: A Study of "Cymbeline" and the Last Plays* (Durban, 1964); Robert Kimbrough, *Shakespeare's "Troilus and Cressida" and Its Setting* (Cambridge, Mass., 1964); Northrop Frye, *A Natural Perspective: The Development of Shakespearean Comedy and Romance* (New York, 1965); T. W. Baldwin, *On the Compositional Genetics of "The Comedy of Errors"* (Urbana, Ill., 1965); R. G. Hunter, *Shakespeare and the Comedy of Forgiveness* (New York, 1965); E. M. W. Tillyard, *Shakespeare's Early Comedies* (London, 1965); David Lloyd Stevenson, *The Achievement of Shakespeare's "Measure for Measure"* (New York, 1966); Peter G. Phialas, *Shakespeare's Romantic Comedies* (Chapel Hill, N.C., 1966); David P. Young, *Something of Great Constancy: The Art of "A Midsummer Night's Dream"* (New Haven, 1966); A. D. Nuttall, *Two Concepts of Allegory: A Study of Shakespeare's "The Tempest" and the Logic of Allegorical Expression* (London, 1967); Joseph G. Price, *The Unfortunate Comedy: A Study of "All's Well That Ends Well" and Its Critics* (Toronto, 1968); M. Bradbury and D. J. Palmer, eds., *Shakespearian Comedy*, Stratford-upon-Avon Studies 14 (London, 1972); L. G. Salingar, *Shakespeare and the Traditions of Comedy* (Cambridge, 1974); and Alexander Leggatt, *Shakespeare's Comedy of Love* (London, 1974).

XIII. CRITICAL STUDIES OF THE ENGLISH HISTORY PLAYS. *An Essay on the Dramatic Character of Sir John Falstaff* (1777), Maurice Morgann, in his *Shakespearian Criticism*, ed. D. A. Fineman (Oxford, 1972); A. W. Pollard, ed., *Shakespeare's Hand in the Play of "Sir Thomas More"* (Cambridge, 1923); J. Dover Wilson, *The Fortunes of Falstaff* (Cambridge, 1943); E. M. W. Tillyard, *Shakespeare's History Plays* (London, 1944); Lily B. Campbell, *Shakespeare's "Histories": Mirrors of Elizabethan Policy* (San Marino, Calif., 1947); Irving Ribner, *The English History Play in the Age of Shakespeare* (Princeton, 1957; rev., London, 1965); M. M. Reese, *The Cease of Majesty: A Study of Shakespeare's History Plays* (London, 1961); Arthur Colby Sprague,

Shakespeare's Histories: Plays for the Stage (London, 1964); H. M. Richmond, Shakespeare's Political Plays (New York, 1967); Wolfgang H. Clemen, A Commentary on Shakespeare's "Richard III" (London, 1968); H. A. Kelly, Divine Providence in the England of Shakespeare's Histories (Cambridge, Mass., 1970); David Riggs, Shakespeare's Heroical Histories: "Henry VI" and Its Literary Tradition (Cambridge, Mass., 1971); Robert Ornstein, A Kingdom for a Stage: The Achievement of Shakespeare's History Plays (Cambridge, Mass., 1972); Moody E. Prior, The Drama of Power: Studies in Shakespeare's History Plays (Evanston, Ill., 1973); Edward I. Berry, Patterns of Decay: Shakespeare's Early Histories (Charlottesville, Va., 1975).

XIV. CRITICAL STUDIES OF THE TRAGEDIES AND ROMAN PLAYS. A. C. Bradley, Shakespearean Tragedy (London, 1904); M. W. MacCallum, Shakespeare's Roman Plays and Their Background (London, 1910); Elmer Edgar Stoll, Hamlet: An Historical and Comparative Study (Minneapolis, 1919); Lily B. Campbell, Shakespeare's Tragic Heroes: Slaves of Passion (Cambridge, 1930); A. J. A. Waldock, Hamlet: A Study in Critical Method (Cambridge, 1931); J. Dover Wilson, What Happens in "Hamlet" (Cambridge, 1935); Robert B. Heilman, This Great Stage: Image and Structure in "King Lear" (Baton Rouge, La., 1948); H. B. Charlton, Shakespearian Tragedy (Cambridge, 1948); Ernest Jones, Hamlet and Oedipus (London, 1949); John F. Danby, Shakespeare's Doctrine of Nature: A Study of "King Lear" (London, 1949); H. N. Paul, The Royal Play of "Macbeth" (New York, 1950); Willard Farnham, Shakespeare's Tragic Frontier (Berkeley, Calif., 1950); D. G. James, The Dream of Learning: An Essay on "The Advancement of Learning," "Hamlet," and "King Lear" (Oxford, 1951); Peter Alexander, Hamlet, Father and Son (Oxford, 1955); Robert B. Heilman, Magic in the Web: Action and Language in "Othello" (Lexington, Ky., 1956); Franklin M. Dickey, Not Wisely but Too Well: Shakespeare's Love Tragedies (San Marino, Calif., 1957); Adrien Bonjour, The Structure of "Julius Caesar" (Liverpool, 1958); Bernard Spivack, Shakespeare and the Allegory of Evil: The History of a Metaphor in Relation to His Major Villains (New York, 1958); H. S. Wilson, On the Design of Shakespearian Tragedy (Toronto, 1959); Harry Levin, The Question of Hamlet (New York, 1959); L. C. Knights, An Approach to "Hamlet" (London, 1960); Irving Ribner, Patterns in Shakespearian Tragedy (New York, 1960); Marvin Rosenberg, The Masks of Othello: The Search for the Identity of Othello, Iago, and Desdemona by Three Centuries of Actors and Critics (Berkeley, Calif., 1961); Maurice Charney, Shakespeare's Roman Plays: The Function of Imagery in the Drama (Cambridge, Mass., 1961); John Holloway, The Story of the Night: Studies in Shakespeare's Major Tragedies (London, 1961); Morris Weitz, "Hamlet" and the Philosophy of Literary Criticism (Chicago, 1965); Maynard Mack, "King Lear" in Our Time (Berkeley, Calif., 1965); William R. Elton, King Lear and the Gods (San Marino, Calif., 1966); Northrop Frye, Fools of Time: Studies in Shakespearean Tragedy (Toronto, 1967); Nicholas Brooke, Shakespeare's Early Tragedies (London, 1968); Dennis Bartholomeusz, Macbeth and the Players (Cambridge, 1969); Maurice Charney, Style in "Hamlet" (Princeton, 1969); Reuben A. Brower, Hero and Saint: Shakespeare and the Graeco-Roman Tradition (Oxford, 1971); Nigel Alexander, Poison, Play, and Duel: A Study in "Hamlet" (London, 1971); Marvin Rosenberg, The Masks of King Lear (Berkeley, Calif., 1972); Kenneth Muir, Shakespeare's Tragic Sequence (London, 1972); and E. A. J. Honigmann, Shakespeare: Seven Tragedies: The Dramatist's Manipulation of Response (London, 1976).

XV. CRITICAL STUDIES OF THE POEMS AND SONNETS. Edward Hubler, The Sense of Shakespeare's Sonnets (Princeton, 1952); G. Wilson Knight, The Mutual Flame: On Shakespeare's Sonnets and "The Phoenix and the Turtle" (London, 1955); J. B. Leishman, Themes and Variations in Shakespeare's Sonnets (London, 1961); Brents Stirling, The Shakespeare Sonnet Order (Berkeley, Calif., 1968); Stephen Booth, An Essay on Shakespeare's Sonnets (New Haven, 1969); and Giorgio Melchiori, Shakespeare's Dramatic Meditations (Oxford, 1976).

XVI. RECORDINGS. The Marlowe Society of Cambridge, with professional players, has recorded the complete works under the direction of George Rylands in Dover Wilson's text for Argo. Most of the works have been recorded by professional players in G. B. Harrison's text on the Caedmon label. There are other recordings of individual plays and extracts that may be traced through the catalogs of the record companies.

BEN JONSON
(ca. 1572-1637)

J. B. Bamborough

I

BEN JONSON suffered the worst fate that can overtake a creative writer. Himself a man of great talent or minor genius—his real place is on the frontier where the terms become virtually indistinguishable—he had the misfortune to live and work at the same time and in the same field as a genius acknowledged by the world as supreme—William Shakespeare. However devotedly his admirers have labored to rescue him from this position, their efforts have never succeeded in saving him from being overcast by that mighty shadow. For a time, in the seventeenth century, he was considered Shakespeare's equal—even, by some, his superior—but from the time of Dryden onward his reputation has become more and more eclipsed. It must seem very unjust and unfair to his ghost, and also very irritating. Not that he did not admire Shakespeare; although he occasionally made fun of him, Jonson wrote about Shakespeare more warmly than he wrote about any other contemporary writer. Yet his love for Shakespeare was, as he said himself, "this side idolatry." He thought that Shakespeare had many faults and made many mistakes; above all, he thought that Shakespeare had not reflected deeply enough on the nature and purpose of drama, nor taken sufficient care to observe its laws. To find himself ranked below a writer seemingly so careless and unserious would have been a very bitter pill to swallow. Yet however hard we try to avoid it, we almost automatically find ourselves comparing the two, and Jonson nearly always comes off the worse.

In some respects the comparison is illuminating. Their social origins were not dissimilar: Shakespeare's father was a tradesman; Jonson's father, who died before Jonson was born, was a priest, but his mother soon married again, and her second husband was a bricklayer or builder. Both, then, belonged to the lower middle class, that vast and rather ill-defined reservoir of talent from which so many English writers have come. But Shakespeare was a countryman, and his knowledge and love of the country are shown in countless images in his poetry from country life; Jonson, at least from early years, was a Londoner, and his interests and memories were predominantly urban. We know nothing of Shakespeare's education (although modern research has shown that he possessed more book learning than he was at one time given credit for); Jonson was educated at Westminster, one of the largest and most important English public schools, under William Camden, the greatest Elizabethan scholar and antiquary, and there he acquired not only an impressive store of knowledge—mainly, of course, of classical literature—but scholarly habits of mind that never deserted him. In later life he was able to consort on equal terms with the most famous scholars of his age, men like Sir Walter Ralegh (to whose son he acted as tutor), Sir Robert Cotton, and John Selden, and he thought of himself as a scholar as much as a creative writer.

When he left Westminster, Jonson did not proceed, as he might have been expected to do, to one of the universities. Perhaps his family was too poor; indeed, according to one not very well supported story, he did spend a few weeks at Cambridge, but had to leave for lack of money. Instead he worked for a time as a bricklayer in his stepfather's firm; then, tiring of this, he volunteered as a soldier, and went in one of the English expeditionary forces to the Netherlands, fighting the Spanish; this would have been in the early 1590's. After this he appears to have become an actor, possibly in one of the second-rate touring companies which traveled around England putting on shows in town halls, marketplaces, or gentlemen's houses—wherever they could find an audience; and from this he graduated to playwriting. This again is rather what Shakespeare did, but there is an important difference. Shakespeare, at least by the time he was thirty, had established himself not only as an actor and playwright, but as a "sharer" or partner in the activities of one particular theatrical company with which he became identified and for which he wrote all his plays. Jonson never took part in the business side of the theater, and always maintained his position as a freelance writer. Indeed, for the greater part of his life his income came as much from the king or noble patrons as from the popular audience, and he always made it clear that he was a playwright from necessity rather than from choice. There is little doubt that he would have preferred to earn his living another way, if he had not been hampered by his lack of powerful connections and by his religion; for a long period of his life he was a Roman Catholic, and this in itself prevented him from taking up certain kinds of employment. The stage was really the only opening for him if he was to win his independence by his pen, but he never forgot, as he put it later in life in *Ode to Himself*, written when one of his plays had been hissed off the stage by the audience (it begins: "Come, leave the loathéd Stage!"), that

They were not meant for thee, less, thou for them,

and he always preferred to be regarded as a gentleman who happened to write for the stage rather than as a professional playwright. (One of the charges made against him by his enemies was that he was always boasting of his grand friends.)

There is still one more important comparison between Shakespeare and Jonson to be made. Shakespeare was born in 1564, Jonson probably in the summer of 1572; and that difference of eight years meant a great deal. Shakespeare was 25 in 1589 and probably began his work in the theater about the same time. At that period the great literary figures were Sidney and Spenser, and in the theater the big names were Lyly, Kyd, Marlowe, and the rest of the so-called uni-

versity wits; the influence of all these men can be seen in Shakespeare's early work. Jonson reached maturity in 1597, which is also the year in which he is first recorded as writing for the stage, and his generation was that of Donne, Middleton, Webster, and Marston. The mere mention of these names indicates the quite different atmosphere in which Jonson was working. The earlier generation had been high-minded and courtly, sometimes flamboyant and extravagant, but always idealistic and romantic. By the middle of the 1590's a new kind of writer had appeared; one is tempted to call them the Elizabethan "angry young men," and the comparison is not without point. Like their predecessors, the "university wits," they were intellectuals; but unlike Marlowe and his friends they were not natural bohemians, politically suspect, and accustomed to living only one jump ahead of the bailiff. Instead, they were the sons of professional men or of the minor gentry, and many of them had been trained as lawyers in the Inns of Court, the legal colleges in London that formed almost a third university in England. Instead of being high-minded and idealistic, they were down-to-earth, flippant, sometimes cynical in their approach to life; at the same time they were scholars and fundamentally serious-minded (many of them ended in the church). Above all their mood was satirical; what they most wanted to do was to attack society, to puncture pretense and reveal folly and corruption. Jonson readily absorbed their tone. He had in any case, we may suspect, the irascibility, the strong sense of the ridiculous, and the deep conviction of his own rightness that go to the making of the born satirist, but in addition the time was ripe for his development. His home in Westminster was not far from the Inns of Court, many of the students were old schoolfellows of his, and his first major success, *Every Man in His Humor* (staged in 1598), was very much to their taste. We know that before this he had written or had a share in writing several other plays, but this was the first he saw fit to preserve, and clearly he regarded his career as a playwright as beginning with it. In the following year he followed it with his second important play, *Every Man out of His Humor*. Put on, like its predecessor, by Shakespeare's company (according to tradition it was Shakespeare who first recognized Jonson's gifts and urged his fellows to employ him), *Every Man out of His Humor* had an even greater success. Jonson made it something like a manifesto of his artistic intentions, and published it in 1600—the first of his plays to see print—with the air of offering a sample of a new art form. From that time onward his position as a major dramatist was recognized, though not for a long time was it unchallenged.

II

JONSON was a proud and self-confident man. Circumstances might force him to take up playwriting, a despised occupation looked down on by the scholars and gentlemen among whom he felt his right place to be; very well, he would make it his business to render it an accepted and valued profession. Time and again he asserts the high place of poetry, which for him meant all forms of creative writing. One of the earliest and also one of his finest defenses occurs in the original version of *Every Man in His Humor*. A father tries to dissuade his son from writing by pointing out to him how low a place poets and poetry hold in the world's opinion, and the son bursts out:

> Opinion? O God let gross opinion
> Sink and be damned as deep as Barathrum.[1]
> If it may stand with your most wished content,
> I can refell opinion, and approve
> The state of poesy, such as it is,
> Blessed, eternal, and most true divine:
> Indeed if you will look on poesy,
> As she appears in many, poor and lame,
> Patched up in remnants and old worn rags,
> Half starved for want of her peculiar food,
> Sacred invention, then I must confirm,
> Both your conceit and censure of her merit.
> But view her in her glorious ornaments,
> Attirèd in the majesty of art,
> Set high in spirit with the precious taste
> Of sweet philosophy, and which is most,
> Crowned with the rich traditions of a soul,
> That hates to have her dignity profaned,
> With any relish of an earthly thought;
> Oh then how proud a presence doth she bear.
> Then is she like her self, fit to be seen
> Of none but grave and consecrated eyes.
> (V. iii. 312–333)

[1] The pit of Hell.

Bad poets might have brought poetry into disrepute, and given cause for her enemies to attack her; it was Jonson's aim to

> raise the despised head of *poetry* again, and stripping her out of those rotten and base rags, where with the times have adulterated her form, restore her to her primitive habit, feature and majesty, and render her worthy to be embraced, and kissed of all the great and master-spirits of our world.

It was a bold claim, but Jonson had no doubts of his ability to fulfill it. A man who could write a play for presentation before the queen, and end it with the injunction:

> By God 'tis good, and if you lik't, you may!

did not suffer from lack of self-confidence.

One aspect of Jonson's resolve to raise the status of his art was his determination that his plays should be considered as literature. Elizabethan plays were usually thought of as acting vehicles only, and were printed, if at all, as an afterthought. Jonson wrote his plays with his eye on the reader as much as on the spectator, and he had them printed with remarkable (and unique) care. The crowning point of his campaign came in 1616, when a collection of his plays, masques, and poems was printed in folio—a format hitherto reserved for serious works of learning—as *The Works of Benjamin Jonson*. This caused great mirth: for a writer to call his plays "works" was absurd—"works" meant works of philosophy, theology, or science. Even thirty years later Sir John Suckling made fun of Jonson by representing him as claiming his right to be crowned by Apollo above other poets:

> For his were called works, where others were but
>   plays.

Yet Jonson carried his point. Not only did his example cause a general rise in the standard of printing plays (and very likely gave Heming and Condell the idea of collecting Shakespeare's works in folio); since his time nobody has seriously denied the right of plays to be considered as literature.

Jonson had not merely to establish plays as literature; he had to demonstrate the correct way of writing them. He knew quite well what was wrong with the plays of his contemporaries. Wherever he looked he saw them full of errors: they were badly written, stuffed with stale jokes and senseless bombast, marred by obscenity and blasphemy—"all licence of offence to God and man"; their plots were absurd, full of improbabilities and coincidences, and such stale tricks as mistaken identity and the "cross-wooing" of dukes, duchesses, and their servants (as in *Twelfth Night*); their characters were incredible and there were too many clowns and servant-monsters (such as Caliban); they contained far too many violent, pointless, and noisy incidents—battles, storms, shipwrecks, and so on. All this was partly the fault of authors, partly of the audience, whose poor taste Jonson frequently reproved (no dramatist, not even Shaw, has been so consistently rude to his audience as Jonson was). Jonson's audiences could expect none of all this; instead, they were to be given models of correctly formed, correctly written drama. Late in life Jonson wrote a prologue for a play by a former servant of his, Richard Brome. In it he congratulates Brome on having achieved success

> By observation of those comic laws
> Which I, your master, first did teach the age,

and it was as a lawgiver, a pioneer in drama, that he saw himself.

This did not mean, as it so often meant in the later Renaissance, that he was a slave to the "laws of drama" derived by neoclassical theorists from Aristotle and the practice of the ancient dramatists. Jonson was very firm about this. The ancients, he said, were there as guides, not masters, and just as they had modified and improved their own drama, so it was open to modern dramatists to modify their practice and improve upon them. This is why arguments as to whether Jonson is more correctly regarded as a "classical" writer on the Continental model or as a "romantic" English writer are beside the point. In fact he was both; he deliberately set out to combine the best in both traditions. He wished to have the seriousness of purpose, the polish, the concentration, and the precise construction of the classics, without losing the richness, the vitality, and the raciness of

the freer English native drama. Because of this he may seem, to a critic accustomed to the loose, often haphazard, architecture of other Elizabethan drama, to be very classical; while to a French critic, brought up on the severity of Corneille and Racine, he will seem characteristically English and undisciplined.

Jonson observed the rules as far as he thought necessary, and ignored them when he thought fit. One thing he did absorb from his study of classical and neoclassical drama, and that was the beautiful articulation of his plots. No praise can be too high for the construction of his comedies. Nothing in them happens by chance and no loose ends are ever left dangling; it is not too much to say that every character who appears is given an intelligible motive for his actions, and his every entrance and exit is accounted for. Alongside the plays of his contemporaries, which often seem like heaps of broken parts, Jonson's plays resemble well-oiled, smoothly running machines.

More important to Jonson, however, than the formal qualities of drama was the aim which it shared with all literature, that of being morally instructive. No tag is more frequently quoted by him than Horace's dictum that poetry should either instruct or delight, or, as it was usually taken by the Renaissance, should instruct *and* delight. This was the justification for the high place which Jonson claimed for poetry and also why he so many times insisted that to be a good poet it was first necessary to be a good man. He saw it as his duty to instruct his audience, and he carried out that duty. As a comic writer it was not his place to give examples of right behavior—that was more the function of tragedy—and in fact there are very few characters in his comedies who are held up for admiration. His mode was satire, and his method of teaching was to attack the faults he saw in men, and by ridicule to shame them out of their vices and follies. In *Every Man out of His Humor* the character Asper (who to some extent is Jonson himself) proclaims his intention:

> with an arméd and resolvéd hand
> I'll strip the ragged follies of the time,
> Naked, as at their birth . . .
> . . . and with a whip of steel,
> Print wounding lashes in their iron ribs.

I fear no mood stamped in a private brow,
When I am pleased t' unmask a public vice:
I fear no strumpet's drugs, nor ruffian's stab,
Should I detect their hateful luxuries:
No broker's, usurer's, or lawyer's gripe,
Were I disposed to say, they're all corrupt.

(Ind., 16–26)

This bold and independent attitude made Jonson famous, but it also made him many enemies. Other writers resented his arrogant suggestion that only he was truly moral and only he knew how to write comedies, and not long after the publication of this play he found himself attacked in plays and pamphlets. He tried to ward off these attacks by writing a play—*Poetaster*, staged in 1601—in which he parodied his opponents and defended his methods; this had some success, but in the end Jonson was defeated. He retreated from the theater in a huff, loudly proclaiming that the age was not capable of understanding his drama, and for the next few years he wrote no comedies. When he resumed in 1605, with *Volpone*, his tone was noticeably more moderate, though no less self-assured.

Although in effect he abandoned his claim to be the sole censor or moral conscience of his age, Jonson never gave up his didactic purpose. All his life he was engaged in attacking affectation and pretentiousness, and the eccentricities which the age called "humors." Strictly speaking, the humors were the four secretions which the human body was thought to contain—blood, phlegm, choler, and "black bile." A man's "temperament" depended on which of these was present in the greatest quantity in him: if it was blood, then he would be sanguine; if phlegm, phlegmatic; if choler, choleric; and if black bile predominated, then he would be melancholy. We still use these terms, of course, to mean very much what they meant in Jonson's day. By the end of the sixteenth century, however, "humor" was being used as a slang term very much as "complex" is used today. A man would say that it was his humor to dislike cats, or that it was his humor to trim his beard in a particular way. Jonson objected to this use of the term, and also to the belief that it was smart to have a particular affectation. At the beginning of *Every Man out of His Humor* he in-troduces three characters called Asper, Cordatus, and Mitis. Asper afterward takes a part in the play, while Cordatus and Mitis remain on the stage and act as a kind of chorus, commenting for the benefit of the audience on Jonson's purpose and technique. At their first appearance one of them happens to use the word "humor" and Asper immediately picks the term up. He gives a little lecture on what the word really means, and then goes on to describe some of the silly habits that get dignified by the popular use of the word:

But that a rook, in wearing a pied feather,
The cable hat-band, or the three-piled ruff,
A yard of shoetie, or the Switzer's knot
On his French garters, should affect a humor!
O, 'tis more than most ridiculous.

(Ind., 110–114)

He finishes by threatening to expose these fops:

Well I will scourge those apes;
And to these courteous eyes oppose a mirror,
As large as is the stage, whereon we act:
Where they shall see the time's deformity
Anatomized in every nerve, and sinew,
With constant courage and contempt of fear.

(Ind., 117–122)

When Jonson called his plays "comedies of humors," then, he did not mean that he was only going to represent the humors in their limited medical sense; if he had, he would have had a total cast of only four characters. What he meant was that he was going to satirize the follies and affectations of his age, and this he certainly did; there are in his plays a vast number of foolish, vain, affected, and pretentious people, as well as a few who are not quite sane, like Morose in *Epicoene* (Morose's "humor" is that he cannot bear noise, and his servants have to communicate with him by gesture only). All of them, by the end of the plays in which they appear, have been taken "out of their humor"—that is, ridiculed or shocked into realizing their folly, and cured of it. The danger of this, of course, is that it may strike us today as rather out of date; it is not very easy to get excited over an exposure of the absurdities of people's behavior three hundred and fifty years ago. Some critics have also felt that Jonson spent so much time attacking stupidity that he neglected much more serious faults. This is not quite fair, for he does deal in several plays with important human sins—pride, luxury, ambition, and greed, for example—although it is true that there are some failings which he hardly mentions at all. The real object of Jonson's attack, however, was deception, including deception of oneself. Like Swift (though perhaps not as bitterly as Swift) he resented all the means we use in order to feed our vanity and disguise from ourselves that our real value depends on our moral worth and nothing else. His aim was to bring man to a sense of his real nature, and to make him realize that right action can only be based on reason and a recognition of truth. To see vanity and folly as ridiculous is a first step in the right direction.

III

But it is, after all, not for his moral teaching that we are likely to value a comic writer. Rightly or wrongly (wrongly, in Jonson's eyes), we are more interested in delight than in instruction, more concerned with the sugar than with the pill. What has Jonson to offer us in his comedies? In the first place, great energy and exuberance. We usually associate seriousness of artistic purpose and scrupulous attention to form with thinness of inspiration and content, but this is not so with Jonson. He always provides a multitude of characters and a variety of incidents, and his humor is lively and boisterous, sometimes even rough and crude. He has a liking for practical jokes; at the end of *Poetaster*, for example, he brings on his chief enemy, the poet and playwright John Marston, and the other characters give him a pill which makes him vomit up specimens of his vocabulary, which Jonson thought pedantic and obscure. It is hardly a refined scene, but it is a very funny one, as Marston with difficulty regurgitates words like "turgidous," "bolatrant," "furibund," and "prorumped." There is no use in coming to Jonson's plays looking for refinement and delicacy of feeling, for he had little; on the other hand he was rarely bitter or mean in his ridicule.

The wealth of character and incident makes Jonson's plays sometimes rather difficult to read and follow, but when they are put on the stage this difficulty disappears, and his skill in handling a mass of material is revealed. His most remarkable achievement in this respect is *Bartholomew Fair*, which has a cast of over forty speaking parts, and really requires a large number of "extras" as well if it is to be properly staged. Its plot is quite impossible to describe briefly; in fact it is built up not so much around a plot as by interlocking a large number of episodes. The scene is the great yearly fair at Smithfield, near London; some of the characters are the showmen and stallholders of the fair, and the others are the visitors to whom they sell their trumpery wares (and whose pockets they pick). The whole play is full of color, movement, and excitement, and it comes wonderfully alive on the stage; it might be even more successful as a film.

Jonson had an acute sense of the theater—he had, after all, been an actor himself—and a good many scenes which one hardly notices in reading his plays are very effective on the stage. In *Every Man in His Humor* the intriguing servant Brainworm makes the lawyer's clerk Formal drunk, and steals his clothes. When Formal sobers up, all he can find to put on is an old suit of rusty armor, in which he later makes an entrance. The eye may easily slip over this on the printed page, but in the theater Formal clanking on with great difficulty, with his pale face peering out of a battered helmet, makes a very happy moment. Jonson's comic scenes, however, are not usually simple like this one, but complex and cumulative. In *The Alchemist*, one of his best plays, Face the servant is left in charge of the house while his master has gone to the country to escape the plague. He brings in two accomplices—Subtle, whose speciality is to masquerade as a magician or alchemist, and a girl, Doll Common—and between them they defraud a wide selection of "gulls" of their money. The action of the play only covers a few hours and everything takes place at great speed, as the victims arrive hot on each other's heels. Face, Subtle, and Doll display breathtaking virtuosity in taking advantage of every opportunity. One customer brings a load of scrap metal which he wants turned into gold, and they promptly sell this to another customer as goods belonging to some poor orphans; a country squire arrives to be taught the manners of the town, bringing his sister with him, and in no time they are offering her favors to another customer, who has come in the belief that they are running a bawdy-house. Trick is piled on trick until eventually Face's master returns unexpectedly, and the whole house of cards collapses.

In *Epicoene* the surly Morose, who hates noise, decides to get married in order to disinherit his nephew, whom he detests. The problem is to find a woman who will not upset him by her chatter. One is produced who is reported never to talk at all, and he marries her; as soon as they are married, however, she finds her voice and nags him all the time, and, what is more, invites all her friends to a noisy party. In despair, Morose sends for a lawyer and a priest to see if they can find some way of declaring his marriage invalid. In fact they are Otter and Cutberd, both frauds, sent along by his nephew, and they argue with each other in a wonderful mixture of dog-Latin and sheer gibberish:

Ott.   Your *impotentes*, I should say, are *minime apti ad contrahenda matrimonium*.
True. Matrimonium! we shall have most unmatrimonial Latin with you: *matrimonia*, and be hanged.
Daup. You put them out, man.
Cut.   But then there will arise a doubt, master parson, in our case, *post matrimonium*: that *frigid itate proeditus*—do you conceive me, sir?
Ott.   Very well, sir.
Cut.   Who cannot *uti uxore pro uxore*, may *habere eam pro sorore*.
Ott.   Absurd, absurd, absurd, and merely apostatical!
Cut.   You shall pardon me, master parson, I can prove it.
Ott.   You can prove a will, master doctor, you can prove nothing else. Does not the verse of your own canon say

Haec socianda vetant connubia, facta retractant?

Cut.   I grant you; but how do they *retractare*, master parson?
Mor.   O, this was it I feared.
Ott.   *In aeternum*, sir.
Cut.   That's false in divinity, by your favor.
Ott.   'Tis false in humanity to say so. Is he not

prorsus inutilis ad thorum? Can he *proestare fidem datam?* I would fain know.
Cut.   Yes; how if he do *convalere?*
Ott.   He cannot *convalere*, it is impossible.

(V. iii. 188–213)

This quarrel is funny in itself; it is also torture for Morose, across whom the disputants are shouting. The real point, however, as some at least of the audience will have guessed (and the rest will shortly find out), is that Morose's "wife" is not a woman at all, but a boy planted on him by his nephew, and the whole business is absolutely absurd because he has never been married at all.

This cumulative effect seems to be the result of the way Jonson worked—deliberately and carefully, rather than impulsively and by inspiration. He seems to have been a slow writer; indeed his enemies taunted him that his brain, like an elephant, took a year to gestate. His method appears to have been to hit upon the original idea or theme for a play and then work over it at leisure, building it up piece by piece into a whole. The strength of the constructions made in this way is always noticeable, and also their originality, notwithstanding the fact that he borrowed much from other writers—mainly from the classics. This was no crime in his day, when imitation was a recognized and accepted method of writing; the only rule was that one should always try to improve on one's original. This Jonson nearly always succeeds in doing: as Dryden said, "he invades authors like a monarch, and what would be theft in other poets is only victory in him." In fact he transformed all he took, and if we read his plays without looking up any notes (or better still, see them on the stage), what strikes us most is how much of a piece they seem, and how unlike any other comedies. One never feels with Jonson, as one sometimes does with Molière, that he is merely engaged in reshuffling plots and characters that have been the common stock of European comedy for centuries.

Just as Jonson's comic effects depend on piling up incident upon incident, his characteristic style is the result of an accumulation of words and phrases. He is not a witty writer in the sense that Congreve or Sheridan or Wilde is witty; he does not have the unexpected

341

adroitness of phrasing that causes a single remark to be greeted with a shout of laughter in the theater and remain fixed in the memory. Nor for that matter does he have (and this is a great relief) more than a little of the tiresome wordplay and still more tedious obscenity which mar so many Elizabethan comedies; in fact he disapproved strongly of both. His habit is to let his characters overwhelm us with a flood of words, and he is happiest with a quarrel or a tirade. He seems to have been fascinated by contemporary tricks of speech, and particularly by the cant or jargon of different professions. In *The Alchemist*, for example, Subtle holds forth at great length on the mysteries of alchemy in speeches which modern producers usually cut—wisely, for although they are technically remarkable, they go on rather too long. The same play, however, begins with a splendid quarrel between Face and Subtle, with Doll vainly trying to restrain them:

Face: Do but 'collect, sir, where I met you first.
Subtle. I do not hear well.
Face. Not of this, I think it.
But I shall put you in mind, sir, at Pie Corner,[2]
Taking your meal of steam in from cooks' stalls,
Where, like the father of hunger, you did walk
Piteously costive, with your pinched-horn-nose,
And your complexion, of the Roman wash,[3]
Stuck full of black and melancholic worms,
Like powder corns,[4] shot, at th'artillery-yard.[5]
Subtle. I wish, you could advance your voice, a little.
Face. When you went pinned up, in the several rags,
You'd raked, and picked from dunghills, before day,
Your feet in mouldy slippers, for your kibes,[6]
A felt of rug,[7] and a thin threaden cloak,
That scarce would cover your no-buttocks—
Subtle. So, sir!
Face. When all your alchemy, and your algebra,
Your minerals, vegetals, and animals,

[2] A well-known inn near Smithfield.
[3] Swarthy; a hint also of a lotion for skin disease.
[4] Grains of powder.
[5] A public place for weapon practice.
[6] Chilblains.　　[7] Coarse hat.

Your conjuring, cozening, and your dozen of trades,
Could not relieve your corpse,[8] with so much linen
Would make you tinder, but to see a fire;
I ga' you countenance, credit for your coals,
Your stills, your glasses, your materials,
Built you a furnace, drew you customers,
Advanced all your black arts; lent you, beside,
A house to practice in—
Subtle. Your master's house?
Face. Where you have studied the more thriving skill
Of bawdry, since.

. . .

Face. I will have
A book, but barely reckoning thy impostures,
Shall prove a true philosopher's stone, to printers.
Subtle. Away, you trencher-rascal.
Face. Out you dog-leech,
The vomit of all prisons—
Doll. Will you be
Your own destructions, gentlemen?
Face. still spewed out
For lying too heavy o' the basket.[9]
Subtle. Cheater.
Face. Bawd.
Subtle. Cow-herd.
Face. Conjurer.
Subtle. Cut-purse.
Face. Witch.
(I. i. 23–49; 100–107)

As well as this gift for vituperation, Jonson had a fine vein of nonsense. In *Bartholomew Fair* Justice Overdo, the central character, in order to keep an eye on the criminals at the fair, disguises himself as a lunatic called Mad Arthur of Bradley, and in this disguise he delivers a sermon against ale and tobacco (in the original this is broken up by interruptions from the other characters on the stage):

Thirst not after that frothy liquor, ale; for who knows when he openeth the stopple, what may be in the bottle? Hath not a snail, a spider, yea, a newt been found there? Thirst not after it, youth; thirst not after it. . . . Neither do thou lust after that tawny weed, tobacco. . . . whose complexion is like the Indian's

[8] Body.
[9] Alludes to the greed of prisoners who seize more than their share of the scraps of food sent in by basket.

that vents [sells] it. . . . and who can tell, if before the gathering and making up thereof, the alligator hath not pissed thereon? . . . The creeping venom of which subtle serpent, as some late writers affirm, neither the cutting of the perilous plant, nor the drying of it, nor the lighting or burning, can any way persway [mitigate] or assuage. . . . Hence it is that the lungs of the tobacconist [smoker] are rotted, the liver spotted, the brain smoked like the backside of the pig-woman's booth here, and the whole body within, black as her pan you saw e'en now, without.

(II. vi. 11– 44)

Much of the vitality and excitement of Jonson's comedies resides precisely in these glittering heaps of words, but they are by no means careless and haphazard effusions. Jonson was very much concerned with language and style; indeed he wrote one of the first English grammars. Since he meant his plays to be read as literature, he was extremely careful in writing them. There was another reason for this care, for he believed that character was revealed most clearly in speech; in his notebooks he jotted down the tag from Quintilian: "Speech most shews a man; Speak, that I may know thee." He portrays his characters more through what they say than what they do, and this is why he took so much interest in contemporary colloquial speech. In his portrayal of character Jonson was much influenced by the Renaissance principle of decorum, which (in brief) laid it down that the persons of a drama must always be types, with the typical characteristics belonging to their age, sex, social class, profession, and so on, and that they must never do anything which a person of their type would not do. The result is not that his characters never impress us as individuals, for this they frequently do, but it does mean that they often strike us as one-sided and limited. Bobadil, the boastful, cowardly soldier in *Every Man in His Humor*, is one of Jonson's best creations, but he is far less complex and rounded than Falstaff, who belongs to the same general type. A better way of putting it would be to say that Bobadil is a vivid representation of the type, while Falstaff can surprise us with some of the things he says and does; Bobadil cannot and does not. Decorum also demanded that characters should be consistent from their first appearance to their last, and this means that Jonson's people never develop in the course of the plays in which they appear. It is this fact, together with their tendency to have some marked idiosyncrasy or "humor," that led Coleridge to remark that they were like "the hopeless patients of a mad doctor." This is overstating the case, but it is true that Jonson's characterization lacks subtlety and depth. Yet he was wonderfully faithful to the appearance and manners of his contemporaries and in "holding the mirror up to Nature"; in his plays we have, as Dryden said of *The Canterbury Tales*, "our forefathers and great-grandames all before us."

What *is* difficult is to feel much affection for Jonson's characters, and this is the direct result of his decision to instruct by ridicule. There are few really likable people in Jonson's plays, and curiously enough those that are most likable are very often rogues—which hardly assists his moral purpose. This makes his comedies different from most English comedies, and they are different, too, in that they contain almost no mixture of the pathetic or tragic. This again was a matter of principle; it was the business of comedy to deal only with laughable events, or as Jonson put it, to

Sport with human follies, not with crimes;

anything more serious was the province of tragedy. Only once, in his greatest play, does Jonson verge on the tragic in a comedy. In *Volpone* the hero is a magnifico of Venice and a rich man, but he delights in adding to his wealth by pretending to be sick and dying, thus inducing other rich men to give him presents in the hope of being made his heirs. One of these suitors is even persuaded to prostitute his wife to Volpone in the hope of cutting out his rivals, and the scene in which Volpone tries to seduce the shrinking girl is more like what we expect to find in Elizabethan tragedy than anything else in Jonson. The speech in which she begs for mercy is truly moving:

If you have ears that will be pierced; or eyes,
That can be opened; a heart, may be touched;
Or any part, that yet sounds man, about you:
If you have touch of holy saints, or heaven,
Do me the grace, to let me scape. If not,
Be bountiful, and kill me. You do know,
I am a creature, hither ill betrayed,
By one, whose shame I would forget it were.

If you will deign me neither of these graces,
Yet feed your wrath, sir, rather than your lust;
(It is a vice, comes nearer manliness)
And punish that unhappy crime of nature,
Which you miscall my beauty: flay my face,
Or poison it, with ointments, for seducing
Your blood to this rebellion. Rub these hands,
With what may cause an eating leprosy,
E'en to my bones, and marrow: anything,
That may disfavour[10] me, save in my honour.
And I will kneel to you, pray for you, pay down
A thousand hourly vows, sir, for your health,
Report, and think you virtuous—

                                          (III. vii. 240–260)

This is fine, but it is quite untypical of Jonson, and elsewhere he restricted himself to what he considered the true matter of comedy. To an Englishman, accustomed to the pathetic, often sentimental, comedy of Chaucer, Shakespeare, or Dickens, Jonson as a result often seems strange and un-English, despite the raciness of his scenes and characters. His is a hard, tough, quite unsentimental comedy, and it belongs more in the tradition of European comedy than to the peculiarly English stream. In that tradition it takes a high place; not perhaps as high as Molière's, but nearly so; and that is in itself no mean achievement.

IV

JONSON's comedies, however, are only part of his work, although to us by far the most important part. He himself would have put equal or greater weight on his masques and tragedies, to say nothing of his nondramatic verse. The masque was a dramatic form which in England reached its peak in the reign of King James, and Jonson was its foremost practitioner. Magnificently spectacular, it was also inordinately expensive—too expensive for the frugal Elizabeth. James was naturally extravagant, and felt it part of his duty as a great prince to have these "shows" staged for the entertainment of his court. Jonson wrote his first court masque in 1605; it was a great success, and from then onward his services were in steady demand. He produced an average of one masque a year until King James's death in 1625. Writing these

[10]Disfigure.

masques not only provided him with a good income, it gave him enhanced social position and literary prestige. He was able to regard himself as "the King's poet," and there is evidence that he hoped to be given the (as yet nonexistent) post of poet laureate. So secure did he feel that for ten years, from 1616 to 1626, he gave up writing for the public stage altogether and devoted himself entirely to poetry and to his work for the court and his noble patrons. This must have seemed to him the crown of his career, after his early struggles to make his name and the period from 1605 to 1616 in which he was consolidating his reputation (and in which, as we now see, he was writing his greatest plays). The death of King James, however, broke his connection with the court. Although he wrote a few more masques, he was never as highly regarded by Charles I as by his father, and in consequence he had to turn back to the public stage in order to support himself. The three or four plays he wrote from 1626 onward were unkindly described by Dryden as his "dotages"; the description is unduly harsh, but not quite unjustified, for they undeniably represent a decline of his great powers. When he wrote them he was in sickness and in poverty, not without friends but surrounded by powerful enemies, and whatever we may think of these last plays as literature, it is impossible not to admire the courage with which he maintained a bold and confident front. He went on writing up to his death in 1637—at least a manuscript of a half-finished play was found among his papers after he died, and curiously enough this (*The Sad Shepherd*) is one of his most serene, light-hearted, and beautiful works.

It is more pleasant to turn back to Jonson at the height of his success. Yet even here there is an element of sadness in watching Jonson devoting his gifts to so transitory and ephemeral an art form as the masque. For all their great cost, and the splendor of their scenery and costumes, the masques were very rarely staged more than once, and in the performance of them there must have been something of the air of brief glory that hangs over a great ball. Jonson captured this feeling of pathos and finality at the end of *Oberon*, one of his best masques; Phosphorus, the Day Star, appears and bids the dancers end their revels:

To rest, to rest; the herald of the day,
Bright Phosphorus commands you hence; obey.
The moon is pale, and spent; and wingéd night
Makes head-long haste, to fly the morning's sight:
Who now is rising from her blushing wars,
And, with her rosy hand, puts back the stars.
Of which my self, the last, her harbinger,
But stay, to warn you, that you not defer
Your parting longer. Then, do I give way,
As night hath done, and so must you, to day.

*After this, they danced their last dance, into the work.
And with a full song, the star vanished, and the whole
machine closed.*

SONG

O yet, how early, and before her time,
The envious morning up doth climb,
    Though she not love her bed!
What haste the jealous sun doth make
His fiery horses up to take,
    And once more shew his head!
Lest, taken with the brightness of this night,
The world should with it last, and never miss his
    light.   (434– 455)

Moreover, the poet's part in the masque was not all-important. The scenery and the costumes, which were the work of the designer (usually, in Jonson's masques, Inigo Jones), the music, and above all the dances, which were performed by members of the court (including, on occasion, some of the royal family), were the main source of interest to the audience, and all the poet was required to do was to provide a story and some speeches which would hold everything together. Despite the pomp of their staging, the masques were really amateur theatricals (though some professionals took part in them), and what could be printed was only a fragment of the whole. What is left to us of Jonson's masques, in fact, is something like the libretto of a grand opera. Yet they illuminate aspects of his genius which we would hardly guess at from his comedies—above all, a gift of delicate lyrical grace and fantasy. Here as an example is a song sung by the Nymphs in *Pan's Anniversary*, a minor masque written to celebrate one of the king's birthdays (James is figured under the name of Pan, the god of shepherds):

Thus, thus, begin the yearly rites
Are due to Pan on these bright nights;
His morn now riseth, and invites
To sport, to dances, and delights:
    All envious and profane, away,
    This is the shepherds' holiday.

Strew, strew, the glad and smiling ground
With every flower, yet not confound
The primrose drop, the spring's own spouse,
Bright daisies, and the lips of cows,
    The garden-star, the queen of May,
    The rose, to crown the holiday.

Drop, drop, you violets, change your hues,
Now red, now pale, as lovers use;
And in your death go out as well
As when you lived, unto the smell;
    That from your odor all may say,
    This is the shepherds' holiday.   (5–24)

This is far removed from the boisterousness of Jonson's comedies, and many similar passages could be quoted; they are a useful corrective to the tendency to think of Jonson as a purely urban writer.

Less need be said of Jonson's two tragedies, *Sejanus* and *Catiline*. They were failures when they were first staged, and they have never found many admirers since, although *Catiline* enjoyed a brief run of popularity at the time of the Restoration. It is not difficult to account for their lack of success. Jonson made them monuments to his scholarship; they are very accurate re-creations of Roman life, and in the original editions their margins are studded with references to the Roman historians and other authorities. They are also serious studies of the effects of ambition, corruption, and power-lust in the state, and their moral intention is always apparent. Their characters are powerfully and clearly drawn, but they are also, unfortunately, verbose and static; they have a marked tendency to orate at each other without getting anything done. This is especially true of *Catiline*, where whole scenes are taken up with translations of Cicero's orations. We know that these bored the Jacobean audience, and we cannot but sympathize with them; no amount of seriousness of purpose or obedience to the formal rules of drama will make up for sheer dullness. But to us a more deep-seated failing is a failing in the writing itself, and it could be expressed by saying that Jonson failed because he tried to write poetic tragedy without writing poetry.

This is to oversimplify grossly, yet there is truth in it. As a poet Jonson had many gifts. He was excelled only by Shakespeare in the art of playing off the rhythms of colloquial speech against the regular beat of blank verse, and his best dramatic poetry is clear, strong, and full of movement. Here is a character in one of his later and less well-known plays speaking on that common Elizabethan theme, the wickedness of luxury:

> Who can endure to see
> The fury of men's gullets, and their groins?
> What fires, what cooks, what kitchens might be
> spared,
> What stews, ponds, parks, coopes, garners, maga-
> zines,
> What velvets, tissues, scarfs, embroideries,
> And laces they might lack! They covet things—
> Superfluous still; when it were much more honor
> They could want necessary! What need hath nature
> Of silver dishes, or gold chamberpots?
> Of perfumed napkins, or a numerous family
> To see her eat? Poor and wise, she requires
> Meat only; hunger is not ambitious:
> Say, that you were the emperor of pleasures,
> The great dictator of fashions, for all Europe,
> And had the pomp of all the courts, and kingdoms,
> Laid forth unto the show? to make your self
> Gazed, and admired at? You must go to bed
> And take your natural rest: then, all this vanisheth.
> Your bravery was but shown; 'twas not possessed:
> While it did boast it self, it was then perishing.
> (*The Staple of News*, III. iv. 45–66)

This is flexible, sinewy, athletic writing, but in no way exceptional in Jonson; and it is a great contrast to the flaccid and nerveless verse of many of his contemporaries in the drama. In the same play the hero describes his emotions at first meeting his mistress:

> My passion was clear contrary, and doubtful,
> I shook for fear, and yet I danced for joy,
> I had such motions as the sunbeams make
> Against a wall, or playing on a water,
> Or trembling vapour of a boiling pot
> (II. v. 63–67)

Simple, vivid images of this kind abound in Jonson's plays; even in the somber, more rhetorical verse of the tragedies there come snatches like this, in which one character describes how the conspiring senators whisper together:

> Ay, now their heads do travail, now they work;
> Their faces run like shuttles, they are weaving
> Some curious cobwebs to catch flies.
> (*Sejanus*, III. 22–24)

Jonson's dramatic verse, like his prose, is always meaningful and pointed, never empty or conventional.

Of his poems outside his plays Jonson himself valued his epigrams most highly, but to us the best are found among his vigorous odes, his grave and manly verse letters:

> Tonight, grave sir, both my poor house, and I
> Do equally desire your company:
> Not that we think us worthy such a guest,
> But that your worth will dignify our feast,
> (*Inviting a Friend to Supper*, 1–4)

and in a handful of lovely lyrics. *Drink to Me Only with Thine Eyes* is too familiar to need quotation; this *Hymn to Diana* from *Cynthia's Revels* is less well known, and equally good:

> Queen and huntress, chaste, and fair,
> Now the sun is laid to sleep,
> Seated, in thy silver chair,
> State in wonted manner keep:
>   Hesperus entreats thy light,
>   Goddess, excellently bright.
>
> Earth, let not thy envious shade
> Dare itself to interpose;
> Cynthia's shining orb was made
> Heaven to clear, when day did close:
>   Bless us then with wishèd sight,
>   Goddess, excellently bright.
>
> Lay thy bow of pearl apart,
> And thy crystal-shining quiver;
> Give unto the flying hart
> Space to breathe, how short soever:
>   Thou, that mak'st a day of night,
>   Goddess, excellently bright.

It was the exquisite finish and smoothness of this type of lyric that Jonson handed on to his "sons," the group of younger poets—the best known of them is Herrick—who accepted him as their master.

Yet for all the vigor, dignity, polish, and sweetness of which Jonson's poetry is capable, we become in the end aware of something lacking in it. It is not merely that he shows a marked preference for concrete images, drawn (sometimes awkwardly) from everyday life, and avoids anything vague, exotic, or "romantic." This indeed should be of positive value to him today, when the vaguely "poetic" is so much out of favor. It is not even that his poetry for the most part is passionless, and lacks urgency. The later seventeenth-century critics always note, when they are discussing Jonson, that he was surprisingly unsuccessful as a love poet, and he himself began his verse collection, *The Forest*, with a little humorous poem called *Why I write not of Love*. As a matter of fact this is not quite true, for he wrote several love poems, and some of them are very fine—for instance this, one of a group of poems in *The Underwood* dedicated to a lady he called Charis:

See the chariot at hand here of Love
　Wherein my lady rideth!
Each that draws, is a swan, or a dove,
　And well the car Love guideth.
As she goes, all hearts do duty
　Unto her beauty;
And enamoured, do wish, so they might
　But enjoy such a sight,
　That they still were, to run by her side,
Thorough swords, thorough seas, whither she would
　ride.

Do but look on her eyes, they do light
　All that Love's world compriseth!
Do but look on her hair, it is bright
　As Love's star when it riseth!
Do but mark her forehead's smoother
　Than words that sooth her!
And from her archèd brows, such a grace
　Sheds itself through the face,
　As alone there triumphs to the life
All the gain, all the good, of the elements' strife.

Have you seen but a bright lily grow,
　Before rude hands have touched it?
Ha' you marked but the fall o' the snow
　Before the soil hath smutched it?
Ha' you felt the wool o' the beaver,
　Or swansdown ever?

Or have smelt o' the bud o' the briar,
　Or the nard in the fire?
　Or have tasted the bag of the bee?
O so white! O so soft! O so sweet is she!

(Her Triumph)

Yet although this is exciting and moving, it is not exactly personal—certainly not in the way that Donne's and Burns's love lyrics are personal, and this is generally true of Jonson's poetry. He put a good deal of himself into his poems, but always with a certain reserve and a sense of himself as a public figure speaking in public. There is never any question of Jonson's pouring forth his full heart in profuse strains of unpremeditated art; he is always the conscious artist fully in control of his medium.

This restraint can indeed be a great advantage, as it is, for example, in Jonson's elegies, particularly the poems he wrote on his two eldest children, who died young, and in his *Epitaph on Salomon Pavy*. Pavy was a boy actor (he acted in *Cynthia's Revels*) who died before he grew up; it is a subject which would lend itself very easily to sentimentality, but Jonson with his exquisite control makes his poem tender, yet never in the least mawkish:

Weep with me all you that read
　This little story,
And know, for whom a tear you shed,
　Death's self is sorry.
'Twas a child, that so did thrive
　In grace and feature,
As Heaven and Nature seemed to strive
　Which owned the creature.
Years he numbered scarce thirteen
　When Fates turned cruel,
Yet three filled zodiacs had he been
　The stage's jewel;
And did act (what now we moan)
　Old men so duly,
As, sooth, the Parcae[11] thought him one,
　He played so truly.
So, by error, to his fate
　They all consented,
But viewing him since (alas, too late)
　They have repented;
And have sought (to give new birth)
　In baths to steep him;
But, being so much too good for earth,
　Heaven vows to keep him.

(Epigram CXX)

[11] Fates.

This is a poem that can hardly be faulted, and in the face of it, it is perhaps churlish to wish that Jonson had sometimes been prepared to drop his guard and speak more directly from his heart.

But Jonson's main limitation as a poet lies elsewhere, and much nearer to the heart of poetry. It is, quite simply, that while Jonson's use of words is always precise, vigorous, and meaningful, he almost always brings into play only their immediate denotatory or dictionary significance, and only rarely calls up their complete range of suggestion, evocation, or emotive power. His verse, that is, lacks texture or richness of overtone and verbal harmony, and it is this that distinguishes it so sharply from the work of most of our major poets, and especially from the poetry of Shakespeare. This is the major reason why Jonson's tragedies are failures: unlike Shakespeare's they fail to establish through their poetry an atmosphere in which their characters can have their being, and they do not stir us imaginatively and emotionally. In comedy this limitation is less severe, and it is not so apparent in the masques, but it imposes throughout an all-important restriction on the praise which can be given Jonson as a master of language.

Here again qualification is necessary. There are indeed passages of poetry in Jonson of a profoundly moving kind; one of them—Celia's plea for mercy—has already been quoted. Characteristically, however, they are passages expressing two emotions not usually thought of as "poetic"—scorn and greed. In vituperation Jonson's manipulation of language is really creative or (to use Coleridge's term) esemplastic, and here, too, his sharp sense of the realistic and the sordid strengthens his vigor (see, for example, Face's description of Subtle in his poverty, given above). He has yet finer passages which communicate the desire for possession or power. At the beginning of *Volpone* the hero expounds his credo, rejoicing that he does not, as other men do, win wealth by toil or by the oppression of others, but by the exercise of a superior intelligence, and delivers a paean of praise to his idol, gold:

Good morning to the day; and, next, my gold!
Open the shrine, that I may see my saint.

Hail the world's soul, and mine! More glad than is
The teeming earth to see the longed-for sun
Peep through the horns of the celestial Ram,
Am I, to view thy splendor, darkening his;
That, lying here, amongst my other hoards,
Show'st like a flame, by night; or like the day
Struck out of Chaos, when all darkness fled
Unto the center. O, thou sun of Sol,
But brighter than thy father, let me kiss,
With adoration, thee, and every relic
Of sacred treasure, in this blessed room.
Well did wise Poets, by thy glorious name
Title that age, which they would have the best;
Thou being the best of things; and far transcending
All style of joy in children, parents, friends,
Or any other waking dream on earth.
Thy looks when they to Venus did ascribe,
They should have given her twenty thousand Cupids;
Such are thy beauties, and our loves! Dear saint,
Riches, the dumb god, that giv'st all men tongues;
That canst do nought, and yet mak'st men do all things;
The price of souls; even hell, with thee to boot,
Is made worth heaven! Thou art virtue, fame,
Honor and all things else!

(I. i. 1–26)

This is powerful poetry, but it should be noticed that part at least of its power comes from its subject; it is about something which stirs some of our strongest if not our most noble feelings—wealth and the possession of wealth. In a subtle way, then, it is the same sort of poetry as the song about Charis, and also the Nymphs' *Song from Pan's Anniversary*; in all of them the subject—the gold, the woman, the flowers—moves us in itself, of its own nature. The subject, that is, is giving force to the verse, rather than the verse to the subject. We may doubt whether Jonson could through his language alone make poetry about something to which we previously have felt indifferent (as Coleridge claimed that Wordsworth did), and it is not an accident that the two emotions, desire and scorn, which Jonson found it easiest to communicate, demand the actual presence of people or things in themselves desirable or contemptible. Jonson, that is, is a poet of the actual, the real, solid world about us, and not often of the inner world of hopes and ideals, velleities and doubts.

V

DRYDEN concluded his famous comparison between Jonson and Shakespeare in his *Essay of Dramatic Poesy* by saying "I admire him, but I love Shakespeare," and this has been the common response to Jonson. He certainly did not lack "personality"—indeed he lives for us in his work as a singularly vivid, robust, and even aggressive figure—but he did lack charm, and not many readers have taken him to their hearts. To the general public, in fact, he is known, if at all, as a literary figure rather similar to (and, one suspects, sometimes confused with) his namesake Samuel Johnson. Yet his best plays—*Volpone, Epicoene, The Alchemist,* and *Bartholomew Fair*—are always successful whenever they are performed. No other playwright except Shakespeare and Shaw has added so many plays to the national repertory, and it is not irrelevant to wonder how many of Shaw's plays will still be holding the stage in three hundred years' time. If Jonson must be thought of as a considerable rather than as a great poet, he did at least write one of the best-known lyrics in the English language, and he is a prose writer of very great distinction—a fact which is not always recognized. His range as a master of prose is wide, from the racy, colloquial dialogue of the comedies to the grave, dignified, harmonious prose of some of his prefaces and of the descriptive passages in the masques, and just as his poetry had a profound influence on the development of much later seventeenth-century verse, he had a part to play in the reformation of English prose style. Without ever losing the vigor of Elizabethan language, that is, he looked forward to the clear, smooth, yet pointed English of the eighteenth century. He has considerable importance, too, as a critic. Much of his criticism is incidental to his plays, but he left behind a critical notebook—*Timber, or Discoveries*—in which he had set down from time to time his considered thoughts on literature. These observations show him as virtually the first Englishman to have thought deeply about writing as a craftsman and practitioner rather than as a grammarian or moralist, and in this he anticipates Dryden. We have, too, some notes of his everyday conversation, made by the Scots poet Drummond of Hawthornden, whom Jonson visited in 1619; they form an odd mixture of scraps of gossip, anecdotes, and pieces of biographical information, but among them there are many snap judgments of men and books. No doubt Jonson would be horrified to find some of them quoted solemnly by scholars and literary historians, as they often are today, but they reveal much of his mind, and from them one thing emerges clearly: although he was often harsh and brusque in his condemnation of bad writing, he was very ready to praise what he thought good, and he recognized quality when he saw it.

Jonson answers better than most English writers to the description of a man of letters—that is, a writer who has thought deeply and read widely about his art, and tries to carry out his work according to his own principles. The English tend to prefer wilder and less self-conscious geniuses, and to associate artistic care with aestheticism and effeteness. Nothing could be less true of Jonson. He cared as much for his art as any other English writer, and more than all but a few, but there is nothing in him of the *petit maître*. Together with his fine sense of form and love of solid construction went a great vitality and creative vigor, and the two together give him his unique power. He belongs, as Milton does, to that class of serious and dedicated artists of whom Virgil (whom he admired so much) is the supreme example, and if he is not among the greatest, he is not unworthy of their company.

SELECTED BIBLIOGRAPHY

I. BIBLIOGRAPHY. H. L. Ford, *Collation of the Ben Jonson Folios, 1616–31–1640* (London, 1932); S. A. Tannenbaum, *Ben Jonson: A Concise Bibliography* (New York, 1938), Elizabethan Bibliographies, Supplement (New York, 1947), supplement no. 3 to the series adds a section on Jonson covering the years 1947–1965, compiled by G. R. Goffey (London, 1968); W. W. Greg, *A Bibliography of the English Printed Drama to the Restoration*, 4 vols. (Oxford, 1940–1959); D. Heyward Brock and J. M. Welsh, *Ben Jonson: A Quadricentennial Bibliography, 1947–1971* (Metuchen, N.J., 1974); S. Wells, ed., *English Drama (excluding Shakespeare)*, Select Bibliographical Guides (London, 1975), ch. 5.

II. COLLECTED WORKS, FIRST FOLIO. *The Workes* (1616), contains (date of first performance in parentheses): *Every Man in His Humor* (1598); *Every Man out of His Humor* (1599), *Cynthias Revells* (1600); *Poetaster* (1601); *Sejanus* (1603); *Volpone* (1605); *Epicoene* (1609); *The Alchemist* (1610); *Catiline* (1611); *Part of the Kings Entertainment* (15 March 1604); *A Panegyre on the Happie Entrance of James* (19 March 1604); *Entertainment at Althrope* (25 June 1603); *Entertainment at Highgate* (1 May 1604); *The Masque of Blackness* (6 Jan. 1605); *Hymenaei* (3 Jan. 1606); *Entertainment of the King of Denmark* (24 July 1606); *Entertainment at Theobalds* (22 May 1607); *The Masque of Beautie* (10 Jan. 1608); *Lord Haddington's Masque* (9 Feb. 1608); *The Masque of Queenes* (2 Feb. 1609); *Prince Henry's Barriers* (6 Jan. 1610); *Oberon* (1 Jan. 1611); *Love Freed from Ignorance and Folly* (3 Feb. 1611); *Love Restored* (6 Jan. 1612); *A Challenge at Tilt* (1 Jan. 1614); *The Irish Masque* (9 Dec. 1613); *The Golden Age Restor'd* (6 Jan. 1615); *Mercury Vindicated* (1 Jan. 1616); *Epigrammes; The Forrest* (poems).

III. COLLECTED WORKS, SECOND FOLIO. *The Workes,* 2 vols. (1640), vol. I reprints the First Folio, vol. II adds (date of first performance in parentheses) *Bartholomew Fayre* (31 Oct. 1614); *The Divell Is an Asse* (1616); *The Staple of News* (1626); *The Magnetick Lady* (1632); *A Tale of a Tub* (1633); *The Sad Shepherd* (unfinished); *Christmas His Masque* (1616); *Lord Hay's Masque* (*Lovers Made Men*) (22 Feb. 1617); *The Vision of Delight* (6 Jan. 1617); *Pleasure Reconciled to Virtue* (6 Jan. 1618); *For the Honour of Wales* (17 Feb. 1618); *Newes from the New World Discover'd in the Moon* (17 Jan. 1620); *Pans Anniversarie* (19 June 1620); *The Gypsies Metamorphos'd* (3 Aug. 1621); *The Masque of Augures* (6 Jan. 1622); *Time Vindicated* (19 Jan. 1623); *Neptunes Triumph* (planned for 6 Jan. 1624 but never performed); *The Masque of Owles* (19 Aug. 1624); *The Fortunate Isles* (9 Jan. 1625); *Loves Triumph through Callipolis* (9 Jan. 1631); *Chloridia* (22 Feb. 1631); *Entertainment at Welbeck* (21 May 1633); *Love's Welcome at Bolsover* (30 July 1634); *Underwoods* (poems); *Mortimer His Fall* (an unfinished tragedy); *Horace, His Art of Poetrie* (translation); *The English Grammar; Timber, or Discoveries* (critical notes).

IV. OTHER COLLECTED WORKS. W. Gifford, ed., *Works,* 9 vols. (London, 1816), repr. with corrections by F. Cunningham, 9 vols. (London, 1875); F. E. Schelling, ed., *Complete Plays,* 2 vols. (London 1910), in Everyman's Library. C. H. Herford, P. Simpson, and E. M. Simpson, eds., *Works,* 11 vols. (Oxford, 1925–1952), the definitive ed. with ample intro. and full critical and textual notes, a masterpiece of scholarship; A. B. Kernan and R. B. Young, eds., *The Yale Ben Jonson,* (New Haven, 1962–   ).

V. SELECTED WORKS. M. Castelain, ed., *Timber; or Discoveries* (London, 1889; Paris, 1906); G. B. Harrison, ed. (London, 1923); H. Morley, ed., *Masques and Entertainments* (London, 1890); B. Nicholson, ed.,

Ben Jonson, 3 vols. (London, 1893–1894), with intro. by C. H. Herford, Mermaid Dramatists Series, contains *Every Man in His Humour; Every Man out of His Humour; Poetaster; Bartholomew Fair; Cynthia's Revels; Sejanus; Volpone; Epicoene; The Alchemist;* B. H. Newdigate, ed., *The Poems* (Oxford, 1936), I. Donaldson, ed., Oxford Standard Authors (Oxford, 1975), G. Parfitt, ed., Penguin modern spelling ed. (Harmondsworth, 1975); H. Levin, ed., *Selected Works* (New York, 1938); *Five Plays* (Oxford, 1953), in the World's Classics Series, contains *Every Man in His Humour; Sejanus; Volpone; The Alchemist; Bartholomew Fair;* S. Orgel, ed., *The Complete Masques* (New Haven–London, 1969).

VI. SEPARATE WORKS. *The Comicall Satyre of Every Man out of His Humour* (1600), comedy, facs. rep. of the first of the quarto eds. of 1600, W. W. Greg and F. P. Wilson, eds., Malone Society (London, 1920); *Every Man in His Humour* (1601), comedy, the quarto ed. revised by Jonson before inclusion in the First Folio, Facsimile, H. H. Carter, ed. (New Haven, 1921), M. Seymour-Smith, ed., New Mermaids Series (London, 1966), J. W. Lever, ed., Regents Renaissance Drama Series (London, 1972); *The Fountain of Self-Love, or, Cynthia's Revels* (1601), comedy, edited from the quarto of 1601 by W. Bang and L. Krebs (Louvain, 1908); *Poetaster, or, the Arraignment* (1602), comedy, H. de Vocht, ed. (Louvain, 1934); *Part of King James His Royal and Magnificent Entertainment . . . also, a Brief Panegyre of His Majesties Entrance to Parliament . . .* (together with) *the Entertainment of the Queene and Prince to Althrope* (1604), masque; *Sejanus His Fall* (1605), tragedy, H. de Vocht, ed. (Louvain, 1935), W. F. Bolton, ed., New Mermaids Series (London, 1968); *Hymenaei* (1606), masque; *Volpone, or, The Foxe* (1607), comedy, H. de Vocht, ed. (Louvain, 1937), P. Brockbank, ed., New Mermaids Series; *The Characters of Two Royall Masques, the One of Blackness, the Other of Beautie* (1608); *The Description of the Masque . . . Celebrating the Happy Marriage of . . . Viscount Haddington* (1609), F. E. Schelling, ed. (New York, 1926); *The Case Is Alter(e)d* (1609), comedy, not included in the First Folio, first included in *Works,* P. Whalley, ed. (1756), W. E. Selin, ed. (New Haven, 1919); *The Masque of Queens* (1609), facs. with Inigo Jones's designs, G. Chapman, ed. (London, 1930); *Catiline His Conspiracy* (1611), tragedy, W. F. Bolton and J. F. Gardner, eds., Regents Renaissance Drama Series (London, 1973); *The Alchemist* (1612), comedy, Noel Douglas Replicas (London, 1927), D. Brown, ed., New Mermaids Series (London, 1966), F. H. Mares, ed., Revels Plays (London, 1967); *Lovers Made Man* (1617), masque; *Epicoene, or, the Silent Woman* (1620), comedy, R. Beaurline, ed. (London, 1967), Regents Renaissance Drama Series (London, 1967); *The Masque of Augures* (1621); *Time Vindicated* (1623), masque; *The Fortunate Isles and Their Union* (1624), masque; *Neptunes Triumph* (1625), masque; *Loves Triumph Through Callipolis* (1630), masque; *Chloridia* (1630), masque; *The New Inne, or, the Light Heart* (1631); *Bartholomew Fair: A Comedy* (1631), E. A. Horsman, ed., Revels Plays (London, 1960), E. B. Partridge, ed., Regents Renaissance Drama Series (London, 1964), M. Hussey, ed., New Mermaids Series (London, 1964); *Execration Against Vulcan . . . Epigrams* (1640), verse; *The Masque of Gypsies* (1640), W. W. Greg, ed. (London, 1952); *The Divell Is an Asse: A Comedie* (1641).

VII. SOME BIOGRAPHICAL AND CRITICAL STUDIES. R. F. Patterson and G. B. Harrison, eds., *Conversation with William Drummond* (London, 1623), a Scottish poet's notes on the visit Jonson paid him at Hawthornden in 1618; B. Duppa, ed., *Jonsonus Virbius*, (London, 1638), memorial verses by some of Jonson's friends; J. Dryden, *An Essay of Dramatick Poesie* (London, 1668), contains critical remarks on Jonson, and an "Examen" of *Epicoene, or, the Silent Woman*; W. Hazlitt, *Lectures on the English Comic Writers* (London, 1819), includes an essay "On Shakespeare and Ben Jonson"; S. T. Coleridge, *Literary Remains*, vol. I (London, 1836); A. C. Swinburne, *A Study of Ben Jonson* (London, 1889); F. E. Schelling, *Ben Jonson and the Classical School* (Baltimore, 1898); M. Castelain, *Ben Jonson: L'homme et L'oeuvre* (Paris, 1907); G. G. Smith, *Ben Jonson* (London, 1919), in English Men of Letters Series; T. S. Eliot, *The Sacred Wood* (London, 1920), includes an essay on Ben Jonson, repr. in *Selected Essays* (London, 1932); E. Welsford, *The Court Masque: A Study in the Relationship Between Poetry and the Revels* (Cambridge, 1927); J. Palmer, *Ben Jonson* (1934); R. G. Noyes, *Ben Jonson on the English Stage 1660–1776* (Cambridge, Mass., 1935); U. M. Ellis-Fermor, *The Jacobean Drama: An Interpretation* (London, 1936; 2nd ed., 1947; 3rd ed., 1953); F. R. Leavis, *Revaluation* (London, 1936); L. C. Knights, *Drama and Society in the Age of Jonson* (London, 1937); O. J. Campbell, *Comicall Satyre and Shakespeare's "Troilus and Cressida"* (San Marino, Calif., 1938); A. H. King, *The Language of the Satirized Characters in "Poetaster": A Socio-stylistic Analysis*, Lund Studies in English, no. 10 (London, 1941); G. E. Bentley, *Shakespeare and Jonson: Their Reputations in the 17th Century Compared*, 2 vols. (Chicago, 1945); G. B. Johnson, *Ben Jonson: Poet* (New York, 1945); F. L. Townsend, *Apologie for Bartholo-*

mew Fayre: The Art of Jonson's Comedies (New York, 1947); A. II. Sackton, *Rhetoric as a Dramatic Language in Jonson* (New York, 1948); E. V. Pennanen, *Chapters on the Language of Ben Jonson's Dramatic Works* (Turku, Finland, 1951); Edmund Wilson, *The Triple Thinkers* (2nd ed., 1952), includes an essay, "Morose Ben Jonson"; A. C. Partridge, *Studies in the Syntax of Jonson's Plays* (Cambridge, 1953); A. C. Partridge, *The Accidence of Jonson's Plays, Masques and Entertainments* (Cambridge, 1953); M. Chute, *Ben Jonson of Westminster* (New York, 1953; London, 1954); M. C. Bradbrook, *The Growth and Structure of Elizabethan Comedy* (London, 1955); P. Simpson, *Studies in Elizabethan Drama* (Oxford, 1955); G. Walton, *Metaphysical to Augustan: Studies in Tone and Sensibility in the Seventeenth Century* (Cambridge, 1955); J. J. Enck, *Jonson and the Comic Truth* (Madison, 1957); E. B. Partridge, *The Broken Compass: A Study of the Major Comedies of Ben Jonson* (London, 1958); W. T. Furniss, *Ben Jonson's Masques*, Yale Studies in English, no. 138 (New Haven–London, 1958), pp. 89–179; J. A. Barish, *Ben Jonson and the Languages of Prose Comedy* (Cambridge, Mass., 1960); W. Trimpi, *Ben Jonson's Poems: A Study of the Plain Style* (Stanford, 1962); J. A. Barish, *Ben Jonson: A Collection of Critical Essays* (Englewood Cliffs, N.J., 1963); C. G. Thayer, *Ben Jonson: Studies in the Plays* (Norman, Okla., 1963); R. E. Knoll, *Ben Jonson's Plays: An Introduction* (Lincoln, Neb., 1964); S. K. Orgel, *The Jonsonian Masque* (Cambridge, Mass., 1965); J. C. Meagher, *Methods and Meaning in Jonson's Masques* (Notre Dame–London, 1966); B. Gibbons, *Jacobean City Comedy: A Study of Satiric Plays by Jonson, Marston and Middleton* (London, 1968); G. B. Jackson, *Vision and Judgement in Ben Jonson's Drama*, Yale Studies in English, no. 166 (New Haven–London, 1968); J. G. Nichols, *The Poetry of Ben Jonson* (London, 1969); J. B. Bamborough, *Ben Jonson* (London, 1970); Ian Donaldson, *The World Upside-Down* (Oxford, 1970); Ian Donaldson, "Ben Jonson," in *English Drama to 1710*, edited by C. Ricks, Sphere History of Literature in the English Language, vol. 3 (London, 1971); H. C. Dessen, *Jonson's Moral Comedy* (Evanston, Ill., 1971); J. A. Bryant, Jr., *The Compassionate Satirist* (Athens, Ga., 1972); G. Parfitt, *Ben Jonson: Public Poet and Private Man* (London, 1976); L. A. Beaurline, *Ben Jonson and Elizabethan Comedy* (San Marino, Calif., 1978).

JOHN DONNE

(1572-1631)

Frank Kermode

TO HAVE read Donne was once evidence of a curious taste; now (though the vogue may be fading) it is a minimum requirement of civilized literary talk. We have seen the history of English poetry rewritten by critics convinced of his cardinal importance. This change was partly the effect of the reception into England of French symbolist thought and its assimilation to the native doctrines of Blake, Coleridge, and Pater. Poets and critics were struck by the way Donne exhibits the play of an agile mind within the sensuous body of poetry, so that even his most passionate poems work by wit, abounding in argument and analogy; the poetry and the argument cannot be abstracted from each other. And this was interesting because the new aesthetic was founded on a hatred for the disembodied intellect, for abstract argument, for what the French called *littérature.* A series of poets, culminating in T. S. Eliot, proclaimed their affinity with Donne. They also searched the past in order to discover the moment when the blend of thought and passion that came so naturally to Donne, and with such difficulty to themselves, developed its modern inaccessibility. One answer was that this occurred during the lifetime of Milton, who helped to create the difficulties under which modern poetry labors. This very characteristic symbolist historical myth is usually called by the name that Eliot gave it, the "dissociation of sensibility." Eliot altered his views on Donne and Milton, but his later opinions have been less successful in the world than his earlier ones; and it remains true that to write of the fortunes of Donne in the past seventy years is, in effect, to write less about him than about the aesthetic preoccupations of that epoch.

Donne has been distorted to serve this myth; but it is true that earlier criticism had treated him harshly. As Ben Jonson suggested, his kind of poetry runs the risk of neglect, especially in periods that value perspicuity. Dryden thought of him as a great wit, rather than as a poet, and a normal late seventeenth-century view of Donne was that this "eminent poet . . . became a much more eminent preacher." Dr. Johnson's brilliant critique occurs more or less accidentally in his *Life of Cowley.* Coleridge and Lamb, Browning and George Eliot admired him—indeed he enjoyed a minor vogue in the middle of the last century—but Edmund Gosse, in what was, until the publication in 1970 of R. C. Bald's *Life,* the standard biography, is patronizing about the poetry and calls Donne's influence "almost entirely malign." The revaluation of Donne has certainly been radical. The present is probably a favorable moment for a just estimate. The past half-century has provided the essential apparatus, and though the time for partisan extravagance has gone, so has the time for patronage.

LIFE

DONNE was born early in 1572, in the parish of St. Olave, Bread Street, in the City of London, of Roman Catholic parents. His mother was of good family; and since she numbered among her kinsmen Mores, Heywoods, and Rastells, Donne could well claim, in his *apologia* at the beginning of the anti-Jesuit *Pseudo-Martyr,* that his family had endured much for the Roman Catholic doctrine. His own brother was arrested for concealing a priest and died in prison. His father, a prosperous City tradesman, died when Donne was not yet four, leaving him a portion of about £750. A more enduring legacy was his early indoctrination by Jesuits. To his intimate acquaintance with their persecution under

Queen Elizabeth he attributes his interest in suicide (*Biathanatos*) and his right to characterize as mistaken the Jesuit thirst for martyrdom by the hostile civil power (*Pseudo-Martyr*). In fact, his whole life and work were strongly affected by this circumstance of his childhood. He suffered materially; for example, as a Roman Catholic he was disabled from taking a degree at Oxford. But, more important, his mind was cast in the mold of learned religion. We know that during his years at the Inns of Court, in the early 1590's, he read much besides law; that he explored many fields and many languages; and—though described as a great visitor of ladies—rose at four every morning and rarely left his chamber before ten. Much, if not most, of this reading must have been theological in character.

Donne traveled in Italy and Spain, and in 1596 and 1597 took part in naval expeditions. In 1598 he became secretary to the influential Sir Thomas Egerton; but his secret marriage to Lady Egerton's niece, Ann More, in December 1601, put an end to his hopes of worldly success. Her father had Donne imprisoned and dismissed from his post; he even tried to have the marriage annulled. Donne's dignified apologies prevailed, but he did not achieve reinstatement, and for some years lived somewhat grimly and inconveniently in what he called "my hospital at Mitcham," burdened and distracted by illness, poverty, and a growing family. A letter describes him writing "in the noise of three gamesome children; and by the side of her, whom . . . I have transplanted into a wretched fortune." He complained, in dark and memorable phrases, of his hated inactivity. He sought patronage, and had it of the countess of Bedford, of the king's favorite, Carr, and of Sir Robert Drury. He worked as assistant to Morton, later bishop of Durham, in anti-Romanist polemic, but refused to take orders when Morton requested it. The belated payment of his wife's dowry gave him a period of relief, in which he wrote more and published for the first time—*Pseudo-Martyr* in 1610, *Ignatius His Conclave* in 1611, and the two poems for Elizabeth Drury's death in 1611 and 1612. *Biathanatos,* which he forbade "both the press and the fire," belongs to this time, and the *Essays in Divinity* were written in 1614.

When James I had made it plain that he would advance Donne only within the Church, the poet finally took orders (January 1615). In 1616 he was appointed reader in divinity at Lincoln's Inn, where, over the years, he both gave and received great satisfaction. A learned audience suited Donne, although this one must have been well informed about those youthful indiscretions concerning which the lack of evidence has never impeded warm speculation; he was accepted as the penitent he claimed to be, and the audience would remember St. Augustine. Donne had found his true genre.

His wife died in 1617, her memory celebrated by a fine sonnet and a great sermon; Donne was left with seven children. He was made dean of St. Paul's in 1621 and became the most famous of preachers, invested with a somber sanctity and happy in the rejection of "the mistress of my youth, Poetry" for "the wife of mine age, Divinity." In 1623 he was seriously ill, and during his illness wrote *Devotions Upon Emergent Occasions*, a series of religious meditations on the course of his disease that is striking evidence of his continuing ability to be witty on all topics; with all its solemnity it has a macabre playfulness and hospital wit.

His sermons are often surprisingly personal; we learn of his family anxieties (the death of a daughter, a son missing in action, his own departure abroad in 1619) and his remorse for past sins. In the end he brought his own death (on March 31, 1631) into the pulpit (having wished to die there) and preached the appalling sermon called *Death's Duel* before Charles I in Lent, 1631. His ordering of the monument which survived the Fire and is still in St. Paul's, and his almost histrionic composure on his deathbed, Walton has made famous. This aspect of Donne has perhaps been overstressed; he and death are a little too closely associated. This can be corrected only by prolonged reading in the sermons, or perhaps by reminding oneself of his marked interest in life: his desire for success, which made him the dependent of the dubious Carr, or his rich and varied friendships—with Goodyere, with the scientist earl of Northumberland, with Lady Danvers and her sons, George and Edward Herbert, with Jonson and Wotton—many of them central to the intellectual life of their time. But it is still true that he was a somber man, a melancholic even, at a time when this quality was associated with the highest kind of wit.

CONCEPTS AS "CONCEITS"

WIT is a quality allowed Donne by all critics, of all parties. In his own time people admired his "strong lines," and perhaps the best way of giving a general account of his wit is to try to explain what this expression meant. Donne is notoriously an obscure poet—in fact his obscurity is often overestimated, but he is never easy—and this is often because his manner is tortuous and, in his own word, "harsh." Thomas Carew's famous tribute emphasizes the strain he put on language: "to the awe of thy imperious wit Our stubborn language bends." Carew speaks of his "masculine expression"; Donne himself of his "masculine persuasive force." There was a contemporary taste for this kind of thing, related probably to an old tradition that it was right for some kinds of poetry to be obscure. And Donne was not writing for the many. He expected his readers to enjoy difficulty, not only in the scholastic ingenuity of his arguments, but in the combination of complicated verse forms and apparently spontaneous thought—thought that doubled back, corrected itself, broke off in passionate interjections. This kind of writing belongs to a rhetorical tradition ignored by much Elizabethan poetry, which argued that language could directly represent the immediate play of mind—style as the instantaneous expression of thinking. And this is why Donne—if I may translate from Mario Praz what I take to be the best thing ever said about Donne's style—will always appeal to readers "whom the *rhythm of thought* itself attracts by virtue of its own peculiar convolutions."

Obviously this is a limited appeal. Ben Jonson, himself not a stranger to the strong line, was only the first to accuse Donne of overdoing it. He recommended a middle course between jejune smoothness and a manner conscientiously rough. But for a while "strong lines"—applied to prose as well as verse—was a eulogistic term; so Fuller could praise those of Cleveland, saying that "his Epithetes were pregnant with metaphors, carrying in them a difficult plainness, difficult at the hearing, plain at the considering thereof." But there was opposition to what Walton called "the strong lines now in fashion"; witness, for example, Corbet's good nonsense poem *Epilogus Incerti Authoris*, a heap of paradoxes beginning "Like to the mowing tone of unspoke speeches," and ending

> Even such is man who died, and yet did laugh
> To read these strong lines for his epitaph—[1]

which not only parodies Donne, but foretells the fate of the strong line: it degenerated into a joke and until recently recurred only in comic poetry. Hobbes, legislating for a new poetry in the 1650's, called strong lines "no better than riddles." The taste for them is not universal, nor are the powers they require of poets.

As strong lines directly record mental activity, they contain concepts, or, in the contemporary form of the word, "conceits." The meaning we now attach to this word is a specialization directly due to the vogue for strong lines. The value of such lines obviously depends on the value (and that is almost the same thing as the strangeness) of the concepts they express, and these were usually metaphors. A high valuation was placed on metaphor, on the power of making what Dr. Johnson, who understood without approving, called the *discordia concors*. The world was regarded as a vast divine system of metaphors, and the mind was at its fullest stretch when observing them. Peculiar ability in this respect was called *acutezza* by the Italians and, by the English, wit. But although the movement was European in scope, it is unnecessary to suppose that Donne owed much to its Spanish and Italian exponents; they were known in England, but they conspicuously lack Donne's colloquial convolution, and his argumentativeness. Johnson's mistake in reporting Marino as a source has often been repeated. Marino has strength but not harshness, not the masculine persuasive force. We cannot think of

[1] All quotations, in modern spellings, are from A. J. Smith, ed., *The Complete English Poems of John Donne* (Harmondsworth, 1971).

Donne without thinking of relentless argument. He depends heavily upon dialectical sleight of hand, arriving at the point of wit by subtle syllogistic misdirections, inviting admiration by slight but significant perversities of analogue, which reroute every argument to paradox. Still, in view of the lack of contemporary English criticism on these points, it is wise to learn what we can from Continental critics of witty poetry; and the most important lesson, brilliantly suggested by S. L. Bethell, is that they regarded the conceit of argument—making a new and striking point by a syllogism concealing a logical error—as the highest and rarest kind of conceit. This is Donne's commonest device. Of course we are aware that we are being cleverly teased, but many of the love poems, like *The Ecstasy* or *The Flea*, depend on our wonder outlasting our critical attitude to argument. Consider the progression of ideas in *The Flea*:

Mark but this flea, and mark in this,
How little that which thou deny'st me is;
Me it sucked first, and now sucks thee,
And in this flea, our two bloods mingled be;
Confess it, this cannot be said
A sin, or shame, or loss of maidenhead,
    Yet this enjoys before it woo,
    And pampered swells with one blood made of two,
    And this, alas, is more than we would do.

Oh stay, three lives in one flea spare,
Where we almost, nay more than married are.
This flea is you and I, and this
Our marriage bed, and marriage temple is;
Though parents grudge, and you, we're met,
And cloistered in these living walls of jet.
    Though use make you apt to kill me,
    Let not to this, self murder added be,
    And sacrilege, three sins in killing three.

Cruel and sudden, hast thou since
Purpled thy nail, in blood of innocence?
In what could this flea guilty be,
Except in that drop which it sucked from thee?
Yet thou triumph'st, and say'st that thou
Find'st not thyself, nor me the weaker now;
    'Tis true, then learn how false, fears be;
    Just so much honour, when thou yield'st to me,
    Will waste, as this flea's death took life from thee.

This poem, which was enormously admired by Donne's contemporaries, is cited here merely as an example of his original way of wooing by false syllogisms. So in *The Ecstasy*: the argument, a tissue of fallacies, sounds solemnly convincing and consecutive, so that it is surprising to find it ending with an immodest proposal. The highest powers of the mind are put to base use but are enchantingly demonstrated in the process.

Part of Donne's originality lies precisely in the use of such methods for amorous poetry. Properly they belong to the sphere of religion (of course there is always much commerce between the two). This human wit suggests the large design of God's wit in the creation. It is immemorially associated with biblical exegesis and preaching, sanctioned and practiced by St. Ambrose and St. Augustine, and blended in the patristic tradition with the harshness of Tertullian, as well as with the enormous eloquence of Chrysostom. The Europe of Donne's time had enthusiastically taken up witty preaching; but the *gusto espagnol*, as it was called, though associated with the Counter-Reformation, is essentially a revival of what Professor Curtius would call the "mannerism" of the patristic tradition. Now this tradition was venerated by the Church of England, a learned Church that rejected the Puritan aphorism "so much Latin, so much Flesh." And the Fathers could provide not only doctrine but examples of *ingenium*, that acuity of observation by which the preacher could best illustrate and explicate the Word. Donne's youthful examination of "the whole body of divinity controverted between the churches of England and Rome" provided him not only with a religion but with a style. Some aspects of his Jesuit training would help him in the business of analogy; but primarily the conceit of his secular poetry is derived from his later religious studies. It is, in fact, a new, paradoxical use, for amorous purposes, of the *concetto predicabile*, the preacher's conceit. As usual, we see him all of a piece, yet all paradox; Donne the poet, with all his "naturalist" passion, knowingness, obscenity indeed, is *anima naturaliter theologica*. What made him a poet also made him an Anglican: the revaluation of a tradition.

NATURAL AND DIVINE KNOWLEDGE

I⊤ is for this reason that the old emphasis on the "medieval" quality of Donne's thought, though in need of qualification, is more to the point than the more recent stress on his modernity. A great deal has been made of his interest in the "new philosophy," and the disturbance supposed to have been caused him by such astronomical discoveries as the elliptical movement of planets, the impossibility of a sphere of fire, the corruptibility of the heavens, the movement of the earth, and so on. Certainly, as we know from *Ignatius* and elsewhere, Donne was aware of such developments, aware that it was no longer humanly satisfactory to look at the heavens through the spectacles of Ptolemy. But it is the greatest possible misunderstanding of Donne to suppose that he took this as any more than another proof, where none was needed, of the imperfection of human intellect. Mutability reached higher toward heaven than one had thought; but this only shows how unreliable human knowledge must always be. In *Ignatius*, Donne does not recount the new discoveries for their own sakes, but only as part of the sneering. "Kepler . . . (as himself testifies of himself) ever since Tycho Brahe's death, hath received into his care, that no new thing should be done in heaven without his knowledge." Kepler himself called this "impudent," not "flattering." When the devil sees that he can find no worthy place in hell for Ignatius, he decides to get Galileo to draw down the moon (an easy matter for one who had already got close enough to see its imperfections) so that the Jesuits can get on to it—they will "easily unite and reconcile the *Lunatic Church* to the *Roman Church*," and a hell will grow in the moon, for Ignatius to rule over. At times Donne uses "new philosophy" more seriously, to illustrate some moral or theological assertion. The new astronomy, for example, is "applicable well" because it is right that we should move toward God, not He to us. Or, the Roman church is like Copernicanism—it "hath carried earth farther up from the stupid Center" but carried heaven far higher. When he wants, for the sake of some argument, to disprove the sphere of fire, he does not use the new scientific argument from optics, but the old-fashioned opinion of Cardan

(God would not make an element in which nothing could live). In a serious mood he often forgets that the earth moves: "the Earth is not the more constant because it lies still continually" (*Devotions*); or, it is a wonderful thing that "so vast and immense a body as the Sun should run so many miles in a minute" (sermon of 1627). The famous passage in *The First Anniversary*:

> And new philosophy calls all in doubt,
> The element of fire is quite put out;
> The sun is lost, and the'earth, and no man's wit
> Can well direct him where to look for it,

is merely part of the demonstration of "the frailty and decay of this whole World" mentioned in the title of the poem—a theme enforced by many illustrations taken from a wide variety of subjects, including the "old" philosophy. And this is Donne's way with new or old knowledge. It would be very unlike him to be much affected by the new philosophy; "if there be any addition to knowledge," he says in a sermon of 1626, "it is rather new knowledge, than a greater knowledge." For, if you know as much as Socrates, you know nothing, and "S. Paul found that to be all knowledge, to know Christ." There is always an antithesis, in Donne, between natural and divine knowledge, the first shadowy and inexact, the second clear and sure. New philosophy belongs to the first class. What we really know is what is revealed; later we shall know in full:

> up unto the watch-tower get,
> And see all things despoiled of fallacies:
> Thou shalt not peep through lattices of eyes,
> Nor hear through labyrinths of ears, nor learn
> By circuit, or collections to discern.
> In heaven thou straight know'st all, concerning it,
> And what concerns it not, shalt straight forget.

THE AMOROUS POEMS

A mind habituated to such discriminations between the light of nature and "light from above, from the fountain of light," as Milton calls it, may, in some spheres of knowledge, earn the epithet "skeptical." Donne deserted a church that, as he and Hooker agreed, had mistaken mere custom for law. Liberated from the tyranny of custom, he turns, in his erotic poetry, a professionally disenchanted eye on conventional human behavior. We may speak confidently of a "libertine" or "naturalist" Donne only if we use the terms as applying to literature and thought rather than to life; but it remains true that the *Songs and Sonnets* are often (though without his shocking coolness) akin to the franker pronouncements of Montaigne. Consider, for example, his essay *Upon Some Verses of Virgil*, where he professes his contempt for "artised" love; he prefers the thing itself and, in accordance with his preference, argues that amorous poetry also should be "natural," colloquial, "not so much innovating as filling language with more forcible and divers services, wrestling, straining, and enfolding it . . . teaching it unwonted motions." This is Donne to the life:

> Who ever loves, if he do not propose
> The right true end of love, he's one who goes
> To sea for nothing but to make him sick.

Donne openly depises the ritual and indirection of Platonic love; he will follow nature and pluck his rose (or roses; for love's sweetest part is variety). The enemies of nature are such fictions as honor; in the good old times, before custom dominated humanity, things were very different: see *Love's Deity* and *Elegy xvii*:

> How happy were our sires in ancient time,
> Who held plurality of loves no crime!
>   . . .
> But since this title honour hath been used,
> Our weak credulity hath been abused;
> The golden laws of nature are repealed,

This is the sense in which Donne often celebrates the passion of love—as immediate and natural, but constricted by social absurdities:

> Love's not so pure and abstract, as they use
> To say, which have no mistress but their muse.

But of course we must allow for an element of formal paradox. Donne found this very congenial—it is in a way a theological, a liturgical, device—and his *Juvenilia* contain such joke par-

adoxes as a defense of woman's inconstancy, an argument that it is possible to find some virtue in women, and so on, worked out with the same half-serious, half-ribald ingenuity that we find in some of the *Songs and Sonnets*:

> Go, and catch a falling star,
>   Get with child a mandrake root,
> Tell me, where all past years are,
>   Or who cleft the Devil's foot,
> Teach me to hear mermaids singing,
>   Or to keep off envy's stinging,
>   And find
>   What wind
> Serves to advance an honest mind.
>
> If thou be'est born to strange sights,
>   Things invisible to see,
> Ride ten thousand days and nights,
>   Till age snow white hairs on thee,
> Thou, when thou return'st, wilt tell me
> All strange wonders that befell thee,
>   And swear
>   No where
> Lives a woman true, and fair.
>
> If thou find'st one, let me know,
>   Such a pilgrimage were sweet;
> Yet do not, I would not go,
>   Though at next door we might meet,
> Though she were true, when you met her,
> And last, till you write your letter,
>   Yet she
>   Will be
> False, ere I come, to two, or three.

To take these poems too seriously, as moral or autobiographical pronouncements, is to spoil them; though some are clearly more serious than others.

THE SECULAR POEMS

THIS may suggest the possibility of dividing the secular poems into groups other than their obvious genres; but it is a highly conjectural undertaking. There is a similar difficulty about their chronology; attempts to determine this depend on hypothetical links with events (and women) in Donne's life. We can say that the *Satires* were written in the 1590's; we can place many verse letters over a twenty-year period; epithalamia and obsequies are datable; one or two references in the love poems hint at dates. But in these last the evidence is scanty. Jonson's testimony, that Donne did his best work before he was twenty-five, depends on what he thought good—all we know is that he admired *The Calm* and *The Storm* (verse letters) and *Elegy xi,* a frantically witty poem but not among the most admired today. Only exceptionally can we say with certainty that this poem is addressed to his wife, that to another woman; this is witty with a stock situation (*The Flea,* for example, or *The Dream*), while that is drawn from life. Gosse actually invented a disastrous affair to explain some poems and absurdly supposed *Elegy xvi* to be addressed to Donne's wife; another critic has argued passionately that *The Ecstasy* is a husband's address to his wife. Even Herbert Grierson supposes that the *Nocturnal* must be connected with the countess of Bedford, whose name was Lucy; and a whole set of poems, some of them full of racy double entendre, has been associated with Lady Danvers, ten years Donne's senior and the mother of his friends the Herberts. All we may be sure of is that Donne, with varying intensity, passion, and intellectual conviction, exercised his wit on the theme of sexual love, and that he was inclined to do this in a "naturalist" way. We need not concern ourselves with dates or with identities of mistresses celebrated, cursed, or mourned.

The *Songs and Sonnets* were read only in manuscript in Donne's lifetime, and by a small and sophisticated circle. They certainly exhibit what Donne, in the little squib called *The Courtier's Library,* calls "itchy outbreaks of far-fetched wit"; and the wit is of the kind that depends both upon a harsh strangeness of expression and upon great acuity of illustration and argument. We are asked to admire, and that is why the poet creates difficulties for himself, choosing arbitrary and complex stanza forms, of which the main point often seems to be that they put tremendous obstacles in his way. Without underestimating the variety of tone in these poems, one may say that they all offer this kind of pleasure—delight in a dazzling conjuring trick. Even the smoothest, simplest song, like "Sweetest love, I do not go," is full of mind. Donne would have despised Dryden's distinc-

tion between poets and wits. True, some of these poems deserve the censure that when we have once understood them they are exhausted: *The Indifferent, The Triple Fool,* and a dozen others fall into this class. Others, like *The Flea* and "A Valediction: of my name, in the window," are admired primarily as incredibly perverse and subtle feats of wit; yet others, like *The Apparition,* as examples of how Donne could clothe a passion, in this case hatred, in a clever colloquial fury. This is the inimitable Donne; sometimes, as in *The Broken Heart,* we might be reading Cowley's sexless exercises.

One should here dwell at rather more length on one or two poems. I almost chose *The Damp,* a fine example of Donne's dialectical wit (the main argument is attended by a ghost argument, supported by slang double meanings); and *Farewell to Love,* which would have pleased Montaigne by its grave obscenity; and, for its wide-ranging metaphor and brilliant farfetched conclusion, *Love's Alchemy. Lovers' Infiniteness* has the characteristic swerving argument, its stanzas beginning "If . . . Or . . . Yet . . ."; compare *The Fever,* with its "But yet . . . Or if . . . And yet . . . Yet . . ." For his best use of "the nice speculations of philosophy," *Air and Angels* and *The Ecstasy* commend themselves:

> Where, like a pillow on a bed,
>   A pregnant bank swelled up, to rest
> The violet's reclining head,
>   Sat we two, one another's best;
> Our hands were firmly cemented
>   With a fast balm, which thence did spring,
> Our eye-beams twisted, and did thread
>   Our eyes, upon one double string;
> So to intergraft our hands, as yet
>   Was all the means to make us one,
> And pictures in our eyes to get
>   Was all our propagation.
>   . . .
> But O alas, so long, so far
>   Our bodies why do we forbear?
>   . . .
> As our blood labours to beget
>   Spirits, as like souls as it can,
> Because such fingers need to knit
>   That subtle knot, which makes us man:
>
> So must pure lovers' souls descend
>   T'affections, and to faculties,

358

Which sense may reach and apprehend,
  Else a great prince in prison lies.

To our bodies turn we then, that so
  Weak men on love revealed may look;
Love's mysteries in souls do grow,
  But yet the body is his book.

But *The Curse* is both characteristic and neglected, and *A Nocturnal upon S. Lucy's Day* is
Donne's finest poem; so there follow some
scanty remarks on these.

The Curse has the usual complex rhyme
scheme and rather more than the usual energy
in that Irish ingenuity of malediction which reminds us that Donne was one of the early
satirists:

Whoever guesses, thinks, or dreams he knows
Who is my mistress, wither by this curse;
    His only, and only his purse
      May some dull heart to love dispose,
And she yield then to all that are his foes;
    May he be scorned by one, whom all else
      scorn,
    Forswear to others, what to her he hath
      sworn,
    With fear of missing, shame of getting,
      torn:

The syntactical conciseness of lines 3–5 is remarkable: "May he win only a mercenary love,
yet may he have to spend all he has to get her
(and may she be dull in the bargain). Then,
wretched mistress though she be, let her betray
him—and do so with everybody who dislikes
him (presumably a large number of people)."
This only begins the cursing. "May he suffer
remorse, not of conscience because he has
sinned (too noble a passion for him), but because the reputation of the only woman he was
able to get makes him everybody's butt" . . .
and so on. The poem ends with an inventory of
hatred and poison, provisions for further additions to the curse as they may occur to the poet,
and finally—as often in Donne—a light, epigrammatic couplet to place the poem on the witty
side of passion: you can't curse a woman more
than she is naturally "cursed" (forward, fickle,
uncertain of temper) already:

The venom of all stepdames, gamesters' gall,
What tyrants, and their subjects interwish,

What plants, mines, beasts, fowl, fish,
Can contribute, all ill which all
Prophets, or poets spake; and all which shall
  Be annexed in schedules unto this by me,
  Fall on that man; for if it be a she
  Nature before hand hath out-cursed me.

(lines 25–32)

So much of the effect depends on the control of
syntactical and rhythmic emphasis, on devices
like the repeated "all" (28–29), on the impressive catalog, the compression of meaning in line
26 that calls forth the neologism "interwish,"
the formal streak of legal diction, and the
minatory solemnity of "Fall on that man"—that
paraphrase breaks down into inoffensive jesting
a poem that gets its effect by an impression of
qualified but dangerous loathing. This is pure
Donne; as a matter of opinion good, as a matter
of fact unique.

This last is true, a fortiori, of the *Nocturnal*,
which has the additional interest of involving
some of his known intellectual problems and
convictions. The imagery is predominantly alchemical; the argument goes in search of a
definition of absolute nothingness; yet the cause
of the poem is grief at the death of a mistress.
This is the most solemn and difficult of Donne's
poems, superficially slow in movement, but
with a contrapuntal velocity of thought. It begins as a meditation on the vigil of his saint; St.
Lucy's day is chosen because it is the dead day
of the year, as midnight is the dead hour of the
day:

'Tis the year's midnight, and it is the day's,
Lucy's, who scarce seven hours herself unmasks,
    The sun is spent, and now his flasks
    Send forth light squibs, no constant rays;
      The world's whole sap in sunk:
The general balm th'hydroptic earth hath drunk,
Whither, as to the bed's-feet, life is shrunk,
Dead and interred; yet all these seem to laugh,
Compared with me, who am their epitaph.

That which preserves life, the "general balm,"
is shrunk into the frozen earth. Darkness, which
is Nothing to light's All, and death, which is
Nothing to life's All, reign in the great world;
yet the little world, the poet, is far deader and
darker, an abstract of death, an epitaph. The
world will be reborn in spring, and there will be

359

JOHN DONNE

lovers; but he is "every dead thing." His deadness is enforced by a remarkable alchemical figure, based on the idea that the alchemist deals in the quintessence of *all things,* "ruining" (abstracting form from) metals in order to reconstitute them as gold, by means of the quintessence. But this "new" alchemy, on the contrary, works with a quintessence of *nothing,* privation, and imposes on the poet's "ruined" matter the "form" of absolute nothingness—"absence, darkness, death." Alchemical and theological figures come as it were naturally to Donne; he uses alchemy to push the notion of absolute privation beyond human understanding. The poet has less being than the primordial Nothing that preceded Chaos, which preceded Creation; he is a quintessence of Nothing: "I am none." The internal rhyme with "sun" (meaning light, and All, as well as the woman responsible for his state of nonbeing) brings us back, at the end, to the commonplace lovers whose activity will be restored in spring, when the commonplace sun returns:

> But I am none; nor will my sun renew.
> You lovers, for whose sake, the lesser sun
>   At this time to the Goat is run
>   To fetch new lust, and give it you,
>   Enjoy your summer all;
> Since she enjoys her long night's festival,
> Let me prepare towards her, and let me call
> This hour her vigil, and her eve, since this
> Both the year's, and the day's deep midnight is.

The witty sneer about the object of the sun's journey to the Tropic of Capricorn helps to distance these inferior loves; and we return to darkness, the perpetual sleep of the other sun, and the propriety of this saint's day as the type of darkness and lifelessness.

This is a very inadequate account of a marvelous poem. My main object is to make a point about Donne's use, in poetry, of ideas that he clearly regarded as important. The general balm, the alchemical ruin, the violent paradoxes on All and Nothing, belong to Donne's mental habit. There is, for instance, a fine examination of the All-Nothing paradox in the exegetical passages on Genesis in *Essays in Divinity,* and it occurs in the sermons. As he extracted the notion of absolute privation in alchemical terms, Donne must have been thinking of the cabalistic de-

scription of God as the nothing, the quintessence of nothing; here a keen and prejudiced ear might discover one of his blasphemies. But it is more interesting, I think, that Donne the poet is claiming what Donne the theologian calls impossible; he constantly recurs to the point that the man cannot desire annihilation. So the wit of the poem (using the word in its full sense) really derives from its making, by plausible argument, the impossible seem true. And he does it by the use of figures from alchemy, an art traditionally associated with the resurrection of the body, the escape from annihilation—he spoke in his own last illness of his physical decay as the alchemical ruining of his body before resurrection; here, with vertiginous wit, he uses the same analogy to prove the contrary. It is not inappropriate that the finest of the *Songs and Sonnets* should also be the most somberly witty and the most difficult.

Of Donne's twenty *Elegies* I have room to say little. They are love poems in loose iambic pentameter couplets, owing a general debt, for tone and situation, to the *Amores* of Ovid; the Roman poet loses no wit but acquires harshness, masculinity. These poems are full of sexual energy, whether it comes out in frank libertinism or in the wit of some more serious attachment. *The Anagram (ii)* is an example of the wit that proved all too imitable, all too ready to degenerate into fooling—it is a series of paradoxes on somebody's foul mistress, a theme current at the time. *Elegy viii* is a similar poem, comparing one's own and another's mistress, with plenty of unpleasant detail. But the *Elegies* have a considerable variety of tone, ranging from the set pieces on change and variety (*iii* and *xvii*) which are paralleled by several of the *Songs and Sonnets,* to the passionate *xvi* and the somber *xii,* on the theme of parting:

> Nor praise, nor dispraise me, nor bless nor curse
> Openly love's force, nor in bed fright thy nurse
> With midnight's startings, crying out, "Oh, oh
> Nurse, O my love is slain, I saw him go
> O'er the white Alps alone;

The *Elegies* have always had a reputation for indecency, and they certainly exploit the sexual puns so much enjoyed by Elizabethan readers. Among the poems excluded from the first edi-

360

tion is the magnificently erotic *Elegy xix, Going to Bed:* too curious a consideration of some of the metaphors in this poem (such as the passage about "imputed grace") has led critics to charge it with blasphemy, a risk Donne often runs by the very nature of his method. Montaigne might have complained that Donne here substitutes a new mythology and metaphysics of love for those he had abandoned, new presbyter for old priest. But it is impossible not to admire the translation of sexual into mental activity. *Elegy xix* was later regarded as the poet's own epithalamion, a fancy as harmless as it is improbable, except that it has perhaps resulted in the acceptance of a very inferior reading in line 46.[2] One beautiful and exceptional poem is *Elegy ix, The Autumnal* to lady Danvers; but even this would not, I think, quite escape Herbert Grierson's criticism, that Donne (especially in the *Elegies*) shows "a radical want of delicacy"; for it has the wit and fantastic range of reference that mark the erotic *Elegies*.

The *Satires* belong to the same phase of Donne's talent as the work I have been discussing. They are, as Elizabethan satire was supposed to be, rough and harsh, written in that low style that Donne so often used, though here it is conventional. *Satire iii* I shall discuss later; of the others we may say that they have the usual energy, a richness of contemporary observation rather splenetic, of course, in character. Pope thought them worth much trouble; but it is doubtful if, except for *iii,* they play much part in anybody's thinking about Donne. The same may be said of the epicedes and obsequies, funeral poems that in this period were often, when they were not pastoral elegies, poems of fantastically tormented wit. So Donne proves, in the elegy on Prince Henry, that "we May safelier say, that we are dead, then he." The form suited him only too well. The same cannot be said of the epithalamion; Spenser is the poet to thrive here. Yet there are fine things in

Donne's poem for the marriage of the Princess Elizabeth in 1613:

> Up, up, fair Bride, and call,
> Thy stars, from out their several boxes, take
> Thy rubies, pearls, and diamonds forth, and make
> Thyself a constellation, of them all,
>   And by their blazing signify,
> That a great Princess falls, but doth not die;

Donne could not speak without wit; it is this naturalness that often redeems him.

Of the occasional verse included under the title *Letters to Several Personages* a word must suffice. There is a mistaken view that they are negligible because they occasionally flatter. They were written over many years, and not all for profit; notice the little-known verses to Goodyere (Grierson, I,183), which have the strong Jonsonian ring; and the charming "Mad paper, stay" to Lady Herbert before her remarriage. The best, probably, are to the countess of Bedford, dependant though Donne may have been; and the poem beginning "You have refined me" is a great poem, certainly no more "blasphemous" in its compliment than *Elegy xix* in its persuasions.

This matter of blasphemous allusion comes to a head in the two *Anniversaries,* written for Sir Robert Drury on the death of his daughter Elizabeth, and published in 1611 and 1612. These are amazingly elaborate laments for a girl Donne had never seen. The first he called *An Anatomy of the World,* announcing in his full title that the death of Elizabeth Drury is the occasion for observations on the frailty and decay of the whole world, and representing the dead girl as Astraea, as the world's soul, as the preservative balm, and so on; her departure has left it lifeless, and he dissects it. The second, describing "the Progress of the Soul" after death, is similar: "By occasion of the religious death of Mistress Elizabeth Drury, the incommodities of the soul in this life, and her exaltation in the next, are contemplated." From Jonson forward, critics have complained of the faulty taste of such hyperbolical praise of a young girl, and Donne defended himself more than once, though without much vigor; he would have little patience with this kind of misunderstanding. All we may say here is that these poems—now known to be

---

[2]"There is no penance due to innocence," the reading of 1669, is represented in most manuscripts by "There is no penance, much less innocence." The received reading makes the poem slightly more appropriate if the woman is a bride. But clearly she is no more innocent than she is penitent, and ought not to be wearing the white linen that signifies either innocence or penitence.

planned in a highly original way as a series of formal religious meditations—are essential to the understanding of Donne; they come near to giving us a map of the dark side of his wit. The deathbed meditation in the second poem is comparable with the *Holy Sonnets* on the same topic:

Think thyself laboring now with broken breath,
And think those broken and soft notes to be
Division,[3] and thy happiest harmony.
Think thee laid on thy death-bed, loose and slack;
And think that, but unbinding of a pack,
To take one precious thing, thy soul, from thence.

The *Anniversaries* lead us into a consideration of Donne's religious life. But we shall find that the poet and the religious were the same man.

ACCEPTANCE OF ANGLICANISM

DONNE'S acceptance of the established church is the most important single event of his life, because it involved all the powers of his mind and personality. His youthful sympathies must have been with the persecuted Romanists, and his *Satires* contain bitter allusions to "pursuivants," tormentors of Jesuits; the odious Topcliffe is mentioned by name in some manuscripts. But he was familiar with the fanaticism as well as with the learning of Jesuits; and he later decided that the first of these was the hardest affliction of Christendom, though the second was to serve him well. No one can say exactly when he left one church for the other; it was a gradual process. According to Walton, he was about nineteen when, "being unresolv'd what religion to adhere to, and, considering how much it concern'd his soul to choose the most Orthodox," he abandoned all studies for divinity. Donne himself, in *Pseudo-Martyr*, claims to have done this with "an indifferent affection to both parties." Particularly, he consulted Bellarmine, "the best defender of the *Roman cause*" (Walton), and Hooker, whose *Laws of Ecclesiastical Polity* appeared in 1593, when Donne was twenty-one—though his famous sermon *Of Justification*,

which must have appealed to all moderate Romanists, had long been available. Hooker triumphed; but as late as 1601 the unfinished satirical extravaganza, *The Progress of the Soul*, treats the queen as the last of a line of archheretics, and more dubious references suggest that Donne's recusancy persisted in some form up to the time of *Pseudo-Martyr*. When Walton says he treated the problem as urgent, he is paraphrasing the remarkable *Satire iii*, which must belong to the 1590's. What makes this poem odd is the brisk impatience of its manner, an exasperated harshness proper to satire but strange in a deliberative poem about religion. It has often been misunderstood. The main theme is simply the importance of having a religion; without it, one is worse off than "blind [pagan] philosophers":

shall thy father's spirit
Meet blind philosophers in heaven, whose merit
Of strict life may be imputed faith, and hear
Thee, whom he taught so easy ways and near
To follow, damned?

But which religion? Rome is loved because true religion was once to be found there; Geneva out of a perverse love for the coarse and plain; the English church from inertia. Such divisions encourage on the one hand abstinence from all, and on the other a mistaken belief that they are all true. It is necessary to choose one; and the best course is to "Ask thy father which is she, Let him ask his." Above all, do not rest; no business is as important as this. This is a tentative assertion of the Catholic tradition invoked by all Anglicans—the true, not the Roman, Catholicism. Donne had in fact to choose only between these two churches; though he was to develop a great respect for Calvin, he was never concerned with extreme Protestantism. Of the two communions—"sister teats of his graces" he called them, "yet both diseased and infected, but not both alike"—he was to choose the one truer to the Catholic tradition as he understood it. Like his learned contemporary Casaubon, he found this to be the Church of England—episcopal and sacramental, but divested of the Romanist accretions. *Satire iii* is a poem about his search, not about its end. He still had much to do before he could think of "binding his conscience to a local religion."

---

[3] A musical term, meaning a variation on a melody, made by dividing each of its notes into shorter ones.

One consequence of this deliberation was that Donne was unusually moderate in later allusions to Rome. In *Pseudo-Martyr* he speaks frankly of its long hold over him and is charitable to "all professors of Christian Religion, if they shake not the Foundation." All his animus is against the Jesuits, for a false doctrine of martyrdom and inculcating for opening up, by their intransigence, deplorable breaches in the church. He attacks and satirizes them as enemies of tolerance: "that Church," he says in *Essays in Divinity*, "which despises another Church, is itself no other than that of which the Psalm speaks, *Ecclesia Malignantium*." Here we are at the heart of his religious position. Donne had convinced himself that reform had made the English church more truly Catholic than any other. It was not only a middle way but the ground on which, he hoped, the longed-for reunion of the churches might be accomplished. Given tolerance, given an abatement of "that severe and unrectified zeal of many, who should impose necessity upon indifferent things, and oblige all the world to one precise form of exterior worship, and ecclesiastic policy," Donne saw a chance of ending the division of the church.

In this aspiration he was at one with James I, though the prospect of success was much smaller than it had been when the Gallican party in France hoped for something from the Council of Trent. With the king, and his friend Wotton, Donne had expected much of the dispute between Venice and the papacy in 1606; Wotton, as English ambassador in Venice, had played an active part, and for a while there was excited speculation about the chance of Venice turning to a sort of Anglicanism. Wotton was acquainted with Paolo Sarpi, the canonist who conducted the Venetian case; and Sarpi's *History of the Council of Trent* was published first in London. In it he deplores the rigidity and extremism of that council and, as Frances Yates has said, "indirectly suggests that if the right course had been pursued at Trent, the Church as a whole would have been reformed somewhat on the model of the Anglican reform." Wotton sent home several portraits of Sarpi for his English admirers; and it was presumably one of these that hung, as Donne's will testifies, in his study. It was an emblem of his hopes,

and Donne completely accepted Sarpi's view of Trent. Preaching before Charles I in April 1626, on the text "In my Father's house are many mansions," he deplores its intolerance, its coming "to a final resolution in so many particulars"; as a result the Scriptures themselves are slighted and reduced in authority, and men are the readier to call each other heretics, "which is a word that cuts deep, and should not be passionately used." Both these consequences are disastrous. The priest is ordained to preach the Word—Donne's favorite quotation is St. Paul's *vae mihi si non*, "woe unto me if I do not so." "Nothing," he says in 1618, "is to be obtruded to our faith as necessary to salvation, except it be rooted in the Word," and he constantly complains that Rome "detorts" the Word, as the Puritans do. As for the frequent charges of heresy, he warns his own congregation to "be not apt to call opinion false, or heretical, or damnable, the contrary whereof cannot be evidently proved." Early and late, Donne the preacher insists upon the prime importance of the Word and on the great need for tolerance; only thus may the church in England be the matrix of a new universal church. So, in an early sermon: "For all this separation, Christ Jesus is amongst us all, and in his time will break down this wall too, these differences among Christians, and make us all glad of that name." And in 1627 he prays that God "in his time bring our adversaries to such moderation as becomes them, who do truly desire, that the Church may be truly *Catholic, one flock in the fold, under one Shepherd*, though *not all of one color*, of one practice in all outward and disciplinary points." This last was after the setback to the cause in 1626, when the defeat of the elector of Bohemia elicited from Donne the sonnet "Show me, dear Christ, thy spouse."

Donne, then, accepted the Church of England because it was truly Catholic. He rejoiced to discover a Reformed church that cultivated the Fathers and was slow to come "to a final resolution" in "particulars." He wanted tradition but without its errors: Aquinas, but not the Scholastic nonsense; the Fathers, but not their mistakes. The Catholic heritage was enormously more important to him than any "new" knowledge, theological or physical, and he has little distinction as a speculative theologian, though his age is one of dogmatic controversy. He detested, for instance, the Calvinist teaching on predestination, which had the intellectual presumption to dishonor God by suggesting that He could "make us to damn us"; when it was necessary to pronounce on the matter he fell back on Aquinas ("God has appointed all future things to be, but so as they are, that is necessary things necessarily, and contingent things contingently") but he disliked the whole argument: "*Resistibility*, and *Irresistibility*, of grace, which is every Artificers wearing now, was a stuff that our Fathers wore not, a language that pure antiquity spake not." "The best men," he says, "are but Problematical, only the Holy Ghost is Dogmatical." Though by no means a complete skeptic, he knew the limits of reason and often defined its relation to faith (in *Essays in Divinity, Biathanatos*, a verse letter to the countess of Bedford, the Christmas sermon for 1621). His position is not dissimilar from Hooker's (e.g. *Laws* I, 8). The limitations of human learning he sets forth in the famous *Valediction Sermon* of 1619, and the contrast between natural and heavenly knowledge (see the passage quoted earlier from *Anniversaries*) is developed in a splendid passage of the 1622 Easter sermon: "God shall create us all Doctors in a minute." Obviously the fierce certainties of some contemporaries were not for Donne. "It is the text that saves us," he says. "The interlineary glosses, and the marginal notes, and the *variae lectiones*, controversies, and perplexities, undo us." He was content with his church's restoration of a good, lost tradition, just as, in his capacity as poet, he had used a traditional but neglected style that had its roots in the same great body of learning, the teaching of the Fathers.

THE SERMONS

No one, then, will read Donne for theological novelties; even in the *Essays*, which are full of curious applications, Donne's regard for authority puts him at the opposite pole from the radically speculative Milton. And whatever may be offered by the vast array of sermons, it is not that kind of excitement.

It is not easy to give a general account of the sermons. They were preached on all manner of occasions, over fifteen years, and they take their color from the audience, and from Donne's mood, as well as from the text and from the ecclesiastical occasion. Some were for a great audience, some for a small; some for lawyers, some for the court; some for Lent and some for Easter; some were preached when the preacher had private reason for joy, some when he was miserable. The tone varies widely. There is truth in the often repeated charge that Donne was preoccupied with sin and death; he confesses his melancholy temperament (calling it "a disease of the times") and constantly quotes St. Paul's *cupio dissolvi* (Phil. 1 : 23), "having a desire to depart and be with Christ." "If there were any other way to be saved and to get to Heaven," he says, "than by being born into this life, I would not wish to have come into this world." There are terrible sermons on death, full of the poetry of charnel house and worm. There are lamentations for the sins of youth: "I preach the sense of Gods indignation upon mine own soul." There are even rather grim sermons on apparently joyous occasions; a wedding sermon for personal friends is a forbidding, though orthodox, account of the church's teaching on marriage, with many gloomy strictures on women. But one can overdo this aspect of the sermons. Death and sin are fully presented, but perhaps not inordinately. And, to balance them, there is a massive insistence on the theme of resurrection and far more humanity than one is led to expect; see, for example, the moving passages on the death of Augustine's son, and that of his own daughter, in the superb Easter sermon for 1627:

He was but a heathen that said, if God love a man, *Iuvenis tollitur*, He takes him young out of this world; and they were but heathens that bestowed that custom, to put on mourning when their sons were born, and to feast and triumph when they died. But thus much we may learn from these heathens, that if the dead, and we, be not upon one floor, nor under one story, yet we are under one roof. We think not a friend lost, because he is gone into another room, nor because he is gone into another land; and into another world, no man is gone; for that heaven, which God created, and this world, is all one world. If I had fixed a son in court, or married a daughter into a plentiful fortune, I were satisfied for that son and that daughter. Shall I not be so, when the King of heaven hath taken that son to himself, and married himself to that daughter, for ever? I spend none of my faith. I exercise none of my hope, in this, that I shall have my dead raised to life again.

This is the faith that sustains me, when I lose by the death of others, or when I suffer by living in misery myself, that the dead, and we, are now all in one Church, and at the resurrection, shall be all in one choir.

It could well be argued that the sermon suited Donne's talents perfectly. That patristic learning which had settled his Anglican convictions and given him his style as a poet equipped him also with the matter and the manner of his preaching; and for the style that he adopted he needed all his mastery of the techniques of wit. The preacher's basic duty was simply, as Augustine said, "to teach what is right and refute what is wrong, and in the performance of this task to conciliate the hostile, and rouse the careless." This was to be done according to a general scheme that both preacher and congregation took for granted. But within this scheme there could be enormous variation. Donne was of the party that cultivated "the learned manner of preaching"; not for him the doctrinal plainness of the Puritan. He was, as hostile witnesses put it, "a strong-lin'd man" and "a bad edifier."

How did "strong lines" go with the preaching of the Word? First, their cultivation did not mean that the Word was neglected. It was stated, divided, illuminated, fantastically explicated. For example, Donne makes much of the expression "let us make man" (Gen. 1 : 26): no other act of creation involved a conference; therefore, the Trinity was concerned in this one alone. Secondly, the Word itself gives warrant for all the devices of the learned preacher. The style of the Scriptures is "artificial"; indeed the Psalms are poems. "There are not in the World so eloquent Books as the Scriptures . . . they mistake it much, that think, that the Holy Ghost hath rather chosen a low, and barbarous, and homely style, than an eloquent, and powerfull manner of expressing himself." The Scriptures use metaphor of "infinite sweetness, and infinite latitude," though they have, when necessary, concision as well as eloquence, simplicity as well as highly wrought wit. All these

qualities are found in the Fathers whom the Reformed church revived. Ambrose and Augustine—to whom Donne owed most—are ancestors of mannerist wit; Tertullian Christianized the Latin strong lines of Seneca. Nearer in time to Donne was the Continental revival of witty preaching, which, as I have said, had much to do with the new poetic wit; but ultimately all depended on the Fathers and on the wit and eloquence of the Holy Ghost in Scripture.

One famous and passionate page must serve to illustrate Donne's habitual eloquence:

Let me wither and wear out mine age in a discomfortable, in an unwholesome, in a penurious prison, and so pay my debts with my bones, and recompense the wastefulness of my youth, with the beggary of mine age; let me wither in a spittle under sharp, and foul, and infamous diseases, and so recompense the wantonness of my youth, with that loathsomeness in mine age; yet if God withdraw not his spiritual blessings, his grace, his patience, if I can call my suffering his doing, my passion his action, all this that is temporal, is but a caterpillar got into one corner of my garden, but a mildew fallen upon one acre of my corn; the body of all, the substance of all is safe, as long as the soul is safe. But when I shall trust to that, which we call a good spirit, and God shall deject, and impoverish, and evacuate that spirit, when I shall rely upon a moral constancy, and God shall shake, and enfeeble, and enervate, destroy and demolish that constancy; when I shall think to refresh myself in the serenity and sweet air of a good conscience and God shall call up the damps and vapours of hell itself, and spread a cloud of diffidence, and an impenetrable crust of desperation upon my conscience; when health shall fly from me, and I shall lay hold upon riches to succour me, and comfort me in my sickness, and riches shall fly from me, and I shall snatch after favour, and good opinion, to comfort me in my poverty; when even this good opinion shall leave me, and calumnies and misinformations shall prevail against me; when I shall need peace, because there is none but thou, O Lord, that should stand for me, and then shall find that all the wounds that I have come from thy hand, all the arrows that stick in me, from thy quiver; when I shall see that because I have given myself to my corrupt nature, thou hast changed thine; and because I am all evil towards thee, therefore thou hast given over being good towards me; when it comes to this height, that the fever is not in the humours, but in the spirits, that mine enemy is not an imaginary enemy, fortune, nor a transitory enemy, malice in great persons, but a real, and an

365

JOHN DONNE

irresistible, and an inexorable, and an everlasting enemy, The Lord of Hosts himself, the Almighty God himself, the Almighty God himself only knows the weight of this affliction, and except he put in that *pondus gloriae*, that exceeding weight of an eternal glory, with his own hand, into the other scale, we are weighted down, we are swallowed up, irreparably, irrevocably, irrecoverably, irremediably.

But in addition to such tremendous sentences we find a hopping Latin wit, as of Tertullian: "He came, and *venit in mundum*, He came into the world; it is not *in mundam*, into so clean a woman as had no sin at all, none contracted from her parents, no original sin . . . yet *per mundam in mundum*, by a clean woman into an unclean world." And we find startling conceits and paradoxes. Can man be the enemy of God, even as the mouse is of the elephant? Man is nearly nothing, but God is "not only a multiplied elephant, millions of elephants multiplied into one, but a multiplied World, a multiplied All. . . . Man cannot be allowed so high a sin, as enmity with God." But Donne can also be simple, like the parables. So on irresistibility of grace: "Christ beats his drum, but he does not press men; Christ is served with voluntaries." For "no metaphor, no comparison is too high, none too low, too trivial, to imprint in you a sense of God's everlasting goodness towards you." To such a preacher the "metaphysical conceit" was a natural mode of thought. Laud, addressing from the scaffold a hostile crowd, spoke of "going apace . . . towards the Red Sea . . . an argument, I hope, that God is bringing me into the land of promise." Here, at such a moment—though the conceit has a long history—we have precisely those qualities of deliberate false argument essential to the wit of Donne's poems.

As a preacher Donne is guilty, by modern standards, of pedantry. His style is artificial; he would have been angry to have been told otherwise. The pedantry was partly a matter of fashion, but also a token of his confidence in a truly Catholic tradition. The sermons are inconceivable without it; so is Donne himself. And if he makes our flesh creep, that was still part of his duty; if he almost ignores the ecstatic religion that flourished in his day, that was a defect of his central merit. If we want Donne as a modern poet we may find it tiresome that he was capable of so much archaic quibbling, so much jargon and flattery. But, while it is perfectly proper to read the *Songs and Sonnets* and ignore the sermons, it is improper to construct an image of Donne without looking at them; and many such caricatures still circulate.

THE DIVINE POEMS

It was Donne's habit, in later life, to speak slightingly of his poetry; and although he considered, for a brief moment before his ordination, the possibility of publishing his poems, it seems he did not even possess copies of them. There are signs that it was regarded as slightly improper, after his ordination, for "a man of his years and place" to be versifying, and indeed Donne wrote little verse as a priest. The *Elegies* on his death often allude to the exercise of his great wit in both secular and religious spheres—"Wit He did not banish, but transplanted it"—but Chudleigh, in these lines, has in mind not verse but sermons:

> Long since, o poets, he did die to you,
> Or left you dead, when wit and he took flight
> On divine wings, and soared out of your sight.
> Preachers, 'tis you must weep.

In fact it now appears that the bulk of the divine poems belongs to 1607–1615. These years produced the *Corona* sequence, most of the *Holy Sonnets*, the *Litany*, *Upon the Annunciation and Passion*, *Good Friday, 1613*, and probably *The Cross*. The poem addressed to Tilman, the *Lamentations of Jeremy*, the lines on Sidney's *Psalms*, the three great *Hymns*, three Sonnets, and *An hymn to the Saints, and to Marquess Hamylton*, which Donne wrote reluctantly in 1625, make up the extant poetical work of the priest. Most of the religious poetry, therefore, belongs to the period of many of the verse letters, and the *Anniversaries*.

It is verse of remarkable originality. *Satire iii* shows that even in his youth Donne considered the language of passionate exploration and rebuke appropriate to religious themes; and even when he is working in strict forms like the sonnet, and on devotional topics, we recognize at once that turbulent diction which spontaneously records the pressure of fervent and excited thought. But though he rejected some of the formalities in his secular poetry, Donne was habituated in matters of devotion to certain schematic disciplines. He had been taught to pray; and when his poems are prayers they are formed by this early training. When he undertook "a serious meditation of God," he tended to do so by employing these meditative techniques.

Here a learned man committed to the reformed religion occupies himself with papist devotion; but we should not exaggerate the paradox. Donne's church did not reject what it found good in the tradition; many devotional practices were retained, and some were revived. Donne's *Corona* sonnets are an ingenious adaptation of an old Dominican system of meditation, based on an obsolete type of rosary called the *corona*. A Puritan might condemn this, but to Donne it was, theologically, an indifferent matter and good in that it concentrated the devotional powers of a man easily distracted from prayer. More remarkable, perhaps, is the fact that some of the *Holy Sonnets*, and the *Anniversaries*, are indebted to meditative techniques defined and propagated by Ignatius Loyola and the Jesuits; yet these were so widely disseminated, and apparently so fruitful, that it was by no means exceptional for enemies of the order to adopt them.

The *Corona*, with its linked sonnets and carefully balanced ingenuity, may strike us as "mixt wit"; the Ignatian method is more interesting. The purpose of the technique is to concentrate all the powers of the soul, including the sensual, in the act of prayer. So a man might present as vividly as possible to himself the scene of the Nativity or the Crucifixion, or his own deathbed. There is no doubt that this technique, the most considerable contribution of Jesuit piety to European art, affects the *Holy Sonnets*; Helen Gardner presents twelve of them as a sequence, the first six being a formal meditative series on the Last Things. The method is to achieve a vivid image, enforce it with appropriate similitudes, and then to pray accordingly. So, in "O my black Soul! now thou art summoned," Donne imagines his deathbed in the octave and

compares the sinful soul to an exile afraid to return to his country, or a prisoner afraid to be freed; then in the sestet he prays for grace to repent, so that death may not, after all, be like such miseries. The meditation is here forcefully assimilated to the sonnet form, which Donne uses with virtuosity; and the complexities of the form coexist with that sense of immediate and poignant spiritual effort, that tormented natural diction, which was his great, and sometimes abused, discovery. The sonnets are not reports of spiritual exercises; they are the exercises themselves. There is little sense of contrivance, "artificial" though the form is; Donne reconciles the prescribed form with the true word, just as he reconciles ecclesiastical tradition with the supremacy of Scripture. It is true that the wit of these poems occasionally ventures where we are reluctant to follow, as in "Show me, dear Christ, thy spouse." This last complaint for the division of the church is couched in terms of a traditional image carried to the point where we feel uneasy about its taste:

> Betray kind husband thy spouse to our sights,
> And let mine amorous soul court thy mild dove,
> Who is most true, and pleasing to thee, then
> When she' is embraced and open to most men.

Perhaps we dislike this metaphor (Christ as *mari complaisant*) because the image of the church as the Bride is no longer absolutely commonplace; but having accepted the image we are still unwilling to accept its development, even though we see that the main point is the *glorious* difference of this from a merely human marriage. Something is asked of us that we can no longer easily give. Many of the *Holy Sonnets* have this perilous balance; their wit is always likely to seem indelicate as well as passionate. So in one of the greatest, "Batter my heart, three-personed God":

> Batter my heart, three-personed God; for, you
> As yet but knock, breathe, shine, and seek to mend;
> That I may rise, and stand, o'erthrow me, and bend
> Your force, to break, blow, burn and make me new.
> I, like an usurped town, to another due,
> Labour to admit you, but oh, to no end,
> Reason your viceroy in me, me should defend,
> But is captived, and proves weak or untrue,
> Yet dearly I love you, and would be loved fain,

But am betrothed unto your enemy,
Divorce me, untie, or break that knot again,
Take me to you, imprison me, for I
Except you enthrall me, never shall be free,
Nor ever chaste, except you ravish me.

I turn my back to thee, but to receive
Corrections, till thy mercies bid thee leave.
O think me worth thine anger, punish me,
Burn off my rusts, and my deformity,
Restore thine image, so much, by thy grace,
That thou mayst know me, and I'll turn my face.

This is a great poem, certainly; but what, we wonder, has "three-personed" to do with the passion of the opening? Yet the poem is another of Donne's exercises in the paradoxes of his religion, and the Trinity is one of the greatest of them. The epithet is obliquely justified by the intensity of the rhythmical conflicts throughout; in the opposition between the heavy "Batter" and the weak, cadential "knock, breathe, shine, and seek to mend"; in the divine absurdity of heaven troubling to take the sinner by storm, laying him low that he may stand; finally, by the imagery of rape. Love is figured as lust because it is to be rough and irresistible; God is a monster of mercy (but the Scripture compares him to a thief). The powerful paradoxes of the last couplet suggest an infinite series of such: God as infant, God as malefactor, justice as mercy, death as life, and so forth. We respond crudely to this kind of challenge, and such a reading as this is clumsy and overly explicit. Similarly we are inclined to think of a poem that celebrates the coincidence of Lady Day and Good Friday as a toy; but for Donne it was a motive to reverence, a piece of calendar wit that challenged a Christian poet to prayer. We are usually content to be more clever about the love of women than the love of God; therefore the *Songs and Sonnets* keep better. But Donne was clever about both, and sometimes in much the same way; our awkwardness here leads us to charge *Elegy xix* with blasphemy, and "Show me, dear Christ" with indelicacy. Donne himself was not blind to some of the dangers of his method; in the *Litany* he writes, "When we are moved to seem religious Only to vent wit, Lord deliver us."

The finest of the other preordination poems is *Good Friday, 1613*. Here too Donne starts from a paradox; on this day of all days he is turned away from the east. This plunges him into that paradoxical series where he moves with such assurance; and his wit binds up the paradoxes, with just the neatness and passion of the love poems, in a fine conclusion:

Of the poems written after ordination, only the sonnets of the Westmoreland manuscript and the three *Hymns* are of the best of Donne. The little group of sonnets includes the moving poem about the death of his wife, and "Show me, dear Christ." The *Hymns* are justly admired. "A Hymn to Christ, at the Authors last going into Germany" records a moment of intense personal feeling and is a companion to the beautiful *Valediction Sermon* of 1619. The other two belong to the period of Donne's serious illness in 1623, when he also wrote *Devotions*. "Thou art a metaphysical God," he says in that work, "full of comparisons." And although these poems abjure harshness in favor of the solemnity proper to hymns, they nevertheless live by their wit. "A Hymn to God, my God, in my sickness" is founded on a favorite conceit; the poet is a map over which the physicians pore.

As west and east
In all flat maps (and I am one) are one,
So death doth touch the resurrection.

The "Hymn to God the Father" contains the famous play on the poet's name (but so does the inscription on the portrait of the author in his shroud, prefixed to *Death's Duel*); what in our time would be only a puerile joke is thrice repeated in this solemn masterpiece.

Donne's wit, of course, depends on the assumption that a joke can be a serious matter. Wit, as he understood it, was born of the preaching of the Word, whether employed in profane or in religious expression. "His fancy," as Walton says, "was unimitably high, equalled only by his great wit. . . . He was by nature highly passionate." It will never be regretted that the twentieth century, from whatever motive, restored him to his place among the English poets, and wit to its place in poetry.

JOHN DONNE

SELECTED BIBLIOGRAPHY

I. BIBLIOGRAPHY. G. L. Keynes, *Bibliography of the Works of Dr. John Donne* (Cambridge, 1914; rev. 1932, 1957).

II. COLLECTED AND SELECTED EDITIONS. *Poems, by J. D[onne]. With Elegies on the Author's Death* (London, 1633), repr. with additions (some spurious) and alterations, 1635, 1639, repr. with some alteration 1649, 1650, 1654, repr. with alterations and important additions 1660; H. J. C. Grierson, ed., *Poems*, 2 vols. (Oxford, 1912); J. Hayward, ed., *Complete Poetry and Selected Prose* (London, 1929; rev. 1936); H. Gardner, ed., *The Divine Poems* (Oxford, 1952); G. R. Potter and E. M. Simpson, eds., *Sermons*, 10 vols. (Berkeley, Calif., 1953–1962); F. Manley, ed., *The Anniversaries* (Baltimore, 1963); H. Gardner, ed., *The Elegies, and the Songs and Sonnets* (Oxford, 1965); W. Milgate, ed., *The Satires, Epigrams and Verse Letters* (Oxford, 1967); E. M. Simpson, ed., *Selected Prose* (Oxford, 1967); A. J. Smith, ed., *The Complete English Poems* (Harmondsworth, 1971).

III. LETTERS. *Letters to Severall Persons of Honour* (London, 1651); E. W. Grosse, ed., *The Life and Letters of John Donne*, 2 vols. (London, 1899).

IV. BIOGRAPHICAL AND CRITICAL STUDIES. Izaak Walton, "The Life and Death of Dr. Donne" in *The Lives of Dr. John Donne, Sir Henry Wotton, Mr. Richard Hooker, Mr. George Herbert . . .* (London, 1640; enl. 1658), many modern reprints; M. P. Ramsay, *Les doctrines medievales chez Donne* (London, 1917; 2nd ed. 1924); E. M. Simpson, *A Study of the Prose Works of John Donne*, 2nd ed. (Oxford, 1948); M. Praz, *Secentismo e marinismo in Inghilterra; John Donne–Richard Crashaw* (Florence, 1925); P. Legouis, *Donne the Craftsman* (Paris, 1928); G. Williamson, *The Donne Tradition* (Cambridge, Mass., 1930); T. Spencer, ed., *A Garland for John Donne* (Cambridge, Mass., 1931); W. F. Mitchell, *English Pulpit Oratory from Andrewes to Tillotson* (London, 1932); H. C. White, *The Metaphysical Poets: A Study in Religious Experience* (New York, 1936); C. M. Coffin, *John Donne and the New Philosophy* (New York, 1937); R. L. Sharp, *From Donne to Dryden: The Revolt Against Metaphysical Poetry* (Chapel Hill, N.C., 1940); R. Tuve, *Elizabethan and Metaphysical Imagery: Renaissance Poems and Twentieth Century Critics* (Chicago, 1947); M. H. Nicolson, *The Breaking of the Circle: Studies in the Effect of the "New Science" Upon Seventeenth Century Poetry* (Evanston, Ill., 1950); L. L. Martz, *The Poetry of Meditation* (New Haven, 1954; rev. 1962); J. E. Duncan, *The Revival of Metaphysical Poetry* (Minneapolis, 1959); A. Alvarez, *The School of Donne* (London, 1961); H. L. Gardner, ed., *John Donne: A Collection of Critical Essays* (Englewood Cliffs., N.J., 1962); F. Kermode, ed., *Discussions of John Donne* (Boston, 1962); A. J. Smith, *John Donne, the Songs and Sonnets* (London, 1964); N. J. C. Andreasen, *John Donne, Conservative Revolutionary* (Princeton, 1967); R. C. Bald, *John Donne: A Life* (Oxford, 1970); A. J. Smith, *John Donne, the Critical Heritage* (London, 1975); J. R. Roberts, ed., *Essential Articles for the Study of John Donne's Poetry* (Hamden, Conn., 1975).

THE ENGLISH BIBLE

Donald Coggan, Archbishop of Canterbury

No ONE can write on so large a theme as that of the English Bible within so short a compass as that prescribed here without being very conscious of omissions that he cannot but regret. For example, I have written practically nothing in the following pages about the Apocrypha, that collection of books often bound up with the Old and New Testaments, and regarded by Roman Catholics as a true part of their Bible and by Anglicans as books that "the Church doth read for example of life and instruction of manners; but yet doth it not apply them to establish any doctrine . . ." (Article VI). Nor have I written about those apocryphal books that failed, sometimes by only a narrow margin, to gain access to the canon of the New Testament. The standard source in English for these works is now *New Testament Apocrypha* by Edgar Hennecke: vol. I, material about Jesus; vol. II, the Apostles (Philadelphia, 1963–1965). The corrected edition (Oxford, 1953) of the 1924 *The Apocryphal New Testament*, by Montague Rhodes James, is still useful as an introduction, but does not contain some of the more recent and extremely significant discoveries, and gives less background information. Nor have I entered the field of the Dead Sea Scrolls, which in recent years have acquired an extensive literature of their own. To embark on any of these themes would be to use space that is better given to the main theme.

Even within the compass of the story of the English Bible, the theme is so large as to call for an outline, rather than a detailed treatment. For example, when dealing with translations of the sixteenth century, I have not even mentioned Matthew's Bible (1537) nor Taverner's of about the same date, nor the Douay-Rheims Version. It is to be hoped that the select bibliography which appears at the end of the article will help those who wish to do so to make up certain of these deficiencies.

THE ENGLISH BIBLE

ANYONE picking up the Bible for the first time, or sampling at random its contents, is likely to be bewildered by the variety and often the strangeness of the individual books that go to make it up. This will almost certainly be so if the English version is a modern one; perhaps less certainly if it is a classic like the King James Version, since for some people the very beauty and "old world" quality of such a work can obscure these variations and neutralize the flavor of an individual writer's purpose and circumstances. In fact, the books, sixty-six in all (thirty-nine in the Old Testament and twenty-seven in the New), vary in content from ancient history of Near Eastern peoples to poems (some of war, others of love, others expressive of deep religious experience); from books of prophecy, long and short, to wide-ranging collections of popular proverbs and sophisticated reflections on life, ethics, and the ordering of the universe; from ancient fragments of a people's lore to that strange apocalyptic writing that looks beyond the confines of time; from records of the life and work of Jesus that are unlike anything that we moderns describe as biography, to pastoral letters called forth by the exigencies of day-to-day difficulties; from the first great book of the history of the early church, to a treatise on the ascended Christ as that subject bears on the life of a particular Christian community.

It is a *library* of books. Are we justified in calling this library, this heterogeneous collection of writings, *the* Bible, as if it were something of a unity? This is a question of considerable importance, to which some attention must be given before we turn to consider those English versions of it which have so deeply influenced the life and letters of the British people. And, through them, have molded the religion, government, and thought of peoples the world over.

The Bible has been more minutely studied, especially during the last 150 years, than any other comparable quantity of literature. There have been four main branches of investigation: textual criticism, which has attempted to recover as far as possible the precise words of the original writers; source criticism—most notably in the first five books of the Old Testament (the Pentateuch), in the prophets, and in the Gospels—which has attempted to identify the earlier documents from which the present texts were constructed; form criticism, which has sought to deepen our understanding of the material by identifying the various literary "forms" used not only by the writers but often by the oral tradition on which they drew; and redaction criticism, which brings out the creative contribution of the final writers by studying the way in which they used and arranged their material, or, as in the case of Matthew and Luke, who both incorporate the greater part of Mark into their own Gospels, the changes they made in it. All this analysis having been done, however, the student of the Old and New Testaments has a right to ask whether there emerges from the books any central theme or themes that justify the binding together of those sixty-six books under the title "The Bible."

The question becomes all the more pressing when it is realized that a variety of national cultures and religions have made their contribution to the books of this little library. The people who above all others "made" these books are the people of Israel. It was Israel's seers and kings and wise men and poets who gave us the Old Testament. But they were by no means uninfluenced by the nations that surrounded them. (Sometimes their prophets wished they were *less* influenced, particularly in the direction of the worship of gods and goddesses and in the practices that the prophets could only consider immoral or ungodly.) The peoples of Canaan, of Babylon, of Persia, and of Greece

were forces to be reckoned with, and their influence on the thinking and the habits of Israel must not be underestimated. As to the New Testament, most of the writers of its books were themselves Jews, who were deeply indebted to their Scriptures; and indeed the central figure of the New Testament was a Jew. But all the writers of the New Testament books grew up in a Graeco-Roman environment, influenced to greater or lesser degree by the culture and beauty of Greece and the order and authority of Rome. For example, the Fourth Gospel, profoundly Hebraic as it is in its essence, is deeply influenced by Greek thought and vocabulary. No one could write as St. John did who had not lived in an atmosphere where Hellenism held sway. Even St. Paul, that most Hebrew of all Hebrew writers, could not spend his boyhood in the distinguished town of Tarsus, predominantly Greek yet having synagogues within it, without being stimulated, as he was at times shocked, by the fresh winds of Greek philosophy and by the activities of gymnasium and theater. It is not without significance that all his letters were written in Greek, the *lingua franca* of the world of his day. And in addition to that, he held Roman citizenship, a privilege that acted as a kind of passport wherever he traveled and more than once got him out of a tight corner.

Here is the Bible, then, the product of centuries of time; of varying theological, philosophical, linguistic, and cultural backgrounds; many of its books themselves composite works. Variety, yes. But unity?

During the first half of the twentieth century many scholars, dissatisfied with purely analytical study, addressed themselves to this question of the underlying unity of the Bible. One obvious unifying factor has already been noted, namely that the writers of the Bible were all connected in one way or another with the history of a particular nation and people—Israel and the Jews. The movement that has come to be known as "Biblical theology," which was immensely influential until the late 1950's, saw the deeper unity of thought in the Bible also in historical terms, as presenting a "salvation history." The story of God's mighty acts for redemption of his human children from evil and death was interpreted as having been carried out through the history of one people, Israel, and as having culminated in the life, death, and resurrection of Jesus Christ, before spreading out for the benefit of the whole world through the activity of God's Spirit, no longer in Israel but in the church. This is undoubtedly a very important theme in the Bible as a whole, apparent in its fullness of course only in the New Testament as the writers look back on the whole sequence of events and see them prefigured and prophesied in the ancient Jewish Scriptures, but also glimpsed and hinted at in many places in the Old Testament. It cannot be said, however, to be the unifying theme common to all the biblical writers, since some of them, such as Job and Ecclesiastes in the Old Testament, or James in the New, hardly think in terms of history at all. In the end we are forced to recognize that the unifying factor in the Bible is not an idea or a series of events but a Person, the Person of God. The Bible is an anthology of attempts by members of a common tradition to understand all existence as God's Kingdom, of sometimes anguished wrestling with the problems this raises, and of the vision that came to men through Jesus Christ and that enabled them to believe in this Kingdom, to transcend many of the problems, and so to live with a new kind of faith, hope, and love.

Story. History. His story. This is the heart, the unity, the crux of the Bible. We may well call it the *crux,* for the Cross is at the center of the story. The message of the Bible is expressed in a great series of indications—"God spoke; God created; God sent; Christ came; He died; He rose; He sent the Holy Spirit; He promised to be with His church." Indicative first, and only then imperatives. For the central message is not primarily a new philosophy nor a new code of ethics, but a declaration of God's mighty acts in Christ "for us men and for our salvation." The ethics of gratitude and obedience follow, of course; but it is the gracious activity and power of God which come first.

THE NEW TESTAMENT

It was this message that made a *New* Testament necessary at all. The early church went out into the world with a book in its hand—the Old Testament as we know it, from the sacred Scriptures of the Jewish people. The members of the church were soon to see that much that was contained in those Scriptures was no longer obligatory on them. For example, many of the old food laws of the Pentateuch were seen to be irrelevant; so were the instructions in regard to sacrificial worship (the Jerusalem Temple was destroyed by Titus in A.D. 70). There were elements in the Old Testament picture of God that had to be rethought radically in the light of the teaching of Jesus, although the *general* Old Testament descriptions of God as the Father, King, Shepherd, Savior of His people had been formative for their whole "theology." They did not abandon the Old Testament. They held on to it, and again and again were able to see in the events in which they had recently taken part in Galilee and Jersualem the "fulfillment" of what had been adumbrated there. "This," they said, "is that which was spoken by the prophet . . ." (Acts 2 : 16).

But it was not long before a new group of writings began to come together. First there was a group of letters written by St. Paul and others, which probably circulated among the little companies of Christians that met for worship and encouragement and for the planning of a Christian strategy of advance. Then there may well have been a collection of the sayings of Jesus on certain issues of pressing importance. And—perhaps about the time when Peter and Paul were martyred (*ca.* A.D. 62) and when the original eyewitnesses were beginning to get scarce—the first of those four Gospels (St. Mark) which, while giving a fair measure of biographical material about Jesus, leave so many questions unanswered which we should love to ask. Dating the various parts of the New Testament is never easy and in some cases frankly impossible. We just do not have the necessary evidence—for example, none of the letters bears a date or refers to an event known in world history. Recent discussion shows scholars varying widely in their conjectures. But we shall not be far wrong if we say that the majority of the New Testament was written before A.D. 100, and that the little which may possibly—although this is far from certain—come from the second century falls into its first quarter. We know rather more about the different but very important matter of the canon of the New Testament, that is, by what period it was decided which books were to have the same status of sacred and authoritative Scripture as that accorded to the Old Testament. By the year 200 the recognized list of books was virtually that which we now have, although one or two items remained contentious for some time longer. So the Christian church was equipped with two volumes in one—the story of God's old covenant (testament) with His people was now accompanied by the story of the New Covenant made in Christ with the New Israel.

THE FIRST TRANSLATIONS

THE young church was essentially a missionary movement. It took for granted that if you are the possessor of incredibly good news, you do not keep it to yourself: you spread it. You may be imprisoned (as were St. Peter and St. Paul and St. James); you may be temporarily driven to the catacombs in times of persecution. But the principle holds good: "We cannot but speak the things which we have seen and heard" (Acts 4 : 20). Had not the Master said: "As My Father hath sent Me, even so send I you?" (St. John 20 : 21).

The Old Testament which the members of the Christian church took with them on their missionary task had already been translated into Greek (the Septuagint). So the secrets of Judaism had been opened to great numbers of non-Jews who had, as it were, formed an outer ring around the synagogues where Jews met in predominantly Gentile centers. Those godly Gentiles, many of whom were tired of the stories of polytheism and the laxity of morals which marked society in the years just before the beginning of the Christian era, looked longingly toward the monotheism and the high ethical code of Judaism. The Septuagint helped to introduce them. It has been described as "the first apostle to the Gentiles." The New Testament was, as we have seen, all in Greek. So in most parts of the world, the Scriptures of both Testaments were available in the *lingua franca* used in the opening centuries of the Christian era. "The babel of tongues was hushed in the wonderful language of Greece." This was not the least part of that *preparatio evangelica* of which other evidences were to be seen in a remarkable network of Roman roads which served as highways for the Gospel; and in the *pax Romana* without which it would have been impossible for the message of *pax Christi* to be widely proclaimed.

But there were certain corners of the world where Greek was not the natural language of the people. They probably knew quite a sprinkling of Greek words—they might, indeed, be able to "get along" with it in the conduct, say, of a business deal. But if they were to understand a story, such as that of the beginnings of the Christian movement; if they were to read the Apostles' letters and really understand them; then it would be necessary for the original documents to be translated. So it was that the *Versions* were called for and were supplied. For example, around Edessa, where a form of Aramaic continued to be spoken, it soon became a matter of some urgency to have the New Testament in Syriac; as in North Africa, where Latin was spoken, a Latin version was needed. So there came into being a number of versions, and a variety of copies all made by hand (manuscripts—for the day of printing was many centuries later) which to the textual critic today present so many problems but which are such an invaluable part of his "apparatus" in the achieving of an accurate text of his documents.

Further afield than the Euphrates valley or North Africa, the work of translation went on. Egypt and the Nile Delta got its versions, Ethiopia too; and as early as the fourth century Ulfilas, bishop of the Goths (312–380), translated the Bible into Gothic for the sake of the Gothic tribes then moving through Bulgaria and Serbia. So the good work went on that eventually led to the great versions of the Vulgate (Latin), Peshitta (Syriac), and so on.

THE BIBLE IN BRITAIN: CAEDMON

IF it seems a far cry to carry the story of the Bible from the Near East to Britain, we must recall that the Gospel spread at first as much by the faithful witness of "lay" Christians as by any carefully made "ecclesiastical" plan. A soldier on duty here; a trader pursuing his work there; a prisoner bearing his witness in his cell—it was thus that the Gospel spread. The Scriptures soon followed in the wake of the Christians. Of this we may be sure, although the actual beginnings of the Bible in Britain are wrapped in the mists of obscurity. That the Christian faith was planted in these islands very early is, of course, well established. For the last hundred years of Roman occupation Christianity was anyway the official religion; and as early as 314, at the Council of Arles, Britain was represented by three bishops, those of York, London, and (probably) Caerleon on Usk. Mention should also be made of two major pieces of archaeological evidence: the Christian chapel in the Roman villa excavated at Lullingstone and the mosaic pavement at Hinton St. Mary in Dorset, discovered in the early 1960's, which has as its centerpiece a picture of Christ the King.

That the Scriptures first appeared in Britain in very fragmentary form is altogether probable. Almost certainly the Bible stories were told more often in picture or in dramatic form and by preaching than in translated documents. The picture of those days is by no means clear, nor is it likely ever to be so. But one who has had the privilege of serving as archbishop of York may be pardoned if he feels a glow of pride in recording the story, which is more than probably true, that it was in that diocese, in the monastery at Whitby, some thirteen hundred years ago, that one of the monks turned much of the Scriptures into verse in the vernacular. In Whitby, St. Hilda presided over a double community of men and women. Bede tells us that Caedmon, a herdsman connected with this community, until an advanced age

had never learned anything of versifying, for which reason being sometimes at entertainment, when it was agreed for the sake of mirth that all present should sing in their turns, when he saw the instrument come towards him, he rose up from the table and returned home.

But once, when this had happened, he had a vision in the stable where he slept. "A person appeared to him in his sleep, and saluting him by his name, said, 'Caedmon, sing some song to me.' " To his surprise he found that he was able to do so—"to praise the Maker of the heavenly Kingdom, the power of the Creator and his counsel, the deeds of the Father of glory." The abbess and her advisers perceived that this was a gift from God, and Caedmon was taken into the monastery as a brother. The scholars of the monastery taught him passages of Scripture, and he turned them into verse. Bede goes on with the story:

Thus Caedmon, keeping in mind all he heard, and as it were chewing the cud, converted the same into the most harmonious verse; and sweetly repeating the same, made his masters in their turn his hearers. He sang the creation of the world, the origin of men, and all the history of Genesis: and made many verses on the departure of the children of Israel out of Egypt, and their entering into the land of promise, with many histories from holy writ; the incarnation, passion, resurrection of our Lord, and His ascension into heaven; the coming of the Holy Ghost, and the preaching of the apostles; also the terror of future judgment, the horror of the pains of hell, and the delights of heaven; besides many more about the divine benefits and judgments, by which he endeavored to turn away all men from the love of vice, and to excite them in the love of, and application to, good actions.

It is hardly to be wondered at that Caedmon came to be known as the father of English poetry.

THE VENERABLE BEDE

THE real glory of the North of England of that time was, however, not so much Caedmon as his biographer, the Venerable Bede (673–735). Although, as he tells us, all his years were spent in the monastery at Jarrow, he became a writer of European reputation. A student of Latin, Greek, and Hebrew, he was "ever intent upon the study of the Scriptures. In the intervals between the duties enjoined by the disciplinary rule and the daily care of chanting in the church, I took sweet pleasure in always learning, teaching or writing." To exactly what extent Bede translated the Scriptures into the vernacular, it is impossible to say. Margaret Deanesly tells us that there is "no evidence that a complete translation,

THE ENGLISH BIBLE

even of the four gospels, was made till the time of Aelfric, in the eleventh century. . . . Generally speaking, the text of the Bible was studied only by the monks, and it was studied in Latin." (*The Lollard Bible*, p. 132). But that he did translate the Scriptures is clear from the delightful and well-known story that his disciple Cuthbert tells of the master's closing days. The year was 735, and Bede was at work on translating excerpts from Isidore of Seville and the Gospel of St. John.

Ascension Day drew near. His illness increased, but he only labored the more diligently. On the Wednesday, his scribe told him that one chapter alone remained, but feared that it might be painful for him to dictate. "It is easy," Bede replied. "Take your pen and write quickly." The work was continued for some time. Then Bede directed Cuthbert to fetch his little treasures, pepper, scarves and incense, so that he might distribute them among his friends. So he passed the rest of the day to the evening in holy and cheerful conversation. His boy-scribe at last found an opportunity to remind him, with pious importunity, of his unfinished task: "One sentence, dear master, still remains unwritten." "Write quickly," he answered. The boy said, "It is completed now." "Well," Bede replied, "thou hast said the truth: all is ended. Take my head in thy hands, I would sit in the holy place in which I was wont to pray, that so sitting I may call upon my Father." Thereupon, resting on the floor of his cell, he chanted the *Gloria*, and his soul immediately passed away while the name of the Holy Spirit was on his lips.

JOHN WYCLIFFE

It is a long journey in time from Bede to John Wycliffe (1320?–1384), but any story, however brief, of the English Bible must delay over this extraordinary character. Knowles describes his mind as one "to which personal affection was a stranger." It was, nevertheless, a mind that moved along the lines of inexorable logic which led him to question most of what the medieval church held sacred. Bishop Stephen Neill questions his right to be called "The Morning Star of the Reformation," but, he adds, "one thing in Wyclif is genuinely new—the basis on which his criticisms were made. It was his aim to restore the Scriptures to their position as the

unique and sole authority for life and doctrine in the Church" (*Anglicanism*, p. 21). It would seem to be a fact that only part of the Wycliffe Bible is actually the work of John Wycliffe himself—Nicholas Hereford at Oxford translated much of the Old Testament. But the impetus was Wycliffe's, and the whole work appeared two years before his death. G. M. Trevelyan has well described it as "an admirable and scholarly piece of work, a great event in the history of the English language as well as religion."

The translations of the Bible into the tongue of the people brought light—clear and liberating light. Indeed it was needed, for many of the clergy of the day could not construe nor expound the Lord's Prayer, nor the Creed, nor the Ten Commandments. If this was the case with the clergy, the plight of the laity must have been desperate. The copies of the Wycliffe Bible still extant are small, unadorned, and closely written, indicating that they were meant not for the wealthy and the privileged, but for the man in the street.

It is hard to exaggerate the importance of Wycliffe and his colleagues in the story of the English Bible. Some forty-four years after his death, the pope ordered the bishop of Lincoln "to proceed in person to the place where John Wycliffe was buried, cause his body and bones to be exhumed, cast far from ecclesiastical burial and publicly burnt, and his ashes to be so disposed of that no trace of him shall be seen again." "Thus," commented Thomas Fuller, the historian, "this brook [the river Swift] hath conveyed his ashes into Avon; Avon into Severn; Severn into the narrow seas; they into the main ocean. And thus the ashes of Wycliffe are the emblem of his doctrine, which now is dispersed all the world over." The claim would seem to be little more than sober fact.

WILLIAM TYNDALE
THE FIRST ENGLISH PRINTED BIBLES

It is hard for us who live in a world of printed books to realize how far-reaching a revolution the invention of printing brought about. In 1476 William Caxton set up his press under the shadow of Westminster Abbey. (In 1456 Guten-

375

berg had issued the first book printed in Europe, a Latin Bible.) Caxton's version of *The Golden Legend*, issued in 1483, contained a great part of the Bible. What a weapon this new process was to be for the dissemination of literature and in particular of the English Bible. No longer would it be necessary laboriously to copy out each Gospel and Epistle by hand. Wycliffe's Bible of the previous century and Tyndale's of the next would be rolled off in their thousands by means of this stupendous invention.

The achievement of William Tyndale, to which we may now turn, must be put firmly within its historical setting. The Renaissance had as one of its results not only the revival of the Greek and Roman classics but—indirectly, perhaps, but none the less certainly—the revival of deep interest in the documents of the New Testament. Thus, when about the year 1500 John Colet returned from Italy, it was not only the classics that had come alive to him. In Oxford, his lecture room was crowded to the doors by men who heard him lecture on the Epistles of St. Paul, bringing them to life in a way that the old scholasticism had entirely failed to do. Colet at Oxford and Erasmus at Cambridge helped men to see that the great doctrines of, for example, the Epistle to the Romans were not the relics of a bygone age nor the property of the scholars only, but the word of God to those who had ears to hear. The expository skill of such men, married to the technical achievement of Caxton and his successors, placed the Bible firmly in the hand, and in the hearts, of the English people.

William Tyndale (1492?–1536) was driven by a great passion. It was, to use his own words, a desire to "cause a boy that driveth the plough to know more of the Scripture" than did many of the clergy of his day. In similar vein, Erasmus wrote:

I wish that even the weakest woman should read the Gospel—should read the Epistles of Paul. And I wish these were translated into all languages, so that they might be read and understood, not only by Scots and Irishmen, but also by Turks and Saracens. . . . I long that the husbandman should sing portions of them to himself as he follows the plough, that the weaver should hum them to the tune of his shuttle, that the traveller should beguile with their stories the tedium of his journey.

Here were two great minds thinking alike, and it was Erasmus' edition of the Greek Testament that Tyndale used in his great translation. Great it certainly was, if only on the ground of its influence on later versions. It has been reckoned that 90 percent of Tyndale's translation stands unaltered in the King James Version of 1611 (the so-called Authorized Version), and some 80 percent or more in the Revised Versions of 1881 and 1885. S. L. Greenslade has justly called him "the man who more than Shakespeare even or Bunyan has molded and enriched our language." But Tyndale's translation was great because of his almost uncanny gift of simplicity in the use of the English language. His was a true nobility of homeliness. Phrases of almost monosyllabic grandeur which have become part and parcel of our literary inheritance we owe to Tyndale. For example, "in Him we live and move and have our being," or, "until the day dawn and the day-star arise in our hearts"; or, "for here we have no continuing city, but we seek one to come."

Tyndale sealed his work with his blood. Much of his work he had been obliged to do on the Continent, for he had been driven out of London. From the Continent, copies of his work were smuggled out, some in bales of cotton and some by other surreptitious means. He met his death in 1536, when he was martyred at Vilvorde by strangulation and burning. His letter to the governor of the castle is an epic document. The prison was damp.

"If I am to remain here during the winter," he writes, "you will request the Procureur to be kind enough to send me from my goods which he has in his possession a warmer cap, for I suffer extremely from cold in the head, being afflicted with a perpetual catarrh which is considerably increased in this cell. A warmer coat also, for that which I have is very thin; also a piece of cloth to patch my leggings; my overcoat is worn out. He has a woollen shirt of mine, if he will be kind enough to send it. I have also with him leggings of thicker cloth for putting on above; he also has warmer caps for wearing at night. I wish also his permission to have a lamp in the evening, for it is wearisome to sit alone in the dark. But above all, I entreat and beseech your clemency to be urgent with the Procureur that he may kindly permit me to have my Hebrew Bible, my Hebrew Grammar and Hebrew Dictionary, that I may spend my time with that study."

"Lord"—such was the martyr's dying prayer—"Lord, open the King of England's eyes." That prayer was to be answered in the very next year by the royal recognition of the Coverdale Bible, which itself was vastly indebted to Tyndale's.

MYLES COVERDALE: THE GENEVA BIBLE: THE BISHOPS' BIBLE

To Myles Coverdale (1488–1568) belongs the distinction of producing the first *complete* Bible to be printed in the English language. A native of York and a graduate of Cambridge, he was not a scholar of the caliber of Tyndale; but he devoted the major part of his life to making the Bible available to his fellow countrymen. In 1535 appeared the Bible to which I have just referred, deeply indebted to the work of Tyndale, as well as to the Vulgate, and to Luther, etc. But Coverdale also edited the Great Bible of 1539, which was to occupy a prominent position in every parish church in the land. He had a share in the preparation of the Geneva Bible which was to be published in 1560. And he produced diglots—that is to say, bilingual editions in Latin and English, of the New Testament in 1538 and of the Psalter in 1540. But for the average Anglican, Coverdale's fame rests on the fact that it is his version of the Psalms that is incorporated in the Book of Common Prayer. If he was not always accurate, if, indeed, parts of his version of the Psalms are nonsense (for example, Psalms 68: 13, "though ye have lien among the pots, yet shall ye be as the wings of a dove"), he had a sensitive ear for beauty of rhythm. It has been well said of him that "he sings his way through the Psalter like a choirboy enjoying his anthem." It is a tribute to his greatness that when in 1958 the then archbishops of Canterbury and York appointed a commission to revise the Psalter, part of the terms of reference that they gave was that the new version should "retain, as far as possible, the general character in style and rhythm of Coverdale's version and its suitability for congregational use."

Mention has been made of the Geneva Bible, popularly known as the "Breeches Bible" from the statement in Genesis 3 : 7, that Adam and Eve sewed fig leaves together and made themselves "breeches" (the Authorized Version has "aprons"). This Bible, dedicated to Queen Elizabeth I, represents, so far as the Old Testament is concerned, a thorough revision of the Great Bible; in the New Testament it leans heavily on Tyndale's latest edition, revised with the aid of Beza's Latin version. Published with notes representing a radical Reformed position, it won, and for long retained, widespread popularity, particularly as the household Bible of English-speaking Protestants. Although it was never appointed to be used in the churches of England, it was so in Scotland, and held its own there for some time, even after the appearance of the Authorized Version in 1611. Not least among its claims to fame is the fact that it was the Bible of Shakespeare.

Eight years after the publication of the Geneva Bible came the Bishops' Bible, in 1568. The Geneva Bible was unacceptable for use in the churches of England, its annotations being too Calvinistic in tone. So in 1561 Archbishop Matthew Parker submitted to the bishops of his province a proposal to revise the Great Bible of 1539. With Parker as editor in chief, the work was done by a number of bishops and some other scholars and was submitted to the queen and her chief minister, Sir William Cecil, in the autumn of 1568. Three years later, the Convocation of Canterbury ordered that "every archbishop and bishop should have at his house a copy of the holy Bible of the largest volume as lately printed at London . . . and that it should be placed in the hall or large diningroom, that it might be useful to their servants or to strangers," and that a copy should be procured by every cathedral and, as far as possible, by every church. Some nineteen editions were published between 1568 and 1606.

THE AUTHORIZED OR KING JAMES VERSION

IT was in 1604, the year after the death of Queen Elizabeth I, that at the Hampton Court Conference, with the full approval and encouragement of King James I, a new translation of the Bible was decided on.

The King James Version (or, as it is also

known, although less accurately, the Authorized Version) is the final answer to those who maintain that no good thing can come out of the deliberations of a committee.

This version was the result of the work of a committee, itself divided into six subcommittees, two sitting at Westminster, two at Oxford, and two at Cambridge. The members were the cream of the scholarship of the day. It was said, for example, of Bishop Launcelot Andrewes, who headed the Westminster group, that "he might have been interpreter general at Babel . . . the world wanted learning to know how learned he was." But the committee was marked not only by culture and learning—it was marked also by humility and piety. In the "Preface of the Translators," the members wrote, rather delightfully: "We never thought from the beginning, that we should need to make a new Translation, nor yet to make of a bad one a good one . . . but to make a good one better, or out of many good ones, one principal good one, not justly to be excepted against, that hath been our endeavour, that our mark."

It is easy to look back from the vantage point of the passage of 350 years and to detect errors in scholarship that the research of later years has brought to light. We know much more today about the Hebrew language and about Greek manuscripts than did Launcelot Andrewes and his colleagues. But Macaulay was right when he described the 1611 version as "a book which, if everything else in our language should perish, would alone suffice to show the whole extent of its beauty and power."

It was a matter of extreme good fortune that the King James Version came into being just when it did, for this was the period when our language reached what G. M. Trevelyan has called "its brief perfection." It was the age of Shakespeare and Marlowe, of Spenser, Hooker, and Bacon. There is a kind of monosyllabic simplicity and yet majesty about much of the language. Consider this: "Thus will I bless Thee while I live: I will lift up my hands in Thy name." Or: "The Son of Man is come to seek and to save that which was lost." Or again: "The flowers appear on the earth; the time of the singing of birds is come, and the voice of the turtle is heard in our land." For sheer beauty, it would be hard to improve on sentences such as these. It was this kind of English that fixed the standard for centuries to come.

It was hard to improve—impossible perhaps—on the language of the Bible and of the Prayer Book and of Shakespeare. There had been a steady progress and enrichment from Chaucer to Elizabeth, and the peak was reached in the early years of the seventeenth century. Even today, three and a half centuries later, our common speech is vastly enriched by the cadences and proverbs of this version. Very often those who use such phrases as "the skin of my teeth," "heap coals of fire on his head," "the fat of the land," "the salt of the earth," "the powers that be," "the pearl of great price," "hip and thigh," do not realize to what extent they are indebted to this most formative of all translations. Moreover there are numberless phrases or proverbial sayings to be met with again and again in ordinary converse. From Ecclesiastes we get "Cast thy bread upon the waters" (11 : 1); "there is no new thing under the sun" (1 : 9); "Whatsoever thy hand findeth to do, do it with thy might" (9 : 10). Or from the Gospel According to St. Matthew: "No man can serve two masters" and "Ye cannot serve God and mammon" (6 : 24); "Sufficient unto the day is the evil thereof" (6 : 34). We often hear of the wolf "in sheep's clothing" (7 : 15) or of building a "house upon the sand" (7 : 26); and the frequent allusions to a thing being as difficult to do as for "a camel to go through the eye of a needle" comes from the Gospel According to St. Mark (10 : 25), while "Eat, drink, and be merry" we owe to both Ecclesiastes and St. Luke.

We have spoken of the influence of the Bible on the English language. But as a matter of fact, it had an influence far deeper on character, religion, and social history. In a famous sentence, J. R. Green wrote of the time of Queen Elizabeth I: "England became the people of a book and that book was the Bible." G. M. Trevelyan, who perhaps better than any other Englishman has described British social history, says that "when Elizabeth came to the throne, the Bible and Prayer Book formed the intellectual and spiritual foundation of a new social order. . . . For every Englishman who had read Sidney or Spenser, or had seen Shakespeare acted at the Globe, there were hundreds who had read or heard the Bible with close attention as the word of God."

Many of the Biblical stories have been used as subject matter by poets, the greatest instances being Milton's *Paradise Lost* and *Paradise Regained;* Browning's *Saul* may be quoted as another, and Frederick Temple, archbishop of Canterbury, described his *Death in the Desert* as "the most penetrating interpretation of St. John that exists in the English language." Not only the subject matter but much of the actual libretti of oratorios, such as Handel's *Messiah,* are taken from the biblical text, while the cinema, television, and the theater prove year after year that the life of Jesus as reflected in the Gospels retains its compulsive hold on Christian and non-Christian alike. But all through English literature there are constant allusions to Biblical stories or sayings, and much of the point of the literary work is lost if the allusion is not recognized. The title of Shakespeare's *Measure for Measure* loses its significance if we do not have in mind the reference to the Gospel According to St. Matthew (7 : 1–2) "Judge not, that ye be not judged. For with what judgment ye judge, ye shall be judged: and with what measure ye mete, it shall be measured to you again." Further, in the text of the play we read, as statement of much of the Christian faith:

Why, all the souls that were were forfeit once,
And He that might the vantage best have took
Found out the remedy.
(*Measure for Measure,* II. ii. 73–74)

Throughout the centuries we find the reader's acquaintance with the Bible being taken for granted; for example, we find that a knowledge of 2 Samuel at once gives us the clue to what Dryden meant in his *Absalom and Achitophel.* The whole sense of Ecclesiastes serves as a comment on Thackeray's *Vanity Fair,* when he cries out at the end "Ah! *Vanitas Vanitatum,*" implying that all is vanity and vexation of spirit (1 : 2). Ernest Hemingway drew also on Ecclesiastes, indeed just three verses further along, in *The Sun Also Rises* (1 : 5), and when Henry James entitled a book *The Golden Bowl,* he expected everyone to hear echoing in his mind Ecclesiastes 12 : 6, "Or ever the silver cord be loosed, or the golden bowl be broken." Kipling also took the title of his book *Many Inventions* from that work, "Lo, this only have I found,

that God hath made man upright; but they have sought out many inventions" (7 : 29).

In Kipling—to take one example among many writers—Biblical phrases and allusions continually recur, as in the famous poem "Recessional," when he speaks of "an humble and a contrite heart," expecting his readers to remember "a broken and a contrite heart, O God, thou wilt not despise" in Psalms 51 : 17. When he wrote a bitter poem on a political scandal he named it "Gehazi," confident that all would have read the story of Naaman the Syrian in 2 Kings 5. He ended the story "The Gardener" with these words: "When Helen left the cemetery she turned for a last look. In the distance she saw the man bending over his young plants; and she went away supposing him to be the gardener." The reference to the Gospel According to St. John (20 : 15) enables the reader to feel the deep implications of the tale. Many of Kipling's later stories cannot be fully understood without a knowledge of the Bible.

The "effect of the continual domestic study of the book upon the national character, imagination, and intelligence for nearly three centuries to come, was greater than that of any literary movement in our annals, or any religious movement since the coming of St. Augustine." So Trevelyan said. It is a stupendous claim, but it is one that can be amply justified. Let us look at two illustrations.

Some sixty or seventy years after the 1611 version appeared, a tinker in Bedford was writing prose of extraordinary power. His education had been very slight, his reading limited mainly to the Bible, the Book of Common Prayer, and Foxe's *Book of Martyrs.* John Bunyan's most famous book, *The Pilgrim's Progress,* opens like this:

I dreamed and behold I saw a man clothed with rags, standing in a certain place, with his face from his own house, a Book in his hand, and a great burden upon his back. I looked, and saw him open the Book and read therein: and as he read, he wept and trembled: and not being able longer to contain, he broke out with a lamentable cry, saying: "What shall I do?"

"A Book in his hand"—that was true not only of John Bunyan but of tens of thousands of his fellow countrymen. The days were long past when they had to be dependent on the mystery plays for a knowledge of the drama of biblical events, or on strolling preachers such as the Lollards, or on a visit to the local church to read from a Bible chained to the lectern. The Bible was available to practically every man, and available in lucid English. "A man, with a Book in his hand," from which he learnt the secret of forgiveness and of life—this was an apt description of multitudes from the early decades of the seventeenth century on.

The second illustration is drawn from an engraving. The scene of Edward Prentis' "Evening Prayer" is set in a middle-class home of about 1850. The table has been cleared except for a vase of flowers. At the table sits the head of the house, a book open in front of him. He has his glasses on, and he is reading to the family, including a small child and an old lady with her workbasket beside her. Near the door sit the maid and a working man. There is no question what the book is. It is the Bible, which in this way, by daily reading and pondering, became a powerful influence in tens of thousands of homes. A nation's character was largely molded not only by what was heard in church, but by what was read and reverently listened to at home.

EIGHTEENTH-CENTURY VERSIONS

IT would be both tedious and unnecessary to trace in any detail here the story of those translations that followed in the wake of the King James Version. The seventeenth and eighteenth centuries saw many—one could almost say too many—of these. Many of them by their banality only served to show up the simple splendor of the Authorized Version. Fortunately, by the kindly operation of the law of the survival of the fittest, many of these versions proved ephemeral. A very few examples will suffice to show the kind of thing that was perpetrated in those centuries.

In 1729, Daniel Mace published anonymously *The New Testament in Greek and English . . . Corrected From the Authority of the Most Authentic Manuscripts*. Whereas, for example, in the Authorized Version, St. James 2 : 3 reads, ". . . ye

have respect to him that weareth the gay clothing, and say unto him, Sit thou here in a good place," Mace makes the verse run, ". . . you should respectfully say to the suit of fine cloths, sit you there, that's for quality." Whereas St. James 3 : 5–6 reads in the Authorized Version, "Even so the tongue is a little member, and boasteth great things. Behold, how great a matter a little fire kindleth! And the tongue is a fire, a world of iniquity: so is the tongue among our members, that it defileth the whole body, and setteth on fire the course of nature; and it is set on fire of hell," Mace makes them read, "The tongue is but a small part of the body, yet how grand are its pretensions! a spark of fire! What quantities of timber will it blow into a flame! The tongue is a brand that sets the world in a combustion: it is but one of the numerous organs of the body, yet it can blast whole assemblies: tipped with infernal sulphur it sets the whole train of life in a blaze."

In 1764 Anthony Purver, a Quaker, produced *A New and Literal Translation*. We may contrast the lovely simplicity of the Authorized Version of The Song of Solomon 2 : 12, "The flowers appear on the earth;/The time of the singing of birds is come,/And the voice of the turtle is heard in our land"; with Purver's version: "Earth's Lap displays her infant Flowers,/The warbling Spring is welcomed in,/And hark how the Turtledove cooes in our Clime."

Again, in 1768 Edward Harwood went to work. True, he attempted to produce something more than a translation. He called his work *A Literal Translation of the New Testament: Being an Attempt to translate the Sacred Writings with the same Freedom, Spirit, and Elegance, with which other English Translations from the Greek Classics have lately been executed*. In the Authorized Version, St. Matthew 5 : 17–18 reads thus: "Think not that I am come to destroy the law, or the prophets: I am not come to destroy, but to fulfil. For verily I say unto you, Till heaven and earth pass, one jot or one tittle shall in no wise pass from the law, till all be fulfilled." In Harwood, this is the rendering: "Do not think that the design of my coming into the world is to abrogate the law of Moses, and the prophets—I am only come to supply their deficiencies, and to give mankind a more complete and perfect system of morals. For I tell you that the precepts of morality are of eternal and immutable obligation, and their power and efficiency shall never be relaxed or annulled, while the world endures." In the Authorized Version, St. Matthew 6 : 7 reads: "But when ye pray, use not vain repetitions, as the heathen do: for they think that they shall be heard for their much speaking." In Harwood it reads: "Think not the design of prayer is by the dint of importunity to tease the Deity into a compliance with your requests—Carefully avoid therefore the error of the heathen who think that the supreme Being can be prevailed upon by enthusiastic clamors, and a constant unvaried repetition of noisy expressions."

It should not go without mention that in 1768 John Wesley produced a version of the Authorized Version with notes "for plain, unlettered men who understand only their Mother Tongue." Wesley was, of course, a man who knew his Greek Testament well, and an evangelist who longed that the Bible should be understood by the common people. He divided the text into paragraphs, "a little circumstance," he said, "which makes many passages more intelligible to the Reader."

THE REVISED VERSION

WE come now to the last two chapters in the history of the English Bible, namely, the story of the Revised Version, and the period of modern versions.

The Revised Version (New Testament 1881, Old Testament 1885, Apocrypha 1895) was indeed a landmark in the long story of the evolution of the Bible, but from certain points of view it proved to be a disappointment. Nor was this by any means entirely the fault of the revisers. History has shown that its production was badly timed in regard to discoveries in the realm of biblical scholarship—but none of us is gifted with the gift of prescience to know what is "around the corner."

Shortly after the Revised Version came out, the dry sands of the Near East, and especially of Egypt, threw up thousands upon thousands of ostraca (old pieces of broken pots and vessels) and papyri (sheets, some fairly large and others no more than little scraps, of papyrus reeds glued together, rubbed smooth with pumice, and used as bits of paper). On these ostraca and papyri were written, in the Greek of the street, the marketplace, and the home, all kinds of things, for example, lists of names or articles, and messages of all sorts. (One such, in atrocious Greek, is from a schoolboy asking his father for money; another is from a husband on military service, writing to his wife who is expecting the birth of their child. "If it is a boy," he writes, "well and good; if it is a girl, cast it out.") At first sight one would not think that such discoveries would have much bearing on biblical scholarship. As a matter of fact, they were of the greatest importance. For, as these little scraps of writing were gathered together, deciphered, and compared with the Greek in which the New Testament was written, it became clear that the New Testament documents, so far from being written (as many had previously thought) in a kind of special "language of the Holy Ghost," were, as a matter of fact, written in the ordinary language used by the people of the first century Graeco-Roman world. True, the themes with which the documents dealt had an ennobling effect on the language and, as it were, lifted it out of the street on to a higher plane. True, the Hebraic thought of many of the writers and the use of the Greek Version of the Old Testament, the Septuagint, influenced the style of the Greek. True, some of the writers of the New Testament were men of culture and great literary skill—St. Luke especially and the unknown author of the Epistle to the Hebrews. But *basically* the language was that of the *lingua franca* which was the chief means of intercourse among the peoples of the Mediterranean world of the time of Christ. Many of the discoveries were in themselves of no great importance. (For example, the Authorized Version of St. Luke 15 : 13 says the Prodigal son "gathered all together" before he went into the far country. The papyri have shown that the verb can mean "realize goods into ready cash." This is precisely what he needed if he was to have a good time.) But taken together, they opened up something of a new epoch in New Testament textual study.

All this was "around the corner" when the revisers got busy with their work. But the time had not arrived when such discoveries could be used and incorporated in the work of revision. The result was the production of a volume which, while it was to be used, especially by students, for several decades to come, yet fell disappointingly short of what it might have been had it appeared early in the twentieth century instead of late in the nineteenth.

That having been said, however, the achievement was notable as a joint work of scholarship on the part of the most outstanding biblical scholars of the day. The initiation of the scheme was due to a motion of the Upper and Lower Houses of the Convocation of Canterbury in 1870 to appoint a committee "to report upon the desirableness of a revision of the Authorized Version. . . ." Another committee was set up which in turn separated into two companies, one to work at the Old Testament and one at the New. The choice of scholars was catholic, the Church of Scotland and the English and Scottish Free Churches being well represented. John Henry Cardinal Newman was invited to join the company, but declined. A Unitarian scholar, Dr. G. Vance Smith, was invited—and accepted. Among the most distinguished and learned scholars were B. F. Westcott and F. J. A. Hort, who were working at their famous edition of the Greek text of the New Testament (which appeared five days before the Revised New Testament).

The terms of reference under which the committees worked were cautious. "We do not contemplate any new translation of the Bible," the committees of the Canterbury Convocation had said, "or any alteration of the language, except when in the judgment of the most competent scholars such change is necessary." When such changes were made, "the style of the language employed in the existing version" (i.e., the Authorized Version) was to "be closely followed." If the revision proved sometimes to be somewhat pedantic (partly as a result of the attempt always to translate a Greek word by the same English word wherever it occurred); and if the New Testament part of it leaned too heavily on the Vatican and Sinaitic codices (technically known as B and Aleph respectively) owing to the influence especially of Westcott and Hort, still the Revised Version was an immense improvement on the Authorized, especially in ob-scure parts of the Old Testament; in the paragraphing according to the sense of the passage; and in the marginal notes which deal with alternative renderings and variant readings. It is true that the Authorized Version was so securely established in the affections of the people that the Revised Version never dislodged it. To many then (as indeed now) the Authorized Version *was* the Bible. But where a text of the Bible in English was required by students, there the Revised Version came into its own, particularly after the University Presses of Oxford and Cambridge produced an edition with marginal references in 1898. Austin Farrer remarked that these references, linking ideas and phrases in one part of the Bible with kindred ones in another, were the truly inspired part of this particular revision.

TWENTIETH-CENTURY VERSIONS

SINCE the appearance of the Revised Version, there has been a spate of new translations. By no means all of them can be mentioned here, but those who wish to go further into this particular chapter in the story of the English Bible will find the matter well treated in E. H. Robertson's *The New Translations of the Bible*.

R. F. Weymouth's *New Testament in Modern Speech* should not go unmentioned. First published in 1902, it met a real need among students of the Bible, as is witnessed by the fact that it passed through many editions. It shows the marks of scholarship and at the same time of reverence. It is still worth referring to.

Passing by with only a mention of the translation of J. N. Darby and *The Modern Reader's Bible* by R. G. Moulton (1907), we come to the famous and outstanding translation of James Moffatt. The production of this work (New Testament 1913, Old Testament 1924, whole Bible finally revised in 1935) was a landmark in the story of modern biblical translations. Moffatt was a biblical theologian and church historian of international reputation. In his translation, he tried to break away from old styles of translation, and to give us the biblical books in the idiom of modern English. Moreover, he tried to incorporate, insofar as was possible, some of the results of modern source criticism. Very often he did not hesitate to rearrange the order of the text in order to show how, in his opinion, such a rearrangement would improve the sense (a device adopted, if less extensively, by the Old Testament panel of the *New English Bible*.) Moreover, poetry was printed in verse form, an immense improvement. In these as in other important respects, the credit of being something of a pioneer rests with this great Scotsman.

The English-speaking world is indebted to the committee of thirty-two American scholars who in 1946 put out the Revised Standard Version of the New Testament. The whole Bible appeared in 1952. The language is modern but dignified, and reads more easily in public than do some of the more radical translations. Basing their work on the American Standard Version of 1901, the committee thoroughly revised it, and embodied the results of modern scholarship, preserving "those qualities which have given to the King James Version a supreme place in English literature."

In 1949 Ronald Knox's translation of the Old and New Testaments was published, "from the Latin Vulgate at the request of the Cardinal Archbishop of Westminster—for private use only." It was an astonishing achievement, including as it did the Apocrypha and, just for good value, two translations of the Psalms. Knox's biographer makes clear how big a place the task occupied in the translator's life. The disadvantage of a translation from the Vulgate is, in part, offset by the notes which make it abundantly clear that Knox kept a very careful eye on the original languages. The Latin form of the proper names (Neomi for Naomi, and Booz for Boaz) may be annoying to non-Roman Catholic readers. But there is a dignity and power of style about Knox's translation that make it worthy of constant reference.

The publication of J. B. Phillips' *Letters to Young Churches,* with an introduction by C. S. Lewis (1947), was an exciting event. It was followed by *The Gospels in Modern English* (1952), by *The Young Church in Action* (The Acts of the Apostles, 1955), and by *The Book of Revelation* (1957). The whole *New Testament in Modern English* appeared in 1958. This was the work of an Anglican clergyman who was convinced that the New Testament has a living message for the people of today, but that the message is dimmed and dulled by the kind of English in which they are compelled to read it. His work is not by any means a word-for-word translation. Nor is it wholly a paraphrase. F. F. Bruce says that "what he gives us is a meaning-for-meaning translation" (*The English Bible,* p. 214). It has had a phenomenal success on both sides of the Atlantic, and has succeeded in tearing aside for multitudes the veil that has hidden from them the meaning of the New Testament books. The message has become "contemporaneous." Mention should also be made of the distinguished work of E. V. Rieu in the realm of the translation of the classics. In 1952 he produced a translation of *The Four Gospels,* with an admirable introduction. This was followed in the same series by a translation of the *Acts of the Apostles,* by his son, C. H. Rieu (1957).

It might be thought that the market for English renderings of the Bible would by now have been saturated, but since 1960 there have been no fewer than three major new versions of the whole Bible in English, and our survey cannot conclude without some mention of them, however inadequate.

The first is the *New English Bible,* of which the New Testament appeared in 1961, and the Old Testament and Apocrypha, together with a corrected version of the New Testament, in 1970. This translation, like the Authorized and Revised Versions, was the result of committee work, although the procedures adopted differed significantly from those used on former occasions. Under the guidance of a Joint Committee, there was an Old Testament panel, a New Testament panel, an Apocrypha panel, and (since sound scholarship does not necessarily carry with it a delicate sense of English style) a fourth panel of literary advisers, to whom all the work of the translating panels was submitted for scrutiny. Passages of peculiar difficulty might on occasion pass repeatedly between the panels, but in no instance was the final version settled until all concerned had agreed.

The quality of the scholarship available to this Version was formidable. C. H. Dodd, one of the greatest New Testament scholars in the world, was director of the project throughout; Sir Godfrey Driver, an internationally acclaimed Semitist, was Joint Director from 1965; and W. H.

McHardy was deputy director from 1968. The result of the expertise brought to bear by these men and by the interdenominational teams that worked under them is that passage after passage is seen in its true meaning for the first time, like a freshly cleaned picture, even by comparison with the Revised Standard Version of only fifteen or twenty years earlier. The version has its defects, even from an academic point of view, notably in a tendency to inject a particular scholarly theory about the background or implications of the text into the rendering, when the original does not justify it (see, for example, Hosea 3 : 2, where "got her back" is pure conjecture, and not at all, as the footnote suggests, on a par with "bought her," the literal sense.) There are also books, such as the Epistles of John, where the translators seem to have found it hard to grasp the logic of the writer's thought. But there can be no question that this version is an overwhelming gain to the serious understanding of the Bible in the English-speaking world.

Stylistically, the aim of the translators was "to render the Greek . . . into the natural vocabulary, constructions and rhythms of contemporary speech," avoiding "archaism, jargon, and all that is either stilted or slipshod" ("Introduction to the New Testament") and "phrases likely soon to become obsolete" ("Introduction to the Old Testament"). How far they have succeeded is a judgment that it will take time to make. But two things may be said with some assurance: first, that the Old Testament reads better than the New, not because the one panel was more skilled than the other but simply because Hebrew renders more easily into English than does Greek; secondly, that many complaints about the version are due to the inability of readers in church to deliver it in the natural manner appropriate to a modern book instead of with the stylized solemnity conventional for the Authorized Version. Our age does not have a delicate ear for English cadences; and that of the translators of the New English Bible undoubtedly failed from time to time. But in parts of their work they rise nobly to the challenge of the original, for example, in the fifty-third chapter of Isaiah, which here succeeds as well in its own manner as the traditional rendering.

In the years 1966–1968 appeared another translation that has secured widespread popularity. The Jerusalem Bible is so called because it was the work of a team of Roman Catholic scholars under Alexander Jones, who made their rendering direct from the ancient languages but "in doubtful points preserved the text established and (for the most part) the interpretation adopted" by the École Biblique at Jerusalem in their French version, *La Bible de Jérusalem*, some years earlier. This translation, like the New English Bible, is prone to the vice of overtranslating. While it is inevitable that any rendering, however seemingly literal, contains a degree of interpretation, it is still a sound rule that to resort needlessly to expansion and paraphrase is always to increase the risk of distortion. Nevertheless, here again there are many excellent things to be thankful for. As in the New English Bible the Old Testament often comes up very well indeed, in particular, the patriarchal narratives in Genesis, the court history in Samuel–Kings, and the wisdom books, especially Ecclesiastes. In the New Testament, interestingly enough, the Jerusalem Bible fares better in the Synoptic Gospels, where the New English Bible is perhaps least happy. It is worth recording that both the Jerusalem Bible and the New English Bible are now in use officially in many churches for liturgical reading.

The third major translation to be launched in this period came out in 1976 and was known by the name of *Today's English Version*, a title which, fortunately, has now been dropped in favor of the *Good News Bible*. The purpose of this rendering was to make the message of the Bible immediately clear and comprehensible to people of little educational background. While totally applauding the aim, one must reserve judgment on the quality of the execution. There have already been anxieties that clarity has been purchased at the cost of oversimplification. As for the style, it is perhaps worth remarking that the Authorized Version found its way into the hearts and minds of the simple and uneducated without becoming flat or banal in the process.

Finally, mention must be made of a version of the New Testament which only appeared in 1973, issued by the British and Foreign Bible Society under the title, *The Translator's New Testament*. This rendering has been designed specifically to help those engaged in translating the

Scriptures into little-known languages and dialects in Asia, Africa, and elsewhere, but who cannot be expected to be experts in Greek as well. Disputed passages therefore carry translational notes, explaining the version adopted, and giving a selection of other published renderings. But in the main the work is done by the actual text; and the need to think hard to produce the simplest and yet most precisely equivalent word or phrase in each case has resulted in a genuine translation in the classic sense, not a paraphrase or hidden commentary, and one moreover which, though it has lapses like every other rendering (including the Authorized Version!), communicates with a fresh and simple dignity.

It will be seen that the story of the English Bible is by no means over. Rather it has entered on a new creative phase. The variety of new versions is not to be regretted. But what will be wanted before too long, surely, is that, as happened in the sixteenth century, when so many interesting renderings were in competition, once use has freed us from the superficial charm of what is merely new and has taught us which turns of phrase "work" and which do not, a version should be produced that will aim simply to bring together the best inspirations of each. If this were done, not only would it be a worthwhile exercise in Christian cooperation, but it might well be that the twenty-first century would open, like the seventeenth, with an English Bible that would be both serviceable and inspiring for many generations to come.

CONCLUSION

In the course of the previous pages, reference has more than once been made to the influence of the English Bible on the writers of our literature.

A giant work, still to be done, perhaps in the old manner by committees of committees, is to trace the penetration of English religious and secular life by the substance and idiom of the English Bible. The prayers of Bishop Launcelot Andrewes and Doctor Samuel Johnson, the poetry of Shakespeare and Milton, the fiction of Bunyan, the lyrics of Blake and Hardy are but milestones on a long and fascinating journey.

So J. Isaacs ends his essay on "The Authorized Version and After" in *Ancient & English Versions of the Bible* (p. 234). It would not be an exaggeration to say that it is impossible really to appreciate the literature of the English-speaking people without a knowledge, an understanding, an appreciation of the English Bible.

But, of course, the influence of the Bible has been far deeper than a literary influence only. The influence on religion, on ethics, on character has been even more profound than it has been in the realm of literature. Explain it as you will, it appears to be a fact that when, for example, the message of Saint Paul is grasped, when it springs into new life, then there is a quickening of mind and conscience among men. Augustine, living in an age when the old order was crashing into ruins, seizes upon the truths of the Pauline gospel and writes in such a way as mightily to influence the Western world in all succeeding generations. Luther labors in his cell at the Epistle to the Galatians (which Lightfoot used to describe as the rough model of which Romans is the finished statue), and the Reformation begins to shake Europe. Colet lectures at Oxford on the Epistles of Saint Paul; Erasmus feeds on the truths of the New Testament at Cambridge; and the light shines out over England. Wesley, Oxford don and returned missionary, meets with a little group of godly men studying Luther's commentary on the Epistle to the Galatians, and finds his heart "strangely warmed." The warmth which glowed within him was not selfishly contained. It drove him on horseback up and down the length and breadth of England, to preach the message that had revolutionized his own life. That message played no small part in averting in England the kind of revolution that had drenched France in blood.

The names mentioned above are the names of intellectual and religious giants—Augustine, Luther, Colet, Erasmus, Wesley. One could mention names in our own day—a Karl Barth on the Continent, a William Temple in England, a Niebuhr in America—all men whose have been stimulated and their the massive message of another phenomenon that calls for mention. The Bible speaks, not only to the intellectually powerful, but also to the unlettered and the simple. Perhaps this is not wholly to be wondered at, for as Saint Paul remarked, in writing to the Corinthians, "Few of you are men of wisdom, by any human standard; few are powerful or highly born" (1 Corinthians 1 : 26 [*New English Bible*]). The writer of the Acts of the Apostles says that their opponents noticed that the early Christians at Jerusalem were "unlearned and ignorant men" (Acts 4 : 13). And Celsus, one of the opponents of the Christian movement in the second century, mocked at the lowly social status of many of the adherents of Christianity in his day. Certain it is that those who are most experienced in the exercise of ordinary pastoral duties among all kinds of people find that there is about the Bible a kind of *universal* appeal. There may, for example, be many problems to the scholar about the precise meaning—even about the precise translation—of the opening verses of the fourteenth chapter of the Gospel According to St. John. But anyone whose task it is to minister to sorrowing or fearful people will tell you that verses such as these have brought comfort and strength to men and women of all kinds of social and educational background. The first chapter of St. John is one of the profoundest documents ever penned; but again and again it has proved a source of nourishment and inspiration to the simple. The fifty-third chapter of Isaiah is to the scholar a passage full of difficulties of interpretation—almost every sentence is patient of more than one translation. But again and again it has lit up for the simplehearted the meaning of the Passion of Jesus and something of its significance in the salvation of the world.

Nor is this the case in English-speaking countries only. We may explain it as we will, but the fact remains that for scholar and ignoramus, for Eastern and Western, for black and white, the Bible has a message that is always fresh and alive. Albert Einstein bore witness to the fact that when all other movements, universities included, bowed the knee to Hitler, it was the Christian church that stood up to him. It is to be noted that the church that opposed Hitler and did so much to break his power was a church ~oly indebted to and nourished on the Word of God. Particularly in times of stress and strain, the Scriptures have a way of stating their message in a way almost unbelievably relevant to the particular situation. The Psalms, for example, from one point of view are ancient national poems, marred, in parts, by a vengeful spirit which the Christian mind rejects in any literal sense. They were written out of national agony and personal stress centuries before the Christian era dawned. They reflect the persecution and perplexities of a pre-Christian age. But the voice of the experience of the church is unanimous in averring that, in times of stress, national and personal, these Psalms have a way of rising above their original local application, of "speaking to our condition," of forming the prayer of Christians who, with fuller knowledge, worship the same God as did the writers of the Psalms many centuries ago. The Scriptures have a way of being the material on which the Holy Spirit of God breathes, and from which He brings forth light and truth to the Christian conscience.

It is facts such as these that prompt the Christian church in many countries to spend large sums of money every year in the translation and dissemination of the Bible throughout the world. Millions of dollars are spent annually on such projects. Under the aegis of the United Bible Societies, some twenty-four national bible societies of the world think and plan together for the accurate translation and for the speedy spreading of the Bible in whole or in part. Similarly, such agencies as the Bible Reading Fellowship and the Scripture Union distribute every month hundreds of thousands of booklets aimed at expounding, in ways suitable for all levels of age and education, the message of the Bible. The immense labor entailed in carrying out these tasks is prompted by the knowledge that the Bible is more than an ancient document, more than one of the classics of world literature. It has a way of becoming the word of God to the man of faith.

SELECTED BIBLIOGRAPHY

I. BIBLIOGRAPHY. J. I. Mombert, *A Handbook of the English Versions of the Bible* (New York, 1883; rev. ed., New York, 1890); T. H. Darlow and H. F. Moule,

Historical Catalogue of the Printed Editions of Holy Scripture, 2 vols. (London, 1903–1911), the standard bibliography, commonly known as Darlow and Moule; vol. I covers the English editions; A. W. Pollard, *Records of the English Bible: The Documents Relating to the Translation and Publication of the Bible in English 1525–1611* (Oxford, 1911), an essential bibliographical study of the early translation; H. A. Guppy, *A Brief Sketch of the History of the Transmission of the Bible Down to the Revised English Version of 1881–95* (Manchester, 1925).

II. Versions.

?1380: Wycliffe's version.
—the first translation of the complete Vulgate. First printed, Oxford, 1850.

1525–1526: Tyndale's version of the New Testament.

1530: Tyndale's version of the Pentateuch.

1525: Coverdale's version.
—printed on the Continent. First edition printed in England, 1537.

1537: Matthew's edition (combining the Tyndale and Coverdale versions).
—the primary version of the English Bible.

1539: Taverner's revision of Matthew's edition.

1539: The Great Bible or Cranmer Bible.

1548–1549: Erasmus' paraphrase of the New Testament.

1557–1560: The Geneva version or Breeches Bible.
—translated by Whittingham and other refugees.

1568: Parker's version or the Bishops' Bible.

1582: The first Roman Catholic version of the New Testament. Printed at Rheims.

1609–1610: The first Roman Catholic (Douay) version of the Old Testament. Printed at Douay.
—revised edition of the Douay Bible, by Challoner, 1750.

1611: King James Version. The Authorized Version (AV).

1729: Mace's version of the New Testament.

1764: Purver's version. The Quaker Bible.

1808: Thomson's version. Printed in Philadelphia.

1833: Webster's expurgated version.

1881–1895: The Revised Version (RV) of King James Version.

1901: American Standard Version.

1924: Moffatt's version.

1938: *The Bible, An American Translation*, by E. J. Goodspeed and J. M. Powis Smith.

1944–1950: Knox's version.

1946–1952: Revised Standard Version (RSV) of King James Version.

1948: Lattey's Roman Catholic version.

1950: Basic English version.

1958: Phillips' New Testament in Modern English.
—portions published separately as *Letters to Young Churches*, 1947; *The Gospels in Modern English*, 1952; *The Young Church in Action*, 1955; *The Book of Revelation*, 1957.

1961: The New English Bible: the New Testament.

1963: Phillips' *Four Prophets* (Amos, Hosea, First Isaiah, Micah).

1966: The Jerusalem Bible.

1967: The Jerusalem Bible New Testament Reader's Edition.

1967: The New Testament in Four Versions (King James Version; Revised Standard Version; Phillips' Modern English; New English Bible).

1968: The Jerusalem Bible Reader's Edition.

1968: The New Testament, a New Translation. Vol. I: The Gospels and the Acts of the Apostles, William Barclay.

1970: The New English Bible, with the Apocrypha.

1973: The Translator's New Testament.

1976: The Good News Bible: Today's English Version.

III. Studies. The literature is so extensive that the following selective list is limited mainly to recent works. Many of these contain bibliographies or reading lists as aids to further study.

B. F. Westcott, *A General View of the History of the English Bible* (London, 1968), a standard work, revised by W. Aldis Wright (London, 1905) and in 1916; J. B. Lightfoot, *On a Fresh Revision of the English New Testament* (London, 1871); H. W. Hoare, *The Evolution of the English Bible* (London, 1901; 2nd ed., 1902); G. Milligan, *Selections From the Greek Papyri* (Cambridge, 1910); A. Souter, *The Text and Canon of the New Testament* (New York, 1913; 2nd ed., London, 1954); M. Deanesly, *The Lollard Bible* (Cambridge, 1920); H. G. Meecham, *Light From Ancient Letters* (London–New York, 1923); C. H. Dodd, *The Bible and the Greeks* (London, 1935); J. F. Mozley, *William Tyndale* (New York–London, 1937); S. L. Greenslade, *The Work of William Tyndale* (London, 1938); H. W. Robinson, ed., *The Bible in Its Ancient and English Versions* (Oxford, 1940; repr. 1954); C. C. Butterworth, *The Literary Lineage of the King James Version, 1340–1611* (Philadelphia, 1941); D. Daiches, *The King James Version of the English Bible* (Chicago, 1941); H. J. C. Grierson, *The English Bible* (London, 1943); F. G. Kenyon, *The Reading of the Bible as History, as Literature, and as Religion* (London, 1944); C. H. Dodd, *The Bible Today* (Cambridge, 1946); *An Introduction to the Revised Standard Version of the New Testament* (New York, 1946), by Members of the Revision Committee; R. A.

Knox, *On Englishing the Bible* (London, 1949); L. A. Weigle, *The English New Testament From Tyndale to the Revised Standard Version* (New York, 1949); C. S. Lewis, *The Literary Impact of the Authorized Version* (London, 1950); J. F. Mozley, *Coverdale and His Bibles* (London, 1953); H. G. G. Herklots, *Back to the Bible* (London, 1954), also published as *How Our Bible Came to Us: Its Texts and Versions* (New York, 1954); London Times, *The Bible Today, Historical, Social, and Literary Aspects of the Old and New Testaments, Described by Christian Scholars* (New York, 1955); R. A. Knox, *On English Translation* (Oxford, 1957); F. G. Kenyon, *Our Bible and the Ancient Manuscripts*, 5th ed., rev. and enl. by A. W. Adams (London, 1958); E. H. Robertson, *The New Translations of the Bible* (London, 1959); G. MacGregor, *The Bible in the Making* (Philadelphia, 1959; London, 1961); F. F. Bruce, *The English Bible: A History of Translations* (New York–London, 1961); *The Cambridge History of the Bible*, vol. III, *The West From the Reformation to the Present Day*, S. L. Greenslade (Cambridge, 1963); H. von Campenhausen, *The Formation of the Christian Bible*, J. A. Baker, trans. (Philadelphia, 1972); J. Barr, *The Bible in the Modern World* (London, 1973); J. Finegan, *Encountering New Testament Manuscripts* (London, 1975).